KING JAMES
BIBLE
WORD
BOOK

KING JAMES
BIBLE
WORD
BOOK

Edited by
Martin H. Manser

Assistant Editors:
Natasha B. Fleming   Kate Hughes

THOMAS NELSON PUBLISHERS
Nashville

Publisher's Preface

Despite the availability of many new translations and paraphrases of God's Word, the venerable King James Version still posts significant sales each year. Wholly apart from its achievement as an accurate translation accessible to the ordinary people of its day, the King James (or Authorized) Version lives as a specimen of the English language unsurpassed in its grace and beauty.

But even as time and history refuse to stand still, so also the living English language refuses to freeze in time. Words and expressions once common become fully obsolete, or they take on new meanings—meanings at times opposite to those of an earlier time. Especially in such cases, the casual reader of today may read a word from the sixteenth century but give to it a contemporary meaning and think nothing of doing so. The reader's current meaning may still make sense within the sentence, but it will not be the sense intended by the sixteenth-century writer. To the extent that this is true, communication breaks down, and what the writer wished to say is, in part or whole, lost.

Readers of the King James Version want to understand it accurately and fully. And because the English language has changed a great deal in the last four centuries, they need an authoritative guide that will help them make proper sense of the words and phrases that are rarely or never used by speakers of English today, as well as alert them to expressions whose common meanings today differ from those of the past.

To meet this need, Thomas Nelson is pleased to release this fully revised and updated edition of a volume that has provided such information for all users and lovers of the King James Bible. Originally published in 1960 as *The Bible Word Book*, this volume served as a dictionary dedicated specifically to the King James Version. Its 800 articles on the King James words and phrases most affected by changes in English offered casual readers and students, ministers, and scholars unique and valuable information not available in any other volume. This edition adds more than 300 new entries, including a large number of phrases commonly heard in everyday speech but not often recognized as having been used in the King James Bible.

Authors' Preface

This book is concerned with words and phrases used in the King James Version of the Bible. The King James Version has had a profound effect on the English language, and this volume seeks to describe two aspects of such an effect.

First, it describes those words that have become obsolete or archaic, or have changed in meaning or acquired new meanings, so that they no longer convey to the reader the sense which the King James translators intended them to express. Most of these words were accurate translations in 1611, but they have become ambiguous or misleading.

Secondly, it describes many phrases that have become an established part of the English language and which are often used without the speaker or writer being aware of their biblical origins.

The language of the King James Version of the Bible was sixteenth-century English, for it was a revision of English versions that went back to Wycliffe in the late fourteenth century and to Tyndale and his successors from 1525 on. And it was sixteenth-century English at its best—"the noblest monument of English prose." There is general agreement with the verdict of its revisers in 1881, who expressed admiration for "its simplicity, its dignity, its power, its happy turns of expression . . . the music of its cadences and the felicities of its rhythm."

Yet the development of biblical studies, the discovery of ancient manuscripts, and the new knowledge of Bible lands and languages gained by archaeology have made its revision desirable; and the changes in English usage have made it necessary. The Revised Version was published in 1881–1885, the American Standard Version in 1901, and the Revised Standard Version in 1946–1952. In more recent years many contemporary translations have been published: the New American Standard Bible (1960–1977, 1995), the New International Version (1973, 1978, 1984), the New King James Version (1979, 1980, 1982, 1990), the New Century Version (1987, 1988, 1991), the New Revised Standard Version (1989), the Contemporary English Version (1995), and the New Living Translation (1996).

The original 1960 edition of this volume owed its title to *The Bible Word-Book* by William Aldis Wright, the second edition of which was published in England in 1884, succeeding a first edition prepared with the help of the Reverend J. Eastwood, published in 1866. Wright had articles on 2,316 archaic words and phrases in the King James Version of the Bible and the Book of Common Prayer. He gave for each a brief definition and statement of etymological derivation, then quoted examples of its use in English literature, chiefly of the sixteenth century. For these illustrations, his book is of lasting value.

Today the situation is different. Several revisions of the King James Version have been published, and there have been notable new translations of the Bible into modern English. The twenty-volume *Oxford English Dictionary* (second edition, 1989) affords a wealth of illustration for the varied senses of English usage. The etymology of the English words is indicated in all of the larger dictionaries.

The King James Bible Word Book bears little resemblance, therefore, to the

Bible Word-Book of one hundred years ago. It is intended for the general public and is meant to be read as well as to be used for reference. Its purpose is (1) to explain what the King James translators meant when they used a word or phrase which is now obsolete or archaic, (2) to state what word or phrase is used to replace it in the revised versions or contemporary translations, and (3) to explain the meaning, use, and contemporary renderings of phrases and expressions that have become part of the English language. Illustrations from general literature are cited where they seem to be helpful; and these are taken from, for example, Shakespeare, Ben Jonson, or Milton, on the assumption that their works will be readily available to readers.

This revised and updated edition contains articles on 1,100 words and phrases, including more than 300 new entries: words (e.g., "engine," "pitiful") whose meanings have changed since the KJV was first published, and phrases (e.g., "a fly in the ointment," "the salt of the earth") that have become part of the English language. Further, the entire text of the 1960/1994 editions of the *King James Bible Word Book* has been revised to include renderings of the contemporary versions listed above. It can be seen that the range of translations bring out different shades of meaning.

The articles are drawn from the language of the Old and New Testaments. The book makes occasional reference to the language of the Apocrypha, the Book of Common Prayer, and the Preface to the King James Version entitled "The Translators to the Reader."

Quotations from the King James Version and later versions—particularly the contemporary versions of the CEV, NASB, NCV, NIV, NKJV, NLT, NRSV, and RSV—are marked as such. Other translations are cited where these are helpful.

The comprehensive Index at the back of the book lists more than 2,500 additional words and phrases. These are words that do not appear in the King James Version but are used by the contemporary translations instead of the archaic KJV terms. This Index also includes the key words or phrases used in the King James Version. The Index will guide readers to the pages in this book on which each of these Bible words or phrases appears or is discussed.

Acknowledgments

Martin H. Manser, as editorial reviser, acknowledges with gratitude the help of the following people in the preparation and publication of this book:

Natasha Fleming and Kate Hughes for their assistance in revising and updating the text.

Rosalind Desmond for bringing together the diverse texts.

Lynda Drury, and Ben and Hannah Manser for secretarial assistance.

Martin Selman and Greta Chang for their advice on particular theological and stylistic points.

Ward Allen for pointing me to useful bibliographical sources.

Frank Harper, Geoffrey Hunt, and Anthony Gray for their help on computerization.

Harper Collins Publishers for permission to adapt certain sections of my book, *Amazing Book of Bible Facts.*

Lee Hollaway and the staff of Thomas Nelson Publishers for their encouragement in the preparation of this book.

Sources Consulted and Abbreviations Used

The *Bible Word-Book* by William Aldis Wright was published by The Macmillan Company, London, 1884.

The translations of the Bible referred to in the present book are those by John Wycliffe and his associates, made between 1380 and 1400; William Tyndale, 1525–1535; Miles Coverdale, 1535; "Thomas Matthew," a pseudonym of John Rogers, 1537; Richard Taverner, 1539; the Great Bible, 1539; the Geneva Bible, 1560; the Bishops' Bible, 1568, revised 1572; the Rheims New Testament, 1582; the Douay Bible, 1609; the King James Version (KJV), 1611; the Revised Version (RV), 1881–1885; the American Standard Version (ASV), 1901; the Revised Standard Version (RSV), 1946–1952.

Translations of the New Testament into modern English are *The Twentieth Century New Testament*, 1898–1904, and individual translations by R. F. Weymouth, 1903; James Moffatt, 1913; Edgar J. Goodspeed, 1923; William G. Ballantine, 1923; Charles B. Williams, 1949; J. B. Phillips, 1947–1958.

New translations of the Gospels are by Charles C. Torrey, 1933, revised 1947; and E. V. Rieu, 1952.

Translations of the Bible into modern speech are by James Moffatt, finally revised in 1935; by J. .M. P. Smith and associates for the Old Testament, with Goodspeed's New Testament, in *An American Translation*, 1931; by S. H. Hooke in *The Basic Bible*, 1949; by Ronald Knox, 1944–1954; and by the Confraternity of Christian Doctrine, 1948–1959, and the following contemporary translations whose publication details appear on the copyright page: Contemporary English Version (CEV), New American Standard Bible (NASB), New Century Version (NCV), New International Version (NIV), New King James Version (NKJV), New Living Translation (NLT), New Revised Standard Version (NRSV), and Revised Standard Version (RSV).

The reference work to which this book owes most is the *Oxford English Dictionary* (OED); next to it, *Webster's New International Dictionary*, and *Merriam-Webster's Collegiate Dictionary* (Tenth Edition). There are excellent articles on words in the four-volume Hastings' *Dictionary of the Bible*. The volumes of *The Interpreter's Bible* are of great value for comparison of KJV and later versions. The Oxford Hebrew lexicon referred to in this book is by Brown, Driver, and Briggs (BDB), published by the Clarendon Press in 1907, corrected impression 1952. The Greek lexicons are by J. H. Thayer, 1885, fourth edition, reprinted 1953; and by W. F. Arndt and F. W. Gingrich, 1957.

Valuable concordances are by John Bartlett for the works of Shakespeare; by James Strong and by Robert Young for the King James Version of the Bible; by M. C. Hazard for the American Standard Version of the Bible; and hard copy and computerized concordances on contemporary versions. Especially useful is *Nelson's Electronic Bible Reference Library* (Nashville: Thomas Nelson Publishers, 1997).

A, AN

The indefinite article "a" or "an" is one of the most frequently used words in the English language. In the KJV the archaic uses of "a" and "an" occur most familiarly in "an hungred" ["hungered," Matthew 4:2; 25:35, 37, 42, 44; Luke 6:3], which appears in Matthew 12:1, 3 and Mark 2:25. This expression, in each of these cases, comes from Tyndale. The contemporary versions render "an hungred" as "hungry" (occasionally "very hungry," and Matthew 4:2, NRSV, "famished.")

The use of "a" as a "worn-down proclitic form of preposition" (OED) with a verbal noun, to denote a process or continued action, occurs in Luke 8:42, "she lay a dying"; Luke 9:42, "as he was yet a coming"; John 21:3, "I go a fishing"; Hebrews 11:21, "when he was a dying"; 1 Peter 3:20, "while the ark was a preparing." These expressions also come originally from Tyndale.

The contemporary versions generally translate them by "-ing" forms, e.g., "I am [NLT, "I'm"] going fishing" (John 21:3, NASB, NKJV, NRSV, RSV). Variations include the NLT of Luke 9:42, "As the boy came forward"; the NIV of John 21:3, "I'm [NCV, "I am"] going out to fish"; the CEV of Hebrews 11:21, "when Jacob was about to die"; the NASB of 1 Peter 3:20, "during the construction of the ark."

The phrase "in building" occurs in the KJV at 1 Kings 6:7; Ezra 5:16; and John 2:20 in the passive sense of "being built"; and it occurs in the active sense in 1 Kings 6:12, 38; Ezra 4:4. The "worn-down" form of this phrase, "a building," appeared in the 1611 edition of the KJV, 2 Chronicles 16:6, "the timber thereof, wherewith Baasha was a building." It so remained until 1769, when Dr. Blayney deleted the "a." In 1873, Dr. Scrivener, editor of the Cambridge Paragraph Bible, restored the "a"; but subsequent publishers of the KJV have not followed his example.

Other prepositional uses of "a" are in 2 Chronicles 2:18, "set the people a work," and 1 Corinthians 9:7, "Who goeth a warfare any time at his own charges?" The NASB, NKJV, NRSV, and RSV read, "make the people work" and the NCV and NIV, "to keep the people working." For 1 Corinthians 9:7 the NIV and RSV read, "Who serves as a soldier at his own expense?"; the NRSV reads, "Who at any time pays the expenses for doing military service?" Other adjectival uses are 2 Corinthians 10:6, "having in a readiness to revenge" (NKJV, RSV, "being ready to punish"; NCV, NIV, "are ready to punish") and Luke 9:28, "about an eight days" (all contemporary versions except NASB, "about eight days," NASB, "Some eight days.").

A glimpse of the English language in the making can be seen by comparing Acts 13:36, "David . . . fell on sleep," and 7:60, "he fell asleep." The Greek verb is identical in these two cases; the difference in rendering goes back to Coverdale and the Great Bible, which had "fell on slepe" and "fell a slepe." The NASB, NIV, NKJV, and RSV retain "fell asleep"; and the CEV, NCV, NLT, and NRSV translate as "died." Compare also "laying await" and "lying in wait" (Acts 9:24; 20:19), rendered in the contemporary versions by the noun "plot(s)" or "plan(s)."

In the parable of the Last Judgment, Matthew 25:31–46, Tyndale and Geneva had "thursted" (vv. 35, 42) and "a thurst" (vv. 37, 44); the KJV has "athirst" (v. 44) but otherwise (vv. 35, 37, 42) "thirsty." All the contemporary versions have "thirsty" for all these verses.

ABHOR

"Abhor" now means "to hate vehemently," "to abominate," "to regard with loathing or disgust." Once it had the meanings derived from the Latin *abhorreo*, "to shrink from," "to be averse to," "to differ from," "to be inconsistent with." We should understand in this way the dictum of Spinoza or Samuel Johnson that "nature abhors a vacuum," or the line in the *Te Deum,* "Thou didst not abhor the Virgin's womb." But these meanings are now obsolete.

The KJV uses "abhor" forty-three times, to represent fourteen different Hebrew or Greek words. In most cases the contemporary versions have changed it. In Exodus 5:21 the KJV "made our savour to be abhorred" is changed to "made us abhorrent" (NKJV), "made us offensive" (RSV), "brought us into bad odor" (NRSV), "made us a stench" (NIV).

In 2 Samuel 16:21 the KJV "abhorred of thy father" is changed to "odious to your father" (NRSV), "publicly disgraced your father" (CEV), "insulted him beyond hope of reconciliation" (NLT). The statement, in connection with the sin of the sons of Eli, that "men abhorred the offering of the LORD" does not refer to a general public consequence of their misdeeds, but simply describes the sin of these two men. The NRSV reads, "treated the offerings of the LORD with contempt" (1 Samuel 2:17); the CEV has "did not show any respect for the sacrifices"; the NASB "despised the offering of the LORD."

The KJV has "I abhor myself" (Job 42:6); the NRSV, RSV, NIV have "I despise myself"; the CEV and NCV render it as "I hate myself." In Isaiah 66:24 "an abhorring" (KJV) means a thing that is abhorred: "they shall be an abhorrence to all flesh" (NKJV, NRSV, RSV); "an abhorrence to all mankind" (NASB); "loathsome to all mankind" (NIV); "the sight will be disgusting to everyone" (CEV).

In Psalm 10:3 the KJV has "blesseth the covetous, whom the Lord abhorreth" This is now translated, referring to the wicked, "He blesses the greedy and renounces the LORD" (NKJV); "hate and curse you, LORD" (CEV); "curses and spurns the LORD" (NASB); "reviles the LORD" (NIV). The Lord's word to Ahaz (Isaiah 7:16), "the land that thou abhorrest shall be forsaken of both her kings," (KJV) is "the land before whose two kings you are in dread will be deserted"

(NRSV); "the land that you dread will be forsaken by both her kings" (NKJV). Other versions have "the two kings you fear so much" (NLT); "You are afraid of the kings of Israel and Aram" (NCV).

ABIDE

In contemporary language "abide" is most commonly used in the sense "to hold to," "to remain true to," "to abide by the rules," and in the sense "to tolerate" (used in the negative as in "I will not abide such language"). But from the twelfth century onwards "abide" meant "to wait," "stay," "remain," with other senses developing over the centuries.

From the thirteenth century onwards, these senses included "to endure," "to bear," for example in Numbers 31:23 (KJV), "Every thing that may abide the fire," rendered in the NASB and RSV as "everything that can stand the fire." The contemporary versions generally replace the KJV "abide" with "endure" in the cry of the prophets: "Who can endure the day of his coming?" "Who can endure the heat of his anger?" (Malachi 3:2; Nahum 1:6; see also Joel 2:11; Jeremiah 10:10).

In the negative use of "abide" meaning "tolerate," as Coverdale rendered Job 19:17, "Myne owne wyfe maye not abyde my breth," the KJV translates "My breath is strange to my wife"; the NLT, NRSV translate as "my breath is repulsive to my wife," the NASB, NIV, NKJV as "my breath is offensive to my wife"; the CEV "my breath disgusts my wife."

Tyndale's rendering of John 8:43, "ye cannot abyde the hearynge of my wordes," is rendered by the KJV as "ye cannot hear my word"; Tyndale's sense of the passage is seen in the RSV, "you cannot bear to hear my word" and the CEV "stand to hear what I am saying."

The related word "bide" is not used in contemporary Bible translations but Tyndale used it in Mark 10:7, "And for this thingis sake shall a man leve father and mother and byde by his wyfe." The KJV reads "cleave to his wife," the NKJV, NLT, NRSV, RSV, "joined to his wife," the NCV, NIV, "be united" to his wife.

In addition to the Hebrew word for "stay" or "remain," thirteen other Hebrew words are occasionally translated "abide" in the KJV. Their primary meanings are such as: go in, sojourn, whirl, encamp, bear, spend the night, stand still, stand up, sit, dwell, cleave to, remain.

The Greek words translated "abide" in the New Testament are not so scattered in meaning. An interesting passage is Acts 20:23, where Tyndale had Paul say concerning his journey to Jerusalem that "bondes and trouble abyde me." The KJV has "abide me," but added a note "Or, wait for me." The NASB, NKJV, and RSV have "await me"; the NRSV, "are waiting for me," the NIV, "are facing me."

The KJV translation of Ecclesiastes 8:15, "for that shall abide with him of his labour the days of his life," could be thought to be misleading, for it seems to say that food, drink, and mirth are the only abiding results of labor. But the writer is referring to them as its cheering accompaniment—for this will "go with" (RSV, NRSV; NASB, "stand by"; NIV, "accompany"; NKJV, "remain with") people in their toil through the days of life which God gives.

"Abide" is retained in most of the contemporary versions of Psalm 91:1, "abide" in the shadow of the Almighty; the NIV renders this "rest," the NLT "find rest."

In the New Testament "abide" is retained in John 5:38, KJV, "ye have not his word abiding in you." The NASB, NKJV, NRSV, and RSV retain "abide" here; the NIV has "nor does his word dwell in you," the NLT, "you do not have his message in your hearts," and the CEV, "You have not believed his message."

In John chapter 15, KJV "abide" (beginning "Abide in me, and I in you," John 15:4), is retained by the NASB, NKJV, NRSV, and RSV and translated "remain" by the NCV, NIV, and NLT and "stay joined" by the CEV and NLT. The KJV for 1 Corinthians 13:13 has, "And now abideth faith, hope, charity." The NASB, NKJV, NRSV, and RSV retain "abide," the NIV translates as "remain," the NLT as "endure." 1 Peter 1:23 in the KJV reads, "the word of God, which liveth and abideth for ever." The NKJV retains the verb "abide"; the CEV has "lives on"; other contemporary versions (NASB, NIV, NRSV) have adjectives "the living and enduring word of God;" (NLT) "the eternal, living word of God."

Throughout 1 John and 2 John, the KJV "abide" is retained by the NASB, NKJV, NRSV, and RSV (except 1 John 2:17 where the NASB and NRSV have the verb "live"). The NCV, NIV, and NLT generally translate the KJV "abide" as "live." The NIV also has "remain" or "continue"; the NLT also has "continue to live." The CEV paraphrases, for example, 1 John 2:14, "God's message is firm in your hearts" (KJV, "the word of God abideth in you"); 1 John 2:24, "Keep thinking about the message you first heard" (KJV, "Let that therefore abide in you, which ye have heard from the beginning").

ABJECT

The word "abject" is currently used as an adjective to refer to a situation that is wretched or hopeless ("live in abject poverty") or to a person who is considered worthless or contemptible ("an abject coward"). In the KJV, however, "abject" is used as a noun in this latter sense, to refer to a worthless or contemptible person, one cast off, an outcast, from the Latin *abjectus*, cast aside.

The word occurs once in the KJV, at Psalm 35:15, "But in mine adversity they rejoiced, and gathered themselves together: yea, the abjects gathered themselves together against me, and I knew it not; they did tear me, and ceased not." The contemporary versions render "abjects" in this verse as: "attackers" (NIV, NKJV), "smiters"

(NASB), "ruffians" (NRSV), "cripples" (RSV), and "worthless liars" (CEV).

In *King Richard III* (I, 1, 106), Shakespeare used this word in the same sense: "We are the queen's abjects, and must obey."

ABRAHAM'S BOSOM

"Abraham's bosom" is an archaic phrase that refers to the sleeping place of the blessed who are dead. It occurs in the KJV in the story of Lazarus and the rich man at Luke 16:22: "The beggar Lazarus died, and was carried by the angels into Abraham's bosom." The NASB, NKJV, and RSV retain the phrase "Abraham's bosom"; the other contemporary versions have that Lazarus was carried by the angels "to be with Abraham" (NLT, NRSV); "to Abraham's side" (NIV); "to the place of honor next to Abraham" (CEV); and "to the arms of Abraham" (NCV). Shakespeare used the expression in *King Richard III* (IV, 3, 38): "The sons of Edward sleep in Abraham's bosom."

ABROAD

In modern English, "abroad" means "away from one's home" or "to or in foreign lands." It was a popular word with Elizabethan writers, including Shakespeare, for broadly, widely, at large, or for outside the house, in the streets, away from home. The KJV uses it in this sense. For example, Jeremiah 6:11 reads, "I am full of the fury of the LORD; I am weary with holding in: I will pour it out upon the children abroad." The NASB, NCV, NIV, NRSV, RSV have "in the street," the NLT, "in the streets," the NKJV, "outside."

"Abroad" simply means "outside"—and is generally rendered in this way in all the contemporary versions—in the sanitary provisions of Deuteronomy 23:10, 12, 13 and the rules governing loans (24:11). The marriages "abroad" of the thirty daughters and the thirty sons of one of the ancient judges of Israel were merely marriages "outside his clan" (Judges 12:9, CEV, NIV, NLT, NRSV, RSV), "not in his family groups" (NCV).

"Come abroad" stands for the Hebrew word which means "be made known" (Esther 1:17, as NRSV and RSV), and for the Greek phrase which means "come to light" (Mark 4:22; Luke 8:17 in NASB, NKJV, NRSV, and RSV). "His name was spread abroad" is more literally translated "his name had become known" (Mark 6:14, NRSV and RSV); "well known" (NASB, NCV, NIV, NKJV); "people everywhere were talking about him" (NLT).

ACCEPT

In modern English, "accept" means "to take something offered," "to agree or approve," or "to recognize as true." The KJV sometimes uses "accept" with the modern meaning, for example in "the owner shall accept thereof [i.e., the oath]" (Exodus 22:11), rendered "accept" by all the contemporary versions except the CEV and "not accepting deliverance" (Hebrews 11:35, KJV, NKJV), "refusing to accept release" (NRSV, RSV). The passage which the KJV renders "accept of the punishment of their iniquity" (Leviticus 26:41) is translated "make amends for their iniquity" (NASB, NRSV, RSV), "accept their guilt" (NKJV), and "pay for their sin" (NIV).

Usually, however, the KJV uses "accept" in an archaic sense of "implying approval and pleasure in receiving," for example in the expression "accept the person" (a translation of the Hebrew "lift up the face" of another person). In various contexts this expression means "to show favor," "be gracious to," "grant a request," or "show partiality." In 1 Samuel 25:35, David is represented as saying to Abigail, "I have accepted thy person." This is translated in the NASB and the NIV as "granted your request," in the NRSV and the RSV "granted your petition" and in the CEV, "I'll do what you asked."

"God accepteth no man's person" (Galatians 2:6, KJV) is rendered "God shows no partiality" (NASB, NRSV, RSV), "God has no favorites" (NLT), "God doesn't have any favorites!" (CEV), "God shows personal favoritism to no man" (NKJV), and "God does not judge by external appearance" (NIV). A similar KJV phrase is "God is no respecter of persons" (Acts 10:34). (See PERSON)

ACCEPTABLE

According to contemporary usage, "acceptable" has a range of meanings including "capable" or "likely to be accepted," agreeable," "well-pleasing," "barely satisfactory," or "adequate." In the KJV, however, the word means "capable of being accepted," "pleasing," "gratifying," with the implication that what is acceptable is "well-pleasing." (This is in contrast to the contemporary sense of the word which can mean barely satisfactory, i.e., less than the best.) In certain cases the contemporary versions bring out the implication of pleasure or favor: Ecclesiastes 12:10, the KJV "acceptable words"; the NASB, "delightful words"; the NRSV, RSV "pleasing words"; Isaiah 49:8, the KJV, "In an acceptable time"; the NASB, "In a favorable time"; the NRSV, RSV, "In a time of favor"; the NIV, "In the time of my favor"; Isaiah 61:2, the KJV, "the acceptable year of the LORD"; the NIV, NRSV and RSV, "the year of the LORD's favor."

In Deuteronomy 33:24, in the KJV Asher is blessed as "acceptable to his brethren"; in the CEV, NCV, NRSV and RSV as the "favorite"; in the NIV and NKJV "favored" by his brothers. In Esther 10:3, Mordecai is, according to the KJV, "accepted of the multitude of his brethren"; this is translated by the NIV and NLT as "held in high esteem" and as "popular" in the CEV, NRSV, and RSV.

In the New Testament, in 2 Corinthians 5:9, the KJV "accepted" is rendered "well pleasing" (NKJV, "Therefore we make it our aim, whether present or absent, to be well pleasing to Him"), "pleasing" (NASB) and "to please" God (CEV, NCV, NIV, NLT, NRSV, RSV).

The KJV for Ephesians 1:6 reads, "To the praise of the glory of his grace, wherein he hath made us accepted in the beloved." The NKJV retains "made us accepted in the

Beloved." The NASB, NRSV, and RSV render the final phrase describing grace as that which he "freely bestowed on us in the Beloved," the NIV as "the glorious grace, which he has freely given us in the One he loves."

ACQUAINT

In contemporary English "acquaint" means "to cause to know personally" ("I am acquainted with the Congressman"). In contrast, in the KJV "acquaint" was used in the obsolete sense of "accustom," "habituate." In Job 22:21, Eliphaz calls upon Job: "Acquaint now thyself with him, and be at peace" (KJV; "acquaint" is retained in the NKJV) translated in the NRSV and RSV as "Agree with God," in the NIV, "Submit to God," in the CEV, "Surrender to God," in the NASB, "Yield," in the NLT, "Stop quarreling with God!" In itself, that is good counsel; but in the context of Eliphaz' groundless accusations of Job (22:5–11) it suggests that he surrender his integrity.

In Ecclesiastes 2:3 "yet acquainting mine heart with wisdom" (KJV) is rendered by the NIV, NRSV, and RSV as "my mind still guiding me with wisdom."

ADDICTED

The word "addicted" is now generally used of bad habits ("addicted to drugs and alcohol"). Shakespeare uses "addict" and its cognates similarly, always of trivial or less desirable habits.

> "But, if 't be he I mean, he's very wild;
> Addicted so and so."
> *—Hamlet* (II, 1, 19)

In the sixteenth and seventeenth centuries, however, "addicted" was usually used to describe good qualities, as these KJV examples show: "they have addicted themselves to the ministry of the saints" (1 Corinthians 16:15, KJV), rendered in the contemporary versions as "devoted themselves" to the service of the saints (NASB, NIV, NKJV, NRSV, RSV); "They have done all they can for God's people" (CEV), "spending their lives in service to other Christians" (NLT).

ADMIRE, ADMIRATION

These words refer to liking and respecting someone or something very much. They were used in the seventeenth century simply to denote wonder or astonishment, without any implication of praise or approval. Thomas Fuller, the church historian, writing in 1639, said of Islam that it was "admirable how that senseless religion should gain so much ground on Christianity"—by which he meant that this fact was amazing. He elsewhere told of Cardinal Pole delivering "a dry sermon . . . many much admiring the jejuneness of his discourse"—that is, they were astonished at its emptiness. In Milton's *Paradise Lost* (Book II, line 677), Satan was confronted at the gates of hell by a monster Shape, and "the Undaunted Fiend what this might be admired"—that is, Satan wondered what this might be.

In Shakespeare's *Hamlet* (I, 2, 192), when Horatio tells Hamlet that he had seen the ghost of "the king your father," Hamlet responds with a startled exclamation of surprise, to which Horatio answers (I, 2, 195):

"Season your admiration for a while
With an attent ear, till I may deliver,
Upon the witness of these
    gentlemen,
This marvel to you."

This evidence is enough to show that when the writer of Revelation 17:6, as reported in the KJV, expressed "great admiration" for the woman arrayed in scarlet, "drunken with the blood of the saints, and with the blood of the martyrs of Jesus," he meant simply to declare his wonder and astonishment at her. The contemporary versions translate as follows: the NASB, "When I saw her, I wondered greatly"; the NRSV, "I was greatly amazed"; the NIV, "I was

greatly astonished"; the NKJV, "I marveled with great amazement."

The other occurrences are 2 Thessalonians 1:10, rendered in the KJV and NKJV as "to be admired" (NASB, NIV, NRSV, RSV "to be marveled at"); and Jude 16, in the KJV, "having men's persons in admiration because of advantage," translated as "flattering people" (NASB, NRSV, RSV) to gain an advantage; they "flatter others" (CEV, NCV, NIV, NLT) to get what they want.

ADVENTURE

"Adventure" is used as a noun today to refer to an undertaking involving excitement or risk. But from the fourteenth century and beyond it was used as a verb meaning "to venture," "to expose to danger." In the KJV of Deuteronomy 28:56, "adventure to set the sole of her foot upon the ground" is rendered in the NASB, NIV, NKJV, NRSV and RSV as "venture." Similarly, in Acts 19:31, where Paul's friends at Ephesus were "desiring him that he would not adventure himself into the theatre" (KJV), is rendered "venture" in the NASB, NIV, NKJV, NRSV, and RSV. Jotham's statement, "my father fought for you, and adventured his life far, and delivered you out of the hand of Midian," reads in the NASB, NCV, NIV, NKJV, NLT, NRSV, and RSV, "risked his life" (Judges 9:17).

ADVERTISE

The marketing and promotion of products and services that is so much part of modern life is a far cry from the language of the KJV. "Advertise" appears twice in the KJV, Numbers 24:14 and Ruth 4:4. Its meaning in the KJV is simply to tell or inform without any of its contemporary connotations of wide public notice. Balaam's statement, "I will advertise thee what this people shall do to thy people," is rendered "I will let you know" (RSV), "I will advise you" (NASB, NKJV), "let me warn you" (NIV), "let me advise you" (NRSV).

The statement of Boaz to the kinsman of

Ruth, "I thought to advertise thee," was not a threat; what he said was simply, "I thought I would tell you of it" (NRSV and RSV); "I thought I should bring this matter to your attention" (NIV); "I thought to inform you" (NASB, NKJV); "I am telling you about this" (CEV). Shakespeare uses "advertise" and "advertisement" a dozen times in this sense.

> "I have advertised him by secret
> means
> That if about this hour he make this
> way,
> Under the color of his usual game,
> He shall here find his friends with
> horse and men
> To set him free from his captivity."
> —*King Henry VI, Part III* (IV, 5, 9–13)

ADVICE, ADVISE

In contemporary English, "advice" is something that is given to help a person who is in difficulty, needs assistance, or needs to make a decision; "advise" is the verb meaning "to give advice." But in the KJV, "take advice" is used in the obsolete sense of "deliberate," "consult," "take counsel" (Judges 19:30; 2 Chronicles 25:17).

The contemporary versions in these passages use the verbs "take counsel" (NASB, NRSV, and RSV); Judges 19:30 is rendered by the NKJV as "confer," by the NIV as "Consider it!"; in 2 Chronicles 25:17 the NKJV and NIV use the verb "consult."

When the prophet Gad, in the name of the Lord, offered to David his choice of three punishments—seven years of famine, three months of flight before his enemies, or three days of pestilence—his final word was, "Now advise, and see what answer I shall return to him that sent me" (2 Samuel 24:13, KJV). The parallel account in 1 Chronicles 21:12 (KJV) has "Now advise thyself." In both accounts the verb "advise" is used in the obsolete sense of "consider and decide."

The Hebrew verbs are different; the current translations render 2 Samuel 24:13 as "consider" (NASB, NKJV, NRSV, RSV), "think it over" (NIV); 1 Chronicles 21:12 as "decide" (NCV, NIV, NRSV, RSV), "think about it and decide" (CEV), "consider" (NASB, NKJV); for both verses, the NLT has "think this over."

In the story of Nabal, Abigail, and David, the KJV and NKJV word "advice" is a translation of the Hebrew word *ta'am* which means discretion or discernment (1 Samuel 25:33). David recognizes in Abigail's plea the restraining voice of the Lord. He expresses thanks and praise for her "good sense" (CEV, NLT, NRSV), "good judgment" (NIV), "discernment" (NASB, RSV).

ADVISEMENT

In formal contexts in modern English, if people take a matter under advisement they decide that the matter needs to be considered more carefully, especially by experts. In the KJV the word is used similarly. In 1 Chronicles 12:19 the KJV reads, "the lords of the Philistines upon advisement sent him [David] away." The phrase "upon advisement" in the KJV rendering means that they consulted and took counsel together, as a result of which they reached the decision to send him away.

Contemporary translations read "after consultation" (NASB, NIV), "[the rulers of the Philistines] took counsel" (NRSV, RSV), and "by agreement" (NKJV). In current language, to have something "under advisement" usually implies more leisurely consideration than the rulers of the Philistines could give in David's case.

AFFECT

In modern English the verb "affect" means "have an influence on," or "pretend that something is natural or real" ("to affect an interest"). From the fifteenth century, the verb "affect" meant "to aim at," "aspire to," "try to obtain or do." Shakespeare used it frequently in this sense, e.g., in *Two Gentlemen of Verona* (III, 1, 81): "There is a lady of Verona here whom I affect." The OED notes that as late as 1776, Thomas Jefferson wrote in his memoirs, "He has affected to render the military independent of, and superior to, the civil power." This meaning is now obsolete.

In the KJV "affect" is used in the sense of "make a display of liking," sometimes connoting a "pretense." In this sense, the word is used three times in the KJV in Galatians 4:17–18. "They zealously affect you but not well; yea, they would exclude you, that ye might affect them. But it is good to be zealously affected always in a good thing, and not only when I am present with you."

The contemporary versions translate the verb "affect" as "be zealous" and "zealously court" (NKJV), "be zealous" [for, to win you over] (NIV), "eagerly seek" (NASB), "pay/give [a bit of] attention" (CEV), and "make much of" (NRSV, RSV).

In Acts 14:2 the KJV translation "made their minds evil affected against the brethren" is translated, "poisoned their minds against the brothers" (NIV, NRSV), "against the brethren" (NKJV, RSV), "embittered them against the brethren" (NASB), "saying all sorts of evil things about them" (NLT).

AFFECTION

The word "affection" refers today to feelings of fondness and love. From the thirteenth century, the word was applied to a mental state, and it is sometimes used in the KJV for those who are dishonorable. "Vile affections" (Romans 1:26, KJV) is translated as follows: "degrading passions" (NASB, NRSV), "dishonorable passions" (RSV), "vile passions" (NKJV), "shameful lusts" (NIV), "shameful desires" (NLT), "evil desires" (CEV). "Inordinate affection" (Colossians 3:5, KJV) is "passion" (NASB, NKJV, NRSV, RSV) and "lust" (NIV, NLT). "Affections and lusts" (Galatians 5:24, KJV) is "passions and desires" (NASB, NIV, NKJV, NLT, NRSV, RSV).

The expression "Be kindly affectioned" in the command in Romans 12:10 (KJV), "Be kindly affectioned one to another with brotherly love" is translated, "Love each other" (CEV, NCV, NLT), "love one another" (NRSV, RSV), "Be devoted to one another" (NASB, NIV), "Be kindly affectionate to one another" (NKJV).

With reference to Titus, "his inward affection is more abundant toward you" (2 Corinthians 7:15, KJV) is rendered in the contemporary versions, "his heart goes out all the more to you" (NRSV, RSV), "His affection abounds all the more toward you" (NASB), "his affections are greater for you" (NKJV), "his affection for you is all the greater" (NIV), "he cares for you more than ever" (NLT), "Titus loves all of you very much" (CEV). "Affectionately desirous" (1 Thessalonians 2:8, KJV) is translated "We loved you so much" (NIV, NLT), "So deeply do we care for you" (NRSV), "We cared so much for you" (CEV), and "Having so fond an affection for you" (NASB).

In David's statement, "because I have set my affection to the house of my God" (1 Chronicles 29:3, KJV) "affection" (also in the NKJV) is translated in the NIV and NLT as "devotion" and in the NASB as "delight."

AFFINITY

In current English "affinity" refers to a close relationship or likeness. But in the KJV it refers to a relationship by marriage, the sense derived from the Latin *affinitas*. "Solomon made affinity with Pharaoh king of Egypt" (1 Kings 3:1, KJV) is rendered in the contemporary translations: "made an alliance" (NIV, NLT), "made a marriage alliance" (NRSV, RSV), "formed a marriage alliance" (NASB), and "made a treaty" (NKJV).

So also "Jehoshaphat . . . joined affinity with Ahab" (2 Chronicles 18:1, KJV) is translated in the contemporary versions: "he allied himself" by marriage (NASB, NIV, NKJV) and "made a marriage alliance" (NRSV, RSV). (The OED lists this text as an example of affinity by inclination or attraction rather than as the marriage alliance.)

In the prayer of Ezra, "Should we again break thy commandments, and join in affinity with the people of these abominations?'' (9:14, KJV), ''join in affinity'' is rendered by the verb ''intermarry'' (NASB, NIV, NLT, NRSV, RSV) and ''join in marriage'' in the NKJV.

AFORE

This word is now archaic or used in English dialects to refer to prior time. It survives as a prefix in ''aforesaid'' and ''aforementioned.'' ''Afore'' appears seven times in the KJV. These are generally translated ''before'' or ''beforehand'' (Romans 1:2, NASB, NIV, NRSV, RSV; Romans 9:23, NASB, NKJV, NRSV) or ''long ago'' (Romans 1:2, CEV, NCV, NLT).

AFOREHAND

This archaic word for ''beforehand'' appears once in the KJV: ''she is come aforehand to anoint my body to the burying'' (Mark 14:8). The contemporary translations (NASB, NIV, NKJV, NRSV, RSV) generally render the word as ''beforehand''; the NLT has ''ahead of time.''

AFORETIME

Now archaic, ''aforetime'' means ''formerly,'' ''previously,'' or ''of old.'' It appears seven times in the KJV, and is generally rendered in the contemporary versions as ''before,'' ''formerly,'' ''previously,'' or ''long ago.'' Job 17:6, KJV has ''He hath made me also a byword of the people; and aforetime I was as a tabret.'' The Hebrew phrase which means ''before'' in the sense of ''in the presence of'' was taken by the KJV translators to mean ''before'' in the sense of ''formerly,'' and they understood the word for the act of spitting, *topheth*, to be a form of *toph*, which means tabret, timbrel, or tambourine. (See TABRET)

The contemporary translations all take the expression to refer to the act of spitting, e.g., the NRSV translates the verse: ''He has made me a byword of the peoples, and I am one before whom people spit,'' the NIV has ''a man in whose face people spit.''

AFTER

The KJV uses ''after'' in the established sense denoting a later time or following in place or order, but it also frequently uses ''after'' in the archaic sense of ''according to,'' ''like,'' or ''as.'' In these cases it usually represents the Hebrew preposition *k* or the Greek preposition *kata*. In Genesis 1 and 6—8 ''after his (their) kind(s)'' means ''according to'' its (their) kind(s), and this is the rendering that is most frequently given by the contemporary versions.

Of the many Old Testament examples, the following may be cited, giving the rendering of the KJV followed by the rendering(s) most frequently found in the contemporary versions: Exodus 21:9, ''after the manner of daughters'' (''as with a daughter,'' NRSV, RSV; ''according to the custom of daughters,'' (NASB, NKJV); Exodus 28:15, ''after the work of the ephod'' (''like the work of the ephod,'' NASB, RSV); Exodus 30:13, ''after the shekel'' (''according to the shekel,'' NASB, NKJV, NRSV, RSV); Exodus 34:27, ''after the tenor of these words'' (''in accordance with these words,'' NASB, NIV, NRSV, RSV); Numbers 4:2, ''after their families'' (''by their families,'' NASB, NKJV, RSV); 2 Kings 8:2, ''after the saying'' (''according to the word,'' NASB, NRSV, RSV); 2 Chronicles 10:14, ''after the advice'' (''according to the advice,'' NASB, NKJV); Isaiah 44:13, ''maketh it after the figure of a man'' (''like [RSV, ''into''] the figure of a man,'' NKJV, RSV; ''like a person,'' CEV, NCV).

Examples from Shakespeare are:

''frame the business after your own wisdom''

—*King Lear* (I, 2, 107)

and the Queen's word to Imogen:

''No, be assured you shall not find me, daughter,
After the slander of most stepmothers,
Evil-eyed unto you . . .''

—*Cymbeline* (I, 1, 70–72)

Among New Testament examples: Luke 2:27, "after the custom of the law" ("according to the custom of the law," NKJV, RSV); Acts 15:1, "after the manner of Moses" ("according to the custom of Moses," NASB, NKJV, NRSV, RSV); Acts 26:5, "after the most straitest sect" ("according to the strictest sect," NASB, NIV, NKJV); Romans 8:4, "after the flesh" ("according to the flesh [NIV, "sinful nature"]," NASB, NIV, NKJV, NRSV, RSV); Titus 1:1, "the truth which is after godliness" ("the truth which accords with godliness," NKJV, RSV).

In some situations this older use of "after" survives in the language of today. We still name a son after his father, or name a building after the person for whom we wish it to be a memorial. This phrasing is used in Genesis 4:17; Deuteronomy 3:14; 2 Samuel 18:18; Luke 1:59; and the contemporary versions almost invariably retain "after."

Exceptions are: Deuteronomy 3:14, NCV, "that land was named for Jair"; 2 Samuel 18:18, NRSV, "he called the pillar by his own name"; Luke 1:59, NKJV, "they would have called him by the name of his father." Exodus 25:40, KJV "after the pattern" is generally rendered "according to the pattern" in the contemporary translations.

In the description of David, "a man after mine [God's] own heart" (Acts 13:22, KJV, cf. 1 Samuel 13:14), "after" is retained in the NASB, NIV, NKJV, NLT, NRSV, RSV. The CEV has, "the kind of person who pleases me most!"; the NCV, "the kind of man I want." In "After the order of Melchizedek" (Psalm 110:4, KJV, cf. Hebrews 5:6; 7:17), the RSV retains "after"; other translations have "according to" (NASB, NKJV, NRSV), "like" (CEV, NCV), "in" ("in the order of," NIV; "in the line of," NLT).

In Hebrews 7:15–16 three occurrences of "after" are rendered by a range of expressions: the KJV "after the similitude of Melchisedec" is rendered as "like" (CEV, NCV, NIV, NLT); the KJV "after the law of a carnal commandment" is rendered "according to" (NKJV, RSV) and "on the basis

of" (NASB, NIV); the KJV "after the power of an endless life" is rendered "according to" (CEV, NKJV), "by [NRSV, "through"] the power of" (NLT, NRSV, RSV); "on the basis of" (NIV).

The adverb "after," used to indicate a later event, is translated in a variety of ways, e.g., in Genesis 33:7, KJV, "and after came Joseph near and Rachel" as "finally" (CEV, NLT, NRSV), "last of all" (NCV, NIV), "afterward" (NASB, NKJV); in 1 Kings 17:13, KJV, "and after make for thee" as "afterward" (NASB, NKJV, NLT, RSV), "afterwards" (NRSV), "then" (NCV, NIV).

AGAINST

The word "against" means "opposite," "on a background of." In a few instances in the KJV its sense may not be easily understood. In "Take all the heads of the people, and hang them up before the LORD against the sun" (Numbers 25:4), "against the sun" is rendered in the contemporary translations: "in broad daylight," (NASB, NIV, NLT) and "in [NKJV, "out in"] the sun" (NKJV, NRSV, RSV).

The instruction to Aaron, "When thou lightest the lamps, the seven lamps shall give light over against the candlestick" (Numbers 8:2), is generally rendered in the contemporary versions, "in front of the lampstand" (NCV, NIV, NKJV, NRSV, RSV). As Abigail rode on her mission of goodwill, David and his men came down, not "against her" (KJV) but "toward her" (1 Samuel 25:20, NASB, NCV, NIV, NKJV, NLT, NRSV, RSV).

The KJV "over against" is generally rendered "opposite" in the contemporary versions in Deuteronomy 34:6, 2 Samuel 16:13, 1 Kings 20:29, and Esther 5:1. In Mark's account of the crucifixion of Jesus, "the centurion, which stood over against him" (Mark 15:39, KJV), "over against" is rendered "in front of" (CEV, NASB, NCV, NIV), "facing" (NLT, NRSV, RSV), and "opposite" (NKJV). In the account of Paul's voyage to Rome, "against Cnidus" and "against Salmone" (Acts 27:7, KJV) are generally translated "off Cnidus" and "off Salmone" in the contemporary versions.

In the KJV rendering of Romans 2:5, "But after thy hardness and impenitent heart treasurest up unto thyself wrath against the day of wrath and revelation of the righteous judgment of God," "against" is replaced by "on" (CEV, NCV, NRSV, RSV), "in" (NASB, NKJV), and "for" (NIV).

The KJV uses "against" in the sense relating to time or preparation in Genesis 43:25, "against Joseph came," translated in contemporary versions as "for Joseph's coming" (NASB, NKJV, NRSV, RSV) and "for Joseph's arrival" (NIV, NLT); Exodus 7:15, "against he come," in contemporary translations as "to meet him" (NASB, NIV, NKJV, NRSV); and 2 Kings 16:11, "against king Ahaz came," in contemporary translations as "before King Ahaz came back" (CEV, NCV, NKJV), "before King Ahaz arrived" (NRSV, RSV), and "before King Ahaz returned" (NIV). Shakespeare used "against" in this sense:

> "I'll charm his eyes against she do appear."
> —*A Midsummer Night's Dream*
> (III, 2, 99)

AGONE

"Agone," meaning "ago," is an old form of the past participle of the verb "go," similar to the Old English *agan*. As early as 1300 it was contracted to "ago," and from Caxton on this has been the ordinary form in printed prose; but "agone" has remained as an archaic and poetic variant. It is used once in the KJV, "three days agone I fell sick" (1 Samuel 30:13). The same book, 9:20, has "three days ago." It seems that the choice of "agone" was for euphony, because of the succeeding vowel "I." All the contemporary translations render "agone" as "ago."

AGREE

In the KJV in the sense "to correspond," "to be similar," the verb "agree" is linked with "to." "Thou art a Galilean, and thy speech agreeth thereto" (Mark 14:70) is Tyndale's rendering, kept by subsequent versions made from the Greek. But the translations from the Latin Vulgate, Wycliffe, and Rheims do not have the last clause. Tyndale's rendering is retained in the KJV but the clause is omitted in all the contemporary versions except the NKJV, which translates it as, "and your speech shows it."

Acts 5:40, KJV reads, "And to him they agreed." In the contemporary versions this is rendered, "they agreed with him" (NKJV), "They took his advice" (NASB, RSV), "The council accepted his advice" (NLT), and "His speech persuaded them" (NIV).

AHA

This word is an interjection expressing joy, satisfaction, or triumph. This may be innocent, as in Isaiah 44:16, KJV, "he roasteth meat, and is satisfied . . . he warmeth himself and saith, Aha, I am warm, I have seen the fire." Or it may be an expression of malicious joy, of satisfaction over the misfortune of an enemy or rival, as in the psalmist's prayer that his enemies may not rejoice over him (Psalm 35:21, 25; see also Psalms 40:15; 70:3; Ezekiel 25:3; 26:2; 36:2).

In all these instances the contemporary translations generally retain the KJV, "Aha." Some contemporary versions, however, expand on and paraphrase the sense, for example, Psalm 40:15, "Let them be horrified by their shame, for they said, 'Aha! We've got him now!'" (NLT); "Embarrass and shame all those who say, 'Just look at you now!'" (CEV); Ezekiel 36:2, "This is what the Sovereign LORD says: 'Your enemies have taunted you, saying, "Aha! Now the ancient heights belong to us!"'" (NLT); "I, the LORD God, am saying: Your enemies sneered and said that you mountains belong to them" (CEV).

The Hebrew interjection thus translated is *he'ah*, which in one passage the KJV represents by "Ha, ha." This passage (Job 39:24–25) is about the war horse: "He swalloweth the ground with fierceness and rage: neither believeth he that it is the sound of the trumpet. He saith among the trumpets, Ha, ha; and he smelleth the battle afar off, the thunder of the captains, and the shouting."

The RV changed the "Ha, ha" in this passage to "Aha!" This was criticized for giving the horse a human cry. But "Ha, ha" is also human, and expresses laughter. The older translations were even more "human." Coverdale, the Great Bible, and the Bishops' Bible had the horse saying "tush." The Geneva Bible was the first to use "Ha, ha," which the KJV adopted. The Douay Bible simply used the Latin "Vah." The contemporary translations generally have, "Aha!", with the NCV, NIV, and NLT adding the verb "snorts," e.g., the NIV, "At the blast of the trumpet he snorts, 'Aha!'"

In Mark's account of the crucifixion of Jesus (15:29–30), the KJV reads, "And they that passed by railed on him, wagging their heads, and saying, Ah, thou that destroyest the temple, and buildest it in three days, Save thyself, and come down from the cross." The Greek interjection here is *oua*, which the Latin represents by *vah;* the Geneva Bible translated it by "Hey." The contemporary translations translate it as "Ha!" (CEV, NASB, NLT), "Aha!" (NKJV, NRSV, RSV), and "So!" (NIV).

ALARM

In modern English "alarm" is, firstly, a feeling of apprehension that something dangerous or unpleasant is about to happen and, secondly, an automatic device, e.g. a bell, that warns of danger. In the KJV, however, "alarm" refers to a call to arms, as in 2 Chronicles 13:12, "God himself is with us for our captain, and his priests with

sounding trumpets to cry alarm against you." In this verse, "cry alarm" is rendered in the contemporary versions as: "sound the alarm" (NASB, NKJV), "sound the call to battle" (NRSV, RSV), "sound the battle cry" (NIV), and "sound the signal" (CEV). The word "alarm" comes from the Italian *all' arme*, "To arms!"

The Mosaic Law with respect to the trumpets is given in Numbers 10:1–10, and verse 9 enjoins their use in war: "blow an alarm" (KJV), translated in the contemporary versions as: "sound an alarm" (NASB, NKJV, NRSV, RSV), "sound the alarm" (NLT), "sound a blast" (NIV), and "give a warning signal" (CEV). Shakespeare used the word "alarm" in this sense, and often spelled it "alarum."

> "Sound, sound alarum! we will rush on them."
> —*King Henry VI, Part I* (I, 2, 18)

> "Now,—when the angry trumpet sounds alarum,
> And dead men's cries do fill the empty air."
> —*King Henry VI, Part II* (V, 2, 3–4)

ALBEIT

"Albeit" is a formal or old-fashioned word which is used to mean "although" ("what redeemed the play, albeit somewhat belatedly, was the culmination of events in the final act"). It is an old word, made by combining "all" with the subjunctive mood of the verb "be" and a following subject "it." It appears twice in this sense in the KJV. In Ezekiel 13:7 the word of the Lord condemns the lying prophets who "say, The LORD saith it; albeit I have not spoken." The contemporary versions have: "but" (NASB, NKJV), "although" (RSV), "though" (NIV), "even though" (NRSV), and "when" (NLT).

Asking Philemon to receive Onesimus not just as a returned slave but as a Christian brother, Paul goes on to write: "If he hath wronged thee, or oweth thee ought, put that on mine account; I Paul have written it with mine own hand, I will repay it: albeit I do not say to thee how thou owest unto me even thine own self besides" (KJV).

The "albeit" appeared in the Geneva Bible and was accepted by the KJV translators. Tyndale had, "So that I do not saye to thee." Rheims had, "I will repay it: not to say to thee that thou owest me thine owne self also." The contemporary translations render the expression with "not to mention" (NASB, NIV, NKJV) and "say nothing about" [RSV, "of"] (NCV, NRSV, RSV), e.g., "I will repay—not to mention to you that you owe me even your own self besides" (NKJV).

ALIKE

If two or more things are alike, they are similar. The word is used in the KJV in this sense. In Ecclesiastes 11:6, the KJV has, "Whether they both shall be alike good"; the contemporary translations render this "both [NASB, "both of them"] alike will be good" (NASB, NKJV, NRSV, RSV), "both will do equally well" (NIV). The question is not whether their goodness will be in all respects identical, but whether both, the one as well as the other, will be good.

The basic idea of the Hebrew word which usually underlies the KJV use of "alike" is "together," and the KJV translates it in this way more than one hundred times. In the KJV "they lie down alike in the dust" (Job 21:26), "alike" is retained by the NKJV, NLT, NRSV, and RSV; the NASB has "together," the NIV "side by side," and the NCV "next to each other."

The KJV "all things come alike to all" (Ecclesiastes 9:2) implies the common fate of mortal human beings, a meaning that is brought out in the contemporary translations, e.g., "all share a common destiny" (NIV), "all things come alike to all" (NKJV), "the same destiny ultimately awaits everyone" (NLT), and "the same fate comes to all" (NRSV).

The KJV rendering of Psalm 33:15, "He fashioneth their hearts alike," is translated

"the hearts of [NASB, NRSV, RSV "of them"] all" (NASB, NIV, NRSV, RSV), "individually" (NKJV), and "each" (CEV). In Psalm 139:12, KJV "the darkness and the light are both alike to thee," "alike" is retained by the NASB, NKJV, and NLT; the NIV, NRSV, and RSV have "darkness is as light."

ALL

"All" is used in contemporary English to refer to the whole of something or every one of a group. As well as retaining this sense, the KJV also uses "all" in the sense of "any," as in Hebrews 7:7, "without all contradiction the less is blessed of the better," rendered by the contemporary translations as "beyond all contradiction" (NKJV), "beyond dispute" (NRSV, RSV), "without any dispute" (NASB), "without doubt" (NIV), and "without question" (NLT). In Deuteronomy 22:3, KJV, "with all lost thing of thy brother's" is translated "any lost thing" (NKJV, RSV) and with "anything" (CEV, NASB, NCV, NIV, NLT, NRSV).

The word "all" in Peter's statements, in the KJV, "we have forsaken all" (Matthew 19:27) and "we have left all" (Mark 10:28; Luke 18:28), is translated in the Matthew and Mark passages as "everything" in the CEV, NASB, NCV, NIV, NLT, NRSV, and RSV; the NKJV retains "all" in both passages. In Luke, the KJV "all" is retained by the NIV and the NKJV. The CEV and NCV have "everything" and the NLT, NRSV, and RSV translate the phrase as "we have left our homes"; the NASB, "we have left our own homes."

The intensive expression "all manner of" is frequently used in the KJV, for example, 1 Peter 1:15, "in all manner of conversation." This is rendered "in all your conduct" in the NKJV, NRSV, and RSV; "in all your behavior" in the NASB; and as "in everything you do" in the NLT.

Occasionally the KJV introduces ambiguity by the position it gives to the word "all." It represents Jesus as saying when he offered the cup to his disciples at the Last Supper, "Drink ye all of it" (Matthew 26:27).

Jesus did not tell his disciples to drink all of the contents of the cup; he invited all of them to drink, a meaning that was expressed in some of the earlier English translations. Tyndale had, "Drink of it every one." The Geneva Bible had, "Drink ye every one of it." The contemporary translations have, "Drink from [RSV, "of"] it, all of you" (NASB, NIV, NKJV, NRSV, RSV). The NCV has, "Every one of you drink this"; the NLT, "Each of you drink from it."

In James 3:2 the KJV reads, "For in many things we offend all." That seems to mean that we are offensive to everybody. This is rendered, "we all [NRSV, "all of us"] make many mistakes" (NCV, NLT, NRSV, RSV); "we all stumble in many ways" [NKJV, "things"] (NASB, NIV, NKJV); "all of us do many wrong things" (CEV).

ALL IS VANITY
See VANITY.

ALL THE DAYS OF ONE'S LIFE
See DAYS OF ONE'S LIFE.

ALL THINGS IN COMMON
See THINGS IN COMMON.

ALL TO

The KJV records that when Abimelech approached the door of the tower of Thebez to set it on fire, "a certain woman cast a piece of a millstone upon Abimelech's head, and all to brake his skull" (Judges 9:53). Modern readers, unless they are acquainted with Old and Middle English, are not sure what the last clause means. Does it state the woman's purpose or tell the result of her action? If the result, what was it? Does "all to brake" mean "almost broke" or "quite broke"?

Referring to the expression in Judges 9:53, the OED notes that this was "etymologically and historically all-to-brake, i.e., 'all-to-pieces-broke', but may have been understood as all-to brake, i.e., 'altogether' or 'completely broke'"—cf. the prefix

"to-," like the German "*zer-*" and the Latin and English "dis-," expressing separation, and the archaic verb "to-break" meant break asunder or in pieces.

This prefix came also to be used with verbs containing no idea of separation, and with these verbs it simply emphasized or intensified their meaning—for example "to-establish" meant establish perfectly or entirely. The word "all" was often used with the prefix "to-," as adding further emphasis or intensity. In time, from the sixteenth century, "all to" and "all-to" began to be regarded as adverbs meaning completely or entirely.

A literal translation of the Hebrew of Judges 9:53 is "crushed his skull," and the NASB, NCV, NKJV, NLT, NRSV, and RSV all have "crushed [NASB, "crushing"] his skull"; the CEV and NIV have "cracked his skull."

Coverdale's rendering of Proverbs 6:15 was, "Sudenly shal he be al tobroken, and not be healed." The KJV translators did not retain the "all to" expression in this verse, which they rendered: "suddenly shall he be broken without remedy"; the contemporary versions translate by "broken" (NASB, NKJV, RSV) or "destroyed" (NIV, NLT), and the noun "damage" (NRSV), and with, the adverbial clause, retaining the KJV translation "without remedy" (NIV, NKJV), or "beyond repair" (NRSV) and "beyond healing" (RSV). The CEV renders the whole expression, "left without a hope."

Milton wrote of Wisdom that her wings "were altoruffled, and sometimes impaired" (*Comus*, 380). In Bunyan's *Pilgrim's Progress* (1684), Christiana tells the Interpreter about the efforts of Mrs. Timorous to persuade her not to undertake the journey, and says, "She all-to-be-fooled me."

There are treatments of this now obsolete usage in the OED, under *all*, C, 14 and 15; *to-, prefix²*; and *to-break*.

ALLEGE

To "allege" now means "to claim" or "to assert," especially without proof ("he is alleged to have collaborated with the company's competitors"), but in the sixteenth century it meant to mention or cite as a source of authority, to adduce evidence. That is what it means in Acts 17:2–3, where we are told by the KJV that for three weeks Paul "reasoned with them out of the scriptures, opening and alleging, that Christ must needs have suffered, and risen again from the dead."

The contemporary translations for the verb "allege" generally use the verb "prove" (NCV, NIV, NLT, NRSV, RSV). For "alleging" the NASB has "giving evidence" and the NKJV "demonstrating."

ALLIED

If people or things are "allied" to others, they are joined in an alliance of kinship, marriage, or treaty or are associated with or linked in some way. The KJV uses the word in this way. Nehemiah 13:4 states that Eliashib, a priest in the time of Nehemiah, "was allied unto Tobiah," the Ammonite who did all that he could to hinder Nehemiah's work. This alliance probably refers to some connection by marriage. Both Tobiah and his son had married women of Judah (6:17–19), and Eliashib's grandson had married the daughter of Sanballat, Tobiah's associate.

Yet just how Eliashib and Tobiah were connected, and to what extent they were allied, are nowhere stated. The Hebrew simply means "near to," in the sense of a close personal relationship. The contemporary versions refer to the relationship in different ways: the NKJV retains "allied with"; other translations are: "related to" (NASB, NRSV), "a relative of" (CEV, NLT), "connected with" (RSV), "closely associated with" (NIV), and "friendly with" (NCV).

ALLOW

In contemporary English "allow" means "to permit." But in the sixteenth and seventeenth centuries this verb also had the meaning "to approve" or "to accept," a

meaning derived from the Latin *allaudare,* "to praise." Jesus' accusation (Luke 11:48), "ye allow the deeds of your fathers," does not imply any power to permit or prohibit what their fathers did. The contemporary versions generally use the verb "approve" (NASB, NCV, NIV, NKJV, NRSV); the RSV has "consent"; the NLT, "agree with"; the CEV, "think that was the right thing."

When the KJV translators used the word "allow" in Paul's vivid description of the predicament of the sinner (Romans 7:15, KJV), "that which I do I allow not: for what I would, that do I not; but what I hate, that do I," they used it in the sense of approve. Every contemporary translation uses the verb "understand," e.g., "For what I am doing, I do not understand" (NASB, NKJV).

Paul's statement in 1 Thessalonians 2:4, KJV, "but as we were allowed of God to be put in trust with the gospel," does not mean merely that God permitted them to be entrusted with the preaching of the gospel, but that they had been "approved by God" (NASB, NIV, NKJV, NLT, NRSV, RSV). The CEV and NCV change the passive to an active verb: "God was pleased to trust us" (CEV) and "We speak the Good News because God tested us and trusted us to do it" (NCV).

Romans 14:22, KJV has, "Happy is he that condemneth not himself in that thing which he alloweth." For the verb "allow" here, the NASB, NIV, NKJV, NRSV, and RSV all use the verb "approve." Acts 24:15, KJV has, "And have hope toward God, which they themselves also allow, that there shall be a resurrection of the dead." For the verb "allow" here, the NKJV, NRSV, and RSV all have "accept"; the NASB translates, "having a hope in God, which these men cherish themselves"; and the NIV translates, "I have the same hope in God as these men."

ALPHA AND OMEGA

The alpha and omega of something is its start and end, its first and last, including its most important aspects. The expression occurs four times in the KJV, in Revelation at 1:8, 11; 21:6; and 22:13, to refer to God's eternity. The expression denotes the first and last letters of the Greek alphabet. At all the references in Revelation, except 1:11, the contemporary versions retain "Alpha" and "Omega"; at 1:11, all the contemporary versions except the NKJV omit this expression. Before the KJV, Wycliffe and Tyndale had used this phrasing.

The expression also occurs in literature, especially from the nineteenth century onwards and in secular contexts. For example, in *Jane Eyre* (chap. 37) by Charlotte Brontë, Rochester confesses that "the Alpha and Omega of my heart's wishes broke involuntarily from my lips in the words— 'Jane! Jane! Jane!' "

ALWAY

Originally spelled as two words ("all way"), this term was probably first used to refer to the space traversed, but was "already in the oldest Eng. transferred to an extent of time" (OED). "Alway" now exists only in poetic and archaic use, being replaced by "always" in standard usage.

In the KJV, "alway" appears twenty-three times and "always" sixty-two times. Attempts have been made to show that the KJV translators observed a distinction, writing "Lo, I am with you alway" (Matthew 28:20) and "without ceasing I make mention of you always in my prayers" (Romans 1:9). But in most cases no such distinction can be discerned. The KJV has "set upon the table shewbread before me alway" (Exodus 25:30) and "cause the lamp to burn always" (27:20). It has "The Cretians are alway liars" (Titus 1:12) and "I foresaw the Lord always before my face" (Acts 2:25).

In the contemporary translations "always" is generally used; alternatives used occasionally include "at all times" (Exodus 25:30, NASB, NIV) and "continually" (Exodus 27:20, NASB, NKJV, NLT, RSV). In Romans 1:9 the contemporary translations include "I never stop praying for you" (CEV) and "Day and night I bring you and your needs in

prayer to God" (NLT). Shakespeare did not use "alway."

AMAZE

In contemporary English, to "amaze" is "to surprise greatly," but from the thirteenth century onwards, to "amaze" was "to stun or stupefy," as by a blow on the head, "to bewilder or perplex," or "to overcome with fear," "to terrify." In accounts of old battles many a warrior fell to the ground "amazed." He was not astonished; he was knocked cold. Isaak Walton's *The Compleat Angler* (1653) warns that "the sight of any shadow amazes the fish."

The four Hebrew verbs which the KJV represents by "amazed" mean "to be dismayed," "terrified," "dumbfounded," "appalled." Contemporary translations use these stronger terms in the Old Testament. Examples are: Exodus 15:15 and Judges 20:41, in which contemporary translations generally render the KJV "amazed" as "dismayed" (e.g., NRSV, RSV) or "terrified" (e.g., NIV, NLT). The NKJV for Judges 20:41 reads, "The men of Benjamin panicked." In Ezekiel 32:10, the NASB, NIV, NRSV, and RSV have "appalled"; the CEV has "horrified"; the NLT, "bring terror"; and the NKJV, "astonished."

In Isaiah 13:8 for KJV, "they shall be amazed one at another," the contemporary versions have a variety of translations: "They will look aghast at one another" [NIV, "at each other"] (NIV, NRSV, RSV); "they will stare at each other with horror on their faces" (CEV); "they look helplessly at one another" (NLT); NASB has "in astonishment" and the NKJV retains the KJV "amazed."

In the New Testament, the KJV generally uses "amaze," "amazement," "astonish," and "astonishment" with the contemporary sense. Two passages in the KJV are exceptions: in the statement that Jesus in Gethsemane "began to be sore amazed, and to be very heavy" (Mark 14:33), "sore amazed" is rendered "sad [NCV, "very sad"] and troubled" (CEV, NCV); "very [NIV, "deeply"]; RSV, "greatly"] distressed and troubled" (NASB, NIV, RSV); "troubled and deeply distressed" (NKJV); "distressed and agitated" (NRSV); and "filled with horror and deep distress" (NLT).

Peter's counsel to the women to be "not afraid with any amazement" (1 Peter 3:6) is rendered, "don't let anything frighten you" (CEV); "let nothing terrify you" (RSV); "without being frightened by any fear" (NASB); "do not give way to fear" (NIV); "never let fears alarm you" (NRSV); and "not afraid with any terror" (NKJV).

AMBASSAGE

This is an archaic word for a group of people sent on a mission. In the KJV it appears in Luke 14:32. The same Greek word is used in Luke 19:14, where the KJV translates it by "message." The contemporary translations render this word in both contexts as "delegation" (NASB, NIV, NKJV, NLT, NRSV), "embassy" (RSV), and "messengers" (CEV).

AMERCE

"Amerce" is an archaic word meaning "to punish by an arbitrary fine," the amount of which is stated by a court. It derives from the Old French . . . à merci. Shakespeare has the angry Prince Escalus say in *Romeo and Juliet* (III, 1, 195):

"But I'll amerce you with so strong
  a fine
That you shall all repent the loss
  of mine."

In the one passage where it occurs in the KJV, "they shall amerce him in an hundred shekels of silver" (Deuteronomy 22:19), there is nothing arbitrary about the fine. It is part of the Deuteronomic code of law, which prescribes the exact amount to be imposed under certain conditions. The NASB, NIV, NKJV, NLT, NRSV, and RSV all have the verb "fine."

AMIABLE

Someone who is described today as "amiable" is friendly and pleasant. In the sixteenth and seventeenth centuries, however, it was applied to things as well as to people. "They keep their churches so cleanly and amiable" is a quotation from Howell (1644) cited by the OED. This echoes the one appearance of the word in the KJV: "How amiable are thy tabernacles, O LORD of hosts!" (Psalm 84:1).

All the contemporary versions translate "amiable" as "lovely"; Moffatt has "dear." The Rheims New Testament had "whatsoever holy, whatsoever amiable" in Philippians 4:8; the KJV has "whatsoever things are pure, whatsoever things are lovely." The contemporary versions (NASB, NIV, NKJV, NLT, RSV) generally have "lovely"; the CEV has "friendly"; the NCV has "beautiful"; and the NRSV has "pleasing."

ANCIENT

"Ancient" is used in the Old Testament, as in literature generally, to refer to times long past and to the people who lived in those times. Generally the contemporary translations retain the KJV "ancient" in "ancient mountains" (Deuteronomy 33:15), "ancient times" (Isaiah 46:10), "ancient kings" (Isaiah 19:11), "an ancient nation" (Jeremiah 5:15), "the ancient landmark" (Proverbs 22:28).

The NCV simplifies, with "old" for Deuteronomy 33:15, Proverbs 22:28, and Jeremiah 5:15; "a long time ago" (Isaiah 46:10); and "the old family of kings" (Isaiah 19:11). In the KJV "the proverb of the ancients" (1 Samuel 24:13) is rendered "old proverb" in the CEV and NLT and "old saying" in the NCV and NIV.

The KJV also uses "ancient" to refer to older people. For example, the "ancient men" of Ezra 3:12 were "old men" (NASB, NKJV, RSV), "older priests" (CEV, NCV, NIV, NLT), "old people" (NRSV) who had seen the first house of God and wept with joy at the laying of the foundation for the second. In Isaiah 3:5, KJV, "The child shall behave himself proudly against the ancient," "the ancient" is rendered "the elder" (NASB, NKJV, NRSV, RSV), "the elders" (CEV), "the old" (NIV), "older people" (NCV), and "authority" (NLT).

In Psalm 119:100, KJV "I understand more than the ancients," "the ancients" (retained by the NKJV) is rendered "the aged" (NASB, NRSV, and RSV), "elders" (NIV, NLT), "older leaders" (NCV), and "those who have lived a long time" (CEV). Similarly, in Job's statement, "With the ancient is wisdom" (12:12), "the ancient" is rendered "the aged" (NIV, NLT, NRSV, RSV), "aged men" (NASB), "older people" (NCV), and "those who have lived a long time" (CEV).

In the book of the Apocrypha entitled "The History of Susanna," the KJV introduces "two of the ancients of the people," and refers to them as "ancient judges," in verse 5. But in verse 8 and thereafter they are "the two elders" or "the elders." The same Greek word, *presbuteros*, is used in verses 5 and 8 and all the other cases in the book of Susanna. The RSV and NRSV have "elders" throughout.

"Ancient of days" appears in the vision of Daniel 7, first as an anthropomorphic description (v. 9), and then as a title (vv. 13, 22), of God. This translation of the Aramaic phrase came from the Geneva Bible, was adopted by the KJV translators, and has entered into English literature and hymnology. Notable hymns which contain this expression include Robert Grant's "O Worship the King"; Charles Wesley's "Come, Thou Almighty King"; William Cullen Byrant's "Ancient of days, except thou deign"; and Bishop William C. Doane's "Ancient of Days, who sittest throned in glory."

"Ancient of Days" is retained by the NASB, NIV, NKJV, and RSV (lowercase "ancient of days," Daniel 7:9, RSV) and is also rendered the "Ancient One" (NLT, NRSV); the "Eternal God" (CEV); and "God, who has been alive forever" (NCV). These translations are con-

sonant with other Old Testament passages, such as Job 36:26; Psalms 90 and 102:24–27; and Isaiah 41:4 that describe the eternity of God.

AND, AND IF

"And" is now used as a coordinating conjunction. In a now obsolete use, "and" was a conditional conjunction; when so used "and" means "if"; it is sometimes strengthened by adding "if," so that "and if" constitutes a repetitious, double-barreled introduction to the supposition or condition. The OED gives examples from Shakespeare of the use of both "and" and "and if" in the sense of "if":

"And you will not, sir, I'll take my heels."
—*Comedy of Errors* (I, 2, 94)

"A sheep doth very often stray,
And if the shepherd be awhile away.
—*Two Gentlemen of Verona* (I, 1, 75)

In the 1525 edition of Tyndale's New Testament, the last sentence of Matthew 19:17 reads, "But and thou wilt enter into life, keep the commandments." In the revised edition of 1534, Tyndale omitted the "and," changing the rendering to "But if thou wilt." In the 1525 edition Matthew 6:14–15 read: "For and if ye shall forgive other men their trespasses, your father in heaven shall also forgive you. But and ye will not forgive men their trespasses, no more shall your father forgive your trespasses."

This rendering was retained in 1534, except that "your heavenly father" was substituted for "your father in heaven." The KJV and all of the contemporary translations for Matthew 6:14–15 and 19:17 have simply "if."

The expression "But and if" is used by the KJV in five passages: "But and if that evil servant shall say in his heart" (Matthew 24:48); "But and if that servant say in his heart" (Luke 12:45); "But and if we say" (Luke 20:6); "But and if thou marry" (1 Corinthians 7:28); "But and if ye suffer" (1 Peter 3:14). Generally, the contemporary translations have simply "but if" for the first three verses, although the CEV, NCV, and NIV have "but suppose" for the verses in the Gospels. For 1 Peter 3:14, all the contemporary translations except the CEV have "but even if"; the CEV has simply, "even if."

The conditional "and" may be used with a concessive force, meaning "even if" or "though." Tyndale has the example: "that they might touch, and it were but the edge of his vesture" (Mark 6:56). The "and it were but" was retained by subsequent sixteenth-century versions until the Rheims New Testament, which was simply "but." The KJV has "if it were but," and the RSV and the NRSV "that they might touch even the fringe" of his garment; the NIV, "touch even the edge of his cloak"; the NASB and NKJV, "might just touch the fringe" [NKJV, "the hem"]; the NLT, "at least touch the fringe." The Greek word is *k'an*, which means "even if."

In Acts 5:15, KJV, "they brought forth the sick into the streets, and laid them on beds and couches, that at the least the shadow of Peter passing by might overshadow some of them," the English versions from Tyndale on translate *k'an* by some form of "at least." The NASB, NCV, and RSV have "at least his shadow might fall on."

The conditional "and" may appear as "an." Some of the examples cited in the OED are:

"There, an 't shall please you."
    —*Love's Labour's Lost* (V, 2, 584)

"If an she be a rebel."
    —Fielding, *Tom Jones* (II, 2, 154)

"But an if this will not do."
    —Coleridge, *Sibylline Leaves* (273)

In the KJV, however, it is consistently spelled "and."

ANGLE

As a noun, an "angle" in contemporary English is a V-shaped corner between two lines or surfaces that is measured in degrees. But in the KJV "angle" is used in the sense of "a fishhook," a meaning that can be traced back to about the ninth century. "All they that cast angle into the brooks" (Isaiah 19:8, KJV) refers, according to the contemporary translations, to those "who cast hooks" (NIV, NKJV, NRSV), "cast a line" (NASB), or "fish with hooks" (NLT). In "They take up all of them with the angle" (Habakkuk 1:15, KJV) "angle" is translated "hook" (NASB, NKJV, NRSV, RSV) and "hooks" (NCV, NIV, NLT).

The Hebrew word for "angle" is the one which the KJV, NKJV, and NLT translate "hook" in Job 41:1, KJV, "Canst thou draw out leviathan with an hook?" All other contemporary translations have "fishhook." The English word "angle" came to be used for the rod and line as well, and was in this sense used by Shakespeare in Cleopatra's speech:

"Give me mine angle,—we'll to the
    river: there,
My music playing far off, I will
    betray
Tawny-finn'd fishes; my bended
    hook shall pierce
Their slimy jaws; and, as I draw
    them up,
I'll think them every one an Antony,
And say 'Ah, ha! you're caught.'"
    —*Antony and Cleopatra* (II, 5, 10–
                                                                    15)

ANON

In contemporary English, "anon" is used as an abbreviation of "anonymous" and also as an adverb to mean "soon," "presently," or "later." In the KJV, "anon" meant "immediately," e.g., in Mark 1:30, KJV, "But Simon's wife's mother lay sick of a fever, and anon they tell him of her." The modern reader could get the impression that they did some visiting first, but the sense is that they told Jesus about her "immediately" (NASB, RSV), "at once" (NKJV, NRSV), or "right away" (NLT).

In Matthew's account of the parable of the sower, Jesus' statement concerning the hearer who is like stony ground (13:20–21) reads in the KJV: "But he that received the seed into stony places, the same is he that heareth the word, and anon with joy receiveth it; Yet hath he not root in himself, but dureth for a while: for when tribulation or persecution ariseth because of the word, by and by he is offended."

The Greek adverb for "anon" and "by and by" in each of these verses is *euthus*, which means "immediately." The same adverb appears in the corresponding verses of Mark's account, 4:16–17, where the KJV translates it in both cases by "immediately." The use of "anon" and "by and by" in Matthew goes back to Tyndale's translation, which was retained by subsequent versions.

The contemporary versions generally have "immediately"; or the expression is recast with the adverb "quickly," e.g., "When trouble or persecution comes because of the word, he quickly falls away" (Matthew 13:21, NIV).

Tyndale also gives an early example of the use of "anon" which gradually changed its meaning from "immediately" to "soon" or "after a while." It is in Revelation 11:14, which he translated: "The seconde woo is past, and beholde the thyrd woo wyll come anon." Here the Greek adverb is *tachu*, which means "quickly"; and here the KJV did not follow Tyndale, but used "quickly." The KJV, NASB, and NKJV retain "quickly"; the CEV, NCV, NIV, and RSV have "soon"; the NRSV "very soon."

"Anon" was a favorite word with Shakespeare. In the drinking scene at the Boar's Head tavern, *King Henry IV, Part I* (II, 4), he uses it sixteen times for the response of a servant to a call for immediate attention.

ANOTHER

This word means "an additional one of the same sort" or "one that is different." Two notable examples of the use of "another" in these distinct senses are 2 Corinthians 11:4 and Galatians 1:6–7. These passages read in the KJV: "For if he that cometh preacheth another Jesus, whom we have not preached, or if ye receive another spirit, which ye have not received, or another gospel, which ye have not accepted, ye might well bear with him." "I marvel that ye are so soon removed from him that called you into the grace of Christ unto another gospel: Which is not another; but there be some that trouble you, and would pervert the gospel of Christ."

In 2 Corinthians 11:4, the NASB, NKJV, NRSV, and RSV translate "another" (NIV, "other") where the Greek has *allos*, and "different" where the Greek has *heteros*, e.g., "For if he who comes preaches another Jesus whom we have not preached, or if you receive a different spirit which you have not received, or a different gospel which you have not accepted—you may well put up with it!"

In Galatians 1:6–7, the contemporary versions generally have "different" for the Greek *heteros* and "another" for the Greek *allos*, e.g., "I am astonished that you are so quickly deserting the one who called you in the grace of Christ and are turning to a different gospel—not that there is another gospel" (NRSV). There are also other renderings for the Greek *allos*, e.g., Galatians 1:7, NIV, "which is really no gospel at all"; CEV, "there is really only one true message."

Examples of the use of the KJV "another" in contexts which modern English expresses differently are: "divided them in the midst, and laid each piece one against another," Genesis 15:10; contemporary versions generally translate as "opposite"; "every one helped to destroy another," 2 Chronicles 20:23; contemporary versions translate as "one another" (NASB, NIV, NKJV, NRSV, RSV) or "each other" (NCV, NLT); "eat every one the flesh of another," Zechariah 11:9; contemporary versions translate as "one another" (CEV, NASB, NIV, NRSV, RSV) or "each other" (NCV, NKJV, NLT).

ANSWER

The expression "answered and said" or "answered, saying" appears frequently in the KJV. The OED says that it is archaic, and that it is "a Hellenism of the New Testament"; but it was a common Hebrew phrase, which passed into the Greek of the New Testament by way of the Septuagint. Of the contemporary translations, only the NKJV and the RSV retain the expression "answered and said" in, e.g., Numbers 22:18; 1 Samuel 4:17; and 1 Kings 3:27.

Both in the Hebrew and in the Greek the word for "answered" may be used in cases where no prior question or charge or remark is recorded. In these cases the "answer" is not to anything that has been said, but is called forth by some factor or circumstance in the situation. Examples are the accounts of the five spies inciting their fellow tribesmen to rob Micah (Judges 18:14), the angel at the empty tomb (Matthew 28:5), Peter's question to Sapphira (Acts 5:8), and the elder's question in Revelation 7:13.

The contemporary versions usually eliminate "answered" in such cases; but the NKJV retains "answered" in all these instances. In Luke 7:40, where Jesus speaks in response to Simon's unspoken thought, the NASB, NIV, NLT, and RSV use the verb "answer," e.g., the NLT, "Then Jesus spoke up and answered his thoughts."

ANY

With reference to people, the word "any" may refer to any one person or any number of people. In Acts 9:2, the KJV has "any of this way." Although the context makes it clear that a plural is referred to, most contemporary translations retain "any," adding "belonged" (NIV, NRSV) or "belonging" (NASB) to the Way, or "any followers" (NCV, NLT) of the Way. In Mark 11:25, KJV, "When ye stand praying, forgive, if he have ought against any," the Greek is singular, and most contemporary versions translate this as "anyone."

Acts 4:34, KJV, "Neither was there any among them that lacked" is generally rendered in the contemporary translations, "There was not a needy person [NIV, "There were no needy persons"] among them" (NASB, NIV, NRSV, RSV). First Corinthians 1:15, KJV, "Lest any should say that I had baptized in mine own name," leaves the number of "any" indeterminate. The NASB, NCV, NIV, and NRSV rephrase the "lest any" expression to "so [NASB, NCV, NRSV, "so that"] no one."

In James 5:19, KJV, "If any of you do err from the truth," the word "any" is singular and this is brought out in the contemporary translations: "if anyone among you" (NKJV, NLT, NRSV); "if one of you" (NCV, NIV).

ANY MAN

See NO MAN.

ANY THING

This term is used as an adverb in the KJV of Judges 11:25, "And now art thou any thing better than Balak?" The contemporary translations render the KJV "any thing better" as "any better" (NASB, NCV, NKJV, NLT, NRSV, RSV) or, simply, "better" (CEV, NIV).

In Numbers 17:13, the KJV "Whosoever cometh any thing near unto the tabernacle of the LORD shall die" is expressed by a literal translation of the repetition which is in the Hebrew, as in the NASB and RSV, "Everyone [RSV, "Every one"] who comes near, who comes near to the tabernacle" or with the adverb "even" to show emphasis: "Anyone [NKJV, "Whoever"] who even comes near" (NCV, NIV, NKJV); "Everyone who even comes close" (NLT).

Paul's statement before Festus (Acts 25:8,

KJV), "Neither against the law of the Jews, neither against the temple, nor yet against Caesar, have I offended any thing at all," is recast in the contemporary versions: "nor against Caesar have I offended in anything at all" (NKJV); "I have in no way committed an offense" (NRSV); "I have committed no offense" (NASB); "I have done nothing wrong" (NCV, NIV).

APOTHECARY

In contemporary English, this word refers to a person who prepares and sells drugs for medicinal purposes. In the KJV the word refers to a perfume maker and occurs six times: Exodus 30:25, 35; 37:29; Nehemiah 3:8; Ecclesiastes 10:1. In the contemporary versions, it is generally rendered as "perfumer"; the NLT has "incense maker" at Exodus 30:35 and Exodus 37:29; for Nehemiah 3:8 the CEV and NCV have "perfume maker" and the NIV, "one of the perfume-makers."

APPARENTLY, EVIDENTLY

Originally these were strong words referring to sight. They meant "visibly," "manifestly," "clearly," "plainly," "distinctly." But usage has changed the meaning of both words, so that "apparently" may now mean "seemingly," and "evidently" may be used in cases of inference as well as with respect to the presence of visible signs.

In Shakespeare's *Comedy of Errors* (IV, 1, 78) Angelo angrily orders:

"arrest him, officer.—
I would not spare my brother in this case,
If he should scorn me so apparently."

Hobbes, in *Government and Society* (1651), refers to "the Prophets . . . who saw not God apparently like unto Moses."

But the statement that God "apparently" spoke to Moses (Numbers 12:8, KJV) means to most people today that he only seemed

to do so. The contemporary versions translate this as "clearly" (NCV, NIV, NRSV, RSV); "perfectly clear" (CEV); "openly" (NASB); "plainly" (NKJV); "directly" (NLT).

In the statement about Cornelius, "He saw in a vision evidently about the ninth hour of the day an angel of God coming in" (Acts 10:3, KJV), "evidently" is generally translated as "clearly" by the contemporary versions; the NIV has "distinctly."

In Galatians 3:1, KJV, "before whose eyes Jesus Christ hath been evidently set forth, crucified among you," "evidently set forth" is translated as "clearly portrayed" (NIV, NKJV); "publicly portrayed" (NASB, RSV); "publicly exhibited" (NRSV); the NLT paraphrases: "For you used to see the meaning of Jesus Christ's death as clearly as though I had shown you a signboard with a picture of Christ dying on the cross."

APPLE OF ONE'S EYE

If one or something is the "apple of one's eye," he or it is a very precious or treasured possession. The apple was a metaphor for the pupil of the eye, since both were round. The association of the eye—itself very precious—with a person or thing that is highly valued lies behind this expression. The phrase occurs three times in the KJV, at Deuteronomy 32:10, Psalm 17:8, and Proverbs 7:2.

At these verses the NIV, NKJV, NRSV, and RSV retain the KJV "apple of his eye" with minor stylistic modifications; the NASB retains it for the two final references and translates Deuteronomy 32:10 as "the pupil of His eye"; and the NLT has "apple of your eye" at Psalm 17:8.

Contemporary paraphrases include: Deuteronomy 32:10, "God became your fortress, protecting you as though you were his own eyes"(CEV); "He surrounded them and brought them up, guarding them as those he loved very much" (NCV); Proverbs 7:2, "Guard my teachings as your most precious possession" (NLT).

APPOINT

In contemporary English, to appoint someone to a job is formally to choose that person for the post. It can also mean officially "to set or arrange," e.g., a date. In the KJV, "appoint" is used as a translation for thirty different Hebrew words and twelve different Greek verbs which cover such meanings as "to grant," "to determine," "to establish," "to ordain," as well as the contemporary meanings of "to choose," "to arrange."

For example, Laban says to Jacob, "Appoint me thy wages" (Genesis 30:28, KJV), generally translated "name" in the contemporary versions; Solomon asks Hiram to "appoint" the wages to be paid to his men (1 Kings 5:6, KJV), translated "set" in the NIV, NRSV, and RSV and "say" in the CEV, NASB, and NKJV. In 2 Samuel 15:15, David's servants declare that they are ready to do whatever "the king shall appoint" (KJV); for the verb "appoint" the contemporary versions use the verb "choose" (NASB, NIV); "decide" (NRSV, RSV); and "say" (CEV, NCV).

In 2 Samuel 17:14 the KJV "appointed" in "the LORD had appointed to defeat" is translated "ordained" (NASB, NRSV, RSV), "decided" (CEV), "planned" (NCV), "determined" (NIV), "purposed" (NKJV), and "arranged" (NLT). "To appoint unto them that mourn in Zion" (Isaiah 61:3, KJV) is, in the contemporary versions, to "grant" (NASB, RSV), "provide for" (NIV, NRSV), "help" (NCV), and "console" (NKJV).

The six hundred Danites, "appointed with weapons of war," (Judges 18:11, 16, KJV) are "armed," according to most of the contemporary versions.

In "Appointed to death" (Psalm 102:20, KJV), "appointed" is retained by the NKJV and translated "doomed" (CEV, NASB, NRSV, RSV), "condemned" (NIV, NLT), and "sentenced" (NCV). In "Appointed to death" in the KJV of 1 Corinthians 4:9 "appointed" is "condemned" (NASB, NIV, NKJV, NLT); "sentenced" (NCV, NRSV, RSV); the CEV paraphrases the whole expression as "We are like prisoners on their way to death."

In "God hath not appointed us to wrath" (1 Thessalonians 5:9, KJV), "appointed" is translated "destined" (NASB, NRSV, RSV), "decided" (NLT), "intend" (CEV); the NIV and NKJV retain the verb "appoint." In "Appoint him his portion with the hypocrites" (Matthew 24:51, KJV; compare Luke 12:46) "appoint" is retained by the NKJV but rendered "assign" (NASB, NIV), "put" (NRSV, RSV), "send . . . away" (NCV), and "banish" (NLT).

In Job 7:1 and 14:14 the KJV phrase "appointed time" is an erroneous translation for the Hebrew word which means "warfare," which is so translated in the KJV of Isaiah 40:2. The verses in Job are rendered as follows: Job 7:1, "hard service" (NIV, NKJV, NRSV, RSV), "struggle" (NLT); Job 14:14; "struggle" (NASB, NCV, NLT), "hard service" (NIV, NKJV), "service" (NRSV, RSV).

APPOINTMENT

An appointment today is the choice of a person to a particular job ("appointment to the post of professor") or an arrangement to meet someone ("an appointment with your accountant"). In the KJV an "appointment" is "a request," "a direction," or "an agreement." In "That which they have need of . . . according to the appointment of the priests which are at Jerusalem" (Ezra 6:9, KJV), "appointment" is translated by the noun "request" in the NKJV and by the verb "request" (NASB, NIV), "require" (NRSV, RSV), and "need" (CEV, NLT).

In "At the appointment of Aaron and his sons" (Numbers 4:27, KJV) "appointment" is translated "command" (NRSV, RSV) and "direction" (NIV). In "By the appointment of Absalom" (2 Samuel 13:32, KJV), "appointment" is translated "command" (NKJV, RSV), "intent" (NASB), "expressed intention" (NIV).

Job's three friends "made an appointment together" (Job 2:11, KJV) to come to comfort him. The expression "made an appointment together" is retained by the NASB and the NKJV. The other contemporary versions have "agreed to [NCV, "agreed to meet and"] visit" (CEV, NCV), "meet together" (NRSV), and "meet together by agreement" (NIV). The Hebrew verb used here is translated "let us meet together" in two passages in Nehemiah (6:2, 10, KJV), translated as "meet" or "meet together" in the contemporary versions.

It occurs also in Amos 3:3, KJV: "Can two walk together, except they be agreed?" The NASB, NRSV, and RSV translate this final clause as "unless they have made an appointment?" The other contemporary versions use the verb "agree": "without agreeing to meet?" (CEV); "unless they are agreed?" (NKJV); "unless they have agreed to do so?" (NIV); "without agreeing on the direction?" (NLT).

APPREHEND

The word "apprehend" today means "to arrest a person in the name of the law" and "to understand." In the KJV, "apprehend" is used in the senses of "to arrest someone" and also in the now obsolete sense of "to take possession of."

Examples of the use of "apprehend" in the sense of "arrest" are Acts 12:4, where it is recorded that Herod apprehended Peter and put him in prison, and in 2 Corinthians 11:32, where Paul writes of the attempt of the governor of Damascus to apprehend him. For these, the contemporary versions generally use the verbs "seize" or "arrest"; for 2 Corinthians 11:32, the CEV has "capture" and the NLT "catch."

"Apprehend" is used in the obsolete sense, "to take possession of," in Philippians 3:12–13, where it translates the Greek verb which means "to obtain," take possession of," "make one's own."

The contemporary translations render the verb "apprehend" by use of the phrases "make one's own" (NRSV, RSV); "take hold of" (CEV, in Philippians 2:12 only; NIV); and "lay hold of" (NKJV, in Philippians 2:12 only; NASB); e.g., "Not that I have already obtained it or have already become perfect, but I press on so that I may lay hold of that for which also I was laid hold of by Christ Jesus. Brethren, I do not regard myself as having laid hold of it yet" (NASB).

ARK

In contemporary English the word "ark" is used to refer to the large boat that God commanded Noah to build and to the ark of the covenant that symbolized the presence of the Lord. The KJV uses the word in both these senses. The use of this word to denote the ark built by Noah (*tebah*) and the ark of the covenant (*'aron*), tends to make the reader forget that "ark" was once a common English noun meaning a "chest," "box," or "coffer." The ark was a household fixture in English homes for centuries, and its manufacture provides the family name Arkwright.

The ark that God commanded Noah to build is called "ark" in the NASB, NIV, NKJV, NRSV, and RSV; and a "boat" in the CEV, NCV, and NLT. The ark of the covenant is called the "sacred chest" in the CEV; "ark" in the NASB, NIV, NKJV, NRSV, and RSV; and "Ark" in the NCV and NLT.

ARMAGEDDON

The name "Armageddon" is sometimes used today to refer to a vast and intensely destructive conflict, especially the final war between good and evil. In the KJV the word is found only at Revelation 16:16. Here it is the meeting-place in the apocalyptic scene of the great day of God Almighty. The word "Armageddon" may stand for Har Magedon, the mountain of Megiddo.

The contemporary versions retain "Armageddon" (NCV, NIV, NKJV, NLT, and RSV); the CEV has "Armagedon," the NASB, "Har-Magedon," and the NRSV, "Harmagedon."

ARMHOLE

In contemporary English an armhole is an opening for the arm in a garment. But from the fourteenth century, "armhole" meant "armpit." It is used in that now obsolete sense in Jeremiah 38:12, KJV: "Put now these old cast clouts and rotten rags under thine armholes under the cords."

The contemporary versions (NASB, NKJV, NLT, NRSV, and RSV) translate as "armpits"; the CEV, NCV, and NIV as "arms." The Hebrew word here translated "armpits" means "joints of the arms," and may be applied to elbows or wrists. In Ezekiel 13:18 in the expression "sew pillows to all armholes," "armholes" is generally rendered "wrists" (CEV, NASB, NCV, NIV, NLT, NRSV, RSV) and "sleeves" (NKJV). (See KERCHIEF; PILLOW)

ARTILLERY

The word "artillery" in modern usage refers to large, powerful guns, but from the fifteenth century the word was applied to any implements of war, e.g., bows and catapults. The OED cites a sixteenth-century diarist as listing under artillery "drumes, flutes, trumpetes." And it quotes from Samuel Williams's *History of Vermont* (1794): "A club made of hard wood, a stake hardened in the fire, a lance armed with a flint or a bone, a bow and an arrow constituted the whole artillery of an Indian war."

When Jonathan went to the field where David was hiding, and shot three arrows for his little lad to gather, he "gave his artillery unto his lad, and said unto him, Go, carry them to the city" (1 Samuel 20:40, KJV). The use of "artillery" here was an innovation of the KJV, for Tyndale and Coverdale had "weapons," Geneva had "bowe and arrowes," and the Bishops' Bible had "instruments." All the contemporary versions except the NLT have returned to the rendering of Tyndale and Coverdale, "weapons"; the NLT has "bow and arrows."

AS

In contemporary English and in the KJV, "as" is used in phrases that express similarity or comparison. The KJV expression

"like as," meaning "like," is generally translated "like" in the contemporary versions, e.g., Jeremiah 23:29, KJV, "Is not my word like as a fire?"; NIV and NRSV, "Is not my word like fire"; Deuteronomy 17:14, KJV, "When thou art come unto the land which the LORD thy God giveth thee, and shalt possess it, and shalt dwell therein, and shalt say, I will set a king over me, like as all the nations that are about me"; NASB, NIV, NKJV, NRSV, and RSV, "like all the nations."

The KJV of Genesis 3:5, "ye shall be as gods," is translated in all the contemporary versions except the CEV as "like God"; the CEV has "just as God does." The KJV of Luke 18:17, "Whosoever shall not receive the kingdom of God as a little child shall in no wise enter therein," is rendered "as a little child" (NKJV, NRSV); "like a little child" (NIV); "like a child" (CEV, NASB, RSV). Luke 10:18, KJV, "I beheld Satan as lightning fall from heaven," is rendered, "like lightning" (NASB, NCV, NIV, NKJV, RSV), "like a flash of lightning" (CEV, NRSV), "as a flash of lightning" (NLT). Judges 6:5, KJV, "they came as grasshoppers for multitude," is translated, "like swarms of locusts" (NCV, NIV); "as thick as locusts" (NLT, NRSV); "as numerous as locusts" (NKJV); and "like locusts for number" (NASB).

Occasionally the contemporary versions expand the expression to a clause with "as," following the principle that "as" may be used to introduce a clause but "like" may not. For example, Isaiah 26:17, KJV, "Like as a woman with child, that draweth near the time of her delivery, is in pain, and crieth out in her pangs"; the NIV and NKJV have: "As a woman with child" is in pain.

The expression "as it were" is translated in the contemporary versions as simply "like," e.g., "sweat was as it were great drops of blood" (Luke 22:44; KJV); "A certain vessel descending unto him, as it had been a great sheet" (Acts 10:11, KJV). The council that condemned Stephen "saw his face as it has been the face of an angel" (Acts 6:15,

KJV); this is rendered with "like" (CEV, NASB, NCV, NIV, NRSV, RSV); the NKJV has "saw his face as the face of an angel"; the NLT has "his face became as bright as an angel's."

The word "as," in the KJV use of "as it were" and "as it had been," has the sense of "as if" or "as though"—an archaic use which is described in the OED article on *as*, adv B, 1b and 9. An example from Shakespeare is *King Henry VI, Part II* (I, 1, 103), where the Duke of Gloucester protests against

> "Defacing monuments of
> conquer'd France,
> Undoing all, as all had never been!"

Examples in the KJV are Revelation 5:6, "a Lamb as it had been slain," rendered "as if" (CEV, NASB, NCV, NIV, NRSV) and "as though" (NKJV); Revelation 13:3, "one of his heads as it were wounded to death," rendered "as if it had been" (NASB, NCV, NKJV) and "seemed to have" (CEV, NIV, NRSV, RSV); Revelation 15:2, "I saw as it were a sea of glass," rendered "something like" (NASB, NKJV); "something that looked like" (CEV); "what looked like" (NCV, NIV); "what seemed to be" (NLT); "what appeared to be" (NRSV, RSV).

AS CONCERNING

This is a somewhat awkward phrase for "with regard to." In Leviticus 4:26 the KJV has "an atonement for him as concerning his sin," and in 5:6, "an atonement for him concerning his sin."

The contemporary translations use "for" (NIV, RSV); "concerning" (NKJV); the expression "on [someone's] behalf" (NRSV, and the NASB at Leviticus 5:6); and "in regard to" (NASB, Leviticus 4:26). "Of whom as concerning the flesh Christ came" (Romans 9:5, KJV) is rendered "according to the flesh" (NASB, NKJV, NRSV, RSV); the whole expression is rendered in the NLT as, "as far as his human nature is concerned" and in the NIV as, "from them is traced the human ancestry of Christ."

In Paul's statement to the Philippians (4:15), "no church communicated with me as concerning giving and receiving, but ye only" (KJV), "as concerning" is rendered "in the matter of" (NASB, NIV, NRSV) and "concerning" (NKJV). Other contemporary renderings of this KJV expression include the expressions "as for the fact that" (NASB, RSV; the NRSV has "as to") for Acts 13:34, KJV, "And as concerning that he raised him up from the dead"; "as regards" (the NRSV and RSV of Romans 11:28; which in the KJV reads, "As concerning the gospel." Here, the NASB has "from the standpoint of the gospel"; the NIV has "as far as the gospel is concerned."

The KJV of 2 Corinthians 11:21 reads, "I speak as concerning reproach." This is rendered, "To my shame" (NASB, NIV, NRSV, RSV), "To our shame" (NKJV), "It is shameful to me to say this" (NCV); "I'm ashamed to say" (NLT).

AS YET

In contemporary English and in the KJV, "as yet" means "up to this time," and implies the expectation or possibility of coming change. It is used in Exodus 9:17, KJV, the LORD's words to Pharaoh, "As yet exaltest thou thyself against my people, that thou wilt not let them go?"; generally rendered by "still" in the contemporary versions (CEV, NASB, NCV, NIV, NLT, NRSV, and RSV) e.g., "You are still exalting yourself against my people"; the NKJV retains "as yet."

In John 20:9, "For as yet they knew not the scripture, that he must rise again from the dead," KJV "as yet" is retained by the NASB, NKJV, NRSV, and RSV; the CEV has "at that time"; the NIV, "still"; the NLT, "until then."

In 2 Corinthians 1:23, "Moreover I call God for a record upon my soul, that to spare you I came not as yet unto Corinth," KJV, the NASB and NRSV have, "I did not come again"; the NIV and NLT, "I did not [NLT, "didn't"] return"; the CEV, "I stayed away from"; and the NKJV, "I came no more."

In Jeremiah 31:23 it is a mistranslation

of the Hebrew word which in the context means "once again" (as in the CEV, NASB, NIV), "once more" (NRSV, RSV), or simply "again" (NCV, NKJV, NLT).

ASSAY

In modern technical English, "assay" is used as a noun to refer to a test of the chemical composition of a substance. In the KJV, however, "assay" occurs six times as a verb in the archaic sense of "attempt" or "venture": Deuteronomy 4:34; Acts 9:26; 16:7; Hebrews 11:29.

The contemporary versions generally render this verb by using the verbs "try" or "attempt," e.g., Acts 9:26, KJV, "And when Saul was come to Jerusalem, he assayed to join himself to the disciples," rendered in the NIV and NKJV as "he tried to join the disciples" and in the NRSV and RSV as "he attempted to join the disciples."

When the youth David volunteered to fight with Goliath, King Saul gave him a helmet of bronze, a coat of mail, and a sword. "And David girded his sword upon his armour, and he assayed to go; for he had not proved it." All the contemporary versions except the NLT use the verb "try"; the NLT has, "David put it on, strapped the sword over it, and took a step or two to see what it was like, for he had never worn such things before."

Eliphaz begins his attempt to comfort Job by inquiring, "If we assay to commune with thee, wilt thou be grieved?" (Job 4:4, KJV). The contemporary versions have, "If one [NIV, "someone"] ventures a word with you" (NASB, NIV, NRSV, RSV); the NKJV has, "If one attempts a word with you."

The NASB, NKJV, and RSV use the noun "assayer" in Jeremiah 6:27 (the other contemporary translations simplifying this word to e.g., "tester of metals," NIV, NLT), where the figure is drawn from the assaying of metals. the KJV's rendering—"I have set thee for a tower and a fortress among my people"—is due to confusion between the Hebrew word *baḥon*, which

means *assayer,* and a similar Hebrew word which means "tower."

ASSWAGE

This is the old spelling of "assuage," "to pacify," "to quieten." It appears in the KJV as an intransitive verb, in the obsolete sense of "to grow less," "abate," "subside" (Genesis 8:1). The contemporary translations have "the waters [NASB, "the water"] subsided" (NASB, NKJV, NRSV, RSV); the NIV, "the waters receded"; the CEV, "the water started going down"; the NLT, "the floods began to disappear."

Job 16:5-6, KJV reads, "But I would strengthen you with my mouth, and the moving of my lips should asswage your grief. Though I speak, my grief is not asswaged: and though I forbear, what am I eased?" For the KJV "asswage grief," the NRSV and RSV use the expression "assuage pain"; the NASB has "lessen pain"; the NKJV has "relieve grief"; the NIV has "bring you relief . . . my pain is not relieved."

The CEV simplifies the whole verse: "But I would offer hope and comfort instead. If I speak, or if I don't, I hurt all the same. My torment continues."

ASTONIED, ASTONISHED, ASTONISHMENT

In contemporary English "astonish" means "to surprise greatly" ("I am always astonished by their insularity"). The KJV "astonied," "astonished," and "astonishment" are derived from the obsolete verb "astone," which meant "to stun," "strike senseless," or "to overwhelm with amazement," "to astound." The KJV words have stronger connotations, especially in the Old Testament, than "astonish" now has.

In place of "astonied," the NKJV has "astonished," except Jeremiah 50:13, "horrified" and Ezekiel 4:17, "dismayed"; the other contemporary versions often render KJV "astonied" as "appall," "shock," or "horrify," e.g., Jeremiah 50:3, KJV, "every one that goeth by Babylon shall be astonished";

NRSV, "everyone who passes by Babylon shall be appalled"; NCV, "Everyone who passes by Babylon will be shocked"; NASB, "Everyone who passes by Babylon will be horrified."

Other contemporary translations include in the NASB "perplexed," for Daniel 5:9, KJV, "and his lords were astonied"; "dismayed" in the NKJV for Ezekiel 4:17, KJV, "That they may want bread and water, and be astonied one with another"; NKJV, "that they may lack bread and water, and be dismayed with one another"; "confused" in the NRSV for Jeremiah 14:9, KJV, "Why shouldest thou be as a man astonied"; NRSV, "Why should you be like someone confused."

The variety of renderings is demonstrated in the translations of Isaiah 52:14: KJV, "As many were astonied at thee"; CEV, "Many were horrified at what happened to him"; NASB, "Just as many were astonished at you"; NCV, "Many people were shocked when they saw him"; NIV, "Just as there were many who were appalled at him"; NKJV, "Just as many were astonished at you"; NLT, "Many were amazed when they saw him"; NRSV, "Just as there were many who were astonished at him."

Turning to the noun "astonishment," e.g., regarding the prophecy of the fate of Babylon, "Babylon shall become heaps, a dwellingplace for dragons, an astonishment, and a hissing, without an inhabitant" (Jeremiah 51:37, KJV), the most frequently used translation (e.g., NASB, NIV, NLT, NRSV) is "object of horror."

The NKJV generally has "astonishment," with the exception of Jeremiah 51:41, KJV, "how is Babylon become as astonishment among the nations!"; NKJV, "How Babylon has become desolate among the nations!"

Similar expressions are rendered in other ways: Deuteronomy 28:37, KJV, in describing curses for disobedience in "And thou shalt become an astonishment, a proverb, and a byword, among all nations whither the LORD shall lead thee"; CEV,

"People of nearby countries will shudder when they see your terrible troubles, but they will still make fun of you"; Jeremiah 44:12, KJV, "Ye shall be . . . an astonishment"; NCV, "People will be shocked by what will happen to you."

"The cup of astonishment" (Ezekiel 23:33, KJV) is a "a cup of [CEV, "filled with"] horror" (CEV, NASB, NKJV, NRSV, RSV); "the cup of ruin" (NIV). "The wine of astonishment" (Psalm 60:3, KJV) is "drink that made us reel" (NRSV, RSV), "that makes [CEV, "made"] us stagger" (CEV, NASB, NIV). The prophecy concerning Jerusalem, "they shall drink water by measure, and with astonishment" (Ezekiel 4:16, KJV, compare 12:19), is rendered with the following nouns: "despair" (NIV, "utter despair," NLT of Ezekiel 12:19); "dismay" (NLT, NRSV); "horror" (NASB); "shock" (NCV); "dread" (NKJV).

"Astonishment of heart" (Deuteronomy 28:28, KJV) is "confusion of mind" (NIV, NRSV, RSV), "confusion of heart" (NKJV); "bewilderment of heart" (NASB), "panic"(NLT). In the prophecy in Zechariah 12:4, "I will smite every horse with astonishment," "smite . . . with astonishment" is rendered: "strike . . . with panic" (NIV, NRSV); "cause . . . to panic" (NLT); "make . . . panic" (CEV); "strike . . . with bewilderment" (NASB); "strike . . . with confusion" (NKJV).

AT

The preposition "at" is used in contemporary English and in the KJV to show the place where something happens. In the KJV, obsolete uses of the preposition "at" appear in Exodus 19:15, "come not at your wives," rendered: "do not go near a woman" (NASB, NRSV, RSV); "do not come near your wives" (NKJV); "abstain from sexual relations" (NIV); "abstain from having sexual intercourse" (NLT); and Numbers 6:6, KJV, "he shall come at no dead body," rendered "not go near" a dead body (NASB, NCV, NIV, NKJV, NLT, NRSV, RSV), "never go close to" (CEV).

In Numbers 30:4, KJV, compare verse 7, "hold his peace at her" is rendered "says nothing to her" (NASB, NIV, NRSV, RSV) and "makes no response to her" (NKJV). "David enquired at the LORD" (1 Samuel 30:8, KJV) is "inquired of" (NASB, NIV, NKJV, NRSV, RSV) or "asked" (CEV, NCV, NLT).

When King Nebuchadnezzar demanded that his magicians tell him what the dream was which he had forgotten, they protested that only the gods could do this and that no king had "asked such things at any magician" (Daniel 2:10); the NASB, NIV, NKJV, NLT, NRSV and RSV have "asked . . . of."

When the plotters against Daniel were themselves cast into the den of lions, "the lions had the mastery of them, and brake all their bones in pieces or ever they came at the bottom of the den" (6:24, KJV) is rendered "reached the bottom" [NIV, "floor"] (CEV, NASB, NIV, NRSV, RSV) and "hit the floor" (NCV, NLT).

Shakespeare's *The Winter's Tale* (II, 3, 31) was played at the Globe Theatre on May 15, 1611, which was the year in which the King James Version was published. It contains the lines:

"Madam, he hath not slept to-night; commanded
None should come at him."

AT THE HANDS OF

See HAND.

AT THE LENGTH

"At the length" is an obsolete form of the phrase "at length," which means "finally" or "in the end." It is used in the KJV just once, Proverbs 29:21, as a translation for the Hebrew word which denotes the end or ultimate issue of a course of action. The NASB, NIV, NKJV, and RSV translate the expression as "in the end"; the NCV and NLT as "later"; for the whole verse the NRSV has, "A slave pampered from childhood, will come to a bad end."

ATTENDANCE

In contemporary English "attendance" is the fact of being present ("regular attendance at church services"). "Attendance" in the KJV, however, also meant "attention." To "give attendance" to something was to give attention to it, to apply one's mind or effort to it. The KJV uses the word twice in this obsolete sense.

In Paul's direction to Timothy to "give attendance to reading, to exhortation, to doctrine" (1 Timothy 4:13, KJV), "give attendance to" is rendered "give attention to" (NASB, NKJV, NRSV); "devote yourself to" (NIV); "focus on" (NLT); and "be sure to" (CEV).

In the letter to the Hebrews, affirming that the priesthood of our Lord is superior to the priesthood of Aaron and his descendants, in "pertaineth to another tribe, of which no man gave attendance at the altar" (Hebrews 7:13, KJV), "gave attendance at" is rendered with the verbs "serve at" (NIV, NLT, NRSV, RSV); "serve as a priest at" (CEV, NCV); and "officiate at" (NASB, NKJV).

The word "attendance" is retained in the account of the visit of the queen of Sheba to King Solomon—"the attendance of his ministers" (1 Kings 10:5; 2 Chronicles 9:4, KJV) is retained by the NASB and changed to "the attendance of his servants" (NRSV and RSV); "the attending servants" (NIV), and "the service of his waiters" (NKJV).

ATTENT

This is an obsolete word, derived from the Latin *attentus* and the French *attentif,* meaning "attentive." "Attent" is used by the KJV in King Solomon's prayer of dedication and the Lord's reply (2 Chronicles 6:40; 7:15). The NASB, NIV, NKJV, NLT, NRSV, and RSV all have "attentive" in both verses; the CEV and NCV paraphrase 2 Chronicles 6:40: "Lord God, hear us when we pray in this temple" (CEV); "Now, my God, look at us. Listen to the prayers we pray in this place" (NCV).

The KJV does, however, use "attentive"

elsewhere, e.g., Nehemiah 1:6, 11 and Psalm 130:2.

When the chief priests and their friends sought to destroy Jesus, they did not find anything they could do, "for all the people were very attentive to hear him" (Luke 19:48, KJV). The NKJV retains "attentive." The other contemporary translations render this with the expression "hang on/upon" his words (NASB, NIV, NLT, RSV); the CEV has "everyone else was eager to listen to him"; the NRSV has "all the people were spellbound by what they heard."

The adverb "attentively" is used when Elihu, seeking to impress Job with the wondrous works of God, describes a thunderstorm (Job 37:1–5, KJV). But the exhortation to "hear attentively" (retained by the NKJV) could be thought to be incongruous in a passage which has the heavens crashing in one's ears. There is no Hebrew word for "attentively"; it is simply the translators' attempt to express the intensive force of the repetition of the verb. So the NCV, NIV, and NRSV repeat the word "Listen"; the NASB has "Listen closely"; the NLT, "Listen carefully."

AUDIENCE

In modern usage an audience is a group of people who are watching or listening to a play, film, etc. In the KJV, "audience," however, refers to the act or state of hearing. The NASB, NIV, NKJV, NRSV, and RSV generally translate this as "hearing," e.g., Nehemiah 13:1, KJV, "On that day they read in the book of Moses in the audience of the people"; NASB, "On that day they read aloud from the book of Moses in the hearing of the people."

Variants include: Genesis 22:13, KJV, "in the audience of the people of the land"; CEV, "in front of these witnesses"; NLT, "as everyone listened"; in Abigail's words to David in 1 Samuel 25:24, KJV, "let thine handmaid, I pray thee, speak in thine audience," "in thine audience" is rendered "in your ears" (NKJV, NRSV, RSV).

For the KJV expression "give audience" (Acts 13:16; 15:12; 22:22), the contemporary versions use the word "listen," e.g., Acts 13:16, KJV, "Paul stood up, and beckoning with his hand said, Men of Israel, and ye that fear God, give audience"; CEV, "Paul got up. He motioned with his hand and said: People of Israel, and everyone else who worships God, listen!" An example from Shakespeare's *As You Like It* (V, 4, 157) is, "Let me have audience for a word or two."

AVOID

In contemporary English, "avoid" is a transitive verb that means "to prevent" or "keep away from." As well as uses in these senses, "avoid" is used once in the KJV as an intransitive verb, in the sense of "to go away," "withdraw." When Saul cast a javelin at David, thinking to pin him to the wall, "David avoided out of his presence twice" (1 Samuel 18:11). This use of the word "avoid," which is now obsolete, was common in the sixteenth century.

The NASB, NCV, and NKJV translate "avoided" as "escaped"; the NIV and NRSV as "alluded"; the RSV as "evaded." The NLT has "David jumped aside and escaped"; the CEV, "David dodged and got away." Coverdale's translation of Matthew 16:23, "Auoyde fro me, Sathan" is rendered as "get behind" me (NASB, NIV, NKJV, NRSV, RSV) and "get away from me" (CEV, NLT).

AWAY WITH

The expression "away with" can be used today as a slogan expressing disapproval ("away with old ideas and in with the new!"). In the KJV, however, in Isaiah 1:13 the phrase means "put up with," "tolerate," "endure": "the new moons and sabbaths, the calling of assemblies, I cannot away with." The contemporary translations render "I cannot away with" as: "I can't stand" (CEV, NCV); "I cannot endure" (NASB, NKJV, NRSV, RSV); "I cannot bear" (NIV); and "I want nothing more to do with" (NLT).

"Away with" was a well-established idiom in the sixteenth and seventeenth centuries. Tyndale's translation of Matthew 19:11 was "all men can not awaye with that sayinge," rendered "receive" in the KJV and RSV and "accept" by all the other contemporary translations.

The OED quotes from a sermon of Bishop Sanderson (1621): "He being the Father of lyes . . . can away with the Truth." In Shakespeare's *King Henry IV, Part II* (III 2, 213), Justice Shallow says of Jane Nightwork, "She never could away with me," and Falstaff answers, "Never, never; she would always say she could not abide Master Shallow."

BABEL

In contemporary English a babel is a confusion of sounds or voices or a noisy or confused scene. The expression comes from the biblical tower of Babel (Genesis 11:9), built with the proud intention of reaching to heaven.

The actual name "Babel" means "gate of God." God confounded the efforts of the builders by causing them to speak in different languages so they could not understand one another. The link with the idea of the confusion of languages is based on the Hebrew word for "confuse" (*balal*) which has a similar sound to *babel*.

All the contemporary versions retain the name "Babel."

BACKBITE, BACKBITING, BACKBITER

These are terms which, in contemporary language, have to do with gossip of a negative or bitter kind. They occur four times in the KJV, where the emphasis on deceit as an inherent element is more pronounced than in current usage.

The Hebrew verb *ragal* means "to go about slandering," and is translated "slander" by the KJV in 2 Samuel 19:27, where Mephibosheth complains that his servant Ziba had deceived him and openly lied about him (16:1–4): "he hath slandered thy servant unto my lord the king; but my lord the king is as an angel of God"(KJV; CEV and NCV, "he lied about me"). Consequently, the NRSV translates Psalm 15:3 (KJV, "He that backbiteth not with his tongue") as "who do not slander with their tongue";

other contemporary versions follow the KJV in rendering the word as "slander," except for the NCV which has "tell lies about others," the CEV which has "spread gossip," and the NKJV which retains the KJV "backbite."

However, in Proverbs 25:23 the RSV and NRSV retain "a backbiting tongue" because here the Hebrew literally means "a tongue of secrecy," and secrecy—"behind one's back"—is the distinctive element in the sort of slander which is also backbiting. The CEV has "cruel words," the NIV "a sly tongue," and the NLT "a gossiping tongue."

In 2 Corinthians 12:20 and Romans 1:30 the Greek words mean "slander" (NCV, "evil talk"; NLT, "backstabbing") and "slanderers" (CEV, "say cruel things about others"; NLT "backstabbers").

BACKSLIDING

In contemporary English, to backslide means "to relapse into sin or error," and in common usage can refer to any stage of such a relapse—from slackness in spiritual discipline to open apostasy.

The word occurs sixteen times in the KJV: thirteen times in Jeremiah and three times in Hosea. In both prophetic books it is a term for Israel's turning away from God. It implies deliberate sinfulness (Hosea 17:7, KJV, "my people are bent to backsliding from me"), a sense brought out strongly in contemporary renderings of this verse: "My people are determined to reject me" (CEV), "My people have made up their minds to turn away from me" (NCV);

"determined to turn from me" (NIV); "determined to desert me" (NLT).

The RSV and NRSV generally use "faithless" or "faithlessness" (cf. e.g., Jeremiah 3:6, 8, 11, 12, 14; 31:22) and "apostasy" or "apostasies" (cf. Jeremiah 2:19; 14:7). The RSV retains the KJV "our backslidings are many" in Jeremiah 14.7, and both the RSV and NRSV change the KJV "slidden back by a perpetual backsliding" to "turn away in perpetual backsliding" (8:5).

Isaiah 57:17, KJV, "he went on frowardly," is rendered, "he went on backsliding" by the RSV and NKJV; the NRSV has, "they kept turning back to their own ways," NLT, "they went right on sinning"; NIV, "he kept on in his willful ways"; NASB, "he went on turning away"; CEV, "you kept returning to your old sinful ways."

But in Hosea 4:16 a quite different Hebrew word appears, which means "stubborn" (translated thus by all the contemporary versions). In the KJV the verse reads, "For Israel slideth back as a backsliding heifer: now the LORD will feed them as a lamb in a large place." The NRSV has:

"Like a stubborn heifer, Israel is
    stubborn;
can the LORD now feed them like
    a lamb in a broad pasture?"

BAKEMEATS

The chief baker, in his dream, was carrying on his head three cake baskets, in the uppermost of which were "all manner of bakemeats for Pharaoh" (Genesis 40:17, KJV). The word "bakemeat" became obsolete after the sixteenth century, though "sweetmeat" (used of confectionery) has survived. The context of the now obsolete word was "bakery," and literally translated, the Hebrew means "all sorts of food made by a baker."

The NASB, NRSV, and RSV render the expression in this verse "all sorts of baked food"; the CEV, "all kinds of baked things"; the NIV and NKJV, "all kinds of baked goods";

the NLT, "all kinds of bakery goods." Shakespeare used "baked meats" in the same sense as sweetmeat.

"Look to the baked meats, good
    Angelica:
Spare not for cost."
                —Romeo and Juliet (IV, 4, 5)

"Thrift, thrift, Horatio! the funeral
    baked meats
Did coldly furnish forth the
    marriage tables."
                —Hamlet (I, 2, 180–181)

BALM IN GILEAD

The expression "balm in Gilead" is sometimes used today to refer to something that is healing or soothing. It derives from Jeremiah 8:22, KJV, "Is there no balm in Gilead." The prophet Jeremiah is questioning whether there is an effective means of healing the distress of Judah.

Of the contemporary versions, the NASB, NIV, NKJV, NRSV, and RSV retain the KJV expression "no balm in Gilead"; the CEV has, "If medicine . . . may be found in Gilead" and the NLT has, "Is there no medicine in Gilead?"

BALTHAZAR

A balthazar is a large bottle equivalent to sixteen standard wine bottles, about twelve liters, named in allusion to King Belshazzar (the spelling adopted by the KJV and all the contemporary versions) of Babylon who gave a great feast for one thousand of his lords and drank wine with them (Daniel 5:1). The OED lists variant spellings of the wine bottle as Balthasar and Belshazzar. (See JEROBOAM; METHUSELAH; NEBUCHADNEZZAR)

BAND

In the sense of that by which a person or thing is bound, the word "bond" occurs twenty-seven times in the KJV. Most versions, including the RSV and NRSV, retain in Daniel 4:15 (KJV, "a band of iron and brass") and in Hosea 11:4—though this latter verse is rendered "bonds of love" by the NASB, "ties of love" by the NIV, and "ropes of love" by the NCV.

Elsewhere the various Hebrew and Greek terms so represented are rendered in the contemporary versions by "bonds" (Judges 15:14, NKJV, NRSV, RSV; Job 39:5, NASB, NKJV, NRSV, RSV; Psalm 2:3, NKJV, NRSV, RSV; 107:14, NRSV, RSV; Isaiah 28:22; 52:2; 58:6, NKJV, NRSV, RSV; Jeremiah 2:20, NASB, NIV, NKJV, NRSV, RSV; Luke 8:29, NASB, NKJV, NRSV, RSV); "cords" (Psalm 119:61, NASB, NKJV, NRSV, RSV; Ezekiel 3:25; 4:8, NRSV, RSV); "fetters" (Ecclesiastes 7:26, NKJV, NRSV, RSV; Isaiah 28:22, NASB; Acts 16:26, RSV); "binding" or "bindings" (Exodus 39:23, NKJV, NRSV, RSV; Judges 15:14, NIV); "bars" (Leviticus 26:13, NASB, NIV, NRSV, RSV; Ezekiel 34:27, NASB, NCV, NIV, NRSV, RSV); "ropes" (Judges 15:14, NCV, NLT; Job 39:10, NASB, NKJV, NRSV, RSV; Psalm 2:3, CEV, NCV; Acts 27:40, NASB, NIV, NRSV); "ligaments" (Colossians 2:19, NASB, NKJV, RSV; CEV has "muscles" and NIV and NRSV, "sinews").

Psalm 119:61 in the KJV reads, "The bands of the wicked have robbed me," a rendering taken from the Geneva Bible. This had appeared in Coverdale and the Great Bible in the form of "The congregations of the wicked have robbed me," and had come from Luther's German Bible. The RSV and the NRSV render the verse:

> "Though the cords of the wicked ensnare me,
> I do not forget thy law."

Other contemporary versions have "The cords of the wicked have encircled me," NASB; "The wicked bind me with ropes," NIV. The NCV and NLT translate more loosely, "Wicked people have tied me up" and "Evil people try to drag me into sin."

The KJV rendering of Psalm 73:4, "For there are no bands in their death" may not be clear to contemporary readers. It came, in fact, from the Geneva Bible; other sixteenth-century versions had "they are in

no peril of death"—a rendering which Coverdale took from Luther. The RSV renders the word "bands" as "pangs," as does the NKJV; the NRSV and NASB have "pains" and "pain," while the NIV reads "they have no struggles."

The prophet's symbolic staffs, "Beauty" and "Bands" (Zechariah 11:7–14, KJV), are rendered in the contemporary versions: "Mercy" and "Unity" (CEV), "Favor" and "Union" [NRSV, "Unity"] NASB, NIV, NLT, NRSV; and "Grace" and "Union" (RSV).

BANQUET

A banquet is something to look forward to—and probably to dress up for. It is a lavish feast, usually prepared for honored guests in celebration of some special occasion such as a wedding or a meeting of heads of government. At ceremonial banquets, pomp, ceremony, and speeches are the order of the day. The Hebrew word *mishteh* can mean "a feast of food and drink" or simply "a drinking bout"; consequently, the exact meaning of the word in translation is not always easy to determine.

In the book of Esther, where it occurs most often, the KJV translates it as "banquet" ten times and "feast" or "feasting" ten times. Four times the Hebrew word for "wine" is added; so the KJV has "banquet of wine" and the RSV, "as they were drinking wine." The RSV uses "dinner" for Queen Esther's invitation to the king and Haman.

For Herod's birthday party, the NIV and NASB follow the RSV in using "banquet" rather than "supper" (KJV) for Mark 6:21. In Luke 14:12, Jesus' advice to the disciples is rendered, "When you give a dinner or a banquet" ["supper," KJV] in the RSV and CEV alone; other contemporary versions have "luncheon or dinner" (NASB, NIV, NLT, NRSV). A few verses later, in the parable of the invited guests, the KJV's "a great supper" is rendered "a great banquet" by the NIV and RSV, and "a great dinner" by the NRSV (Luke 14:16–17, 24).

In Amos 6:7 we read, "The banquet of

them that stretched themselves shall be removed" (KJV), which could be interpreted as meaning little more than that the feast will come to an end and the plates and glasses removed.

The NKJV translation emphasizes that it is "those who recline at banquets [who] shall be removed," while other contemporary versions suggest that it is the feasting and revelry which will end (NRSV, "the revelry of the loungers shall [NASB, "the sprawlers' banqueting will"] pass away"; NIV, "feasting and lounging will end"; NLT, "all your revelry will end." The RSV translates, "the revelry of those who stretch themselves shall pass away."

A confusion of similar Hebrew verbs has resulted in the KJV's rendering of Job 41:6 ("Shall the companions make a banquet of him?"); contemporary versions have "Will traders bargain over [NIV, "barter for"] him?" (NASB, NIV, NRSV, RSV).

In 1 Peter 4:3 "walked in . . . banquetings" is translated by the contemporary versions as "living in . . . carousing" (NIV); "walked in . . . drinking parties" (NKJV); and "pursued a course of . . . drinking parties" (NASB).

BARABBAS

It was the custom of the governor to release one prisoner chosen by the crowd at the Passover Feast (Matthew 27:15–26). Barabbas was the robber who was released in response to the crowd's request to crucify Jesus in his place.

The expression "Now Barabbas was a publisher" is often attributed to the English poet Lord Byron (1788–1824). Byron, so the story goes, received a copy of a magnificent edition of the Bible from the publisher John Murray as an expression of thanks for a favor. Byron, it is said, returned the copy, having substituted the word "publisher" for "robber" in the text of John 18:40, "Now Barabbas was a robber" (KJV).

Of the contemporary versions, "robber" is retained by the NASB, NCV, NKJV, and RSV;

the CEV has "terrorist," the NLT, "criminal," the NRSV, "bandit," and the NIV, "had taken part in a rebellion."

BARBARIAN, BARBAROUS

The word "barbarian" has rather unfavorable connotations today; people speak of barbarous behavior when they mean behavior that is rude or uncivilized. In its original meaning, however, the term *barbaros* was applied to all non-Greek-speaking peoples, who were regarded as foreigners. In time it acquired the additional meaning of rude or uncivilized, and began to be more widely used. It was applied by Romans to non-Romans. In 2 Maccabees it is applied by Jews to the Greeks, and is also used in the sense of "savage" as an adjective describing a wild beast.

In the New Testament *barbaros* is used only in its original sense. The NRSV, NASB, and NKJV retain "barbarians" in Romans 1:14 (the NIV has "non-Greeks"; the NCV, "those who are not Greeks") and Colossians 3:11 (also the NIV; the NCV has "people who are foreigners"), but without the capital B which the KJV uses. In Acts 28:2 (KJV, "barbarous people") the NRSV and NASB translate the word as "natives" (NIV, "islanders"; NLT, "people of the island"). In 1 Corinthians 14:11 most contemporary versions have "foreigner" (CEV, NCV, NIV, NKJV, NRSV), but the NASB retains "barbarian."

BASE

This word has different meanings in different contexts. We hear it used in baseball ("first base") and elsewhere to refer to a starting point or some sort of center of operations. It can mean an object's lowest point or support, but it is also used as an adjective in a moral sense to imply inferiority or a lack of worth ("a base joke"; "the base metals"). The adjective is used by the KJV in the archaic sense of "low in rank or position," "lowly," "humble." "The basest of men" (Daniel 4:17) does not mean the most worthless or most wicked of human beings, but those of lowest position: "the lowliest of human beings" (NRSV).

Similarly, in Ezekiel 29:15 "the basest of the kingdoms" (KJV) is rendered "the most lowly of kingdoms" by the NRSV; the NASB has "the lowest of the kingdoms" and the NKJV and NIV have "the lowliest of kingdoms." Paul's reference to himself in 2 Corinthians 10:1 as "who in presence am base among you, but being absent am bold toward you" (KJV) is rendered, "I who am humble when face to face with you, but bold to you when I am away!" in the NRSV; in the NASB "base" is rendered "meek," while the NIV has "timid." The NKJV uses the word "lowly."

In 1 Corinthians 1:26–29 the word occurs frequently in a passage contrasting human wisdom with God's wisdom. Here the NKJV and NASB follow the KJV rendering, "the base things of the world" (v. 28); the NIV has "the lowly things of this world," while the NCV and CEV have "what the world thinks is worthless [NCV, "is unimportant"]."

Acts 17:5 speaks of "certain lewd fellows of the baser sort" (KJV) who raised an uproar in Thessalonica. The word which the KJV represents by "lewd" is the common Greek word for "wicked," and it gives to the phrase its moral connotations. The word represented by "the baser sort" simply means the crowd in the marketplace.

In contemporary versions the text is rendered "some wicked fellows of the rabble" (RSV); "some ruffians in the marketplaces" (NRSV); "some wicked men [NIV, "bad characters"] from the market place" [NIV, "marketplace"] (NASB, NIV); and "some worthless fellows from the streets" (NLT). C. B. Williams translates the phrase "some wicked loafers about the public square."

BE

The KJV frequently uses "be" with a plural subject, where modern usage would say "are." An interesting passage is Genesis 42:31–32, "We are true men; we are no spies: We be twelve brethren."

Other examples are Delilah's cry to Samson, "The Philistines be upon thee" (Judges 16:9, 12, 14, 20); Elisha's assurance to his servant, "They that be with us are more than they that be with them" (2 Kings 6:16), and Zechariah's question to the angel, "What be these? And he answered me, These are the horns" (Zechariah 1:19). In these cases the contemporary versions use "are" instead of "be."

The KJV translators have "thy sins be forgiven thee" in Matthew 9:2 and "thy sins are forgiven thee" in Luke 5:20, though the Greek text which they used is the same in the two cases. The contemporary versions have "your sins are forgiven," although in the RSV, NRSV, and NASB Luke 5:20 reads "your sins are forgiven you." In Jeremiah 17:5 the KJV has "Cursed be" and "Blessed is" for parallel constructions.

In many cases the word "be" as used in the KJV is the subjunctive mood of the verb. Many of these are retained by the contemporary versions, in expressions such as "Blessed be the Lord!" In accordance with modern usage, however, the subjunctive form of the verbs is less often used than in the seventeenth century.

In Genesis 27:21, for example, the blind Isaac's word to Jacob, "Come near, I pray thee, that I may feel thee, my son, whether thou be my very son Esau or not," is expressed by the NRSV, NASB, and NKJV, "whether you are really [NIV, "you really are"] my son Esau or not"; NLT, "to make sure you really are Esau."

BE FRUITFUL AND MULTIPLY
See FRUITFUL AND MULTIPLY.

BEAM IN ONE'S OWN EYE

The "beam in one's own eye" is a serious fault in one's nature which one ignores while at the same time criticizing less important faults in other people. The expression derives from Jesus' saying in the Sermon on the Mount in Matthew 7:3, "And why beholdest thou the mote that is in thy brother's eye, but considerest not the beam that is in thine own eye?"

The contemporary versions render the lesser "mote" as "speck" (CEV, NASB, NKJV, NLT, NRSV, RSV), "speck of sawdust" (NIV), and "little piece of dust" (NCV) and the greater "beam" as "log" (CEV, NASB, NLT, NRSV, RSV), "plank" (NIV, NKJV), and "big piece of wood" (NCV).

The expression is often alluded to in literature. Shakespeare has in *Love's Labour's Lost* (IV, 3, 162):

"You found his mote; the king your
    mote did see;
But I a beam do find in each of
    three."

And Latimer, recorded in *Sermons and Remains* (1845, 314) wisely notes, "Learn from your own beams to make allowances for your neighbour's motes."

BEAR THE BURDEN AND HEAT
OF THE DAY

The expression "bear the burden and heat of the day" means to perform the longest and hardest part of a task and is often used in a contrast with others' share in a task which is thought to be easier or shorter.

The expression comes from Jesus' parable of the workers in the vineyard, in which the groups of workers who have worked differing lengths of time are all paid the same amount. Those who have borne the burden and heat of the day—those who have worked the longest—felt that they had been unfairly treated.

The contemporary versions render the expression as: "borne the burden of the day and scorching heat" (NRSV, RSV); "borne the burden and the [NASB, "the scorching"] heat of the day" (NASB, NKJV); "borne the burden of the work and the heat of the day" (NIV); "worked all day in the scorching heat" (NLT); "worked in the hot sun all day

long" (CEV); and "worked hard all day in the hot sun" (NCV).

BEAST

In contemporary English "beast" is a word for "a wild animal," although the word "animal" tends to be more commonly used. "Beast" also suggests a wild or unruly nature ("the beast in him"), and as a result has come to be used of a brutal or uncivilized person.

The word "animal" does not appear in the KJV, which uses "beast" as a general term for living creatures other than human beings. "Cattle" is used as a collective name for all live animals held as property or reared for some use. The word "reptile" does not appear, for it was a relatively new word, just beginning to be current in 1611; the KJV used the older term "creeping thing."

"Fowl" is used twice as often as "bird," and for the same Hebrew and Greek words. Here again, "fowl" was the old generic term for feathered vertebrates, which had begun to be displaced by "bird."

The contemporary versions use both "beasts" (Genesis 1:30, RSV, NRSV, NASB, NIV) and "animals" (1 Kings 4:33, RSV, NRSV, NASB, NIV); at Psalm 148:10 the RSV and NASB have "beasts of the field," and the NRSV and NIV have "wild animals."

In Acts 10:12, Peter's vision is of "animals" (RSV, NASB, NIV; NRSV, "creatures"), reptiles and birds. In the Old Testament the KJV's "creeping things" is retained, in places, by the RSV (Genesis 1:30, NRSV, "everything that creeps upon the earth"), NRSV, and NASB (Psalm 148:10).

In Leviticus 5:2 these versions render the KJV's "creeping things" as "swarming things" [NRSV, "swarming thing"]. Elsewhere the RSV and NRSV use "winged insects" (Leviticus 11:21, KJV, "flying creeping thing") or "reptiles" (Acts 10:12; NASB, "crawling creatures of the earth"). The NIV has "creatures that move along (Genesis 1:30, "on") the ground" (Leviticus 5:2; Ezekiel 38:20).

The KJV's "fowls of the air" is now generally rendered as "birds of the air" (Psalm 148:10, NRSV, "flying birds"; here the NASB retains "winged fowl").

In the book of Revelation the word "beast" is used frequently by the KJV. John's vision of heaven showed to him, around the throne of God, twenty-four elders and four living creatures who worship him and sing his glory. The Greek word for "living creature" is *zoon;* it is used twenty times to refer to these heavenly beings (chaps. 4—7, 14—15, 19). Later, he saw a beast rising out of the sea and another which rose out of the earth, and was told of the beast that ascends from the bottomless pit.

These beasts are the enemies of God and the objects of his wrath. The Greek word that refers to them is *therion;* it is used twenty-seven times between chapters 11 and 20.

The KJV uses the word "beast" as a translation both for *zoon* and *therion.* The Latin Vulgate makes a distinction between the two, using *animal* for the heavenly beings and *bestia* for the infernal beasts.

The contemporary versions render the heavenly beings as "living creatures" [NLT, "beings"] and the hellish beasts who come up from the earth and the sea as "beasts." The KJV itself uses "living creatures" for the Hebrew term of similar import in chapters 1, 3, and 10 of Ezekiel.

BEAT SWORDS INTO PLOWSHARES

The expression "beat swords into plowshares" refers to changing one's implements of warfare into instruments of peace. The expression occurs in the KJV at Isaiah 2:4 and Micah 4:3. Isaiah 2:4, KJV, reads, "And he shall judge among the nations, and shall rebuke many people: and they shall beat their swords into plowshares, and their spears into pruninghooks: nation shall not lift up sword against nation, neither shall they learn war any more."

The NIV, NKJV, NLT, NRSV, and RSV retain the KJV expression. The other contemporary versions render the expression "beat swords into plowshares" as "hammer their swords into plowshares" (NASB), "make their swords into plows" (NCV at Isaiah 2:4), and "pound their swords . . . into rakes" (CEV).

In Joel 3:10, the reverse process is recorded: "Beat your plowshares into swords" (KJV, NASB, NIV, NKJV, NLT, NRSV, and RSV); the CEV has "Make swords out of plows" and the NCV, "Make swords from your plows."

BECAUSE

This was originally a phrase, "by (bi, bie, be) cause," often followed by of, why, or that. "Because of" is in common use today, meaning "for the reason that." "Because that" occurs in Genesis 2:3, Numbers 11—20, and twenty other passages in the KJV, but in contemporary versions is replaced by "because."

From the fifteenth to the seventeenth century, "because" was used not only to express a cause or reason, but also to express a purpose. The following quotations from Tyndale illustrate the variety of seventeenth-century usage:

Luke 1:7: "They had no chylde, because that Elizabeth was barren."

Luke 13:14: "the ruler of the sinagoge answered with indignacion (be cause that Iesus had healed on the sabbath daye)."

Matthew 12:10: "they axed him sayinge: ys it lawfull to heale apon the saboth dayes? because they might accuse him."

Matthew 20:31: "the people rebuked them, be cause they shulde holde their peace."

John 16:1: "these thinges have I sayde unto you, because ye shuld not be offended."

In the first two of these passages "because that" and "be cause that" translate the Greek *hoti,* which means "because"; in the last three passages "because" and "be cause" represent the Greek *hina,* which means "in order that." The KJV changed Tyndale's wording in two of these last three passages, but kept it in Matthew 20:31. The contemporary versions change to modern usage in all cases where "because" was used in the sense of "in order that."

"For because" is an archaic and redundant expression which simply means "because." It is used in the KJV in Genesis 22:16 and Judges 6:22.

BEGGARLY

The adjective "beggarly" is currently used to refer to something, especially a sum of money, that is paltry or scant or to something extremely poor, as a beggar typically is.

In the KJV the word occurs once with the meaning "intellectually poor," "destitute of meaning or intrinsic value" (OED). The word occurs in the KJV at Galatians 4:9, "But now, after that ye have known God, or rather are known of God, how turn ye again to the weak and beggarly elements, whereunto ye desire again to be in bondage?"

Of the contemporary versions, the NKJV, NRSV, and RSV retain the KJV "beggarly"; the other contemporary versions render "beggarly" as "useless" (NCV, NLT), "worthless" (NASB), "miserable" (NIV), and "pitiful" (CEV).

BENEVOLENCE

This is a rich word which suggests kind intentions, generosity, and charitableness; a benevolent person is a person with a heart of gold. Today we might speak of a benevolent organization, or of someone having offered us a benevolent smile. The word occurs in the KJV rendering of 1 Corinthians 7:3: "Let the husband render unto the wife due benevolence."

The expression "due benevolence" came from Tyndale, who had: "Let the man geve unto the wyfe due benevolence. Lykwyse also the wyfe unto the man." "Benevolence" is here used in the sense of affection or good will toward a particular person. The ancient Greek manuscripts read simply, "Let the husband give to his wife her due, and likewise the wife to her husband." The Greek word is *opheile*, which the KJV translates as "debt" in Matthew 18:32 and "due" in Romans 13:7. Paul here uses it for the mutual obligations of husband and wife.

Some copyist of the Greek text must have felt that it was not explicit enough, and inserted the Greek word *eunoia*, "good will"; this addition was picked up by other copyists and appears in most of the late medieval manuscripts. It has been eliminated from contemporary editions of the Greek text, and from contemporary versions generally, as early as those by John Wesley and Alexander Campbell.

Of the contemporary versions, the NASB, NIV, NKJV, and NLT bring out the connotations of indebtedness and obligation present in the Greek word *opheile:* the husband is to "fulfill his [NIV, "his marital"] duty to his wife" (NASB); "render to his wife the affections due her" (NKJV); "not deprive his wife of sexual intimacy" (NLT). The RSV and NRSV have "give to his wife her conjugal rights."

BESOM

Archaic for "broom," the word "besom" occurs once in the KJV, where the Lord says of Babylon, "I will sweep it with the besom of destruction" (Isaiah 14:23). Literally translated, the Hebrew is "I will sweep it with the sweeper of destruction." Contemporary versions all have "I will sweep it [NIV, "her"; NLT, "the land"; NCV, "Babylon as"] with the [NCV, "a"] broom of destruction," except the CEV which paraphrases, "The LORD will sweep out the people."

Shakespeare used "besom" just once, in the angry speech of the rebel Jack Cade to Lord Say in *King Henry VI, Part I,* (IV, 7, 34): "I am the besom that must sweep the court clean of such filth as thou art."

BESTEAD

"Bestead" is an archaic word which originally meant "placed" or "situated," but which came to be used only in cases of difficulty, disadvantage, hostility, ill fortune, and the like. It thus acquired such meanings as "beset" or "hard pressed." In its one appearance in the KJV, Isaiah 8:21, "hardly bestead" represents a Hebrew verb which means "hard-pressed." The ASV translated it as "sore distressed."

Contemporary versions have "greatly distressed" (RSV, NRSV; the NIV has simply, "Distressed"), "hard-pressed" (NASB), "hard pressed" (NKJV), "weary" (NLT), "troubled" (NCV), and "in great pain" (CEV).

The word is used in KJV fashion by Shakespeare in *King Henry VI, Part II* (II, 3, 56):

"I never saw a fellow worst bested,
Or more afraid to fight, than is the
    appellant."

BESTOW

This is a word we most often hear in the context of gifts or awards. Institutions confer honorary titles and awards, or other recognitions of achievement, upon deserving individuals. Only a higher person or institution can "bestow" gifts on others; hence, the word implies superiority and condescension on the part of the giver.

In the KJV it has a variety of meanings, and is used to render no less than six different Hebrew verbs and five Greek verbs.

In 1 Kings 10:26 and 2 Chronicles 9:25 we read of fourteen hundred chariots and twelve thousand horsemen that King Solomon "bestowed in the cities" (KJV).

The contemporary versions say simply that they were "stationed" (NASB, NKJV, NRSV, RSV) or "kept" (CEV, NCV, NIV) there. When Gehazi took the gifts from Naaman and "bestowed them in the house" (2 Kings 5:24, KJV) the Hebrew means that he "put them [NIV, "put them away"] in the house"

(RSV; NASB, "deposited them"; NKJV, "stored them away").

The rich fool who worried over where to "bestow" his crops was not thinking of giving them away; he meant to keep them, and his problem was where to "store" them (Luke 12:17–18, rendered thus by the contemporary versions).

"Thou shalt bestow that money for whatsoever thy soul lusteth after" (Deuteronomy 14:26, KJV) is rendered "and spend the money for whatever you desire" in the RSV; "spend the [NKJV, "that"] money" is also the rendering in the CEV, NASB, NKJV, and NRSV, while the NIV and NCV have "use the silver [NLT, "money"]."

The word "bestow" is applied by the KJV to the payment of workers (2 Kings 12:15; RSV and NRSV, "to pay out to" the workers); to the use for the Baals of things dedicated to the Lord (2 Chronicles 24:7; most contemporary versions have "used," although the NKJV has "presented"); and to Ezra's authorization to "provide" what is required for the house of God (Ezra 7:20, rendered thus by all contemporary versions).

In three passages, the KJV uses "bestow labour" for the Greek word which it elsewhere translates "labour" or "toil." These passages are John 4:38 (RSV, NRSV, "for which you did not labor"), Galatians 4:11 (RSV, "labored over you in vain"), and Romans 16:6 (NASB, "who [RSV, NRSV, NASB, NLT, "who has"] worked hard [NLT, CEV, "so hard"; NIV, NCV, "very hard"] for you" [RSV, NRSV, "among you," NLT, "for your benefit"]). The KJV wording came from Tyndale.

BETHINK THEMSELVES

This word is an archaic expression occurring in 1 Kings 8:47 and in the parallel text 2 Chronicles 6:37, "if they shall bethink themselves . . . and repent, and make supplication unto thee . . . saying, We have sinned." The phrase is used here in a sense equivalent to "when he came to himself" (KJV, NKJV, NRSV, RSV) in the parable of the prodigal son (Luke 15:17), and the NKJV translates the words accordingly ("when they come to themselves").

The RSV translates the Hebrew more literally, "if they lay it to heart . . . and repent"; the NRSV has "if they come to their senses," and the NIV, "if they have a change of heart." Other occurrences of the same Hebrew idiom are Deuteronomy 4:39; 30:1; Isaiah 44:19; 46:8; Lamentations 3:21.

BETIMES

This is archaic word. It was a common word in Elizabethan English, and meant "early," "soon," "in good time." Shakespeare used it frequently, as in *Macbeth* (IV, 3, 162):

"Good God, betimes remove
The means that makes us strangers!"

In *Hamlet* (IV, 5, 49), Ophelia says:

"To-morrow is Saint Valentine's day,
All in the morning betime,
And I a maid at your window,
To be your Valentine."

This meaning is clear in the KJV's rendering of Genesis 26:31 ("And they rose up betimes in the morning"); contemporary versions translate "betimes" as "early." Elsewhere in the KJV "betimes" is used for other Hebrew words as the renderings in the following verses show.

In 2 Chronicles 36:15, the words which the KJV translates as "rising up betimes" ("The LORD God of their fathers sent to them by his messengers, rising up betimes, and sending") have the sense of "repeatedly," and are rendered "persistently" by the RSV and NRSV, and "again and again" by the NASB, NCV, NIV, and NLT. In Proverbs 13:24 (KJV, "He that spareth his rod hateth his son: but he that loveth him chasteneth him betimes"), "chasteneth him betimes" is now rendered as "diligent [NIV, "careful"] to discipline him" (NIV, NRSV, RSV).

In Job 8:5 and 24:5, the KJV uses the word "betimes" when the words "seek" and "seek-

ing" carry the full meaning without its addition.

BEWRAY

"Bewray" is an archaic word for "reveal" or "disclose." It had almost the same range of meanings as "betray," except that it lacked the connotation of treachery or disloyalty that "betray" almost always has. Shakespeare used "betray" sixty-seven times and "bewray" ten times; the KJV uses "betray" forty-two times and "bewray" four times. "Betray" is the word for the act of Judas, and "thy speech bewrayeth thee" (Matthew 26:73, KJV) describes Peter's unintentional disclosure of his identity.

But the distinction between the two words has not been maintained in English usage. "Bewray" has fallen into disuse, and we now use "betray" for "reveal" or "disclose," as well as for acts of treachery or disloyalty. As early as 1588, Shakespeare wrote in *Love's Labour's Lost* (I, 2, 138), "I do betray myselfe with blushing." In 1711, Addison wrote, "If be coughs, or betrays any Infirmity of Old Age" (Spectator No. 106. See OED, *betray*, 6 and 7).

The result is that "bewray" does not appear in the contemporary versions. In Proverbs 29:24, they have "disclose nothing" (RSV), and "tells nothing" (NASB); the NIV has "dare not testify," and the NCV has "afraid to say anything." In Isaiah 16:3, the majority of the contemporary versions have "do not betray [RSV, "betray not"] the fugitive." In Matthew 26:73, we find "the way you talk [NIV, "your accent"] gives you away" (NASB, NIV), and "your accent betrays you" (NRSV, RSV).

Proverbs 27:16 is an obscure text. The KJV has "Whosoever hideth her hideth the wind, and the ointment of his right hand, which bewrayeth itself." The words "which bewrayeth itself," or their equivalent, are not found in the contemporary renderings of the verse.

BLAIN

This word makes us think of blisters and ulcers, since we are familiar with the compound "chilblain." "Blain" was indeed the old word for a blister or large pustule. It appears in the account of the plagues of Egypt, "a boil breaking forth with blains upon man, and upon beast" (Exodus 9:9, 10, KJV), which contemporary versions translate as "boils breaking out in [NASB, "with"] sores on man and beast" (NASB, RSV), and "festering boils" breaking out on humans and animals (NRSV, NIV).

Wycliffe's first translation of Job 2:7 was "He smot Job with the werste stinkende bleyne from the sole of the fot unto the nol." The NRSV has "inflicted loathsome sores on Job from the sole of his foot to the crown of his head." The NASB has "sore boils"; the NIV, NCV, CEV, "painful sores."

BLASTED, BLASTING

When we read these words today, we imagine strong gusts of wind, or explosions which produce noise and turbulence of some kind. The KJV, however, uses "blasted" where today we would use the word "blighted," i.e., as a term for plant diseases of atmospheric or unknown origin. "Blight" did not enter the language until the seventeenth century and so may not have been available to the KJV translators.

In Genesis 41:6, 23, 27 Pharaoh dreams of seven thin ears of corn, "blasted with the east wind" (KJV). Isaiah refers to the victims of Sennacherib, king of Assyria, as "the grass on the housetops, and as corn blasted before it be grown up" (2 Kings 19:26; Isaiah 37:27, KJV).

In these passages for "blasted," the NASB and NIV use "scorched," and the RSV and NRSV use "blighted." These versions also use "blighted" instead of "blasting" in passages that connect it with mildew and pestilence as scourges of the land and people (1 Kings 8:37; 2 Chronicles 6:28; in Amos 4:9

and Haggai 2:17 the NASB has "scorching wind" and "blasting wind" respectively).

BLIND LEADING THE BLIND

The expression "the blind leading the blind" refers to inexperienced people who try to guide others who are similarly inexperienced, with the result that neither group is helped. The expression derives from Jesus' comment about the Pharisees, recorded in Matthew 15:14 (KJV), "Let them alone: they be blind leaders of the blind. And if the blind lead the blind, both shall fall into the ditch."

John Bunyan used the expression in *Pilgrim's Progress:* "that ditch . . . into which the blind have led the blind in all ages." In place of the KJV "blind leaders," the NASB, NIV, NLT, NRSV, and RSV have "blind guides."

BLOW UP

This term conjures up images of buildings flattened by explosives or fits of anger. In the KJV, the expression is a retention of the older usage of a redundant "up" or "out" with "blow." "Blow up the trumpet" (Psalm 81:3) is rendered "Blow the trumpet" in the NASB, NCV, NKJV, and NRSV and "Sound the trumpet" by the NIV, NLT, and CEV.

There is no difference in the Hebrew wording between this verse and other verses about trumpet blowing in which the word "up" has not been inserted. Coverdale had "They blewe out the trompettes" in 1 Maccabees 3:54, but the KJV did not retain the "out."

BODY OF HEAVEN

When Moses, Aaron, Nadab, Abihu, and seventy of the elders of Israel saw the God of Israel, "there was under his feet as it were a paved work of a sapphire stone, and as it were the body of heaven in his clearness" (Exodus 24:10, KJV).

The NRSV translates this, "under his feet there was something like a pavement of sapphire stone, like the very heaven for clearness." Smith and Confraternity have "as clear as the sky itself" (as does the NASB); Moffatt, "clear as the sky itself" (as does the NIV).

BOLLED

"Bolled" is archaic. As a result of the hail which the Lord rained upon the land of Egypt, the flax and the barley were ruined, "for the barley was in the ear, and the flax was bolled" (Exodus 9:31, KJV). Tyndale added to his translation a marginal note to the effect that "boulled," as he spelled the word, meant "swollen, i.e. grown into buds."

The Hebrew word means "bud"; the NIV and NLT translate as "the flax was in bloom," and the RSV, NRSV, and NASB as "the flax was in bud."

BONE OF MY BONES

When God made a woman from the man's rib and God brought the woman to Adam, Adam said, "This is now bone of my bones, and flesh of my flesh: she shall be called Woman, because she was taken out of Man" (Genesis 2:23, KJV). This expression is an example of the Hebrew genitive superlative, a phrase that gives emphasis or intensity or renders the greatest example of a particular quality (e.g., "holy of holies").

The NASB, NIV, NKJV, NRSV, and RSV retain the KJV "bone of my bones"; the NCV has "this is someone whose bones came from my bones."

BOOK

Today we think of a "book" as a bound copy of a printed manuscript, but the word was formerly applied to any written document of legal significance, and some traces of this usage remain in the Bible. At Mark 10:4, Wycliffe's version of 1382 had "a libel, that is, a litil boke of forsakyng," which was condensed in the 1388 revision to "a libel of forsakyng"; Tyndale and his successors had "a testimoniall of devorsement"; Rheims took "a bill of divorce" and the KJV "a bill of divorcement."

Contemporary versions have "a certifi-cate of divorce" [NRSV, "of dismissal"] (RSV, NKJV, NIV, NASB, NRSV); the CEV and NCV have "divorce papers." In Isaiah 50:1, where Wycliffe had "boc of forsakyng," the KJV has "bill of . . . divorcement"; the RSV and NRSV have "bill of divorce"; the NIV, "certificate of divorce."

Numbers 5:23 reads in the KJV, "And the priest shall write these curses in a book, and he shall blot them out with the bitter water." Wycliffe's first version had "in a libel," and the second "in a litil book"; Tyndale and Coverdale used "bill"; and in the Geneva Bible and thereafter it is "book." In *The Interpreter's Bible* (vol. 2, p. 169), John Marsh remarks that the word "may mean anything useful for writing on, and here may well indicate a stone, from which ink could be easily washed off."

Most of the contemporary versions have "wash them [NCV, "the words"] off" for the KJV's "blot them out," thus clarifying the fact that the purpose of the priest's action is to wash the curses off into the water, which acquires and conveys their potency, rather than to "blot" them out.

"The book of the purchase" (Jeremiah 32:12) is the deed of the purchase, and is so translated by the majority of contemporary versions.

"Let him that is my contrary party, sue me with a lybell," was Coverdale's translation of the last clause of Job 31:35. In time this was toned down to the KJV's "my desire is . . . that mine adversary had written a book." The NRSV translates the verse:

"O that I had one to hear me!
(Here is my signature! Let the
    Almighty answer me!)
O that I had the indictment written
    by my adversary!"

The word "libel," which originally had the same meaning as "book," does not appear in the KJV.

BOOTIES

This is not a misspelling of the word for baby shoes, but are the articles carried away following the plunder of an enemy's goods. "Booties" is the plural, now obsolete, of "booty"; today we might refer to such plundered goods as "the spoils of war." The word appears once in the KJV: "Shall they not rise up suddenly that shall bite thee, and awake that shall vex thee, and thou shalt be for booties unto them" (Habakkuk 2:7).

The NRSV reads, "Will not your own creditors suddenly rise, and those who make you tremble wake up? Then you will be booty for them."

The word "booties" occurs once in Shakespeare, in *The Winter's Tale* (IV, 3, 863), where the rogue Autolycus says, "If I had a mind to be honest, I see Fortune would not suffer me: she drops booties in my mouth."

BORN AGAIN

In contemporary English, the expression "born again" is used to describe an enthusiastic conversion to a particular cause or even simply to mean "renewed, new." The origin of the expression is Jesus' answer to Nicodemus: "Verily, verily, I say unto thee, Except a man be born again, he cannot see the kingdom of God" (John 3:3, KJV). Nicodemus had to undergo a radical transformation by the Spirit of God in order for him to see the kingdom of God.

Most of the contemporary versions retain the KJV's expression "born again"; the CEV and the NRSV have "born from above"; the RSV, "born anew."

BOSS

In the modern workplace, "boss" is a familiar term for someone in charge; "bossy" is a word for someone with an overbearing or dictatorial manner. But the word "boss" can also mean a knob or stud, such as those seen on ornamental ceilings,

and shields, or some other projection in a casting (*emboss*). This meaning is nearer the KJV's usage.

In the one passage where the word appears (Job 15:25–26), a boss is the convex projection in the center of the face of a shield. The KJV rendering of this passage is: "For he stretcheth out his hand against God, and strengtheneth himself against the Almighty. He runneth upon him, even on his neck, upon the thick bosses of his bucklers." The "he" which is the subject of these sentences is "the wicked man" of verse 20, who is here represented as running upon God, even on God's neck, upon the thick bosses of God's bucklers.

The ASV translates verse 26:

"He runneth upon him with a stiff
    neck,
With the thick bosses of his
    bucklers."

Today, the NRSV translates the two verses as one sentence:

"Because they stretched out
    their hands against God,
and bid defiance to the Almighty,
running stubbornly against him
    with a thick-bossed shield."

Other contemporary versions render "bosses of his buckler" as "strong, embossed shield" (NKJV); "strong shield" (NLT); "thick, strong shield" (NIV); and "massive shield" (NASB).

BOTCH

When we see the word "botch" today, we are likely to think of something being ruined or made a mess of ("they made a botch of that job"). In fact, it is also an obsolete word for "boils" or "sores." As "the botch of Egypt" it appears in the curse pronounced by Moses upon Israel if it should forsake the Lord (Deuteronomy 28:27, 35, KJV). From Wycliffe and Tyndale through the sixteenth-century translations to the KJV, this expression persisted and suggested that "the botch of Egypt" was a distinct and especially fearsome disease.

The Hebrew word represented by "botch" really means a "boil" or "boils," and is so translated by the KJV in every other occurrence; the contemporary versions all have the word "boils" at Deuteronomy 28:27. "The botch of Egypt" was the plague of boils referred to in Exodus 9:9–11. The Hebrew word also appears in Leviticus 13:18–20, 23; in the account of Hezekiah's illness, 2 Kings 20:7 (and its parallel Isaiah 38:21); and in Job 2:7.

BOTTOM

The word "bottom" has several meanings including "lowest part, side, or position," "the buttocks," and the part of a set of clothes for the lower part of the body. In the KJV the word is used in the sense of "lowest part, side, or position" and also in the sense of "low-lying land; a valley." This latter sense occurs at Zechariah 1:8: "I saw by night, and behold a man riding upon a red horse, and he stood among the myrtle trees that were in the bottom; and behind him were there red horses, speckled, and white."

The contemporary versions render "bottom" as "ravine" (NASB, NCV, NIV); "glen" (NRSV, RSV); "valley" (CEV); "small valley" (NLT); and "hollow" (NKJV).

Shakespeare used the word in this sense in As You Like It (IV, 3, 79): "West of this place, down in the neighbour bottom."

BOTTOMLESS PIT

A "bottomless pit" is a hole or chasm that has or seems to have no end. The expression is sometimes used figuratively in contemporary English ("the amount of money in public funds is not a bottomless pit").

The expression occurs six times in the book of Revelation in the KJV: 9:1–2, 11; 11:7; 17:8; 20:1, 3 to refer to the place of torment and punishment. Of the contemporary versions, the NCV, NKJV, NLT, and NRSV

retain the KJV expression "bottomless pit" (the NRSV has "pit" at 20:3); the CEV translates as "deep pit" ("pit" at Revelation 20:3); the NASB retains "bottomless pit" at 9:1–2 but translates as "abyss" at the other references; and the NIV has "Abyss" throughout.

The same Greek word is found in Luke 8:31 (KJV, "the deep"); NASB, NKJV, NRSV, "the abyss"; NIV, "the Abyss"; NCV, "eternal darkness"; NLT, "The Bottomless Pit" and Romans 10:7 (KJV, NIV, "the deep"); NASB, NKJV, NRSV, "the abyss"; CEV, "the world of the dead"; NLT, "the place of the dead"; NCV, "the world below."

The Greek word abyssos, translated as "bottomless," is also used in the Septuagint (the Greek translation of the Old Testament) to render the Hebrew word for the primeval deep (Genesis 1:2).

BOW

As a verb, "bow" occurs often in the KJV and is usually used with the modern meaning of "bend" or "stoop." "A bowing wall" (Psalm 62:3, KJV) is rendered by the majority of the contemporary versions as "a leaning wall." "They have set their eyes bowing down to the earth" (Psalm 17:11) is translated as "they set their eyes to cast me to the ground" by the NRSV, and similarly by the other contemporary versions.

In prayer to God, the expression "bow down thine ear" is used by the KJV in Psalms 31:2 and 86:1 for the Hebrew idiom which it translates as "incline thine ear" in Psalms 17:6; 71:2; 88:2; 102:2; Daniel 9:18. The NRSV and NASB have "Incline your ear" in all these references. Hezekiah's prayer (2 Kings 19:16, KJV) has "bow down thine ear," but the same prayer in the parallel account (Isaiah 37:17) is translated "incline thine ear." For this Hebrew idiom the KJV uses "incline (one's) ear" twenty-two times and "bow down (bow) thine ear" five times.

BOWELS

This word has a specific anatomical definition today: the bowel is the part of the alimentary canal beneath the stomach. Occasionally the word is still used more loosely to refer to the inward parts, or to deep feelings: someone might say "I feel it in my bowels" when they have a strong inner sense of something. The KJV uses the word in all these ways. It occurs twenty-eight times in the Old Testament.

"Bowels" is used literally in Numbers 5:22; 2 Samuel 20:10; 2 Chronicles 21:15, 18–19; Psalms 22:14; 109:18. It is used for the stomach in Job 20:14 and Ezekiel 3:3; 7:19. It denotes the womb in Genesis 25:23; Psalm 71:6; Isaiah 49:1. It denotes the male organs of procreation in Genesis 15:4; 2 Samuel 7:12; 16:11; 2 Chronicles 32:21; Isaiah 48:19.

"He that shall come forth out of thine own bowels" (Genesis 15:4, KJV) is translated more simply "your own son" by the RSV and "your very own issue" by the NRSV. The NASB retains a longer form, "one who will come forth from your own body," and "body" is the contemporary rendering for "bowels" in many of the passages just cited.

In ten cases the word "bowels" is used by the KJV to denote feelings or emotions. Jeremiah's cry, "My bowels, my bowels!" (Jeremiah 4:19, KJV) is rendered "My anguish, my anguish!" by the RSV, NRSV, and NIV; "My soul, my soul!" by the NASB. Job's lamentation, "My bowels boiled" (Job 30:27, KJV), is rendered "My heart is [NRSV, "My inward parts are"] in turmoil" by the RSV and NRSV; "I am seething within" by the NASB; and "The churning inside me never stops" by the NIV. Similarly, "My bowels are troubled" (Lamentations 1:20; 2:11, KJV) is translated "my soul is in tumult" by the RSV; "my spirit is greatly troubled" by the NASB; but "my stomach churns" by the NRSV.

The rendering of Song of Solomon 5:4, "my bowels were moved for him," is changed by the ASV to "my heart was moved for him." The RSV, relying upon a slightly different Hebrew text, reads "my heart was thrilled within me"; the NRSV has "my inmost being

yearned for him"; the NIV, "my heart began to pound for him."

"The sounding of thy bowels" as an expression concerning God (Isaiah 63:15, KJV) is rendered "the yearning of your heart" by the NRSV; the entire verse is recast and restated in the contemporary versions, e.g., "Look down from heaven, and see from Your holy and glorious habitation; where are Your zeal and Your mighty deeds? The stirrings of Your heart and Your compassion are restrained toward me" (NASB). See also Isaiah 16:11.

It is said of Joseph (Genesis 43:30, KJV) that "his bowels did yearn upon his brother," which is now translated "his heart yearned for his brother" (RSV); "he was overcome with affection for his brother" (NRSV); "he was deeply stirred over his brother" (NASB); and "Deeply moved at the sight of his brother" (NIV). Similar expressions are found in 1 Kings 3:26 and Jeremiah 31:20.

When Judas fell headlong, his body burst open and "all his bowels gushed out" (Acts 1:18, KJV). This is the only New Testament passage in which the KJV uses the word "bowels" in its literal physical meaning. In eight other cases it is used in the sense of affection or compassion.

BOWELS OF COMPASSION

The Greek word which the KJV translates by "bowels" does not refer to the intestines specifically but to the "inward parts" or internal organs generally. Like the Greek word for "heart," this word was also used for the feelings and affections. It is translated "inward affection" by the KJV in 2 Corinthians 7:15, where the contemporary versions simply have "affection" (NIV, NASB; NKJV, "affections") or "heart" (RSV, NRSV).

In the English language of 1611 both "bowels" and "heart" had this double reference to physical organs and to the emotions of which these organs were supposed to be the seat.

The NRSV renders "Ye are not straitened

in us, but ye are straitened in your own bowels" (2 Corinthians 6:12, KJV) as "There is no restriction in our affections, but only in yours." Paul's words to the Philippians that he longs for them "in the bowels of Jesus Christ," (1:8, KJV) are rendered "with the affection [NRSV, "with the compassion"] of Christ Jesus" by the RSV, NASB, NIV, and NRSV. Again, in Philippians 2:1 "bowels" has this meaning of affection or compassion.

In Colossians 3:12 "bowels of mercies" is now translated "a heart of compassion" (NASB), "tender mercies" (NKJV; NLT, "tenderhearted mercy"), or simply "compassion" (RSV, NRSV, NIV). "Shutteth up his bowels of compassion from him" (1 John 3:17) is rendered as "closes his heart against him" in the RSV and NASB, and "has no pity on him" in the NIV. In the short letter of Paul to Philemon, the contemporary versions generally substitute "heart" for "bowels" in verses 7, 12, and 20.

The Greek verb derived from the noun which the KJV translates "bowels" is used twelve times in the New Testament, and is always translated by the KJV as "have compassion" or "moved with compassion."

BRAVERY

Today we use the word "bravery" of courage in the face of difficult or threatening circumstances. The word occurs once in the KJV, in Isaiah 3:18, where its meaning is quite different. It refers to feminine finery: "In that day the Lord will take away the bravery of their tinkling ornaments about their feet."

Shakespeare uses the word once in this sense, and, like Isaiah (cf. vv.18–23), lists some of the items:

"and now, my honey love,
Will we return unto thy father's house.
And revel it as bravely as the best,
With silken coats, and caps, and golden rings,
With ruffs, and cuffs, and fardingales, and things;

With scarfs, and fans, and double change of bravery,
With amber bracelets, beads, and all this knavery."
—*The Taming of the Shrew*
(IV, 3, 52–58).

The NASB, RSV, and NRSV replace the KJV's rendering, "the bravery of their tinkling ornaments," with "the finery [NASB, "the beauty"] of their anklets." Other translations also use the word "finery" (NIV, NKJV); the NLT has "artful beauty," while the NCV has "everything that makes them proud."

BRAY

The word "bray" conjures up the loud, harsh sound of a donkey's cry. In the KJV the word is used in this sense but also in the etymologically distinct and rarer sense of "crushing or grinding something to powder."

In the latter sense, it occurs at Proverbs 27:22: "Though thou shouldest bray a fool in a mortar among wheat with a pestle, yet will not his foolishness depart from him." The contemporary versions render "bray" as "grind" (NIV, NKJV, NLT), "crush" (NRSV, RSV), "pound" (NASB), and "beat" (CEV). The OED quotes this use in a figurative sense with several citations, including Ben Jonson's *The Alchemist* (1611): "Sir, with an Argument, He'll bray you in a mortar."

BREACH

As a noun, the word "breach" describes "a break" or "rupture." While today we might think of a breakdown in a business contract, or a violation of a law or code, the KJV uses the term to mean "a break," "a broken place," or "an injury." The word is retained by the RSV and the NASB where it refers to breaches in fortifications or city walls (1 Kings 11:27; Nehemiah 4:7; 6:1; Psalm 60:2; Isaiah 22:9; Ezekiel 26:10; Amos 9:11).

Other versions use "gap" (e.g., 1 Kings 11:27, NIV, NRSV), "fractures" (e.g., Psalm 60:2, NIV), "cracks" (e.g., Psalm 60:2, NRSV), and "broken places" (e.g., Amos 9:11, NIV). The idioms "stood in the breach" (Psalm 106:23, KJV) and "the repairer of the breach" (Isaiah 58:12, KJV) are also retained by the RSV, NRSV, and NASB, although at Isaiah 58:12 the NIV has "Repairer of Broken Walls."

The expression "a breach in the tribes of Israel" (Judges 21:15, KJV) is kept by the RSV, NRSV, and NASB, but "breach" in "bindeth up the breach of his people" (Isaiah 30:26, KJV) is reworded "the hurt" (RSV), "injuries" (NRSV), "fracture" (NASB), "bruises" (NIV), "bruise" (NKJV).

The KJV rendering of Proverbs 15:4, "A wholesome tongue is a tree of life: but perverseness therein is a breach in the spirit," is now rendered as "A gentle tongue is a tree of life, but perverseness in it breaks the spirit" in the RSV and NRSV. In the other contemporary versions, the KJV's "breach in the spirit" is rendered as "crushes the spirit" (NASB, NIV, NLT); the CEV paraphrases as "deceitful words can really hurt."

Tyndale's translation of Leviticus 24:20 was "broke for broke, eye for eye and toth for toth: euen as he hath maymed a man, so shall he be maymed again." In a marginal note he gave "breach" and "fracture" as alternate readings for "broke." The Geneva Bible changed to "breach for breach," and was followed by the Bishops' Bible and the KJV.

The NRSV returns to the other word in Tyndale's margin and reads, "fracture for fracture, eye for eye, tooth for tooth; the injury inflicted is the injury to be suffered." The majority of the contemporary versions use the word "fracture" for the KJV's "breach" in this verse.

In Judges 5:17, the KJV uses "breaches" to render a Hebrew word which means "landing places," rendered "harbors" (CEV, NCV, NLT), "landings" (RSV, NRSV, NASB), "inlets" (NKJV), and "coves" (NIV) by the contemporary versions. In Amos 6:11, the KJV uses the words "with breaches" to translate the Hebrew which reads "into fragments" (NIV, RSV, NCV, "into bits"; NRSV, NLT, CEV, "to pieces"; NASB, "to fragments").

The only context in which the KJV use of "breach" might cause serious confusion is Numbers 14:34, where the Lord sentences the Israelites to forty years in the wilderness, and says, "ye shall know my breach of promise." Today, this phrase has become common for a kind of lawsuit and leaves us with the uncomfortable inference that the Lord has not only broken his promise to the Israelites but is admitting it in a flint-hearted judgment.

The Hebrew phrase rendered "my breach of promise" by the KJV means "my opposition." Tyndale's translation was "ye shall fele my vengeaunce." The Great Bible had "ye shall know my displeasure." The Geneva Bible introduced the idea of "breach of promise," and was followed by the Bishops' Bible and the KJV.

The RSV and NRSV return to the rendering of the Great Bible, "you shall know my displeasure." Moffatt reads "That will teach you what it is to have me against you"; Confraternity has "Thus you will realize what it means to oppose me." Other contemporary versions have "you will know My opposition" (NASB); "You will know me as your enemy" (NCV); "know what it is like to have me against you" (NIV); and "you shall know My rejection" (NKJV).

BREAD ALONE

Satan tempted Jesus after Jesus had fasted for forty days and forty nights, saying, "If You are the Son of God, command that these stones become bread" (Matthew 4:3, NKJV). Jesus answered, quoting from Deuteronomy 8:3, "Man shall not live by bread alone but by every word that proceedeth out of the mouth of God" (Matthew 4:4, KJV).

The KJV expression "man shall not live by bread alone" is retained by the NKJV and RSV; the NASB has "on bread alone"; the NIV, "Man does not live on bread alone"; the CEV, "No one can live only on food"; the NRSV, "One does not live by bread alone"; the NLT, "People need more than bread for their life."

The poet, essayist, and philosopher Ralph Waldo Emerson alluded to this expression when he noted, "Man does not live by bread alone, but by faith, by admiration, by sympathy" *(Lectures and Biographical Sketches. The Sovereignty of Ethics).*

BREAK UP

This expression today implies severance or destruction: to break up a meeting is to effectively end it. The expression occurs nine times in the KJV, and it represents seven different Hebrew or Greek verbs. "Break up your fallow ground" (Jeremiah 4:3; Hosea 10:12, KJV) remains current English; "when the congregation was broken up" (Acts 13:43, KJV) is now rendered "when the meeting of the synagogue broke up" in the NRSV.

Elsewhere, however, the expression is used in an obsolete sense for which we now say "break in," "break into," or "break through." The KJV itself uses "break through" in Matthew 6:19–20 and Luke 12:39 as a translation for the same Greek verb which it renders "broken up" in Matthew 24:43. The majority of the contemporary versions have "break in" in Matthew 6:19–20, and "broken into" in Luke 12:39 and Matthew 24:43.

The KJV rendering of Job 38:10, "And brake up for it my decreed place" is a literalism which may not be readily understood. Translations in the Tyndale-Coverdale line used "gave it my commandment." The RV and ASV have "marked out for it my bound"; contemporary versions have "prescribed bounds for it" (RSV, NRSV); "placed boundaries on it" (NASB); and "fixed limits [NKJV, "fixed My limit"] for it" (NKJV, NIV).

BRICKS WITHOUT STRAW

To "make bricks without straw" means to require work to be done without the proper materials or to be done under unreasonable conditions. The expression alludes to the time when Moses and Aaron asked Pharaoh to allow the people of Israel to celebrate a religious festival to the Lord in the wilderness. Pharaoh would not allow them but made their task even more difficult, in that the straw—used to bind the clay in making bricks—would no longer be supplied to them.

The phrase "make bricks without straw" alludes to Exodus 5:7, KJV, "Ye shall no more give the people straw to make brick, as heretofore: let them go and gather straw for themselves."

The current form and usage of the phrase have moved beyond the text of the biblical narrative. It was not that the Israelites had to make bricks without straw, but that the straw would not be supplied to them—they had to gather their own straw on their own time.

BRIGANDINE

This is a term for a coat of cloth or leather with rings or little plates sewed on to make it a lightweight coat of mail. It was invented in the Middle Ages to increase mobility, and was worn by "brigands," who were light-armed foot soldiers, equipped for duty as scouts or skirmishers. This meaning of "brigand" is now obsolete; a brigand today is a bandit, and brigandines have long since passed into history. A "brigantine" was originally a light skirmishing for which "brig" was simply a colloquial abbreviation.

"Brigandine" occurs only twice in the KJV, in Jeremiah 46:4 and 51:3, and is variously rendered by the contemporary versions as "scale-armor" (NASB), "coat [or: coats] of mail" (RSV, NRSV), or simply "armor" (NKJV, NIV, NCV, NLT). The Geneva Bible had called Goliath's coat of mail a "brigandine" (1 Samuel 17:5), but its weight of five thousand shekels made the term inappropriate.

BRIM

The word "brim" today suggests the edge of something hollow ("the volcano's brim"). The KJV uses it in this sense in 1 Kings 7:23–24, 26; 2 Chronicles 4:2, 5; John 2:7. But "the brim of the water"

(Joshua 3:15, KJV) is archaic. In Old English "brim" was a poetical word for the sea or flood, which then came to be used for the edge of the water or for its surface.

In Joshua 3:15 the Hebrew word represented by "brim" in the KJV means edge or border. The NRSV translates, "So when those who bore the ark had come to the Jordan, and the feet of the priests bearing the ark were dipped in the edge of the water." The majority of the contemporary versions replace the KJV's "brim" with "edge" in this verse.

BROKEN REED

A "broken reed" is a person or thing that is weak or likely to fail. The expression comes from Isaiah 36:6 (KJV), in which the prophet tells Hezekiah, "Lo, thou trustest in the staff of this broken reed, on Egypt." The contemporary versions render this expression as "broken stick" (CEV); "broken reed of a staff" (NRSV); "the staff of this crushed reed" (NASB); "splintered reed of a staff" (NIV); "splintered walking stick" (NCV); the NKJV retains the KJV rendering, "the staff of this broken reed."

The parallel passage in 2 Kings 18:21 has "the staff of this bruised reed" (KJV) but otherwise follows the renderings above.

Jesus quoted from Isaiah 42:1–4, describing the ministry of the Servant of the Lord: "A bruised reed shall he not break" (Matthew 12:20, KJV). The contemporary versions render "bruised reed" as "bent reed" (CEV), "battered reed" (NASB), and "crushed blade of grass" (NCV); the NIV, NKJV, and NRSV retain the KJV "bruised reed"; and the NLT paraphrases the whole expression as "He will not crush those who are weak."

BROTHER'S KEEPER

In contemporary English the phrase "brother's keeper" is used to mean one who accepts responsibility for another person's behavior or welfare. The phrase derives from Cain's reply, "Am I my brother's keeper?" (Genesis 4:9, KJV) to God after Cain had killed his brother Abel.

The phrase "Am I my brother's keeper?" is retained by the NASB, NIV, NKJV, NRSV, and RSV; the CEV, NCV, and NLT paraphrase as "Am I supposed to look after my brother?" (CEV), "Is it my job to take care of my brother?" (NCV), "Am I supposed to keep track of him wherever he goes?" (NLT).

BRUIT

This is an archaic word which means "a report noised abroad," "a rumor," or "tidings." "All that hear the bruit of thee shall clap the hands over thee," says Nahum in a prophecy against Nineveh (Nahum 3:19, KJV); the NRSV has "All who hear the news about you clap their hands over you."

Jeremiah 10:22, addressed to Judah, reads in the KJV: "Behold, the noise of the bruit is come, and a great commotion out of the north country, to make the cities of Judah desolate, and a den of dragons." The NRSV has "Hear, a noise! Listen, it is coming—a great commotion from the land of the north to make the cities of Judah a desolation, a lair of jackals." For the KJV's "the noise of the bruit," other contemporary versions have "a rumor" (RSV); "the noise of the report" (NKJV); "the report" (NIV); "the sound of a report" (NASB); "the news" (NCV); "sounds of destruction" (CEV); and "the terrifying roar" (NLT).

Shakespeare used "bruit" both as a noun and as a verb. Examples are:

> "The bruit thereof will bring you
> many friends."
> —*King Henry VI, Part III* (IV, 7, 64)

> "I find thou art no less than fame
> hath bruited."
> —*King Henry VI, Part I* (II, 3, 68)

> "By this great clatter, one of greatest
> note
> Seems bruited."
> —*Macbeth* (V, 7, 29)

BUCKLER

This word refers to a small, round shield with a knob or "boss" in the center, which is carried or strapped to the arm for use in hand-to-hand fighting. The Hebrew word *magen* denotes a buckler, and *tsinnah* a large shield covering the whole body, but the KJV does not distinguish between the two. It translates *magen* as "shield" forty-seven times and "buckler" only eight times; and it renders *tsinnah* by "shield" ten times, "buckler" five times, and "target" five times.

The "thousand bucklers" hanging on the tower of David (Song of Solomon 4:4, KJV) are retained by the RSV, NRSV, and NKJV, but are rendered "shields" by the other contemporary versions. "Lift up the buckler against thee" (Ezekiel 26:8, KJV) is replaced by "raise a roof of shields against you" in the NRSV and RSV, "shield" or "shields" also appearing in the majority of the other contemporary versions.

In the great song of faith, Psalm 91, the person who trusts in God is given assurance that "his faithfulness is a shield and buckler" (v. 4, KJV). The RSV, NRSV, and NKJV retain "shield and buckler"; the NASB has "shield and bulwark"; the NIV, "shield and rampart"; and the NCV and NLT, "shield [NLT, "armor"] and protection."

BULLOCK

As used in the KJV, the word "bullock" means "a young bull." The term is nowadays limited to bulls that have been castrated. Since the animals offered for sacrifice were required to be "without blemish" (Leviticus 1:3, 10, KJV), the word "bullock" can be misleading. The contemporary versions use the term "bull" or "young bull."

BUNCH

We use the noun "bunch" today for a group of things ("a bunch of flowers") or colloquially for a group of people ("a fine bunch of people"). But "bunch" is also an obsolete term for the hump on the back of a camel or of a deformed person, and the KJV uses the word in this sense only. The KJV rendering of Isaiah 30:6 is: "they will carry . . . their treasures upon the bunches of camels" (Isaiah 30:6).

Today this is rendered "they carry . . . their treasures on the humps of camels" by the NRSV, RSV, NKJV, and NIV; the NASB similarly has "on camels' humps" for "the bunches of camels," and the NCV has "on the backs of camels."

Shakespeare used this word in *King Richard III*. The humpbacked Richard is called "that poisonous bunchback'd toad" (I, 3, 246) and "that foul bunchback'd toad" (IV, 4, 81).

BURDEN

Today we speak of a "burden" when referring to something heavy or awkward to carry or when describing a significant responsibility. The Hebrew verb *nasa'* means "to lift, carry, take." The related noun *massa'* means "a burden that is carried," but it also means "an oracle," that is the message of a prophet who lifts up his voice in formal and solemn utterance of the word or vision which has come to him. The KJV uses "burden" for both these senses of *massa'*.

The RSV and NASB use "oracle" where that is the meaning (2 Kings 9:25; Isaiah 13:1; Ezekiel 12:10; Nahum 1:1; Habakkuk 1:1; Zechariah 9:1; 12:1; Malachi 1:1), although the NASB occasionally retains "burden" (e.g., Zechariah 9:1; 12:1; Ezekiel 12:10). The NRSV and NIV usually translate as "oracle"; the NLT, NCV, and CEV usually have "message."

In Jeremiah 23:33–40 there is vivid, pointed wordplay upon the double meaning of *massa'*, which is expressed by using "burden" in the same double meaning (KJV, RSV, NRSV).

BURN

This word leads us to imagine fire and its effects. Where it occurs in the KJV, however, this is not the meaning—although it is easy to see how Paul's thought, "It is better to marry than to burn," could be misunderstood as meaning "burn in hellfire." The text in 1 Corinthians 7:9 reads in the KJV, "If they cannot contain, let them marry: for it is better to marry than to burn."

The word "burn" here translates a Greek passive infinitive which since the days of the poet Anacreon had been used in the sense of "to be inflamed or on fire with emotion," usually with lust or anger. The translation of the NRSV—"If they cannot exercise self-control they should marry. For it is better to marry than to be aflame with passion"—is justified by all lexicons of the Greek language, and adopted in some form by all the contemporary versions.

The word "better" does not mean that marriage is the less of two evils; it expresses Paul's judgment that to marry is not a sin (vv. 28 and 36), while Jesus taught that to burn with lustful desire is sinful (Matthew 5:28).

The same Greek word is used in 2 Corinthians 11:29, where the KJV has "Who is weak, and I am not weak? who is offended, and I burn not?" The word "offended" is here used in an obsolete sense which may not be clear to the modern reader. The NRSV translates the second half of the verse, "Who is made to stumble, and I am not indignant?" Goodspeed's translation has "fired with indignation"; Knox's translation, "ablaze with indignation."

This word is used three times in 2 Maccabees (4:38; 10:35; 14:45), where its reference to anger is made explicit.

BURNT OFFERING

"Burnt offering" is sometimes used humorously to refer to a burnt meal. The phrase derives from the name of the Old Testament sacrifice of a bull, ram, or male bird to be burnt on an altar, as a gift to God, in thanksgiving or as an atonement for sin. The first example of a burnt offering in the Bible is recorded in Genesis 8:20 (KJV), "And Noah builded an altar unto the LORD; and took every clean beast, and of every clean fowl, and offered burnt offerings on the altar."

Here the NASB, NIV, NKJV, NRSV, and RSV retain the KJV "burnt offerings"; the CEV has "Noah built an altar where he could offer sacrifices to the LORD. Then he offered on the altar one of each kind of animal and bird that could be used for a sacrifice"; and the NLT translates as "Then Noah built an altar to the LORD and sacrificed on it the animals and birds that had been approved for that purpose."

BURSTING

This word is used today of something's having reached its maximum holding capacity ("a suitcase bursting at the seams"). The word "burst" is used nine times in the KJV with this modern meaning; it is retained by the contemporary versions in every case. But in Isaiah 30:14 "bursting" is used for a Hebrew noun derived from the verb which means "to beat," "break into pieces," or "crush." Here "in the bursting" means in the breakage; the word "burst" simply means "break," as it does in Shakespeare's *The Taming of the Shrew* (Induction, 1, 8): "You will not pay for the glasses you have burst?"

Alongside the KJV's use of a now obsolete meaning in this verse is the question of the meaning of the Hebrew noun which the KJV renders as "in the bursting of it." The noun denotes the *results* of the breaking, rather than the process, and contemporary versions render it as "among its pieces" (NASB, NIV) or "among its fragments" (NKJV, RSV).

The older versions likewise brought out this meaning. The Vulgate has "de fragmentis eius," and the Septuagint, as translated by Thomson, reads, "the fragments of which are so small that there cannot be found among them." Martin Luther's translation into German had *von seinen Stücken*.

The rendering which found its way into the KJV goes back to the Great Bible, from which it passed to the Bishops' Bible and so to the KJV. The entire verse reads, in the NRSV:

> "its breaking is like that of a potter's
> vessel that is smashed so ruthlessly
> that among its fragments not a sherd
> is found for taking fire from the
> hearth, or dipping water out of the
> cistern."

BUSINESS

This word is used today of an enterprise of some sort ("the car business"), or to refer to affairs or matters with which someone is concerned. In the Old Testament the KJV uses the word in the same senses for which we would naturally use it today. In the New Testament, however, the KJV uses it five times, in each case to represent a different Greek term.

Jesus' answer to his parents' anxiety (Luke 2:49, KJV), "Wist ye not that I must be about my Father's business?" is translated by the NRSV, "Did you not know that I must be in my Father's house?" The Greek means literally "in the (things) of my Father," an expression used repeatedly in the Greek papyri for "in the house of." This translation was adopted by the Revised Version of 1881, and by almost all subsequent translations of the New Testament, including the contemporary versions.

In 1 Thessalonians 4:11 and Romans 16:2, the contemporary versions attempt to reproduce the very general and comprehensive character of the expressions used in the Greek. "Do your own business" (1 Thessalonians 4:11, KJV) is rendered "mind your [NLT, "minding your"] own business" by the NKJV, NIV, and NLT, but the RSV, NRSV and NASB change to "mind [NASB, "attend to"] your own affairs."

In Romans 16:2, "assist her in whatsoever business she hath need of you" (KJV) is rendered "help her in whatever [NASB, "whatever matter"] she may require from you" [NASB, "she may need of you"] in the NRSV, RSV, and NASB.

On the other hand, a specific Greek term is used in Acts 6:3, and "appoint over this business" (KJV) is rendered as "appoint to this duty" (NRSV, RSV) and "put in charge of this task" (NASB).

In his biography of Charles W. Eliot, president of Harvard University, 1869–1909 (Boston: Houghton-Mifflin, 1930), Henry James states that "the Puritan believed, as in a cardinal tenet, that it was consonant with the divine order that he should pursue his own private gain and 'be not slothful in business.'" But the word "business" in this text (Romans 12:11) is used in the sense of "diligence."

The list of meanings which the word "business" had up to the seventeenth century, but which then became obsolete, is long. It includes "diligence," "activity," "briskness," "officiousness," "eagerness," "earnestness," "importunity," "anxiety," "solicitude," "care," "attention," "trouble," "difficulty," "commotion" (OED). Tyndale's translation of Galatians 6:17 was "From hence forth, let no man put me to busynes," and this was retained by Coverdale, the Great Bible, and the Geneva Bible. The same versions had "When Pilate sawe . . . that more busines was made" (Matthew 27:24).

The Greek word in Romans 12:11 is *spoude*, which means "haste," "zeal," or "earnestness." The NASB has "diligence"; the NIV, NRSV, and RSV, "zeal."

BUT

We hear the word "but" today in connection with exceptions or excuses ("I would like to pay for our meal, but I've lost my wallet"). The KJV use of the word conforms to our modern-day usage. In Amos 3:7, however, we find "but" being used with the archaic meaning of "unless": "Surely the Lord GOD will do nothing, but he revealeth his secret unto his servants the prophets."

We could be forgiven for understanding this to be two statements of fact, contrasting with each other—that is, to mean that instead of doing anything God reveals something. In fact, the word "but" here means "unless." The ASV has "except he reveal." The NRSV rendering is "Surely the Lord GOD does nothing, without revealing his secret to his servants the prophets." Wycliffe often used "but" in this sense of unless. Examples are:

Matthew 5:20: "I seie to you that but your riytfulnesse be more plenteuous, thanne of scribis . . . ye schulen not entre in."

John 3:2: "no man mai do these signes that thou doist, but god be with hym."

John: 3:3: "truli truli I seie to thee, but a man be born again, he mai not se the kyngdom of god."

John 12:24: "truli truli I seie to you. But a corne of whete fall into the erthe and be deed: it dwelleth aloone."

This use of "but" was beginning to be archaic when Tyndale made his translation, and he substituted for it "except," which remains the usage of the KJV in these and similar cases. The NRSV and other contemporary versions use "unless."

BY

The word "by" is a familiar preposition with a number of different meanings. To name just a few, we might use it in the sense of near to ("a house by the river"); or to refer to a route ("she came by the highway"); to refer to the means by which something is done ("sent by express mail"); or to mean not later than ("by six o'clock"). The KJV, however, uses "by" in ways which may be unfamiliar to us. Paul's statement in 1 Corinthians 4:4 (KJV), "I know nothing by myself," means "I know nothing against myself." This is an obsolete use of "by" which occurs in Shakespeare's *All's Well That Ends Well* (V, 3, 237): "By him and by this woman here what know you?"

In Foxe's *Book of Martyrs,* an inquisitor accuses Elizabeth Young, "Thou hast spoken evil words by the queen"; and she answers, "No man upon earth can prove any such things by me."

The preposition "by" is used in the sense of "during" or "for" as part of the phrase "by the space of"—"this continued by the space of two years" (Acts 19:10, KJV; see also Acts 7:42; 13:21; 20:31). When the KJV New Testament uses the word "space," it usually refers to a period of time. (See SPACE)

"By" is so commonly used in forms of swearing or adjuration (see Matthew 26:63) that this might seem to be its function in 2 Thessalonians 2:1: "Now we beseech you, brethren, by the coming of our Lord Jesus Christ" (KJV). But it is here used as a translation for the Greek word which means "concerning."

The NRSV and RSV read: "Now concerning [NRSV, "As to"] the coming of our Lord Jesus Christ and our assembling to meet [NRSV, "our being gathered together to"] him, we beg you, brethren [NRSV, "brothers and sisters"], not to be quickly shaken in mind or excited [NRSV, "in mind or alarmed"]." "Every man is brutish by his knowledge" (Jeremiah 51:17) represents the Hebrew which the KJV translates as "Every man is brutish in his knowledge" in Jeremiah 10:14. Neither of these renderings is found in the revised versions or contemporary versions, however. The NRSV reads in both cases, "Everyone is stupid and without knowledge."

The KJV occasionally uses "by" to translate the Greek preposition which means "because of" or "for the sake of." In John 6:57, "by the Father" and "by me" mean "because of the Father" and "because of me." "By your tradition" (Matthew 15:3, 6) is "for the sake of your tradition."

"For the earth which drinketh in the rain that cometh oft upon it, and bringeth forth herbs meet for them by whom it is dressed, receiveth blessing from God" (Hebrews 6:7, KJV) is rendered by the NRSV as "Ground that drinks up the rain falling on it repeatedly, and that produces a crop useful to those for whom it is cultivated, receives a blessing from God."

BY AND BY

This is an adverbial phrase which meant "immediately" in the fifteenth and sixteenth centuries. Like "anon" and "presently," it gradually lost this sense and came to mean "soon," "after a while," or "at some indefinite time in the future." When we hear the phrase today, it tends to have a procrastinating ring to it.

In Mark's account of the beheading of John the Baptist, we find in the KJV a contrast between the haste of Salome's coming before the king, the immediacy of the king's answering command to the executioner, and the leisurely tone of Salome's request that the head of John the Baptist be given her "by and by" (6:25, 27).

In the Greek, the adverb for Salome's coming in (v. 25) and that for the king's command (v. 27) are the same—*eutheōs*, which means immediately. But the adverb which Salome uses is even stronger—*ex-autes*, which means "at once," "instantly," "at this very hour."

The NASB, NKJV, NRSV, and RSV thus render the word as "at once"; the NIV, CEV, NCV, and NLT have "right now."

In the parable of the sower (Matthew 13:21), Jesus says of the hearer who is like stony ground that when persecution comes he immediately falls away; the KJV has "by and by he is offended." In Luke 17:7, the KJV reads, "Which of you, having a servant plowing or feeding cattle, will say unto him by and by, when he is come from the field, Go and sit down to meat?"

But the adverb, here rendered as "by and by," belongs to the last clause. The NRSV translates as "Who among you would say to your slave who has just come in from plowing or tending sheep in the field, 'Come here at once and take your place at the table'?"

In Luke 21:9, the KJV reads "the end is not by and by." "By and by" is here an adverbial phrase which translates the Greek adverb *eutheos* The RSV reads "the end will not be at once"; the NRSV and NASB have "the end will not [NASB, "does not"] follow immediately."

BY COURSE

In its one occurrence in the KJV, "by course" means "in turn" (1 Corinthians 14:27). The KJV rendering of this verse is, "If any man speak in an unknown tongue, let it be by two, or at the most by three, and that by course; and let one interpret."

The contemporary versions render "by course" here as "one at a time" (NLT, NIV), "one after the other" (NCV), and "each in turn" (RSV, NRSV, NASB). The whole verse in the NRSV reads, "If anyone speaks in a tongue, let there be only two or at most three, and each in turn; and let one interpret."

C

CAB

We are familiar with the "cab," a shortened form of "taxicab," from the word "cabriolet." In the KJV, however, the word is used to refer to a unit of measurement, such a word being etymologically distinct from the word for the vehicle used in transportation in our cities.

The word "cab" occurs only once in the KJV—at 2 Kings 6:25: "And there was a great famine in Samaria: and, behold, they be-sieged it, until an ass's head was sold for fourscore pieces of silver, and the fourth part of a cab of dove's dung for five pieces of silver." The unit was a dry measure of capacity, equivalent to one-fifth or one-sixth of a seah. It is uncertain what its equivalent in contemporary measures is, with cited equivalents for a cab ranging from one to two liters.

The NASB, NKJV, NRSV, and RSV render the KJV "cab" with the alternative spelling "kab," while the NIV retains the KJV spelling "cab." For the KJV measure "fourth part of a cab," the NCV has "half a pint"; the CEV has "small bowl"; and the NLT has "cup."

CABIN

In modern times, a "cabin" is a small room in a ship, an area inside an airplane, or a small simple wooden hut. In contrast, in the fourteenth to sixteenth centuries "cabin" was used in the sense of "cell." When Jeremiah was put in prison by the princes of Judah, according to the KJV, he "was entered into the dungeon, and into the cabins" (Jeremiah 37:16).

The contemporary translations render the KJV "the cabins" as "vaulted cell" (NASB, NIV), "cell" (NCV), "dungeon cell" (NLT), "cells" (NKJV, NRSV), and "dungeon cells" (RSV). Shakespeare made a verb of it in *Macbeth* (III, 4, 24): "But now I am cabin'd, cribb'd, confin'd, bound in To saucy doubts and fears." In 1616 *The Country Farm* described bees as "busie making combes, and building of little Cabbins."

CAMEL THROUGH AN EYE OF A NEEDLE

Jesus' response after the rich young ruler went away sadly was, "It is easier for a camel to go through the eye of a needle, than for a rich man to enter into the kingdom of God" (Matthew 19:24, KJV). For a camel—the largest animal in Palestine—to pass through the tiny eye of a needle—the smallest opening—is impossible. But even this, impossible though it is, is easier than for a rich person to enter the kingdom of heaven. All the contemporary versions retain this same illustration.

Shakespeare used this expression in *King Richard II* (V, 5, 16–17)

> "It is as hard to come as for a camel
> To thread the postern of a small
>   needle's eye."

CANDLE, CANDLESTICK

A "candlestick" today is a holder that has a socket for a candle. In the KJV, however, the word "candlestick" referred to a lampstand. The "candlestick" which Moses was commanded to make for the tabernacle weighed about 108 pounds. It was of pure gold, hammered, with a base and shaft and six branches (Exodus 25:31–40). It had no candles. "Thou shalt make the seven lamps thereof," verse 37 says. Again and again, in the books of Exodus and Numbers, reference is made to the candlestick of pure gold, with its seven lamps, its vessels, and the oil for the light.

This "candlestick" was a massive, beautifully wrought stand for seven lamps. All the contemporary versions render the KJV "candlestick" as "lampstand." So also the seven candlesticks which stood for the seven churches to which John was commissioned to write (Revelation 1:10–20).

In Proverbs 20:27 the KJV "candle" is rendered "lamp" by most of the contemporary versions; the NLT has "The LORD's searchlight penetrates the human spirit, exposing every hidden motive." In Proverbs 24:20 the KJV "the candle of the wicked" is "the lamp of the wicked" (NASB, NIV, NKJV, NRSV, RSV); the NLT has "light"; the CEV has "the flame of a lamp."

CANKER

In present-day English and in the KJV, "canker" is used to refer to a spreading sore, a gangrene. Second Timothy 2:17, in the KJV reads, "their word will eat as doth a canker." The word for "canker" translates the Greek word from which the Latin *gangrena* and the English "gangrene" are derived. The NASB, NIV, NRSV, and RSV render the word as "gangrene"; the NKJV and NLT as "cancer"; the CEV as "a sore that won't heal."

CANKERED

In modern English "cankered" means infected with (a) canker, a spreading sore or a plant disease. In the KJV it is used in the now obsolete sense of "rusted," translating a Greek verb which means "to become rusty," "tarnished," "corroded."

In James 5:3, the CEV, NASB, NCV, NRSV, and RSV substitute "rusted" for "cankered"; the NIV and NKJV have "corroded"; the NLT has "become worthless." The NRSV reads, "Your gold and silver have rusted, and their rust will be evidence against you, and it will eat your flesh like fire. You have laid up treasure for the last days."

Shakespeare used "canker'd" in this sense in *King Henry IV, Part II* (IV, 5, 71):

"For this they have engrossed and
piled up
The canker'd heaps of
strange-achieved gold."

CANKERWORM

A cankerworm is a kind of moth, the larvae of which destroy the buds and leaves of plants. In the KJV, "cankerworm" is used to refer to a kind of locust. The word occurs as a rendering for the Hebrew word *yeleq* in Joel 1:4; 2:25 and Nahum 3:15–16. In all these cases the reference is to locusts, and the contemporary versions render this word as follows: "hopping locust" (NCV, NLT, NRSV, RSV); "hopper" (Joel 2:25, NRSV, RSV); "creeping locust" (NASB); "crawling locust" (NKJV); and "young locust" (NIV). In Nahum 3:15–16 the multiplication is likened to that of "grasshoppers" in the CEV, NIV, NLT, and NRSV. (See PALMERWORM)

CAPTIVITY

In contemporary English "captivity" refers to a state of imprisonment, subjection, or exile. In the KJV, the word is used not only in this sense but also in the now obsolete sense of a group of captives restrained by imprisonment, subjection, or exile. For example, "the whole captivity" in Amos 1:6, KJV, "they carried away captive the whole captivity," is rendered "whole communities" (NIV), "entire communities" (NRSV),

"all the people" (NCV), "my people" (NLT), and "an entire population" (NASB).

The KJV phrase "bring again the captivity of" is translated by the NRSV as "restore the fortunes of," in e.g., Amos 9:14: "I will bring again the captivity of my people of Israel" (KJV) becomes "I will restore the fortunes of my people Israel" (NRSV). Other translations adopt this latter rendering at, e.g., Jeremiah 30:3 (NASB, NLT) and Jeremiah 30:18 (NASB, NIV, NLT).

The KJV of Jeremiah 33:11, "return the captivity of," is rendered in the NCV as "do good things for" and in the NLT as "restore the prosperity of." The Hebrew idiom in these verses is used more than thirty times in the Old Testament, and is applied even to Job, who had not been in captivity or exile—"the LORD turned the captivity of Job" (42:10). This is rendered as the LORD "restored the fortunes of Job" (NASB, NRSV, RSV); "restored his fortunes" (NLT), "restored Job's losses" (NKJV), "made him prosperous again" (NIV), and "gave him success again" (NCV).

In "arise, Barak, and lead thy captivity captive" (Judges 5:12, KJV), the Hebrew has here the repetition involved in a cognate accusative, the literal rendering of which would be "lead captive your captives." This is expressed as "take captive your captives" in the NIV, "lead [NASB, "take"] away your captives" (NASB, NRSV, RSV), and "lead your captives away" (NKJV, NLT). The same construction appears in Psalm 68:18, and in the quotation of this verse in Ephesians 4:8.

These are rendered he "led a parade of captives" (NCV), "led a crowd of captives" (NLT), "led captives in your [or: his] train" (NIV), "led captivity captive" (NKJV), and "made captivity itself a captive" (Ephesians 4:8, NRSV). By his death Jesus Christ conquered all the host of spirits that had conspired against him. He is pictured as leading them captive in his train when he ascended.

CARE, CAREFUL, CAREFULNESS

In English "care" now refers to a sense of concern or regard or, usually in the plural "cares," to problems or worries. In the KJV both meanings are seen, for example 1 Peter 5:7 in the KJV reads, "Casting all your care upon him; for he careth for you." The contemporary translations all retain the verb "care" in the second part of the verse but in the first part of the verse the noun "care" is translated "anxiety" (NASB, NIV, NRSV), "anxiety" (RSV), "worries" (CEV, NCV), and "worries and cares" (NLT); the NKJV retains "care" as a noun.

When Paul wrote in 2 Corinthians 11:28 of "that which cometh upon me daily, the care of all the churches," he was writing of his "concern" (NASB, NCV, NIV, NKJV), "anxiety" (NRSV, RSV), or "worrying" (CEV).

When Jesus gently reproved Martha for being "careful . . . about many things" (Luke 10:41, KJV), it was because she was "worried and upset" (CEV, NCV, NIV), "worried and bothered" (NASB), "worried and troubled" (NKJV), or "worried and distracted" (NRSV). "Be careful for nothing" (Philippians 4:6, KJV) is rendered "Don't [NCV, NRSV, "Do not"] worry about anything" (CEV, NCV, NLT, NRSV); "be anxious for nothing" (NASB, NKJV); and "Do not be anxious about anything" (NIV).

In "I would have you without carefulness" (1 Corinthians 7:39, KJV), "carefulness" is rendered "worry" (CEV, NCV), "concern" (NASB, NIV), "concerns" (NLT), "anxieties" (NRSV, RSV), and "care" (NKJV).

"Carefulness" is used in 2 Corinthians 7:11 to translate the Greek *spoude,* which means "haste," "diligence," "zeal." This is rendered as "earnestness" (NASB, NIV, NLT), "eagerness" (NRSV, RSV), and "diligence" (NKJV).

CARELESS

"Careless" is most frequently used today to mean "not paying enough attention"; "done without sufficient attention to de-tail." The word is used rarely today in the sense of "free from troubles." In the KJV the word is used in this latter sense, sometimes with the connotations of complacency.

For example, the KJV for Judges 18:7 reads: "Then the five men departed, and came to Laish, and saw the people that were therein, how they dwelt careless, after the manner of the Zidonians, quiet and secure"; for the KJV "careless" the contemporary versions have "in safety" (NIV, NKJV); "safely" (NKJV); "in security" (NASB, RSV); "securely" (NRSV); and "carefree" (NLT). The adverb "carelessly" at Isaiah 47:8, Ezekiel 39:6, and Zephaniah 2:15 in the KJV is generally rendered in the contemporary versions as "securely," "in security," or "in safety."

The connotation of complacency and the modern sense of neglect is brought out in Isaiah 32:9–11: "Rise up, ye women that are at ease; hear my voice, ye careless daughters; give ear unto my speech. Many days and years shall ye be troubled, ye careless women: for the vintage shall fail, the gathering shall not come. Tremble, ye women that are at ease; be troubled, ye careless ones: strip you, and make you bare, and gird sackcloth upon your loins."

"Careless" in these verses is rendered as "complacent" (NASB, NKJV, RSV), or with the phrase "feel safe" (NCV) and "feel secure" (NIV). The NLT for verses 10–11 reads, "you careless ones will suddenly begin to care . . . throw off your unconcern"; the CEV for the whole passage is: "Listen to what I say, you women who are carefree and careless! You may not have worries now, but in about a year, the grape harvest will fail, and you will tremble. Shake and shudder, you women without a care! Strip off your clothes—put on sackcloth."

In the *Merry Wives of Windsor* (V, 5, 56), Shakespeare used the word "careless" in the sense of "free from troubles": "Sleep she as sound as careless infancy."

CARRIAGE

A "carriage" refers today to a small passenger vehicle that is pulled by horses. In the KJV, however, the word referred to baggage, i.e., what people carry, rather than the vehicle that carries them. For example, when the six hundred Danites who despoiled the house of Micah departed, they "put the little ones and the cattle and the carriage before them" (Judges 18:21, KJV). The Hebrew word represented by "carriage" means "abundance" or "riches"; and the contemporary versions render this as "possessions" (CEV, NIV, NLT), "goods" (NKJV, NRSV, RSV), or "valuables" (NASB).

The KJV for Acts 21:15 has "After those days we took up our carriages and went up to Jerusalem." The use of the word "carriages" in this verse is peculiar to the KJV. The Great Bible and the Bishops' Bible had "took up our burdens"; the Geneva Bible, "trussed up our fardels." An objector to the reliability of the Acts of the Apostles asks, "How could they have taken up their carriages, when there was no road for wheels, nothing but a mountain track, between Caesarea and Jerusalem?"

The Greek word means simply "to get ready" or "prepare for." Tyndale's translation was "After those days we made ourselves ready, and went up to Jerusalem." The contemporary versions render this as "got ready" (CEV, NASB, NCV, NIV, NRSV), "packed" (NKJV), and "packed our things" (NLT).

"Carriages" in the KJV for Isaiah 10:28, "laid up his carriages," is rendered in the contemporary versions as "baggage" (NASB, NRSV, RSV) "equipment" (NKJV, NLT), and "supplies" (CEV, NIV).

"Carriages" in Isaiah 46:1, "your carriages were heavy loaden," is rendered "things [NASB, "things that"] you carry" (NASB, NRSV, RSV). Other versions are more specific, e.g., the NIV, "the images," and the NCV, "the statues."

CAST DOWN

This adjective means that people are worried. In the KJV in Daniel 7:9, however, "cast down" is used as a verb to mean "were placed." This is part of Daniel's description of his vision: "I beheld till the thrones were cast down, and the Ancient of days did sit." Coverdale, Matthew, and the Great Bible had "till the seates were prepared." The Geneva Bible and the Bishops' Bible had "till the thrones were set up." The Greek Septuagint and the Latin Vulgate have verbs which mean "were placed." Martin Luther had "bis dass Stühle gesetzt wurden." The KJV stands alone in the rendering "cast down."

The contemporary versions have "set up" (CEV, NASB), "put in place" (NKJV, NLT), and "set in place" (NIV).

CAST IN HIS TEETH

The expression "cast in his teeth" is used in Matthew 27:44, KJV: "The thieves also, which were crucified with him, cast the same in his teeth." It means "revile" or "insult." The contemporary versions translate this expression as "insulted" (NASB, NCV), "heaped insults" (NIV), "shouted . . . insults" (NLT) "reviled" (NKJV, RSV), and "taunted" (NRSV). The parallel passage in Mark 15:32 has the same Greek verb, but the KJV translates this as "reviled." The discrepancy goes back to Tyndale, who used "cast in his teeth" in Matthew and "checked him" in Mark.

Tyndale translated James 1:5 as "If any of you lack wisdom, let him ask of God which giveth to all men indifferently, and casteth no man in the teeth: and it shall be given him." His rendering of Mark 16:14 was: "After that he appeared unto the eleven as they sat at meat, and cast in their teeth their unbelief and hardness of heart, because they believed not them which had seen him after his resurrection." These texts in Tyndale are the earliest to be cited in the OED as examples of the idiom "cast in the teeth." The form used in James, to cast a person in the teeth, is marked as obsolete, with no example cited later than 1642.

Mark 16:14 is translated as "upbraided" (KJV, NRSV, RSV), "rebuked" (NIV, NKJV, NLT), and "reproached" (NASB). James 1:5 is translated "without reproach" (NASB, NKJV), "without finding fault" (NIV), and "ungrudgingly" (NRSV).

CAST ONE'S BREAD UPON THE WATERS

The expression "cast one's bread upon the waters" means "to give generously" and "do good," as one's kindness may well be repaid in the future. The saying comes from Ecclesiastes 11:1 (KJV), "Cast thy bread upon the waters: for thou shalt find it after many days."

The contemporary versions render this expression as follows: the first clause as "Cast [NRSV, "Send out"] your bread upon the [NASB, "the surface of"] waters," (NASB, NIV, NKJV, NRSV, RSV), "Be generous," (CEV); "Give generously," (NLT); and "Invest what you have" (NCV); the second clause as "for you shall find it after many days" (NASB, NKJV, RSV), "for after many days you will get it back" (NRSV), "for after many days you will find it again" (NIV), "for after a while you will get a return" (NCV), "for your gifts will return to you later" (NLT).

CAST PEARLS BEFORE SWINE

See PEARLS BEFORE SWINE.

CAST THE FIRST STONE

The expression "cast the first stone" alludes to the woman caught in the act of adultery. The scribes and Pharisees pointed out to Jesus that according to the Law of Moses, such women should be stoned. Jesus said, "Let anyone among you who is without sin be the first to throw a stone at her" (NRSV), that is if any one of them was not guilty of that sin themselves, then such a person—and only such a person—would

be qualified to condemn the woman according to the law's just demands.

The KJV has "He that is without sin among you, let him first cast a stone at her." Here is a good example of how the KJV wording ("first cast a stone") has been slightly changed over the years to "cast the first stone."

The other contemporary versions have "be the first to throw a stone at her" (NASB, NIV, RSV); "throw a stone at her first" (NKJV); "throw the first stone at her" (CEV, NCV); the NLT paraphrases as "All right, stone her. But let those who have never sinned throw the first stones!"

CASTAWAY

"Castaway" evokes stories of a shipwrecked mariner, a person who has succeeded in swimming to a desert island after a shipwreck. In the KJV, however, the noun "castaway" is a translation of the Greek adjective *adokimos*, which means "rejected" or "unfit." This adjective was applied to metals or coins that failed to meet the test.

In 1 Corinthians 9:24–27 the dominant metaphor that Paul uses is that of a race, and in verse 26 comes a reference to boxing: "I therefore so run, not as uncertainly; so fight I, not as one that beateth the air: But I keep under my body, and bring it into subjection: lest that by any means, when I have preached to others, I myself should be a castaway."

The word translated "preach" also means "proclaim." Paul is saying that he does not want to be rejected or disqualified for the race to which he has exhorted others. All the contemporary versions except the CEV use the verb "disqualified" to render the noun "castaway"; the CEV has "lose out."

CERTAINTY

In contemporary English as well as in the KJV, "certainty" is used in the sense of "the truth," "the actual facts," "the real circumstances." For example, from the KJV: "That thou mightest know the certainty of those things, wherein thou hast been instructed" (Luke 1:4), rendered "the truth" in the CEV, NLT, NRSV, and RSV, "the exact truth" in the NASB, with the NIV and NKJV retaining "certainty"; "When he could not know the certainty for the tumult" (Acts 21:34), rendered with "the truth" (NIV, NKJV, NLT) and "the facts" (NASB, NRSV, RSV).

In Proverbs 22:21—"That I might make thee the certainty of the words of truth; that thou mightest answer the words of truth to them that send unto thee"—the expression "the certainty of the words of truth" is retained by the NASB and NKJV, but is translated as "true and reliable words" in the NCV and NIV and "what is right and true" in the NRSV and RSV.

Shakespeare used "certainty" in this sense in *Hamlet* (IV, 5, 140): "If you desire to know the certainty Of your dear father's death." Laertes did not doubt that his father was dead, but he did not know the facts concerning his death.

CERTIFY

Modern accounts are certified as correct; documents are certified as meeting all the requirements. Thus, "certify" means "to state officially" or "to state that something is true." In the Old Testament of the KJV, "certify" simply means "to inform." For example, "certified" in "Esther certified the king thereof" (Esther 2:22) is translated "inform" in the NASB and NKJV and "told" in the NCV, NLT, NRSV, and RSV; the NIV has "reported." The word "certify" also occurs in 2 Samuel 15:28 and Ezra 4:14, 16; 5:10; 7:24; other contemporary translations include "let know," "make known," and "notify."

In Galatians 1:11, KJV, "But I certify you, brethren, that the gospel which was preached of me is not after man," is rendered "I want you to know" (CEV, NCV, NIV, NRSV), "I would have you know" (NASB, RSV), "I make known to you" (NKJV), and "I solemnly assure you" (NLT).

CHAFED

"Chafed" now means "rubbed" or, in figurative usage, "irritated." From the fourteenth century "to chafe" meant "to heat"; it early developed the abstract meaning of "heating the mind or soul," hence "to enrage," then by a lessening of intensity of the meaning it came to suggest "fretting," and later "irritation by rubbing."

The KJV has one example of "chafed" in the sense of "enraged," the Hebrew word being *mar*, which means "bitter." It occurs in Hushai's counsel to Absalom, 2 Samuel 17:8, KJV: "thou knowest thy father and his men, that they be mighty men, and they be chafed in their minds, as a bear robbed of her whelps in the field." The sense is of a she-bear, robbed of her cubs—or whelps—as being "chafed" over it. The contemporary versions have "enraged" (NKJV, NLT, NRSV, RSV) and "fierce" (CEV, NASB, NIV).

CHALLENGE

As a verb in modern English, "challenge" means "to question the validity of a person" or "to invite someone to fight."

The word is used once in the KJV in the obsolete sense of "to claim," "to assert one's right to something." It occurs in Exodus 22:9, "any manner of lost thing, which another challengeth to be his." The contemporary versions translate this with the verb "claim" (CEV, NKJV), or with the expression "this is mine" (NCV, NIV, NRSV) or "this is it" (NASB, RSV).

Shakespeare uses "challenge" with this sense in *King Richard II* (II, 3, 134): "I am a subject, And I challenge law." The OED quotes Sir Thomas Herbert: "I challenge no thankes for what I publish" (1634) and also Smollett: "An injured friend!—who challenges the name? If you, what Title justifies the claim?" (1746).

CHAMBERING

"Chambering" is an obsolete word, dating from Tyndale, that refers to sexual excesses. It appears in Romans 13:13, KJV: "Let us walk honestly, as in the day; not in rioting and drunkenness, not in chambering and wantonness, not in strife and envying." The Greek word here is a euphemism for sexual indulgence: it appears in the plural and is linked with the Greek word for "licentious behavior," also in the plural.

The contemporary translations render the word "chambering" as "debauchery" (NRSV, RSV), "sexual promiscuity" (NASB), "sexual immorality" (NIV), "adultery" (NLT), "lewdness" (NKJV). (See LASCIVIOUSNESS)

CHAMPAIGN

This is an old French word for "open level country," "a plain." It appears only in Deuteronomy 11:30, KJV, where it was spelled "champion" in the 1611 edition. It serves as translation for the Hebrew *arabah,* and the NASB, NIV, NRSV, and RSV render this word as the proper name "Arabah"; the NKJV has "the plain."

The KJV uses this word as a proper name in Joshua 18:18, and elsewhere translates it as "desert," "plain," or "wilderness." For example, Deuteronomy 4:49 in the KJV has "the sea of the plain"; this is rendered "the Sea [NASB, "sea"] of the Arabah" in the NASB, NIV, NKJV, NRSV, and RSV and the "Dead Sea" in the NCV and NLT.

CHANGEABLE

If something such as the weather is said to be changeable, then it is likely to change many times. In the KJV the word "changeable" is used to describe clothes that could be worn or taken off and laid away as the occasion required. In the KJV the word occurs at Isaiah 3:22, "changeable suits of apparel," in Isaiah's list of feminine finery. These were outer garments for festal occasions. The contemporary versions describe them as "festal robes" (NASB, NRSV, RSV), "fine robes" (NCV, NIV), "outer garments" (NKJV), and "party clothes" (NLT).

The same Hebrew word is used in Zechariah's vision of the high priest being accused by Satan before the angel of the Lord (Zechariah 3:4). It is contrasted with filthy clothes and is translated "change of raiment" by the KJV, "festal apparel" by the NRSV, "festal robes" by the NASB, "rich robes" by the NKJV, and "rich garments" by the NIV.

CHAPITER

This is an architectural term for the capital of a column, the head or upper part of the column that in classical architecture supports the entablature. The word appears twenty-eight times in the KJV, most often in 1 Kings 7:16–42, in describing the building of Solomon's temple. All the contemporary translations except the CEV use "capital" in its place; the CEV uses "cap." The OED states that "chapiter" is still an occasional equivalent of "capital."

CHAPMEN

"Chapman" is an archaic term for an itinerant peddler or trader. The KJV uses this word once (2 Chronicles 9:14), in a passage which states that "the weight of gold that came to Solomon in one year was six hundred and threescore and six talents of gold; beside that which chapmen and merchants brought." These men were the traveling buyers and sellers, the explorers and adventurers, of Solomon's far-flung commercial interests.

The contemporary versions render "chapmen" as "traders." In the NKJV of 2 Chronicles 9:14 the expression "chapmen and merchants" is translated "traveling merchants and traders." In the parallel passage (1 Kings 10:15) the Hebrew expression for "chapmen" is translated "merchantmen" in the KJV and "traders" in the contemporary versions.

The cheap reputation of chapmen is reflected in Shakespeare's lines:

> "Not utter'd by base sale of
>   chapmen's tongues."
>   —*Love's Labour's Lost* (II, 1, 16)

"Fair Diomed, you do as chapmen
do,
Dispraise the thing that you desire
to buy."
—*Troilus and Cressida* (IV, 1, 75)

CHAPT

If your skin is chapped, then it is dry and cracked, from, perhaps, the cold wind. The word "chapt" appears once in the KJV, in Jeremiah 14:4: "The ground is chapt." This is a descriptive detail of Jeremiah's picture of the drought in Judah. It is peculiar to the KJV, for the translations from Coverdale to the Bishops' Bible had "dryed up," the Geneva Bible had "destroyed," and the revised versions of 1885–1901 used "cracked."

The contemporary versions render the word as "cracked" (NASB, NIV, NRSV), "parched" (NKJV), and "parched and cracked" (NLT). The original Hebrew employed its own figure of speech, "the ground is dismayed," the rendering adopted by the RSV.

CHARGE

In contemporary English as well as in the KJV, the word "charge" has a number of different senses. Three senses call for particular discussion.

First, "charge" refers to an amount or money that has to be paid for a service. For example, the KJV has "at his own charges" (1 Corinthians 9:7) and "be at charges with them" (Acts 21:24); the contemporary versions have "at his own expense" (NASB, NIV, NKJV, RSV) and "pay their expenses" (NASB, NCV, NIV, NKJV, RSV).

Secondly, "charge" sometimes means "to impose a responsibility" or "to instruct." This is seen in a number of expressions—for example, "charge with an oath" in Numbers 5:21 and 1 Samuel 14:28. The first of these passages is generally rendered as "put the woman under the [NLT, "this"] oath" (NIV, NKJV, NLT) or "make the woman take the oath" (NRSV, RSV). In the second passage "charge" is retained by the NKJV, NRSV, and RSV; the NASB has "put the people

under oath"; and the NIV, "bound the army under a . . . oath."

"Let not the church be charged" (1 Timothy 5:16, KJV) is translated let the church not "be burdened" (NASB, NIV, NKJV, NRSV, RSV). The expression "I charge you" occurs four times in the KJV of the Song of Solomon (2:7; 3:5; 5:8; 8:4) and is translated "adjure" by the NASB, NRSV, and RSV; the NIV and NKJV retain the KJV rendering, and the NCV and NLT use the verb "promise."

Thirdly, "charge" in the legal sense of "being blamed or accused for something" occurs in the expression, "lay . . . to their charge." This is rendered in the contemporary versions by using the phrasal verb "hold against," in e.g., Stephen's dying prayer, "Lord, lay not this sin to their charge," rendered as, "Lord, do not hold this sin against them" in the NASB, NCV, NIV, NRSV, and RSV.

Romans 8:33, KJV, "Who shall lay any thing to the charge of God's elect?" is rendered in the contemporary versions as, "Who will bring any [NKJV, "a"] charge against" God's elect (NASB, NIV, NKJV, NRSV, RSV).

CHARGEABLE

If something is chargeable, then you have to pay money for it: ("rooms not vacated by midday are chargeable as whole days"). In the KJV, "chargeable" means "burdensome." For example, when King David refused Absalom's invitation to his sheepshearing "lest we be chargeable unto thee" (2 Samuel 13:25, KJV), "chargeable" is translated "burdensome" in the NASB, NRSV, and RSV; "a burden" in the NIV and NKJV; and "too expensive" in the CEV.

The governors before Nehemiah "were chargeable unto the people" (Nehemiah 5:15, KJV), which is rendered as those who had "laid burdens [NLT, NRSV, RSV, "heavy burdens"] on the people" (NASB, NKJV, NLT, NRSV, RSV).

Paul reminds the Thessalonians that he worked night and day, that he "might not be chargeable" to any of them (1 Thessalonians 2:9, KJV); translated as "not be [NASB, NIV, "not to be"] a burden" to them (NASB, NIV, NKJV, NLT). He continues similarly in 2 Thessalonians 3:8, translated in the NCV as "so we would not be an expense to any of you." Second Corinthians 11:9, KJV, "I was chargeable to no man," is translated with the word "burden" in the NASB, NIV, NKJV, NRSV, and RSV; the CEV has "I still didn't bother you" and the NLT has "I did not ask you to help me."

CHARGER

In modern times, a "charger" is a device that recharges batteries; and also a horse that is ridden in battle. In the KJV, however, a charger is a term for "a large platter" for carrying a large joint of meat. The daughter of Herodias, prompted by her mother, asked Herod to give her the head of John the Baptist on such a platter (Matthew 14:8, 11; Mark 6:25, 28). All the contemporary versions except the NLT have "platter"; the NLT has "tray."

A "silver charger" which headed the offerings of each of the twelve tribes of Israel for the dedication of the altar (Numbers 7) was a "plate" (NIV, NRSV, RSV); a "platter" (NKJV, NLT), and "dish" (NASB). The "thirty chargers of gold" (Ezra 1:9–11, KJV) at the head of the list of the vessels which Cyrus king of Persia restored to the house of the Lord in Jerusalem were "dishes" (CEV, NASB, NCV, NIV), "basins" (NRSV, RSV), "platters" (NKJV), and "trays" (NLT).

CHARITY

See LOVE.

CHECK

The noun "check" has a number of meanings today, including "testing," "a sudden stop or restraint," or "a piece of paper indicating an amount to pay." In the KJV, the noun "check" is used once (Job 20:3), in the obsolete sense of "reproof," "censure," or "rebuke." "The check of my reproach"

is rendered by the contemporary versions as "censure that insults me" (RSV), "the reproof which insults me" (NASB), "a rebuke that dishonors me" (NIV), and "the rebuke that reproaches me" (NKJV).

Shakespeare used the word "check" in this sense in *King Lear* (I, 3, 20), when Goneril says concerning her father,

"Old fools are babes again; and must be used
With checks as flatteries."

CHIDE

In contemporary English "chide" means "to rebuke." The word appears seven times in the KJV, with the present-day meaning of "rebuke" and also the obsolete sense of "to use loud and angry words," "to contend," "wrangle," or "scold."

The translation "rebuke" is retained by one contemporary version, the RSV, only once—"He will not always chide, nor will he keep his anger for ever" (Psalm 103:9, RSV).

In the other passages, "chide" is used in the obsolete sense of contend, wrangle, or scold. The renderings of the contemporary translations include: "quarreled" (e.g., Numbers 22:3, NIV, NRSV; Exodus 17:2, NASB, NCV, NIV, NRSV; Exodus 17:7, NIV, NRSV); "contended" (the NASB at Genesis 31:36 and Judges 8:1); "upbraided" (the NRSV and RSV at Genesis 31:36 and Judges 8:1); "took . . . to task" (Genesis 31:36, NIV); "rebuked" (Genesis 31:36, NKJV); "criticized" (Judges 8:1, NIV); and "argued heatedly" (Judges 8:1, NLT).

For the past tense, the KJV employs "chode" twice (Genesis 31:36; Numbers 20:3 and "did chide" twice (Judges 8:1; Exodus 17:2).

CHIEFEST

The OED quotes Samuel Johnson's definition of "chief" as "of the first order," and states that in this use it had the comparative "chiefer" and the superlative "chiefest." This usage is now obsolete. The superlative is used eight times in the KJV, representing seven different Hebrew and Greek terms. Doeg, "the chiefest of the herdmen that belonged to Saul" (1 Samuel 21:7, KJV), was "the chief" (NASB, NCV, NKJV, NLT, NRSV, RSV); the NIV has "head."

"The chiefest" when referring to the sin of the sons of Eli, "to make yourselves fat with the chiefest of all the offerings of Israel my people" (1 Samuel 2:29, KJV), is described by the contemporary versions as "the choicest" parts (NASB, NRSV, RSV); "the choice parts" (NIV); and "the best" parts (NCV, NKJV, NLT).

Samuel placed Saul "in the chiefest place" (1 Samuel 9:22, KJV), rendered "the head" in the NASB, NIV, NLT, NRSV, and RSV; the NKJV has "the place of honor." For "the chiefest of the sepulchres" (2 Chronicles 32:33, KJV), the NRSV and RSV have "the ascent of the tombs"; the NASB, NKJV, and NLT refer to the "upper" area of the tombs; and the CEV refers to "the section of the royal tombs that was reserved for the most respected kings."

The young woman in the Song of Solomon declares that her beloved is "the chiefest" among ten thousand (5:10); the contemporary versions render this as "outstanding" (NASB, NIV), "the most outstanding" (CEV), "chief" (NKJV), and "distinguished" (NRSV).

In Mark 10:44 the "chiefest" is referred to in all the contemporary versions as the "first" among you: e.g., the NKJV, "And whoever of you desires to be first shall be slave of all." In Paul's claim to be not at all inferior to "the very chiefest apostles" (2 Corinthians 11:5; 12:11), "the chiefest" is rendered as "super" (CEV, NIV, NLT, NRSV, RSV; used as a prefix in NIV and NRSV); and "most eminent" in the NASB and NKJV.

CHIMNEY

In contemporary English a chimney is a vertical structure enclosing a flue through which smoke goes up into the air through the roof of a building. In the KJV, however, the word "chimney" may be used to refer to an opening in the wall.

The word occurs at Hosea 13:3: "Therefore they shall be as the morning cloud, and as the early dew that passeth away, as the chaff that is driven with the whirlwind out of the floor, and as the smoke out of the chimney." Of the contemporary versions, the CEV, NASB, NKJV, and NLT retain "chimney," while the NCV, NIV, NRSV, and RSV translate as "window."

The Hebrew word here is *arubbah,* which may mean either a latticed wall opening (i.e., a window) or a chimney on the roof. It occurs in the plural also, for example, at Isaiah 60:8, where the KJV, RSV, and NRSV translate as "windows"; the NASB has "lattices."

CHOLER

This word is rarely used in modern English. It is used in the obsolete senses of "bile" and "the state of being bilious"; in occasional modern use it refers to "irascibility" or "anger." This last use is found in the KJV, in Daniel 8:7, "he was moved with choler," and 11:11, "the king of the south shall be moved with choler."

The contemporary versions' renderings of "choler" include the words "enraged" (Daniel 8:7, NASB, NRSV), "furiously" (Daniel 8:7, NIV, NLT, e.g., the NLT, "The goat charged furiously at the ram"), and the expression "moved with rage" (Daniel 11:11, NKJV, NRSV).

Derived from the Greek *cholos* or *chole,* which meant both "bile" and "bitter anger," "choler" has the same double meaning. It was one of the "four humors" of the body, according to early physiology, the other three being sanguis, melancolia, and phlegma. The relative balance of these "cardinal humors," which were bodily fluids, was believed to determine a person's temperament and disposition.

Shakespeare often used this word, for example in *King Henry V* (IV, 7, 188): "I do know Flueullen valiant, And, toucht with choler, hot as gunpowder."

CHOSEN FEW

The phrase "the chosen few" is used to refer to a relatively small group of people who are in a specially favored position ("I see that only the chosen few were invited to the party"). The expression comes from Jesus' statement in Matthew 22:14 (KJV), "For many are called, but few are chosen." The NASB, NKJV, NLT, NRSV, and RSV retain the KJV wording; the NIV has "For many are invited, but few are chosen"; the CEV, "Many are invited, but only a few are chosen." (See also MANY ARE CALLED, BUT FEW ARE CHOSEN)

CHOSEN INSTRUMENT

In contemporary English, a "chosen instrument" is a person to whom a special task has been entrusted. The expression derives from Acts 9:15, the Lord's words to Ananias concerning Saul: "Go thy way: for he is a chosen vessel unto me, to bear my name before the Gentiles, and kings, and the children of Israel" (KJV). The contemporary versions render the KJV's "chosen vessel" (retained in the NKJV) as "chosen instrument" (NASB, NIV, NLT, RSV), "an instrument whom I have chosen" (NRSV); the CEV has "I have chosen him."

CHOSEN PEOPLE

The phrase "chosen people" is usually used to refer to the Jews, chosen by God in the Old Testament to fulfill his purposes, or, more generally, to all believers—those whom God has chosen for salvation. The expression derives from 1 Peter 2:9 (KJV), "But ye are a chosen generation, a royal priesthood, an holy nation, a peculiar people."

Of the contemporary versions, the NCV, NIV, and NLT render the beginning of this quote as "you are a chosen people"; the CEV has "you are God's chosen and special people"; the NKJV has "But you are a chosen generation, a royal priesthood, a holy

nation, His own special people"; the NRSV and RSV, "But you are a chosen race, a royal priesthood, a holy nation, God's own people"; the NASB, "But you are a chosen race, a royal priesthood, a holy nation, a people for God's own possession."

CHURCH

The word "church" translates the Greek word *ekklesia*. The word is used in the Septuagint (the Greek translation of the Old Testament) for the congregation of the Israelites, and in the New Testament for the congregation of Christian believers. It applies to a local congregation or to the church universal, the body of Christ, to which all who have faith in Christ belong.

The word is not used in the Bible as a name for the building in which believers gather for worship. Paul's advice to some to "keep silence in the church" refers not to a building but to an assembly of Christians for prayer and edification (1 Corinthians 14:28); the NCV and NLT render this as "church meeting." For the congregation of the Israelites, "the church in the wilderness" (Acts 7:38, KJV) is translated as "the congregation in the wilderness" (NASB, NKJV, NRSV, RSV); "the assembly in the desert" (NIV); and "the assembly of God's people in the wilderness" (NLT).

The Greek word which the KJV translates as "robbers of churches" (Acts 19:37) is rendered "robbers of temples" (NASB, NKJV), "temple robbers" (NRSV), or those who have "robbed temples" (CEV, NIV).

CHURL, CHURLISH

A person who is churlish is unfriendly, bad-tempered, and rude. This adjective fits the fool Nabal perfectly (1 Samuel 25:3), as the translation of a Hebrew adjective which means "hard," "severe," "stubborn," "rough," or "rude." The contemporary translations render this as "harsh" (NASB, NKJV), "surly" (NIV, NRSV), and "rough" (CEV). For the corresponding Greek adjective the expression "a hard man" may be thought to be equally appropriate in the parable of the talents (Matthew 25:24), rendered "hard" in all the contemporary translations except the NRSV; the NRSV has "harsh."

The noun "churl" is occasionally used in contemporary English to refer to a rustic person or one who is rude or mean. It appears twice in the KJV, in Isaiah 32:5-7. The Hebrew word which it is intended to represent in these passages means one who is crafty, wily, deceitful, or knavish. The contemporary translations render this as "rogue" (NASB) "wicked" (NCV), "scoundrel" (NIV), "villain" (NRSV), and "knave" (RSV).

Instead of "the instruments . . . of the churl" (Isaiah 32:7, KJV), three translations reproduce the wordplay of the Hebrew, where *kelai* means "villain" and *keli* means "instrument, implement, or weapon." The NKJV has "the schemes of the schemer"; the NLT has "the villainies of the villains"; and the RSV has "the knaveries of the knave."

CIEL, CIELING

These words are obsolete spellings of "ceil," and "ceiling." "Ciel" is a rare verb that means "to furnish with a lining or ceiling." In the KJV "cieled" is used four times in the sense of "lining or paneling walls with wood." In the description of Solomon's temple, it is said that "the greater house he cieled with fir tree" (2 Chronicles 3:5).

The Hebrew verb which is represented here by "cieled" means "to cover or overlay," and is translated by "overlaid" in the second clause of this verse and also in verses 7, 8, and 9. The contemporary versions translate verse 5 with the word "paneled" (NIV, NKJV, NLT), "lined" (NRSV, RSV), and "overlaid" (NASB).

The temple in Ezekiel's vision, "cieled with wood round about" (Ezekiel 41:16, KJV), was "paneled" (NASB, NKJV, NLT, NRSV, RSV) or "covered" (NIV) with wood all around. In the word of the Lord by Haggai the prophet, "Is it time for you, O ye, to dwell in your cieled houses, and this house lie waste?" (Haggai 1:4, KJV), "cieled" is translated as "paneled" in the NASB, NIV, NKJV, NRSV, and RSV; the NCV has "fancy"; the NLT, "luxurious." The KJV "cieling" at 1 Kings 6:15 is "ceiling" in its modern sense, with this spelling adopted by all the contemporary versions.

CLEAN

As an adverb, "clean" is used both in modern English ("the knife went clean through his thumb") and also in the KJV to mean "completely," "entirely." In Joshua 3:17; 4:1, 11 it is used for the Hebrew verb which means "finish." "Were clean passed over Jordan" (Joshua 4:1, KJV) is translated "had finished crossing [NRSV, "crossing over"] the Jordan" (NASB, NCV, NIV, NRSV, RSV).

In three passages, Zechariah 11:17, Joel 1:7, and Isaiah 24:19, "clean" is used to express the emphasis or intensity of meaning which the Hebrew conveys by repeating the verb, using both the absolute infinitive and a finite form. For example, "His arm shall be clean dried up" (Zechariah 11:17, KJV) is translated as "completely withered" (NIV, NRSV).

In 2 Peter 2:18, "those that were clean escaped from them who live in error" (KJV), "clean" is reworded by the contemporary translations as "barely" (CEV, NASB, RSV); the NCV, NIV, NLT, and NRSV have "just"; the NKJV has "actually."

CLIFT

This word is an earlier form of "cleft," meaning "a narrow opening in a rock." It occurs twice in the KJV: "I will put thee in a clift of the rock" (Exodus 33:22), and "in the valleys under the clifts of the rocks" (Isaiah 57:5). The contemporary versions generally use "cleft" and "clefts." The CEV and NCV at Exodus 33:22 have "a large crack"; the NIV at Isaiah 57:5 has "overhanging crags."

CLOSE

As an adjective, the word "close" has a range of meanings in contemporary English, including "enclosed," "shut up," "stuffy," and "intimate." In the KJV, however, its senses are more limited. Two senses call for special comment. First, the phrase "close places," which occurs in Psalm 18:45 (and its parallel 2 Samuel 22:46): "The strangers shall fade away, and be afraid out of their close places." The KJV's "close places" is translated "strongholds" (NIV, NLT), "fortresses" (CEV, NASB), and "hideouts" (NKJV).

Secondly, in Luke 9:36, the KJV reads: "They kept it close, and told no man in those days any of those things which they had seen." "Kept it close" is rendered in the contemporary translations as "kept silent" (NASB, NRSV), "kept quiet" (CEV, NKJV); the NIV has "kept it to themselves." This sense is also seen in the preface to the KJV, entitled "The Translators to the Reader," in which the question is put, "But how shall men meditate in that which they cannot understand? How shall they understand that which is kept close in an unknown tongue?"

CLOSET

In contemporary English a closet is a cabinet for storing things and also the condition of secrecy ("he came out of the closet"), whereas in the KJV the word means "a private room." It is used three times in the KJV. The Hebrew word in Joel 2:16, KJV, "and the bride out of her closet," is rendered "chamber" by the NIV and RSV, "bridal chamber" by the NASB, "dressing room" by the NKJV, "private room" by the NLT, and "canopy" by the NRSV.

The same Hebrew word occurs in Psalm 19:5, which the KJV translates as "chamber" ("a bridegroom coming out of his chamber"). The contemporary versions use the same translation in that verse as in Joel 2:16, except the NIV which has "pavil-

ion" and the NRSV which has "wedding canopy"; it is untranslated in the NLT.

The Greek word for which the KJV has "closet" in Matthew 6:6 and Luke 12:3 means "private room," or "inner room." For Matthew 6:6 all the contemporary translations have "room," except the NASB, which has "inner room."

For Luke 12:3, "closets" in "that which ye have spoken in the ear in closets shall be proclaimed upon the housetops" is rendered "inner rooms" (NASB, NIV, and NKJV); "closed room" (CEV). The NLT and NRSV render the KJV expression "in closets" as "behind closed doors."

CLOTHED AND IN ONE'S RIGHT MIND

To be "clothed and in one's right mind" means "to be fully prepared in mind and body to undertake the tasks one faces." The expression comes from the story of Jesus' healing of a demon-possessed man. The KJV at Luke 8:35 records, "Then they went out to see what was done; and came to Jesus, and found the man, out of whom the devils were departed, sitting at the feet of Jesus, clothed, and in his right mind: and they were afraid."

The contemporary versions (NASB, NCV, NKJV, NRSV, and RSV) retain the KJV expression "clothed and in his right mind"; the NIV has "dressed and in his right mind"; the CEV, "He had clothes on and was in his right mind"; the NLT, "clothed and sane." In the parallel passage, Mark 5:15, the renderings are similar, including the NLT, "fully clothed and perfectly sane."

CLOTHED UPON

The KJV expression "to be clothed upon," which does not occur in today's English, is a somewhat awkward literalism for the Greek verb which means "to put on a garment over other garments." It occurs twice in the KJV, at 2 Corinthians 5:2, 4. Wycliffe used "clothed above," and Rheims "overclothed." Tyndale used "clothed with" in verse 2 and "clothed upon" in verse 4 and was followed by the other sixteenth-century versions.

For 2 Corinthians 5:2, the NASB, NIV, NKJV, and NRSV have simply "clothed"; the NLT and RSV have "put on." For 2 Corinthians 5:4, the NASB has "clothed"; the NKJV, NRSV, and RSV have "further clothed"; and the NIV, "clothed with our heavenly dwelling." The NLT expresses it as "We want to slip into our new bodies."

CLOUD NO BIGGER THAN A MAN'S HAND

The expression "a cloud no bigger than (or: no bigger than the size of) a man's hand" is used to refer to a small sign of an impending significant event or change of circumstances. The phrase derives from the account of Elijah on Mount Carmel. After the destruction of the prophets of Baal, Elijah's servant is commanded to look out for the coming rain in response to Elijah's prayer. On the seventh occasion of looking, the servant reported, "Behold, there ariseth a little cloud out of the sea, like a man's hand" (1 Kings 18:44, KJV).

The contemporary versions render this phrase as, "a cloud as small as a man's hand" (NASB, NIV, NKJV); "a little cloud about the size of a hand" (NLT); "a little cloud no bigger than a person's hand" (NRSV); "a small cloud . . . no bigger than a fist" (CEV); and "a small cloud, the size of a human fist" (NCV).

CLOUT (noun)

As a noun in contemporary English, "clout" means "a strike or hit" or, in figurative uses, "influence." It also occurs in certain northern English and Scottish dialects to refer to "a rag," "a piece of cloth that has been torn off." Such words as "dishclout" are not yet completely obsolete, but have been almost displaced by "dishcloth."

This current dialectal usage is found in the KJV in Jeremiah 38:11. The reference is to Ebed-Melech the Ethiopian, who found "old cast clouts and old rotten rags" which he lowered to Jeremiah in the dungeon. The revised versions of 1885–1901 call these "rags and worn-out garments"; the NCV, NIV, NRSV, and RSV render as "old rags and worn-out clothes." The NASB has "worn-out clothes and worn-out rags"; the NKJV has "old clothes and old rags"; the NLT has "some old rags and discarded clothing."

Shakespeare used the word in *King John* (III, 4, 58), "a babe of clouts," which means "a rag doll."

CLOUTED (verb)

As a verb in contemporary English, "clout" means "to strike or hit." It also occurs in certain northern English and Scottish dialects to mean "to cover or patch." The inhabitants of Gibeon, pretending to have come from a far country, went to Joshua with "old shoes and clouted upon their feet, and old garments upon them" (Joshua 9:5). The contemporary versions refer to "worn-out, patched sandals" (NLT, NRSV, RSV), "worn-out and patched sandals" (NASB), "old and patched" sandals (CEV, NKJV), and "worn and patched sandals" (NIV).

The rebel Jack Cade, in Shakespeare's *King Henry VI, Part II* (IV, 2, 182), exhorts his followers:

"And you that love the commons,
    follow me.
Now show yourselves men; 'tis
    for liberty.
We will not leave one lord, one
    gentleman:
Spare none but such as go in
    clouted shoon."

COAST

In contemporary English, the coast is the area of land that is next to the sea. In the KJV, however, the coast referred to a border or a region, senses that are now obsolete in English. For example, when the KJV states that Paul "passed through the upper coasts" on his way to Ephesus (Acts 19:1), he did in fact traverse the high land which lies in the interior of Asia Minor. The contemporary versions render "upper coasts" as "upper country" (NASB, RSV); "upper regions" (NKJV); "hill country" (CEV); the NIV has "interior"; the NLT "interior provinces"; and the NRSV, "interior regions."

In the Gospels, when we read of Jesus visiting "the coasts of Tyre and Sidon" (Matthew 15:21; Mark 7:31), we naturally think of the seacoast, knowing these to be maritime cities, whereas the word refers to the area. For Matthew 15:21 the NASB, NRSV, and RSV have "district" and the NIV, NKJV, and NLT have "region." The word occurs twice in Mark 7:31, with the contemporary versions generally rendering the word as "region"; the NIV also has "vicinity."

The KJV also has that Capernaum is situated "upon the sea coast" (Matthew 4:13). The NASB, NKJV, NRSV, and RSV translate this as "by the sea"; the NIV has "by the lake"; the CEV, "beside Lake Galilee"; and the NLT, "beside the Sea of Galilee."

COCKATRICE

A cockatrice is a mythical serpent that was hatched by a reptile from a cock's egg, said to kill by its mere glance. This is the word which the KJV uses in Isaiah 11:8; 14:29; 59:5 and Jeremiah 8:17 for the Hebrew *tsepha* or *tsiphoni,* "a venomous serpent." The RV changed this to "basilisk."

The contemporary translations render as follows: the NIV and NKJV have "viper"; the NRSV and RSV have "adder"; the NASB has "viper" and "adder"; the CEV has "poisonous snake"; the NLT has "deadly snake," "poisonous snake," and "viper."

The OED notes that "the sense-history of this word is exceedingly curious," and summarizes it in a full column of fine print describing the vagaries of human credulity. In heraldry it was figured as "a hybrid monster with the head, wings, and feet of a cock, terminating in a serpent with a barbed tail." Shakespeare refers to "cockatrice" or "basilisk" a dozen times. Tarquin delivers

his threat to Lucrece "with a cockatrice' dead-killing eye" (*Rape of Lucrece,* 540).

Wycliffe, translating from the Latin Vulgate, used "cockatrice" in the Isaiah texts and in Psalm 91:13. Coverdale, following Martin Luther's *Basilisken,* used "cockatrice" in the Isaiah texts and Jeremiah 8:17. The Geneva Bible was the only sixteenth-century version to use "cockatrice" in Proverbs 23:32 as well: "In the end thereof it wil bite like a serpent and hurt like a cockatrise." The Great Bible and the Bishops' Bible used "adder" in Isaiah 14:29, but the KJV reverted to the practice of Coverdale.

COLLECTION

In a religious context, a "collection" is an offering of money that is given by people during a service of worship. In the KJV this word occurs in a slightly different sense, for the tax that Moses levied upon Israel in the wilderness, as described in Exodus 30:11–16. The word occurs twice in the KJV, at 2 Chronicles 24:6, 9: "And they made a proclamation through Judah and Jerusalem, to bring in to the LORD the collection that Moses the servant of God laid upon Israel in the wilderness" (2 Chronicles 24:9).

The contemporary versions render "collection" as "tax" (NIV, NRSV, RSV; the NLT also has "taxes"); "taxes" (CEV); "levy" (NASB); the NKJV retains "collection."

In 1 Corinthians 16:1–2 the KJV "collection" and "gatherings" stand for the singular and plural of the same Greek word, and refer to the contribution for the poor among the saints at Jerusalem—the relief fund to which Paul gave much attention. The NASB, NIV, NKJV, and NRSV have "collection/collections"; the RSV has "contribution/contributions"; the CEV and NCV use the verb "collect" and the noun "collection"; the NLT uses only the verb "collect."

COLLEGE

A college is an educational institution; in the KJV the word was used to translate the Hebrew *mishneh,* meaning "second quarter" or "second district." It occurs in the KJV at 2 Kings 22:14 and 2 Chronicles 34:22, when the text states that Huldah the prophetess "dwelt in Jerusalem in the college." The contemporary versions render the word "college" as "Second Quarter" (NASB, NKJV, NRSV, RSV); "Second District" (NIV); "northern part" (CEV); "the newer Mishneh section" (NLT); and "new area" (NCV).

The word occurs also in Zephaniah 1:10, where the KJV translates it as "the second." The contemporary translations render the word here as noted above, except for the NIV which translates it as "New Quarter," and the CEV which has "New Town."

The rendering "college" came from the Geneva Bible, and is ultimately traceable to confusion of *mishneh* with the post-biblical word *mishnah*, the collection of binding precepts that is the basis of the Talmud and embodies the oral law of Judaism.

In justice to the KJV translators of 1611, it should be stated that while they took "in the colledge" for the text, they added a marginal note, "Or, in the schoole, or in the second part."

COLLOPS

The word "collops" refers to slices of meat, rashers of bacon, or thick folds of fat upon the body. "Maketh collops of fat on his flanks" (Job 15:27) is a vivid translation of Hebrew for which the NRSV and RSV have "gathered fat upon his loins"; the NASB has "made his thighs heavy with flesh"; the NKJV, "made his waist heavy with fat"; and the NIV, "his waist bulges with flesh." (See FLANKS)

COME BY

In contemporary English if you come by something, you obtain or find it. The OED notes that the phrase originally implied "effort," but in later use was often used of "getting things by chance or involuntarily."

"Come by" occurs in the KJV at Acts 27:16, when Paul's ship was caught and driven by a tempestuous northeaster: "we

had much work to come by the boat" (Acts 27:16). That seems to mean that the boat had broken loose and was adrift. The Greek means that it was hard to control the boat and make it secure.

The NASB and the NRSV have "we were scarcely able to get the ship's boat under control"; the NIV, "we were hardly able to make the lifeboat secure"; the NKJV, "we secured the skiff with difficulty"; the NLT, "with great difficulty we hoisted aboard the lifeboat"; and the CEV, "We had a hard time holding the lifeboat in place."

COMFORT

As a verb in contemporary English, "comfort" means "to console"—to make someone feel less anxious or troubled, to relieve from distress, by, for example, speaking kind words to them. As a noun, "comfort" means "a state of ease" or "something that brings ease and happiness" ("just talking to you is a great comfort").

As verb and noun, the word "comfort" is used more than one hundred times in the KJV. It is retained in the contemporary versions where the meaning is "to console or relieve from distress"; but it is replaced in the many cases where the meaning is "to strengthen, refresh, encourage, exhort, or cheer."

Examples of contemporary translations are: by the "encouragement" of the scriptures (Romans 15:4, NASB, NCV, NIV, NLT, NRSV, RSV; the NKJV retains the KJV "comfort"); all may learn and be "encouraged" (1 Corinthians 14:31, all the contemporary versions except for the NASB, which has "exhorted"); "encourage" the fainthearted (1 Thessalonians 5:14, all the contemporary versions except for the NKJV, which retains the KJV "comfort"); that their hearts may "be encouraged" (Colossians 2:2, NASB, NIV, NKJV, NLT, NRSV, RSV; the NCV has "strengthened"; the CEV has "I do it to encourage them.").

The KJV expression, "that I also may be of good comfort" (Philippians 2:19), is rendered by "encouraged" in the CEV, NASB, and NKJV; "cheered" by the NIV, NRSV, and RSV, and "cheer . . . up" by the NLT. In "any comfort of love" (Philippians 2:1, KJV), the word "comfort" is retained by the CEV, NCV, NIV, NKJV, and NLT; the NASB and the NRSV have "consolation"; and the RSV has "incentive."

Paul's closing greeting at 2 Corinthians 13:11, "be of good comfort" (KJV and NKJV), is rendered "be comforted" by the NASB, "encourage each other" by the NLT, "listen to my appeal" by the NIV and NRSV, "pay attention to what I have said" by the CEV; and "heed my appeal" by the RSV.

The word "comfort" comes from the Latin *conforto,* which means "to strengthen." Though it was sometimes applied to things or animals, the primary reference of the word is to the strengthening of human beings in body and spirit. Hence the verb "comfort" has various meanings: "strengthen," "encourage," "support," "aid," "refresh," "relieve," "soothe," "console," "make comfortable." The first six of these meanings are now obsolete, except especially for legal usage.

Early usage is seen in these examples from Wycliffe: Isaiah 41:1, "he coumfortide hym with nailes"; Psalm 147:13, "he coumfortede the lockis of thi gatis"; Luke 1:80, "the child wexed, and was counfortid in spirit"; Philippians 4:13, "I may alle thingis in him that comfortith me."

In these passages Tyndale and Coverdale used "fastened," "strengthened," "waxed strong," "strengtheneth," and were followed by the KJV. The contemporary versions have "fastened," "strengthen," "fortify," "make strong," and "become strong."

COMFORTABLE

If a piece of furniture or garment is comfortable, it makes you feel relaxed and at ease; a comfortable income is one where you have enough money to be able to live without financial difficulties. In the KJV the word "comfortable" occurs twice, mean-

ing "comforting" and "giving rest." "Comfortable words" (Zechariah 1:13) are words that are "comforting," the rendering of all the contemporary versions.

In 2 Samuel 14:17, however, "the word . . . shall now be comfortable" is used to represent a different Hebrew expression, which is translated by the contemporary versions as, "the word . . . will set me at rest" (NRSV, RSV); "the word . . . bring me rest" (NIV); the NASB and NKJV have "the word . . . be comforting."

In the Order for Holy Communion in the Book of Common Prayer, "the most comfortable Sacrament of the Body and Blood of Christ" and "what comfortable words our Saviour Christ saith," the word "comfortable" is used in the sense of "strengthening" and "inspiring." Though the note of consolation is present, it is not primary. The same is to be said of the words of invitation, "take this holy Sacrament to your comfort."

COMFORTABLY

The adverb "comfortably" in contemporary English is used to refer to physical relaxation ("lying comfortably in bed"). The word is used five times in the KJV, always with the verb "speak." It stands for a Hebrew phrase which means "to the heart." The contemporary translations allow the renderings to be determined by the context, e.g., "speak kindly" (2 Samuel 19:7, NASB, NRSV, RSV); "spoke encouragingly" (2 Chronicles 30:22, NASB, NIV, NRSV, RSV); "encouraged" (2 Chronicles 32:6, NCV, NIV, NLT); and "speak tenderly" (Isaiah 40:2; Hosea 2:14, NIV, NLT, NRSV, RSV).

The CEV uses the verb "thank" for 2 Samuel 19:7 and 2 Chronicles 30:22. The NKJV retains the KJV "speak comfort" for three verses and has "gave encouragement" for the others, 2 Chronicles 30:22; 32:6.

COMFORTER

In modern English, a comforter is a thick, quilted bedcover or a person or thing that comforts. In the KJV, "Comforter" is a title of the Holy Spirit, translating the Greek term *parakletos,* used four times in Jesus' parting talk with his disciples (John 14:16, 26; 15:26; 16:7). Jerome left it untranslated in the Latin Vulgate, and the word has passed into the English language as "Paraclete." Wycliffe translated it as "coumfortour," however, and Tyndale as "comforter." It was capitalized in the Geneva Bible and the KJV.

The NIV, NLT, and RSV translate this word as "Counselor"; the NASB, NCV, and NKJV as "Helper"; the NRSV as "Advocate"; the CEV expands to "the Holy Spirit will help you."

In 1 John 2:1 the Greek word *parakletos* is applied to Jesus Christ himself. In the KJV and NRSV it is translated "advocate"; in the NKJV and NASB, "Advocate"; in the NIV, "one who speaks to the Father in our defense"; in the NCV, "a helper in the presence of the Father"; in the CEV Jesus Christ is described as one who "will speak to the Father for us"; and in the NLT, "someone to plead for you before the Father." *Parakletos,* means "one who is called." Bishop Samuel Hinds wrote that the call may be "for any purpose of need, whether to strengthen, to console, to guide, to instruct, to plead and intercede for, or otherwise to aid."

COMFORTER, JOB'S

The expression "a Job's comforter" refers to someone who intends to sympathize with an unhappy person but in actual fact makes that person even more unhappy. Haven't we all met them? Job's comforters have that uncanny knack of telling us how hopeless our situation really is—as if we didn't know already! The expression "Job's comforter" comes from Job's three so-called "friends," who offered him joyless comfort in his affliction. Job's response: "Miserable comforters are ye all" (Job 16:2).

The modern translations mostly retain the expression "miserable comforters" except the NASB, "Sorry comforters," the NCV,

"You are all painful comforters!" and the CEV which renders the expression as "it offers no comfort."

COMFORTLESS

This word, meaning "destitute," "without comfort" is rarely used today. It is found in the KJV rendering of John 14:18, "I will not leave you comfortless," which goes back to the beginning of the fifteenth century.

The Greek word for "comfortless" is *orphanos,* and the contemporary translations render this "as orphans" (CEV, NASB, NIV, NLT; the NLT has "I will not abandon you as orphans"); "like orphans" (CEV, NCV; the NCV has "I will not leave you all alone like orphans"); the NRSV has "I will not leave you orphaned"; the RSV, "I will not leave you desolate."

COMMUNE

In contemporary English the verb "commune" means "to communicate intimately," "to meditate" ("to commune with nature"). The KJV uses the word mostly in the now obsolete sense of "talk over" or "discuss," as well as in the sense of "meditate." For example, where the Psalmist says of the wicked: "They encourage themselves in an evil matter; they commune of laying snares privily" (64:5, KJV), the contemporary versions have "talk of" (NASB, NKJV, NRSV, RSV), "talk about" (NCV, NIV), and "plan" (NLT).

When the scribes and Pharisees were angered by Jesus' attitude toward the Sabbath (Luke 6:11), the KJV states that "they were filled with madness, and communed with one another what they might do to Jesus." All the contemporary versions except the CEV use the word "discuss"; the CEV has "started saying."

The account in the KJV of Judas' bargain to betray Jesus reads (Luke 22:3–4): "Then entered Satan into Judas surnamed Iscariot, being of the number of the twelve. And he went his way, and communed with the chief priests and captains, how he might betray him unto them." For the KJV "communed," the NKJV, NRSV, and RSV have "conferred"; the NASB, NIV, and NLT use the word "discuss"; the CEV has "talk with."

In the two passages that concern meditation (Psalms 4:4 and 77:6), the NASB and NKJV have "meditate" with the NRSV and RSV having "meditate" at Psalm 77:6. At both passages, and at Psalm 4:4 in the NLT, the NCV uses the verb "think." Other renderings of Psalm 4:4 are "search your heart" [NIV, "hearts"] (CEV, NIV); "ponder" (NRSV), with the RSV retaining the KJV "commune." At Psalm 77:6 for the KJV, "I commune with mine own heart," the NIV has "My heart mused."

COMMUNICATE, COMMUNICATION

Communications and technological innovations for staying in touch are so much a part of modern living that it is almost impossible to imagine life without these means of exchanging information. In the KJV, however, "communicate" is usually used with the meaning "to share," a sense that is now archaic in English.

In the KJV the verb "communicate" is used six times and the noun "communication" seven times; but in nearly every case the contemporary versions have chosen another word. Generally, the contemporary versions render the KJV "communicate" by using the word "share." For example, "communicate" in "to do good and to communicate forget not" (Hebrews 13:16, KJV) is rendered "share what you have" (NLT, NRSV, RSV). In Paul's injunction to the Galatians (6:6), "Let him that is taught in the word communicate unto him that teacheth in all good things" (KJV), "communicate" is rendered "share" by all the contemporary versions except the NLT, which has "help."

When Paul wrote to the Philippians (4:14) "Ye have well done, that ye did communicate with my affliction" (KJV), he did not refer to letters of sympathy, but to gifts of material aid, as the succeeding verses make clear. "Communicate" in this verse is translated using the verb "share" in all the contemporary versions (except the NCV, which has "helped"), e.g., the NRSV, "it was kind of you to share my distress."

In the use of the word "communication" in "evil communications corrupt good manners" (1 Corinthians 15:33), "evil communications" does not mean profane or obscene language. The Greek word used here is more comprehensive; it refers to all social influences, companionships, and associations, in which spoken conversation and written communications play only a part. And what is at stake is more than good manners; it is moral character.

The contemporary versions render "evil communications" as "bad company" (NASB, NIV, NLT, NRSV, RSV); "bad friends" (CEV, NCV); and "evil company" (NKJV).

When Paul "communicated" to the heads of the church in Jerusalem the gospel which he was preaching among the Gentiles (Galatians 2:2, KJV), the Greek says that he "laid it before them" with a view to coming to an agreement concerning the most far-reaching question of principle and policy that the church ever faced.

The NRSV and RSV have "laid before"; the NIV has "set before"; the NASB has "submitted"; the CEV, "explained"; the NLT, "talked"; and the NKJV retains the KJV "communicated."

COMPACTED

In contemporary English, to "compact" something means "to compress it" or "to press something together so that it become more dense" ("the soil is compacted over a period of time"). In the KJV, the verb occurs in the form "compacted" in a slightly different sense, "to knit together, to combine."

"Compacted" occurs in one passage, Ephesians 4:16, "From whom [Christ] the whole body fitly joined together and compacted by that which every joint supplieth." The KJV expression "fitly joined together and compacted" is translated "joined and knit together" by the NKJV, NRSV, and RSV; "joined and held together" by the NCV and NIV; "fitted and held together" by the NASB. The CEV and NLT paraphrase as "Christ holds it together" (CEV) and "the whole body is fitted together perfectly" (NLT).

COMPASS

In contemporary English "compass" is used as a noun to refer firstly to a device that is used for finding directions, secondly to a V-shaped instrument for drawing circles ("a pair of compasses"), and thirdly in a figurative sense to a range or limit of something. In the KJV the second meaning occurs and also the now obsolete meaning of "circumference" or "circle."

The second meaning—an instrument for taking measurements and drawing circles—is seen in Isaiah 44:13: "The carpenter stretcheth out his rule; he marketh it out with a line; he fitteth it with planes, and he marketh it out with the compass, and maketh it after the figure of a man, according to the beauty of a man; that it may remain in the house." The NASB, NKJV, and NRSV retain "compass"; the NIV has "compasses."

The now obsolete meaning of "circumference" or "circle" is seen in several usages.

First, it occurs at Exodus 27:5 and 38:4 when referring to the burnt offering, e.g., "And he made for the altar a brasen grate of network under the compass thereof beneath unto the midst of it" (38:4, KJV). The contemporary versions render this as "ledge" (CEV, NASB, NIV, NLT, NRSV) and "rim" (NCV, NKJV).

Secondly, it occurs in Proverbs 8:27, KJV, "When he prepared the heavens, I was there: when he set a compass upon the face of the depth." The contemporary versions render "compass" as "horizon" (NCV, NIV, NLT) and "circle" (NASB, NKJV, NRSV).

Thirdly, it occurs in the expression "fetch a compass" in the sense of "make a circuit" or "go round." (See FETCH A COMPASS)

"Compass" is not used as a verb in contemporary English; its modern equivalent is "encompass" with the meanings "to surround" or "to include." In the KJV the verb "compass" has the basic meaning of "to go round" and is generally rendered as "surround" by the contemporary versions.

For example, in Judges 16:2, "And it was told the Gazites, saying, Samson is come hither. And they compassed him in, and laid wait for him all night in the gate of the city" (KJV); the NASB, NCV, NIV, NKJV, and RSV translate as "surrounded the place" and the NRSV as "circled around"; in Luke 21:20, "When ye shall see Jerusalem compassed with armies" (KJV), rendered as "surrounded" by the CEV, NASB, NIV, NKJV, NLT, NRSV, and RSV.

Other renderings are given, depending on the context. For example, Joshua 6:3 (KJV), "And ye shall compass the city," which all the contemporary versions translate as "march around"; Matthew 23:15, "Woe to you, scribes and Pharisees, hypocrites! for ye compass sea and land to make one proselyte" (KJV), which the contemporary versions translate as "cross" (NLT, RSV), "travel over" (CEV, NIV), "travel around on" (NASB), "travel across" (NCV), "travel" (NKJV), and "traverse" (NRSV); Hebrews 5:2 (KJV), "he [every high priest] himself also is compassed with infirmity"; the contemporary versions render "compassed with" as "subject to" (NIV, NKJV, NLT, RSV) and "beset with" (NASB).

COMPEL

To "compel" someone to do something means "to force" that person to do it. The word is used in this sense in the KJV and also in the sense "to urge." For example, the KJV says that King Saul's servants "compelled" him to eat (1 Samuel 28:23).

All the contemporary versions except the NCV translate this by using the word "urge"; the NCV has simply "asked." Paul, before his conversion, "compelled" (Acts 26:11, KJV, NKJV) the early Christians to blaspheme; in the other contemporary versions this is rendered that he "tried to make" (CEV, NCV, RSV), "tried to force" (NASB, NIV, NRSV), "tried to get" (NLT) them to do so.

COMPREHEND

In contemporary English, "comprehend" is a more formal word for "understand" or "include." The word occurs in the KJV in these senses.

Its occurrence in John 1:5 in the KJV, "The light shineth in darkness; and the darkness comprehended it not" is retained by the NASB and the NKJV as "comprehend"; but it is rendered in different ways by other versions. The ASV has "apprehended"; other contemporary versions use the verb "overcome" (NRSV, RSV); the NCV, Weymouth, Twentieth Century, and Williams have "overpowered"; Rieu, "conquer"; Moffatt, "master"; the NLT, "extinguish"; the CEV, Goodspeed; Phillips, "put . . . out"; the NIV, "understood."

The word comes from a Latin verb which means "to seize or grasp." The primary reference of the Latin *comprehendere* was to the physical laying hold of something; but it also acquired a secondary meaning, and was applied to the intellectual grasp or understanding of a matter. In the sixteenth century the English word "comprehend" was employed in both the physical and the intellectual senses, as was also the related word "apprehend." Today the physical sense of "comprehend" is obsolete, while "apprehend" retains both senses.

CONCEIT

In present-day English, "conceit" refers to an excessive sense of pride in one's abilities or worth that others consider to be undeserved. In the KJV, however, it is mainly used in the sense of "thought," "opinion," or "imagination."

For example, the expression "wise in his own conceit" occurs five times in Proverbs. In four of these cases, the Hebrew word means "eyes," and the contemporary versions generally translate literally as "wise in his own eyes" (26:5, 12, 16; 28:11). Variants include: people who "think they are wise" (Proverbs 26:12, NCV, NLT), "wise in their own estimation" (Proverbs 26:5, NLT), "wise in self-esteem" (Proverbs 28:11, NRSV), those who say "I am smarter than everyone else" (Proverbs 26:16, CEV).

The other case is Proverbs 18:11, where the KJV has "The rich man's wealth is his strong city, and as an high wall in his own conceit." Here the Hebrew word is different, and the contemporary versions translate it with "imagination" (NASB, NRSV); the NIV and NLT have "imagine"; the NKJV has "esteem." As well as meaning "imagination," the word may mean "cover." The RSV has "protection" and follows the Greek and Latin versions and Martin Luther's German translation: "A rich man's wealth is his strong city, and like a high wall protecting him." Similarly, the CEV has "The rich think their money is a wall of protection."

The KJV expression "wise in your own conceits" (Romans 11:25, retained by the RSV) is rendered "be conceited" (NIV); "wise in your own opinion" [NASB, "estimation"] (NASB, NKJV); "claim to be wiser than you are" (NRSV); "be too proud of yourselves" (CEV); and "feel proud and start bragging" (NLT).

CONCISION

This is an archaic word meaning "cutting to pieces." It is used once (Philippians 3:2, KJV) as a contemptuous term for those advocates of Jewish circumcision who would require Gentile Christians to submit to this rite. Instead of the KJV beware of "the concision," the contemporary versions read, "those who mutilate the flesh" (NRSV, RSV), "the false circumcision" (NASB), "those mutilators of the flesh" (NIV), "the mutilation" (NKJV), and those who "cut the body" (NCV).

This is one of the rare cases where a play on words can be reproduced in different languages. The Latin has *circumcisio—concisio*; Greek, *peritome—katatome*; English, *circumcision—concision*. The contrast in the contemporary versions is with the "true circumcision" (v. 3, NASB, RSV) or those who are "truly circumcised" (CEV, NCV, NLT), those who "worship God in the Spirit, rejoice in Christ Jesus, and have no confidence in the flesh" (NKJV).

CONCLUDE

In contemporary English, "conclude" means "to decide," "to settle," "to end." In the English language at the time of the KJV, the word was used not only in these senses, but also in the now obsolete sense of "shut up," "restrict," "confine." The word occurs twice in this sense in the KJV, in Romans 11:32: "For God hath concluded them all in unbelief, that he might have mercy upon all," and Galatians 3:22: "But the scripture hath concluded all under sin, that the promise by faith of Jesus Christ might be given to them that believe."

The contemporary versions translate "concluded" in these verses as follows: "shut up" (NASB), "imprisoned" (NRSV, and NLT at Romans 11:32), "consign" (RSV). The NKJV for Romans 11:32 is "For God has committed them all to disobedience" and for Galatians 3:22, "But the Scripture has confined all under sin"; the NIV for Romans 11:32 is "For God has bound all men over to disobedience" and for Galatians 3:22, "But the Scripture declares that the whole world is a prisoner of sin"; the CEV for Romans 11:32 is "All people have disobeyed God, and that's why he treats them as prisoners"; and for Galatians 3:22, "But the Scriptures say that sin controls everyone."

In two other passages the KJV "conclude" refers to the holding of an opinion or to the coming to a decision. "We conclude that a man is justified by faith without the deeds of the law" (Romans 3:28), in which the verb "conclude" is rendered as "maintain" by the NASB and the NIV and "hold" by the NRSV and the RSV; the NKJV retains the KJV word "conclude." "Concluded" in Acts 21:25, "we have written and concluded," is expressed as "decided" by the NASB and NKJV; the NIV, NRSV, and RSV rephrase with a noun: the NIV has "our decision" and the NRSV and RSV "our judgment."

CONCUPISCENCE

A word rarely used today, "concupiscence" means "strong desire." The Latin *concupiscentia* was one of a list of ninety-nine Latin words and phrases from the Vulgate which Bishop Gardiner presented to the Convocation of 1542, insisting that "for the sake of their germane and native meaning and for the majesty of the matter in them contained," these words should be retained in any translation of the Scriptures or be rendered into English with the least possible change. In the New Testament the Vulgate had used *desiderium* twenty-four times and *concupiscentia* fourteen times as translation for the Greek noun *epithumia*. (See LUST)

Tyndale, translating from the Greek, used "concupiscence" four times; the Rheims New Testament, translating from the Vulgate, used "concupiscence" fifteen times, including one passage where it has "in concupiscences" for the Vulgate *in desideriis*.

The King James translators followed Tyndale, except in James 1:14, where they replaced his "concupiscence" with "lust." In the three verses where the KJV retains "concupiscence," the contemporary versions have rendered it as follows, e.g., Romans 7:8: "covetousness" (NRSV, RSV), "covetous desire" (NIV) "evil desire" (NKJV); Colossians 3:5: "desire" (NASB, NKJV, NRSV, RSV), "desires" (NIV, NLT), "thoughts" (CEV); the KJV "lust of concupiscence" in 1 Thessalonians 4:5 is rendered "lustful passion" by the NASB, NLT, and NRSV; "passion of lust" by the NKJV and RSV, and "passionate lust" by the NIV.

CONDESCEND

To condescend to other people is to behave toward them in a way which shows that you think you are superior to them. The OED defines "condescend" as "to stoop from one's position of dignity or pride," and quotes Samuel Johnson's definition: "to depart from the privileges of superiority by a voluntary submission; to sink willingly to equal terms with inferiors." There is something patronizing about such actions. The people who condescend never forget their "superiority" and usually succeed in reminding others of it.

The word appears only once in the KJV, in Romans 12:16: "Mind not high things, but condescend to men of low estate." It is included in the OED with a parenthetical note to its quotation of the passage: "The meaning of the translators in 1611 is not clear."

The possible connotation of "snobbishness" is not found in the contemporary versions which render the word as "associate with" (NASB, NKJV, NRSV, and RSV); the NIV has "be willing to associate with"; the CEV and the NCV have "make friends with"; and the NLT has "enjoy the company of."

CONFECTION, CONFECTIONARY

These words now refer to candy and sweetmeats, things that are good to eat because of their sweetness or sugar. As used in the KJV, however, they refer to compounds of spices, things good to smell, whether for perfume or for incense. "Confection" occurs in the instructions given to Moses for the making of the holy incense: "Thou shalt make it a perfume, a confection after the art of the apothecary" (Exodus 30:35, KJV).

The RSV and NRSV have "make an incense blended as by the perfumer"; for the KJV "confection" the NKJV has "a compound"; the NIV, "a fragrant blend of incense." This was to be used only in the worship of the Lord.

"Confectionary" occurs in 1 Samuel 8:13, where the prophet Samuel warns the people who were asking for a king: "he will take your daughters to be confectionaries, and to be cooks, and to be bakers" (KJV). For the KJV "confectionaries" the NASB, NIV, NKJV, NRSV, and RSV have "perfumers."

CONFIDENCES

In contemporary English as well as in the language of the KJV, "confidence" is trust or faith; and a "confidence" is a secret that you tell another person. In Jeremiah 2:37, "the LORD hath rejected thy confidences," the use of the word could be thought to be ambiguous. It may be taken to mean that Israel had confided in the Lord and had been rejected or that Israel was putting its confidence in others, and the prophet is saying that the Lord has rejected these others.

This second sense is brought out by the contemporary versions: "the LORD has rejected those [NASB, NRSV, RSV, "those in whom"] you trust" (NASB, NIV, NRSV, RSV); "the LORD has rejected the nations you trust" (NLT); "the LORD has rejected your trusted allies" (NKJV).

CONFOUND

The word "confound" means "to confuse" or "to surprise" someone. The word is used in this sense is in the KJV, but is used more commonly in the sense "put to shame."

Examples of the sense "put to shame" are 1 Corinthians 1:27 and 1 Peter 2:6. First Corinthians 1:27, KJV, reads: "But God hath chosen the foolish things of the world to confound the wise; and God hath chosen the weak things of the world to confound the things which are mighty." For the two occurrences of "confound," the contemporary versions have "put . . . to shame" (CEV, NKJV), and the verb "shame" (NASB, NCV, NIV, NLT, NRSV, RSV).

First Peter 2:6, KJV, reads, "he that believeth on him shall not be confounded." For the KJV "confounded," the contemporary versions have "disappointed" (CEV, NASB,

NCV, NLT) and "put to shame" (NIV, NKJV, NRSV, RSV).

In Genesis 11:7, 9 the KJV "confound" ("confound their language," v. 7) is used in the sense of "confuse," the translation generally adopted by the contemporary versions.

In the account of Pentecost, Acts 2:6, the successive versions from Wycliffe to Rheims had "were astonied," and the KJV changed this to "were confounded." The contemporary versions have "surprised" (CEV, NCV), "confused" (NKJV), "bewildered" (NASB, NLT, NRSV, RSV), "in bewilderment" (NIV). The statement that Paul "confounded the Jews which dwelt at Damascus, proving that this is very Christ" (Acts 9:22, KJV) goes back to Wycliffe and appears, with minor variations in wording and spelling, in the NASB, NKJV, NRSV, and RSV; the CEV has "confused," the NIV, "baffled."

In Jeremiah 1:17, the KJV "confound" is rendered as "dismay" (NASB, NKJV, RSV); the NIV has "terrify"; the CEV, "make you terrified"; the NLT, "make . . . look foolish"; the NRSV, "break."

CONFUSION

In contemporary English "confusion" is used to refer to a state of disorder or a state in which things are mixed up. The word is used in the New Testament in this sense. The city of Ephesus was "filled with confusion" (Acts 19:29, KJV).

The NASB, NKJV, NLT, NRSV, and RSV retain the rendering "confusion"; the CEV and the NIV state that the whole city was "in an uproar" (NIV) and "in a riot" (CEV). Paul writes to the Corinthians that "God is not the author of confusion, but of peace" (1 Corinthians 14:33, KJV "Confusion" is retained by the NASB, NCV, NKJV, and RSV and translated as "disorder" in the NIV, NLT, and NRSV.

In the Old Testament, "confusion" is the KJV translation of Hebrew words which mean "shame," "dishonor," and "disgrace." Examples are: "confusion of face" (Ezra 9:7,

KJV), translated by the NRSV and RSV as "utter shame," and by the NIV as "humiliation"; "My confusion" (Psalm 44:15, KJV), translated by the NASB, NIV, NRSV, and RSV as "disgrace," and by the NASB and NKJV as "dishonor"; "The city of confusion" (Isaiah 24:10, KJV and NKJV), translated by the NASB, NRSV, and RSV as "the city of chaos," and by the NCV and NIV as "the ruined city"; "Their everlasting confusion" (Jeremiah 20:11, KJV), translated by the NIV, NLT, NRSV, and RSV as "dishonor."

CONSENT

If you give your consent to something, you give permission to someone to do it; if you consent to something, you agree to do it or allow it to be done. In the seventeenth century the word was used in this sense and also in a stronger sense, meaning "to be of the same mind," "to think and feel alike."

A clear example of the KJV's use of "consent" in this stronger sense is Psalm 50:18: "When thou sawest a thief, then thou consentedst with him." The Hebrew verb means "be pleased with," "take pleasure in." The contemporary versions render "consentedest" as "made [NRSV, "make"] friends" (CEV, NRSV); "join" (NCV, NIV); "are pleased with" (NASB); and "help" (NLT); the NKJV has "consented."

The phrase "with one consent" in Psalm 83:5, KJV, "they have consulted together with one consent," is translated by the NRSV and RSV as "with one accord," and as "with one mind" by the NASB and NIV; the CEV has "All of them fully agree in their plans"; the NCV has "They are united in their plan"; the NLT has "This was their unanimous decision," and the NKJV retains "consent."

"The fear of the LORD fell on the people and they came out with one consent" (1 Samuel 11:7, KJV) is changed by the NASB, NIV, and RSV to read "as one man," which is a literal translation of the Hebrew; the NRSV has "as one"; the CEV has "together"; and again the NKJV retains the KJV "with one consent."

When Stephen was stoned to death, the "witnesses," who were also the prosecutors and the executioners, laid their clothes at the feet of a young man named Saul, "and Saul was consenting unto his death" (Acts 8:1, KJV). Years later, when Paul recounted this in the face of the mob at Jerusalem, he said, "I also was standing by, and consenting unto his death" (Acts 22:20, KJV). The Greek verb in both passages means "join in thinking well of."

The contemporary versions render these verses with the verbs and phrases "agree" (NCV), and "giving approval" (NIV), "approved" (NRSV); the NKJV retains "consenting to his death." Other significant renderings are Acts 8:1, NASB, "Saul was in hearty agreement with putting him to death" and Acts 22:20, CEV, "I stood there and cheered them on."

The phrase "to his death" is part of the ancient text in Acts 8:1, but not in Acts 22:20.

CONSIDER THE LILIES

The expression "consider the lilies" is sometimes used in contemporary English as a saying that a person should trust in God's care and providence to supply what is needed instead of worrying about material goods. The saying derives from Jesus' saying in the Sermon on the Mount: "And why take ye thought for raiment? Consider the lilies of the field, how they grow; they toil not, neither do they spin: And yet I say unto you, That even Solomon in all his glory was not arrayed like one of these" (Matthew 6:28–29, KJV).

"Lilies of the field" are flowers generally or could refer to a particular flower. According to the *Illustrated Bible Dictionary* (IVP), "The 'lilies of the field' . . . could refer to any of the spectacular and beautiful flowers of the Palestinian countryside. Many have been suggested, including the poppy anemone *Anemone coronaria* and the white daisy *Anthemis palaestina* or the crown marguerite *Chrysanthemum coronarium.*"

Of the contemporary versions, the NKJV, NRSV, and RSV retain the KJV "consider the lilies of the field, how they grow"; the NASB has "Observe how the lilies of the field grow"; the NIV, "See how the lilies of the field grow"; the NLT, "Look at the lilies and how they grow"; the CEV, "Look how the wild flowers grow."

CONSIST

This word occurs only twice in the KJV. It has its standard sense of "to have its essence in"; "to be composed of." In Luke 12:15, "a man's life consisteth not in the abundance of the things he possesseth" (KJV), the NASB, NIV, NKJV, NRSV, and RSV have "consist"; the NCV and NLT render the whole expression as "life [NLT, "real life"] is not measured by how much" one owns.

In Colossians 1:17, KJV, "he is before all things, and by him all things consist," Tyndale and the sixteenth-century versions had "in him all things exist." Rheims rendered the clause as "in him all things consist," and the KJV adopted this, changing "in" to "by." The NASB, NIV, NKJV, NRSV, and RSV have a literal rendering of the Greek, "in him [NASB, NKJV, "Him"] all things hold together" [NKJV, "consist"]; the CEV has "by him everything is held together"; the NCV has, "all things continue because of him"; and the NLT has "he holds all creation together."

CONSORT WITH

The meaning of "consort" is "to associate with" or "to keep company with." The one appearance of the word in the KJV is in Acts 17:4, "And some of them believed, and consorted with Paul and Silas." Its use was an innovation in Bible translation. Wycliffe and Rheims had "joyned to"; Tyndale and the Great Bible, "came and companyed with"; Coverdale and the Bishops' Bible, "joyned with"; the Geneva Bible, "joyned in companye with."

Except for the revised versions of 1881–1901, no modern English translators retain "consorted with." John Wesley in 1755 translated it "were joined to"; Alexander Campbell in 1826, "adhered to." The Twentieth Century New Testament (1904), taking its clue from the etymology of the Greek verb, translated it "threw in their lot with Paul and Silas," and this has been accepted by Moffatt, Knox, and Phillips. Weymouth and Ballantine have "attached themselves to." Goodspeed returns to the word which was used by most of the sixteenth-century versions, and reads, "joined Paul and Silas."

This simple, direct translation of the Greek is used also by Confraternity, Williams, and the NASB, NCV, NIV, NKJV, NRSV, and RSV. The CEV has "became followers with Paul and Silas"; the NLT has "became converts."

"Consort" was a relatively new word when the KJV translators were at work. As a verb, its earliest occurrences recorded in the OED were in 1588. Shakespeare used it often, as well as the related verb "sort":

> "They wilfully themselves exile
> from light,
> And must for aye consort with
> black-brow'd night."
> —*A Midsummer Night's Dream* (III, 2, 386–387)

> "What will you do? Let's not consort with them."
> —*Macbeth* (II, 3, 141)

CONSTANT, CONSTANTLY

"Constant" is mainly used today as an adjective to describe something that continually occurs or is always there ("a constant reminder"). In the KJV, however, the main emphasis of the word is "with firmness or steadfastness."

For example, when Rhoda "constantly affirmed" (Acts 12:15, KJV) that Peter was at the door, the Greek does not mean "contin-

ually," but "confidently": "she insisted" that it was so (NLT, NRSV, RSV); "kept insisting" (NASB, NIV, NKJV); and "kept [NCV, "kept on"] saying" (CEV, NCV).

"These things I will that thou affirm constantly" (Titus 3:8, KJV) is "I desire that you insist on these things" (NRSV); "I want you to insist" on them (CEV, NLT); "I want you to stress these things" (NIV); "I want you to speak confidently" (NASB); the NKJV retains the KJV "affirm constantly."

"If he be constant to do my commandments and my judgments, as at this day" (1 Chronicles 28:7, KJV) is rendered by the NRSV and RSV as "if he continues resolute in keeping my commandments and my ordinances, as he is today"; the CEV, NCV, and NLT have "if he continues to obey"; the NASB, "if he resolutely performs"; the NIV, "if he is unswerving in carrying out," and the NKJV, "if he is steadfast to observe."

CONSULT

In modern usage, "consult" means "to ask the opinion and advice of someone who has more knowledge than yourself" or "to look in a reference book, map, etc., for information." The word is used in this sense in the KJV and also in the obsolete sense of "plan" or "devise." In this latter sense it is used twice. "Thou hast consulted shame to thy house" (Habakkuk 2:10, KJV) is rendered "You have devised shame to your house" (NRSV, RSV); "bring shame on" (CEV); "shamed your name" (NLT); "devised a shameful thing" (NASB); "give shameful counsel" (NKJV); and "plotted the ruin" (NIV). "What Balak . . . consulted" (Micah 6:5, KJV) is what Balak "counseled" (NASB, NIV, NKJV), "devised" (NRSV, RSV), or "the evil plans" (CEV, NCV) of Balak.

CONTAIN

In contemporary English, if you cannot contain a feeling such as delight or anger, you are unable to restrain yourself from showing that feeling. This sense is found intransitively in the KJV, at 1 Corinthians 7:9, "If they cannot contain," with reference to sexual behavior, where it means "cannot be continent and chaste."

The contemporary versions have "cannot exercise self-control" (NKJV, RSV), "cannot [NLT, "can't"] control themselves" (NIV, NLT), "not practicing self-control" (NRSV), "don't have enough self-control" (CEV), and "do not have self-control" (NRSV). (See BURN)

CONTENT

In contemporary English the adjective "content" means "pleased," "happy," or "satisfied." It is used in this sense in the KJV, but also in the imperative expression "be content," in the obsolete sense of "be pleased." This phrase occurs four times in the KJV.

When Gehazi, the servant of Elisha, ran after Naaman's chariot and asked him for a talent of silver, Naaman replied, "Be content, take two talents" (2 Kings 5:23, KJV). It is obvious that Naaman was not advising Gehazi to restrain his desires or urging him to be contented with only two talents. His reply is an immediate and generous gift of twice what Gehazi asked.

The contemporary versions translate it as "Be pleased" (NASB, RSV) to accept two talents; other translations reflect present-day idiomatic language: "Please" (NCV, NKJV, NRSV), "By all means" (NIV, NLT); and the CEV has "Sure . . . But why don't you take twice that amount of silver?" In these expressions is seen the language of polite diplomacy, between the commander of the army of the king of Syria and the servant of the man of God who represented the king of Israel.

The other passages, with renderings in the contemporary versions, are: Judges 19:6, "Please stay" (NCV, NIV, NLT); the NRSV has, "Why not spend the night?"; 2 Kings 6:3, "Please come" (NLT, NRSV); Job 6:28, "be pleased to look at me" (NKJV, NRSV, RSV); "please look at me" (NASB, NCV); "now be so kind as to look at me" (NIV). The idiomatic expression "be content" is recorded in the

OED under the adjective *content* (I, 3) and "please" under the verb *please* (I, 4 and II, 6).

CONTRARIWISE

This word may refer to contrary dispositions or to perverse, self-willed opposition—attitudes in which one is unwilling to accept control from others, or, more simply, it may mean "on the contrary." It has this latter meaning in the three passages in which it appears in the KJV: 2 Corinthians 2:7, Galatians 2:7, and 1 Peter 3:9.

The contemporary versions generally translate this expression by "on the contrary." Variants include: "instead" (2 Corinthians 2:7, NIV, NRSV; 1 Peter 3:9, NLT); "rather" (2 Corinthians 2:7, RSV).

CONTROVERSY

The phrase "without controversy," a literal translation of the Latin *sine controversia*, was current in the sixteenth century in the sense of "undeniably," "unquestionably," "indisputably." The KJV translators used it in their Preface, "The Translators to the Reader," when they referred to "St. Hierome, a most learned Father, and the best linguist without controversy of his age, or of any other that went before him." They used it in 1 Timothy 3:16, "without controversy great is the mystery of godliness." The Greek adverb here means "most certainly," as all would agree. The Latin Vulgate translates it by *manifeste*.

The contemporary versions render it "without [NRSV, "without any"] doubt" (NCV, NRSV); "without question" (NLT); "beyond all question" (NIV); "by common confession" (NASB); the NKJV retains the KJV, "without controversy."

CONVENIENT

The OED records that from the fourteenth century "convenient" meant "fitting," "becoming," "appropriate," "proper," or "right." But these meanings of the word are now obsolete, and "convenient" is applied to what suits one's personal ease or comfort or lies near at hand. It is used in the older sense in the KJV, and is generally given different renderings in the contemporary versions.

For example, "convenient" in "Feed me with food convenient for me" (Proverbs 30:8, KJV) is the food "that I need"; "that is my portion" (NASB), "allotted to me" (NKJV), "enough" (NCV); "just enough" (NLT); "what I need" (CEV); "only my daily bread" (NIV).

When Jeremiah is told that he may "go wheresoever it seemeth convenient unto thee to go" (Jeremiah 40:5, KJV; compare verse 4), the contemporary versions render "convenient" as "right" (NASB, NRSV, RSV); "anywhere you please" (NIV), "wherever you like" (NLT); the NKJV retains the KJV "convenient."

"Not convenient" (Ephesians 5:4) is rendered "not fitting" by the NASB, NKJV, and RSV; "out of place" by the NIV; "entirely out of place" by the NRSV; and "not for you" by the NLT. "To do those things which are not convenient" (Romans 1:28, KJV) is expressed by the contemporary versions as "indecent things" (CEV); "improper conduct" (RSV); "those things which are not proper" (NASB); "those things which are not fitting" (NKJV); "things that should never [NRSV, "should not"] be done" (NLT, NRSV); "what ought not to be done" (NIV).

"To enjoin thee that which is convenient" (Philemon 8, KJV) is rendered by the contemporary versions as what is "proper" (NASB); "right" (NASB); "the right thing for you to do" (NLT); to do "your duty" (NRSV); "what you ought to do" (NIV); "what is required" (RSV).

In four New Testament passages, the Greek word underlying the use of "convenient" or "conveniently" means "opportunity" (Mark 6:21; 14:11; Acts 24:25; 1 Corinthians 16:12), and the contemporary versions generally use "opportunity" (e.g., Mark 6:21, NRSV, RSV; 1 Corinthians 16:12, NASB, NCV, NIV, NRSV, RSV), "opportune time" (e.g., Mark 6:21, NIV).

Other noteworthy renderings are: "stra-tegic" (Mark 6:21, NASB), "perfect" (Mark 6:21, NCV), "a good chance" (Mark 14:11, CEV); "the best time" (Mark 14:11, NCV); and "the right time" (Mark 14:11, NLT). The KJV "convenient" is retained on occasions, e.g., Acts 24:25, NIV, NKJV, NLT.

CONVERSANT

In contemporary English if you are conversant with something, then you are familiar with it. In the KJV, however, "conversant" meant "dwelling habitually or frequently, accustomed to live or abide, passing much of one's time, in a place" (OED). The word occurs twice in the KJV, at Joshua 8:35 and 1 Samuel 25:15.

At Joshua 8:35 the KJV reads "the strangers that were conversant among them." For "conversant among," all the contemporary versions except the CEV and NRSV have "lived [NASB, NKJV, "living"] among"; the NRSV has "resided among," and it is untranslated in the CEV.

The KJV at 1 Samuel 25:15 reads "But the men were very good unto us, and we were not hurt, neither missed we any thing, as long as we were conversant with them, when we were in the fields." For "we were conversant with them," the contemporary versions have: "we were with them" (NRSV); "we were . . . with them" (NCV); "we were . . . near them" (NIV); "we went with them" (RSV); "we accompanied them" (NKJV); and "they were with us" (NLT).

CONVERSATION

In the KJV "conversation" always refers to conduct, behavior, or way of life, and is never used in the sense that it has today as a term for "talk" or "exchange of views."

"Conversation" in "the end of their conversation" (Hebrews 13:7, KJV) is translated by the contemporary versions as "way of life" (NIV, NRSV); "conduct" (NASB, NKJV); and "life" (RSV). "Conversation" in the "vain conversation received by tradition from your fathers" (1 Peter 1:18, KJV) is "way of life"

(CEV, NASB, NIV); "conduct" (NKJV); "ways" (NRSV, RSV); and "life" (NLT).

Lot is said to have been "vexed with the filthy conversation" of Sodom and Gomorrah (2 Peter 2:7, KJV), rendered in the contemporary versions as "conduct" (NASB, NKJV); "lives" (NCV, NIV); "licentiousness" (NRSV, RSV); and "immorality" (NLT).

The injunction to the Christian wives of unbelieving husbands expressed in the KJV of 1 Peter 3:1–2 may well be confusing to contemporary readers: "Likewise, ye wives, be in subjection to your own husbands; that, if any obey not the word, they also may without the word be won by the conversation of the wives; while they behold your chaste conversation coupled with fear."

This conveys the impression that these wives are to talk their husbands into becoming Christians, though it seems strange that husbands are to behold the conversation rather than listen to it, and one can only wonder what being coupled with fear has to do with it. But there is no word in the Greek for "coupled." The word "fear" stands for the reverent fear of God which is the mark of a good Christian; and the "conversation" of these wives (v. 1) is their "behavior" (NASB, NIV, RSV), their "conduct" (NKJV, NRSV).

The NRSV translates the passage: "Wives, in the same way, accept the authority of your husbands, so that, even if some of them do not obey the word, they may be won over without a word by their wives' conduct, when they see the purity and reverence of your lives."

Other examples of this archaic use of the word "conversation" include the following.

In Galatians 1:13, KJV, Paul refers to his "conversation in time past in the Jews' religion," now rendered as "life" (NCV, NRSV, RSV); "manner of life" (NASB); "way of life" (NIV); and "conduct" (NKJV).

He urges the Ephesians (4:22, KJV) to "put off concerning the former conversation the old man," rendered as "way of life" in the CEV, NIV, NLT, and NRSV and "manner of life" in the NASB and RSV.

Earlier in Ephesians (2:3, KJV) Paul wrote "among whom also we all had our conversation in times past." This is rendered with the verb "live" by all the contemporary versions except the CEV and NKJV; the NKJV has "conducted ourselves."

Paul exhorts the Philippians (1:27, KJV) to let their "conversation be as it becometh the gospel of Christ," rendered in the contemporary versions as "conduct yourselves" (NASB, NIV), "live in a way that" (CEV, NCV), "live [NRSV, "live your life"] in a manner" (NLT, NRSV).

Paul declares that "our conversation is in heaven" (3:20, KJV), rendered "citizenship" by the NASB, NIV, NKJV, and NRSV; "homeland" by the NCV; and "commonwealth" by the RSV; the CEV and NLT change the sentence structure to "we are citizens of heaven."

Timothy is encouraged by Paul to "be thou an example of the believers, in word, in conversation" (1 Timothy 4:12, KJV), rendered in the contemporary versions as "conduct" (NASB, NKJV, NRSV, and RSV); "actions" (NCV); "the way you live" (NLT); and "what you . . . do" (CEV).

Among the injunctions in the letter to the Hebrews is, "Let your conversation be without covetousness" (13:5, KJV), rendered in the contemporary versions as "lives" (NCV, NIV, and NRSV); "conduct" (NKJV); and "character" (NASB); the CEV has "Don't fall in love with money."

If a person is wise and understanding (James 3:13, KJV), "let him shew out of a good conversation his works," rendered in the contemporary versions as "life" (NIV, NLT, NRSV, and RSV); "living right" (CEV, NCV); "behavior" (NASB); and "conduct" (NKJV).

Peter counsels his readers (1 Peter 1:15; 2:12, KJV) to be holy "in all manner of conversation" and "having your conversation honest among the Gentiles," rendered in the contemporary versions as "conduct" (NKJV, NRSV, and RSV); "behavior" (NASB);

with the other versions rephrasing, e.g., "in everything [NIV, "in all"] you do" (1 Peter 1:15, NIV, NLT). He encourages them (2 Peter 3:11, KJV) to "holy conversation and godliness," rendered in the contemporary versions as "lives" (NCV, NIV, NLT, NRSV, and RSV); "conduct" (NASB, NKJV); and "the way you live" (CEV).

CONVINCE

To convince someone of something is to make that person certain that something is true ("they succeeded in convincing him that they were not to blame") or to persuade that person to do it. In the KJV, however, the word is used in two senses that are now obsolete: firstly, "to convict or prove to be guilty or in the wrong," and secondly, "to prove to be in error."

In the sense of "convict" or "prove to be guilty or in the wrong," the word is used four times in the KJV: John 8:46, "Which of you convinceth me of sin?"; 1 Corinthians 14:24, "convinced of all"; James 2:9, "If ye have respect to persons, ye commit sin, and are convinced of the law as transgressors"; and Jude 15, "to convince all that are ungodly."

The contemporary versions generally translate "convince" in these verses as "convict," e.g., John 8:46, NRSV, "Which of you convicts me of sin?" Other noteworthy renderings include: John 8:46, NLT, "Which of you can truthfully accuse me of sin?"; NIV, "Can any of you prove me guilty of sin?"; 1 Corinthians 14:24, CEV, "They will realize that they are sinners"; NRSV, "an unbeliever or outsider who enters is reproved by all." At this verse the NIV and NKJV retain the KJV verb "convince."

In the second sense of "to prove to be in error," the word is used three times in the KJV: Job 32:12, "there was none of you that convinced Job"; Acts 18:28, "he [Apollos] mightily convinced the Jews"; and Titus 1:9, "Holding fast the faithful word as he hath been taught, that he may be able by

sound doctrine both to exhort and to convince the gainsayers."

The contemporary versions generally translate "convince" in these verses as "confute" or "refute," e.g., Acts 18:28, NKJV, "he vigorously refuted the Jews publicly"; RSV, "he powerfully confuted the Jews in public." Other noteworthy renderings of these expressions include: "prove Job wrong" (Job 32:12, NCV and NIV; the NKJV at this verse retains the KJV "convince"); "he got into fierce arguments with the Jewish people" (Acts 28:18, CEV); and "convict those who contradict" (Titus 1:9, NKJV).

Shakespeare uses "convince" in the sense of "convict" in *Troilus and Cressida* (II, 2, 129):

"Else might the world convince of
     levity
As well my undertakings as your
     counsels."

He uses "convince" in a further, now obsolete, sense of "conquer" or "overcome" in *Macbeth* (I, 7, 64):

"his two chamberlains
Will I with wine and wassail so
     convince
That memory, the warder of the brain,
Shall be a fume, and the receipt of
     reason
A limbeck only."

CORN

This word means "grain," first as a small granular object, and second as a cereal crop. The word is used once by the KJV in the sense of a single seed: "Except a corn of wheat fall into the ground and die, it abideth alone" (John 12:24).

The contemporary versions generally have "a grain of wheat" (CEV, NASB, NCV, NKJV, NRSV, RSV) or "a kernel of wheat" (NIV, NLT). We still refer to a "barleycorn" or a "peppercorn," and formerly it was common to refer to a corn of gunpowder, an apple corn, or a corn of salt—from which we retain "corned beef."

An outstanding difference between British usage and American usage is that "corn" in America means maize or Indian corn, while in British usage it is a general term for grain, including all the cereal plants and their seed. This difference is seen, for example, in the NIV at Matthew 12:1: the North American edition has "grain" and "grainfields" whereas the Anglicized edition has "corn" and "cornfields."

CORNERS OF THE EARTH

The "four corners of the earth" are the extremities or ends of the earth; the areas of the world that are considered distant from a supposed central position. The expression comes from Isaiah 11:12 (KJV), "[the Lord] shall assemble the outcasts of Israel, and gather together the dispersed of Judah from the four corners of the earth."

Of the contemporary versions, the NASB, NKJV, and NRSV retain the KJV phrasing "four corners of the earth"; the NIV has "the four quarters of the earth"; the CEV, "all over the earth"; the NCV, "all parts of the earth." The earliest citation of this usage in the OED is Coverdale's translation of Psalm 95, "In his honde are all ye corners of the earth."

CORRUPT

People who are corrupt behave in a morally wrong or dishonest manner, often in order to gain power, money, or other advantage. As a verb, "corrupt" means to encourage someone to behave in such a way. The KJV uses the word in this sense and also in referring to physical decay or rotting, a sense that has become archaic.

For example, "corrupt" in "Where moth and rust doth corrupt" (Matthew 6:19, KJV) is generally rendered in the contemporary versions as "destroy" (CEV, NASB, NCV, NIV, NKJV) and "consume" (NRSV, RSV); in "Neither moth corrupteth" (Luke 12:33) as "destroy"; and in "Your riches are corrupted"

(James 5:2) as "rotted" (CEV, NASB, NCV, NIV, NRSV, and RSV); the NLT has "rotting"; while the NKJV retains the KJV "corrupted."

The distinction in the KJV of Romans 1:23 between "the uncorruptible God" and "corruptible man" is not, according to the Greek terms, the difference between God as morally incorruptible and human beings as corruptible, but the difference between God as imperishable and humans as perishable. The same distinction between *phthartos,* "perishable," and *aphthartos,* "imperishable," appears in 1 Corinthians 9:25; 15:42, 50–54; 1 Peter 1:4, 18, 23. These passages are concerned with the resurrection of the dead to eternal life.

The contemporary versions generally have "perishable" and "imperishable." For example, "For this perishable must put on the imperishable, and this mortal must put on immortality" (1 Corinthians 15:53, NASB). In all those passages except 1 Corinthians 9:22, the NKJV uses words based on "corrupt," e.g., 1 Peter 1:23, "having been born again, not of corruptible seed but incorruptible, through the word of God which lives and abides forever."

Occasionally in the contemporary versions, the verb "corrupt" is expanded, e.g., to "die or decay" in 1 Corinthians 15:53, CEV, "Our dead and decaying bodies will be changed into bodies that won't die or decay."

Other occurrences of "corrupt" in the KJV are rendered differently in the contemporary versions: "corrupt" in, for example, "They are corrupt" (Psalm 73:8), is "scoff" (NIV, NKJV, NLT, NRSV, RSV); "My breath is corrupt" (Job 17:1) is in the NASB, NCV, NIV, NKJV, NRSV, and RSV, "My spirit is broken"; and in "I will corrupt your seed" (Malachi 2:3), "corrupt" is rendered "rebuke" (NASB, NIV, NKJV, NLT, NRSV, RSV) and "punish" (CEV, NCV).

The KJV also uses "corrupt" in a moral sense, for example at Genesis 6:12, "God saw the earth, and behold, it was corrupt;

for all flesh had corrupted their way upon the earth."

The contemporary versions generally retain "corrupt," e.g., "So God looked upon the earth, and indeed it was corrupt; for all flesh had corrupted their way on the earth" (NKJV) and at 2 Peter 2:19, describing people who are "servants of corruption"; rendered "slaves of corruption" by the NASB, NKJV, NRSV, and RSV, "slaves to sin and corruption" by the NLT, "slaves of depravity" by the NIV, and "slaves of filthy living" by the CEV.

COUNT THE COST

To "count the cost" of something means "to consider its risks, disadvantages, advantages, etc., before deciding to do it." The expression is a figurative extension of the sense of "considering the financial implications of a project." This latter sense is found in Luke 14:28 in Jesus' comparison with the cost of being a disciple: "For which of you, intending to build a tower, sitteth not down first, and counteth the cost, whether he have sufficient to finish it?" (KJV).

The contemporary versions render the KJV "counteth the cost" as "count the cost" (NKJV, RSV); "estimate the cost" (NIV, NRSV); "calculate the cost" (NASB); "figure out how much it will cost" (CEV); and "first getting estimates and then checking" (NLT).

COUNTERVAIL

The word "countervail" means "to compensate" or "make up for." It occurs most frequently these days as "countervailing," meaning "having an equally strong, but opposite, effect" ("a countervailing force"). When Esther protested to the king against the edict to destroy her people, she added, "If we had been sold for bondmen and bondwomen, I had held my tongue, although the enemy could not countervail the king's damage" (Esther 7:4, KJV).

The contemporary versions, except the NKJV and the NRSV, regard the subject of the last clause as "distress" or "affliction" rather than "enemy." Hebrew has two nouns,

from different roots, but spelled alike, *tsar*, one of which means "distress" while the other means "adversary." The RSV reads "for our affliction is not to be compared with the loss to the king." The NIV has "because no such distress would justify disturbing the king."

The NLT has "for that would have been a matter too trivial to warrant disturbing the king." The CEV has "if we were merely going to be sold as slaves, I would not have bothered you." The Basic Bible has "for our trouble is little in comparison with the king's loss." The NRSV renders as "but no enemy can compensate for this damage to the king." The NKJV has "although the enemy could never compensate for the king's loss."

COUNTRY

The KJV reads "a country" in John 11:54, "Jesus therefore walked no more openly among the Jews; but went thence unto a country near to the wilderness." "A country" here could mean a different land or nation; "the country" (the rendering of the NASB, NKJV, RSV) is equivalent to "the countryside."

All English translations from Wycliffe on had "a" here until the Rheims version (1582) used "the." The KJV reverted to "a." This was changed to "the" by John Wesley (1755) and Alexander Campbell (1826), and by the NASB, NKJV, and RSV, which have "the country"; the NCV and NLT have "a place"; the NIV, "a region"; and the NRSV, "the region." Weymouth has "the district," and Phillips, "the countryside."

COUSIN

A cousin is the child of your uncle or aunt. In the KJV, however, a cousin was simply a relative, a kinsman or kinswoman. When the angel told Mary that her "cousin" Elizabeth had also conceived a son (Luke 1:36, KJV), the Greek word meant "relative" (all the contemporary versions except the RSV) or "kinswoman" (RSV). When Elizabeth gave birth to her son, the KJV has that it was "her neighbours and her cousins" that rejoiced with her (1:58), rendered in the contemporary versions as "her neighbors" and "relatives" (all the contemporary versions except the RSV) and "her neighbors and kinsfolk" (RSV).

"Uncle's son" in Leviticus 25:49 and Jeremiah 32:8–9, 12 is rendered "cousin" or retained by the contemporary versions, except the NLT at Leviticus 25:49, which has "nephew." Mark's relation to Barnabas, according to the KJV, was "sister's son" (Colossians 4:10), rendered in all the contemporary versions as "cousin."

COVER A MULTITUDE OF SINS

If something covers a multitude of sins, it compensates for or hides many different things, especially faults and weaknesses. The phrase is sometimes used humorously ("his official job title is 'educational adviser' but that description covers a multitude of sins"). The phrase has its origin in 1 Peter 4:8–9 (KJV), "And above all things have fervent charity among yourselves: for charity shall cover the multitude of sins."

Of the contemporary versions, the NASB, NIV, NKJV, NLT, NRSV, and RSV have "love covers [NKJV, "will cover"] a multitude of sins"; the CEV has "love wipes away many sins"; the NCV, "love will cause many sins to be forgiven."

James 5:20 (KJV) reads "Let him know, that he which converteth the sinner from the error of his way shall save a soul from death, and shall hide a multitude of sins."

The contemporary versions render "hide a multitude of sins" as "cover a multitude of sins" (NASB, NIV, NKJV, NRSV); the CEV has "many of their sins will be forgiven"; the NLT has "bring about the forgiveness of many sins."

COVER HIS FEET

"Cover his feet" is the literal translation of a Hebrew euphemism for evacuating the bowels. It was derived from the posture as-

sumed, screening the feet with long garments (*Oxford Hebrew Lexicon*). The contemporary versions generally translate it with the phrase "relieve himself" (Judges 3:24; 1 Samuel 24:3), except the NKJV which has "attend to his needs"; the NLT at Judges 3:24 has "using the latrine."

COVET

This word means "to have inordinate desire for what belongs to someone else." Covetousness is consistently denounced in the Bible, from the Ten Commandments (Exodus 20:17; Deuteronomy 5:21, with the contemporary versions generally retaining the KJV "covet"; the CEV has "want"; the NCV, "want" and "want to take") to the Second Epistle of Peter (2:3, 14, where "covetousness" is generally translated by the contemporary versions as "greed").

The characteristic word for "covetousness" in the Old Testament is *betsa,* which means "unjust gain"; and in the New Testament it is *pleonexia,* which means "greed," "the desire for more and more." Bishop Lightfoot, commenting on "covetousness" in Romans 1:29 (KJV, NKJV, NRSV, RSV; the NASB, NIV, and NLT have "greed") defined *pleonexia* as "the disposition which is ever ready to sacrifice one's neighbour to oneself in all things, not in money dealings merely."

The verb "covet" has also been used in the simple sense of "desire" or "long for," without any sinister implications. It appears twice in this good sense, in Paul's first letter to the Corinthians: "Covet earnestly the best gifts" (12:31) and "Wherefore, brethren, covet to prophesy" (14:39). The Greek verb here is *zeloute,* an imperative which means "desire," "strive for." The noun *zelos* has entered the English language as "zeal."

In 1 Corinthians 12:31 the contemporary versions have "earnestly desire" (NASB, NKJV, RSV), "eagerly desire" (NIV), "I want you to desire" (CEV), "you should desire" (NLT), and "strive for" (NRSV). In 1 Corinthians

14:39 the contemporary versions have "be eager to" (CEV, NIV, NLT, NRSV), "desire earnestly" (NASB, NKJV), and "truly want" (NCV).

CRACKNEL

"Cracknel" is defined by the OED as "a light, crisp kind of biscuit," with citations which show that the word has been used in English since the fifteenth century. When King Jeroboam sent his wife in disguise to consult the prophet Ahijah, he said she should take with her "ten loaves, and cracknels, and a cruse of honey" (1 Kings 14:3, KJV). All the contemporary versions except the CEV render "cracknels" as "some cakes"; the CEV has "some small cakes."

Just what the cakes (neqqudim) were is a mystery. The word is translated "mouldy" in Joshua 9:5, KJV; "moldy" by the NCV, NIV, NKJV, NLT, NRSV, RSV. The Hebrew dictionary inclines toward "crumbly"—the rendering followed by the CEV; the NASB has "had become crumbled." An adjective from the same Hebrew root describes the "speckled" (KJV and all the contemporary versions) sheep and goats that Jacob acquired (Genesis 30:32—31:12).

The conjecture has been made that neqqudim may have been cakes sprinkled on the surface with aromatic seeds. But we do not know. It is clear, however, that to call these cakes "cracknels" was a piece of modernization about as justifiable as it would be to call them "pretzels" or "ginger snaps" today.

CREATURE

In contemporary English a "creature" is a created living being—a human being, animal, insect, etc. In the KJV at Romans 8:19–22 the word "creature" is employed in the now obsolete sense of "the created universe"—"the whole creation"—as the KJV itself translates the same Greek word in verse 22. The contemporary versions generally use "creation" throughout this passage; the NCV has "everything God made."

This passage closes with Paul's great af-firmation of faith (Romans 8:38–39): "For I am persuaded, that neither death, nor life, nor angels, nor principalities, nor powers, nor things present, nor things to come, nor height, nor depth, nor any other creature ("nor any other created thing," NASB, NKJV; "nor anything else in all creation," NIV, RSV; "nothing in all creation," CEV, NLT; "nor anything else in the whole world," NCV), shall be able to separate us from the love of God, which is in Christ Jesus our Lord."

"Creature" also means anything created, and is not limited to living beings. The KJV at 1 Timothy 4:4 has "For every creature of God is good"; the contemporary versions render "every creature of God" as "everything created by God" (NASB, NRSV, RSV); "everything God created" (CEV, NIV, NLT); and "everything God made" (NCV); the NKJV retains the KJV translation.

At 2 Corinthians 5:17, "a new creature" (KJV and NASB) is rendered "a new creation" (NCV, NIV, NKJV, NRSV, RSV), "a new person" (CEV), and "new persons" (NLT). At Galatians 6:15, "a new creature" (KJV) is rendered "a new creation" (NASB, NIV, NKJV, NRSV, RSV), "a new person" (CEV), "new and different people" (NLT), and "new people God has made" (NCV).

CREEK

In British English, a creek is a narrow inlet of the sea; but in American English a creek is a small tributary or branch of a river. The KJV "a certain creek with a shore" (Acts 27:39) is in the contemporary versions "a bay with a beach"; in the NIV, "a bay with a sandy beach."

CRUMBS THAT FALL FROM THE RICH MAN'S TABLE

The expression "crumbs that fall from the rich man's table" is used to refer to what is available to the poor after a rich man has finished with it.

The expression has its source in two passages in the Gospels: Matthew 15:27, in which a Gentile woman shows her faith,

"And she said, Truth, Lord: yet the dogs eat of the crumbs which fall from their masters' table" (KJV) and Luke 16:20–21, the story of the rich man and Lazarus, "And there was a certain beggar named Lazarus, which was laid at his gate, full of sores, And desiring to be fed with the crumbs which fell from the rich man's table: moreover the dogs came and licked his sores" (KJV).

The contemporary versions render the first passage in very similar ways to the KJV, with only minor stylistic alterations; in the second passage the KJV "the crumbs which fell from the rich man's table" is rendered as "the scraps that fell" (CEV), "the small pieces of food" (NCV), and "what fell from the rich man's table" (NIV, NRSV, RSV).

CUMBER

"Cumber" is rare word in modern English. It means "to hinder" or "to encumber" and also "to clutter up." In the KJV the word is used in this final meaning and also in the sense of "to trouble, harass, or distress." The KJV "cumbered" in "Martha was cumbered about much serving" (Luke 10:40) is rendered by the contemporary versions: "distracted" (NASB, NIV, NKJV, NRSV, RSV); "worried" (CEV), "worrying" (NLT), and "busy" (NCV).

The owner of the barren fig tree is represented as saying, "Cut it down; why cumbereth it the ground?" (Luke 13:7). The KJV "cumbereth" here is a translation of a different Greek verb which is rendered in the contemporary versions as "use up" (NASB, NIV, NKJV, RSV), and by the verbs "take up" (CEV, NLT) and "waste" (NCV, NRSV).

CUMBRANCE

This word is now obsolete, meaning "hindrance," "burden," or "encumbrance." It appears once in the KJV, at Deuteronomy 1:12: "How can I myself alone bear your cumbrance, and your burden, and your strife?" "Cumbrance" was Tyndale's word here. The Hebrew word *ṭoraḥ* simply means burden. In this verse *ṭoraḥ* is cou-

pled with the more common word for "burden," *massa'*.

The contemporary versions translate "cumbrance" as "problems" (CEV, NCV, NIV, NKJV), "load" (NASB), and "quarrels" (NLT). The word *ṭoraḥ* is used in one other passage (Isaiah 1:14), rendered in the KJV and NKJV as "trouble" and generally translated in the other contemporary versions as "burden."

CUNNING

Today if people are described as "cunning," they are able to deceive people in a clever way in order to achieve what they want. The word is used in this sense in the KJV in the New Testament and in a now obsolete, positive, sense of "skillful" or "expert" in the Old Testament. In this latter sense, the contemporary versions generally replace the KJV "cunning" with "skilled" or "skillful."

For example, Esau is described as a "skillful" rather than "cunning" hunter (Genesis 25:27) in the NASB, NCV, NIV, NKJV, NLT, and NRSV. David was a "skillful player of the harp" (1 Samuel 16:16, NASB, NKJV). Hiram of Tyre was "filled with wisdom and understanding and skill" (1 Kings 7:14, NASB, NKJV). The "cunning artificer" of Isaiah 3:3 was "skillful" (NASB, NKJV, NRSV) and "skilled" (NCV, NIV, NLT)

In the chapters of Exodus and Chronicles dealing with the furnishings of the tabernacle and the temple, "cunning men" (e.g., at 2 Chronicles 2:14, KJV) are "skilled men" (NASB), "skillful men" (NKJV), "craftsmen" (NIV, NLT), "artisans" (NRSV). "Cunning work" (e.g., at Exodus 35:33, KJV) is "craft" (NRSV), "skilled craft" (RSV), "artistic craftsmanship" (NIV), "artistic workmanship" (NKJV), and "inventive work" (NASB).

In the New Testament, "cunning" is used in the pejorative sense which is now its prevalent meaning. In Ephesians 4:14, the KJV (and also NKJV) "cunning craftiness" is rendered "craftiness" (NASB, NRSV, and RSV), and "cunning and craftiness" (NIV). The

NLT translate the whole verse as "Then we will no longer be like children, forever changing our minds about what we believe because someone has told us something different or because someone has cleverly lied to us and made the lie sound like the truth."

In 2 Peter 1:16, the KJV (and also NKJV) "cunningly devised" fables is rendered as "cleverly devised" (NASB, NCV, NRSV, RSV); the CEV has "clever stories that someone had made up."

CUP IS FULL

The expression "one's cup is full" or "one's cup runneth over" means that "a person has an abundance of something, especially good fortune or other joys." The expressions derive from Psalm 23:5 in Coverdale's translation (in the Book of Common Prayer), "my cup shall be full" and (KJV), "my cup runneth over."

The contemporary versions render this as "My cup overflows" (NASB, NIV, NRSV, RSV), "My cup overflows with blessings" (NLT), "My cup runs over" (NKJV), "you fill my cup until it overflows" (CEV), and "you fill my cup to overflowing" (NCV).

CURIOUS

Today if you are "curious" about something, you want to know more about it; if something is described as "curious" then it is unusual, strange, or difficult to understand ("a curious mixture of traditional and futuristic styles of architecture"). It is used in two senses in the KJV, both of which are now obsolete.

The first sense is "made with care and skill." The "curious girdle of the ephod" (Exodus 28:8, KJV) was a "skillfully woven band" (NASB, NRSV), a "skillfully woven waistband" (NIV), or an "intricately woven band" (NKJV). The "curious works" (Exodus 35:32, KJV) which Bezalel devised were "artistic designs" (NIV, NRSV, RSV) or "artistic works" (NKJV). The KJV "curiously wrought in the lowest parts of the earth" (Psalm 139:15) is

rendered "woven together" (CEV, NIV, NLT), "skillfully wrought" (NASB, NKJV), "intricately woven" (NRSV), and "intricately wrought" (RSV).

The *Bible Word-Book*, 1884, quotes from *Taylor's Concordance* the following statement concerning the expression "curiously wrought in the lowest parts of the earth": "The word is the same which is usually translated 'embroidered'; the adjusting and formation of the different members of the human body being by a bold and beautiful metaphor compared to the arranging the threads and colours in a piece of tapestry."

The second sense, defined by the OED as "recondite, occult," occurs once in the New Testament at Acts 19:19: "curious arts" (KJV) is "magic" (NASB, NCV, NKJV, NLT, NRSV), "magic arts" (RSV), "sorcery" (NIV), or "witchcraft" (CEV).

CURSE OF CAIN

See MARK OF CAIN.

CUSTOM

In contemporary English "custom" refers to a usual or traditional way of behaving or to business patronage ("withhold one's custom"); the plural "customs" refers to the taxes on goods that come into a country or to the organization or place where such taxes are collected. The KJV uses the word in both these senses; however, in the meaning referring to taxes it is used only in the singular. The KJV also uses the expression to refer to a woman's period.

In the New Testament, the KJV "receipt of custom" at which Jesus saw Matthew (Levi) (Matthew 9:9; Mark 2:14; Luke 5:27) is the "tax collector's booth" (NCV; NIV in Matthew and Mark); "tax-collection booth" (NLT); "tax booth" (NASB, NRSV; NIV in Luke), "tax office" (NKJV, RSV), "place for paying taxes" (CEV).

In Matthew 17:25, Jesus' question to Peter is recorded, "What thinkest thou, Simon?

of whom do the kings of the earth take custom or tribute? of their own children, or of strangers?" (KJV). The contemporary versions render the KJV expression "custom or tribute" as "customs or poll-tax" (NASB), "customs or taxes" (NKJV), "duty and taxes" (NIV), "toll or tribute" (NRSV), and "taxes and fees" (CEV).

In Paul's injunctions to submit to human authorities, believers are instructed to pay "custom to whom custom" (Romans 13:7, KJV, NASB); this tax is rendered as "customs" (NKJV), "revenue" (NIV, NRSV, RSV), "fees" (CEV), and "import duties" (NLT).

In the Old Testament, "custom" is used three times in Ezra in the KJV (4:13, 20; 7:24) in the expression "toll, tribute, and [7.24: "or"] custom." Of the contemporary versions for 4:13 and 20, the KJV "custom" is retained by the NASB, NKJV, NRSV, and RSV; the NLT has "customs"; and the NIV has "duty." The CEV and NCV do not distinguish between the different kinds of tax.

In Genesis 31:35 (KJV) the "custom of women" is rendered as "the manner of women" (NASB, NKJV), "the way of women" (NRSV, RSV), "my monthly period" (NCV, NLT), and "my period" (CEV, NIV).

D

DAILY BREAD

The expression "one's daily bread" refers to the food that one needs every day, or more generally, to all the physical necessities that one requires in order to live. ("There must be better ways of earning one's daily bread than this.") The phrase has its origin in the Lord's Prayer in Matthew 6:11 (KJV), "Give us this day our daily bread."

This rendering is retained by the NASB, NKJV, NRSV, and RSV; the CEV and NLT have "Give us our food for today"; the NIV has "Give us today our daily bread"; and the NCV, "Give us the food we need for each day."

DAMASCUS ROAD EXPERIENCE

See ROAD TO DAMASCUS EXPERIENCE.

DAMNATION, DAMNED

When we hear these words today we think of hell and of those consigned to it. At the time of the KJV, however, "damn" was a general word which meant "condemn," and "damnation" meant "condemnation"— senses in which these words are now obsolete. The KJV uses the word "damnation" ten times, and "damned" three times, as translations of words connected with the

Greek *krino*, which means "to judge," "pass sentence," or "condemn."

The revised versions do not use "damnation" and "damned" in these contexts, but use terms which the KJV elsewhere uses to render the same Greek words: "judge" (used eighty-seven times in the KJV), "judgment" (forty-one times), "condemn" (twenty-two times), and "condemnation" (eight times).

The scribes who devour widows' houses are said in the KJV to receive "greater damnation" (Matthew 23:14; Mark 12:40; Luke 20:47); the contemporary versions speak of their receiving "greater condemnation" (NASB, NKJV, RSV, NRSV), or "greater punishment" (NCV; NLT, "their punishment will be the greater"; NIV, "they will be punished most severely").

In Romans 13:2 the penalty of resisting the authorities is to "receive damnation" (KJV), which the contemporary versions render as to "receive condemnation" (NASB), "incur judgment" (NRSV, RSV), and "bring judgment [NCV, "bring punishment"] on themselves" (NCV, NIV, NKJV).

In the KJV rendering of 1 Corinthians 11:29, "he that eateth and drinketh unworthily, eateth and drinketh damnation to himself," the word which is rendered "damnation" is the same as that which is rendered "condemnation" in verse 34. The NRSV has "eat and drink judgment against themselves," and the majority of the contemporary versions use the word "judgment" for the KJV's "condemnation" in the verse.

In 1 Timothy 5:12, Paul writes that the younger widows who wish to marry incur "damnation, because they have cast off their first faith" (KJV); the NRSV translates this as "condemnation for having violated their first pledge." The other contemporary versions use either "condemnation" (NASB, NKJV), or "judgment" (NIV; NCV, "they will be judged") to render "damnation" (KJV). The CEV and NLT paraphrase as "guilty of breaking" a previous pledge. "How can ye escape the damnation of hell?" (Matthew 23:33, KJV) is now "How can you escape being sentenced to hell?" (NRSV).

DAMSEL

This word evokes memories of legends and fairy stories, where the damsel in distress wins the attention of knights and dragons alike. The word appears fifty-one times in the KJV, representing Hebrew and Greek words which mean "young woman," "child," "little girl," "maiden," or "maid." It was spelled "damsell" and more often "damosell" in the 1611 edition of the KJV. Since the seventeenth century it has not been in ordinary spoken use. It is archaic and literary or playful (OED).

The contemporary versions use "girl" (NASB, NIV, NRSV), "maiden" (RSV), and "young woman" (NKJV) for Rebecca and Dinah (Genesis 24 and 34). In Deuteronomic law (22:15–29) the NASB and NIV again use "girl," while the NKJV, NRSV, and RSV have "young woman." Salome (Matthew 14:11; Mark 6:22, 28) is referred to as a "girl" by all the contemporary versions, and the daughter of the ruler of the synagogue (Mark 5:39–42) is referred to as a "child" and "girl," following the Greek.

For the Greek *paidiske*, a maidservant,

the RSV uses "maid" where the majority of the contemporary versions have "servant girl" or "slave girl" (Matthew 26:69; John 18:17), although in Acts 12:13 the NRSV also uses "maid" to refer to Rhoda. In Acts 16:16, the young woman who dogs Paul's steps at Philippi is referred to as a "slave girl" by the contemporary versions.

DAN TO BEERSHEBA

The expression "from Dan to Beersheba" is sometimes used to mean "from one end of the country to another." The phrase refers to the most northerly city (Dan) and the most southerly town (Beersheba) of Palestine (Judges 20:1): "Then all the children of Israel went out, and the congregation was gathered together as one man, from Dan even to Beer-sheba, with the land of Gilead, unto the LORD in Mizpeh."

The contemporary versions retain the expression "from Dan to Beersheba," except the CEV, which has "from Dan in the north, Beersheba in the south" and the NRSV and RSV spell the name of the southerly town "Beer-sheba."

DANGER

The word "danger" means the "risk or threat of harm." The KJV, however, uses the word in the now obsolete sense of "legal liability." In Matthew 5:21, Jesus quotes a saying which warns that "whosoever shall kill shall be in danger of the judgment," and the word "danger" is here used in its original meaning as "the power that an authority has over those subject to it." In 1611 it was a good translation of the Greek *enochos*, which was a legal term meaning "bound by," "liable to," or "subject to."

In Shakespeare's *Merchant of Venice* (IV, 1, 180), Portia's first question to Antonio is concerning Shylock's bond: "You stand within his danger, do you not?" The NRSV translates the saying in Matthew 5:21 as "whoever murders shall be liable to judgment"; the NASB renders it as "Whoever commits murder shall be liable to the court." The NIV and NLT have "subject to judgment."

In the translation of the New Testament which Alexander Campbell published in 1826, he used in Matthew 5:21 what seems to us now to be a strange word: "whosoever commits murder shall be obnoxious to the judges." "Obnoxious" once meant "subject to" or "answerable to," but that meaning is now obsolete.

In Mark 3:29, the KJV reads "is in danger of eternal damnation," which the NASB, NIV, NRSV, and RSV now render as "is guilty of an eternal sin." The KJV translates *enochos* by "subject to" in Hebrews 2:15, and by "guilty of" in four other cases. (See GUILTY OF)

DARKNESS, OUTER

The expression "outer darkness" occurs three times in the New Testament, in Matthew's Gospel, to represent God's judgment upon individuals and unfaithful Israel.

In the parable of the wedding feast, the king says to his servants concerning the guest who was not wearing a wedding garment, "Bind him hand and foot, and take him away, and cast him into outer darkness; there shall be weeping and gnashing of teeth" (22:13, KJV). In the parable of the talents, the master says to the man who hid his one talent in the ground, "cast ye the unprofitable servant into outer darkness: there shall be weeping and gnashing of teeth" (25:30); to unfaithful Israel Jesus said, "But the children of the kingdom shall be cast out into outer darkness: there shall be weeping and gnashing of teeth" (8:12).

Of the contemporary versions, the NASB, NKJV, NLT, NRSV, and RSV retain the KJV expression "outer darkness"; the NIV has "outside, into the darkness" at all three references, and the CEV has "[thrown out] into the dark" at 8:12 and 22:13.

DARLING

This word in modern usage is an affectionate term of endearment. We also sometimes use it to mean "things which we like or appreciate," or "things which have won our hearts in some way" ("a darling puppy"; "a darling dress"). In the KJV, however, the word is used in the sense of "a unique and singular possession."

In Psalms 22:20 and 35:17 "my darling" (KJV) represents the Hebrew word which means "my only." It is the word which is used for Abraham's only son Isaac and for Jephthah's only child, and also occurs repeatedly in references to mourning for an only son. In Psalms 22 and 35, however, the psalmist is not praying for an only son or a loved one, but for himself. "My only" is parallel to "my soul" in the first line of Psalm 22:20. It is a poetic expression for "my life," according to the Hebrew lexicon, "as the one unique and priceless possession which can never be replaced."

The contemporary versions render "my darling" (KJV) in the Psalm as "my life" (NCV, NRSV, RSV), "my only life" (NASB), and "my precious life" (NIV, NKJV, NLT).

DAVID AND GOLIATH

The expression "David and Goliath" alludes to the account in 1 Samuel 17 when David went out against Goliath, the Philistine giant, with no armor but only his staff and five smooth stones and his sling. David trusted in God and used his experience as a shepherd to kill Goliath.

DAVID AND JONATHAN

The expression "David and Jonathan" refers to close friends of the same sex. David was the close friend of Jonathan, Saul's eldest son, and Scripture records their mutual loyalty and affection, e.g., 1 Samuel 18:3 (KJV), "Jonathan and David made a covenant, because he loved him as his own soul."

The NASB, NIV, NKJV, and NRSV retain the word "covenant," the NCV has "agreement";

the CEV has "Jonathan liked David so much that they promised to always be loyal friends"; the NLT, "And Jonathan made a special vow to be David's friend"; David's mourning over Jonathan (2 Samuel 1:26), "I am distressed for thee, my brother Jonathan: very pleasant hast thou been unto me: thy love to me was wonderful, passing the love of women" (KJV), is rendered as "I cry for you, my brother Jonathan. I enjoyed your friendship so much. Your love to me was wonderful, better than the love of women" (NCV).

See also 1 Samuel 20; 23:16–18.

DAY OF SMALL THINGS

The expression "do not despise the day of small things" means "not to condemn and undervalue the occurrence of seemingly insignificant events." The phrase comes from Zechariah 4:10 (KJV), "For who hath despised the day of small things? for they shall rejoice," which was the response of the Lord to Zechariah concerning the rebuilding of the temple, in that some people despised the meager beginnings of the rebuilding work.

The contemporary versions render the expression: "Who has despised the day of small things" (NASB, NKJV); "who despises the day of small things" (NIV); "whoever has despised the day of small things" (NRSV, RSV); "Do not despise these small beginnings" (NLT); "Those who have made fun of this day of small beginnings" (CEV); and "The people should not think that small beginnings are unimportant" (NCV).

DAYS OF ONE'S LIFE

The expression "all the days of one's life" means "for as long as one lives." It comes from Psalm 23:6 (KJV), "Surely goodness and mercy shall follow me all the days of my life: and I will dwell in the house of the LORD for ever." The KJV translation "all the days of one's life" is retained by the NASB, NIV, NKJV, NLT, NRSV, and RSV; the CEV has "each day of my life"; the NCV has "all my life."

DAYSMAN

"Daysman" is an archaic word for "mediator" or "arbitrator." It occurs in the KJV at Job 9:33, "Neither is there any daysman betwixt us, that might lay his hand upon us both." The contemporary versions render this as "umpire" (NASB, NRSV, RSV), "mediator" (NKJV, NLT), "someone to arbitrate" (NIV), and "someone to make peace" (NCV).

The word derives from the obsolete verb "day" meaning "to submit to" or "to decide by arbitration." Spenser wrote in *The Faerie Queene* (II, 8, 28), "For what art thou, That mak'st thy selfe his dayes-man, to prolong The vengeance prest?" And in "If neighbours were are variance, they ran not straight to law: Daysmen took up the matter, and cost them not a straw" (*New Custom*, I, 2; Dodsley's Old English Plays, ed. Hazlitt, III, 14).

DAYSPRING

This is an old and rather romantic word for "daybreak," "dawn," "the spring of the day." It is not often heard today, except in literary or poetic contexts, although it occasionally crops up as a new product title for items such as perfume or bubble bath. In the KJV it occurs in Job 38:12, which reads: "Hast thou commanded the morning since thy days; and caused the dayspring to know his place." The contemporary versions substitute "dawn."

The well-known line in the Benedictus, "whereby the dayspring from on high hath visited us" (Luke 1:78, KJV) is rendered in individual ways by the contemporary versions. The NRSV has "the dawn from on high will break upon us," and the NASB has "the Sunrise from on high will visit us." The NIV speaks of "the rising sun," whereas the NLT has "the light from heaven."

In Milton's *Samson Agonistes* (11), the blind Samson, led out into the open air for a brief rest, expresses joy in "the breath of heaven fresh blowing, pure and sweet, with dayspring born." (See SPRING)

DEAD BURY THEIR DEAD

The phrase "let the dead bury their dead" means that "it is better to be concerned with the present and future than with the past." The expression has its origins in Matthew 8:21–22 (KJV): "And another of his disciples said unto him, Lord, suffer me first to go and bury my father. But Jesus said unto him, Follow me; and let the dead bury their dead."

The contemporary versions generally render the phrase as "Let the dead bury their own dead" (NIV, NKJV, NRSV; the NASB has "Allow the dead"; the CEV follows the KJV; the NLT has "Let those who are spiritually dead care for their own dead." In the parallel passage in Luke (9:60) all the versions except the CEV retain the translation as in Matthew 8:22; the CEV has "Let the dead take care of their dead."

Longfellow alludes to the expression in *A Psalm of Life:*

"Trust no Future, howe'er pleasant!
Let the dead Past bury its dead!"

DEAD CORPSES

In modern usage, the adjective "dead" is unnecessary before the word "corpse" since a corpse is, by definition, a dead body. In Elizabethan English, however, such redundancy was a common form of emphasis. Isaiah 37:36 (and its parallel, 2 Kings 19:35) reads in the KJV: "Then the angel of the LORD went forth, and smote in the camp of the Assyrians a hundred and fourscore and five thousand: and when they arose early in the morning, behold, they were all dead corpses." The Hebrew here also has the redundant equivalent of "dead corpses."

The contemporary versions replace the KJV's rendering with "dead bodies" (CEV, NCV, NIV, NRSV, RSV) or "corpses" (NLT); the NASB states simply that the Assyrians "were dead." An example of redundancy in sixteenth-century English is found in *King Henry IV,* in Shakespeare's report of the death of Mortimer: "Upon whose dead corpse there was such misuse."

DEARTH

This word today means "a scarcity of something." In the sixteenth century, however, it had the sense of "a general scarcity of food," i.e., a famine. Tyndale, portraying the plight of the prodigal son, translated Luke 15:14: "And when he had spent all that he had, ther rose a greate derth thorow all that same londe, and he began to lacke." Tyndale was followed by the subsequent sixteenth-century versions, but the KJV substituted the word "famine."

There remain six passages in the KJV where "dearth" is used for the Hebrew and Greek words which it translates as "famine" in ninety-two other passages. These six passages are Genesis 41:54; 2 Kings 4:38; 2 Chronicles 6:28; Nehemiah 5:3; Acts 7:11; 11:28. The contemporary versions generally use the word "famine" in these passages, or represent the scarcity of food as resulting in "almost nothing to eat" (2 Kings 4:38, CEV; the NCV speaks of "a shortage of food"). The NCV generally paraphrases where the other contemporary versions use "famine": in Nehemiah 5:3 there is "not much food" (NCV); in Acts 11:28 Agabus prophesies that "There will be no food to eat" (NCV).

In Jeremiah 14:1 "the dearth" (KJV) translates a different Hebrew word, which the majority of contemporary versions translate as "the drought."

DEATH, WHERE IS THY STING?

This expression comes from 1 Corinthians 15:55 (KJV), "O death, where is thy sting? O grave, where is thy victory?" "Sting" refers to the painfulness or harmfulness of death. All the contemporary versions except the NCV retain "sting" in this verse; the NCV has "pain."

DEBATE

A "debate" in modern terms is a formal discussion on a subject in which people state differing opinions. In the KJV, however, the word refers to "strife, contention, dissension, quarreling." For example, in Romans 1:29 the KJV lists debate along with envy, murder, deceit, and malignity among the characteristics of the debased mind.

The contemporary versions render the KJV "debate" as "strife" (NASB, NIV, NKJV, NRSV, RSV); and "fighting" (NCV, NLT); and the CEV uses the verb "argue." In 2 Corinthians 12:20 the KJV "debates" is rendered as "quareling" (NIV, NLT, NRSV, RSV), "arguing" (CEV, NCV), "strife" (NASB), and "contentions" (NKJV). In these two verses the word is a translation of the Greek word *eris*, which means "strife."

In Greek legend Eris was the goddess of strife, who threw the golden apple which awakened the jealousy of Hera, Athene, and Aphrodite, and brought on the Trojan War. Turning to the Old Testament, "debate" in Isaiah 58:4, KJV, "ye fast for strife and debate," is rendered by the contemporary versions as "fight" (CEV, NCV, NRSV, RSV), "strife" (NASB, NIV), and "quareling" (NLT); the NKJV retains the KJV "debate."

In Shakespeare's *King Henry IV, Part II* (IV, 4, 2), the king refers to Northumberland's insurrection as "This debate that bleedeth at our doors."

Jesus' answer to his own question, "Do you think that I have come to give peace on earth?" (Luke 12:51) was translated by Tyndale, Coverdale, and Geneva as "I tell you nay, but rather debate." The Great Bible, the Bishops' Bible, and the KJV have "division," and are followed by the NASB, NIV, NKJV, NLT, NRSV, and RSV among the contemporary versions. Weymouth, Moffatt, Ballantine, Torrey, and Knox have "dissension"; the NCV uses the verb "divide"; the CEV renders the whole phrase as "I came to make people choose sides."

DECAY

This word conjures up images of deterioration and rottenness. We use the word both to refer to the breaking down of organic matter ("tooth decay"), and also to refer to a progressive decline of some sort ("the decay at the heart of society"). When the KJV uses the word, however, the sense is the now obsolete one of "to dwindle" or "cause to dwindle."

"Decay" occurs five times in the KJV, and is used to render four different Hebrew verbs, each with its own meaning. "As . . . the flood decayeth and drieth up" (Job 14:11, KJV) is now rendered "As . . . a river wastes away and dries up" by the NRSV. "The decayed places thereof" (Isaiah 44:26, KJV) is rendered "her ruins" by the NASB, and "their ruins" by the NIV, NRSV, and RSV. At Ecclesiastes 10:18, "By much slothfulness the building decayeth; and through idleness of the hands the house droppeth through" (KJV), the NRSV has "Through sloth the roof sinks in, and through indolence the house leaks."

The KJV uses "decay" twice to refer to persons. "The strength of the bearers of burdens is decayed" (Nehemiah 4:10, KJV) is rendered "The strength of the burden bearers [RSV, "burden-bearers"] is failing" by the NASB, NRSV, and RSV. "If thy brother be waxen poor, and fallen in decay with thee, then thou shalt relieve him" (Leviticus 25:35, KJV) is rendered by the NRSV, "If any of your kin fall into difficulty and become dependent on you, you shall support them."

Hebrews 8:13 reads, in the KJV: "In that he saith, A new covenant, he hath made the first old. Now that which decayeth and waxeth old is ready to vanish away." The word for "hath made old" and the word for "decayeth" are active and passive forms of the same Greek verb. The active form means "make old," "treat as obsolete"; the passive form means "become old," "become obsolete."

Tyndale's translation was: "In that he sayth a new testament he hath abrogat the old. Now that which is disannulled and wexed olde, is redy to vannyshe awaye." Geneva accepted this, but substituted "Covenant" for "testament." Coverdale, the Great Bible, and the Bishops' Bible had, with some variations, the rendering which appears in the second edition of the Bishops' Bible: "In that he saith a new Covenant, he hath worne out the first: for that which is worne out and waxed old is ready to vanish away."

The NRSV has "In speaking of 'a new covenant' he has made the first one obsolete. And what is obsolete and growing old will soon disappear."

DECLARE

The word "declare" originally meant "to make clear or plain," and so to explain or to recount in detail. We tend to no longer use the word in these senses, although the original meaning is sometimes implied in our modern usage. "Declare your intentions" means make your intentions clear, and is an expression with a formal tone to it. In fact, we are more familiar with "declare" as a verb for formal, studied, public utterance or for emphatic statement or legal procedure.

This shift in meaning may hide the real meaning of the word "declare" for contemporary readers in many of the contexts where it occurs in the KJV. When Pharaoh told Joseph about his dream and said "there was none that could declare it to me" (Genesis 41:24, KJV), "declare" has the meaning of explain.

The majority of the contemporary versions thus substitute "explain" here, as the NKJV, NLT, and RSV do in Deuteronomy 1:5 where the KJV states, "On this side Jordan, in the land of Moab, began Moses to declare this law." The NASB, NIV, and NRSV render "declare" (KJV) here as "expound."

In the statement of procedure at the cities of refuge, "declare his cause" (Joshua 20:4, KJV) is rendered "explain his case" by the NRSV and RSV, and "state his case" by the NASB and NIV. The request of the disciples that Jesus "declare unto us" the parable (KJV) is generally rendered in the contemporary versions as "explain to us" (Matthew 13:36; 15:15).

In other cases, the contemporary versions also adopt "tell" as a translation of the Hebrew or Greek. Examples are found in Judges 14:12–15; Jeremiah 36:13, Micah 1:10; Colossians 4:7. For other Greek verbs the contemporary versions use "disclose," (NRSV, RSV), "show" (NASB), and "bring to light" (NIV) in 1 Corinthians 3:13; "report" (NRSV, RSV), "describe" (NASB), and "tell" (NIV) in Acts 15:3; "relate" (NASB, RSV) in Acts 15:12, 14; 21:19; and "make known" (NIV, NRSV, RSV) and "show" (NCV) in John 1:18 and 17:26.

In Colossians 1:8 the KJV rendering "Who also declared unto us your love in the Spirit" is now "and he also informed us of your love in the Spirit" (NASB); the NRSV and RSV have "he has made known to us your love in the Spirit."

The suggestion of the messenger sent to summon Micaiah reads in the KJV: "Behold now, the words of the prophets declare good unto the king with one mouth: let thy word, I pray thee, be like the word of one of them, and speak that which is good" (1 Kings 22:13 and its parallel, 2 Chronicles 18:12). In this rendering "declare" and "that which is" were inserted by the translators, and "now" and "I pray thee" represent the Hebrew particle na', an enclitic syllable of polite entreaty or exhortation which has no English equivalent.

The NRSV translates as "Look, the words of the prophets with one accord are favorable to the king; let your word be like the word of one of them, and speak favorably."

In Numbers 1:18, "declared their pedigrees after their families" (KJV) is translated by the NRSV and RSV as "registered themselves in their clans" [RSV, "by families"]; the NASB has "registered by ancestry in their families."

DECLINE

The verb "decline" now means "to become less in quantity or strength," "to refuse," "to slope or move downward." In the time of the KJV "decline" was also used with reference to moral standards, and meant "to turn aside," "turn away," "swerve," "deviate," or "depart," from the right. So when the KJV at 2 Chronicles 34:2 states that Josiah "declined neither to the right hand, nor to the left," the contemporary versions generally render this word with the expression "turn aside" (NASB, NIV, NKJV, NLT, NRSV, RSV).

In Psalm 119 in the KJV, "decline" occurs in verses 51 and 157: "yet have I not declined from thy law" (v. 51) and "yet do I not decline from thy testimonies" (v. 157). Contemporary renderings include "turn aside," (v. 51, NASB, NKJV; v. 157, NASB) "turn away from," (v. 51, NLT, NRSV, RSV) "turn" (v. 51, NIV; v. 157, CEV, NIV, NKJV), and "swerve" (v. 157, NLT, NRSV, RSV).

In Psalm 44:18, "neither have our steps declined from thy way" (KJV), "declined" is rendered "departed" (NKJV, NRSV, RSV) and "strayed" (NIV, NLT).

The CEV generally adopts a positive expression in place of the KJV "not declined," e.g., at Psalm 119:51, "I obey your Law" (CEV).

In Exodus 23:2, KJV, "Thou shalt not follow a multitude to do evil; neither shalt thou speak in a cause to decline after many to wrest judgment," "decline" is translated "turn aside" by the NASB, NKJV, and RSV and with the expression "side with" by the NIV and NRSV.

DEGREE

The word "degree" makes us think of academic awards, a measure or undefined extent of something ("a degree of freedom"), and a distinctive grade of crime ("murder in the first degree"). We are also familiar with the word's geometric meaning. The KJV uses "degree" with the obsolete meaning of "a step," as of a stair, in the

account of Ahaz and the sundial in 1 Kings. It also uses "degree" to refer to a person's status or rank.

Whatever was the form of the sundial of Ahaz, the "degrees" upon it were "steps" (2 Kings 20:9–11; Isaiah 38:8, KJV). The Hebrew word means an "ascent, step, or stair"; and the word "degree" was employed by the KJV translators in the sense, now obsolete, defined by OED as "a step in an ascent or descent; one of a flight of steps; a rung of a ladder." The majority of the contemporary versions replace "degrees" here with "steps"; the NRSV chooses to use the word "intervals."

Applied to persons, the term "degree" in Elizabethan English meant social or official rank. In *King Henry VI, Part II* (V, 1, 73–80) King Henry VI asks of the man who brings him the head of Jack Cade, "What is thy degree?" "A poor esquire of Kent, that loves his king" is the answer, and the esquire is forthwith created knight and given a post in the royal retinue. In *Macbeth* (III, 4, 1), Macbeth says to his guests at the banquet at which he will see the ghost of Banquo: "You know your own degrees; sit down."

The RSV retains the expression "exalted those of low degree" in Luke 1:52, but uses "the lowly brother" in James 1:9. Other contemporary versions render "exalted them of low degree" (KJV) as "exalted those who were humble" (NASB), "lifted up the humble" (NIV), and "lifted up the lowly" (NRSV).

The "brother of low degree" (KJV) in James 1:9 is now "the brother of [NIV, "in"] humble circumstances" (NIV, NASB), "the believer who is lowly" (NRSV), and "Believers [NLT, "Christians"] who are poor" (NCV, NLT). "Purchase a good degree" (KJV) in 1 Timothy 3:13 is now rendered "gain a good [NIV, "an excellent"] standing" in the NIV, NRSV, and RSV, and "obtain . . . a high standing" in the NASB.

The KJV rendering of Psalm 62:9 is "Surely men of low degree are vanity, and men of high degree are a lie: to be laid in the balance, they are altogether lighter than vanity." The NRSV has "Those of low estate are but a breath, those of high estate are a delusion; in the balances they go up; they are lighter than a breath."

The NIV speaks of "lowborn" and "highborn" men in this verse; other contemporary versions have "the least of the people" and "the greatest" (NCV), and the "greatest" and the "lowliest" (NLT). The NKJV and the NASB retain "men of low degree," but the NASB has "men of rank" where the NKJV retains the KJV rendering, "men of high degree."

DELICACY, DELICIOUSLY

These words remind us of choice, finely-prepared foods which are a delight to eat. When the KJV uses the words, however, they have the obsolete sense of "voluptuous, sensual luxury." "Delicacy" and "deliciously" occur in Revelation 18, which portrays the judgment of God upon "Babylon the great."

"The abundance of her delicacies" (v. 3, KJV) is now translated "the wealth of her sensuality" (NASB), "the abundance of her luxury" (NKJV), and "her luxurious living" (NLT). The contemporary renderings thus bring out the sense of Babylon's excessive, sensual luxuries. In verse 9, the KJV speaks of kings who "lived deliciously with her," meaning that they were indulging their lust and greed.

Tyndale and his successors translated it as "lived wantonly with her." The RSV has returned to Tyndale's word. At verse 3 it has "the wealth of her wantonness," and at verse 7 it has "as she . . . played the wanton" where the KJV had "lived deliciously." Similarly in verse 9 we read, in the RSV, "the kings of the earth, who committed fornication and were wanton with her."

Other contemporary versions render "lived deliciously" (v. 7, KJV) as "lived sensuously" (NASB), "lived luxuriously" (NKJV, NRSV), and "lived in luxury" (NLT). The NCV speaks of "rich living," and the NIV has, simply, "luxury."

DELICATELY

In modern usage, the word "delicately" suggests an attitude of care and attention to detail when handling something fine or fragile ("a heavy hand in baking would not result in a delicately-flavoured cake"). The KJV, however, uses "delicately" in the obsolete sense of "sumptuously," "luxuriously." The word occurs three times.

In Lamentations 4:5, we read of "They that did feed delicately" (KJV) and of the contrasting desolation which has befallen them. The NASB and NKJV translate the words as "Those who ate delicacies"; the RSV and NRSV have "Those who feasted on delicacies" [RSV, "dainties"].

In the passage about John the Baptist in Luke 7:25, Jesus speaks of those who are gorgeously appareled, and live delicately" (KJV). Contemporary versions have "those who are splendidly clothed and live in luxury" (NASB); "those who put on fine clothing and live in luxury" (NRSV); and "those who are gorgeously appareled and live in luxury" (RSV).

"He that delicately bringeth up his servant from a child" (Proverbs 29:21, KJV) is now rendered "He who pampers his slave [NKJV, RSV, "servant"] from childhood" (NASB, NKJV, RSV). The majority of the contemporary versions use the word "pampers" or "pampered" to render the sense of "delicately bringeth up" (KJV); the NCV uses the word "spoil," and the CEV paraphrases the verse as "Slaves that you treat kindly from their childhood will cause you sorrow."

The account of Agag coming to Samuel is more difficult. The KJV reads: "Then said Samuel, Bring ye hither to me Agag the king of the Amalekites. And Agag came unto him delicately" (1 Samuel 15:32). Here "delicately" was an innovation of the Bishops' Bible which the KJV adopted.

Various ideas as to the meaning of "delicately" in this verse have been put forward—"mincingly," "tottering," "trembling," "in fear," "cautiously," "slowly," "haughtily," "walking in state." The revised versions return to the rendering of the Geneva Bible, which had "pleasantly," and of Martin Luther's German Bible, which had *getrost* ("confidently"). The NASB, NIV, RSV, and NLT follow these renderings: the NASB and RSV translate "Agag came to him cheerfully," and the NIV has Agag coming to Samuel "confidently." In the NLT Agag arrives "full of smiles," believing the threat of death to have past.

These renderings agree with the RV and ASV, and with certain German translations. Agag did not fear the prophet after he had been spared by Saul and his soldiers. But Samuel "hewed Agag in pieces before the LORD" (v. 33, NRSV). The NKJV and NRSV, however, render "delicately" (KJV) as "cautiously" and "haltingly," respectively.

DELILAH

A "Delilah" is a treacherous and seductive woman. The use of this name alludes to the account of Delilah (Judges 16). Delilah was bribed by the Philistine rulers to discover the secret of Samson's great strength. Samson lied to her on three occasions, but when she continued to ask him, he grew so weary of her nagging that he told her the truth—that the source of his power lay in his long hair. Delilah then betrayed this secret to the Philistines, and while Samson slept upon her lap, his hair was shaved off. So it was that he was deprived of his strength.

DEMAND

The word "demand" in modern usage means "to ask with authority or as a right," or "to ask peremptorily, imperiously, urgently" ("a final demand for payment"; "I demand an increase in salary"). As used in the KJV, however, "demand" does not have these stronger connotations, but is a simple equivalent for "ask." Shakespeare occasionally used the word in this weaker sense.

"*Miranda.* Wherefore did they not
That hour destroy us?
Prospero. Well demanded, wench:
My tale provokes that
question."
—*The Tempest* (I, 2, 139)

"We'll mannerly demand thee of
thy story,
So far as thou wilt speak it."
—*Cymbeline* (III, 6, 92)

Second Samuel 11:7 (KJV) reads, "When Uriah was come unto him, David demanded of him how Joab did." The contemporary versions use "asked" for the KJV's rendering "demanded"; the NRSV translates as "When Uriah came to him, David asked how Joab . . . fared."

Herod "asked" (CEV, NCV, NIV, NLT) or "inquired" (NASB, NKJV, NRSV, RSV), where the Christ was to be born (Matthew 2:4). Luke 3:14 (KJV) reads, "the soldiers . . . demanded of him, saying, And what shall we do?" The contemporary versions use "asked" in this verse, although the NASB renders the verse as "Some soldiers were questioning him, saying, 'And what about us, what shall we do?'" In Luke 17:20, "when he was demanded of the Pharisees" (KJV) is translated "having been questioned by the Pharisees" by the NASB, while the other contemporary versions use the word "asked."

In Acts 21:33, the commander of the Roman battalion at Jerusalem "demanded who he [Paul] was, and what he had done" (KJV). The contemporary versions render this as "asked [NLT, "asked the crowd"] who he was and what he had done" [NCV, "done wrong"] (NCV, NIV, NKJV, NLT). The NASB says of the commander that he "began asking," and the NRSV and RSV use the verb "inquire."

The Lord's words to Job, "I will demand of thee" (Job 38:3; 40:7; 42:4, KJV), are now translated "I will question you" by the NIV, NKJV, NRSV, and RSV. In Exodus 5:14, the words "were beaten, and demanded" (KJV) might seem to suggest that the same persons who were beaten made a demand. The NASB, NKJV, NIV, NRSV, and RSV have "were beaten [NRSV, RSV, "were beaten,"] and were asked."

DEN OF LIONS

To be thrown into "the lions' den" is to be placed in a position of great danger or difficulty: ("facing the reporters at the press conference was like walking into the lions' den"). The expression alludes to the story of Daniel, thrown into the lions' den because he would not stop praying to God (Daniel 6).

The KJV at Daniel 6:16 reads "Then the king commanded, and they brought Daniel, and cast him into the den of lions"; the contemporary versions have "thrown into the den of lions" (NLT, NRSV); "cast [NKJV, "cast him"] into the den of lions" (NKJV, RSV); "cast into the lions' den" (NASB); "thrown into the lions' den" (NCV); "threw him into the lions' den" (NIV); "thrown into a pit of lions" (CEV).

DEN OF THIEVES

The phrase "den of thieves" is used to refer to a place where robbers or rogues meet or to a disreputable business establishment. The expression comes from Jesus' accusation to the money changers in the temple, "It is written, My house shall be called the house of prayer; but ye have made it a den of thieves" (Matthew 21:13).

The contemporary versions render this as "den of robbers" (NIV, NRSV, RSV); "robbers' den" (NASB); "hideout for robbers" (NCV); the NKJV and NLT retain the KJV "den of thieves." In Matthew 21:13, Jesus is quoting from Jeremiah 7:11. In that verse the temple in which Judah trusts is compared to a "den of robbers" (KJV, NASB, NIV, NRSV, RSV), "a den of thieves" (NKJV, NLT), or "a hideout for robbers" (NCV).

The CEV at these verses has "The Scriptures say, 'My house should be called a place of worship.' But you have turned it

into a place where robbers hide" (Matthew 21:13) and "You are thieves, and you have made my temple your hideout" (Jeremiah 7:11).

DENOUNCE

Except for its technical sense, "to give formal notice of the termination of an armistice or a treaty," the verb "denounce" today means "to declare that something is bad," or "to accuse persons of evil": we might denounce an accountant who had defrauded us. But it was used in a wider, more general sense up to the seventeenth century, meaning simply "to proclaim" or "to announce," without implication of evil.

A publication of 1581 is quoted in the OED as saying: "I suppose no man will deny, but that Paule doth denounce men to be Justified by fayth." Wycliffe's translation of the instruction to the Levites concerning the tithes (Numbers 18:26) begins: "Commande thou, and denounce to the dekenes." Tyndale and later translators have "Speak unto the Levites, and say."

Following Wycliffe, the Rheims New Testament (1582) had Paul say "we denounced to you, that if any will not work, neither let him eat" (2 Thessalonians 3:10). Tyndale, the Great Bible, and the Geneva Bible have "we warned you" and the KJV, "we commanded you."

The word "denounce" is used only once in the KJV, where Moses delivers his final exhortation to the people of Israel, warning them what will happen if they turn away from God: "I denounce unto you this day, that ye shall surely perish" (Deuteronomy 30:18). It is used here to represent a general Hebrew verb, *nagad*, which the KJV translates as "declare" sixty-two times, "shew" sixty times, and "tell" 189 times.

The use of the word "denounce" in this verse was an innovation of the KJV translators. Coverdale had used "certify"; Tyndale, the Great Bible, the Geneva Bible, and the Bishops' Bible had used "pronounce"; and the Douay Bible had "foretell." The

NRSV and NASB read, "I declare to you today, that you shall [NASB, "shall surely"] perish."

DEPUTY

The contemporary meaning of "deputy" is "a person appointed to act for another," or "a person elected to represent a constituency." In the KJV it is used with this sense for a regent in Moab (1 Kings 22:47). But in Esther 8:9 and 9:3, "deputy" is used for a Hebrew word which the contemporary versions render as "governor," and is so translated by the KJV in twenty-three other occurrences.

The KJV also uses the word in Acts 13 for the official title of Sergius Paulus, whom the contemporary versions refer to as "governor" (CEV, NCV, NLT) or "proconsul" (NASB, NIV, NKJV, NRSV, RSV) of Paphos, and in 18:12 for the official title of Gallio, again rendered "governor" or "proconsul" of Achaia by the contemporary versions.

In Acts 19:38 the town clerk reminds Demetrius and his fellow craftsmen that "the law is open, and there are deputies" (KJV) before whom legal charges may be brought. The NRSV translates as "the courts are open, and there are proconsuls."

DESCRY

This word is not often heard in contemporary English; it means "to get sight of," "discover," "perceive." It is used by the KJV in the obsolete sense of "investigate," "spy out," "reconnoiter," in Judges 1:23: "the house of Joseph sent to descry Bethel." The NRSV reads as "the house of Joseph sent out spies to Bethel"; the NASB has "The house of Joseph spied out Bethel."

DESERT SHALL BLOSSOM

The expression "the desert shall blossom" is sometimes used today to refer to land reclamation—projects to render poor-quality soil into land suitable for agricultural purposes. It derives from Isaiah 35:1–2 (KJV), "the desert shall rejoice, and blossom as the rose. It shall blossom abundantly, and rejoice even with joy and singing."

For the KJV's phrase "the desert shall . . . blossom" (retained by the NKJV, NRSV, and RSV) the other contemporary versions have: "the desert will . . . produce flowers" (NCV); "the desert will blossom with flowers" (NLT); "the wilderness will . . . blossom" (NIV); "barren lands will blossom with flowers" (CEV); and "the Arabah will . . . blossom" (NASB).

DESIRE

The word "desire" is used by the KJV in much the same way as we use the word today. It refers to a strong want or craving for something ("a desire for success"). In one instance among more than two hundred in the KJV, however, "desire" has a rare old connotation of regret. Second Chronicles 21:18–20 records the death of Jehoram, smitten in the bowels with an incurable disease, in punishment for his evil ways and his infidelity to the Lord. "Thirty and two years old was he when he began to reign, and he reigned in Jerusalem eight years, and departed without being desired." The NRSV, RSV, and NASB read, "he departed with no one's regret."

This is a passage in which the KJV translators showed their sound literary judgment. The preceding English versions had failed to grasp the meaning of the last clause. The Geneva Bible translated it "and lived without being desired"; Coverdale, "and walked not well"; Matthew's Bible, "and he walked not pleasantly"; the Great Bible and the Bishops' Bible, "and lived wretchedly."

DESPITE

This is an old word which we still use for "contempt or scorn, growing into malice, injury, or outrage" ("she acted out of pure despite"). With its adjective and adverb, it appears eight times in the KJV.

In Ezekiel 25:6, the contemporary versions replace it with "malice" (NIV, NRSV, RSV), "disdain" (NKJV), and "insults" (NCV); "rejoiced in heart with all thy despite" (KJV) is rendered "rejoiced with all the scorn of your soul" by the NASB. In verse 15 of the same chapter, the KJV speaks of the Philistines having "taken vengeance with a despiteful heart"; "despiteful heart" is now rendered "malice of heart" by the NRSV and RSV, "strong hatred" by the NCV, and "scorn of soul" by the NASB, and "hateful hearts" (NCV).

In the list of vices in Romans 1:30, the adjective "despiteful," stands for the Greek *hubristes,* which is now translated as "insolent" (NASB, NIV, NLT, NRSV, RSV), and "violent" (NKJV). "Pray for them which despitefully use you" (Luke 6:28, KJV) is now rendered "pray for those who abuse you" by the NRSV and RSV; "pray for those who mistreat you" by the NASB and NIV; and "pray for those who are cruel to you" by the NCV. The NKJV has "those who spitefully use you," and the NLT, "those who hurt you."

The account of the visit of Paul and Barnabas at Iconium closes in the KJV with: "And when there was an assault made both of the Gentiles, and also of the Jews with their rulers, to use them despitefully, and to stone them, They were ware of it, and fled unto Lystra and Derbe" (Acts 14:5–6a). The NRSV translates: "And when an attempt was made by both Gentiles and Jews, with their rulers, to mistreat them and to stone them, the apostles learned of it and fled to Lystra and Derbe."

"To do despite to" is an old idiom which the OED defines as "to treat with injury and contumely; to outrage." In the KJV it appears in Hebrews 10:29: "Of how much sorer punishment, suppose ye, shall he be thought worthy, who hath trodden under foot the Son of God, and hath counted the blood of the covenant, wherewith he was sanctified, an unholy thing, and hath done despite unto the Spirit of grace?"

The NRSV translates it as "How much worse punishment do you think will be deserved by those who have spurned the Son of God, profaned the blood of the covenant by which they were sanctified, and outraged the Spirit of grace?" "Done despite unto the Spirit of grace" (KJV) is rendered "insulted the Spirit of grace" in the NASB, NIV, and NKJV. The CEV and NCV also use the verb "to insult," and the NLT paraphrases the second part of the verse to read: "Such people have insulted and enraged the Holy Spirit who brings God's mercy to his people."

DEVICE

The word "device" is likely to make us think of useful implements and labor-saving devices, such as the garlic crusher, the potato peeler, and other state-of-the-art innovations. But we also use the word in the sense of "a purpose" or "plan" ("the invitation to dinner was merely a device to get them out of the house"), and this is how it was used by both the KJV translators and Shakespeare. So, for example, in *Hamlet* (III, 2, 222) we read:

"Our wills and fates do so contrary run
That our devices still are overthrown;
Our thoughts are ours, their ends
   none of our own."

Except in two cases where the purpose or plan is the Lord's (Jeremiah 18:11; 51:11), the purposes are unworthy and the plans underhanded, so that "scheme" or "plot" is sometimes used as a translation by contemporary versions, e.g., for KJV "devices," the NIV at Job 21:27 has "schemes."

In 2 Chronicles 2:14, Huram the king of Tyre assures King Solomon that the skilled craftsman he is sending is able "to grave any manner of graving, and to find out every device which shall be put to him" (KJV). The NRSV rendering is "to do all sorts of engraving and execute any design that may be assigned him."

Paul's statement to the men of Athens, "Forasmuch then as we are the offspring of God, we ought not to think that the Godhead is like unto gold, or silver, or stone, graven by art and man's device" (Acts 17:29, KJV), is now translated, "Since we are God's offspring, we ought not to think that the deity is like gold, or silver, or stone, an image formed by the art and imagination of mortals" (NRSV).

DEVOTIONS

In modern usage, the word "devotions" refers to traditional religious observances and exercises. The KJV uses the word in this sense in its translation of Paul's speech at Athens in Acts 17:22–23. The statement, "as I passed by, and beheld your devotions," might be understood to imply that he observed a group or groups of Athenians engaged in the act of worship.

But the Greek word which the KJV translates as "devotions" is *sebasmata,* rendered "objects of worship" by the contemporary versions. The NRSV translates Paul's words, "as I went through the city and looked carefully at the objects of your worship."

The Greek word *sebasma,* "object of worship," is used in one other passage in the KJV (2 Thessalonians 2:3–4) where it refers to "the son of perdition, who opposeth and exalteth himself above all that is called God, or that is worshipped; so that he as God sitteth in the temple of God, shewing himself that he is God."

The NRSV reads, "the one destined for destruction. He opposes and exalts himself above every so-called god or object of worship, so that he takes his seat in the temple of God, declaring himself to be God."

DIET

While "diet" might remind us of the need for healthier eating habits, or of efforts to lose weight, the KJV uses the word in the now obsolete sense of "an allowance of food and living expenses."

The freeing of King Jehoiachin from prison is described in 2 Kings 25:27–30 and Jeremiah 52:31–34 in almost identical terms in the KJV. The last verse of the account in 2 Kings reads: "And his allowance was a continual allowance given him of the king, a daily rate for every day, all the days of his life." The corresponding verse in Jeremiah reads: "And for his diet, there was a continual diet given him of the king of Babylon, every day a portion until the day of his death, all the days of his life." Except for the addition of the words for "of Babylon" and "until the day of his death," the Hebrew text of these two verses is identical.

The NASB translates Jeremiah 52:33–34: "So Jehoiachin changed his prison clothes, and had his meals in the king's presence regularly all the days of his life. For his allowance, a regular allowance was given him by the king of Babylon, a daily portion all the days of his life until the day of his death."

DIG UP

This expression is likely to remind us of shovels, perspiration, and hard work ("in the fall, he'll dig up the shrubs in the yard"). The KJV uses the expression in Proverbs 16:27, "An ungodly man diggeth up evil," with the same meaning as it has today. The reference is to scandalmongers who claim to unearth and reveal the misdeeds of others. The Hebrew word, however, refers to the digging of a pit or snare. It is the word used by the KJV in Proverbs 26:27, "Whoso diggeth a pit shall fall therein." It appears also in Psalms 57:6; 119:85 and Jeremiah 18:20, 22.

The RV and ASV have "A worthless man deviseth mischief" at Proverbs 16:27, and the contemporary versions render as "Scoundrels concoct evil" (NRSV), "Worthless people plan trouble" (CEV), and "Useless people make evil plans" (NCV). The NKJV and NASB stay closer to the KJV in their renderings: "A worthless man [NKJV, "An ungodly man"] digs up evil" (NASB, NKJV).

DISALLOW

We understand "disallow" to mean "to refuse to approve, sanction, or accept" ("the board decided to disallow any further talk of mergers or acquisitions"). The KJV uses the word in Numbers 30:3–15, with respect to the vows or pledges made by a woman. At verse 5, for example, the KJV reads as "if her father disallow her in the day that he heareth"; the NASB translates as "if her father should forbid on the day he hears of it." The NRSV has "expresses disapproval to her at the time that he hears of it."

The other appearances of "disallow" in the KJV are 1 Peter 2:4, 7, where Christ is referred to as "the stone which the builders disallowed" (v. 7). In Matthew 21:42, Mark 12:10, and Luke 20:17 the KJV has "the stone which the builders rejected." It has "be rejected of the elders" in Mark 8:31 and Luke 9:22, "be rejected of this generation" in Luke 17:25, and "was rejected" in Hebrews 12:17.

The Greek verb which in all these cases is translated "rejected" is represented by "disallowed" (KJV) in 1 Peter 2:7; the contemporary versions have "tossed aside" (CEV), and "rejected" (NASB, NCV, NIV, NKJV, NLT, NRSV, RSV).

DISANNUL

This is an anomaly among English words. The prefix "dis-" usually means "separation," as in "dismiss" and "dissolve," or negation, as in "disobey" and "displease." In "disannul" the "dis-" is repetitive and intensive, like the prefix "un-" in "unloose" and "unravel." The word means "to utterly annul"; and "annul" means "to abolish," "cancel," "make null and void." We generally choose the shorter form in ordinary speech, and in four of the six passages where "disannul" occurs in the KJV, the RSV does little more than delete the prefix "dis-."

Isaiah 14:27 reads, in the KJV, "For the LORD of hosts hath purposed, and who shall disannul it?" The contemporary versions render "disannul" (KJV) here as "frustrate" (NASB), "stop" (NCV), "thwart" (NIV), "change" (NLT), and "annul" (NRSV, RSV). Isaiah 28:18, "your covenant with death will be an-

nulled" (KJV), is now translated as "Your covenant with death will be canceled" by the NASB, while the NIV, NKJV, NRSV, and RSV use the word "annul."

In Galatians 3:15 the KJV reads "Though it be but a man's covenant, yet if it be confirmed, no man disannulleth, or addeth thereto." The NKJV, RSV, and RSV render "disannulleth" (KJV) as "annul"; the NASB has "sets it aside."

Two passages have been reworded by the contemporary versions. Firstly, "Wilt thou also disannul my judgment?" (Job 40:8, KJV) is now "Will you even put me in the wrong?" (NRSV). Secondly, Hebrews 7:18 reads, in the KJV: "For there is verily a disannulling of the commandment going before for the weakness and unprofitableness thereof." The NASB renders the verse, "For, on the one hand, there is a setting aside of a former commandment because of its weakness and uselessness."

DISCERN

"Discern" is a word that we use to speak of insight, perception, and judgment—both in a physical sense of "recognize" or "apprehend clearly" ("Did you discern a hesitancy in his voice?"), and in the sense of "mental or spiritual astuteness" ("she can discern between the good and the best"). In the KJV the word "discern" occurs eighteen times with these meanings, but on four occasions it is used as a translation for a Hebrew verb which means "to recognize some person or thing as formerly known."

When Jacob presented himself in the guise of Esau, his father Isaac "discerned him not" (Genesis 27:23, KJV). When Laban accused Jacob of stealing his gods, Jacob told him to "discern thou what is thine with me, and take it to thee" (Genesis 31:32, KJV). When Tamar returned to Judah the pledges he had left with her, she said, "Discern, I pray thee, whose are these" (Genesis 38:25, KJV). A wounded man, his face disguised with ashes, condemned Ahab for sparing Benhadad; and when he removed his disguise Ahab "discerned him that he was of the prophets" (1 Kings 20:41, KJV).

The NASB and NRSV use the verb "to recognize" in the first and fourth of these cases, "point out" in the second, and "examine" (NASB) and "Take note" (NRSV) in the third. When Joseph knew his brothers, but they did not know him (Genesis 42:7, 8, KJV), when Obadiah met Elijah and "knew him" (1 Kings 18.7, KJV), and when Job's friends "knew him not," the same Hebrew verb is used which the KJV represents by "discern" in the other cases. The majority of the contemporary versions use the verb "to recognize" in these texts.

DISCOMFIT

This is an old military word. Its primary meaning is "to undo," "throw into confusion," "rout," "to defeat an army or other organized body of attack" or "defense." In non-military contexts, it means "to thwart or defeat the purposes and plans of some individual or group." Applied to an individual, it may mean little more than "to confuse" or "disconcert" him.

"Discomfited" is used nine times in the KJV, always in the military sense. The contemporary versions replace it with "threw... into confusion" (NRSV) and "threw... into... a panic" (NIV) in 1 Samuel 7:10; "confounded" (NASB) and "threw . . . into . . . a panic" (NRSV) in Joshua 10:10; and "routed" (NASB) in Judges 8:12; 4:15; 2 Samuel 22:15; Psalm 18:14.

In Exodus 17:13 the KJV reads, "And Joshua discomfited Amalek and his people with the edge of the sword." The NRSV translates as "And Joshua defeated Amalek and his people with the sword." This verb is translated as "laid low" by the NRSV in Job 14:10 and Isaiah 14:12.

"His young men shall be discomfited" (Isaiah 31.8, KJV) is now rendered "his young men shall be put to forced labor" (NRSV). (See TRIBUTE)

"There was a very great discomfiture" (1 Samuel 14:20) is now translated "there

was very great confusion" by the NASB and NRSV. The Hebrew word here is *mehumah,* which means "confusion," "tumult," "panic." This noun and the verb *hum,* from which it is derived, appear in Deuteronomy 7.23. The KJV renders this verse: "But the LORD thy God shall deliver them unto thee, and shall destroy them with a mighty destruction, until they be destroyed."

The ASV reads, "But Jehovah thy God will deliver them up before thee, and will discomfit them with a great discomfiture, until they be destroyed." The NRSV reads, "But the LORD your God will give them over to you, and throw them into great panic, until they are destroyed."

DISCOVER

The word "discover" makes us think of unexplored worlds, hidden treasure, and a host of computerized learning packages designed to help children learn. We understand the word to mean "to find something new or not previously experienced" ("discover the tropics"), but in the KJV Old Testament the word "discover" is used only in the now obsolete sense of "to uncover or lay bare." It is retained by the NASB, NIV, NKJV, and RSV in only one of these cases, 1 Samuel 22:6: "Saul heard that David was discovered" (KJV). In thirteen instances the RSV uses the word "uncover."

Other typical renderings are: Lamentations 2:14, "exposed your iniquity" (NASB, NRSV, RSV); Proverbs 25:9, "do not disclose another's secret" (NRSV, RSV); 2 Samuel 22:16, "the foundations of the world were laid bare" (NASB, NRSV, RSV); Psalm 29:9, "strips the forests [NRSV, 'forest'] bare" (NASB, NRSV, RSV); 1 Samuel 14:8, "we will show ourselves to them" (NRSV, RSV). For the KJV rendering, "I will discover thy skirts upon thy face" (Nahum 3:5), the NRSV has "I . . . will lift up your skirts over your face." Where the KJV says concerning leviathan, "Who can discover the face of his garment?" (Job 41:13), the NASB and RSV read "Who can strip off his outer garment [NASB, "his outer armor"]?"

In other passages containing the same Hebrew words, the KJV shows that in 1611 the older sense of "discover" was tending to become obsolete. For example, where Wycliffe had "His heed he shal not discouer," the KJV has "he shall not uncover his head" (Leviticus 21:10). It uses "uncover" thirty-five times as translation for these Hebrew words.

In the two instances where "discover" is used in the KJV New Testament, it is rendered by other words in the contemporary versions. In Acts 21:3, "had discovered Cyprus" (KJV) is now "had come in sight of Cyprus" (RSV); "discovered a certain creek with a shore" (Acts 27:39) is rendered "noticed a bay with a beach" (NRSV, RSV).

DISHONESTY

In the one passage where it occurs in the KJV, "dishonest" is used in the obsolete sense of "dishonor," "discredit," "shame." It represents the Greek word *aischune*, which means "shame," "disgrace." In place of "have renounced the hidden things of dishonesty" (2 Corinthians 4:2, KJV), the RSV reads "have renounced disgraceful, underhanded ways"; the NRSV reads "have renounced the shameful things that one hides," and the NASB similarly translates as "have renounced the things hidden because of shame."

The word is used by Shakespeare in *Twelfth Night* (III, 4, 421), where its obsolete meaning is clear: "his dishonesty appears in leaving his friend here in necessity and denying him."

DISORDERLY

This is a word we use today to mean "unruly" or "out of control" ("disorderly behavior"). The KJV uses the word three times in 2 Thessalonians 3, a passage in which Paul cautions against idle living. Verse 6 reads, "Now we command you, brethren, in the name of our Lord Jesus Christ, that

ye withdraw yourselves from every brother that walketh disorderly, and not after the tradition which he received of us" (KJV).

The contemporary versions render "that walketh disorderly" (KJV) in this verse as "leads an unruly life" (NASB); "refuses to work" (NCV); and "living in idleness" (NRSV, RSV). In verse 11, Paul writes, "we hear that there are some which walk among you disorderly, working not at all, but are busybodies" (KJV). The NASB renders this as "we hear that some among you are leading an undisciplined life, doing no work at all, but acting like busybodies."

The corresponding Greek adjective is represented as "unruly" by the KJV in 1 Thessalonians 5:14, but there it also means "idle." Paul's exhortation, which the KJV renders "warn them that are unruly, comfort the feebleminded, support the weak, be patient toward all men," is translated by the NRSV as "admonish the idlers, encourage the fainthearted, help the weak, be patient with all of them."

DISPUTE

By "dispute" today, we mean "a disagreement"; we use the verb in the sense of "to question or challenge" ("I dispute your sales figures"). In the KJV, however, "dispute" often carries the meaning of "reasonable discussion or argument, rather than that of wordy altercation." The verb and its derivatives appear fifteen times in the New Testament.

The contemporary versions have either "dispute" (NKJV, RSV) or "argue" (CEV, NASB, NCV, NIV, NRSV) in Acts 6:9; in Acts 9:29, the NIV says that Stephen "talked and debated" with the Grecian Jews. In Acts 24:12 Paul maintains that he was never found "carrying on a discussion" (NASB), or "arguing" (CEV, NCV, NIV; NLT, "I didn't argue") in the temple; the NKJV, NRSV, and RSV retain "disputing" in this verse.

In Romans 14:1 the KJV reads, "Him that is weak in the faith receive ye, but not to doubtful disputations." The RSV retains the word "disputes" here; the NASB reads, "Now accept the one who is weak in faith, but not for the purpose of passing judgment on his opinions."

In Jude 9 the contemporary versions use the verbs "argue" (CEV, NCV, NASB, NLT) and "dispute" (NIV, NKJV, NRSV, and RSV) in the account of the contention between Michael the Archangel and the devil over the body of Moses. The NRSV uses "argue" in Mark 9:33–34, Acts 17:17 and 19:8–9, and "debate" in Acts 15:2, 7 and 1 Corinthians 1:20. The majority of contemporary versions have "arguing" (RSV, "questioning") in Philippians 2.14. In 1 Timothy 6:5 a quite distinct and rather bitter Greek word is now rendered "wranglings" by the NKJV, NRSV, and RSV where the KJV had "disputings." The NASB and NIV render it as "constant friction."

The one appearance of "dispute" in the KJV Old Testament is in Job's plea for a hearing before God, beginning, "Oh that I knew where I might find him!" (23:3) and ending, "There the righteous might dispute with him; so should I be delivered for ever from my judge" (23:7). The NRSV translates the passage:

> "Oh, that I knew where I might find him, that I might come even to his dwelling!
> I would lay my case before him, and fill my mouth with arguments.
> I would learn what he would answer me, and understand what he would say to me.
> Would he contend with me in the greatness of his power? No; but he would give heed to me.
> There an upright person could reason with him, and I should be acquitted forever by my judge."

DISQUIETNESS

This is an archaic word meaning "uneasiness" or "anxiety." It occurs only once in the KJV, in Psalm 38:8: "I have roared by reason of the disquietness of my heart." The context is that of distress. The NRSV and NASB read, "I groan because of the tumult [NASB, "agitation"] of my heart."

DIVERS, DIVERSE

These were originally two spellings of the same word. Since about 1700 each has had its own pronunciation and meaning— "diverse" meaning "different in character or quality," while "divers" means "various," "sundry," "several," "more than one" without stating how many. In the KJV "diverse" appears eight times, always in the sense of "different" (Leviticus 19:19; Esther 1:7; 3:8; Daniel 7:3, 7, 19, 23, 24).

"Divers" appears thirty-six times in the KJV, and is not used by the contemporary versions. "Divers . . . of the princes of Israel" (2 Chronicles 21:4, KJV) is now translated "some of the officials of Israel" (NRSV), and "divers of Asher" (30:11, KJV) is rendered "a few from Asher" (NRSV). Jesus' expression of compassion for the multitude, "for divers of them came from far" (Mark 8:3, KJV), is rendered "some of them have come from a great distance" (NRSV).

In Acts 19:9, Paul's message in the synagogue at Ephesus is rejected by some of the Jews. The KJV reads "divers were hardened, and believed not." The NASB translates as "some were becoming hardened and disobedient"; the NRSV reads, "some stubbornly refused to believe."

"Thou shalt not sow thy vineyard with divers seeds" (Deuteronomy 22:9, KJV) means "with different [RSV, "with two"] kinds of seed" (NKJV, RSV). The prohibition of "divers weights" and "divers measures" (Deuteronomy 25:13, 14, KJV) refers to "two kinds of weights" and "two kinds of measures" (NRSV).

In passages which speak of Jesus' healing ministry, "divers diseases" (KJV) is now translated "various diseases" (NASB, NIV, NKJV, NRSV, RSV), "every kind of sickness or disease" (CEV), and "different kinds of diseases" (NCV), (Matthew 4:24; cf., also Mark

1:34, Luke 4:40). Similarly "divers places" (KJV) is now generally translated in the contemporary versions as "various places" (Matthew 24:7; Mark 13:8; Luke 21:11). The NRSV has "all kinds of desires" (2 Timothy 3:6), "various passions" (Titus 3:3), "various miracles" (Hebrews 2:4), "various baptisms" (Hebrews 9:10), and "trials of any kind" [RSV, "various trials"] (James 1:2).

One of the oldest poems in the Bible is the Song of Deborah in Judges 5, which ends with the desperate attempt of the mother of Sisera to still her fears because her son has not yet returned from the battle. She seeks to reassure herself by the thought that he is delaying over the division of booty. The KJV reads: "Have they not sped? have they not divided the prey; to every man a damsel or two; to Sisera a prey of divers colours, a prey of divers colours of needlework, of divers colours of needlework on both sides, meet for the necks of them that take the spoil?" The NASB reads:

"Are they not finding, are they not
    dividing the spoil?
A maiden , two maidens for every
    warrior;
To Sisera a spoil of dyed work,
A spoil of dyed work embroidered,
Dyed work of double embroidery
    on the neck of the spoiler?"

DIVES

"Dives" is the name given to the rich man in the story told by Jesus in Luke 16:19–31. In the story, Dives pays no attention to the plight of Lazarus, the beggar at his gate. After death Lazarus is carried to "Abraham's bosom" (see ABRAHAM'S BOSOM) and Dives to hell, and any contact between them is impossible. It is interesting to note that the rich man is not actually named in the English Bible text. In the Vulgate, the Latin version of the Bible, he is called "Dives," the Latin for "rich" or "a rich man," and this word has come to be thought of as a proper noun.

The name Dives has thus become proverbial for a very rich person, especially one who is unconcerned, hard, and insensitive to the needs of others.

DO NOT LET THE SUN GO DOWN ON YOUR ANGER

See SUN GO DOWN ON ONE'S ANGER.

DOCTOR

When we hear the word "doctor" today, we tend to think of someone licensed to practice medicine. But the word originally meant "teacher," and is used with this meaning three times in the KJV. The contemporary versions use "teacher," which is the meaning of the Greek *didaskalos* (Luke 2:46; 5:17; Acts 5:34). In 1 Timothy 1:7 the KJV uses the designation "teacher of the law" for the same Greek term which it renders "doctor of the law" in Luke and Acts. (See TEACH, TEACHER, TEACHING)

DOCTRINE

By "doctrine" in modern terminology, we mean "a principle" or "a dogma" ("the doctrine of the Trinity"). In 1611, however, the word was used of the act of teaching, as well as its content. While the verb *didasko* appears ninety-seven times in the Greek New Testament and is always translated "teach," *didache* and *didaskalia* are translated by the KJV as "learning" once, "teaching" once, and "doctrine" forty-eight times.

This sense of the word is now obsolete, and the revised versions use "teaching" more often than "doctrine." "He said unto them in his doctrine" (Mark 4:2; 12:38) is now rendered "in his teaching he said to them" (Mark 4:2, NRSV), and "As he taught, he said" (Mark 12:38, NRSV). For *didache* and *didaskalia* the RSV has "teaching" thirty-three times, "doctrine" fourteen times, "instruction" twice, and "lesson" once.

DOGS

The term "dogs" immediately makes us think of our much-loved family pets. While we sometimes hear the word used in a pejorative sense ("stay away from that dog" could refer to a growling canine or an undesirable man, depending on the context), in the Bible dogs are always mentioned with contempt.

"Am I a dog," says Goliath, "that you come to me with sticks?" (1 Samuel 17:43, NRSV). "Why should this dead dog curse my lord the king?" growls Abishai when an old retainer of Saul curses David (2 Samuel 16:9, KJV). Dogs licked up the blood of Ahab, and ate the body of Jezebel (1 Kings 22:38; 2 Kings 9:30–37). When the author of Ecclesiastes reflects that life at its worst is yet better than death, he writes, "A living dog is better than a dead lion" (9:4, KJV). The psalmist compares his enemies to dogs (Psalm 22:16). (See GRUDGE)

Paul calls his opponents "dogs" (Philippians 3:2), and John places "the dogs" outside of the holy city, with "sorcerers and fornicators and murderers and idolaters" (Revelation 22:15, NRSV).

There is no trace in the Scriptures of the friendship and loyalty that so commonly exist between a dog and its owner. "The Eastern street dog is a type of all that is cowardly, lazy, filthy, treacherous, and contemptible," says Hastings' *Dictionary of the Bible.*

The only admiring reference is in Proverbs 30:29–31, which reads in the KJV: "There be three things which go well, yea, four are comely in going: A lion which is strongest among beasts, and turneth not away for any; a greyhound; an he goat also; and a king, against whom there is no rising up." The greyhound is a possible rendering of the Hebrew expression, which means "girt in the loins."

Other suggestions are "strutting rooster" (NASB, NIV, NLT, NRSV), and "strutting cock" (RSV). "Cock" is supported by the ancient versions. The Septuagint has "a cock walking proudly among the hens." The NKJV retains the KJV translation, "greyhound."

"The price of a dog" (Deuteronomy 23:18, KJV) is now translated "the wages of a dog" (NASB, RSV), and the reference is to the sodomites or male cult prostitutes who were banned by the commandment in verse 17.

DONE AWAY

We recognize the meaning of removing or getting rid of something from our modern usage ("to do away with free tickets"). In the KJV the expression has a broadly similar meaning, although the emphasis is less on a deliberate removal of something than on its fading or passing away.

"Why should the name of our father be done away from among his family, because he hath no son?" is the question of the daughters of Zelophehad (Numbers 27:4, KJV), for which the NRSV has, "Why should the name of our father be taken away from his clan because he had no son?" Coverdale has "perish"; Tyndale and the other sixteenth-century versions have "taken away."

In 1 Corinthians 13:8–10 prophecies shall "fail," knowledge shall "vanish away," and "that which is in part shall be done away" (KJV). The three verbs go back to Tyndale, but in each of the three clauses the Greek has the same verb. The NASB has "will be done away" in the three instances; the NRSV has "will come to an end." The RSV says of prophecy, knowledge, and the imperfect that each "will pass away."

In 2 Corinthians 3, "done away" appears in verses 7, 11, and 14 in the KJV. The Greek is rendered "fading," "faded [NIV, "fading"] away," "taken away" by the NIV and RSV; "fading," "fades away," and "removed" by the NASB; and "set aside" by the NRSV.

DORCAS SOCIETY

A "Dorcas society" is a Christian charitable society of women who meet to make clothes for the poor. The name derives from Dorcas (or Tabitha), a Christian disciple in Joppa, who was well known for her works of charity. Tabitha was her name in Aramaic; the Greek translation is Dorcas (both words meaning "gazelle"). The fact that this is a translation from the Greek is made explicit in the CEV, NASB, NCV, NLT, and NRSV, e.g., NLT and NRSV, Tabitha, "which in Greek is Dorcas."

When Dorcas died, her friends sent for Peter. Peter prayed, and she was raised from the dead. Her resurrection led many to faith (Acts 9:36–43).

DOTE

In modern usage, "dote" means "to adore" or "to be infatuated with" ("she dotes on that pony"), but sometimes with the associated idea of "foolishness." The OED defines "to dote" as "to be silly, deranged, or out of one's wits; to act or talk foolishly." We might describe someone thus afflicted as "a dotard," "in his dotage," or "a doting fool." When the KJV uses the word, it does so with this meaning of "foolish." When the Lord in anger checked the incipient rebellion of Miriam and Aaron against Moses, Aaron confessed to Moses, "we have done foolishly" (Numbers 12:11, KJV). "The princes of Zoan are become fools" declares Isaiah (Isaiah 19:13, KJV). "They are foolish," says Jeremiah of the inhabitants of Jerusalem (Jeremiah 5:4, KJV). "They shall dote," he says of the "liars" among the inhabitants of Babylon (50:36). In these four cases the Hebrew verb is the same, ya'al. The last verse is rendered, in the NRSV:

"A sword against the diviners, so
    that they may become fools!
A sword against her warriors, so
    that they may be destroyed!"

"Dote" is used with respect to foolish sexual infatuation in Ezekiel 23, where the Lord upbraids Samaria for having played the harlot and having "doted on her lovers, on the Assyrians her neighbours" (v. 5, KJV). The NASB, NIV, and NRSV read "she lusted after her lovers," while the RSV retains the verb "to dote" throughout the chapter.

First Timothy 6:4 reads in the KJV: "He is proud, knowing nothing, but doting about questions and strifes of words." The Greek verb noseo, which is here rendered "doting," means "to be sick." Tyndale had "wasteth his braynes."

The contemporary versions render the KJV phrase "doting about questions and strifes of words" as "a morbid interest in controversial questions and disputes about words" (NASB); "a morbid craving for controversy and for disputes about words" (NRSV); "an unhealthy desire to quibble over the meaning of words" (NLT); "sick with a love for arguing and fighting about words" (NCV); and "Their minds are sick, and they like to argue over words" (CEV).

DOUBT (noun)

As a noun, "doubt" today describes the attitude of questioning or disbelief. In Daniel 5, however, Belshazzar's "doubts" (KJV) are really problems or puzzles, and he appeals to Daniel as one who could solve problems: "I have heard of thee, that thou canst make interpretations, and dissolve doubts" (Daniel 5:16, KJV). The literal meaning of the Aramaic is "to loosen joints or knots."

This Aramaic expression is used literally in Daniel 5:6: "the joints of his loins were loosed" (KJV). It is applied to the knotty problems of the mind in Daniel 5:12 and 16. For "dissolve doubts" (KJV) in verse 16 the CEV, NASB, NIV, and NLT have "solve difficult problems"; the NCV has "find answers to hard problems"; the NKJV has "explain enigmas"; and the RSV has "solve problems."

DOUBT (verb)

As a verb "doubt" is used today in a negative sense to mean "to question the truth or validity of something." To doubt a person's integrity would be to judge it negatively. In 1611, however, the word "doubt" generally stood for indecision, uncertainty, perplexity, suspense of judgment, without as much of a weighting toward the negative as it has now acquired.

The multitude on the day of Pentecost were not so much "in doubt" (Acts 2:12, KJV) as "perplexed" (NIV, NKJV, NLT, NRSV, RSV). Later, when the officers report that the apostles are not to be found in the prison where they had been placed, the KJV states that "when the high priest and the captain of the temple and the chief priests heard these things, they doubted of them whereunto this would grow" (5:24). The NASB reads, "they were greatly perplexed about them as to what could come of this."

In Acts 9:7 Peter "doubted in himself" (KJV) what his vision might mean; the RSV says that he "was inwardly perplexed" (10:17). In all these cases the Greek verb is the one which the KJV itself translates by "was (were) perplexed" in Luke 9:7 and 24:4.

For a different form of the same verb, "doubting" (John 13:22, KJV) is translated as "uncertain" by the NRSV, "at a loss" by the NASB, and "perplexed" by the NKJV. "Because I doubted of such manner of questions" (Acts 25:20, KJV) is rendered "Since I was at a loss how to investigate these questions" (NRSV); and "I stand in doubt of you" (Galatians 4:20, KJV) is now rendered "I am perplexed about you" (NASB, NRSV, NIV).

The question put to Jesus at the feast of dedication as he walked in the temple in Solomon's porch, "How long dost thou make us to doubt?" (John 10:24, KJV), is rendered "How long will you [NASB, "You"] keep us in suspense?" by the NASB, NIV, NRSV, and RSV.

The final word in the phrase "without wrath and doubting" (1 Timothy 2:8, KJV) represents the Greek word *dialogismos*, which in the plural is the last word of the phrase rendered by the KJV, "without murmurings and disputings" (Philippians 2:14). In the text from 1 Timothy the NRSV has "without anger or quarreling," and in the Philippians text has "without grumbling or questioning."

DOUBTFUL

"Doubtful" is a word we would use if something was dubious or uncertain ("it is doubtful that the weather will improve before nightfall"). The word is only used as an adjective in the KJV, which at Luke 12:29 reads "neither be ye of doubtful mind." Here the word is used in the obsolete sense of "full of fear" or "apprehensive." In fact the Greek verb used by Luke, though different from that used by Matthew in the parallel text (Matthew 6:31), also means "do not be anxious." The NASB and NRSV translate as "do not keep worrying"; the RSV has "nor be of anxious mind."

"Him that is weak in the faith receive ye, but not to doubtful disputations" (Romans 14:1, KJV) is worded in the NRSV, "Welcome those who are weak in faith, but not for the purpose of quarreling over opinions."

DOUBTING THOMAS

The phrase "doubting Thomas" is used to refer to someone who is skeptical, particularly someone who refuses to believe until he or she has seen proof of something or has been otherwise satisfied as to its truth.

The expression alludes to Thomas, one of Jesus' apostles, who on the evening of the day of the resurrection refused to believe in Christ's resurrection until he had seen and felt Christ's body for himself (John 20:24–25). A week later, Jesus then satisfied his doubts and Thomas in belief confessed Jesus to be his Lord and his God (John 20:26–29).

DOUBTLESS

This word originally meant "without any doubt," "unquestionably," "certainly"; but usage has weakened it so that, except where used in a concessive clause, it means today little more than "probably." It is more likely to raise doubts than to allay them. "Doubtless thou art our father" (Isaiah 63:16, KJV) reads in the NASB, "For You are our Father."

"I will doubtless deliver the Philistines

into thine hand" (2 Samuel 5:19, KJV) now reads, "I will certainly give the Philistines into your hand" (NASB, NRSV, RSV). In 1 Corinthians 9:2 the contemporary versions use "at least" (NASB, NRSV, RSV), "surely" (NCV, NIV), and "certainly" (NLT) where the KJV has "doubtless."

Philippians 3:7–8a reads, in the KJV: "But what things were gain to me, those I counted loss for Christ. Yea doubtless, and I count all things but loss for the excellency of the knowledge of Christ Jesus my Lord." The NRSV reads: "Yet whatever gains I had, these I have come to regard as loss because of Christ. More than that, I regard everything as loss because of the surpassing value of knowing Christ Jesus my Lord."

In the other three cases where "doubtless" appears in the KJV, it is often omitted by the contemporary versions (Numbers 14:30; Psalm 126:6; 2 Corinthians 12:1).

DRAGON

Dragons are the stuff of legends, and are rarely depicted today outside of children's storybooks. The OED's definition of a "dragon" is "a mythical monster, represented as a huge and terrible reptile, usually combining ophidian and crocodilian structure, with strong claws, like a beast or bird of prey, and a scaly skin; it is generally represented with wings, and sometimes as breathing out fire."

In the New Testament this word occurs only in Revelation, beginning with the appearance in heaven of the "great red dragon" (12:3) and ending with his being bound for one thousand years and thrown into the bottomless pit (20:2–3). It occurs in the KJV Old Testament twenty-two times; the RSV uses the word five times, and on fourteen occasions uses "jackal" as a rendering of the Hebrew. (See SEA MONSTER)

In Ezekiel 29:3 and 32:2 the word "dragon" (KJV) refers to the Pharaoh of Egypt. In Ezekiel 29:3 the NASB, NIV, NKJV, and NLT use the word "monster," the

NCV and CEV have "crocodile," and the NRSV and RSV retain "dragon."

In Psalm 74:13, Isaiah 27:1, and Isaiah 51:9 the references are to ancient Semitic mythology. The Hebrew is rendered as "sea monsters" (Psalm 74:13, NASB), "sea serpents" (Psalm 74:13, NKJV), "the reptile that is in the sea" (Isaiah 27:1, NKJV), and "the dragon of the Nile" (Isaiah 51:9, NLT).

DRAUGHT

In English the spelling "draught" is a variant of the American "draft," with several meanings, including "a current of cold air," and "the amount of liquid swallowed at one time." In the KJV "draught" is used in the sense of "catch of fish," a sense that is rare in current English, and also in the sense of "a latrine."

"Draught" in the sense of a catch of fish is found in the KJV at Luke 5:4, "Now when he [Jesus] had left speaking, he said unto Simon, Launch out into the deep, and let down your nets for a draught," and Luke 5:9, "For he [Simon Peter] was astonished, and all that were with him at the draught of the fishes which they had taken."

The contemporary versions render the KJV "for a draught" in verse 4 as "for a catch" (NASB, NIV, NKJV, NRSV, RSV), "catch some fish" (CEV, NCV), and "catch many fish" (NLT), and the KJV "at the draught" in verse 9 as "at the catch" (CEV, NIV, NKJV, NRSV, RSV). The NLT for this verse reads, "For he was awestruck by the size of their catch, as were the others with him."

In the sense of "latrine," the KJV has "draught house" at 2 Kings 10:27, rendered as "latrine" by the NASB, NIV, NRSV, and RSV, "public toilet" by the CEV and NLT, "refuse dump" by the NKJV, and "sewage pit" by the NCV. As part of Jesus' explanation of what is clean and unclean, Matthew 15:17 in the KJV reads, "Do not ye yet understand, that whatsoever entereth in at the mouth goeth into the belly, and is cast out into the draught?"

The KJV "cast out into the draught" is

rendered as "out of the [CEV, "your"] body" (CEV, NIV), "goes out of the body" (NCV, NLT), "is eliminated" (NASB, NKJV), "passes on" (RSV), and "goes out into the sewer" (NRSV). The parallel verse, Mark 7:19, has similar wordings.

DREADFUL

This word applies strictly to persons, things, or events which inspire fear, reverence, or awe. Like "awful" and "horrid," it has been weakened in common usage so that it may mean little more than "bad," "ugly," or "objectionable." While the KJV uses "dreadful" in its proper sense, the contemporary versions usually employ other terms.

Jacob's exclamation when he awoke from his dream—"How dreadful is this place!" (Genesis 28:17, KJV)—now reads "How awesome is this place!" in the majority of contemporary versions; the CEV has "This is a fearsome place," and the NCV has "This place frightens me."

The word of the Lord by Malachi, "my name is dreadful among the heathen" (Malachi 1:14, KJV), is rendered "my name is reverenced [RSV, "feared"] among the nations" (NRSV, RSV). An identical Hebrew phrase is translated as "the great and the terrible day of the LORD" by the KJV in Joel 2:31, but as "the great and dreadful day of the LORD" in Malachi 4:5. The NIV alone uses the word "dreadful" in the Joel reference, but in Malachi 4:5 the NKJV and NLT use it also. The NRSV and RSV translate the phrase consistently in both verses as "the great and terrible day of the LORD."

The attribute "dreadful" is applied to God by the KJV in Daniel 9:4: "And I prayed unto the LORD my God, and made my confession, and said, O Lord, the great and dreadful God, keeping the covenant and mercy to them that love him, and to them that keep his commandments." The NASB, NIV, NKJV, NLT, and NRSV render "great and dreadful" (KJV) as "great and awesome." The RSV has "great and terrible"; the NCV

paraphrases as "a great God who causes fear and wonder."

The same Hebrew word is translated "terrible" by the KJV in Deuteronomy 7:21; 10:17; Nehemiah 1:5; 4:14; 9:32; Psalms 47:2; 66:3; 68:35; 76:12; 99:3; and Zephaniah 2:11. (See REVEREND).

DROP IN THE BUCKET

The phrase "a drop in the bucket" (or "a drop in the ocean") is used to refer to something very small compared with something considerably larger that is required. For example, a tiny grant of money may be thought to be a drop in the ocean when one considers the total amount that is really needed. The origin of the expression is Isaiah 40:15 (KJV), "Behold, the nations are as a drop of a bucket, and are counted as the small dust of the balance; he taketh up the isles as a very little thing." The insignificance of the earthly nations is compared with the immensity of God.

The contemporary versions render the KJV expression "as a drop of a bucket" as "like a drop from a bucket" (NASB, NRSV, RSV); "like a drop in a bucket" (NIV); "as a drop in a bucket" (NKJV); "but a drop in a bucket" (NLT); "like one small drop in a bucket" (NCV); and "are merely a drop in a bucket"(CEV).

DUKE

The word "duke" is used fifty-seven times in the KJV to denote the chiefs of Edom. It is not a hereditary title of nobility, as in Great Britain, but simply an English rendering of the Latin word dux, "leader."

In the lists of the chiefs of Edom (Genesis 36:15–43; 1 Chronicles 1:51–54; cf. Exodus 15:15), the Latin Vulgate used dux and its plural duces as translation for the Hebrew 'alluph, and both Wycliffe and Tyndale took the word over into English as "duke." The Hebrew word may have meant "the leader of a thousand," since it is derived from 'eleph, the word for "thousand."

The contemporary versions render the

word as "chiefs" (NASB, NIV, NKJV, RSV), "leaders" (NCV), and "clans" (NRSV) at Genesis 36:15–43, and "chiefs" (NASB, NIV, NKJV, RSV), "clans" (CEV, NRSV), and "clan leaders" (NLT) at 1 Chronicles 1:51–54. The only other "dukes" in the KJV Old Testament are the "dukes of Sihon" (Joshua 13:21, KJV), for whom the Latin Vulgate has *duces*, though the Hebrew has the plural of *nasik*, "prince." The majority of the contemporary versions translate the word here as "princes."

Wycliffe translated Matthew 2:6 from the Latin: "And thou bethleem the lond of iuda are not the leest among the princis of iuda, for of thee a duyk schal go out that schal gouerne my puple israel." But Tyndale and his sixteenth-century successors, translating from the Greek, used "captayne" with various spellings. The KJV chose "for out of thee shall come a Governor, that shall rule my people Israel." The NASB, NCV, NIV, NKJV, NLT, NRSV, and RSV use the term "ruler" [NASB, NKJV, "Ruler"]; the CEV has "leader."

DULCIMER

A dulcimer is a musical instrument with strings struck by hammers held in the hands. It was the prototype of the harpsichord and the piano. "Dulcimer" appears in the KJV only as one of the instruments played at the dedication of the golden image which King Nebuchadnezzar had set up (Daniel 3:5, 10, 15).

The Aramaic word *sumponyah* refers to a wind instrument, a kind of bagpipe. It is rendered "bagpipe" by the NASB and RSV, "pipes" by the NCV, NIV, and NLT, and "drum" by the NRSV.

DURE

This word, a verb from the Latin *durare*, is now obsolete. Its place has been taken by "endure," from the Latin *indurare*. "Dure" appears only once in the KJV, at Matthew 13:21, "Yet hath he not root in himself, but dureth for a while." The same Greek verb appears, in the plural number, in Mark 4:17, where the KJV has "And have no root in themselves, and so endure but for a time." The difference in translation goes back to Tyndale, who had "dureth but a season" in Matthew and "so endure but a time" in Mark.

The NRSV, RSV, and NKJV versions use the verb "endure" in both passages; the NASB reads "is only temporary" in Matthew and "are only temporary" in Mark.

What was originally the present participle of "dure" has survived in contemporary English as the preposition "during." And such derivatives as "durable," "durability," and "duration" seem to possess the qualities which they denote, and will doubtless last for more generations to come.

DUST AND ASHES

The phrase "dust and ashes" occurs three times in the KJV to express the humility and insignificance of human beings. It occurs in Genesis 18:27, KJV, "And Abraham answered and said, Behold now, I have taken upon me to speak unto the Lord, which am but dust and ashes." All the contemporary versions except the CEV retain the expression "dust and ashes"; the CEV has "I am nothing more than the dust of the earth."

The phrase occurs twice in Job: 30:19 (KJV): "He that cast me into the mire, and I am become like dust and ashes"; all the contemporary versions except the CEV and NCV retain the expression "dust and ashes"; the CEV has "I have been thrown in the dirt and now am dirt myself" and the NCV, "He throws me into the mud and I become like earth and ashes" and 42:6 (KJV), "Wherefore I abhor myself, and repent in dust and ashes"; here all the contemporary versions retain the expression "dust and ashes" to show Job's repentance.

The phrasing "ashes to ashes, dust to dust" is familiar from the Book of Common Prayer, the service of committal in the burial of the dead, referring to the mortality and perishing of the human physical body: "We therefore commit his body to the ground; earth to earth, ashes to ashes, dust to dust; in sure and certain hope of the Resurrection to eternal life, through our Lord Jesus Christ."

E

EAR

We use the word "ear" today to refer to the organ of hearing, and to the part of the cereal plant that contains the seeds or kernels ("an ear of corn"), but in the KJV we also find it used, as a verb, with the obsolete meaning of "to plow." Ear and plow are both, in fact, old verbs which have the same meaning—"to prepare the soil for sowing by turning it up in furrows."

Thus in the KJV we read, "there shall neither be earing nor harvest" (Genesis 45:6), "in earing time and in harvest" (Exodus 34:21), "neither eared nor sown" (Deuteronomy 21:4), "to ear his ground" (1 Samuel 8:12), and "that ear the ground" (Isaiah 30:24). Elsewhere the KJV uses the word "plow." "Ear" was often used by Wycliffe and the sixteenth-century versions.

For example, Wycliffe had "Whether al day shal ere the erere, that he sowe" (Isaiah 28:24). Tyndale had "earynge" in Genesis 45:6, Exodus 34:21, and Deuteronomy 21:4; his version of 1 Corinthians 9:10 had "he which eareth, shuld eare in hope." But he also had "plowe" in Deuteronomy 22:10 and Luke 9:62, and "plowinge" in Luke 17:7.

Contemporary versions do not retain "ear" in the obsolete sense; they replace it with "to plow" or "to plant." The KJV uses "plough" as a noun once, in Luke 9:62.

EARNEST

An earnest person is one who is very serious and sincere. We may perhaps think of Oscar Wilde's play *The Importance of Being Earnest,* with its courtships, betrothals, and confusions of identity. Indeed the play's subtitle is "A Trivial Comedy for Serious People."

In the KJV (2 Corinthians 1:22; 5:5; Ephesians 1:14), an earnest is money paid to seal an agreement, serving both as a first installment (a down payment) and as a pledge or guarantee that the rest will follow as agreed. Paul is saying in these passages that the gift of the Holy Spirit in our hearts is a foretaste and a guarantee of our heavenly inheritance.

The NCV and NKJV translate it as "guarantee"; the NASB as "pledge"; the NRSV as "first installment" and "pledge"; the NLT as "first installment" and "guarantee"; and the NIV as "a deposit guaranteeing what is to come." The CEV expands on the meaning as follows: The Holy Spirit is given "to show that we belong to him" (2 Corinthians 1:22), "to make us certain that he will do it" (2 Corinthians 5:5), "[to make] us sure that we will be given what God has stored up for his people" (Ephesians 1:14).

Examples of the use of this word in English literature are Shakespeare's *Cymbeline* (I, 5, 65):

> "I prithee, take it;
> It is an earnest of a further good
> That I mean to thee"

and Tennyson's *In Memoriam* (xcvii):

> "The days she never can forget
> Are earnest that he loves her yet."

EASIER FOR A CAMEL TO GO THROUGH AN EYE OF A NEEDLE

See CAMEL THROUGH AN EYE OF A NEEDLE.

EAT, DRINK, AND BE MERRY

The saying "eat, drink, and be merry" sometimes followed by the additional phrase "for tomorrow we die" expresses the philosophy that one should enjoy oneself fully with worldly pleasures at the present time, because the future is uncertain.

The expression is found three times in the KJV: Isaiah 22:13, "let us eat and drink; for to morrow we shall die"; Ecclesiastes 8:15, "a man hath no better thing under the sun, than to eat, and to drink, and to be merry"; and in the parable of the rich fool, Luke 12:19, "take thine ease, eat, drink, and be merry."

The contemporary versions generally follow the traditional wording fairly closely, with some paraphrases, e.g., Isaiah 22:13 in the NLT: " 'Let's eat, drink, and be merry,' " you say. "What's the difference, for tomorrow we die.' "; Ecclesiastes 8:15 in the NCV and NLT, "to eat, drink, and enjoy life" and in the CEV, "to enjoy our food and drink and to have a good time"; Luke 12:19 in the CEV, "Eat, drink, and enjoy yourself" and in the NCV, "eat, drink, and enjoy life!"

EATER, OUT OF THE, CAME FORTH MEAT

See STRONG, OUT OF THE, CAME FORTH SWEETNESS.

EDIFY, EDIFICATION

To "edify," from the Latin *aedificare,* is "to build." The word is rarely used, however, in a material sense. While the word "edifice" usually refers to a large building of wood or stone or steel, the words "edify" and "edification" are used in a figurative sense, to refer to intellectual improvement or moral and spiritual upbuilding.

Jesus said, in answer to Peter's confession, "upon this rock I will build my church" (Matthew 16:18, KJV). Paul took up the verb which Jesus used and made it one of his most characteristic expressions. The KJV sometimes translates it as "build" or "build up" (Acts 20:32; 1 Corinthians 3:10–14; Ephesians 2:20–22; Colossians 2:7; see also 1 Peter 2:5 and Jude 20). But more

often it translates it as "edify" or "edification."

Archbishop Trench, in his *English Past and Present,* held that "our use of 'edify' and 'edification' first obtained general currency among the Puritans," and cited two quotations. One is from the satirist, John Oldham, 1653–1683:

"The graver sort dislike all poetry,
Which does not, as they call it, edify."

The other is from Robert South, 1634–1716, an opponent of the Non-conformists: "All being took up and busied in the grand work of preaching and holding forth, and that of edification, as the word then went."

The words "edify" and "edification" are sometimes used today in less than the high moral and religious sense which has come to be their primary meaning. We might speak of an edifying conversation when all we mean is that it was informing, revealing, or even amusing.

The contemporary versions retain "edify" and "edification" in places (e.g., 1 Corinthians 14:4, NASB, NIV, NKJV, RSV), but also use other renderings such as "the church . . . was built up" [NIV, "was strengthened"] (Acts 9:31, NIV, NRSV); "building up [NASB, "building up of"] the body of Christ" (Ephesians 4:12, NASB, NRSV, RSV); "your strengthening" (2 Corinthians 12:19, NIV), "your benefit" (NLT), and "your upbuilding" (NASB, RSV); "the building up of one another" (Romans 14:19, NASB) and "mutual upbuilding" (NRSV, RSV); and "building itself up in love" (Ephesians 4:16, NRSV).

EITHER

Today we use the conjunction "either" to refer to the first of two alternatives ("either call or write"), but in its obsolete sense it could be used to introduce the second or any later alternative, as well as the first.

So at James 3:12 the KJV reads, "Can the fig tree . . . bear olive berries? either a vine, figs?" The NRSV now renders this "Can a fig tree . . . yield olives, or a grapevine figs?"

"Not as though I had already attained, either were already perfect" (Philippians 3:12, KJV) reads, in the NASB, "Not that I have already obtained it or have already become perfect."

Luke 15:8, "Either what woman having ten pieces of silver" (KJV) begins with the word "Or" in the majority of the contemporary versions. Similarly in Luke 6:42, "Either how canst thou say to thy brother" (KJV), the NASB, NKJV, NRSV, and RSV open the verse with "Or how can you say," as does the KJV in the parallel text, Matthew 7:4.

The old usage is interestingly shown in Wycliffe's phrasing of Matthew 12:33: "ether make ye the tree good and his fruyt good: ether make ye the tree yuel and his fruyt yuel, for a tree is knownun of the fruyt." For the second "ether" Tyndale and his successors had "or else."

ELEVENTH HOUR

If something happens "at the eleventh hour," it occurs at the last possible moment—at a time that is almost, but not quite, too late. The expression refers to the time of hiring of the final group of workers in Jesus' parable about the laborers in the vineyard (Matthew 20:1–16). In the parable, the workers who started work at the eleventh hour received the same wage as the various groups of workers who had started earlier.

The contemporary versions render "the eleventh hour" as "five o'clock" (NCV, NRSV); "five in the afternoon" (CEV); and "five o'clock that evening" (NLT); the NASB, NIV, NKJV, and RSV retain the KJV expression "eleventh hour."

EMERODS

This word is a variant form of "hemorrhoids," a disease also known as "piles," characterized by tumors or painful swellings of the veins about the anus. The three names for this disease were used interchangeably until the seventeenth century, and only "emerods" is used in the KJV. All

but one of its appearances are in the account of the plague which struck the Philistines when they had captured the ark of the Lord (1 Samuel 5—6).

The translation of the Hebrew word is problematic, and is complicated by the fact that the Philistines are described as making an expiatory offering to the Lord of five golden images of their "emerods" (6:3–5, KJV). The phrase "in their secret parts" (5:9) is the KJV translation of the Hebrew verb which the NASB, NRSV, and RSV render as "broke out." It is probable that these were the boils of the bubonic plague. The contemporary versions use "tumors" (NASB, NIV, NKJV, NLT, NRSV, RSV), "growths" (NCV), and "sores" (CEV).

In the context of Deuteronomy 28:27, the RSV translates the Hebrew word by "ulcers": "The LORD will smite you with the boils of Egypt, and with the ulcers and the scurvy and the itch, of which you cannot be healed."

EMINENT

The word "eminent" is likely to make us think of a highly-respected scholar or someone else renowned for his or her achievements. In the KJV, however, the word refers only to physical height, not to persons or qualities. The "eminent place" built by the faithless Jerusalem (Ezekiel 16:24, 31, 39, KJV) is now rendered "a vaulted chamber" (RSV), "a shrine" (NASB, NKJV), "a lofty shrine," "mounds," (NIV), and "a platform" (NRSV). "An high mountain and eminent" (Ezekiel 17:22, KJV) is now rendered "a high and lofty mountain" (NASB, NIV, NRSV, RSV).

On the other hand, the noun "preeminence," which occurs three times in the KJV, refers to persons. "A man hath no preeminence above a beast" (Ecclesiastes 3:19, KJV) reads in the NRSV, "humans have no advantage over the animals." In his third letter, John writes that his words and authority have been rejected by Diotrephes, "who loveth to have the preeminence among them" (3 John 9, KJV); this is now rendered, "who likes to put himself first" (nrsv), and "who loves to be their leader" (ncv).

In Colossians 1:18, where Paul speaks of Christ Jesus, the Son of God, the kjv reads "that in all things he might have the preeminence." This is now rendered "so that He Himself will come to have first place in everything" (nasb); "so that in everything he might have the supremacy" (niv); and "so that he might come to have first place in everything" (nrsv).

EMULATION

"Emulation" is what a young boy might feel toward his sporting heroes: a desire to equal or surpass their achievements. "Emulation" occurs twice in the kjv. In Romans 11:14 Paul writes of stirring his fellow Jews to emulation of the Gentiles, but in Galatians 5:20 the tone is different. Here "emulations" are included with adultery, idolatry, murder, drunkenness and a host of similar evils in a long list of the works of the flesh as contrasted with the fruit of the Spirit.

Like the Latin *aemulatio,* "emulation" could be used in a good sense or a bad sense. It has retained the good sense, its primary meaning, "an honest and fair endeavor to equal or surpass others." The bad sense, "ambitious rivalry leading to contention and ill will," was current in the sixteenth and seventeenth centuries, and it appears a dozen times in Shakespeare's plays.

> "I was advertised their great general slept,
> Whilst emulation in the army crept."
> —*Troilus and Cressida* (II, 2, 212)

> "My heart laments that virtue cannot live
> Out of the teeth of emulation."
> —*Julius Caesar* (II, 3, 14)

This bad sense of "emulation" is now obsolete. The contemporary versions use "jealousy" in the list of works of the flesh in Galatians 5:20.

The Greek verb which the kjv translates as "provoke to emulation" in Romans 11:14 means "to make jealous" and in the contemporary versions is rendered as "move to jealousy" (nasb), "arouse . . . to envy" (niv), and "make . . . jealous" (nrsv).

The nrsv translates Romans 11:13b–14, "Inasmuch then as I am an apostle to the Gentiles, I glorify my ministry in order to make my own people jealous, and thus save some of them." The word "jealous" is here used in the sense which is defined by the oed as "troubled by the belief, suspicion or fear that the good which one desires to gain or keep for oneself has been or may be diverted to another."

The same verb appears in Romans 10:19 and 11:11, where the kjv translates it as "provoke . . . to jealousy." The Rheims New Testament was the first to use "emulate" and "emulation" in these texts, taking the words from the Latin. The kjv took the Rheims rendering in 11:14, but not in 11:11 or in 10:19.

ENABLE

The word "enable" in modern usage means "to make possible" or "to facilitate" ("a new ramp will enable wheelchair access to the gallery"), but in its one occurrence in the kjv it has the meaning of "strengthen": "I thank Christ Jesus our Lord, who hath enabled me" (1 Timothy 1:12, kjv). The Greek verb which it represents is translated by the kjv as "be strong" in Romans 4:20, Ephesians 6:10, and 2 Timothy 2:1; "strengthen" in Philippians 4:13 and 2 Timothy 4:17; and "increased in strength" in Acts 9:22.

Tyndale and his successors here translated it "hath made me strong." The nasb reads, "I thank Christ Jesus our Lord, who has strengthened me"; the rsv has, "I thank him who has given me strength for this, Christ Jesus our Lord."

END

The word "end" is much used in the Bible, and its meaning is usually clear. In Jeremiah 29:11, however, the word occurs in the KJV in a passage which promises a future, rather than an "end" in our usual understanding of the word, to the exiles in Babylon: "For I know the thoughts that I think toward you, saith the LORD, thoughts of peace, and not of evil, to give you an expected end." The Hebrew word is *aharith*, which may mean not only "the termination of a period of time," but also "the latter part of a period of time," or "the future," or "prosperity."

Which of these meanings it has in a particular case depends upon the context; in the Jeremiah text it appears with *tiqwah*, a Hebrew word for "hope." The contemporary versions render "an expected end" (KJV) as "a future and a hope" (NKJV, NASB, NLT, RSV), "a future with hope" (NRSV), and "a future filled with hope" (CEV).

God's assurance, two chapters further on (Jeremiah 31:17), that "there is hope in thine end" (KJV) is now rendered "there is hope for your future" (NASB, NIV, NLT, NRSV, RSV).

Proverbs 23:18 reads in the KJV, "surely there is an end, and thine expectation shall not be cut off." In the following chapter the KJV translates the same Hebrew words differently: "there shall be a reward, and thy expectation shall not be cut off" (Proverbs 24:14). The NRSV reads "Surely there is a future, and your hope will not be cut off" (23:18); "you will find a future, and your hope will not be cut off" (24:14).

In Psalm 37:37–38 the word *aharith* is used in the sense of "posterity," as was recognized by both the Greek Septuagint and the Latin Vulgate. The KJV renderings are "the end of that man is peace" and "the end of the wicked shall be cut off"; the NRSV now reads "there is posterity for the peaceable" and "the posterity of the wicked shall be cut off." The NLT renders the verses as "Look at those who are honest and good, for a won-derful future lies before those who love peace. But the wicked will be destroyed; they have no future."

END IS NOT YET

The expression "the end is not yet" means that "further, often worse, things must happen or be experienced before a process, series of events, etc., is completely finished."

The saying comes from Matthew 24:6: "And ye shall hear of wars and rumours of wars: see that ye be not troubled: for all these things must come to pass, but the end is not yet" (KJV). The contemporary versions render the KJV "the end is not yet" as "that isn't the end" (CEV), "that is not yet the end" (NASB), "the end is still to come" (NIV), "the end won't follow immediately" (NLT); the NKJV, NRSV, and RSV retain the KJV phrasing.

The parallel in Mark (13:7) has the same wordings as Matthew, except the NRSV, "the end is still to come"; the parallel in Luke in the KJV reads "the end is not by and by" (21:9).

ENGINE

An engine is a piece of machinery that changes steam, electricity, or other form of energy into movement. In the KJV, however, the word is used to refer to a military machine or implement of warfare. The word occurs twice in this sense in the KJV. The word "engine" originally meant "genius," "ingenuity" and dates from the fourteenth century.

Second Chronicles 26:15 reports of King Uzziah: "And he made in Jerusalem engines, invented by cunning men, to be on the towers and upon the bulwarks, to shoot arrows and great stones withal. And his name spread far abroad; for he was marvellously helped, till he was strong." The contemporary versions render the KJV "engines" as "machines" (CEV, NIV, NLT, NRSV) and "devices" (NCV, NKJV); the RSV retains the KJV "engines"; the NASB has "engines of war."

In Ezekiel 26:9, the prophecy against

Tyre, the Lord says of Nebuchadnezzar, "And he shall set engines of war against thy walls, and with his axes he shall break down thy towers." All the contemporary versions except the CEV and NCV refer to the use of "battering rams"; e.g., the NIV, "he will direct the blows of his battering rams against your walls"; the CEV has "large wooden poles" and the NCV, "logs." Shakespeare used the word in this sense:

> "So that the ram that batters down
> the wall,
> For the great swing and rudeness
> of his poise,
> They place before his hand that
> made the engine."
> —*Troilus and Cressida* (I, 3, 208)

(See GIN)

ENLARGE

In modern usage, we understand "enlarge" to mean "to make larger," "extend," "widen." In the KJV, however, it is frequently used in ways which may not be familiar. Hannah's prayer of thanksgiving, "my mouth is enlarged over mine enemies" (1 Samuel 2:1, KJV) is rendered "my mouth derides my enemies" by the NRSV and "my mouth speaks boldly against my enemies" by the NASB.

"Thou hast enlarged my steps under me" (2 Samuel 22:37 and its parallel, Psalm 18:36, KJV) now reads "Thou didst give a wide place for my steps under me" (RSV), "You have made me stride freely" (NRSV), "You broaden the path beneath me" (NIV), and "You enlarge my steps under me" (NASB). "Thou hast enlarged me when I was in distress" (Psalm 4:1, KJV) reads, in the NRSV, "You gave me room when I was in distress."

"When thou shalt enlarge my heart" (Psalm 119:32, KJV) is now worded "you enlarge my understanding" (NRSV), while the NIV reads "you have set my heart free." At Habakkuk 2:5, "who enlargeth his desire as hell, and is as death, and cannot be satis-

fied" (KJV), the NIV reads "he is as greedy as the grave and like death is never satisfied."

Isaiah 60, which begins, "Arise, shine; for thy light is come, and the glory of the LORD is risen upon thee" (KJV), is great literature—a poem of sustained beauty and strength. The KJV rendering of the first half of verse 5, however, may not be altogether clear. It reads, in the KJV, "Then thou shalt see, and flow together, and thine heart shall fear, and be enlarged."

Contemporary versions render the passage as follows: "Then you shall [NASB, "you will"] see and be radiant, your heart shall [NASB, "will"] thrill and rejoice" (NASB, NRSV, RSV); "Then you will look and be radiant, your heart will throb and swell with joy" (NIV); "Your eyes will shine, and your hearts will thrill with joy" (NLT). The CEV reads, "When you see this, your faces will glow; your hearts will pound and swell with pride."

The KJV rendering "flow together" at Isaiah 60:5 results from the similarity between the verb *nahar,* which means "be radiant," and a different verb *nahar,* used in Isaiah 2:2 with the meaning "stream" or "flow." The modern translations are anticipated by the Great Bible and the Bishops' Bible, "Then thou shalt see this and be glorious," and by the Geneva Bible, "Then shalt see and shine."

Paul's plea to the Corinthians (2 Corinthians 6:11–13) reads in the KJV: "O ye Corinthians, our mouth is open unto you, our heart is enlarged. Ye are not straitened in us, but ye are straitened in your own bowels." The NRSV reads, "We have spoken frankly to you Corinthians; our heart is wide open to you. There is no restriction in our affections, but only in yours. In return—I speak as to children—open wide your hearts also."

ENLARGEMENT

This word appears once in the KJV, in Mordecai's counsel to Queen Esther: "if thou altogether holdest thy peace at this time, then shall there enlargement and deliverance arise to the Jews from another place" (Esther 4:14, KJV). The word is here used in the sense of release from confinement, bondage, or distress.

The Hebrew uses a word meaning respite or relief, and the NASB, NIV, NKJV, NRSV, and RSV use the word "relief." The NASB reads, "if you remain silent at this time, relief and deliverance will arise for the Jews from another place."

ENSAMPLE

See EXAMPLE.

ENSUE

We use the word "ensue" today to mean "follow" ("ignore this note and a penalty will ensue"), but in the sixteenth and seventeenth centuries it was sometimes used in the sense of "pursue," "seek after," or "strive for." It has this meaning in the KJV rendering of 1 Peter 3:11: "seek peace, and ensue it." This verse is part of a passage (3:10–12) which quotes, with some adaptation, Psalm 34:12–16, in which the KJV had "seek peace, and pursue it."

The "ensue" here comes from Tyndale. The majority of contemporary versions replace it with "pursue."

ENTREAT, INTREAT

The word "entreat" makes us think of pressing requests and the vigor with which they are usually made. In the KJV the word "entreat" is used both in our modern sense of "to plead with," and also as an archaic word for "to treat" or "to deal with."

Thus, Job 24:21 reads, in the KJV, "The evil entreateth the barren that beareth not: and doeth not good to the widow." The NASB renders the verse as "He wrongs the barren woman And does no good for the widow"; the NIV has "They prey on the barren" and the NRSV has "They harm the childless woman."

In the KJV New Testament, "entreat" is used in this obsolete sense in Luke 20:11

(KJV, "entreated him shamefully") and 1 Thessalonians 2:2 (KJV, "we . . . were shamefully entreated"), where the contemporary versions have "treated" (Luke 20:11, NASB, NIV, NKJV, NLT, RSV), "insulted" (1 Thessalonians 2:2, CEV, NIV), and "mistreated" (1 Thessalonians 2:2, NRSV).

In the other instance where the word is used in its obsolete sense, Acts 27:3, the KJV reads, "Julius courteously entreated Paul." Contemporary versions now read, "Julius treated Paul kindly" [NASB, "with consideration"] (NASB, NKJV, NRSV, RSV).

We understand the expression "be entreated" to mean "to be prevailed on or persuaded to grant the object of an entreaty." It is used in the KJV only of God, though in now obsolete English it was applied to human beings as well. The passages are Genesis 25:21; 2 Samuel 21:14; 24:25; 1 Chronicles 5:20; 2 Chronicles 33:13, 19; Ezra 8:23; and Isaiah 19:22.

Contemporary versions' renderings include: "answered his prayer" (Genesis 25:21, NIV), "granted his plea" (Genesis 25:21, NKJV), "was moved by prayer" (2 Samuel 21:14, NASB), "heeded supplications" (2 Samuel 21:14, NRSV), "granted their entreaty" (1 Chronicles 5:20, RSV).

"Easy to be entreated" (James 3:17, KJV) represents a Greek word which contemporary versions now translate as "open to reason" (RSV), "willing to yield" (NRSV, NKJV, NLT), "reasonable" (NASB), and "submissive" (NIV).

The successive translations of 2 Corinthians 8:4 reveal the difficulty of finding the right English to express the meaning of very compact Greek. In modern spelling, Tyndale and his successors had "and prayed us with great instance that we would receive their benefit, and suffer them to be partakers with others in ministering to the saints."

The KJV took a different interpretation of the last clause: "praying us with much intreaty that we would receive the gift, and take upon us the fellowship of the ministering to the saints." The revised versions of 1881–1901 have "beseeching us with much entreaty in regard of this grace and the fellowship in the ministering to the saints."

The contemporary versions return to Tyndale's understanding of the verse; the NRSV translates as "begging us earnestly for the privilege of sharing in this ministry to the saints," and the NASB reads, "begging us with much urging for the favor of participation in the support of the saints."

The corrected editions of the KJV prepared by Dr. Paris (1762) and Dr. Blayney (1769) made a distinction between "entreat," meaning "to deal with," and "intreat," meaning "to ask" or "to pray." This distinction was not present in the original edition of 1611, where the two spellings are used interchangeably—for example, Job 19:16 has "intreated" and 19:17 has "entreated," Job 24:21 has "intreateth," Jeremiah 15:11 has "intreat" in the text and "entreat" in the marginal note, Philippians 4:3 has "entreat." In fact these are simply different spellings of the same word, and the OED so defines "intreat" as an obsolete or archaic spelling of "entreat."

EQUAL

"Equality" is a familiar word today, and the word "equal" is likely to turn our thoughts to opportunities ("equal rights for all"). In the sixteenth and seventeenth centuries, however, the word had a moral meaning. Like the Latin *aequus*, from which it is derived, it was applied to what is fair, just, and therefore right. In this sense it has been superseded by the word "equitable."

Ezekiel protests in the name of the Lord: "Yet ye say, The way of the Lord is not equal. Hear now, O house of Israel; Is not my way equal? are not your ways unequal?" (18:25, KJV; see also 18:29; 33:17, 20). Douay had "right"; Moffatt and Smith use "fair"; contemporary versions use "fair" (CEV, NCV, NRSV), "right" (NASB), and "just" (NIV, NLT, RSV).

"Let thine eyes behold the things that are equal" (Psalm 17:2, KJV) reads in the NRSV, "let your eyes see the right!" The injunction to masters in Colossians 4:1, "give unto your servants that which is just and equal" (KJV), is now rendered "treat your slaves justly and fairly" (NRSV, RSV), and "provide your slaves with what is right and fair" (NIV).

Paul's testimony to the Galatian church in Galatians 1:13–14 reads, in the KJV: "For ye have heard of my conversation in time past in the Jews' religion, how that beyond measure I persecuted the church of God, and wasted it: And profited in the Jews' religion above many my equals in mine own nation, being more exceedingly zealous of the traditions of my fathers."

The word "equals" here is used by the KJV to represent a Greek noun which means "persons of one's own age"; "many my equals in mine own nation" (KJV) reads, in the contemporary versions, "many of my contemporaries among my countrymen" (NASB), "many Jews of my own age" (NIV), and "many among my people of the same age" (NRSV). Verse 14 reads, in the CEV: "I was a much better Jew than anyone else my own age, and I obeyed every law that our ancestors had given us."

The verb "equal" is used in the obsolete sense of "liken" or "compare" in Lamentations 2:13: "what shall I equal to thee, that I may comfort thee, O virgin daughter of Zion?" (KJV). Contemporary versions use "liken" (NASB, NIV, NRSV, RSV) and "compare" (NKJV).

ESCHEW

This word is used in formal texts to mean "to turn away from" or "to shun something unpleasant" ("to eschew evil"). It also has an obsolete meaning, which survives in a proverb from Shakespeare's *King Henry IV, Part II* (II, 4, 49), "What cannot be eschewed must be embraced." The sense here is avoidance or escape from a danger or inconvenience.

In 2 Corinthians 8:20 Tyndale had "For

thys we eschue, that eny man shuld rebuke us in this plenteous distribution that is ministred by us." The Geneva Bible changed this to "Avoyding this," which the KJV adopted. Among the contemporary versions the NKJV retains "avoiding this"; other translations are "taking precaution" (NASB), "being careful" (NCV), "avoid" (NIV), and "guard against" (NLT). The NRSV renders the verse, "We intend that no one should blame us about this generous gift that we are administering."

From Coverdale comes the rendering of Psalm 18:23 which still appears in the Book of Common Prayer: "I was also uncorrupt before him, and eschewed mine own wickedness." The KJV changed this to "I was also upright before him, and I kept myself from mine iniquity"; the NASB has "I was also blameless with Him, And I kept myself from my iniquity."

"Eschewed" is retained by the KJV in two contexts. Job is described as "one that feared God, and eschewed evil" (1:1, 8; 2:3). The contemporary versions translate the word rendered "eschewed" (KJV) with the verbs "turn away from" (NASB, NRSV, RSV), "stay away from" (NCV, NLT), and "shun" (NIV, NKJV). In 1 Peter 3:11 this counsel appears for one who would love life and see good days: "Let him eschew evil, and do good" (KJV). Most of the contemporary versions use the rendering "turn away from evil" in this verse.

ESPOUSED

This word is used by the KJV in an obsolete sense, meaning "betrothed" rather than "married." The contexts are 2 Samuel 3:14, David and Michal; and Matthew 1:18; Luke 1.27; 2:5, Joseph and Mary. In each of these cases the contemporary versions generally use "betrothed," "engaged," "pledged," or "promised." In all other cases, ten in number, the KJV itself, as well as a number of contemporary versions, translates as "betrothed" the word used by David.

Another New Testament occurrence is a figure of speech concerning Christ and the church (2 Corinthians 11:2). This reads in the KJV, "I have espoused you to one husband, that I may present you as a chaste virgin to Christ." The RSV translates, "I betrothed you to Christ to present you as a pure bride to her one husband"; the NRSV reads, "I promised you in marriage to one husband, to present you as a chaste virgin to Christ."

On the other hand, the plural "espousals" is used in the KJV, as it still is, for the formal celebration of a marriage. It is equivalent to "nuptials" or a "wedding." The contexts are Song of Solomon 3:11 and Jeremiah 2:2. The contemporary versions render the KJV of Song of Solomon 3:11 "the day of his espousals" as "the day of his wedding" (NASB, NIV, NKJV, NRSV, RSV) and "his wedding day" (NCV, NLT).

The "love of thine espousals" (Jeremiah 2:2, KJV) is rendered "the love of your betrothal" [NASB, "your betrothals"] (NASB, NKJV), "your love as a bride" (NRSV, RSV), and "as a bride you loved me" (NIV).

ESTATE

In contemporary American English, "estate" is commonly used in the compound "real estate," property in the form of land or houses. In contemporary British English, an estate is an area of buildings or houses ("a post-war housing estate"). Someone's estate is that person's property and possessions, especially left after their death.

In the KJV, "estate" is used in several different ways. The primary meaning of the word in the KJV is "state or condition" as in Ezekiel 16:55, "When thy sisters, Sodom and her daughters, shall return to their former estate, and Samaria and her daughters shall return to their former estate, then thou and thy daughters shall return to your former estate," where "return to their" [or: "your"] former estate" is rendered "return to their" [or: "your"] former estate" by the NASB, NKJV, and RSV and by "return to what they [or "you"] were before" by the NCV and NIV.

The state or condition may be high, "[Thou] has regarded me according to the estate of a man of high degree, O LORD God" (1 Chronicles 17:17, KJV), rendered "a very important person" by the CEV and the NCV, "the rank [NASB, "standard"] of a man of high degree" by the NASB and NKJV, "someone of high rank" (NRSV), "the most exalted of men" (NIV), and "someone very great" (NLT).

Alternatively, the position may be low, as in the words of the Magnificat, "he hath regarded the low estate of his handmaiden" (Luke 1:48, KJV), rendered as "humble state" by the NASB and NIV, "lowly state" by the NKJV, "lowly servant" by the NLT, "humble servant" by the CEV and NCV, and "lowliness" by the NRSV.

Similarly, Psalm 136:23 recalls also the Lord, "Who remembered us in our low estate" (KJV); "estate" is retained by the NASB, NIV, and NRSV; the NKJV has "state"; the CEV and NCV have "trouble" and the NLT, "weakness."

"Estate" can also mean position or place: "let the king give her royal estate unto another that is better than she" (Esther 1:19, KJV), rendered as "position" by the NASB, NIV, NKJV, and NRSV and "place" by the NCV. In Daniel 11:20–21 (KJV) "in his estate" occurs twice, e.g., "Then shall stand up in his estate a raiser of taxes" (Daniel 11:20), rendered as "in his place" by the NASB, NKJV, and NRSV and in Daniel 11:20 by "His successor" in the NIV and NLT and "The next king" by the CEV and NCV.

In Jude 6, "the angels which kept not their first estate" (KJV) is rendered as "domain" (NASB, NKJV), "position" (NRSV), and "positions of authority" (NIV).

Finally, in two references in the KJV, "estate" refers to people: Mark 6:21, "And when a convenient day was come, that Herod on his birthday made a supper to his lords, high captains, and chief estates of Galilee" (KJV), where "chief estates" is rendered as "leading men" (NASB, NIV, RSV), "leaders" (CEV, NRSV), "leading citizens" (NLT), "chief men" (NKJV), and "most important people" (NCV).

Acts 22:5 (KJV) reads "all the estate of the elders," rendered as "all the Council [NKJV, "council"] of the elders" by the NASB and NKJV; "all the Council" (NIV), "the whole council of elders" [NCV, "of older Jewish leaders"] by the NCV and NRSV, "all the council members" (CEV), and "the whole council of leaders" (NLT).

EVEN

As an adverb, "even" is used 1,032 times in the KJV Old Testament, and in 928 of these cases there is no corresponding word in the Hebrew text. In 1611 the translators wrote "even so" for "so," "even as" for "as," and "even unto" where we would now say "to" or "up to" or "as far as."

We also find that they used the word "even" to introduce an additional word or words in order to explain more clearly or fully some preceding word or words. The word "even" was for them a sign of equivalence or identity; it meant that the person or thing or subject referred to in what followed was the same person or thing or subject referred to in what preceded.

For example, for "the men of the city, even the men of Sodom" (KJV) we would say today "the men of the city, the men of Sodom"— the same persons are meant by the two phrases (Genesis 19:4; thus NASB, NKJV, NRSV, RSV). So also "the man, even Lot" means "the man Lot" (Genesis 19:9). "Jacob set up a pillar, even a pillar of stone" (Genesis 35:14) has no "even" in the Hebrew. In such cases, the inserted word "even" in the KJV has a function similar to "namely" or "that is."

The use of "even" in this sense is now obsolete. We use the word today to indicate an extreme case or something not to be expected ("even the bushes are waning in the heat"; "even if we booked flights for this evening we would still be late"). Our modern use of the word might make the sense of the KJV text unclear in places, such as in Genesis 10:21 where we read of Shem that "even to him were children born."

Contemporary versions omit the inserted "even" in most cases. In Genesis, for example, the KJV uses "even" twenty-six times, of which twenty-one were cases of insertion without a corresponding Hebrew word. The NASB and RSV retain "even" in 27:34, 38 and 46:34.

The use of "even" in the KJV New Testament is not so frequent and is rarely retained by the contemporary versions. "God, even the Father" (1 Corinthians 15:24, KJV) is now simply "God the Father" (CEV, NCV, NIV, NKJV, NLT, NRSV, RSV). "God, even our Father" (2 Thessalonians 2:16, KJV) is "God our Father" (CEV, NASB, NCV, NIV, NLT, NRSV, RSV). "The will of God, *even* your sanctification" (1 Thessalonians 4:3, KJV) is rendered "the will of God, your sanctification" in the NASB, NKJV, NRSV, and RSV.

The word is mostly absent from contemporary renderings of John 1:12 (except in the NASB, which retains it); Acts 5:37; Romans 9:10 (except in the NKJV, which retains it); 1 Thessalonians 2:19 (except the NKJV and NASB); and Hebrews 5:14.

EVERY

The word "every" is sometimes used by the KJV in senses we now usually express by "each." "They received every man a penny" (Matthew 20:9, 10, KJV) is a rendering that came from Tyndale; the NRSV has "each of them received the usual daily wage," and the NASB, NKJV, and NIV have "each [NASB, "each one"] received a denarius."

An obsolete use of "every" in the sense of "each of two," occurs in 2 Samuel 21:20: "And there was yet a battle in Gath, where was a man of great stature, that had on every hand six fingers, and on every foot six toes, four and twenty in number." Contemporary versions read "each hand" and "each foot."

EVIDENCE

The word "evidence" makes us think of proof, or a sign of something we can't see ("the dead bird is evidence that the family cat hasn't lost his touch"). In Jeremiah 32 the word is used eight times in the KJV. Jeremiah purchases the field in Anathoth, and the documents recording the transaction are described as "the evidence of the purchase." Here "evidence" is used in a legal sense of the documents themselves, and the contemporary versions use the terms "bill of sale" (CEV), "record of ownership" (NCV), "deed of purchase" (NASB, NIV, NLT, NRSV, RSV), and "purchase deed" (NKJV).

The text which opens the great chapter on faith, Hebrews 11, reads in the KJV: "Now faith is the substance of things hoped for, the evidence of things not seen." The NKJV and NLT retain the word "evidence," while the NASB, NRSV, and RSV translate as "Now faith is the assurance of things hoped for, the conviction of things not seen." The NCV paraphrases as "Faith means being sure of the things we hope for and knowing that something is real even if we do not see it."

EVIDENT

In Job 6:28, Job says to his comforters: "Now therefore be content, look upon me; for it is evident unto you if I lie" (KJV). The Hebrew, which the KJV renders as "evident unto you," reads "to your face," and most contemporary versions render Job's words as a strong negative statement: "I will not [NCV, "I would not"] lie to your face" (NCV, NRSV, RSV); "I would never lie to your face" (NKJV). The NIV has "Would I lie to your face?"

EVIDENTLY

See APPARENTLY.

EXAMPLE, ENSAMPLE

Today we usually understand "example" to be a part of something which shows the character of the whole, or a pattern or model to be imitated ("he set a good example"). We also use it of an instance, especially of punishment, which serves as a warning ("the judge seemed determined to make an example of him"). Examples are thus typical, or good, or bad. The KJV uses "example" nine times, and "ensample" six times, without any distinction of meaning, except that no merely typical instances are included. Of the "examples," five are good and four bad; of the "ensamples," four are good and two bad.

The revised versions of 1881–1901 made an effort to use "ensample" for good instances and "example" for bad, but the effort failed. They could not thus arbitrarily limit the word "example." "Ensample" is archaic, and is not found in the contemporary versions.

Speaking of the punishments which befell the Israelites in the wilderness, Paul writes, "Now all these things happened unto them for ensamples" (1 Corinthians 10:11, KJV). The majority of contemporary versions have "example" or "examples" in their renderings of this verse, although the RSV and CEV read, "These [RSV, "Now these"] things happened to them as a warning."

Israel's failure to act on God's promises is again held up as an object lesson in Hebrews 4:11, where the church is warned against failing to enter God's rest: "Let us labour therefore to enter into that rest, lest any man fall after the same example of unbelief" (KJV). The NRSV has "so that no one may fall through such disobedience as theirs"; the RSV, "that no one fall by the same sort of disobedience"; the NASB, "that no one will fall, through following the same example of disobedience."

Later, in Hebrews 8:5, we read of priests under the Mosaic covenant "Who serve unto the example and shadow of heavenly things" (KJV). The contemporary versions render the KJV's "example" as "copy" (CEV, NASB, NCV, NIV, NKJV, NLT, RSV); the NRSV reads "They offer worship in a sanctuary that is a sketch and shadow of the heavenly one."

In 1 Timothy 4:12 (KJV), Paul urges Timothy to "be thou an example of the believers"; the NRSV reads, "set the believers an example."

In Matthew 1:19 (KJV) we read of Joseph's intentions upon his discovery that Mary was expecting a child: he was "not willing to make her a publick example," and "was minded to put her away privily." The contemporary versions speak of Joseph's "not wanting to disgrace her" (NASB), and of his being "unwilling to expose her to public disgrace" (NRSV). The Greek verb in this case appears also in Hebrews 6:6, where it is translated by the KJV as "put him to an open shame"; the NRSV and RSV have "hold him [NRSV, "holding him"] up to contempt," and the NASB and NKJV have "put Him to [NKJV, "to an"] open shame."

The whole verse reads, in the NIV, "if they fall away, to be brought back to repentance, because to their loss they are crucifying the Son of God all over again and subjecting him to public disgrace."

EXCEED

The word "exceed" is likely to make us think of speed limits and sporting records. It also has an obsolete sense of "pass the bounds of propriety" or "go too far," and it is used at least once with this meaning in the KJV. Job 36:9 reads, "Then he sheweth them their work, and their transgressions that they have exceeded." The Hebrew verb here represented by "exceeded" is the one which is rendered "strengtheneth" by the KJV in Job 15:25: "he strengtheneth himself against the Almighty."

The NRSV translates this as "bid defiance to the Almighty"; and in Job 36:9, "then he declares to them their work and their transgressions, that they are behaving arrogantly." The NKJV reads "they have acted defiantly" in verse 9, and the NASB has "they have magnified themselves."

When Jonathan sent his lad home with his "artillery," and David came out of his hiding place, the two friends "kissed one another, and wept one with another, until David exceeded" (1 Samuel 20:41, KJV). The Hebrew means that he wept "greatly," or, as we would now say, "bitterly." The RSV translates it as "they kissed one another, and wept with one another, until David recovered himself."

The other contemporary versions bring out the sense that David's show of sorrow was greater than Jonathan's: he "wept the more" (NASB, NRSV), "cried louder" (CEV), "cried the most" (NCV). The NKJV reads, "they kissed one another; and they wept together, but David more so."

EXCEEDING

As an adjective, "exceeding" was used in the sixteenth century to connote either "surpassing excellence" or "extreme impropriety." Now obsolete in these senses, the adjective "exceeding" is used only with nouns "denoting quality, condition, or feeling, or including a notion of magnitude or multitude" (OED), and it may mean either "surpassing" or "excessive," in amount or degree. Nowhere in the Bible does it mean excessive or immoderate.

In the Old Testament, the NASB, NKJV, NRSV, and RSV retain "God my exceeding joy" (Psalm 43:4, KJV); the NIV has "God, my joy and delight." In the New Testament, most contemporary versions do not use "exceeding" in the six passages where it served as an adjective in the KJV.

In 2 Corinthians 4:17, "exceeding" (KJV) is rendered "beyond all measure" (NRSV), "beyond all comparison" (RSV, NASB), "much greater" (NCV), and "far outweighs" (NIV). In 2 Corinthians 9:14 "exceeding grace" (KJV) is now "surpassing grace" (NASB, NIV, NRSV, RSV).

The "exceeding greatness of his power to us-ward who believe" (Ephesians 1:19, KJV) reads in the NIV, "his incomparably great power for us who believe." The "exceeding riches of his grace" (Ephesians 2:7, KJV) is rendered "the incredible wealth of his favor" by the NLT. "Be glad . . . with exceeding joy" (1 Peter 4:13, KJV) is now "rejoice with exultation" (NASB), "be overjoyed" (NIV), "be glad and shout for joy" (NRSV), and "rejoice and be glad" (RSV). "With exceeding joy" (Jude 24, KJV) is now "with great joy" (NASB, NCV, NIV, NLT) and "with rejoicing" (NRSV, RSV).

The contemporary versions do not use "exceeding" as an adverb. For example, "An exceeding high mountain" (Matthew 4:8, KJV) is now "a very high mountain" in most versions; "exceeding sorry" (Mark 6:26, KJV) is "exceedingly sorry" (RSV), "very sorry" (CEV, NASB, NLT), and "greatly distressed" (NIV); "exceeding sorrowful" (Matthew 26:22, KJV) is "very sorrowful" (RSV), "deeply grieved" (NASB), "very sad" (CEV, NIV), and "greatly distressed" (NLT, NRSV).

EXCELLENCY

This word is likely to make us think of titles of honor ("Your Excellency") and standards and quality ("they strive for excellency on the sports field"). It is one of many words in English derived from Latin words ending in –ia (arrogancy, continency, innocency, etc.) which are now commonly spelled with a final "e" instead of "y." "Excellency" appears twenty-five times in the KJV. The contemporary versions replace it by other words in all cases, the NKJV alone using the word "excellence."

"The excellency of Jacob" (Psalm 47:4, KJV) is now rendered "the pride of Jacob" (CEV, NIV, NRSV, RSV), "the glory of Jacob" (NASB) and his "proud possession" (NLT). In Amos 6:8 "excellency" (KJV) is rendered "pride" (CEV, NCV, NIV, NKJV, NRSV, RSV), "arrogance" (NASB), and "pride and false glory" (NLT); in Amos 8:7 all the contemporary versions translate it as "pride."

"The voice of his excellency" (Job 37:4, KJV) is now "his [NASB, NKJV, "His"] majestic voice" (NASB, NIV, NKJV, NRSV, RSV). In Isaiah 35:2 the NASB, NRSV, and RSV read "The majesty of Carmel and Sharon. The majesty of our God"; the NIV has "splendor." Job 20:6 reads, in the KJV, "Though his excellency mount up to the heavens, and his head reach unto the clouds." The contemporary versions have "pride" (CEV, NCV, NIV, NLT), "loftiness" (NASB), and "haughtiness" (NKJV). The RSV reads, "Though his height mount up to the heavens."

Philippians 3:8 reads in the KJV, "I count all things but loss for the excellency of the knowledge of Christ Jesus my Lord." The NASB and NRSV render "excellency" (KJV) as "surpassing value"; the NIV has "surpassing greatness," the RSV, "surpassing worth," the NLT, "priceless gain."

EXERCISE

As a verb the word "exercise" is like the verb "to practice." We use it for habitual action and for training. It appears eighteen times in the KJV, translating twelve different Hebrew and Greek verbs. The contemporary versions use other terms in many of these cases.

"I exercise myself" (Psalm 131:1, KJV) is now "I . . . occupy myself" (NRSV, RSV), "I involve myself" (NASB) and "I . . . concern myself" (NIV, NKJV, NLT). In his defense before Felix in Acts 24:16, Paul states "And herein do I exercise myself, to have always a conscience void of offence toward God, and toward men." "I exercise myself" here is rendered "I [NASB, "I . . . do"; CEV, "I try"] my best" (NASB, CEV, NRSV), "I strive" (NIV), and "I . . . take pains" (RSV). "The travail which God hath given to the sons of men to be exercised in it" (Ecclesiastes 3:10, KJV; see also 1:13) is rendered "the business that God has given to everyone to be busy with" by the NRSV. In Ezekiel 22:29, "exercised robbery" (KJV) is now worded "committed robbery" (NASB, NKJV, NRSV, RSV). "Having . . . an heart they have exercised with covetous practices" (2 Peter 2:14, KJV) is rendered "having a heart trained in greed" (NASB).

"Those who by reason of use have their senses exercised to discern both good and evil" (Hebrews 5:14, KJV) reads, in the NRSV, "those whose faculties have been trained by practice to distinguish good from evil." "Train" and "training" are used by the ma-

jority of contemporary versions in Hebrews 12:11 and by the NCV, NIV, NRSV, and RSV in 1 Timothy 4:7–8. The Greek verb is *gymnazo* and the noun *gymnasia*.

EXPECT

The word "expect" is used today in the sense of "to look forward to" or "to anticipate," as well as colloquially for "to suppose" ("I expect he'll turn up later"). In Hebrews 10:13 the KJV uses the word in its obsolete sense of "wait": "From henceforth expecting till his enemies be made his footstool." The contemporary versions use the words "waits" and "waiting"; the NASB reads, "waiting from that time onward until His enemies be made a footstool for His feet."

EXPECTATION

"Expectation" is what we might feel as the date of a much-needed vacation draws near. The word is likely to remind us of the novel by Charles Dickens, *Great Expectations* (1861), and in the plural it is often used of a prospect of future good or profit. As used in the KJV, it means "hope."

"The expectation of the poor" (Psalm 9:18, KJV) is rendered "the hope [NCV, NLT, "hopes"] of the poor" by most of the contemporary versions. "My soul, wait thou only upon God; for my expectation *is* from him" (Psalm 62:5, KJV) is now rendered, "For God alone my soul waits in silence, for my hope is from him" (NRSV).

"Thy expectation shall not be cut off" (Proverbs 24:14, KJV) is now "your hope will not be cut off" (NASB, NIV, NKJV, NRSV, RSV). "To give you an expected end" (Jeremiah 29:11, KJV) is "to give you a future and a hope" (NASB). (See END)

EXPERIENCE

"Experience," both pleasant and unpleasant, is the stuff of life. A child experiences disappointment when she bites off the ear of a chocolate bunny and finds it to be hollow, while the promise of a new, different, or total experience looms large in advertising drives for everything from moisture creams to movie theaters. We recognize this very familiar word to refer to an encounter involving our five senses ("to experience the softness of a new fabric"), and also to knowledge or skill gained through practice ("to learn by experience").

The KJV uses the word in this way in Ecclesiastes 1:16, where the Preacher writes that he had "great experience of wisdom and knowledge" (KJV; NRSV); the NASB reads, "my mind has observed a wealth of wisdom and knowledge," and the NIV, "I have experienced much of wisdom and knowledge." In two other instances, however, the word is rendered very differently by the contemporary versions.

In Genesis 30:27, Laban asks Jacob to remain with him because, he says, "I have learned by experience that the LORD hath blessed me for thy sake" (KJV). The Hebrew word nahash, translated as "experience" here, means "to practice divination," or "to observe signs or omens."

The revised versions of 1881–1901 read, "I have divined that," as does the NASB, but the verb "to divine" is often used today to mean nothing more than "to come to believe that." Goodspeed reads, "I have noted the omens"; Moffatt, "I have learned from the omens." The contemporary versions translate the Hebrew here as "I have learned by divination that the LORD has blessed me because of you" [NLT, "because you are here"] (NLT, NIV, NRSV, RSV).

The verb nahash also occurs in 1 Kings 20:33, where the KJV has "the men did diligently observe"; the NASB has "the men took this as an omen," and the NRSV and RSV have "the men were watching for an omen."

In Romans 5:3–5 we read, in the KJV: "we glory in tribulations also: knowing that tribulation worketh patience; and patience, experience; and experience, hope; and hope maketh not ashamed." The Greek word here translated "experience" is *dokime,* which means "character that has been tested and proved."

The CEV, NCV, NIV, NKJV, NRSV, and RSV render the KJV "experience" of verse 4 as "character"; the NLT as "strength of character" and "character." The NASB renders Paul's words as "we also exult in our tribulations, knowing that tribulation brings about perseverance; and perseverance, proven character; and proven character, hope; and hope does not disappoint."

EXPERIMENT

In contemporary English, an experiment is a scientific test that is carried out in order to discover what happens under certain conditions. In the KJV the word "experiment" is used only with the meaning of "proof" or "proving." It occurs at 2 Corinthians 9:13, referring to the ministry of giving, "Whiles by the experiment of this ministration they glorify God for your professed subjection unto the gospel of Christ, and for your liberal distribution unto them, and unto all men."

The contemporary versions render the KJV "experiment" as "proof" (NASB, NCV, NKJV), as the verbal expression "you have proved yourselves" (CEV, NIV), and as "testing" (NRSV). In his *Merry Wives of Windsor* (IV, 2, 36), Shakespeare used this expression with this meaning, glossed in the OED as "proof; a test, trial," "To make another experiment of his suspicion."

EYE FOR AN EYE

The phrase "an eye for an eye" is used to refer to punishment or harsh treatment that is expressed as the same kind as the offense that has been committed.

The saying, sometimes used to justify retaliation in conflicts, comes from the KJV, Exodus 21:22–24: "If men strive, and hurt a woman with child, so that her fruit depart from her, and yet no mischief follow: he shall be surely punished, according as the woman's husband will lay upon him; and he shall pay as the judges determine. And if any mischief follow, then thou shalt give life for life, Eye for eye, tooth for tooth, and hand for hand, foot for foot." (See also Leviticus 24:20; Deuteronomy 19:21.)

All the contemporary versions except the NLT retain the KJV "eye for an eye"; the NLT has "If an eye is injured, injure the eye of the person who did it."

This principle of retaliation (known as "*lex talionis*") was not so much an expression of vindictiveness as an attempt to set limits on retribution, to indicate a measure of restraint on vengeance. Thus, Jesus in Matthew 5:38–39 urges going beyond this principle in being merciful and to turn the other cheek: "Ye have heard that it hath been said, An eye for an eye, and a tooth for a tooth: But I say unto you, That ye resist not

evil: but whosoever shall smite thee on thy right cheek, turn to him the other also."

The contemporary versions have "An eye for an eye" (CEV, NASB, NCV, NKJV, NRSV, RSV), "Eye for eye" (NIV) and, "If an eye is injured, injure the eye of the person who did it" (NLT).

EYE HATH NOT SEEN

The expression "eye hath not seen" is used to refer to something that is inconceivable to human sight. In the context that Paul writes in 1 Corinthians 2:9, it means the human means of eye, ear, and mind cannot conceive of the wonderful things that God has prepared for those who love him.

The contemporary versions render this KJV expression as "no eye has seen" (NIV, NLT, NRSV, RSV); "eye has not seen" (NASB, NKJV); "no one has ever seen" (NCV); and "more than eyes have seen" (CEV). The quotation in 1 Corinthians 2:9 is based on Isaiah 64:4.

F

FABLE

Parents are well-trained at recognizing "fables" from their children. When we hear the word today, we usually take it to mean "a story or statement which isn't true," but its primary meaning is "a short story devised to convey some special lesson, esp. one in which animals or inanimate things are the speakers or actors" (OED); thus, for example, the fable of the tortoise and the hare.

In the KJV the word appears five times as translation for the Greek *mythos*. Since the word "myth" did not enter the English language until the early nineteenth century, "fable" long carried its meaning. But the favor with which the word "myth" was received and its quick establishment in English usage have tended to restrict the word "fable" to stories more or less akin to the fables of Aesop.

The word *mythos* in the Greek New Testament is now generally translated as "myth,"

which is defined by the OED as "a purely fictitious narrative usually involving supernatural persons, actions, or events, and embodying some popular idea concerning natural or historical phenomena."

Paul instructs Timothy to "refuse profane and old wives' fables" and to warn certain persons not to "give heed to fables and endless genealogies" (1 Timothy 4:7; 1:4, KJV). The contemporary versions translate these as "profane [NIV, "godless"] myths and old wives' tales" (1 Timothy 4:7, NIV, NRSV), and "myths" (1 Timothy 1:4, NASB, NIV, NRSV, NLT, RSV; the NCV has "stories that are not true").

Paul takes a realistic view of human nature, and says that "the time will come when they will not endure sound doctrine; but after their own lusts shall heap to themselves teachers, having itching ears; and they shall turn away their ears from the truth, and shall be turned unto fables" (2 Timothy 4:3–4, KJV). In the letter to Titus, he warns against those "of the circumcision" (1:10, KJV) with their "Jewish fables" (1:14, KJV; the NASB, NIV, NLT, NRSV, RSV read, "Jewish myths").

Peter, in his second letter, declares: "we have not followed cunningly devised fables, when we made known unto you the power and coming of our Lord Jesus Christ, but were eyewitnesses of his majesty" (1:16, KJV). Contemporary versions render "cunningly devised fables" (KJV) as "cleverly devised tales" (NASB), "cleverly invented stories" (NIV), and "cleverly devised myths" (NRSV, RSV).

FAIN

As an adverb, the word "fain" means "gladly." "He would fain have filled his belly with the husks that the swine did eat" (Luke 15:16, KJV) is now translated by the NASB as "he would have gladly filled his stomach with the pods that the swine were eating." (For "pods," see HUSKS.)

The only other occurrence of "fain" in the KJV is in Job 27:22, where "would fain flee" is an attempt, which began with the Geneva Bible, to translate the intensified force of the Hebrew idiom which combines the absolute infinitive and the finite form of the verb for "flee." This is represented in the NRSV by "flees in headlong flight," and in the NIV by "flees headlong."

The three verses, 21–23, are worth comparing in the various versions. "East wind" is the subject of verse 21, and the contemporary versions (including the NKJV) take it as the subject of all three verses. The KJV, on the other hand, inserts "God" as the subject of verse 22, and "Men" as the subject of verse 23. (See GENERALLY and SURELY for explanation of the Hebrew idiom.)

FAINT

To faint is to "temporarily fall into unconsciousness," but we also use the word to mean "to feel, or to look, weak or unsteady." In the KJV it means "to grow weak," whether in body or in spirit. To lose courage is the basic idea. The word refers to

the fainthearted and dispirited more often than to the feeble or exhausted. Shakespeare used it thus in *King Richard II* (II, 1, 297):

> "But if you faint, as fearing to do so,
> Stay and be secret, and myself will go."

The contemporary versions retain "faint" in many of its occurrences in this sense, but replace it in some. Luke 18:1, "ought always to pray and not to faint" (KJV), now reads "at all times . . . ought to pray and not to lose heart" (NASB); "to faint" (KJV) is here also translated as "lose hope" (NCV), and "give up" (NIV). Second Corinthians 4:1, 16, "we faint not" (KJV), similarly reads, "we do not lose heart" (NASB, NIV, NRSV, RSV) and "we never give up" (CEV, NLT).

Hebrews 12:5 reads, in the KJV: "And ye have forgotten the exhortation which speaketh unto you as unto children, My son, despise not thou the chastening of the Lord, nor faint when thou art rebuked of him." The NASB retains "nor faint" in its rendering of this verse, while the other contemporary versions have "don't stop trying" (NCV), "don't be discouraged" (CEV, NLT), and "do not lose heart" (NIV). See also Galatians 6:9 and Ephesians 3:13.

In the KJV Old Testament, "lest his brethren's heart faint" (Deuteronomy 20:8) is now rendered "so that he might not make his brothers' hearts melt" (NASB); "the inhabitants of the land faint because of you" (Joshua 2:9, KJV) is rendered "all who live in this country are melting in fear because of you" (NIV); "they are fainthearted" (Jeremiah 49:23, KJV) is now "They are disheartened" (NIV, NASB) and "they melt in fear" (NRSV, RSV).

In Ezekiel 21:15 God speaks against his people and their rulers: "I have set the point of the sword against all their gates, that their heart may faint" (KJV). Contemporary versions use the word "melt" for the KJV's rendering, "faint." The CEV paraphrases as "They will lose all courage and stumble with fear. My slaughtering sword is waiting at every gate." The Hebrew also expresses bodily weakness or fatigue in Genesis 25:29–30 (NASB, NRSV, "I am famished"); 1 Samuel 30:10, 21 (NASB, NIV, NRSV, RSV, "exhausted"); 2 Samuel 21:15 (NRSV, RSV, "David grew weary"); and Jeremiah 45:3 (NASB, NRSV, RSV "I am weary"). The KJV's rendering, "Therefore shall all hands be faint" (Isaiah 13:7) is now translated, "Therefore all hands will be feeble" [NASB, "will fall limp"] (NASB, NRSV, RSV).

"Faint" does not occur in the sense of "swoon," unless Isaiah 51:20, Jonah 4:8, and Daniel 8:27 are to be so construed. The context in Isaiah 51:17–23 does not support this construction, however; and the NRSV and NASB read, "so that he was [NASB, "he became"] faint" in the description of Jonah's plight, and "was overcome" (NRSV; NASB, "was exhausted") in the account of Daniel's vision.

In Job 4:5 Eliphaz says to Job, "But now it is come upon thee, and thou faintest" (KJV). The contemporary versions render "faintest" (KJV) here as "discouraged" (CEV), "impatient" (NASB, NRSV, RSV), and "weary" (NKJV). Isaiah 10:18, "they shall be as when a standardbearer fainteth" (KJV), is now "it will be as when an invalid wastes away" (NRSV).

David's words in Psalm 27:13, "I had fainted, unless I had believed to see the goodness of the LORD in the land of the living" (KJV), is now rendered, "I believe that I shall see the goodness of the LORD in the land of the living" (NRSV). The NASB rendering is closer to that of the KJV: "I would have despaired unless I had believed that I would see the goodness of the LORD In the land of the living."

In the KJV New Testament, the reason given for Jesus' compassion on the multitudes is that "they fainted, and were scattered abroad" (Matthew 9:36). It appears that in the eighth century an error was made in copying the manuscript of the Greek text and the NRSV, RSV, and NIV use the word "harassed" to translate the Greek

word in the ancient manuscripts, which had been miscopied. "Helpless" (CEV, NCV, NIV, NRSV, RSV) translates a Greek participle which means literally "lying down." The NRSV reads, "When he saw the crowds, he had compassion for them, because they were harassed and helpless, like sheep without a shepherd."

FALL, THE

"The fall" is the term used to describe the first sin—when Adam and Eve disobeyed God—and its consequences, described in Genesis 3. Adam and Eve abused their God-given freedom and disobeyed God's command not to eat the fruit of the tree of the knowledge of good and evil. As the result of that sin, death entered the world and the world suffers the pain of God's curse.

The term "the fall" does not in fact appear in the Bible text itself, although it does occur as "Man's fall and punishment" in the heading at the top of the page in certain editions of the KJV. The contemporary versions render this phrase in the following ways and put the heading before Genesis 3: "The Fall of Man" (NASB, NIV); "The Temptation and Fall of Man" (NKJV); "The Beginning of Sin" (NCV); "The First Sin" (CEV); "The First Sin and its Punishment" (NRSV); and "The Man and Woman Sin" (NLT). (See also FORBIDDEN FRUIT)

FALL AMONG THIEVES

In the parable of the good Samaritan, Jesus spoke of a man who "went down from Jerusalem to Jericho, and fell among thieves, which stripped him of his raiment, and wounded him, and departed, leaving him half dead" (Luke 10:30, KJV).

The phrasal verb "fell among" is rendered "fell into the hands of" by the NIV and NRSV; the NASB, NKJV, and RSV retain the KJV "fell among"; the CEV, NCV, and NLT change the structure of the sentence to "robbers attacked him" (CEV, NCV) and "he was attacked by bandits" (NLT).

FALL BY THE WAYSIDE; FALL ON STONY GROUND

The expressions "fall by the wayside" and "fall on stony ground" come from the parable of the sower and the seed. To "fall by the wayside" is to give up or to fail in an activity; to fail to make progress. If something "falls on stony ground," it is not received or listened to.

The original expressions are: "And when he sowed, some seeds fell by the way side, and the fowls came and devoured them up" (Matthew 13:4, KJV); "And some fell on stony ground, where it had not much earth; and immediately it sprang up, because it had no depth of earth" (Mark 4:5, KJV).

The contemporary versions render these as follows:

Matthew 13:4: "fell by the wayside" (NKJV); "fell along the path" (NIV); "fell on the path" (NRSV); "fell on a footpath" (NLT); "fell along the road" (CEV); "fell beside the road" (NASB); and "fell by the road" (NCV).

Mark 4:5: "fell on the rocky ground" (NASB, NCV, NRSV, RSV); "fell on rocky places" (NIV); "fell on thin, rocky ground" (CEV); the NKJV retains the KJV "fell on stony ground" and the NLT paraphrases the whole sentence as "Other seed fell on shallow soil with underlying rock."

FALL FROM GRACE

To "fall from grace" is to lose one's privileged or favored position. The origin of this expression is Galatians 5:4 (KJV): "Christ is become of no effect upon you, whosoever of you are justified by the law; ye are fallen from grace." The Galatians were trying to put themselves in a right relationship with God by relying on their own efforts to keep the law. They were therefore falling away from receiving God's favor only by grace, and so were rejecting Christ. The expression "fallen from grace" is retained by the NASB and NKJV, and rendered as "fallen away from [NLT, "from God's"] grace" by the NIV, NLT, NRSV, and RSV.

FAME

"Fame" is likely to make us think of the glitter and media attention which surrounds successful individuals, spreading their reputations across the continents. The word's primary meaning, however, is "what people say," "current talk, "a report, rumor, or item of news, whether good or bad," although it is now rarely used in this sense. The KJV uses "fame" twenty-four times, both in the sense of "renown" and in the older, primary sense.

In Genesis 45:16, the KJV reads, "the fame thereof was heard in Pharaoh's house, saying, Joseph's brethren are come"; "the fame" here is rendered as "the news" (NASB, NIV, NLT) and "the report" (NKJV, NRSV, RSV) in contemporary versions. (See also Jeremiah 6:24.)

When the Queen of Sheba has had the opportunity to marvel at Solomon's achievements, she admits to him that "thy wisdom and prosperity exceedeth the fame which I heard" (1 Kings 10:7 and its parallel, 2 Chronicles 9:6, KJV); the NASB, NIV, NRSV, and RSV use the word "report" for "fame" (KJV) here.

With respect to Jesus, the contemporary versions use "fame," "news," or "report" in Matthew 4:24; 9:26, 31; 14:1; Mark 1:28; and Luke 4:14, 37; 5:15.

In the Hymn to Wisdom which constitutes Job 28, verse 22 in the NRSV has "Abaddon and Death say, 'We have heard a rumor of it [KJV, "heard the fame thereof"] with our ears.'" The NASB renders their words as "'With our ears we have heard a report of it.'"

Examples of Shakespeare's use of "fame" in the older sense are:

"Shame hath a bastard fame, well
    managed;
Ill deeds is doubled with an evil word."
    —*The Comedy of Errors* (III, 2, 19–20)

"So is the fame."
    —*Antony and Cleopatra* (II, 2, 166)

"When fame had spread their cursed
  deed."

—*Pericles* (V, 2, 95)

FAMILIAR SPIRIT

A "familiar spirit" is a spirit or demon
believed to be in communication with a
necromancer and responsive, as a servant
(from the Latin, *famulus*), to his call. Those
who "have familiar spirits" are often referred to in the KJV Old Testament, nearly
always in connection with "wizards." The
Mosaic Law required that both be put to
death (Leviticus 20:27).

The NRSV and RSV retain the word "wizard," but for those who have familiar spirits use the term "medium." This was one
of the newest words to appear in the RSV,
for the earliest citation of it in this sense in
the OED is dated 1853, and is concerned
with the "spirit-rappings" which excited
public interest in the middle of the nineteenth century.

Other contemporary versions use the
word "medium" for those who have familiar spirits, and "spiritist" (NASB, NIV), "for-
tune-teller" (NCV), or "psychic" (NLT) for the
term translated "wizard" by the KJV in Leviticus.

FAMILIARS

This word is now obsolete. It occurs in
the KJV, in Jeremiah 20:10, where the prophet
complains, "All my familiars watched for
my halting, saying, Peradventure he will be
enticed, and we shall prevail against him."
The Hebrew expression means literally
"men of my peace," and occurs also in
Psalm 41:9, Jeremiah 38:22, and Obadiah 7.

In Jeremiah 20:10 the contemporary versions read "my so-called friends" (CEV),
"my trusted friends" (NASB), "my old friends"
(NLT), "my close friends" (NRSV), and "my
familiar friends" (RSV). In Psalm 41:9 David's complaint is that his own "familiar
friend" (KJV) has betrayed him; the NLT has
"my best friend, the one I trusted completely." In Obadiah 7, "the men that were
at peace with thee" (KJV) is now rendered
as "your best friends" (CEV) and "your
trusted friends" (RSV, NLT).

FAN, FANNER

A fan is an indispensable item in many
homes, even with the advent of modern air
conditioning. Fans are built into a host of
modern inventions, from fan-assisted ovens
and microwaves to photocopying machines
and motors. In an agricultural context, the
word is also used of "revolving blades which
supply air for winnowing or cleaning grain,"
and this meaning brings us a little closer to
the KJV usage.

The metaphor of the wheat and the chaff
occurs a number of times in the Bible, most
notably in the words of John the Baptist:
"He that cometh after me is mightier than
I, whose shoes I am not worthy to bear: he
shall baptize you with the Holy Ghost, and
with fire: Whose fan is in his hand, and he
will thoroughly purge his floor, and gather
his wheat into the garner; but he will burn
up the chaff with unquenchable fire" (Matthew 3:11–12, KJV).

The NASB translates verse 12 as "His winnowing fork is in His hand, and He will
thoroughly clear His threshing floor; and
He will gather His wheat into the barn, but
He will burn the chaff with unquenchable
fire."

"Fan" appears six times and "fanners"
once in the KJV Old Testament. The contemporary versions generally use the terms
"winnow," "winnowing fork," and "win-
nowers" (Isaiah 30:24; 41:16; Jeremiah 4:11;
15:7; 51:2). The winnowing fan was a six-
pronged wooden fork or a perforated
wooden shovel used to toss the grain in the
air so the wind could blow the lighter chaff
away.

Shakespeare wrote in *Cymbeline* (I, 6, 177):

"The love I bear him
Made me to fan you thus;
  but the gods made you,
Unlike all others, chaffless."

FASHION

The word "fashion" is likely to turn our thoughts to the shopping malls and boutiques which reflect the latest vogues in clothing and design. When the KJV uses the word, however, it has the meaning of "pattern" or "plan." "Rear up the tabernacle according to the fashion thereof" (Exodus 26:30, KJV), is now rendered as "erect the tabernacle according to the plan for it" (NRSV).

In 1 Kings 6:38 we read how Solomon's temple was finished "according to all the fashion of it" (KJV). contemporary versions translate this as "according to all its specifications" [NASB, NKJV, "plans"] (NASB, NKJV, NRSV, RSV). King Ahaz, seeing at Damascus an altar that took his fancy, sent to Urijah the priest "the fashion of the altar, and the pattern of it, according to all the workmanship thereof" (2 Kings 16:10, KJV).

Contemporary versions render this variously as "a model of the altar, and its pattern, exact in all its details" (NRSV, RSV), "the design of the altar and its pattern" (NKJV), and "a model . . . along with the plan for building one" (CEV). The word here rendered as "model" by the CEV, NLT, NRSV, and RSV represents a different Hebrew noun, which is usually translated "likeness."

In Ezekiel 43:11, "the fashion thereof" (KJV) is rendered as "its arrangement" by the NIV, NKJV, NRSV, RSV, translating yet another Hebrew noun.

In the New Testament, the majority of contemporary versions replace "fashion" (KJV) with "appearance" (Luke 9:29); "form" (1 Corinthians 7:31); and "pattern" (Acts 7:44). "The grace of the fashion of it" (James 1:11, KJV) is rendered by most of the contemporary versions as "its beauty"; "on this fashion" (Mark 2:12, KJV) is now "like this."

In the early Christological hymn of Philippians 2, verse 8 reads, in the KJV: "And being found in fashion as a man, he humbled himself, and became obedient unto death, even the death of the cross." The NLT, RSV, and NRSV render the Greek, translated "in fashion as a man" by the KJV, as "in human form," while the NASB, NIV, and NKJV use the words "in appearance as a man."

Dr. William Aldis Wright, in *The Bible Word-Book* (1884), said, "The verb is now rarely used." If that was so, the revisers sixty years later were not aware of it, for they treated the verb "to fashion" as still living English, retaining it in most of the cases where it was used in the KJV.

The outstanding examples of change are 1 Peter 1:14, where "not fashioning yourselves according to the former lusts in your ignorance" (KJV) reads, in the RSV, "do not be conformed to the passions of your former ignorance"; and Philippians 3:21, where "be fashioned like unto" (KJV) is "be like" (RSV).

Contemporary versions render the text from 1 Peter 1:14 as "Don't let your lives be controlled by your desires" (CEV); "do not conform to the evil desires you had when you lived in ignorance" (NIV); and "Don't slip back into your old ways of doing evil" (NLT).

FAST

The word "fast" might make us think of high-speed trains, the periods of life in the fast lane, and the speed of the humble pressure cooker. Our thoughts might also turn to color-fast fabrics, or a fast friendship—by which we would mean, not a quickly-formed attachment, but a deep and permanent one. Another way in which we use the word is in the sense of firmly and securely ("hold it fast or it will slip"), and this usage is also found in the KJV.

For example, in Galatians 5:1 we read, in the KJV, "Stand fast therefore in the liberty wherewith Christ hath made us free" (NRSV, NIV, "Stand firm"; CEV, "hold on"), and in Revelation 3:11 (KJV) Christ admonishes the Philadelphian church to "hold that fast which thou hast, that no man take thy crown" (NASB, NRSV, "hold fast"; NIV, NLT, "Hold on").

However, in the narrative in Ruth 2, the KJV uses the word "fast" to mean "close" or "near." In verse 8, Boaz invites Ruth to "abide here fast by my maidens" (KJV) while she gleans in his field; so she "kept fast by the maidens of Boaz to glean unto the end of barley harvest and of wheat harvest; and dwelt with her mother in law" (v. 23, KJV). This is an archaic meaning of the word, carried on occasionally in such poetic forms as "fast by."

In *Paradise Lost* (II, 725), Milton refers to "the snaky Sorceress that sat fast by Hellgate." Keats' *Lamia* (17) reads, "Fast by the springs . . . were strewn rich gifts." In Ruth the majority of the contemporary versions use "close to" or "close by."

FAT *(adjective)*

When a recipe tells us to "add the fat" we reach for the lard, oil, or butter, but with the drive toward healthy eating fat is becoming a less than popular ingredient. Similarly, the adjective "fat," with its meaning of "plump," "fleshy," or "overweight," is a word with a bad press.

Not so in the KJV Old Testament; the expression "to wax fat" (KJV) occurs in Deuteronomy 31:20, where Israel is promised wealth and abundance as it enters a land "that floweth with milk and honey." The NRSV renders "wax fat" (KJV) in this verse as "grown fat"; the NASB has "become prosperous."

In Isaiah 6:10 "fat" occurs in a different context. The prophet is instructed to "Make the heart of this people fat, and make their ears heavy." (KJV). The NRSV translates this as "Make the mind of this people dull, and stop their ears." The entire verse reads, in the NASB:

" 'Render the hearts of this people
    insensitive,
Their ears dull,
And their eyes dim,
Otherwise they might see with their
    eyes,

Hear with their ears,
Understand with their hearts,
And return and be healed.' "

In verses 12–15 of Psalm 92, the righteous are compared to trees: in place of the KJV "fat and flourishing" (v. 14) the contemporary versions have "full of sap and very green" (NASB), "healthy and fresh" (NCV), and "fresh and flourishing" (NKJV).

Similarly, in Proverbs 11:25 the KJV reads, "The liberal soul shall be made fat"; contemporary versions have, "A generous person will be enriched" (NRSV), and "The generous man will be prosperous" (NASB). "Fat and flourishing" (KJV) is a phrase that comes to the tongue as readily as "fat and sleek" in Horace's *Epistles* (I, 1, 15), and "fat and greasy" in Shakespeare's *As You Like It* (II, 1, 55).

FAT *(noun)*

Fat also appears in an obsolete sense in the KJV, which uses "fats" where the contemporary versions use "vats" (NASB, NIV, NKJV, NRSV, RSV), "barrels" (NCV), "presses" (NLT), and "jars" (CEV) in Joel 2:24 (see also 3:13). "Winefat" (KJV) is translated "wine press" by the NASB, NIV ["winepress"], NRSV, and RSV in Isaiah 63:2 and Mark 12:1. The NKJV has "winepress" in Isaiah 63:2, but "wine vat" in Mark 12:1. Both "fat" and "vat" are old words, but "fat" is the original and "vat" the variant. The song to Bacchus in Shakespeare's *Antony and Cleopatra* (II, 7, 120) contains the lines:

"In thy fats our cares be drown'd,
With thy grapes our hairs be
    crown'd:
Cup us, till the world go round!"

The OED quotes from Bishop Gervase Babington's *Exposition of the Commandments* (1583): "They would have every fatte . . . stand on his owne bottome," and from Bunyan's *Pilgrim's Progress* (1678): "Every Fatt must stand on his own bottom."

FAT OF THE LAND

One of the meanings of fat nowadays is the richest or best part of anything: the expression "the fat of the land" has passed into living English from the KJV rendering of God's promises to Joseph's brothers in Genesis 45:18, "I will give you the good of the land of Egypt, and ye shall eat the fat of the land."

All the contemporary versions, except the CEV and NCV, retain the KJV expression "the fat of the land"; the CEV renders the whole phrase as "they can eat and enjoy everything that grows on it" and the NCV as "they will eat the best food we have here." Today we say that if someone is living off the "fat of the land," that person is enjoying a very luxurious lifestyle, especially without having to work hard for it. Elsewhere, the KJV renders the Hebrew word meaning "fat," as "best" (e.g., Numbers 18:29–30: "the best thereof").

FAT YEARS AND LEAN YEARS

The phrase "the fat years and the lean years" refers to contrasting times of wealth and hardship in the history of a country or in a person's life or business. The origin of the expression is Pharaoh's dream of seven lean cows eating up seven fat cows (Genesis 41:3–4). Seven years of plenty would be followed by seven years of famine (Genesis 41:26–32).

The contemporary versions retain the KJV "fat" (Genesis 41:4, 20) and render the KJV "lean" (Genesis 41:4, 20) as "thin" (NCV, NLT, NRSV), "skinny" (CEV), and "gaunt" (NKJV); the NASB and NIV retain the KJV "lean" at verse 20 and translate as "gaunt" in verse 4.

FATHER, FORGIVE THEM, FOR THEY KNOW NOT WHAT THEY DO

See KNOW NOT WHAT THEY DO.

FATHERS HAVE EATEN A SOUR GRAPE

See TEETH SET ON EDGE.

FEAR AND TREMBLING

If you go to someone "in fear and trembling," you approach that person in a frightened and anxious manner ("The children waited outside the principal's office in fear and trembling"). The origin of the expression is Philippians 2:12 (KJV), "Wherefore, my beloved, as ye have always obeyed, not as in my presence only, but now much more in my absence, work out your own salvation with fear and trembling." Believers are to express their salvation in their ongoing lives with awe, single-minded humility, and reverence.

All the contemporary versions except the NLT retain the KJV "with fear and trembling"; the NLT has "with deep reverence and fear."

FEEBLEMINDED

The word "feebleminded" is used mostly today in a derogatory sense, to mean "ignorant," "mentally slow," or "ill-thought-out" ("a feebleminded attempt to fool the examiners"). In the KJV, however, it has the meaning of "fainthearted," or "discouraged," and appears in the context of Paul's advice to the young church at Thessalonica: "comfort the feebleminded, support the weak, be patient toward all *men*." (1 Thessalonians 5:14, KJV).

Contemporary versions render "comfort the feebleminded" in this verse as "Encourage anyone who feels left out" (CEV), "encourage the timid" (NIV), and "encourage the fainthearted" (NASB, NRSV, RSV).

FEET OF CLAY

Someone who is greatly respected is said to have "feet of clay" when he or she has a fundamental, usually hidden, weakness. The expression comes from Daniel 2:33, where the statue seen in Nebuchadnezzar's dream is described: it had a head made of gold, a chest and arms of silver, a belly and thighs of bronze, legs of iron, and feet of iron and clay. The feet, according to Daniel's explanation, were struck by a stone which broke them to pieces and so smashed the rest of the statue. So to have "feet of clay" means to have a vulnerable or weak point that can be a person's undoing.

The KJV for Daniel 2:33 reads, "His legs of iron, his feet part of iron and part of clay;" the contemporary versions render "his feet part of iron and part of clay" as "its feet partly of iron and partly of [NIV, "of baked"] clay" (NASB, NIV, NKJV, NRSV, RSV) and "its feet were a mixture [NLT, "a combination"] of iron and clay" (CEV, NLT).

FENCED

This word is likely to remind us of enclosures of one sort or another. "Fenced" comes from the word "defence" and is often used in the Old Testament, chiefly in the phrase "fenced cities" (KJV). Contemporary versions generally have "fortified cities." "He fenced it, and gathered out the stones thereof" (Isaiah 5:2, KJV) reads, in the NASB, "He dug it all around, removed its stones"; the majority of contemporary versions use the word "dug" or "digged" where the KJV here had "fenced."

In the KJV rendering of Job 10:11, Job muses, "Thou . . . hast fenced me with bones and sinews"; the contemporary versions use the words "Knit me" (NASB, NKJV, NRSV, RSV, NLT, "you knit my bones and sinews together"), and "sewed me" (NCV).

Later, Job complains, "He hath fenced up my way that I cannot pass, and he hath set darkness in my paths" (Job 19:8, KJV). The NKJV retains "fenced" here, but other versions use the words "walled" (NASB, NRSV, RSV) or "blocked" (NCV, NIV, NLT). The CEV reads, "God has me trapped with a wall of darkness."

In 2 Samuel 23:7, David compares the wicked to thorns: "the man that shall touch them must be fenced with iron and the staff of a spear; and they shall be utterly burned with fire in the same place" (KJV). The NRSV reads, "to touch them one uses an iron bar or the shaft of a spear"; the NASB, "the man who touches them must be armed with iron."

FERVENT

The word "fervent" might make us think of glowing coals on an open fire, and the burning heat they produce. In this physical sense, "fervent" means "boiling," "glowing," "burning." It occurs in this literal sense in one passage of the KJV, where it is twice said that "the elements shall melt with fervent heat" (2 Peter 3:10, 12). The NRSV and RSV have "with fire"; the NIV, "by fire"; the NASB, "with intense heat."

The word is more often used with reference to the passions, aspirations, or actions of persons. It then means "ardent," "glowing," "intensely earnest." In 1 Peter 1:22 and 4:8 the Greek words carry the idea of constancy and earnestness, rather than hot ardor. In the first of these verses we read in the KJV: "see that ye love one another with a pure heart fervently." The NRSV and RSV read, "love one another deeply [RSV, "earnestly"] from the heart."

The KJV rendering of 1 Peter 4:8 is, "And above all things have fervent charity among yourselves: for charity shall cover the multitude of sins." The NASB translates, "Above all keep fervent in your love for one another, because love covers a multitude of sins"; the NRSV reads, "maintain constant love for one another."

In three other passages the Greek words carry the idea of glowing zeal.

For "your fervent mind toward me" (2 Corinthians 7:7, KJV), the contemporary versions have "your zeal for me" (NASB, NKJV, NRSV, RSV), "your great care for me" (NCV), and "your ardent concern for me" (NIV).

Apollos is described by the KJV as "fervent in the spirit" and by the NASB, NKJV, and RSV as "fervent in spirit" (Acts 18:25). The NRSV says that "he spoke with burning enthusiasm."

Paul enjoins the Christians at Rome, according to the KJV, to be "not slothful in business; fervent in spirit; serving the Lord" (Romans 12:11). Many of the contemporary versions take the participles as imperatives; the NIV translates as "Never be lacking in zeal, but keep your spiritual fervor, serving the Lord." The RSV and CEV translate the Greek here as applying to the Spirit of God (RSV, "be aglow with the Spirit"; CEV, "eagerly follow the Holy Spirit"), while other contemporary versions use expressions which refer to the human spirit: "serving the Lord with all your heart" (NCV); "be ardent in spirit" (NRSV); "serve the Lord enthusiastically" (NLT).

Paul's message to the Colossians that Epaphras was "always labouring fervently for you in prayers" (Colossians 4:12, KJV) is now translated as "always wrestling in prayer for you" (NIV), and "always remembering you earnestly in his prayers" (RSV). "The effectual fervent prayer of a righteous man availeth much" (James 5:16, KJV) is now "The effective prayer of a righteous man can accomplish much" (NASB).

FETCH A COMPASS

This phrase appears five times in the KJV, and means "to turn," "to take a roundabout course," "to make a circuit." The invention and wide use of the magnetic compass have caused the phrase to become ambiguous and fall into disuse. The contemporary versions of the Bible use other renderings.

In the description of boundaries, contemporary versions use the verb "turn" in Numbers 34:5, and in Joshua 15:3 "turns [NASB, "turned"] about" (NASB, RSV), "curved around" (NIV), "went around" (NKJV) and "turned toward" (CEV, NLT). "Fetch a compass behind them" (2 Samuel 5:23, KJV) is rendered "go around to their rear" in the NRSV and "circle around behind them" in the NASB.

In 2 Kings 3:9 the kings of Israel, Judah, and Edom joined forces against the king of Moab and "fetched a compass of seven days' journey" (KJV); the NRSV says they "made a roundabout march of seven days" through the wilderness of Edom.

After Paul's shipwreck, he and his guards and companions spent three months on the island of Malta, and then sailed to Syracuse, where they stayed for three days. "From thence we fetched a compass, and came to Rhegium," according to the KJV (Acts 28:13). The RSV has "from there we made a circuit and arrived at Rhegium"; the NKJV reads, "From there we circled round and reached Rhegium"; and the NASB has "From there we sailed around." The other contemporary versions do not translate the expression.

FETCH ABOUT

This word is reminiscent of dog training. In fact, it is an obsolete expression, according to the OED and Webster, for "contrive" or "devise." In some parts of America it is used colloquially, however, with the same meaning as "bring about," that is, "effect" or "accomplish." Just what sense the KJV translators attached to it in 2 Samuel 14:20 is not clear. The KJV rendering is, "To fetch about this form of speech hath thy servant Joab done this thing."

The revised versions of 1885 and 1901 give the translation, "to change the face of the matter." The NRSV and RSV read, "In order to change the course of affairs your servant Joab did this"; the NASB has "in order to change the appearance of things your servant Joab has done this thing."

Other renderings of the expression are "Your servant Joab did this to change the present situation" (NIV), and "He did it to place the matter before you in a different light" (NLT).

FIGHT THE GOOD FIGHT

The expression "fight the good fight" means to act with firm dedication, courage, etc., in the struggle to pursue a goal. The phrase derives from 1 Timothy 6:12: "Fight the good fight of faith, lay hold on eternal life, whereunto thou art also called, and hast professed a good profession before many witnesses."

Of the contemporary versions, the NASB, NCV, and NKJV retain the KJV wording; the NIV, NRSV, and RSV have "Fight the good fight of the faith"; the CEV has "Fight a good fight for the faith" and the NLT, "Fight the good fight for what we believe."

FILE

Today a file is a folder in which documents and other papers are kept in order or, in the language of computers, a set of data with its own name. A file may also refer to a line of people and to a tool used to smooth or sharpen a surface; all of these are historically different words.

In the KJV the word occurs once, at 1 Samuel 13:21. Verses 20 to 21 read: "But all the Israelites went down to the Philistines, to sharpen every man his share, and his coulter, and his axe, and his mattock. Yet they had a file for the mattocks, and for the coulters, and for the forks, and for the axes, and to sharpen the goads."

The word "file" is the Hebrew, *petsirah pim*. Inscribed weights from ancient times indicate that the expression *petsirah pim* refers to a charge based on a "pim" (NKJV, RSV), a unit of weight of about eight grams and equal to two-thirds of a shekel (NASB, NIV, RSV).

FILTHY LUCRE

See LUCRE.

FINE (adjective)

As an adjective, "fine" is used one hundred times in the KJV, always in the sense of "finished," "pure," "of superior quality." We read in it of "fine flour," "fine meal," "fine linen," "fine gold," "fine copper," "fine brass." These expressions are mostly retained by the contemporary versions, ex-cept for "fine brass," which is rendered "burnished bronze" by the NASB, NRSV, and RSV (Revelation 1:15; 2:18); the NCV has "shining bronze"; the NLT, "polished bronze"; the CEV has simply "bronze."

FINE (verb)

As a verb, "fine" is used in the KJV only in the sense of "to make fine or pure," "to refine." "Surely there is a vein for the silver, and a place for gold where they fine it" (Job 28:1, KJV) reads in the NRSV, "Surely there is a mine for silver, and a place for gold to be refined."

"Take away the dross from the silver, and there shall come forth a vessel for the finer" (Proverbs 25:4, KJV) is now rendered, "And there comes out a vessel for the smith" (NASB). The "fining pot" in the KJV is a "crucible" (NIV, NRSV, RSV) or "hot furnace" (NCV) in which silver is refined (Proverbs 17:3; 27:21).

FIRE AND BRIMSTONE

The expression "fire and brimstone" refers to God's extreme judgment on sin. The expressions "fire and brimstone" and "brimstone and fire" occur several times in the KJV, first of all in the punishment sent on Sodom and Gomorrah: "Then the LORD rained upon Sodom and upon Gomorrah brimstone and fire from the LORD out of heaven"; here the contemporary versions render "brimstone and fire" as "burning sulfur" (CEV, NCV, NIV), "sulfur and fire" (NRSV), and "fire and burning sulfur" (NLT); the NASB, NKJV, and RSV retain the KJV expression.

The other references to the expression "fire and brimstone" include Luke 17:29 with reference to the destruction of Sodom and Gomorrah and Revelation, e.g., 20:10: "And the devil that deceived them was cast into the lake of fire and brimstone, where the beast and the false prophet are, and shall be tormented day and night for ever and ever." Here, the contemporary versions render "fire and brimstone" as "burning sulfur" (NCV, NIV), "fire and sulfur" (NRSV), "fire and burning sulfur" (CEV), and "fire that burns with sulfur" (NLT); the NASB and NKJV retain the KJV expression.

In Bunyan's *Pilgrim's Progress,* Christian tells Obstinate and Pliable, who try to deter him from his journey, "you dwell in the City of Destruction, the place also where I was born . . . and dying there, sooner or later, you will sink lower than the grave, into a place that burns with Fire and Brimstone."

In modern usage, a "fire-and-brimstone preacher" is one who emphasizes the torments of hell. (See also SODOM AND GOMORRAH)

FLAG

We are familiar with the flag in the sense of a rectangular piece of fabric bearing the distinctive design of a particular country. In the KJV, however, the word "flag" is an historically different word to denote "a plant." The word "flag" occurs four times in the KJV, at Exodus 2:3, 5; Job 8:11; and Isaiah 19:6.

In the passages in Exodus and Isaiah the word denotes "a reed," "evidently specifically applied to the moisture-loving cattail or reed-mace (*Typha angustata*) still common around the Nile" (*Illustrated Bible Dictionary*). It was in the "flags" (Exodus 2:3, KJV) that the baby Moses was placed in a basket; the contemporary versions render this as "reeds" (NASB, NIV, NKJV, NLT, NRSV, RSV), "tall grass" (CEV), and "tall stalks of grass" (NCV), with the same renderings in the contemporary versions at verse 5, except the NCV which has "tall grass."

At Isaiah 19:6 the KJV "reeds and flags" is rendered by the NASB, NIV, NKJV, NLT, NRSV, and RSV as "reeds and rushes"; the CEV has "reeds and tall grass"; the NCV "all the water plants."

At Job 8:11, the word denotes reed, "a general word for water-loving plants found in swamps and by river-banks" (*Illustrated Bible Dictionary*). It occurs in a rhetorical question posed by Bildad: "Can the rush grow up without mire? can the flag grow without water?" (KJV). The contemporary versions render the KJV "flag" as "reeds" (NCV, NIV, NKJV, NRSV, RSV); "rushes" (NASB); and "bulrushes" (NLT).

Shakespeare used the word "flag" in this sense:

> "This common body,
> Like to a vagabond flag upon the
>   stream,
> Goes to and back, lackeying the
>   varying tide,
> To rot itself with motion."
> —*Antony and Cleopatra* (I, 4, 45)

FLAGON

The phrase "Stay me with flagons, comfort me with apples: for I am sick of love," if taken out of context, seems to be the cry of a disillusioned lover who is seeking solace in drink (Song of Solomon 2:5, KJV). But here, and in 5:8, the speaker is a young woman who is sick with love and longing for her beloved. As early as 1597, to be sick of something was beginning to mean to be "thoroughly tired and weary of it" (OED), and contemporary versions translate the expression as "lovesick" (NASB, NKJV, NLT), and "faint [NCV, "weak"] with love" (NCV, NIV, NRSV). The word represented by "flagon" is *'ashishah,* which means a pressed "cake of raisins" such as King David distributed to the people when he brought the ark of the Lord into the city (2 Samuel 6:19; 1 Chronicles 16:3), and such as were used in Canaanite sacrificial feasts (Hosea 3:1). In Song of Solomon 2:5, the NASB and NKJV read, "Sustain me with raisin cakes" [NKJV, "with cakes of raisins"]; other versions speak simply of "raisins" rather than of the cakes made with raisins.

FLANKS

The word "flanks" has military connotations today, but we also use the word to refer to the side of anything, such as a building, or a human or animal ("a slice of meat from the flank"). In the KJV it is used for the loins of a sacrificial animal (Leviticus 3:4, 10, 15; 4:9; 7:4); the contemporary versions generally render it as "loins," although the NCV refers to "the lower back muscle."

In Job 15:27 we read of the wicked that "he covereth his face with his fatness, and maketh collops of fat on his flanks" (KJV). In the NASB, we read that the wicked "made his thighs heavy with flesh"; in other versions it is the "belly" (NCV), "waist" (NIV, NKJV), or "loins" (NRSV, RSV) which have been fattened.

The Hebrew word which the KJV translates as "flanks" in Job 15:27 is the same as the one it renders as "loins" in Psalm 38:7: "my loins are filled with a loathsome disease: and there is no soundness in my flesh." "Loins" is retained by the NASB, NKJV, NRSV, and RSV, but the CEV and NIV use the word "back."

FLEE FROM THE WRATH TO COME
See WRATH TO COME.

FLESHPOTS OF EGYPT

The word "fleshpots" is often used in modern English to refer to luxurious or self-indulgent living ("regarded with regret or envy" as the OED notes) or to places of lewd entertainment.

The origin of the expression "the fleshpots of Egypt" is Exodus 16:3 (KJV): "And the children of Israel said unto them, Would to God we had died by the hand of the LORD in the land of Egypt, when we sat by the flesh pots, and when we did eat bread to the full; for ye have brought us forth into this wilderness, to kill this whole assembly with hunger."

Of the contemporary versions, the NRSV and RSV have "fleshpots"; the NASB, NIV, and NKJV have "pots of meat"; the CEV and NLT paraphrase the whole verse as: "We wish the LORD had killed us in Egypt. When we lived there, we could at least sit down and eat all the bread and meat we wanted. But

you have brought us out here into this desert, where we are going to starve" (CEV); "'Oh, that we were back in Egypt,' they moaned. 'It would have been better if the LORD had killed us there! At least there we had plenty to eat. But now you have brought us into this desert to starve us to death'" (NLT).

FLOOD

This word is likely to turn our thoughts to insurance claims and freakish weather patterns. It refers to the flowing in of the tide and to flowing rivers, as well as to "deluge," "overflow," and "inundation" ("a flood of mail").

The flood of Noah's time has a special name in Hebrew, *mabbul* (Genesis 6—11; Psalm 29:10), although on one occasion (Isaiah 54:9) it is referred to as "the waters of Noah" (KJV). Outside of these passages and the New Testament references to Noah, "flood" has in the KJV almost the variety of meanings recorded in the OED.

It is generally translated as "streams" (Psalm 78:44; Isaiah 44:3) and "rivers" (Psalms 24:2; 66:6) by contemporary versions. In Job 14:11, "The flood decayeth and drieth up" (KJV) is rendered as "a river wastes away and dries up" (NRSV). Occasionally it refers to a particular river, the Nile, the Euphrates, or the Jordan. "On the other side of the flood" (Joshua 24:2, KJV) is now rendered "beyond the River" by the NASB and NIV, and "beyond the Euphrates" by the NRSV and RSV.

"Thou didst cleave the fountain and the flood" (Psalm 74:15, KJV) reads in the NIV, "It was you who opened up springs and streams."

The hymn concerning wisdom in Job 28 is one of the great poems of the Bible. Verse 4 reads in the KJV: "The flood breaketh out from the inhabitant; even the waters forgotten of the foot: they are dried up, they are gone away from men." The NRSV has "They open shafts in a valley away from human habitation; they are forgotten by travelers, they sway suspended, remote from people." In verse 11, "He bindeth the floods from overflowing" (KJV) is rendered "He dams up the streams from flowing" by the NASB.

Shakespeare used "flood" in a full variety of meanings. Examples are:

"What need the bridge much
broader than the flood?"
—*Much Ado About Nothing*
(I, 1, 318)

"Three times did they drink,
Upon agreement, of swift
Severn's flood."
—*King Henry IV, Part I*
(I, 3, 103)

"Through flood, through fire,
I do wander every where."
—*A Midsummer Night's
Dream* (II, 1, 5)

FLOOR

The word "floor" in the sense of "the floor of a room or building" occurs only seven times in the KJV. It appears thirteen times, however, in the sense of "a threshing floor." The KJV renders the Hebrew word for "threshing floor," *goren*, as "threshing floor" nineteen times and "floor" eleven times.

We find a scattering of other renderings in the KJV: "barn" (Job 39:12); "barnfloor" (2 Kings 6:27); "corn" (Deuteronomy 16:13); "threshingplace" (2 Samuel 24:16); "void place" (1 Kings 22:10 and its parallel, 2 Chronicles 18:9). "Cornfloor" appears in Hosea 9:1, representing Hebrew which adds the word for "corn" to that for "floor."

The contemporary versions generally use "threshing floor" or "threshing place" for all of these cases. (For "floor" in Matthew 3:12 and Luke 3:17, see PURGE.)

FLOWERS

This word conjures up images of summer bouquets and floral meadows—depic-

tions of which are often featured in advertisements for feminine hygiene products. In fact, "flowers," derived from the Latin *fluor* ("a flowing") rather than from *flos, floris* ("a flower"), is an old term, now obsolete, for "menstrual discharges." It appears twice in the list of uncleannesses in Leviticus 15. The KJV renders the Hebrew *niddah* as "flowers" in verses 24 and 33, but as "separation" in verses 20, 25, and 26 of the same chapter as well as in 12:2, 5.

Contemporary versions use a variety of terms for *niddah* in these chapters. For example, at Leviticus 15:33 "her that is sick of her flowers" (KJV) is now "in her monthly period" (NIV), "during her monthly menstrual period" (NLT), "the woman who becomes unclean from her monthly period" (NCV), and "her who is in the infirmity of her period" (NRSV). The "bed of her separation" (KJV) in Leviticus 12:26 is now rendered "the bed of her impurity" (NRSV), and in Leviticus 12:2 "the days of the separation for her infirmity" (KJV) is rendered "at the time of her menstruation" (NRSV, RSV).

FLUX

Because of the contemporary expression, "a state of flux," "flux" is likely to make us think of change and the uncertainties it can create. The word's primary meaning is in fact "a flowing" or "flow." "Flux" was an early English name for "dysentery," and is used by the KJV in Acts 28:8 as translation for the Greek word *dysenteria* (KJV, "bloody flux"): "And it came to pass, that the father of Publius lay sick of a fever and of a bloody flux: to whom Paul entered in, and prayed, and laid his hands on him, and healed him."

The contemporary versions translate *dysenteria* as "dysentery," although the CEV renders it as "stomach trouble."

FLY IN THE OINTMENT

The expression "a fly in the ointment" is used to refer to a person or thing that spoils a situation which is perfect in every other way. The expression derives from Ecclesiastes 10:1 (KJV): "Dead flies cause the ointment of the apothecary to send forth a stinking savour: so doth a little folly him that is in reputation for wisdom and honour." As dead flies give even sweet-smelling perfume a bad odor, so a little folly spoils the virtues of wisdom and honor.

The contemporary versions render the first part of Ecclesiastes 10:1 as "dead flies give perfume a bad smell" (NIV), "Dead flies putrefy the perfumer's ointment" (NKJV), and "Dead flies make the perfumer's ointment give off a foul odor" (NRSV); the whole verse in the CEV is "A few dead flies in perfume make all of it stink, and a little foolishness outweighs a lot of wisdom"; and in the NLT, "Dead flies will cause even a bottle of perfume to stink! Yes, an ounce of foolishness can outweigh a pound of wisdom and honor."

FOLLOW

"Follow" is a word that often occurs in the narratives of the Old Testament and of the Gospels, and in most cases its sense in the KJV is easily understood.

In some instances the KJV uses "follow" to represent the Hebrew word which means "to pursue"; in these cases the contemporary versions use terms other than "follow," such as "pursues righteousness" (Proverbs 21:21, NASB, NIV, NRSV, RSV); "pursues the east wind" (Hosea 12:1, NASB, NIV, NKJV, NRSV, RSV); "runs after gifts" (Isaiah 1:23, NRSV, RSV) and "chases after rewards" (NASB); "in pursuit of strong drink" (Isaiah 5.11, NRSV); "let us press on to know the LORD" (Hosea 6:3, NASB, NRSV, RSV). "I follow the thing that good is" (Psalm 38:20, KJV) is rendered "I follow after good" (NKJV, NRSV, RSV) and "I pursue what is good" (NIV).

In a few cases the KJV uses "follow hard" to represent the Hebrew verb which means "to cling" or "overtake." Where the KJV reads "My soul followeth hard after thee," the NASB, NIV, NRSV, and RSV have "My soul clings to you" [RSV, "thee"] (Psalm 63:8); the NKJV and NLT, however, retain the verb to follow in

their renderings (NLT, "I follow close behind you").

In 1 Samuel 31:2 (and its parallel 1 Chronicles 10:2) the Philistines are said to have "followed hard" upon (KJV) Saul and his sons: this is variously rendered by the contemporary versions as "closed in on" (CEV, NLT), "overtook" (NRSV, RSV), "fought hard against" (NCV), and "pressed hard after" (NIV).

In the Epistles, contemporary versions generally use the words "pursue" or "imitate" to render the Greek words translated "follow" by the KJV. They use the verb "pursue" (NASB, NIV, NKJV, NRSV) and "strive for" (NRSV) at Romans 9:30–31, where the KJV reads: "the Gentiles, which followed not after righteousness, have attained to righteousness . . . But Israel, which followed after the law of righteousness, hath not attained to the law of righteousness."

"Let us . . . follow after the things which make for peace" (Romans 14:19, KJV) is now rendered "let us pursue the things which make for peace" (NASB), and "let us make every effort to do what leads to peace" (NIV).

"Follow peace with all men" (Hebrews 12:14, KJV) now reads "Pursue peace with everyone" (Hebrews 12:14, NRSV), and "Follow after charity" (1 Corinthians 14:1, KJV) reads "Follow the way of love" (NIV), "Pursue love" (NASB, NKJV, NRSV), and "Make love your aim" (RSV).

Similarly, Paul's instruction in 1 Timothy 6:11 and 2 Timothy 2:22, "follow after righteousness" (KJV), is now rendered "pursue righteousness" (NASB, NIV, NKJV, NRSV) and "aim at righteousness" (RSV). The NLT uses both "follow" and "pursue" in its rendering of the verses "follow what is right and good. Pursue a godly life" (1 Timothy 6:11).

Paul did not hesitate to counsel his converts to imitate him. This was not unwarranted pride or self-assertion, because he associated with himself Timothy and Epaphroditus and others, and because the ground of his counsel was that he and his associates sought to imitate Christ. On a number of occasions contemporary versions now use "imitate" and "imitators" in place of the KJV renderings, "follow" and "followers."

Some examples are: 1 Corinthians 4:16, "I beseech you, be ye followers of me" (KJV; NIV, "I urge you, imitate me"); 1 Corinthians 11:1, "Be ye followers of me, even as I also am of Christ" (KJV; NASB, "Be imitators of me, just as I also am of Christ"); Ephesians 5:1, "Be ye . . . followers of God, as dear children" (KJV; NRSV, "be imitators of God, as beloved children"); 1 Thessalonians 1:6, "ye became followers of us, and of the Lord" (KJV; RSV, "you became imitators of us and of the Lord."

Hebrews 13:7 reads in the KJV: "Remember them which have the rule over you, who have spoken unto you the word of God: whose faith follow, considering the end of their conversation." The NRSV translates as "Remember your leaders, those who spoke the word of God to you; consider the outcome of their life, and imitate their faith."

"Follow" is retained in places (e.g., 2 Thessalonians 3:7, CEV, NASB, NIV, NKJV, NLT), or used where the KJV had the noun, "followers" (e.g., 1 Corinthians 11:1, CEV, NCV, NIV, NLT). Other texts are: Philippians 3:17; 1 Thessalonians 2:14; 2 Thessalonians 3:7, 9; Hebrews 6:12; 3 John 11.

The KJV rendering of 1 Thessalonians 5:15 is: "See that none render evil for evil unto any man; but ever follow that which is good, both among yourselves and to all men." The NASB rendering is: "See that no one repays another with evil for evil, but always seek after that which is good for one another and for all people."

In Philippians 3, Paul offers a humble evaluation of his own discipleship and a model for the church at Philippi when he writes: "Not as though I already attained, either were already perfect: but I follow after, if that I may apprehend that for which also I am apprehended of Christ Jesus" (v. 12, KJV). The same Greek verb which is here rendered "I follow after" is translated "I press" by the KJV in verse 14.

Contemporary versions generally render it as "I press on" (NASB, NIV, NKJV "press toward" at v. 14, NRSV, RSV); at verse 12, the CEV reads, "I keep on running and struggling to take hold of the prize, and the NCV has "I continue trying to reach it and make it mine."

"Some men's sins are open beforehand, going before to judgment; and some men they follow after" (1 Timothy 5:24, KJV) is now translated as "The sins of some men are quite evident, going before them to judgment; for others, their sins follow after" (NASB).

FOOTMEN

This word is likely to remind us of the male servants in livery of bygone days, and perhaps of the mice destined to become the beautifully clad attendants of Cinderella's pumpkin carriage. In the KJV, however, footmen are not servants or lackeys but men who are in or available for military service. Of the contemporary versions, the NASB, NRSV, and RSV retain the word only in 2 Kings 13:7, where it stands in context with "horsemen." Elsewhere the Hebrew term is now generally translated as "foot soldiers" or "men on foot."

In 1 Samuel 22:17 a different Hebrew term is translated "guard" by most versions, as the KJV itself does fourteen times in 1 Kings 14, 2 Kings 10 and 11, and 2 Chronicles 12. Guards here are the company of foot soldiers assigned to protect the king, the king's house, or the house of the Lord. "Bodyguard" is a term occasionally used by the CEV (e.g., 1 Samuel 22:17), NCV (2 Kings 11:19), and NLT (2 Chronicles 12:10).

FOR THAT

"For that" is an archaic expression for "because" or "since" in the KJV rendering of such passages as Romans 5:12, 1 Timothy 1:12, and Hebrews 5:2. The contemporary versions render the KJV expression variously, especially by "because," "since," and "for." It appears occasionally in Shakespeare; for example,

"for that
It is not night when I do see your face,
Therefore I think I am not in the
   night."
                   —*A Midsummer Night's Dream*
                                    (II, 1, 220)

FOR TO

This is an obsolete conjunctive phrase indicating "purpose"; the contemporary versions usually replace it with "to." "They pressed upon him for to touch him, as many as had plagues" (Mark 3:10, KJV) now reads, in the NRSV, "all who had diseases pressed upon him to touch him." "All their works they do for to be seen of men" (Matthew 23:5, KJV) reads in the NASB, "they do all their deeds to be noticed by men."

"For to make in himself of twain one new man" (Ephesians 2:15, KJV) is rendered "that he might create in himself one new humanity in place of the two" by the NRSV; the NCV reads, "His purpose was to make the two groups of people become one new people in him."

FORASMUCH AS

"Forasmuch as" is a conjunctional phrase meaning "in view of the fact that," "inasmuch as," "since," "because." It appears forty-three times in the KJV; of the contemporary versions only the RSV retains it, and that only in Jonathan's farewell words to David: "Go in peace, forasmuch as we have sworn both of us in the name of the LORD, saying, 'The LORD shall be between me and you, and between my descendants and your descendants, for ever' " (1 Samuel 20:42, RSV). Elsewhere the contemporary versions use terms such as "inasmuch as," "since," or "because."

"Forasmuch therefore as your treading is upon the poor" (Amos 5:11, KJV) now reads "Therefore because you impose heavy rent on the poor" (NASB). "Forasmuch as thou

sawest" (Daniel 2:41, KJV) is rendered "even as you saw" (NIV). "Forasmuch as he had not to pay" (Matthew 18:25, KJV) reads in the NRSV, "as he could not pay." "Forasmuch as Lydda was nigh to Joppa" (Acts 9:38, KJV) is now "Since Lydda was near Joppa" (NASB, NKJV, NRSV, RSV).

Acts 11:17 reads in the KJV, "Forasmuch then as God gave them the like gift as he did unto us, who believed on the Lord Jesus Christ; what was I, that I could withstand God?" The NRSV renders Peter's words as: "If then God gave the same gift to them as he gave to us when we believed in the Lord Jesus Christ, who was I that I could hinder God?"

Acts 17:29, "Forasmuch then as we are the offspring of God" (KJV), is now "Since we are God's offspring" (NRSV); Acts 24:10, "Forasmuch as I know that thou hast been of many years a judge unto this nation" (KJV), now reads, "Knowing that for many years you have been a judge to this nation" (NASB); and 1 Corinthians 15:58, "forasmuch as ye know that your labour is not in vain in the Lord" (KJV), is rendered by the NASB, as "knowing that your toil is not in vain in the Lord."

The NKJV renders "forasmuch as" (KJV) in Jeremiah 10:6 as "inasmuch as"; other contemporary versions do not render it at all here, and none attempt to render it in 2 Corinthians 3:3, and 1 Peter 1:18.

The phrase appears once in the KJV in the obsolete form "forsomuch as." This is in Jesus' word to Zacchaeus, "forsomuch as he also is a son of Abraham" (Luke 19:9, KJV). The NRSV has "because he too is a son of Abraham."

FORBIDDEN FRUIT

The expression "forbidden fruit" is used to refer to what is attractive because it is prohibited ("forbidden fruit is sweetest," i.e., is the most desirable).

The fruit referred to is the fruit of the tree of the knowledge of good and evil which God forbade Adam and Eve to eat (Genesis

2:9, 17; 3:1–6). The phrase "forbidden fruit" does not itself appear in the Bible text, nor is the fruit identified as an apple. However, the fruit is commonly thought of as an apple, e.g., by Shakespeare in his 93rd sonnet:

"How like Eve's apple doth thy
beauty grow,
If thy sweet virtue answer not
thy show!"

(See also TREE OF THE KNOWLEDGE OF GOOD AND EVIL)

FORETELL

In modern usage, this word means no more than "to predict," but in 2 Corinthians 13:2 the KJV uses the word in the now obsolete sense of "enjoining or warning someone beforehand." In the KJV rendering which follows, "told you before" and "foretell" represent different tenses of the same Greek verb: "I told you before, and foretell you, as if I were present, the second time; and being absent now I write to them which heretofore have sinned, and to all other, that, if I come again, I will not spare."

The NRSV translates this as "I warned those who sinned previously and all the others, and I warn them now while absent, as I did when present on my second visit, that if I come again, I will not be lenient."

Examples of Shakespeare's use of "foretell" in the sense of "warn" are:

"many men that stumble at the
threshold
Are well foretold that danger
lurks within."
—*King Henry VI, Part III* (IV, 7, 11)

"These our actors,
As I foretold you, were all spirits,
and
Are melted into air, into thin air."
—*The Tempest* (IV, 1, 149)

FORTH OF

This expression means "out of" or "from." God's command to Noah, "Go forth of the ark" (KJV), is worded in the NASB, NRSV, and NKJV, "Go out of the ark" (Genesis 8:16). The prophecy of Amos 7:17 that Israel will "go into captivity forth of his land" (KJV) is now rendered "into exile away from its land" (NRSV).

Jehoiada's command concerning Queen Athaliah, "Have her forth without the ranges" (2 Kings 11:15, KJV), appears in the KJV rendering of 2 Chronicles 23:14 as "Have her forth of the ranges." The Hebrew is the same. The NASB, NIV, NRSV, and RSV have "Bring her out between the ranks." (See RANGE)

In Shakespeare's *The Tempest* (V, 1, 160), Prospero "was thrust forth of Milan" and in *Julius Caesar* (III, 3, 3), the poet Cinna had "no will to wander forth of doors."

FORWARD, FORWARDNESS

As applied to a person's disposition and behavior, these words today have an air of pertness or presumption. Not so in the KJV, where they stand for "earnestness," "readiness," or "desire in a good cause." They are used, in fact, only in relation to one particular good cause, the offering organized by Paul for the relief of the saints in Jerusalem. Paul himself was "forward to do" this (Galatians 2:10, KJV); his words read in the NASB, "the very thing I was eager to do."

The other four occurrences, found in Paul's "money letter" (2 Corinthians 8—9), are concerned entirely with the plans for the collection of this offering. In their renderings of the various Greek words, the contemporary versions have "earnestness" (8:8, NASB, NIV, NRSV, RSV) and "diligence" (NKJV); "desire" (8:10, NASB, NIV, NRSV, RSV); "very earnest" (8:17, NASB, RSV), "diligent" (NKJV), "eager" (NRSV), and "with much enthusiasm" (NIV); and "readiness" (9:2, NASB, RSV), "eagerness" (NIV, NRSV), and "willingness" (NKJV).

FOUR CORNERS OF THE EARTH

See CORNERS OF THE EARTH.

FRAME

As a verb, "frame" is familiar to us from thrillers and detective novels, where innocent or unsuspecting parties are set up—usually for harm or arrest. In the KJV it is used once in the obsolete sense of "to manage," "to contrive." This is in the famous Shibboleth passage (Judges 12:6): "Say now Shibboleth; and he said Sibboleth: for he could not frame to pronounce it right."

The Hebrew text of this verse has no word for "frame," and contemporary versions do not render it; e.g., the NASB reads, "for he could not pronounce it correctly." There was no second trial, no time for contriving to reshape his sibilants. If he did not pronounce it right, "they seized him and slew him."

In Shakespeare's *King Henry VI, Part II* (III, 1, 52), the Duke of Suffolk accuses Humphrey, Duke of Gloucester, of planning "by wicked means to frame our sovereign's fall." Another Duke of Gloucester, the hunchback who later became King Richard III, soliloquizes concerning his ambition and his readiness to do anything to get the crown:

> "Why, I can smile, and murder
>   whiles I smile,
> And cry 'Content' to that which
>   grieves my heart,
> And wet my cheeks with artificial
>   tears,
> And frame my face to all occasions."
> —*King Henry VI, Part III* (III, 2, 182)

In Hosea 5:4, "They will not frame their doings to turn unto their God" (KJV), the revised versions and most contemporary translations take "their doings" to be the subject of the verb. The NRSV reads, "Their deeds do not permit them to return to their God."

FRANKLY

In the KJV, "frankly" is used, not in the modern sense of "openly" or "candidly,"

but in the older sense of "freely," "generously," "unconditionally." It appears just once, in Luke 7:42: "he frankly forgave them both." The insertion of the word "frankly" before "forgave" here is unique to the KJV; in nine other cases it translates the Greek verb with a simple "forgive."

The prior versions, from Tyndale on, used no adverb, and contemporary versions omit it. The NASB reads, "he graciously forgave them both"; the NKJV, "he freely forgave them both."

The OED cites Shakespeare's *Measure for Measure* (III, 1, 106):

> "O, were it but my life,
> I'ld throw it down for your deliverance
> As frankly as a pin."

FRAY

This word is likely to make us think of damaged fabric, or of quarrels or skirmishes ("caught in the fray"). In the KJV, however, the word "fray" is a shortened form of the verb "affray," which meant "to frighten," "to make afraid." The familiar adjective "afraid" is simply the modern form of the past participle "affrayed."

In Moses' declaration of blessings and curses, the punishment of the disobedient ends with the abandonment of their dead bodies to be carrion, "thy carcase shall be meat unto all fowls of the air, and unto the beasts of the earth, and no man shall fray them away" (Deuteronomy 28:26, KJV). The NRSV translates: "Your corpses shall be food for every bird of the air and animal of the earth, and there shall be no one to frighten them away." The same punishment is declared in Jeremiah 7:33.

In the KJV account of Zechariah's vision (Zechariah 1:18–21), we read of four "carpenters" who came to "fray" the four horns which had scattered Judah; in contemporary versions we read of "craftsmen" (NASB, NCV, NIV, NKJV) or "blacksmiths" (CEV, NLT, NRSV) who came to "terrify" (NCV, "scare") them. Compare Ezekiel 21:31, where the phrase "skilful to destroy" (KJV) translates the Hebrew which means literally "smiths of destruction."

Shakespeare used the verbs "affright" and "fright," but not "frighten." He uses "fray" only as a noun signifying "a brawl" or "fight." He uses "affray" only once, and as a verb:

"Since arm from arm that voice doth
    us affray."
    —*Romeo and Juliet* (III, 5, 33)

FREELY

This word has several different meanings in the KJV. One meaning is "without restraint or stint," "plentifully," "abundantly." The word is used with this meaning only twice in the KJV, however—in Genesis 2:16, "You may freely eat of every tree of the garden"; and in 1 Samuel 14:30, "How much better if the people had eaten freely."

"Freely" has a different meaning in Numbers 11:5, where it represents the Hebrew word which means "free," "gratis," "without payment" (NCV and NLT, "for free"; NRSV, "for nothing"; NIV, "at no cost"). The Israelites who longed in the desert for the fish they had eaten in Egypt spoke particularly of the fact that it had cost them nothing.

In five passages of the New Testament the KJV uses "freely" to translate the Greek word which means "gratis." "Freely ye have received, freely give" (Matthew 10:8, KJV) is rendered in the NRSV as "You received without payment, give without payment," but other contemporary versions (NASB, NCV, NIV, NKJV) retain the word "freely" here.

"Whosoever will, let him take the water of life freely" (Revelation 22:17, KJV) is paraphrased by the CEV as "If you want life-giving water, come and take it. It's free!" The NRSV reads, "let anyone who wishes take the water of life as a gift" (so also 21:6; compare Isaiah 55:1).

The other passages are Romans 3:24, "being justified freely by his grace" (KJV), which the NASB renders as "being justified as a gift by His grace"; and 2 Corinthians

11:7, "I have preached to you the gospel of God freely" (KJV), which the NRSV translates as "I proclaimed God's good news to you free of charge."

The word "freely" refers to freewill offerings in Psalm 54:6 and Ezra 2:68; 7:15. In Acts 2:29 it represents the Greek phrase which means "with confidence" or "with boldness," and which is so translated by the KJV in Acts 4:29, 31 and 28:31.

The KJV's use of the phrases "freely give" (Romans 8:32) and "freely given" (1 Corinthians 2:12) express the fact that God's gifts to us are at his initiative and of his grace. The verb in these phrases is related to the noun which is translated "free gift" in Romans 5:15–17. The NCV, NLT, NRSV, and RSV omit the adverb "freely" from the verses; the NIV has "graciously" at Romans 8:32. The CEV translation of this verse is: "God did not keep back his own Son, but he gave him for us. If God did this, won't he freely give us everything else?"

First Corinthians 2:12 reads in the NRSV, "Now we have received not the spirit of the world, but the Spirit which is from God, that we might understand the gifts bestowed on us by God."

FRET

The word "fret" makes us think of worry and discontent. In the KJV, however, it occurs four times in the obsolete sense of "eat into," "gnaw," "corrode," or "be eaten away," "become corroded," "decay." "A fretting leprosy" (KJV) appears in Leviticus 13:51–52; 14:44, and "it is fret inward" (KJV) in Leviticus 13:55. These were Tyndale's terms, and were retained by later versions.

For the first of these terms contemporary versions have "a leprous malignancy" (Leviticus 13:51–52, NASB) and "a malignant mark" (14:44, NASB), "an active leprosy" (NKJV), and "a spreading leprous disease" (NRSV). The Hebrew word represented by "fret inward" is a noun which means "leprous decay." The latter part of Leviticus 13:55 reads, in the KJV, "it is fret inward, whether it be bare within or without." The NKJV reads, "it continues eating away, whether the damage is outside or inside."

FROM DAN TO BEERSHEBA
See DAN TO BEERSHEBA.

FROWARD, FROWARDNESS, FROWARDLY

"Froward" is a variant of "fromward," like "to and fro" for "to and from." It is the opposite of "toward," but has been most used as an adjective rather than as a preposition. It means "opposed," "contrary," "perverse," and in the KJV is used also in the sense of "tortuous," "crooked," "devious"— the opposite of sincere, frank, and straightforward.

Seventeen of the twenty-four appearances of "froward" and "frowardness" are in Proverbs, where contemporary versions use terms such as "perverse" (e.g., Proverbs 8:13, NIV), "perverted" (2:12, RSV), "corrupt" (10:32, NLT), "crooked" (6:12, NRSV), "devious" (2:14, NRSV), and "deceitful" (4:24, NKJV).

In the context of Job 5:12–13, "the counsel of the froward is carried headlong" (KJV) is now translated as "the schemes of the wily are brought to a quick end" (NRSV). In 1 Peter 2:18 some masters are referred to as "froward" (KJV), the Greek here meaning harsh or unjust. Contemporary versions refer to such masters as "cruel" (CEV), "unreasonable" (NASB), "dishonest" (NCV), "harsh" (NIV, NKJV, NLT, NRSV), and "overbearing" (RSV).

"Frowardly" appears once in the KJV, in Isaiah 57:17: "he went on frowardly." The NIV has "he kept on in his willful ways"; the RSV and NKJV translate as "he went on backsliding." (See BACKSLIDING)

FRUITFUL AND MULTIPLY

At creation, God spoke to living creatures to "be fruitful, and multiply" (Genesis 1:22, KJV). This same command comes to man in Genesis 1:28; the NASB, NKJV, NRSV, and RSV have "be fruitful and multiply"; the NIV has

"Be fruitful and increase in number"; the NLT, "multiply"; the CEV, "Have a lot of children!"; the NCV, "Have many children and grow in number."

The command is repeated to Noah and his sons (Genesis 9:1, KJV), with the contemporary versions having the same wordings as for Genesis 1:28, except the CEV which has "Have a lot of children and grandchildren."

FRUITS, KNOW THEM BY THEIR

To "know them by their fruits" means that you can recognize a person's real identity by looking at the evidence shown by that person's life. The phrase has its origins in Jesus' warning against false prophets in the Sermon on the Mount (Matthew 7:16–20, KJV): "Ye shall know them by their fruits. Do men gather grapes of thorns, or figs of thistles? Even so every good tree bringeth forth good fruit; but a corrupt tree bringeth forth evil fruit. A good tree cannot bring forth evil fruit, neither can a corrupt tree bring forth good fruit. Every tree that bringeth not forth good fruit is hewn down, and cast into the fire. Wherefore by their fruits ye shall know them."

The KJV "ye shall know them by their fruits" (v. 16) is rendered by the contemporary versions as "you will know them by their fruits" (NASB, NKJV, NRSV, RSV), "by their fruit you will recognize them" (NIV), "you will know these people by what they do" (NCV), "you can tell what they are by what they do" (CEV), and "you can detect them by the way they act" (NLT). (Se also Matthew 12:33; Luke 6:43, 44.)

FRUITS OF ONE'S LABORS

The expression "the fruits of one's labors" refers to the results of one's work ("to enjoy the fruits of one's labor."). The origin of the expression is Philippians 1:22 (KJV), "But if I live in the flesh, this is the fruit of my labour: yet what I shall choose I wot not." The contemporary versions render the KJV "the fruit of my labour" as "fruitful labor"

(NASB, NIV, NRSV, RSV), "fruit from my labor" (NKJV), and "fruitful service for Christ" (NLT).

FURBISH

We are familiar with "furbish" used with the prefix "re-" to mean "to clean," "to redecorate," or "to renovate." In the KJV the verb "furbish" occurs six times in the sense of "remove rust from (a weapon, armour, etc.); to brighten by rubbing, polish, burnish" (OED).

The word occurs four times in Ezekiel 21:9–11; and the contemporary versions generally render the verb as "polish": e.g., NASB,

> "Son of man, prophesy and say,
> 'Thus says the LORD.' Say,
> 'A sword, a sword sharpened
> And also polished!
> Sharpened to make a slaughter,
> Polished to flash like lightning!'
> Or shall we rejoice, the rod of My
> son despising every tree?
> And it is given to be polished,
> that it may be handled; the
> sword is sharpened and
> polished, to give it into the
> hand of the slayer."

The CEV paraphrases:

> "Ezekiel, son of man, tell the
> people of Jerusalem:

> I have sharpened my sword to
> slaughter you; it is shiny and
> will flash like lightning!
> Don't celebrate—punishment is
> coming, because everyone has
> ignored my warnings.
> My sword has been polished; it's
> sharp and ready to kill."

At Jeremiah 46:4 the KJV "furbish with spears" is rendered "polish the spears" by the CEV, NASB, NCV, NIV, NKJV, and RSV; the NLT has "sharpen your spears" and the NRSV, "whet your lances."

FURNITURE

This word is used in the KJV Old Testament for any type of equipment. It refers to the furnishings and utensils of the tabernacle in Exodus 31:7–9; 35:14; 39:33. In Genesis 31:34 we read that Rachel stole her father's images, "and put them in the camel's furniture, and sat upon them" (KJV); contemporary versions refer to the camel's "saddle." "Take ye the spoil of silver, take the spoil of gold: for there is none end of the store and glory out of all the pleasant furniture" (Nahum 2:9, KJV) reads, in the NRSV:

> "Plunder the silver, plunder the
> gold!
> There is no end of treasure!
> An abundance of every precious
> thing!"

G

GADARENE

The adjective "Gadarene" is sometimes used to mean "engaged in a headlong rush." The word refers to the country of the Gergesenes (Matthew 8:28, KJV), where Jesus cast the demons out of two possessed men into a herd of swine. The demons caused the pigs to rush down a steep slope into the sea of Galilee, where they drowned.

The contemporary versions render the KJV "country of Gergesenes" as "the country of the Gadarenes" (NASB, NRSV, RSV), "the region [NLT, "the land"] of the Gadarenes" (NIV, NLT), "the area of the Gadarene people" (NCV), "the town of Gadara" (CEV); the NKJV retains the KJV rendering.

GAIN LOSS

This joining of contradictory terms occurs in the KJV account of the storm which beset the ship carrying Paul toward Rome. When all hope was abandoned, Paul came forward and said that an angel of God had assured him that no lives would be lost, but only the ship. He began by reminding them that he had advised against making the voyage so late in the season: "Sirs, ye should have hearkened unto me, and not have loosed from Crete, and to have gained this harm and loss" (Acts 27:21, KJV).

The primary meaning of the Greek verb *kerdaino* is "to gain," "to derive profit or advantage." But it is also used in a general sense, meaning "to get or obtain"; and even in a bad sense, "to reap a disadvantage" or "to gain someone's ill will." Most scholars regard it as used in a general sense here.

Tyndale's translation was "brought unto us this harm and loss," in which he was followed by Coverdale, the Great Bible, and the first edition of the Bishops' Bible; the revised versions of 1881 and 1901 use "gotten." Alexander Campbell, the Twentieth Century New Testament, Ballantine, and Goodspeed use "incurred," as do the NASB, NKJV, and RSV.

The word "gained" was introduced by the Geneva Bible, where it was accompanied by an explanatory note: "That is, ye should have saved the loss by avoiding the danger." John Wesley translated the clause, "and so have avoided this injury and loss." Other contemporary versions also use "avoided" (NRSV, NLT). The NIV has "spared yourselves."

It has been suggested that we have here an oxymoron, that is, a "pointedly foolish" saying, a deliberate conjoining of contradictory terms to sharpen the speaker's point. But oxymoron is usually a matter of wit or irony, satire or reproach; and it is a figure of speech that does not fit the situation here. Paul did not begin with a wry joke or a bitter jibe as he carried to his shipmates God's assurance that their lives would be saved.

GAINSAY, GAINSAYING, GAINSAYERS

"Gainsay" is not yet obsolete, but it has become a purely literary and slightly archaic word. It is the only word that remains of a set of compound verbs which were common in the Middle Ages. These verbs were formed by prefixing "gain" or "again" (both meaning "against") to the verb root: "again-call" ("to revoke"), "againrise" ("to rebel"), "gainstand" ("to resist").

"Gainsay" means "to speak against," and so "to deny," "contradict," "oppose." Contemporary versions use other terms in each of the word's five KJV appearances.

"Without gainsaying" (Acts 10:29, KJV) is now "without objection" (NKJV, NRSV, RSV) and "without [NASB, "without even"] raising any objection" (NASB, NIV). "A disobedient and gainsaying people" (Romans 10:21, KJV) is "a disobedient and contrary people" (NKJV, NRSV, RSV) and "a disobedient and obstinate people" (NASB, NIV). "Perished in the gainsaying of Core" (Jude 11, KJV) now reads "perish in Korah's rebellion" (NRSV, RSV). "able by sound doctrine both to exhort and to convince the gainsayers" (Titus 1:9, KJV) is rendered, in the NASB, "able both to exhort in sound doctrine and to refute those who contradict."

In Luke 21:15 contemporary versions follow the ancient Greek manuscripts, in which the order of the words differs from the medieval manuscripts available to the KJV translators; "which all your adversaries shall not be able to gainsay nor resist" (KJV) now reads, in the NASB, "which none of your opponents will be able to resist or refute."

GALL

This word is often heard today in the context of "bad feeling," where it is synonymous with "venom" and "spite." Although the word's primary meaning is "bile," the secretion of the liver; it has long been used for "anything bitter to taste" or "to endure," or for "bitterness of spirit." It occurs in the KJV with both meanings.

In Job 16:13, "my gall" (KJV) is translated as "my insides" by the CEV, and as "my blood" by the NCV and NLT. In Job 20:25, the NIV and NCV render "gall" as "liver," but other versions retain the KJV rendering. The word occurs with the meaning of bitterness in Acts 8:23, where Peter rebukes Simon, the former magician, for attempting to purchase the gift of the Holy Spirit with money: "thou art in the gall of bitterness, and in the bond of iniquity" (KJV).

The KJV phrase, "in the gall of bitterness" (KJV), is retained by the NASB, NRSV, and RSV, but is rendered as "full of bitter jealousy" by the NCV, and as "full of bitterness" by the NIV and NLT. Peter's words read, in the NKJV, "you are poisoned by bitterness and bound by iniquity."

Another, more familiar, phrase—"the wormwood and the gall" (Lamentations 3:19, KJV)—is also retained in some contemporary renderings (NKJV, NRSV, RSV). The NASB reads, "the wormwood and bitterness"; the NIV, "the bitterness and the gall." Jeremiah's complaint is paraphrased by the NLT, "the thought of my suffering and homelessness is bitter beyond words."

In Matthew's account of the crucifixion we read, in the KJV, "They gave him vinegar to drink mingled with gall." Here the word "gall" means something bitter and is retained by most of the contemporary versions. Mark's Gospel says that the drink which Jesus refused was "wine mingled with myrrh" (15:23, KJV).

In more than half of its occurrences in the KJV, "gall" has the now obsolete sense of "poison" or "venom" (see paragraph 5 of the OED's treatment of the first noun "gall"). It is in these cases used as a translation of the Hebrew word *rosh,* which means "a bitter, poisonous herb," or "the venom of a serpent."

"The gall of asps" (Job 20:14, KJV) is now rendered as "the venom of asps" [NASB, "cobras"] (NASB, NRSV), and "grapes of gall"

(Deuteronomy 32:32, KJV) is now "grapes of poison" (NASB, NRSV, RSV). In Psalm 69:21 the psalmist says of his enemies, "They gave me . . . gall for my meat." "Gall" is retained by the NASB, NIV, and NKJV here, but replaced with "poison" by the other contemporary versions.

In Amos 6:12, the prophet addresses an apostate nation with the words, "ye have turned judgment into gall, and the fruit of righteousness into hemlock" (KJV). The NLT reads, "you turn justice into poison and make bitter the sweet fruit of righteousness." At Jeremiah 8:14, 9:15, and 23:15, most contemporary versions have "poisoned," or "poisonous" water for "water of gall" (KJV), and "poisonous" for "gall" (KJV) at Deuteronomy 29:18.

GARDEN HOUSE

A "garden house" is defined in the OED as a "summer-house," and this in turn as "a building in a garden or park, usually of very simple and often rustic character, designed to provide a cool shady place in the heat of summer." In 2 Kings 9:27, the KJV says that King Ahaziah fled from Jehu "by the way of the garden house." Scholars are in general agreement that the Hebrew here represents the name of a place, Beth-haggan, which is probably to be identified with En-gannim (Hebrew, "spring of gardens," Joshua 19:21; 21:29).

The NASB follows the KJV rendering. Other contemporary versions have Ahaziah fleeing "in the direction of Beth-haggan" (NRSV, RSV), "along the road to Beth-haggan" (NLT), or "up the road to Beth Haggan" (NIV)—only to be shot in his chariot near Ibleam. The charioteer turned toward Megiddo, where Ahaziah died, and from where his body was carried by chariot to Jerusalem.

GARNISH

This word is likely to make us think of sprigs of parsley showing off a potato dish, or lemon slices succulently embellishing a cake. In the KJV, however, the word is used in its obsolete senses. While garnish in modern usage means "to furnish, adorn, or decorate," originally it was of heavier import, and meant "to furnish a place with the means of defense," "to garrison a town or city." Applied to persons, its passive participle meant "to be furnished with a retinue of attendants" or "to be adorned with any property or quality."

Richard Chancellor, visiting Moscow in 1553, learned to address Ivan the Terrible as "the right High, right Mighty and right Excellent Prince, garnished with all gifts of Nature by God's grace."

In three of its occurrences in the KJV, "garnish" is rendered in the contemporary versions as "decorate" or "adorn." Solomon adorned the house of God with settings of precious stones (2 Chronicles 3:6). In the Revelation to John (21:19) "the foundation stones of the city wall were adorned with every kind of precious stone" (21:19, NASB).

Jesus' accusation of the Pharisees (Matthew 23:29), reads in the KJV: "Woe unto you, scribes and Pharisees, hypocrites! because ye build the tombs of the prophets, and garnish the sepulchres of the righteous." The verse reads in the CEV: "You Pharisees and teachers are nothing but show-offs, and you're in for trouble! You build monuments for the prophets and decorate the tombs of good people."

In the KJV rendering of Jesus' parable in Matthew 12:44 (and its parallel, Luke 11:25), an unclean spirit returns to the house from which he had gone out and finds it "empty, swept, and garnished." The NRSV reads, "empty, swept, and put in order"; the NCV, "[empty] swept clean, and made neat."

Job's statement concerning the Almighty, "By his spirit he hath garnished the heavens" (26:13, KJV), is now rendered "By his wind the heavens were made fair" (NRSV, RSV) and "By his breath the heavens are cleared" (NASB).

GATHER

The word "gather," with its various inflections, appears 461 times in the KJV in the sense of "to collect or assemble," and once in the sense of "to infer, deduce, conclude." This one occurrence is in the account of the vision which led Paul to carry the gospel to Europe: "And after he had seen the vision, immediately we endeavoured to go into Macedonia, assuredly gathering that the Lord had called us for to preach the gospel unto them" (Acts 16:10, KJV).

The two words "assuredly gathering" represent the participle of the Greek verb *sumbibazo*, which the KJV translates as "proving" in Acts 9:22. This Greek verb, like the Latin *colligo* and the English "gather," applies to decisions as well as to physical bringing or coming together. The KJV translators sought to convey its certainty by the word "assuredly."

Contemporary versions use other terms such as "concluding" (NASB, NIV, NKJV, RSV), "understanding" (NCV), and "being convinced" (NRSV). The whole verse reads in the CEV: "After Paul had seen the vision, we began looking for a way to go to Macedonia. We were sure that God had called us to preach the good news there."

GAY

In contemporary usage, "gay" when referring to people means either "homosexual" or "very lively and cheerful," and when referring to things means "attractive and brightly colored." The word occurs only once in the KJV, where it is used in the obsolete sense of "excellent" or "fine." The context is James's warning against partiality in welcoming the poor, and the rich, into the church's gatherings (James 2).

The man in "the gay clothing" (v. 3, KJV) is clothed in "goodly apparel," as verse 2 has it. The clothing is described by the same Greek words in the two verses. The change from "goodly apparel" to "the gay clothing" was one of Tyndale's characteristic touches, and was retained by the KJV. Contemporary versions use "fine clothes" (NASB, NIV, NKJV, NRSV), "fine clothing" (RSV), "fancy clothes" (CEV), and "nice clothes" (NCV).

GENDER

"Gender" refers to the grammatical classification of nouns ("in French the gender of the word 'table' is feminine"). In the KJV "gender" does not, however, occur as a noun but only as a verb with the obsolete meaning of "to breed" (cf. current "engender").

In Leviticus 19:19, the people are instructed not to let their cattle "gender with a diverse kind" (KJV), which the NASB renders as "You shall not breed together two kinds of your cattle." In Job 21:10, the afflicted Job observed how smoothly life seems to run for the wicked. Even their cattle breed successfully: "Their bull gendereth, and faileth not; their cow calveth, and casteth not her calf" (KJV); the contemporary versions generally use the verb "breed."

In Galatians 4:24, Paul depicts Mount Sinai as a woman, representing the Mosaic covenant and thus "bearing children for slavery" (NRSV; KJV, "gendereth to bondage"). In 2 Timothy 2:23, he warns Timothy to avoid "foolish and unlearned questions . . . knowing that they do gender strifes" (KJV).

The NRSV reads, "Have nothing to do with stupid, senseless controversies; you know that they breed quarrels." Other contemporary versions have "produce quarrels" (NASB, NIV), "grow into quarrels" (NCV), "start fights" (NLT), and "generate strife" (NKJV).

GENERALLY

This word occurs only once in the KJV, in 2 Samuel 17:11. Its use in this verse can be better understood if we look, for a moment, at the use of repetition in the Hebrew language. Here, repetition of words is employed to give emphasis or added intensity of meaning. "Justice, justice shalt thou fol-

low" begins Deuteronomy 16:20, which the KJV translates as "That which is altogether just." In Ecclesiastes 7:24 the Hebrew "deep, deep" is translated "exceeding deep" in the KJV. In both of these cases the majority of the contemporary versions retain the repetition—e.g., "Justice, and only justice, you shall follow" and "deep, very deep" (NRSV, RSV).

In the case of verbs, this repetition consists of the absolute infinitive plus a finite form. For example, in Genesis 2:17 a literal translation would be "to die shall die"; in Exodus 21:17, "to be put to death shall be put to death." The KJV has "shalt surely die" and "shall surely be put to death." (See FAIN; SURELY)

When Joseph tells his dream to his brothers, they say, literally, "To reign, shall you reign over us? or to have dominion, shall you have dominion over us?" Here the KJV represents the emphasis of the absolute infinitive by the word "indeed"—"Shalt thou indeed reign over us? or shalt thou indeed have dominion over us?" (Genesis 37:8).

In the one case where the word "generally" is used in the KJV (2 Samuel 17:11), its status is like that of "surely" and "indeed." A literal translation of the Hebrew would be "I counsel to be gathered be gathered to you all Israel." The KJV represents this by "I counsel that all Israel be generally gathered unto thee."

The word "generally" is here employed in the sense of "including every individual without exception"—a sense in which it is now obsolete. The sixteenth-century translations, from Tyndale to the Bishops' Bible, did not represent the infinitive; of the contemporary versions, only the NASB and NKJV do this (NASB, "be surely gathered"; NKJV, "be fully gathered").

GENERATION

The word "generation" appears almost two hundred times in the KJV, almost always in the fifth sense defined by the OED:

"the whole body of individuals born about the same period; also, the time covered by the lives of these." In Matthew 1:1, however, the KJV uses it to translate the Greek word *genesis*. It later renders this as "birth" (1:18). "The generation of Jesus Christ" in 1:1 and "the birth of Jesus Christ" in 1:18 represent the same Greek words.

Contemporary versions render the Greek in verse 1 as "the genealogy of Jesus the Messiah" (NASB, NRSV), and "the genealogy of Jesus Christ" (NIV, NKJV, RSV). The entire verse reads, in the NLT, "This is a record of the ancestors of Jesus the Messiah, a descendant of King David and of Abraham."

First Peter 2:9 reads in the KJV: "But ye are a chosen generation, a royal priesthood, a holy nation, a peculiar people, that ye should shew forth the praises of him who hath called you out of darkness into his marvellous light." The Greek word rendered "generation" by the KJV here is *genos*. The NKJV retains this rendering, but other contemporary versions use "people" (NCV, NIV, NLT; CEV, "God's chosen and special people") and "race" (NASB, NRSV, RSV).

Tyndale translated Paul's quotation from the Greek poet Aratus, "For we are also his generation" (Acts 17:28), and he was followed by subsequent versions up to and including the Geneva Bible. The Bishops' Bible changed it to read, "For we are also his offspring," and the KJV translators accepted this rendering. "Offspring" is retained by the NIV, NKJV, NLT, NRSV, and the RSV; the CEV, NASB, and NCV render the word as "children."

GENERATION OF VIPERS

In Matthew 3:7 and Luke 3:7 the term "generation of vipers" (KJV) appears in a saying of John the Baptist, and in Matthew's Gospel it appears twice in sayings of Jesus (12:34; 23:33). The Greek word is *gennema*, which the majority of the contemporary versions render as "brood" (NASB, NIV, NKJV, NLT, NRSV, RSV). The CEV at Matthew 3:7 has "You bunch of snakes!"

and at 12:34, "You are a bunch of evil snakes." At Matthew 23:33 the NCV reads, "A family of poisonous snakes!" The NLT has "Sons of vipers!"

GET THEE BEHIND ME, SATAN

In the temptation of Jesus in the wilderness, Satan tempted Jesus with the splendor of all the kingdoms of the world if he would worship Satan. Jesus said to the devil "Get thee hence, Satan: for it is written, Thou shalt worship the Lord thy God, and him only shalt thou serve" (Matthew 4:10, KJV).

The contemporary versions render the KJV "Get thee hence, Satan!" as: "Away from me, Satan!" (NIV), "Go, Satan!" (NASB), "Go away Satan!" (CEV), "Go away from me, Satan!" (NCV), "Get out of here, Satan" (NLT).

In Matthew 16:23, in response to Peter's attempt to deflect Jesus from his suffering and death, Jesus said to Peter, "Get thee behind me, Satan" (KJV). The contemporary versions render this as "Get behind me [NASB, NKJV, "Me,"], Satan!" (NASB, NIV, NRSV, RSV), "Get away from me, Satan!" (NLT), "Go away from me, Satan!" (NCV), and "Satan, get away from me!" (CEV).

In Milton's *Paradise Regained,* Satan tempted Christ with "great and glorious Rome" and the "Kingdoms of the world" if he would fall down and worship him as Lord. Jesus answered:

> "Wert thou so void of fear or shame,
> As offer them to me the Son of God,
> To me my own, on such abhorred
>   pact,
> That I fall down and worship thee
>   as God?
> Get thee behind me; plain thou now
>   appear'st
> That Evil one, Satan for ever
>   damn'd."

The phrase "Get thee behind me, Satan" is sometimes said by a person who is tempted to do something wrong.

GHOST

At the time of the preparation of the KJV the word "ghost" meant "the spirit, or immaterial part of a person, as distinct from the body"; and "ghostly" meant "spiritual." In Shakespeare's *Romeo and Juliet* (III, 3, 49), Romeo called Friar Laurence "a ghostly confessor," and the literature of the period abounds in references to priests as "ghostly father," "ghostly adviser," "ghostly director," or "ghostly instructor." "Ghostly counsel" was spiritual counsel, and a "ghostly day" was a day set apart for worship. Hobbes' *Leviathan* refers to "a Ghostly Authority" set up "against the Civill."

These meanings of "ghost" and "ghostly" are now obsolete and by most people forgotten. The American revisers in 1901 used the term "Holy Spirit" instead of "Holy Ghost," and this translation has been widely adopted. Interestingly, the KJV itself renders the Greek word *pneuma* as the "spirit" of man 151 times and as the "Spirit" of God 137 times, but it retains the expression "Holy Ghost" eighty-nine times.

The Greek word *phantasma*, which means "apparition" or "phantom," is used in Matthew 14:26 and Mark 6:49 to express the fear of the disciples when they saw Jesus walking on the sea. Following Tyndale, the KJV has them say, "It is a spirit." The Rhemish Version of 1582 used "ghost," as do the revised versions of 1881–1901 and the majority of contemporary translations.

GHOST, GIVE UP THE

Except for the term "Holy Ghost," the word "ghost" appears in the KJV only in the phrases "give up the ghost" (sixteen times) and "yield up the ghost" (three times). There is no difference in meaning between these phrases, which in most of the cases represent a single Hebrew or Greek word, a verb meaning "die."

For example, in Genesis 25:8 the KJV has "Abraham gave up the ghost, and died in a good old age." For "gave up the ghost," the contemporary versions have "breathed his last" (NASB, NIV, NKJV, NRSV, RSV), "breathed his last breath" (NCV). In Acts 5:5, it is said that Ananias "gave up the ghost" (KJV), and in verse 10 of the same chapter that his wife "yielded up the ghost" (KJV). The difference in wording was Tyndale's, and was retained by the authorized versions including the KJV.

The Greek verb is the same in the two verses; it is rendered as "dropped dead" (Acts 5:5) and "died" (5:10) by the CEV, "breathed his [Acts 5:10, "her"] last" by the NASB and NKJV, and "died" by other contemporary versions.

GIDEONS

The Gideons are an interdenominational Christian group who have the aim of making the Bible available to all people. Originally founded by three Christian commercial travelers—Samuel E. Hill, William J. Knights and John H. Nicholson—in Wisconsin in 1899, the organization places Bibles in hotel rooms, hospital wards, prisons, etc. It is named after Gideon, the Old Testament judge famous for his faithfulness in leading the small army which triumphed over the Midianites (Judges 6—7).

GIN

This word is likely to make us think of the alcoholic beverage, or perhaps of the machine which separates cotton from its seeds ("a cotton gin"). In fact, the word is a contraction of "engine" (see ENGINE), which at first meant "ingenuity," then its products, implements, or tools. One of the word's meanings today is "a trap or snare" (for game, etc.), and it occurs five times in the KJV with this meaning. In four of these passages it refers to the snares which beset people.

In Psalm 140:5 the psalmist complains how the proud "have set gins" (KJV) for him, while in Psalm 141:9 we read of "the gins of the workers of iniquity" (KJV). The

NASB, NRSV, and RSV use "snares" in these verses; the NKJV and NIV, "traps."

In Job 18:9 Bildad muses on the fate of the wicked, saying, "The gin shall take him by the heel" (KJV); the NASB has "snare" here, while other contemporary versions use "trap" (NCV, NIV, NLT, NRSV, RSV). In Isaiah 8:14 it is said of the Lord: "he shall be for a sanctuary; but for a stone of stumbling and for a rock of offence to both the houses of Israel, for a gin and for a snare to the inhabitants of Jerusalem" (KJV).

Contemporary versions read "a snare and a trap" (NASB) and vice versa (NIV, NKJV, NRSV, RSV). In Amos 3:5, "gin" is now rendered as "trap" (NKJV, NRSV, RSV), "snare" (NIV), and "bait" (NASB, NCV, NLT).

In Shakespeare's *King Henry VI, Part III* (I, 4, 60–61), when the Duke of York struggles as his enemies lay hands on him, they comment,

> "Ay, ay, so strives the woodcock with
>   the gin."
> "So doth the cony struggle in the net."

In *Part II* (III, 1, 261) of the same play, Suffolk had counseled that Humphrey, Duke of Gloucester, be put to death:

> "And do not stand on quillets how to
>   slay him:
> Be it by gins, by snares, by subtlety,
> Sleeping or waking, 'tis no matter how,
> So he be dead."

A "quillet" is an old word for a "quibble."

The KJV of 1611 had "ginne" in Isaiah 8:14 and Amos 3:5, but had "grinne" in Job 18:9 and "grinnes" in Psalms 140:5; 141:9. "Grinne" is an Old English word, of independent origin, which means a snare with a running noose. This reading remained in the KJV until the revision by Dr. Paris in 1762, when "gin" and "gins" were substituted in these three texts.

GIRD UP ONE'S LOINS

The phrase "gird up one's loins" means to prepare for energetic action. This old-fashioned idiomatic expression derives from the fact that the Israelites wore loose flowing robes. These were impractical for work or travel unless fastened up with a girdle or belt.

The expression occurs several times in the KJV. For example, 1 Kings 18:46, "And the hand of the LORD was on Elijah; and he girded up his loins, and ran before Ahab to the entrance of Jezreel." Of the contemporary versions, the NASB, NKJV, NRSV, and RSV retain the KJV expression; the NIV and NLT have "tucking [NLT, "He tucked"] his cloak into his belt"; the CEV has "wrapped his coat around himself" and the NCV, "tightened his clothes around him." See also 2 King 4:29, Elisha speaking to his servant Gehazi.

In Job 38:8 when the Lord challenged Job, "Gird up now thy loins like a man; for I will demand of thee, and answer thou me" (KJV), the contemporary versions have: "gird up your loins" (NASB, NRSV), "brace yourself" (NIV, NLT), "prepare yourself" (NKJV), "be strong" (NCV), and "get ready" (CEV).

In the New Testament the expression is used metaphorically to mean to get ready for the difficult tasks to be faced. Luke 12:35, "Let your loins be girded about" (KJV) is rendered: "Be dressed [NCV, "Be dressed,"] for service" (NCV, NIV, NLT), "Be dressed in readiness" (NASB), "Be ready" (CEV), and "Let your waist be girded" (NKJV).

In Ephesians 6:14, Paul describes the whole armor of God, "Stand therefore, having your loins girt about with truth" (KJV). This is rendered in the contemporary versions as "Stand firm therefore, HAVING GIRDED YOUR LOINS WITH TRUTH" (NASB; the small capitals indicating a reference to the Old Testament); "Stand therefore, having girded your waist with truth" (NKJV); "So stand strong, with the belt of truth tied around your waist" (NCV); "Stand therefore, and fasten the belt of truth around your waist" (NRSV); "Stand firm then, with the belt of truth buckled around your waist" (NIV); "Be ready! Let the truth be like a belt around your waist" (CEV); and "Stand your ground, putting on the sturdy belt of truth" (NLT).

In 1 Peter 1:13, Peter writes, "gird up the loins of your mind" (KJV). This is rendered in the contemporary versions as "prepare your minds for action" (NASB, NIV, NRSV), "prepare your minds for service" (NCV), "be alert" (CEV), and "think clearly" (NLT); the NKJV retains the KJV wording.

The phrase occurs in Bunyan's *Pilgrim's Progress*, when Christian had fallen into "musing in the midst of my dumps" at the Strait Gait, he is comforted by Good-will: "Then Christian began to gird up his loins, and to address himself to his journey."

GIVE PLACE

This is an archaic phrase which has a different meaning in each of its four occurrences in the KJV. In Isaiah 49:20 it means "to make room." "Give place to me that I may dwell" (KJV) is now rendered "make room for me" (NASB, NRSV, RSV), "Give us a bigger place" (NCV), and "give us more space" (NIV); the NKJV reads, "Give me a place where I may dwell."

In Matthew 9.24 "Give place" (KJV) represents the Greek verb which means "to go away." Jesus said to the crowd of mourners in the ruler's house, "Give place: for the maid is not dead, but sleepeth" (KJV). The NKJV renders Jesus' words as "Make room, for the girl is not dead, but sleeping"; other contemporary versions have "Go away" (NCV, NIV, NLT, NRSV), "Depart" (RSV), "Leave" (NASB), "Get out of here!" (CEV).

In Ephesians 4:27, "Neither give place to the devil" (KJV) is now rendered as "do not give the devil an opportunity" (NASB), and "do not make room for the devil" (NRSV). The NKJV retains the KJV rendering, and has "nor give place to the devil." In Galatians 2:5 the verb means "to yield." The NKJV reads, "we did not yield submission even for an hour"; the CEV, "we didn't give in to them, not even for a second."

GIVE UP THE GHOST

See GHOST, GIVE UP THE.

GLASS

Except for the book of Revelation, the word "glass" in the KJV means "mirror." In ancient times, mirrors were made of polished metal rather than of coated glass. In Exodus 38:8 we read that "lookingglasses" (KJV) offered by the women as gifts towards the building of the tabernacle were used to make the "laver of brass" (KJV) and its base.

The contemporary versions render "lookingglasses" (KJV) as "mirrors." In Job 37:18 the sky is said to be "strong, and as a molten looking glass" (KJV). The italics indicate that no word for "and" is in the Hebrew; the NASB translates the verse:

"Can you, with Him, spread out
    the skies,
Strong as a molten mirror?"

The "glasses" (KJV) which are listed by Isaiah among the articles of female finery (Isaiah 3:23) may have been hand mirrors, as the revised versions of 1881–1901 translate the word *gillayonim;* of the contemporary versions the NASB, NCV, NIV, and NKJV render them as "mirrors" [NASB, "hand mirrors"].

However, the Septuagint understood it to mean garments of gauzy transparent material, in Laconian style. While the reference to Laconia is probably an anachronism, the adjective which means transparent or translucent fits the context, and the NRSV and RSV follow this lead. They render the Hebrew as "garments of gauze."

GLASS, DARKLY

The contemporary versions use "mirror" in two notable New Testament passages. "For if any are hearers of the word and not doers, they are like those who look at themselves in a mirror" (James 1:23, NRSV). "For now we see in a mirror, dimly, but then face to face" (1 Corinthians 13:12,

NKJV; the KJV has "For now we see through a glass, darkly"). The point of these passages can be missed if we forget that the mirrors to which they refer were simply polished metal surfaces, incapable of the clear, sharply defined reflections from a mirror made of glass.

The phrase "see through a glass darkly" has its origins in 1 Corinthians 13:12 and is sometimes used to express the limitations of present knowledge. In that verse Paul drew a contrast between a present ("now") imperfect knowledge of God having only a poor, indistinct reflection in a mirror, which is as nothing compared with a full ("then face to face") encounter.

The contemporary versions render the KJV "we see through a glass, darkly" as "we see in a mirror dimly" (NASB, NKJV, NRSV, RSV), "we see but a poor reflection as in a mirror" (NIV), "we see things imperfectly as in a poor mirror" (NLT), "we see a dim reflection, as if we were looking into a mirror" (NCV), and "all we can see of God is like a cloudy picture in a mirror" (CEV).

GLISTERING

The word "glistering" is likely to remind us of stars in the night sky and Christmas tree lights. "Glisten," "glister," and "glitter" are old verbs with a common Teutonic base, and at first with no apparent difference of meaning. "Glisten" does not appear in the KJV; "glistering" appears twice, "glitter" once, and "glittering" six times. The KJV had "glistering sword" (Job 20:25) in 1611, but in 1762 this was changed to "glittering sword."

In Shakespeare's *Merchant of Venice* (II, 7, 65), an old proverb was quoted as "All that glisters is not gold" (but in Boswell's *Life of Samuel Johnson* it appears as "All is not gold that glitters"). At Job 20:25 the contemporary versions have "glittering" (NASB, NKJV, NRSV, RSV), "shining" (CEV), "gleaming" (NIV), and "glistens" (NLT).

The "glistering stones" (KJV) listed among the materials that David had provided for the building of the house of God represent

the Hebrew term for "antimony" (1 Chronicles 29:2; compare Isaiah 54:11), and are rendered thus by the NASB, NRSV, and RSV. The NKJV has "glistening stones."

Each of the Synoptic Gospels has its own language to describe the appearance of Jesus' raiment when he was transfigured in the presence of Peter, James, and John. The one word on which the three Gospels agree is "white." The KJV rendering of Luke 9:29 has "white and glistering"; the NLT, NRSV, and RSV have "dazzling white." The Greek word here is the participle of the verb which means "to flash or gleam like lightning," and the NIV reads, "his clothes became as bright as a flash of lightning."

GLORY

As a verb, "glory" is a word which we hear today in the context of proud rejoicing or arrogant boasting ("you should hear him glory in his golfing scores"). The biblical use of the word is likely to be familiar to us from passages such as Isaiah 41:16 ("thou shalt rejoice in the LORD, and shall glory in the Holy One of Israel," KJV) and Galatians 6:14 ("God forbid that I should glory, save in the cross of our Lord Jesus Christ," KJV).

"Glory" is often retained by contemporary versions, for example by the NASB, NIV, NRSV, NLT, and NRSV in their renderings of the Isaiah text. On other occasions, different terms are used. Galatians 6:14 reads, in the NASB, "May it never be that I would boast" and, in the NCV and CEV, "I will never brag."

Romans 15:17 reads in the KJV: "I have therefore whereof I may glory through Jesus Christ in those things which pertain to God." The NASB reads, "I have found reason for boasting"; the NCV, "So I am proud"; the CEV, "I can take pride." The NLT renders Paul's words as "So it is right for me to be enthusiastic about all Christ Jesus has done through me in my service to God."

The renderings of contemporary versions may help to shed light on the word's meaning in Exodus 8:9, which reads, in the KJV: "And Moses said unto Pharaoh, Glory over me: when shall I intreat for thee, and for thy servants, and for thy people, to destroy the frogs from thee and thy houses, that they may remain in the river only?" Moses' first phrase means "Glorify yourself over me." Elsewhere, the KJV translates the verb as "vaunt [themselves]" (Judges 7:2), and "boast [itself]" (Isaiah 10:15). Moses is saying, "Assume the honor over me (to decide) when."

Contemporary versions render Moses' words as "The honor is yours to tell me: when shall I entreat for you" (NASB), "Accept the honor of saying when I shall intercede for you . . . to destroy the frogs from you" (NKJV), and "Kindly tell me when I am to pray for you" (NRSV). The RSV has "Be pleased to command me when I am to entreat . . . that the frogs be destroyed." This is not simply a polite form of address; the real reason for leaving Pharaoh the decision concerning the time for the destruction of the frogs was to manifest more clearly the omnipotence of God. When Pharaoh said, "Tomorrow," Moses answered, "Be it according to thy word: that thou mayest know that there is none like unto the LORD our God" (Exodus 8:10, KJV).

As a noun, "glory" is used in Job 39:19–25 which is a spirited description of the war horse: "Hast thou given the horse strength? has thou clothed his neck with thunder? Canst thou make him afraid as a grasshopper? the glory of his nostrils is terrible" (vv. 19–20, KJV). Contemporary versions render "glory" (KJV) here as "snorting." They have "His [NRSV, "Its"] majestic snorting" (NASB, NKJV, NLT, RSV) and "his [NCV, "its"] proud snorting" (NIV) for "the glory of his nostrils" (KJV).

GLORY, IN ALL ITS

The expression "in all one's/its glory" means "displaying great beauty"; "having a splendid appearance." The expression derives from Matthew 6:29 (KJV), with refer-

ence to the "lilies of the field" (v. 28): "And yet I say unto you, that even Solomon in all his glory was not arrayed like one of these."

Of the contemporary versions the NASB, NKJV, NLT, NRSV, and RSV retain the KJV wording "in all his glory"; the NIV has "in all his splendor"; the CEV, "with all his wealth" and the NCV, "with his riches."

GNASHING OF TEETH

To gnash one's teeth is to grind the upper and lower teeth against each other in anger, pain, frustration, etc. The expression derives from the KJV "weeping and gnashing of teeth" which occurs five times in the Gospels (Matthew 8:12; 13:42; 22:13; 24:51; 25:30; Luke 13:28) and once (Matthew 13:50) as "wailing and gnashing of teeth" to describe pain and anguish of severe punishment.

In all the instances from Matthew's Gospel the KJV phrase "weeping and gnashing of teeth" is retained by the NASB, NIV, NKJV, NLT, and NRSV; the CEV paraphrases as "cry and grit their teeth in pain" and the NCV as "cry and grind their teeth with pain." The translations in the contemporary versions of Luke 13:28 are similar, with the CEV rendering as "you will weep and grit your teeth" and the NCV, "you will cry and grind your teeth with pain."

GO ABOUT

"He that goeth about as a talebearer revealeth secrets" (Proverbs 20:19, KJV). "[They] went about throughout all the cities of Judah, and taught the people" (2 Chronicles 17:9, KJV). "Jesus . . . went about doing good" (Acts 10:38, KJV). These are three of a dozen passages where "go about" is used in the KJV in the natural sense of moving here and there or traveling in various places. In other passages the KJV usage may not be so readily understood.

"Their imagination which they go about, even now" (Deuteronomy 31:21, KJV) is rendered "their intent which they are developing today" by the NASB, and "the purposes which they are already forming" by the RSV. In 1 Samuel 15:12 "is gone about" (KJV) is rendered "turned" (NASB, NIV, RSV), "gone on around" (NKJV), and "returning" (NRSV); and in 2 Kings 3:25 "went about it" now reads, "surrounded it" (CEV, NCV, NIV, NKJV, NRSV, RSV).

"How long wilt thou go about, O thou backsliding daughter?" (Jeremiah 31:22, KJV) is rendered by the NRSV, "How long will you waver, O faithless daughter?" The NKJV has "how long will you gad about?"; the NASB, "How long will you go here and there?" This is in keeping with Jeremiah's earlier prophecy, in chapter 14, where we read that the people "have loved to wander, they have not refrained their feet, therefore the LORD doth not accept them" (v. 10, KJV).

A few verses later, in Jeremiah 14:18, we meet the expression "go about" again: "both the prophet and the priest go about into a land that they know not" (KJV). The NRSV and RSV render "go about" (KJV) as "ply their trade"; the CEV has "go about their business"; the NLT, "continue with their work." The NASB reads, "For both prophet and priest Have gone roving about in the land that they do not know."

"Go about" with a following infinitive is used seven times in the KJV New Testament in the obsolete sense of "endeavor" or "plan." Jesus is represented as asking, "Why go ye about to kill me?" (John 7:19). On Paul's first visit to Jerusalem after his conversion, his opponents "went about to slay him" (Acts 9:29). When the Jews caught him in the temple on his last visit, they "went about to kill" him (Acts 26:21).

In these cases "go about" is used as translation for Greek verbs which contemporary versions render as "seek," "try," or "attempt." In fact, the same Greek verb which the KJV represents by "go about" in Jesus' question is translated by "seek" a few verses later: "Is not this he, whom they seek to kill?" (John 7:25, KJV).

GO AND DO LIKEWISE

"To do likewise" is to do the same or a similar thing. The expression comes at the conclusion of the parable of the good Samaritan, after Jesus had replied to the lawyer's question, "Who is my neighbour?" (Luke 10:29, KJV). Jesus asked the lawyer, "Which now of these three, thinkest thou, was neighbour unto him that fell among the thieves?" And he said, "He that showed mercy on him." Then said Jesus unto him, "Go, and do thou likewise" (Luke 10:36–37, KJV).

The lawyer had to act in the same way—this should be his way of life from now on.

The reply "Go, and do thou likewise" (Luke 10:37, KJV) is rendered as follows in the contemporary versions: "Go and do likewise" (NIV, NKJV, NRSV, RSV), "Go [NLT, "Now go"] and do the same" [CEV, "the same!"] (NASB), and "Then go and do what he did" (NCV). (See GOOD SAMARITAN)

GO ASIDE

This expression has a special meaning in the KJV rendering of Numbers 5:12, 20, 29, where it refers to the behavior of an unfaithful wife. Most contemporary versions use "go astray." The same Hebrew verb appears in Proverbs 7:25, at the close of a vivid description of the seductive wiles of a loose woman.

"Go not astray in her paths," counsels the KJV; the NASB, NKJV, NRSV, and RSV read, "Do not stray into her paths." The NLT reads, "Don't wander down her wayward path."

GO BEYOND

The expression "go beyond" appears in the KJV rendering of 1 Thessalonians 4:6, where Paul urges his new converts to abstain from sexual impurity and fornication, particularly in the context of courtship and marriage: "That no man go beyond and defraud his brother in any matter: because that the Lord is the avenger of all such, as we also have forewarned you and testified."

"Go beyond" is now rendered as "transgress" (NASB, RSV), "wrong" (NCV, NIV, NRSV), and "take advantage" (NKJV). Tyndale and other sixteenth-century translators held the view that verses 3–5 refer to the relations of the sexes, but that verse 6 refers to bargaining or to business in general.

The majority of contemporary translations, however, take verses 3–8 as belonging together, dealing, as they do, with the same subject—abstention from immorality and the sanctity of Christian marriage. Verses 4–6a read, in the NASB: "that each of you know how to possess his own vessel in sanctification and honor, not in lustful passion, like the Gentiles who do not know God; and that no man transgress and defraud his brother in the matter." (See VESSEL)

Contemporary translations differ on the translations of the KJV "his vessel"; the NKJV and NASB have "his own vessel," the CEV and RSV read "your wife" and "a wife," respectively; other translations are "your [NCV, NRSV, "your own"] body" (NCV, NRSV, NLT) and "his own body" (NIV).

GO IT UP

This expression occurs in the KJV rendering of Isaiah 15:5. "For by the mounting up of Luhith with weeping shall they go it up" (KJV) might be taken to imply that the fugitives scamper up in haste. Contemporary versions delete the "it." The NASB reads, "For they go up the ascent of Luhith weeping."

GO THE WAY OF ALL FLESH

The expression "go the way of all flesh" is sometimes used in contemporary English to mean "to die or disappear finally." The phrase, however, is not actually found in the KJV Bible text. The Bible text reads, e.g., at Joshua 23:14 and 1 Kings 2:2, "go [Joshua 23:14, "going"] the way of all the earth" (KJV). This wording is retained by

the NASB, NIV, NKJV, and the NRSV; the CEV at Joshua 23:14 and 1 Kings 2:2 has "I will soon die"; the NCV reads at Joshua 23:14, "It's almost time for me to die" and at 1 Kings 2:2, "My time to die is near."

GO TO

As used in the KJV, "go to" is a mild imperative, which introduces an exhortation or command, and has the force of "Come" in "Come, let us go" (1 Samuel 9:10, KJV); "Come on, let us deal wisely with them" (Exodus 1:10, KJV); or "Come, and let us go up to the mountain of the LORD" (Micah 4:2, KJV). The passages where the KJV uses "Go to" rather than "Come" are Genesis 11:3, 4, 7; 38:16; James 4:13; 5:1. The revised versions omit the now obsolete expression in 2 Kings 5:5 and Judges 7:3.

As an expression of remonstrance, protest, incredulity, or derision, "go to" may still be archaic English, as the dictionaries imply. But it does not have this sense in the KJV.

GO TO THE ANT, THOU SLUGGARD

"Go to the ant, thou sluggard" is sometimes used as a condemnation of laziness. The expression comes from Proverbs 6:6–9 (KJV): "Go to the ant, thou sluggard; consider her ways, and be wise: Which having no guide, overseer, or ruler, Provideth her meat in the summer, and gathereth her food in the harvest. How long wilt thou sleep, O sluggard? when wilt thou arise out of thy sleep?"

The contemporary versions render the KJV expression as "Go to the ant, you [NASB, RSV, "ant, O"] sluggard" (NASB, NIV, NKJV, RSV), "Go to the ant, you lazybones" (NRSV), "Go watch the ants, you lazy person" (NCV), "Take a lesson from the ants, you lazybones" (NLT), and "You lazy people can learn by watching an anthill" (CEV).

GOD AND MAMMON

The expression "serve God and mammon" occurs twice in the KJV: in the Sermon on the Mount (Matthew 6:24), "No man can serve two masters: for either he will hate the one, and love the other; or else he will hold to the one, and despise the other. Ye cannot serve God and mammon" and in the parable of the unjust steward or the shrewd manager (Luke 16:13), "No servant can serve two masters: for either he will hate the one, and love the other; or else he will hold to the one, and despise the other. Ye cannot serve God and mammon."

In both verses the contemporary versions render the KJV "mammon" (also retained by the NKJV and RSV) as "money" (CEV, NLT), "Money" (NIV), "wealth" (NASB, NRSV), and "worldly riches" (NCV). The OED notes that Mammon is "the Aramaic word for 'riches', occurring in the Greek text of Matt. vi. 24 and Luke xvi. 9–13, and retained in the Vulgate. Owing to the quasi-personification in these passages, the word was taken by mediæval writers as the proper name of the devil of covetousness. This use appears in English in the 14th–16th c., and was revived by Milton (*Paradise Lost.* i. 678, ii. 228).

"The word does not occur in the N.T. translations of Wycliffe and Purvey (who substitute *richessis*), but it was used by Tyndale (1526–1534) and subsequent translators, with the exception of those of the Geneva version. From the 16th c. onwards it has been current in English, usually with more or less of personification, as a term of opprobrium for wealth regarded as an idol or as an evil influence."

In Spenser's *The Faerie Queene* (2.7), Sir Guyon encounters Mammon:

"God of the world and worldlings I
  me call,
Great Mammon, greatest god below
  the skye,
That of my plenty poure out unto all,
And unto none my graces do enuye:
Riche, renowne, and principality,
Honour, estate, and all this worldes
  good,

For which men swinck and sweat
  incessantly,
Fro me do flow into an ample flood,
And in the hollow earth have their
  eternal brood."

(See also MAN CANNOT SERVE TWO MASTERS)

GOD FORBID

This expression occurs in the KJV as an expression of strong dissent. Hebrew and Greek expressions which it translates, however, do not refer to the deity. The Hebrew expression is an exclamation, *halilah*, derived from the verb *halal*, which means "to pollute, defile, violate, profane." The exclamation means that the suggestion which calls it forth is so utterly wrong or impious that it is immediately and decisively rejected.

The Latin Vulgate usually translated it as *Absit a me* (*te*, etc.), "Far be it from me (you)," etc.). But Tyndale took "God forbid" as the English translation in the majority of cases, and was followed by the KJV, which has "God forbid" in Genesis 44:7, 17; Joshua 22:29; 24:16; 1 Samuel 12:23; 14:45; 20:2; Job 27:5. It has "The LORD forbid" in 1 Samuel 24:6; 26:11; 1 Kings 21:3, and "My God forbid" in 1 Chronicles 11:19; but in these four texts the word LORD or God is added to *halilah* in the Hebrew. The KJV translates *halilah* as "Be it far from" or "Far be it from" in Genesis 18:25; 1 Samuel 2:30; 20:9; 22:15; 2 Samuel 20:20; 23:17; Job 34:10.

The Septuagint used various Greek phrases to represent *halilah*. Of these, the one which is most often used in the New Testament is *me genoito*, which means literally "May it not be so!" This expression appears ten times in Paul's epistle to the Romans, where it marks the onward course of his argument, as he rejects various wrong inferences and suggestions. It appears also in 1 Corinthians 6:15 and Galatians 2:17; 3:21; 6:14. Tyndale and following versions used "God forbid" in all these cases.

Contemporary versions render *me gen-oito* in various ways. "May it never be!" is the preferred form in the NASB; other versions have "Certainly not!" (e.g., Romans 3:6, NKJV), "Not at all!" (e.g., Romans 3:4, NIV), "By no means!" (e.g., Romans 7:13, NRSV, RSV), "Never!" (1 Corinthians 6:15, NIV, NLT, NRSV, RSV), and "Of course not!" (Galatians 2:17, NLT).

In Luke 20, Luke records Jesus' parable of the wicked tenants, the climax of which comes in verse 16 with the suggestion that the vineyard will be handed over "to others" (KJV). Jesus' listeners react with a shocked "God forbid" (v. 16, KJV). The NLT and RSV retain this rendering, and the NRSV has "Heaven forbid!" Other versions use "May it [NIV, "May this"] never be!" (NASB, NIV), "Let this never happen!" (NCV), and "Certainly not!" (NKJV).

GOD SAVE THE KING

This expression appears in Shakespeare's *Macbeth* (I, 2, 47) as a greeting, in *King Richard II* (IV, 1, 172) as a benediction, and in *King Henry VI, Part II* (IV, 8, 19; 9, 22) as a cry of loyal acclaim. It occurs in the KJV where the people accept Saul as their king (1 Samuel 10:24), and is used in reference to Absalom, Adonijah, Solomon, and Joash (2 Samuel 16:16; 1 Kings 1:25, 34, 39; 2 Kings 11:12; 2 Chronicles 23:11).

The word "God" does not appear in the Hebrew, which reads "may the king live." The same Hebrew expression occurs in 1 Kings 1:31, where the Bishops' Bible had "I pray God that my lord king David may live for ever," which the KJV rendered as "Let my lord king David live for ever."

The revisers in 1901 changed "God save the king" to "Long live the king" in all the passages where the expression occurs, and contemporary versions follow their rendering.

GOD SPEED

To bid one "God speed," says the OED, is "to express a wish for the success of one who is setting out on some journey or enterprise." In 2 John 10–11, however, where the context is arrival rather than departure, we read in the KJV: "If there come any unto you, and bring not this doctrine, receive him not into *your* house, neither bid him God speed: For he that biddeth him God speed is partaker of his evil deeds."

The Greek word is the usual one for "Hail!" The revised versions use "greet" and "greeting," as do the CEV, NASB, NKJV, NRSV, and RSV. The NCV, NIV, and NRSV use "welcome." The NLT reads, "don't invite him into your house or encourage him in any way." Goodspeed has "do not bid him good morning"; Ballantine, "do not bid him welcome."

GOING FORTH

In the KJV, "going forth" occurs in Psalm 19:6 and Isaiah 13:10 where it refers to the rising of the sun. The plural "goings forth" (KJV) occurs in Micah 5:2, where it is retained by the NASB and NKJV; other contemporary versions have "origin" (NRSV, RSV); "origins" (NIV, NLT). This prophecy reads in the NRSV:

"But you, O Bethlehem of Ephrathah,
who are one of the little clans of
   Judah,
from you shall come forth for me
one who is to rule in Israel,
whose origin is from of old,
from ancient days."

In Ezekiel 43:11, the phrases "the goings out thereof, and the comings in thereof" (KJV) is now rendered "its exits and its entrances" (NKJV, NRSV, RSV). The KJV rendering of Ezekiel 44:5, however, may not be so clear. Here Ezekiel is instructed to "mark well the entering in of the house, with every going forth of the sanctuary" (KJV).

A slight emendation of the Hebrew words has led to the rendering offered by the NRSV and RSV: "mark well those who may be admitted to the temple and all those who are to be excluded from the sanctuary." The CEV, NKJV, and NLT echo this rendering, which makes the people entering and exiting the temple the object of the prophet's attention, rather than the entrances and exits themselves, the rendering adopted by the NASB, NCV, and NIV.

GOINGS

The plural of the verbal noun "going" is used six times by the KJV to render Hebrew words which it elsewhere translates as "steps" or "paths." The majority of the contemporary versions have "steps" in Job 34:21, Psalm 17:5, and Proverbs 20:24, and "paths" in Proverbs 5:21.

In Isaiah 59:8 we read of the wicked, that "there is no judgment in their goings" (KJV); the NASB reads, "there is no justice in their tracks." In Psalm 40:2, the psalmist testifies to the Lord's saving action with the words, "He brought me up also out of an horrible pit, out of the miry clay, and set my feet upon a rock, and established my goings" (KJV). The NLT reads, "He set my feet on solid ground and steadied me as I walked along." The meaning in each of these cases is figurative, referring to a course of life.

In Psalm 140:4 "who have purposed to overthrow my goings" (KJV) is now rendered "who have purposed to make my steps stumble" (NKJV). "Thy goings, O God" (Psalm 68:24, KJV) refers either to the procession of worshipers or to the manifestation of God—probably to both. The NRSV translates verses 24–26:

"Your solemn processions are seen,
    O God, the processions of my
    God, my King, into the
    sanctuary—
the singers in front, the musicians
    last, between them girls playing
    tambourines:
'Bless God in the great
    congregation, the LORD, O you
    who are of Israel's fountain!'"

"The sound of [a] going in the tops of the mulberry trees" (2 Samuel 5:24; 1 Chronicles 14:15, KJV) is now "the sound of marching in the tops of the balsam trees" (NASB, NCV, NIV, NRSV, RSV).

GOINGS OUT

The expression "goings out" in Numbers 34 and Joshua 15—16, and 18 stands for the Hebrew word which the KJV renders as "outgoings" in Joshua 17—19. It is rendered as "end" and "termination" by contemporary versions. (See OUTGOINGS)

GOLDEN CALF

While Moses was on Mount Sinai receiving the tablets of the Law, Aaron yielded to pressure from the people to make an idol. Aaron collected the Israelites' gold earrings and melted them "and fashioned it with a graving tool, after he had made it a molten calf" (Exodus 32:4, KJV).

The contemporary versions render this as "made it into an idol cast in the shape of a calf" (NIV), "made a statue of a calf" (NCV), "made a molded calf" (NKJV), "molded and tooled it into the shape of a calf" (NLT), "cast an image of a calf" (NRSV), "made it into a molten calf" (NASB), and "made an idol in the shape of a young bull" (CEV).

In Ben Jonson's *The Alchemist*, Sir Epicure Mammon gives an assurance that he will make Surly rich; he says that no longer shall:

"the sons of Sword and Hazard
    fall before
The golden calf, and on their
    knees, whole nights,
Commit idolatry with wine and
    trumpets . . ."

The "golden calf" has come to stand for money or materialism, considered as an object of worship.

GOLDEN RULE

The "golden rule" is that given by Jesus in the Sermon on the Mount (Matthew 7:12, KJV), "Therefore all things whatsoever ye would that men should do to you, do ye even so to them." The phrase "golden rule" does not, however, appear in the Bible text.

According to the OED, the first usage of this sense of the word "golden" ("Of rules, precepts, etc.: Of inestimable utility") is dated 1674 ("Golden Law"); the first occurrence of "golden rule" in the OED is dated 1807. The phrasing of the golden rule itself in common parlance varies from that of the KJV, ranging from "do as you would done by" (as in the earliest [1674] quotation in the OED noted above) to variants beginning, "Do unto [or: to] others," e.g., "Do to others as you would have them do to you" (Matthew 7:12, NRSV).

The CEV and NASB render the phrase with the verb "treat," e.g., "Treat others as you want them to treat you" (Matthew 7:12, CEV). See also Luke 6:31.

GOOD AND FAITHFUL SERVANT

In the parable of the talents, Jesus commends the servant who had been given five talents and who had used his five talents wisely to gain five more with the words, "Well done, thou good and faithful servant: thou has been faithful over a few things, I will make thee ruler over many things: enter thou into the joy of thy lord."

In the same way, Jesus commends the servant who had been given two talents and who had used his two talents wisely to gain two more. The contemporary versions render the KJV expression "good and faithful servant" as: "good and loyal servant" (NCV), "good and faithful slave" (CEV), and "good and trustworthy slave" (NRSV); the CEV, NIV, NKJV, NLT, and RSV retain the KJV translation.

In Robert Southey's poem *A Vision of Judgment* (1821), King George III appealed to God for pardon:

"Bending forward he spake with
    earnest humility, 'Well done,
Good and faithful servant!' then said
    a voice from the Brightness;
'Enter thou into the joy of thy Lord.'"

GOOD SAMARITAN

A "good Samaritan" is someone who helps others in need. The phrase refers to the parable that Jesus told of the Samaritan who rescued and helped an injured man who had been attacked and robbed—when a priest and a Levite had passed by on the other side without offering any help at all. In the story (Luke 10:30–37), the man from Samaria is nameless; he is described simply as "a Samaritan," but his kind and selfless actions are remembered in the expression "a good Samaritan" that has become part of the language.

Jesus told the parable in response to a lawyer's request for Jesus to say, "who is my neighbour?" (Luke 10:29). The parable shows that a good neighbor may be a person whom one least expects. There was intense rivalry between Samaria and Judea: in Jesus' time the Jews still held the Samaritans in contempt (see, e.g., John 4:9).

So Jesus' hearers would have been shocked: here was a good Samaritan, one who was despised in their eyes (the NLT has "Then a despised Samaritan came along" for Luke 10:33) who was actually the one being compassionate. (See GO AND DO LIKEWISE)

GOOD WORKS

"Good works" are, in common parlance, "charitable work"—acts carried out to improve the well-being of others. The expression occurs sixteen times in the KJV, all in the New Testament, e.g., Acts 9:36, "Now there was at Joppa a certain disciple named Tabitha, which by interpretation is called Dorcas: this woman was full of good works and almsdeeds which she did."

The contemporary versions render the KJV expression "was full of good works" as: "was devoted to good works" (NRSV), "always doing good" (NIV), "was always doing good deeds" (NCV), "was always doing good things for people" (CEV), "was always doing kind things for others" (NLT), "was abounding with deeds of kindness" (NASB); the NKJV and RSV retain the KJV translation.

The KJV "good works" in the other references is retained, translated as "good deeds," or rendered as, for example, "Make your light shine, so that others will see the good that you do and will praise your Father in heaven" (Matthew 5:16, CEV); "For we are God's masterpiece. He has created us anew in Christ Jesus, so that we can do the good things he planned for us long ago" (Ephesians 2:10, NLT).

GOODLY

In contemporary usage, "goodly" is more used in the sense of "substantial" ("a goodly number of people") than in the sense of "pleasantly attractive," its predominant meaning in the KJV. The word is used thirty-six times in the KJV, and it represents nineteen different Hebrew and Greek terms.

The RSV retains "I have a goodly heritage" (Psalm 16:6); "when she saw that he was a goodly child" (Exodus 2:2); and "goodly hill country," "goodly cities," and "goodly houses" (Deuteronomy 3:25; 6.10; 8:12).

Other contemporary versions use "beautiful" (NASB, NCV), "delightful" (NIV), and "wonderful" (NLT) of the psalmist's inheritance (Psalm 16:6); "beautiful" (CEV, NASB, NKJV, NLT) and "fine" (NIV, NRSV) of the child Moses (Exodus 2:2), "good" (NASB, NRSV), "fine" (NIV), and "pleasant" (NKJV) of the hill country beyond the Jordan (Deuteronomy 3:25); and "splendid" (NASB), "flourishing" (NIV), and "prosperous" (NLT) of the cities promised to the Israelites as they enter Canaan (Deuteronomy 6:10). "Goodly houses" (Deuteronomy 8:12, KJV) is now rendered "fine houses" [NLT, "homes"] (NLT, NIV, NRSV).

The KJV uses "goodly" to describe the physical appearance of Joseph (Genesis 39:6), David (1 Samuel 16:12), Adonijah (1 Kings 1:6), and the Egyptian whom Benaiah slew with his own spear (2 Samuel 23:21). The majority of contemporary versions use "handsome" in these contexts.

The KJV says of Saul that he was "a choice young man, and a goodly" (1 Samuel 9:2); the NASB and NKJV describe him as "choice and handsome," while the NIV has "impressive." The "goodly" cedar of Ezekiel 17:23 is now rendered as "stately" (NASB), "great" (NCV), "splendid" (NIV), "majestic" (NKJV), and "noble" (NRSV, RSV), while the cedars of Psalm 80:10 are generally described by the contemporary versions as "mighty."

The "goodly Babylonish garment" which Achan coveted (Joshua 7:21, KJV) is rendered "a beautiful mantle from Shinar" by the NRSV. The NASB and NKJV have "valuable [NKJV, "costly"] articles" for the "goodly vessels" (KJV) of 2 Chronicles 36:10. "Goodly pleasant things" (Joel 3:5, KJV) is now rendered "precious treasures" (NASB, NLT) and "prized possessions" (NKJV); "goodly pearls" (Matthew 13:45, KJV) are now "fine pearls" (NASB, NCV, NIV, NRSV, RSV).

"Goodliness" appears once in the KJV: "All flesh is grass, and all the goodliness thereof *is* as the flower of the field" (Isaiah 40:6). Contemporary versions render "goodliness" (KJV) here as "loveliness" (NASB, NKJV), "glory" (NCV, NIV), "beauty" (NLT, RSV), and "constancy" (NRSV).

GOODMAN

A "goodman" is a husband or the male head of a household. The word is archaic except in Scotland.

In Proverbs 7:19, a harlot tells her quarry, "the goodman is not at home." This translation began with Coverdale. The Geneva Bible and the Douay Bible have "my husband is not at home," as do all the contemporary versions.

"Goodman of the house" is used five times in the Synoptic Gospels to translate the Greek *oikodespotes*. In Matthew 20:11 the majority of the contemporary versions render it as "landowner," but elsewhere other terms are used, such as "homeowner" (e.g., Matthew 24:43, CEV), "owner of the house" (e.g., Mark 14:14, NASB), "head of the house" (e.g., Luke 12:39, NASB), "master of the house" (e.g., Luke 22:11, NKJV), and "house-holder" (e.g., Luke 12:39, RSV).

In the *Concordance to Shakespeare* "good man" and "goodman" are separately listed. The two-word phrase appears in the plays of Shakespeare thirty-seven times, and the word "goodman" thirteen times.

GOVERNOR

The word "governor" is familiar to us today from a range of executive contexts: we have state governors and governors of British Crown colonies, for example. In the KJV the word is also used in the context of government or management—but on a much smaller scale. First Kings 18:3 (KJV) reads, "Ahab called Obadiah, which was the governor of his house" (KJV).

Contemporary versions describe Obadiah as being "in charge" (CEV, NCV, NIV, NKJV, NLT, NRSV), or "over" (NASB, RSV), Ahab's "palace" (CEV, NCV, NIV, NLT, NRSV; NASB, RSV, "household").

In James 3:4, the KJV uses "governor" in the obsolete sense of "the pilot or steers-man of a ship." In Galatians 4.1–2 (KJV), "the heir, as long as he is a child . . . is under tutors and governors until the time ap-pointed of the father." The Greek terms are now rendered "guardians and managers" by the NASB, and "guardians and trustees" by the NIV, NRSV, and RSV.

In the account of the marriage at Cana, "the governor of the feast" and "the ruler of the feast" (John 2.8–9) are the same per-son, the *architriklinos*. He was not the toast-master or "master of the feast"; the Greek word for that was *sumposiarches*. He is now referred to as "the headwaiter" (NASB) or "steward" (NRSV, RSV), who was responsi-ble for managing all the properties and procedures of the affair—tables, seating, courses, and the serving of food and wine.

GRAIN OF MUSTARD SEED

Jesus told the parable of the mustard seed: "The kingdom of heaven is like to a grain of mustard seed, which a man took,

and sowed in his field: Which indeed is the least of all seeds: but when it is grown, it is the greatest among herbs, and becometh a tree, so that the birds of the air come and lodge in the branches thereof" (Matthew 13:31–32, KJV). The Greek has simply "a grain of mustard," meaning "a grain of mustard seed," as in the KJV and RSV, or more simply "a mustard seed" as in all the other contemporary versions.

In the parallel passages, Mark 4:31 and Luke 13:19, the KJV and RSV have "a grain of mustard seed," the NLT has "a tiny mustard seed," and the other contemporary ver-sions have simply "a mustard seed."

GRAVEN IMAGE

A graven image is an image, figure, or other object of worship, usually one that is carved from wood or stone. The second of the Ten Commandments is: "Thou shalt not make unto thee any graven image, or any likeness of any thing that is in heaven above, or that is in the earth beneath, or that is in the water under the earth" (Exo-dus 20:4, KJV).

The expression "graven image" is ren-dered as "idol" by the NASB, NCV, NIV, and NRSV (and the CEV and NLT use "idols") and "carved image" by the NKJV; the RSV retains the KJV term. The parallel passage, Deuter-onomy 5:8, has similar renderings.

The phrase "graven image" or "graven images" occur forty-six times in the KJV; the renderings among the contemporary trans-lations are generally "carved image," "image," or "idol," with the NASB often retaining the KJV rendering "graven image."

GREEN PASTURES

In Psalm 23:2, David writes of the Lord, "He maketh me to lie down in green pas-tures: he leadeth me beside the still wa-ters." The green pastures are the fresh, rich, grassy meadows into which a shep-herd leads his sheep. Of the contemporary versions, the NASB, NCV, NIV, NKJV, NRSV, and RSV retain the KJV expression "green pastures"; the CEV has, "green grass" and the NLT translates as "green meadows."

GRIEF, GRIEVE

The word "grief" is now used only for "deep sorrow" or "regret" but "grief" was more widely applied in Old English. It could mean "any hardship or cause of hardship," "harm or damage," "bodily injury, ailment, disease, or pain," "mental pain or distress." Most of these meanings are now obsolete. The colloquial idiom "come to grief" is an exception. It means "meet with disaster" and may refer to disaster or frustration of any kind.

Even more than "heaviness" and "heavy," the words "grief" and "grieve" are used in the KJV in a great variety of meanings. The KJV uses "grief" or "grieve" as translation for twenty-four different Hebrew words and four Greek words, each of which has its own meaning.

Job, for example, is not a man overcome with grief, in the modern sense of the term. Contemporary versions, with the exception of the NKJV, read "pain" and/or "suffering" in 2:13 and 16:5–6. When, after seven days of silence, Job cursed the day of his birth and Eliphaz ventures to speak, his question reads, in the KJV, "Wilt thou be grieved?" (4:2). "Will you be offended?" is the NRSV and RSV rendering; the NASB and NIV use the word "impatient."

Job's answer begins in 6:2, "O that my grief were thoroughly weighed, and all my calamity laid in the balances together!" (KJV). He uses the Hebrew word (rendered "grief" here by the KJV) which in 10:17 he attributes to God, "thine indignation upon me." The Hebrew word is the same.

The basic meaning of the Hebrew is "vexation" or "anger" in such passages as Genesis 34:7; 1 Samuel 1:16; 15:11; Nehemiah 2:10, 13.8; Psalm 112:10; Ecclesiastes 1:18; 2:23. In Genesis 26:35 we read that Esau's choice of wife from among the Hittites brought "grief of mind unto Isaac and to Rebekah" (KJV). The NRSV and RSV read that

"they made life bitter for Isaac and Rebekah," but the NKJV retains the expression "grief of mind" and other versions have "brought grief" (NASB) and "were a source of grief" (NIV).

Similar references are Ruth 1:13, where the NIV, NLT, NRSV, and RSV have "bitter"; 1 Samuel 30:6, where the NASB reads "embittered"; and Psalm 73:21, where "bitter" and "embittered" are used by most contemporary versions. The Hebrew word is rendered with "loathe," "hate," and "disgust" by many of the contemporary versions in Psalms 95:10; 119:158; and 139:21.

It is rendered as "dread" by the NASB, NIV, NKJV, NRSV, and RSV in Exodus 1:12. It refers to physical attack in Genesis 49:23 (KJV, "The archers have sorely grieved him, and shot at him, and hated him"); and to mere discomfort in Jonah 4:6.

GRIEVOUS, GRIEVOUSLY

Like the noun and verb above, the adjective and adverb are used more widely in the KJV than in contemporary language. They are applied not only to wounds, blows, famine, illness, and sin, but in more general senses to what is heavy, severe, stern, harsh, or displeasing.

"His ways are always grievous" (Psalm 10:5, KJV) is now rendered "His [NRSV, "Their"] ways prosper at all times" (NRSV, NASB, RSV). "Speak grievous things" (Psalm 31:18, KJV) is now "speak insolently" (NRSV, RSV), "speak insolent things" (NKJV), and "speak arrogantly" (NASB). "Grievous revolters" (Jeremiah 6:28, KJV) is rendered "stubbornly rebellious" (NASB, NRSV, RSV).

In a number of instances the contemporary versions replace "grievous" (KJV) with terms such as "savage" (Acts 20:29, NASB, NIV, NKJV, NRSV), "serious" (Acts 25:7, the majority of contemporary versions), "burdensome" (1 John 5:3, NASB, NIV, NKJV, NRSV, RSV), "irksome" (Philippians 3:1, RSV), "painful" (Hebrews 12:11, the majority of contemporary versions), and "malignant" (Revelation 16:2, NASB). "Grievous to be borne" is now rendered "hard to bear" (Matthew 23:4 and its parallel, Luke 11:46, NKJV, NRSV, RSV).

GRIEVOUSNESS

This is a word which we would recognize today as having to do with grief or pain. Its archaic meaning, however, is "burden" or "oppression," and it occurs with this meaning in the KJV rendering of Isaiah 10:1: "Woe unto them . . . that write grievousness which they have prescribed" (KJV). The RSV reads, "Woe to . . . the writers who keep writing oppression."

Other contemporary versions apply the coming doom to those who "constantly record unjust decisions" (NASB), "issue oppressive decrees" (NIV), "write misfortune" (NKJV), and "write oppressive statutes" (NRSV). In its other occurrence in the KJV, grievousness is used in the context of war and the heat of battle: "the grievousness of war" (Isaiah 21:15, KJV) is now rendered as "the press of battle" (NASB, RSV), "the heat of battle" (NIV), "the stress of battle" (NRSV), and "the distress of war" (NKJV).

GRISLED

We might be forgiven for thinking that "grisled" is a form of "grisly," which means "horrible" or "ghastly." In fact, it is an early form of "grizzled" or "grizzly," which means "gray or grayish," "sprinkled, streaked, or mixed with gray." The Hebrew adjective *barod*, which the KJV translates as "grisled," means "spotted" or "marked," as if sprinkled with hail (the word for "a storm of hail" is *barad*). This adjective is applied to Jacob's rams (Genesis 31:10, 12) and to horses in the vision of Zechariah 6:3, 6.

Contemporary versions use "mottled" (NASB, NRSV, RSV) and "spotted" (CEV, NCV, NIV, NLT; NKJV, "gray-spotted") for the rams, and "dappled" (NASB, NIV, NKJV) and "dappled gray" (NRSV, RSV; NLT, "dappled-gray") for the horses.

GRUDGE

In modern terminology, a "grudge" is borne against someone when they have caused resentment or hurt ("he harbored a grudge against him for years"). Originally the word meant "to murmur," "grumble," or complain." Its earlier variant was "grutch"; modern colloquial variants are "grouse" and "grouch." This meaning for "grudge" has been obsolete for more than three centuries; the OED records the date of its last appearance for the noun in 1611, and for the verb in 1632.

Shakespeare used "grudge" along with a new word, "grumbling" (this is the first record of the word) in *The Tempest* (I, 2, 249), where Ariel reminds Prospero that he has

> "Told thee no lies, made thee no
> mistakings, served
> Without or grudge or grumblings."

The KJV uses "grudge" twice in this obsolete sense. "Grudge not one against another" (James 5:9, KJV) is now rendered as "Do not grumble against one another" (NKJV, NRSV) and "Do not complain . . . against one another" (NASB).

The other case is a little more complicated. Psalm 59 is a prayer for deliverance from the psalmist's enemies. Its ancient heading means, "A Miktam of David, when Saul sent men to watch his house in order to kill him" (the meaning of *Miktam*, which appears in the headings of Psalms 16 and 56–60, is uncertain). In two strophes of Psalm 59, verses 6–7 and verses 14–15, he compares his enemies to dogs: "Each evening they come back, howling like dogs and prowling about the city."

The first of these strophes he completes with three lines about their bellowing and snarling, the second with two lines about their foraging for food. The latter are rendered by the KJV, "Let them wander up and down for meat, and grudge if they be not satisfied." The NRSV translates, "They roam about for food, and growl if they do not get their fill." The NASB also uses "growl," but other contemporary versions render the Hebrew as "howl" (NCV, NIV, NKJV).

In three passages the KJV uses the words "grudge," "grudging," and "grudgingly" in their modern sense (Leviticus 19:18; 1 Peter 4:9; 2 Corinthians 9:7). In 1 Peter 4:9 the contemporary versions replace "grudging" (KJV) with "complaining" (NCV, NRSV; NASB, "complaint") and "grumbling" (NIV, NKJV; CEV, "grumble").

In 2 Corinthians 9:7, Paul urges the Corinthians to contribute generously to his collection for the Jerusalem saints: "Every man according as he purposeth in his heart, so let him give; not grudgingly, or of necessity: for God loveth a cheeful giver." The NASB and NKJV retain "grudgingly" in this verse; the NIV, NLT, NRSV, and RSV have "reluctantly." A number of contemporary versions use "grudge" instead of "quarrel" (KJV) in Mark 6:19 (CEV, NIV, NRSV, RSV). (See DOGS; QUARREL)

GUILTY OF

In Numbers 35, the KJV uses the phrases "guilty of blood" (v. 27) and "guilty of death" (v. 31) in the sense in which we would naturally understand these expressions today. When it represents the members of the council of Caiaphas, however, as saying of Jesus, "He is guilty of death" (Matthew 26:66), the expression is used in an obsolete sense.

The KJV translators took it from the Rheims translation, which got it from the Latin Vulgate, *reus est mortis.* Tyndale and his successors had translated the Greek as "He is worthy to die." The revised versions of 1881 and 1901 have "He is worthy of death." Contemporary versions read "deserving of death" (NKJV), "deserves death" (NASB, NRSV, RSV), and "worthy of death" (NIV). Compare Mark 14:64.

H

HABERGEON

This word means "a short, sleeveless hauberk" or "coat of mail." The term is used in the KJV as translation of three Hebrew words: *shiryon, shiryah,* and *tahara.* *Shiryon* occurs in 2 Chronicles 26:14, where its plural is now translated as "coats of mail" (NRSV, RSV), "coats of armor" (NIV), and "body armor" (NASB), and in Nehemiah 4:16, where it is rendered as "body-armor" (NRSV), "armor" (NIV), and "breastplates" (NASB). It is the word for the coat of mail worn by Goliath and for that which Saul put on David and David would not wear (1 Samuel 17:5, 38).

A different word, *shiryah,* occurs in the description of Leviathan in Job 41. The KJV renders verse 26 as "The sword of him that layeth at him cannot hold: the spear, the dart, nor the habergeon." These are offensive weapons, and "habergeon" is now rendered as "javelin" by the NASB, NIV, RSV, and RSV. The NRSV translates as "Though the sword reaches it, it does not avail, nor does the spear, the dart, or the javelin."

The other word is *tahara,* which occurs in the description of "the robe of the ephod" which Aaron wore (Exodus 28:32; 39:23). The meaning of this term is uncertain; the Hebrew lexicons state that it probably means a linen corselet. The robe of the ephod was to be put on over the head and slipped down into place on the body, and *tahara* refers to a garment that had to be put on in the same way.

Exodus 28:32 reads in the KJV: "And there shall be an hole in the top of it, in the midst thereof: it shall have a binding of woven work round about the hole of it, as it were the hole of an habergeon, that it be not rent." The NASB reads: "there shall be an opening at its top in the middle of it;

around its opening there shall be a binding of woven work, as like the opening of a coat of mail, so that it will not be torn."

In the description of the locusts from the bottomless pit (Revelation 9:1–11) Tyndale and the other sixteenth-century translations said that "they had habbergions, as it were habbergions of yron" (v. 9). The KJV changed "habbergions" to "breastplates." The Greek word *thorax*. which is here used twice, separated by the Greek word for "like," means the part of the body which the breastplate covers as well as the breastplate itself.

The NRSV translates as "they had scales like iron breastplates." In verses 2–3, 5, 7c–9 the same simple Greek word *hos* occurs, and means "like." The KJV uses "as" except in verse 9a, where it uses "as it were."

HALE

To one who has been "haled into court" it may come as a surprise that he was "hauled" or "dragged." "Hale" and "haul" are the same word in meaning and origin. "Hale" is the older form, and the only one to appear in the KJV or in Shakespeare. "Haul" is a variant spelling which began in the sixteenth century and has now superseded "hale" except in the language of the law court.

"Hale" occurs twice in the KJV, in Luke 12:58, "lest he hale thee to the judge," and in Acts 8:3, "As for Saul, he made havock of the church, entering into every house, and haling men and women committed them to prison." The Greek verbs imply force rather than law and the majority of contemporary versions use "drag" and "drag off."

The verb *suro*, which appears in Acts 8:3, occurs also in John 21:8, "dragging the net full of fish" (NASB, NRSV, RSV); Acts 14.19, "They hit him with stones and dragged him out of the city, thinking he was dead" (CEV); Acts 17:6, "they dragged Jason and some brethren to the rulers of the city" (NKJV). The KJV translates *suro* in these last two

references as "drew." The Greek verb *kata-suro* used in Luke 12:58 is an intensive form of the same word, which means "to drag forcibly" or even, in some contexts, "to ravage and lay waste."

HALT

The word "halt" is likely to turn our thoughts to highway holdups and border controls. While the contemporary versions use "halt" only in the sense of "stop," the KJV uses the adjective four times to render the Greek adjective which means "lame" or "crippled" (Matthew 18:8; Mark 9:45; Luke 14:21; John 5:3). The KJV translates it as "lame" in ten other passages and as "a cripple" in Acts 14:8.

As an intransitive verb, "halt" is used seven times in the Old Testament, always to render Hebrew terms which mean "to limp," "stumble," or "fall." "Her that halteth" (Micah 4:6, (KJV) is now "the lame" (CEV, NASB, NIV, NKJV, NLT, NRSV, RSV; see also Zephaniah 3:19). "I am ready to halt" (Psalm 38:17, KJV) is rendered "I am ready to fall" (NASB, NKJV, NRSV RSV), and "watched for my halting" (Jeremiah 20:10, KJV) is now "waiting for me to make a [NCV, "make some"] mistake" (NCV, CEV) and "watching for my fall" (NASB, RSV).

The KJV says of Jacob that "he halted upon his thigh" (Genesis 32:31); contemporary versions have him "limping because of his hip" (NIV, NLT, NRSV). Elijah's question to the people of Israel, "How long halt ye between two opinions?" (1 Kings 18:21, KJV) reads in the NRSV, "How long will you go limping with two ifferent opinions?" Other versions have 'How long will you hesitate?" (NASB), "How long will you waver?" (NIV), and "How long will you falter?" (NKJV).

HAND

The word "hand" is used today in a number of different phrases, many of which have to do with help of some sort. We say "lend me a hand," "hand me the screwdriver," "he's always at hand," and "she had a hand in the decorating." Such noun phrases occur also in the KJV.

"An hand weapon of wood" (Numbers 35:18, KJV) means "a weapon of wood in the hand." The Hebrew phrase is parallel to that of verse 17, which the KJV renders as "throwing a stone." The contemporary versions translate as "a stone in the [NIV, "in his"] hand" (NIV, NASB, NKJV, RSV).

"At the hand(s) of" is an old English idiom, still used today, which expresses the immediate source from which something is received or required. "Shall we receive good at the hand of God, and shall we not receive evil?" (Job 2:10, KJV). "When ye come to appear before me, who hath required this at your hand, to tread my courts?" (Isaiah 1:12, KJV). The Hebrew preposition is *min*, which means "from" in both of these texts; the Hebrew word for "hand" is found only in the second.

The NKJV and NRSV retain "hand" in Isaiah 1:12 (NRSV, "who asked this from your hand?"), but other versions have "of": "who has asked this of you?" (NIV), "who requires of you?" (NASB, RSV).

"Out of hand" means "out of control." When it appears in the KJV, however, it means "at once," or "immediately." In the KJV rendering of Numbers 11:15, Moses says to the Lord, "If thou deal thus with me, kill me, I pray thee, out of hand, if I have found favour in thy sight: and let me not see my wretchedness." This is a case where the Hebrew uses repetition as a means of emphasis, adding to the finite verb its absolute infinitive. (See GENERALLY; SURELY)

A literal translation would be "kill me, I pray thee, to kill, if I have found favor in thy sight." The translations from Tyndale on, including the Bishops' Bible, simply ignored the repetitive infinitive; the idea of representing it by the idiom "out of hand" originated with the KJV translators. The NASB and RSV have "at once"; the CEV, NCV, and NKJV, "now"; the NIV, "right now."

"Take in hand" followed by an infinitive means "to undertake" or "to attempt."

Tyndale's translation of the preface to Luke's Gospel reads "many have taken in hand to" and all subsequent versions in the Tyndale-KJV tradition retained the expression. Contemporary versions have "many have undertaken to" (NASB, NIV, NRSV, RSV) and "Many [CEV, "Many people"] have tried" (CEV, NCV).

"With a high hand" in modern usage connotes an overbearing manner. In the KJV, however, it occurs twice as the literal translation of a Hebrew phrase which is applied to the action of the people of Israel in leaving Egypt (Exodus 14:8; Numbers 33:3). It is also applied to the action of a person who despises the word of the Lord and deliberately breaks His commandment, and the RSV retains the expression in its rendering of Numbers 15:30.

The translations in the Tyndale-KJV tradition used "with an high hand" in the first two cases, and "presumptuously" in the latter. The RSV reverses this, using "with a high hand" for the rebel against God, and "defiantly" and "triumphantly" for the departure from Egypt. This reflects the shift in the meaning of the English idiom. "With a high hand" at first simply referred to great power—"High is thy right hand" (Psalm 89:13, KJV), "Our hand is high" (Deuteronomy 32:27, KJV)—but it has come to connote an imperious temper and the overbearing, arbitrary exercise of power.

Other versions render "doeth ought presumptuously" (KJV) in Numbers 15:30 as "does anything defiantly" (NASB), "sins defiantly" (NIV), and "acts high-handedly" (NRSV). Israel's departure from Egypt (Exodus 14:8; Numbers 33:3) is made "proudly" (CEV), "boldly" (NASB, NCV, NIV, NRSV), and "defiantly" (NLT).

HAND, LEFT, DOES NOT KNOW WHAT ONE'S RIGHT HAND IS DOING

"One's left hand does not know what one's right hand is doing" is a saying that is applied in the contemporary world, for example, to a lack of communication between departments or disorganized work methods in a large institution. The saying derives from Jesus' words in the Sermon on the Mount (Matthew 6:3–4): "But when thou doest alms, let not thy left hand know what thy right hand doeth: That thine alms may be in secret" (KJV). The meaning is that one should keep one's giving a secret not only from others but also from oneself.

All the contemporary versions except the CEV and the NCV retain a similar wording to the KJV with a reference to "left hand" and "right hand"; the CEV has "When you give to the poor, don't let anyone know about it" and the NCV, "So when you give to the poor, don't let anyone know what you are doing."

HAND, RIGHT, OFFEND THEE

"If thy right hand offend thee" is a phrase that comes in the Sermon on the Mount: "And if thy right eye offend thee, pluck it out, and cast it from thee: for it is profitable for thee that one of thy members should perish, and not that thy whole body should be cast into hell. And if thy right hand offend thee, cut it off, and cast it from thee: for it is profitable for thee that one of thy members should perish, and not that thy whole body should be cast into hell."

The contemporary versions generally have "If your right hand causes you to sin" (CEV, NASB, NCV, NIV, NKJV, NRSV, RSV); the NLT has "And if your hand—even if it is your stronger hand—causes you to sin." Jesus is saying that radical, drastic action must be taken to remove what may cause sin. The phrase occurs again in Matthew 18:8 and Mark 9:43.

HAND, WHATSOEVER THY, FINDETH TO DO

"Whatsoever thy hand findeth to do" is an expression that comes from Ecclesiastes 9:10 (KJV), "Whatsoever thy hand findeth to do, do it with thy might, for there is no work, nor device, nor knowledge, nor wisdom, in the grave, whither thou goest." The con-

temporary versions render this expression, "Whatever your hand finds to do" (NASB, NIV, NKJV, NRSV, RSV); "whatever you do" (CEV, NLT); and "whatever work you do" (NCV).

HAP

This word means "chance" or "fortune," whether good or bad. The good meanings now cluster around the related words "happy," "happily," "happiness." The neutral meanings are caught up in such terms as "happen," "happening," "haply," "perhaps." The one use of "hap" in the KJV is in Ruth 2:3: "her hap was to light on a part of the field belonging unto Boaz." Contemporary versions have "happened": "She happened to come to the portion of the field belonging to Boaz" (NASB).

In Milton's *Paradise Lost* (9, 421) the serpent "sought them both, but wished his hap might find Eve separate." In *Taming of the Shrew* (IV, 4, 107), Shakespeare has "Hap what hap may."

HAPLY

The word "haply" means "by hap" or "by chance," hence "perchance," "perhaps." It is used six times in the KJV: "if haply" (1 Samuel 14:30; Mark 11:13; Acts 17:27); "lest haply" (Luke 14:29; Acts 5:39; 2 Corinthians 9:4). The majority of the contemporary versions express the element of contingency with a simple "if" or "lest."

When, in Mark's Gospel, Jesus sees a fig tree in the distance, the KJV says that "he came, if haply he might find any thing thereon" (11:13); the NASB and NKJV have "if perhaps," while other versions have "if." "Lest haply, after he hath laid the foundation" (Luke 14:29, KJV) reads, in the NASB, NRSV, and RSV, "Otherwise, when he has laid a foundation."

In Acts 5:38–39, Gamaliel speaks words of caution to the council gathered to decide the fate of the Jerusalem apostles: "if . . . this work be of men, it will come to nought: But if it be of God, ye cannot overthrow it; lest haply ye be found even to fight against

God" (KJV). The final clause is rendered, by the CEV, "unless you want to fight against God."

Other versions have "or else you may be found fighting against God" (NASB), "lest you even be found to fight against God" (NKJV), and "You may even find yourselves fighting against God" (NLT).

It is an interesting fact that the original edition of the KJV (1611) had "happily" in 2 Corinthians 9:4. In the sixteenth century the word "happily" meant the same as "haply," as may be seen in Shakespeare's *Twelfth Night* (IV, 2, 57) or *Hamlet* (II, 2, 402). The latter passage reads:

> "*Hamlet:* That great baby you see there is not yet out of his swaddling-clouts.
> *Rosencrantz:* Happily he's the second time come to them; for they say an old man is twice a child."

HARD

The word "hard" has the variety of meanings in the KJV which it has today. We read of hard bondage, hard labor, hard questions, hard sayings, hard language, hard causes, hard men, hard hearts, and things hard to understand. Some dozen times the adverb "hard" is used in the sense of "close" or "near." When Abimelech "went hard unto the door of the tower" (Judges 9:52, KJV) he, according to the NKJV and RSV, "drew near [RSV, "drew near to"] the door." The NASB and NIV say he "approached the entrance of [NIV, "to"] the tower."

Today we might read the familiar text from Proverbs 13:15, "the way of transgressors is hard" (KJV) as meaning that the path of sinners is difficult and that they have hard times ahead, or that their conduct is unfeeling and cruel. In fact, the Hebrew asserts that the way of the treacherous (or faithless) is enduring (or permanent). The English translators passed from the idea of "enduring" to the idea of "firm," then from "firm" to "hard."

The Greek Septuagint and the Syriac read "destruction," and the Latin Vulgate "whirlpool," where the present Hebrew text has '*eythan*, the word for "enduring." Biblical scholars in general agree that the Hebrew text must have formerly read '*eydham*, which means "destruction."

A number of contemporary versions accept this emendation. According to the CEV, "people without good sense are on the way to disaster," and the NRSV and RSV read, "the way of the faithless is their ruin." The NLT reads, "a treacherous person walks a rocky road."

HARDLY

This word, in modern usage, might make us think of unlikelihood or difficulty ("he's hardly likely to break the record with a sore ankle"). We also use it in the sense of "scarcely" ("the cookies went down well with her visitors: hardly a crumb was left"). In the KJV New Testament, the word's meaning is familiar to contemporary readers. It means "with difficulty" in Matthew 19:23, Mark 10:23 (and its parallel, Luke 18:24), and Acts 27:8.

"How hardly shall they that have riches enter into the kingdom of God!" (Mark 10:23, KJV) now reads "How hard it will be for those who are wealthy to enter the kingdom of God!" (NASB). In the context of Luke's narrative on Paul's travels, "hardly passing it" (Acts 27:8, KJV) is now rendered "with difficulty sailing past it" (NASB) and "Sailing past it was hard" (NCV). In Luke 9:39 "scarcely" is used by the NRSV and NIV; "hardly" is retained by the RSV and NLT.

The word's meaning in the KJV Old Testament may not be so apparent. "Hardly bestead" (KJV) in Isaiah 8:21 is now rendered as "in great pain" (CEV), "hard-pressed" (NASB), and "greatly distressed" (NRSV, RSV). The contemporary versions render the statement "Sarai dealt hardly with her" (Genesis 16:6, KJV) as "Sarai dealt harshly with her" (NKJV, NRSV, RSV) and "So Sarah treated her harshly" (NASB, NLT); the NCV says that "Sarah was hard on Hagar."

Exodus 13:15 reads in the KJV, "when Pharaoh would hardly let us go." Here the KJV reduces the verb for "make hard" to the adverb "hardly." Tyndale had (in modern spelling) "when Pharaoh was loath to let us go," in which he was followed by the Great Bible and the Bishops' Bible, the latter saying "very loath." The Geneva Bible had "when Pharaoh was hard hearted against our departing." The margin of the ASV has "hardened himself against letting us go," and the NIV, NRSV, and RSV read, "when Pharaoh stubbornly refused to let us go."

HARDNESS

"Hardness of heart" is a familiar concept which runs throughout the course of biblical revelation and appears in all translations. On two occasions, however, the KJV use of the word may be unfamiliar. In Job 38:38 we find it applied to the effect of rain upon dust. The context is God's self-revelation to Job, and the list of his mighty works, convincing Job of his own ignorance. Verses 37–38 read, in the KJV:

> "Who can number the clouds in
>   wisdom? or who can stay the
>   bottles of heaven,
> When the dust groweth into
>   hardness, and the clods
>   cleave fast together?"

For those gardeners among us who have to battle with heavy soils in their yards, "hardness" might seem an appropriate word. The NASB, NCV, and NKJV use the adjective "hard" and the verb "to harden." They have "the dust hardens into a mass" (NASB), "the dust becomes hard" (NCV), and "the dust hardens in clumps" (NKJV). The NRSV and RSV have "the dust runs into a mass."

In the injunction to Timothy, "endure hardness as a good soldier of Jesus Christ" (2 Timothy 2:3, KJV), the KJV employs the word in the sense of "hardship"; this is the rendering adopted by the NASB, NIV, and

NKJV. "Troubles" is used by the NCV, all the other contemporary versions choosing to use the word "suffering."

HARNESS (noun)

As a noun, the word "harness" is likely to conjure up images of horses decked out in their working gear. Occasionally we hear the word used, rather negatively, of the grueling routine of work ("to die in harness"). Originally, the word was applied to any sort of gear or equipment. The *Promptorium Parvulorum,* in the fifteenth century, gave four meanings: "raiment," "weapons," "household utensils," "the trappings of a horse."

In the KJV the noun is used only in the sense of "armor." "A certain man drew a bow at a venture, and smote the king of Israel between the joints of the harness" (1 Kings 22:34 and its parallel, 2 Chronicles 18:33, KJV) is rendered, by the NRSV, "A certain man drew his bow and unknowingly struck the king of Israel between the scale armor and the breastplate."

In 2 Maccabees 15:28, the KJV reads, "they knew that Nicanor lay dead in his harness." The NRSV reads, "they recognized Nicanor, lying dead, in full armor." The Greek word here is *panoplia,* from which we get the English word "panoply."

In the list of presents which King Solomon received from other kings, year by year, the KJV has "armour" (1 Kings 10:25) and "harness" (2 Chronicles 9:24) to represent the same Hebrew word.

The contemporary versions have "weapons" (CEV, NASB, NCV, NIV, NLT), "armor" (NKJV), and "weaponry" (NRSV) in both texts; following the Septuagint, the RSV is alone among contemporary versions in rendering the word as "myrrh."

HARNESS (verb)

As a verb, "harness" is used once in the KJV for "horses" (Jeremiah 46:4, "Harness the horses"). Elsewhere the word is applied to people. In Exodus 13:18 we read, "The children of Israel went up harnessed out of the land of Egypt." The same Hebrew word is translated "armed" by the KJV in Joshua 1:14, 4:12, and Judges 7:11.

Contemporary versions, at Exodus 13:18, have "armed for battle" (NIV), "prepared for battle" (CEV, NRSV), "equipped for battle" (RSV), and "in martial array" (NASB).

Tyndale's translation of Numbers 32:20–22 was "Yf ye will do this thinge, that ye will go all harnessed before the Lorde to warre, and will go all of you in harnesse ouer Iordane before the Lorde . . . then ye shall returne and be without sinne agenst the Lorde and agenst Israel." The KJV has "armed" in these verses.

In 1 Maccabees 4:7 the KJV refers to an enemy camp as "strong and well harnessed"; the NRSV has "strong and fortified."

HASTILY

The word "hastily in contemporary usage means "hurriedly." It implies being pressed for time, but also a lack of due consideration. In Elizabethan language, however, the word could be used in the simple sense of "promptly," "without delay." It has this meaning in three KJV passages.

The first is Judges 2:23, where we read that, in order to "prove" Israel (v. 22), "the LORD left those nations, without driving them out hastily" (KJV); contemporary versions have "quickly" (NASB, NCV, NLT), "immediately" (NKJV), and "at once" (NIV, NRSV, RSV).

Then in 1 Kings 20, we have the passage about Ben-Hadad's capture and subsequent release by Ahab. While still in captivity, Ben-Hadad sends to the king of Israel, asking for his life; Ahab's reply is, "Is he yet alive? he is my brother." (v. 32, KJV). Verse 33 reads, in the KJV, "Now the men did diligently observe whether any thing would come from him, and did hastily catch it: and they said, Thy brother Ben-hadad. Then he said, Go ye, bring him."

The NKJV renders the Hebrew as "they quickly grasped at this word"; the majority of contemporary versions also use "quickly" to render "hastily" (KJV) here.

Finally, in John's account of the raising of Lazarus, we read that when the Jews saw Mary rise up "hastily" (John 11:31, KJV) on hearing Jesus' summons, they followed her. Again, contemporary versions use the word "quickly."

HATE

The word "hate" is sometimes used in the KJV in the sense of "to love less." For example, Luke 14:26 (KJV) reads, "If any man come to me, and hate not his father, and mother, and wife, and children, and brethren, and sisters, yea, and his own life also, he cannot be my disciple."

Of the contemporary versions, the NASB, NIV, NKJV, and NRSV retain the verb "hate," with the NASB adding a footnote, "I.e. by comparison of his love for Me"; the CEV, NCV, and NLT render as follows: "You cannot be my disciple, unless you love me more than you love your father and mother, your wife and children, and your brothers and sisters. You cannot come with me unless you love me more than you love your own life" (CEV); "If anyone comes to me but loves his father, mother, wife, children, brothers, or sisters or even life—more than me, he cannot be my follower" (NCV); and "If you want to be my follower you must love me more than your own father and mother, wife and children, brothers and sisters—yes, more than your own life. Otherwise, you cannot be my disciple" (NLT).

In John 12:25 the words of Jesus are recorded: "He that loveth his life shall lose it; and he that hateth his life in this world shall keep it unto life eternal" (KJV). The NASB, NCV, NIV, NKJV, NRSV, and RSV retain the verb "hate"; the NLT has "despise"; the CEV renders the whole verse as "If you love your life, you will lose it. If you give it up in this world, you will be given eternal life."

In the Old Testament, Genesis 29:31 (KJV) has "And when the LORD saw that Leah was hated, he opened her womb: but Rachel was barren"; the RSV retains "hated"; the NASB, NKJV, NLT, and NRSV have "unloved"; the NIV has "not loved"; the CEV and NCV have "Jacob loved Rachel more than [CEV, "more than he did"] Leah."

Deuteronomy 21:15 (KJV) reads, "If a man have two wives, one beloved, and another hated, and they have born him children, both the beloved and the hated; and if the firstborn son be hers that was hated." For the two occurrences of "hated" in the KJV, the NASB and NKJV have "unloved" and the NRSV and RSV, "disliked"; the NIV and NLT have "he loves one but [NLT, "one and"] not the other . . . the wife he does not love."

HATH SHALL BE GIVEN

"To him that hath shall be given" is an expression recorded (with slight variations) several times in the Gospels: in the parable of the sower (Matthew 13:12); the saying about the light under a basket (the lamp on a stand) (Mark 4:25; Luke 8:18); and the parable of the talents (minas) (Matthew 25:29; Luke 19:26).

For example, "For whosoever hath, to him shall be given, and he shall have more abundance: but whosoever hath not, from him shall be taken away even that he hath" (Matthew 13:12, KJV), rendered by the NKJV as "Whoever has, to him more will be given" and by similar phrasing in the NASB, NIV, and NRSV; the NLT has "To those who are open to my teaching, more understanding will be given"; Mark 4:25, "For he that hath, to him shall be given: and he that hath not, from him shall be taken even that which he hath" (KJV); rendered as "everyone who has something will be given more" by the CEV. The expression has passed into the language with the meaning that it is the people who already enjoy a particular benefit or fortunate circumstances who will tend to be the ones who will receive even more good things, in contrast to those who have the greatest need, who will not receive anything.

HAVE

The word "have," followed by an adverb of place, is used in the KJV in the archaic sense of "bring," "lead," "take," "put." Amnon's order, "Have out all men from me" (2 Samuel 13:9, KJV), is rendered "Send out everyone from me" by the NRSV. Jehoiada's command concerning Athaliah, "Have her forth without the ranges" (2 Kings 11:15, KJV), is worded by the NASB, "Bring her out between the ranks."

In 2 Chronicles 35:23, King Josiah is shot by an archer in battle and says to his servants, "Have me away; for I am sore wounded" (KJV); the NASB, NRSV, and RSV render his words as "Take me away, for I am badly wounded."

HE

In Joshua 22:22, "he" occurs in an unusual way in the KJV rendering of the defense of the tribes of Reuben, Gad, and the half-tribe of Manasseh: "the LORD God of gods, the LORD God of gods, he knoweth, and Israel he shall know" (KJV). This is a solemn invocation of the Lord which has the effect of an oath, and "he" here refers not to God but to Israel.

Contemporary versions render the final words as "He knows, and may [NKJV, NRSV, RSV, "and let"] Israel itself know" (NASB, NKJV, NRSV, RSV). Verses 22–23 read, in the full, in the KJV: "The LORD God of gods, the LORD God of gods, he knoweth, and Israel he shall know; if it be in rebellion, or if in transgression against the LORD, (save us not this day,) That we have built us an altar to turn from following the LORD, or if to offer thereon burnt offering or meat offering, or if to offer peace offerings thereon, let the LORD himself require it."

The placing of the words "save us not this day" in parenthesis may make the sense of the passage a little difficult to follow. The verses read, in the NASB: "The Mighty One, God, the LORD, the Mighty One, God, the LORD! He knows, and may Israel itself know. If it was in rebellion, or if in an unfaithful act against the LORD do not save us this day! If we have built us an altar to turn away from following the LORD, or if to offer a burnt offering or grain offering on it, or if to offer sacrifices of peace offerings on it, may the LORD Himself require it."

HEADSTONE

Now the upright stone at the head of a grave, "headstone" occurs once in the KJV in the sense of "the topstone or capstone of a building" (Zechariah 4:7). In the original printing of the KJV, in 1611, it appeared as two words, "head stone," but some later editor or printer ran the two words together, without a hyphen, into one word. This was kept even by Scrivener in *The Cambridge Paragraph Bible* and appears in the present editions of the KJV.

The revised versions, including the NASB, NRSV, and RSV, have "the top stone." Other contemporary versions have "the topmost stone" (NCV), "the capstone" (NIV, NKJV), and "the final stone" (NLT).

The KJV uses the expression "head *stone* of the corner" in Psalm 118:22. The italic type indicates that the English word "stone" was inserted by the translators, and the difference in type doubtless prevented later editors from running the words together. This expression, too, was kept by Scrivener, with cross-references between Psalm 118:22 and Zechariah 4:7.

In fact, Zechariah has *'eben ro'shah,* and the Psalm has *ro'sh pinnah,* which is literally "head of the corner." The NASB, NKJV, and RSV translate Psalm 118:22: "The stone which the builders rejected has become the chief cornerstone [NASB, "corner stone"]." This verse was cited by Jesus (Matthew 21:42; Mark 12:10; Luke 20:17) and by Peter (Acts 4:11; 1 Peter 2:6–7). Taken in conjunction with Peter's citation of Isaiah 28:16 and Paul's "household of God . . . built upon the foundation of the apostles and prophets, Jesus Christ himself being the chief corner stone" (Ephesians 2:19–20, KJV), the context

as a whole tends to point to a cornerstone which enters into the foundation of a building, rather than to a topstone or capstone.

HEADY

This word is likely to turn our thoughts to intoxicating perfumes or passionate romance. In the KJV, however, it is used with its other contemporary sense of "impetuous," "headstrong." It occurs once, among the vices listed in 2 Timothy 3:1–5: "In the last days perilous times shall come. For men shall be . . . traitors, heady, highminded, lovers of pleasures more than lovers of God."

The CEV, NASB, NLT, NRSV, and RSV render the KJV "heady" as "reckless"; the NIV has "rash," and the NKJV, "headstrong." The Greek adjective occurs also in Acts 19:36, where the town clerk urged the citizens of Ephesus "to be quiet, and to do nothing rashly" (KJV).

HEALTH

The word "health" now refers to the soundness and efficient functioning of body and mind. But it had wider meanings in 1611 and before. Then it was used as a synonym for "healing" or "cure"; in the sense of "safety" or "deliverance"; and used in a moral and spiritual sense as the equivalent of "salvation."

Wycliffe wrote of Shammah that "he smote the Philistines, and the Lord made a great health" (2 Samuel 23:12), where Tyndale and subsequent versions read "a great victory." Coverdale has the people say of Jonathan, "that hath done so great health in Israel this night" (1 Samuel 14:45), where the Geneva Bible has "who hath so mightily delivered Israel."

Wycliffe's version of Acts 28:28 is "Therefore be it known to you that this health of God is sent to heathen men." Tyndale rendered it "this salvation of God is sent to the Gentiles"; but at Luke 19:9 his version has Jesus say to Zacchaeus, "This day is health come unto this house." In Ephesians 6:17

Wycliffe had "the helm of health," where subsequent versions have "the helmet of salvation."

In Psalms 42:11 and 43:5 the Geneva Bible reads "my present help and my God"; the Bishops' Bible, "my present salvation and my Lord," which was changed in its second edition to "the help of my countenance and my God." The KJV changed this to "the health of my countenance, and my God."

The NRSV and RSV return to Geneva, with the rendering "my help and my God"; the NKJV and NASB have "The help of my countenance and my God." The NCV, NIV, and NLT replace "help" with "Savior": "my Savior and my God."

One of the most familiar verses of the KJV Old Testament is Psalm 67:2: "That thy way may be known upon earth, thy saving health among all nations." Its wording goes back to Tyndale; in the contemporary versions "saving health" is changed to "saving power" (NLT, NRSV, RSV), "salvation" (NASB, NIV, NKJV), and "power to save us" (CEV).

HEAP BURNING COALS

The command "If thine enemy be hungry, give him bread to eat; and if he be thirsty, give him water to drink: For thou shalt heap burning coals of fire upon his head, and the LORD shall reward thee" (Proverbs 25:21–22, KJV) is quoted by Paul in Romans 12:20, "Therefore if thine enemy hunger, feed him; if he thirst, give him drink: for in so doing thou shalt heap coals of fire on his head."

The meaning generally given to this instruction is that if someone is unexpectedly kind to their enemy, then the enemy is so overcome by the kindness that there is a burning sense of shame and contrition, symbolized by coals of fire. This sense is brought out by the NLT, "If your enemies are hungry, feed them. If they are thirsty, give them something to drink, and they will be ashamed of what they have done to you" (Romans 12:20).

The first examples of this phrase in the OED are from *Piers Plowman* (1377); and Tyndale's translation of Romans 12:20, "In so doynge that shalt heape coles of fyre on his heed."

HEAR

"Hear" is used in the sense of "hear about," "be informed of," in the KJV rendering of Matthew 11:2: "when John had heard in the prison the works of Christ." The NASB has "when John . . . heard of the works of Christ." The elliptical expression "heard say" occurs in Genesis 41:15, where Pharaoh says to Joseph, "I have heard say of thee, that thou canst understand a dream to interpret it" (KJV); and in 2 Samuel 19:2, "the people heard say that day how the king was grieved for his son."

The NIV translates: "I have heard it said of you that when you hear a dream you can interpret it"; and "on that day the troops heard it said, 'The king is grieving for his son.'" A similar expression, "heard tell," appears in Numbers 21:1: "king Arad the Canaanite, which dwelt in the south, heard tell that Israel came by the way of the spies" (KJV). The NRSV translates as "the Canaanite, the king of Arad, who lived in the Negeb, heard that Israel was coming by the way of Atharim." These ways of construing "hear" are still in colloquial use.

Examples from Shakespeare are:

"We have heard your miseries as
    far as Tyre."
                —*Pericles* (I, 4, 88)

"I hear say you are of honourable
    parts."
                —*Pericles* (IV, 5, 80)

"She cannot endure to hear tell
    of a husband."
                —*Much Ado About Nothing*
                (II, 1, 333)

HEAVE OFFERING

This expression is likely to conjure up images of some sort of rite of elevation involving strenuous effort. The expression occurs twenty-four times in the KJV as translation of the Hebrew word *termuah*, rendered elsewhere in the KJV as "oblation" (eighteen times) and "offering" (twenty-eight times).

In Exodus 29 we read about the sacrifice and ceremonies of the consecration of priests; in verse 27, there is reference to "the shoulder of the heave offering, which is waved, and which is heaved up, of the ram of the consecration." This reads, in the NRSV, "the breast that was raised as an elevation offering and the thigh that was raised as an elevation offering from the ram of ordination"; the NASB has "the breast of the wave offering and the thigh of the heave offering which was waved."

Numbers 15:18–20 reads in the KJV: "When ye come into the land whither I bring you, Then it shall be, that, when ye eat of the bread of the land, ye shall offer up an heave offering unto the LORD. Ye shall offer up a cake of the first of your dough for an heave offering: as ye do the heave offering of the threshingfloor, so shall ye heave it." The NASB reads, "When you enter the land where I bring you, then it shall be, that when you eat of the food of the land, you shall lift up an offering to the LORD. Of the first of your dough you shall lift up a cake as an offering; as the offering of the threshing floor, so you shall lift it up."

The injunction to the Levites concerning their offering to the Lord a tenth part of the tithes which they receive concludes with the assurance, "ye shall bear no sin by reason of it, when ye have heaved from it the best of it" (Numbers 18:32, KJV). The CEV translates as "You won't be punished for eating it, as long as you have already offered the best parts to me."

HEAVILY

This word is used in an obsolete sense in the KJV rendering of Psalm 35:14, "I bowed down heavily." The sense of the Hebrew is "bowed down in mourning," and the Hebrew word rendered as "heavily" is translated as "mourning" by the KJV in Psalms 38:6, 42:9, and 43:2.

The contemporary versions have "I bowed down mourning" (NASB), "I bowed in sadness" (NCV), "I bowed my head in grief" (NIV), and "I went about . . . bowed down" (NRSV, RSV). The NKJV retains the KJV rendering.

HEAVINESS

"Heaviness" appears fourteen times in the KJV, but never in the sense of "physical weight." In each case the word has a psychological meaning, as it can have today ("there was a heaviness about him"). It denotes, in the KJV, "a state of mind."

More precisely, in each of these cases it denotes one of a dozen different states of mind: the KJV uses "heaviness" to represent seven different Hebrew words and three different Greek words, each of which has its own distinct meaning. With the exception of the NKJV, which occasionally retains it, contemporary versions replace the word "heaviness" in all of the fourteen cases.

Listing the terms in the order in which they are given in Young's *Concordance*, "heaviness" is rendered as "anxiety" (NASB, NKJV, NRSV, RSV) and "worry"(CEV, NCV, NLT) in Proverbs 12:25; "a faint spirit" (NRSV, RSV) and "a spirit of despair" (NIV) in Isaiah 61:3; "sad countenance"(NASB, NRSV, RSV) in Job 9:27; "lamenting" (NASB), "weeping" (NLT), and "moaning" (NRSV, RSV) in Isaiah 29:2; "sorrow" (CEV, NIV, NRSV, RSV) in Psalm 119:28 and Romans 9:2; "grief" (NASB, NIV, NKJV, NLT, NRSV) in Proverbs 10:1 and 14:13; "fasting" (NKJV, NRSV, RSV), "humiliation" (NASB), and "self-abasement" (NIV) in Ezra 9:5.

It is also rendered as "gloom" (NASB, NIV, NKJV, NLT) and "dejection" (NRSV, RSV) in James 4:9; "painful," (CEV, NIV, NLT, NRSV, RSV) and "in sorrow" (NASB, NKJV) in 2 Corinthians 2:1; "sick" (CEV, NASB), "helpless" (NIV), and "despair" (NLT, NRSV, RSV) in Psalm 69:20; "worried" (CEV, NCV) and "distressed" (NASB, NIV, NKJV, NLT, NRSV, RSV) in Philippians 2:26; and "distressed" (NASB), "sad" (NCV), "suffer grief" (NIV), and "suffer" (NRSV, RSV) in 1 Peter 1:6.

The three examples in Proverbs are: "Heaviness in the heart of man maketh it stoop" (12:25, KJV); the NASB and RSV read, "Anxiety in a man's heart weighs him [NASB, "it"] down." "A foolish son is the heaviness of his mother" (10:1, KJV); the NKJV reads, "a foolish son is the grief of his mother." "The end of that mirth is heaviness" (14:13, KJV) reads in the CEV as "happiness may end in sorrow."

First Peter 1:6 reads in the KJV, "Wherein ye greatly rejoice, though now for a season, if need be, ye are in heaviness through manifold temptations." The NCV translates as "This makes you very happy, even though now for a short time different kinds of troubles may make you sad."

HEAVY

In the KJV we read of heavy yokes, heavy burdens, heavy bondage, heavy hands, heavy hearts, heavy hair, heavy transgression, eyes heavy with sleep, and ears heavy to hear. "Heavy burdens" (KJV) in Isaiah 58:6 is rendered as "chains of prisoners" by the CEV, "bands of the yoke" by the NASB, and "cords of the yoke" by the NIV; the NRSV and RSV have "thongs of the yoke."

In Proverbs 31:6 "those that be of heavy hearts" (KJV) is rendered as "those who have lost all hope" by the CEV, "those who are in anguish" by the NIV, and "those in bitter distress" by the NRSV and RSV.

The KJV uses the same word to express King Ahab's vexation over Naboth's refusal and our Lord's feeling as he approached his agony in the Garden of Gethsemane. Ahab was "heavy," it says, and Jesus began to be "very heavy."

The Hebrew term used concerning Ahab

is rendered "resentful" (NRSV, RSV), "sullen" (NASB, NIV, NKJV), and "angry" (CEV, NCV, NLT) in the contemporary versions, and our Lord's attitude in Gethsemane is expressed by the words "troubled" (CEV, NCV, NIV, RSV), "distressed" (NASB; NKJV, "deeply distressed"), and "agitated" (NRSV). See 1 Kings 20:43; 21:4; Matthew 26:37; Mark 14:33.

HELPMEET

A "helpmeet" is a "companion" or "helper," the word often being applied to one's wife or husband. The word derives from a misreading of Genesis 2:18 in the KJV, "And the LORD God said, It is not good that the man should be alone; I will make him an help meet for him." The word "meet" simply meant "suitable." (See also MEET)

As the Bible text was read aloud, however, the two words "help meet" were thought to be one word: "helpmeet." In the early eighteenth century the word "helpmate" was coined with the thought that "mate" made better sense than "meet."

Other translations bring out different shades of meaning of the KJV "an help meet for him": the NASB and NIV give "a helper suitable for him"; the RSV, "a helper fit for him"; the NCV, "a helper who is right for him"; the NKJV, "a helper comparable to him"; the NRSV, "a helper as his partner"; the CEV, "a suitable partner for him"; and the NLT, "a companion who will help him."

HELPS

The word "help" is likely to make us think of people hired to help with housework or to work on a farm. In the KJV the word means "helpful deeds" (1 Corinthians 12:28) and refers to the ministry of the deacons, who had care of the poor and the sick. In this list of gifts of the Spirit, Paul uses personal terms for the first three—apostles, prophets, teachers—and then turns to impersonal terms—miracles, healings, helps, administrations, tongues.

The NASB and NKJV retain "helps," and

the NRSV has "forms of assistance." Other contemporary versions use personal terms throughout, hence "some to . . . help others" (CEV), "those who can help others" (NCV, NLT), "those able to help others" (NIV), and "helpers" (RSV).

"They used helps, undergirding the ship" (KJV) is a literal translation of the Greek in Acts 27:17. The Arndt and Gingrich lexicon says that the word for "helps" is probably a nautical technical term. A correspondingly technical expression in English would be "they frapped the ship" (Conybeare and Hawson, *Life and Letters of St. Paul,* chap. 23). But just exactly what they did is not clear.

The NRSV and RSV say that "they took measures to undergird the ship"; according to other contemporary versions they "wrapped ropes around the ship" (CEV), "passed ropes under" it (NIV), and "used [NASB, "used supporting"] cables" (NKJV).

HELVE

The word "helve" refers to the handle or wooden part of a tool such as an ax or hammer. It occurs once in the KJV, at Deuteronomy 19:5, "As when a man goeth into the wood with his neighbour to hew wood, and his hand fetcheth a stroke with the axe to cut down the tree, and the head slippeth from the helve, and lighteth upon his neighbour, that he die; he shall flee unto one of those cities, and live."

All the contemporary versions except the NIV render the KJV "helve" as "handle"; it is not translated in the NIV. The word "helve" occurred in the proverb "to throw the helve after the hatchet," meaning to risk losing everything else after having made one extravagant loss.

HEM OF HIS GARMENT

When a woman who was ill "with an issue of blood" for twelve years came behind Jesus, she said to herself, "If I may but touch his garment" (Matthew 9:21, with parallels Mark 5:28 and Luke 8:44), "I shall be whole." Later, in the region around Gennesaret, people brought to Jesus all those who were ill, "that they might only touch the hem of his garment: and as many as touched were made perfectly whole" (Matthew 14:36, parallel Mark 6:56).

The contemporary versions render the KJV "touch the hem of his garment" as, "touch . . . the fringe of his cloak" (NRSV), "touch the fringe of His cloak" (NASB), "touch . . . the fringe of his robe" (NLT), "touch the edge of his cloak" (NIV), and "touch . . . the edge of his coat" (NCV). The parallel in Mark has very similar renderings.

HENCE

In the sense of "therefore," the word "hence" is easily recognized by contemporary readers. It is equally clear in the sense of "away from here." The redundant expression "from hence" has a long history and is used five times in Shakespeare's plays and six times in the KJV. Many of the contemporary versions replace it with "from here."

The devil's third temptation of Jesus was "If You are the Son of God, throw Yourself down from here" (Luke 4:9, NASB). Abraham's answer to the rich man in torment was "between us and you there is a great gulf fixed, so that those who want to pass from here to you cannot, nor can those from there pass to us" (Luke 16:26, NKJV).

With respect to time, "hence" means "from now on"; with respect to origin, it means "from this (which has just been mentioned)." Jesus' answer to Pilate concludes in the KJV, "but now is my kingdom not from hence" (John 18:36). The NASB translates as "My kingdom is not of this realm."

James 4:1 is rendered by the KJV: "From whence come wars and fightings among you? come they not hence, even of your lusts that war in your members?" The NIV reads, "What causes fights and quarrels among you? Don't they come from your desires that battle within you?"

HER

The word "her" is used reflexively, in the sense of "herself," in the KJV rendering of Genesis 21:16, "she went, and sat her down"; and in 38:14, "she put her widow's garments off from her, and covered her with a vail." In the first of these cases the NASB, NKJV, NRSV, and RSV simply omit "her"; in the second the NASB reads, "she removed her widow's garments and covered herself with a veil."

HEREAFTER

In the KJV, as in Shakespeare, "hereafter" is always an adverb, meaning "after this" or "from now on." Examples found in the contemporary versions render it as: "from now on" (Luke 22:69, CEV, NASB, NCV, NIV, NRSV, RSV; NKJV, "hereafter"); "no longer" (John 14:30, NRSV, RSV) and "much longer" (NCV, NIV); "afterward" (John 13:7, RSV), and "later" (CEV, NCV, NIV, NRSV; NASB, "hereafter"); and "after this" (Revelation 4:1, NCV, NIV, NKJV, NRSV, RSV).

"Hereafter" is not used in the Bible as a noun, either in the sense of the future on earth or in the sense of life beyond death, the world to come. Its earliest use in the latter sense, as recorded by the OED, was in 1702. John Wesley's use of "the hereafter" probably popularized the word.

HEREUNTO

"Hereunto" is an archaic adverb which means "to this." "For even hereunto were ye called" (1 Peter 2:21, KJV) is now rendered as "For to this you were called" (NKJV) and "For you have been called for this purpose (NASB)."

The KJV rendering of Ecclesiastes 2:25 may appear a little ambiguous to contemporary readers. The preceding verse reads, "There is nothing better for a man, than that he should eat and drink, and that he should make his soul enjoy good in his labour. This also I saw, that it was from the hand of God." Verse 25 continues, "For

who can eat, or who else can hasten hereunto, more than I?"

With the help of the ancient Greek and Syriac versions, contemporary versions relate the words "hasten hereunto" (KJV) back to the idea of enjoyment in verse 24. Thus the NKJV reads, "For who can eat, or who can have enjoyment, more than I?" and the CEV paraphrases as "no one enjoys eating and living more than I do." Other versions reword "more than I" (KJV, NKJV, CEV) as "without him" [NASB, "Him"] (NASB, NCV, NIV) and "apart from him" (NLT, NRSV, RSV). Thus verses 24–25 read, in the NASB: "There is nothing better for a man than to eat and drink and tell himself that his labor is good. This also I have seen that it is from the hand of God. For who can eat and who can have enjoyment without Him?"

HEROD, TO OUT-HEROD

The expression "to out-herod Herod" means "to exceed someone in a particular quality," especially wickedness or cruelty. The Herod referred to is Herod the Great (73–4 B.C.), king of Judea (37–4 B.C.), and the one who had all the baby boys of Jerusalem killed (Matthew 2:16). The source of the expression itself is Shakespeare's *Hamlet* (III, 2, 16): "I would have such a fellow whipped for o'erdoing Termagant; it out-herods Herod: pray you, avoid it."

The OED notes on this phrase: "to out-herod Herod (represented in the old Mystery Plays as a blustering tyrant) in violence; to be more outrageous than the most outrageous; hence, to outdo in any excess of evil or extravagance. (A casual Shaksperian [sic] expression, which has become current in the 19th c.)."

HEWERS OF WOOD AND DRAWERS OF WATER

When Joshua and the Israelites were conquering Canaan, the Gibeonites, who had heard of the fall of Jericho and the destruction of Ai under Joshua, pretended to be a people from a far country and wanted a peace treaty with Joshua. Joshua and the leaders, not seeking God's counsel, made peace with the Gibeonites. When the Israelites discovered that the Gibeonites were neighbors, the treaty could not be revoked. But Joshua condemned the Gibeonites to permanent menial tasks, "Now therefore ye are cursed, and there shall none of you be freed from being bondmen, and hewers of wood and drawers of water for the house of my God" (Joshua 9:23, KJV).

Of the contemporary versions, the NASB, NRSV, and RSV retain the KJV expression, the NIV and NKJV have "woodcutters and water carriers," the CEV and NLT, those who will "chop [CEV, "cut"] wood and carry water." The expression has now come to refer to those who perform hard menial work. (See also Deuteronomy 29:11.)

The phrase is alluded to in literature, e.g., in *The Knight's Tale* (1.1355–1422) where Chaucer writes of Arcite, "Well koude he hewen wode, and water bere."

HIDE ONE'S LIGHT UNDER A BUSHEL

"To hide one's light under a bushel" means "to conceal or be too modest about one's abilities or talents." The origin of the expression is Jesus' saying in the Sermon on the Mount, "Neither do men light a candle, and put it under a bushel, but on a candlestick; and it giveth light unto all that are in the house" (Matthew 5:15, KJV).

The KJV "bushel" (also in Mark 4:21 and Luke 11:33) is rendered "bowl" by the NCV and NIV; "basket" by the NASB, NKJV, NLT; "bushel basket" by the NRSV [this is in a footnote at Luke 11:33]; and "clay pot" by the CEV; the RSV retains the KJV expression.

The Greek word used in all three references is *modios;* the reference is to a bowl or vessel containing about two gallons or 8.75 liters that was used to measure ground meal or flour.

HIGH

We use this word in all sorts of contexts today, and with a variety of meanings (e.g.,

"he's been in high spirits ever since the canoeing trip"; "he attempted the high jump, but failed"). In the KJV we find it used in the sense of "haughty" in such passages as Psalms 18:27; 101:5; Proverbs 21:4. A typical verse is Isaiah 10:12, where it is said that the Lord "will punish the fruit of the stout heart of the king of Assyria, and the glory of his high looks."

The Hebrew lexicons, taking into account the context, including comparison with 9:9, declare that here the "stout heart" is "pride," and its "fruit" is "arrogant speech," the "high looks" are "haughty," and the "glory" is "glorying" or "boasting." The NIV reads, "I will punish the king of Assyria for the willful pride of his heart and the haughty look in his eyes"; the NRSV, "will punish the arrogant boasting of the king of Assyria and his haughty pride."

"Every high thing that exalteth itself against the knowledge of God" (2 Corinthians 10:5, KJV) now reads, in the CEV, "every bit of pride that keeps anyone from knowing God"; the NASB has "every lofty thing raised up against the knowledge of God." Other contemporary versions have "every proud thing" (NCV), "every pretension" (NIV), and "every proud argument" (NLT).

"The high calling of God in Christ Jesus" (Philippians 3:14, KJV) is now "the upward call of God in Christ Jesus" (NASB, NKJV, RSV) and "the heavenly call of God" (NRSV). The whole verse reads in the NIV: "I press on toward the goal to win the prize for which God has called me heavenward in Christ Jesus."

HIGHMINDED

This is a word that we now almost always use in a good sense. A highminded person is a person who holds and is true to high principles. But in the sixteenth century the word was more often used in a bad sense, and it is so used in the KJV. "Be not highminded" was the common translation of Romans 11:20 and 12:16, and 1 Timothy 6:17.

The contemporary versions have "Do

not be conceited" (NASB), "Do not be proud" (NCV; NRSV, RSV, "do not become proud"), and "Do not be haughty" (NKJV) at Romans 11:20, and "Do not be wise in your own estimation" (NASB), "Do not be conceited" (NIV), and "do not claim to be wiser than you are" (NRSV) at Romans 12:16.

In 1 Timothy 6:17, the rich are warned not to be "proud" (CEV, NCV, NLT), "conceited" (NASB), or "haughty" (NKJV, NRSV, RSV), while in 2 Timothy 3:4 "highminded" appears as one of a long list of evil dispositions of the ungodly. There it represents a Greek word which contemporary versions render as "puffed up with pride" (CEV, NLT), "conceited" (NASB, NCV, NIV), "haughty" (NKJV), and "swollen with conceit" (NRSV, RSV).

HIM

This word is used reflexively, in the sense of "himself," in the KJV rendering of Matthew 9:22, "Jesus turned him about." Most contemporary versions have "Jesus turned." What caused Jesus to turn was the faith of the woman with the long-standing hemorrhage, who touched the fringe of his cloak while saying to herself, "If I may but touch his garment, I shall be whole" (v. 21, KJV).

Verse 22 reads, in the NASB: "But Jesus turning and seeing her said, 'Daughter, take courage; your faith has made you well.' At once the woman was made well."

HIMSELF

The word "himself" is used as the subject of a verb, in place of the nominative pronoun "he," in the KJV rendering of Matthew 8:17, "Himself took our infirmities, and bare our sicknesses." The NASB has "He himself took our infirmities and carried away our diseases"; the NIV, "He took up our infirmities and carried our diseases."

HIS

In the KJV, we occasionally find "his" used where today we would say "its," i.e., for the neuter possessive pronoun. (See IT) "Its" was not in common use in 1611; it

occurs only rarely in Shakespeare, and not at all in the 1611 edition of the KJV.

Consequently we read, for example: "The tabernacle, his tent and his covering" (Exodus 35:11); "they brought in the ark of the LORD, and set it in his place" (2 Samuel 6:17); "Hew down the tree, and cut off his branches" (Daniel 4:14); "if the salt have lost his savour, wherewith shall it be salted?" (Matthew 5:13); "learn a parable of the fig tree; When his branch is yet tender" (Matthew 24:32); "Put up again thy sword into his place" (Matthew 26:52).

In Genesis 1:11 we read that each tree produces "fruit after his kind," and in 1 Corinthians 15:38 that "God giveth it a body as it hath pleased him, and to every seed his own body." Daniel 7:9 reads, "I beheld till the thrones were cast down, and the Ancient of days did sit, whose garment was white as snow, and the hair of his head like the pure wool: his throne was like the fiery flame, and his wheels as burning fire." Contemporary versions use "its" in these cases: e.g., "to each of the seeds a body of its own" (1 Corinthians 15:38, NASB); "its wheels were all ablaze" (Daniel 7:9, NIV).

The original edition of the KJV had "Asa his heart" (1 Kings 15:14) and "Mordecai his matters" (Esther 3:4), but these phrases were changed in 1762 to the modern form, "Asa's heart" and "Mordecai's matters."

HITHERTO

We will recognize "hitherto" as meaning "up to this time," "until now." This is its usual meaning today, but it was formerly also used of "space," meaning "up to this place," "thus far." When David sat before the Lord, and said, "Who am I, O Lord GOD? and what is my house, that thou hast brought me hitherto?" (2 Samuel 7:18 and its parallel, 1 Chronicles 17:16), the Hebrew adverb is one of "place."

The NKJV translates "that you have brought me this far?" The Lord's word to the sea, "Hitherto shalt thou come, but no further" (Job 38:11, KJV), is now rendered

"Thus far you shall come, but no farther" (NASB). The "people terrible from their beginning hitherto" (Isaiah 18:2, KJV) are "a people terrible from their beginning onward" (NKJV) and "a people feared near and far" (NRSV, RSV).

HOLD

The noun "hold" is used twelve times by the KJV in the sense of "stronghold," a word generally used in its place by the contemporary versions (Judges 9:46, 1 Samuel 22:4 etc.).

In Ezekiel 19:9 the captured king of Israel, whom the prophet compares to a lion, is brought "into holds" (KJV). The NCV and NIV have "into [NIV, "in"] prison"; the NLT, "in captivity"; the NRSV and RSV, "into custody." Other versions have "nets" (NKJV) and "hunting nets" (NASB) in place of "holds" (KJV).

In Acts 4:3, the apostles Peter and John were "put . . . in hold unto the next day: for it was now eventide" (KJV). The CEV, NASB, NCV, and NIV say that they were put "in jail"; the NKJV, NRSV, and RSV have "in custody."

The KJV description of the fallen Babylon as "the hold of every foul spirit, and a cage of every unclean and hateful bird" (Revelation 18:2) comes from Tyndale. In this verse the Greek word for "foul" is the same as that for "unclean," and the Greek word for "hold" is the same as that for "cage." The basic meaning of the latter word is a watch or guard. It does not here refer to a prison where foul spirits are under guard or a cage where unclean birds are confined but it is employed in the active sense, and means a station or post of guards, a garrison, or police headquarters. The implication is that the very forces of public safety and defense are prostituted to foul purposes; evil is in control, and is not caged or imprisoned.

The NIV, NRSV, and RSV use the word "haunt." The NRSV translates the passage as "a haunt of every foul spirit, a haunt of every foul bird, a haunt of every foul and hateful beast." The NLT has "the hideout of demons and evil spirits, a nest for filthy buzzards, and a den for dreadful beasts"; other contemporary versions render "hold" as "prison" (NASB, NCV) and "prison" and "cage" (NKJV).

HOLDEN

"Holden" is the old past participle of "hold," which began to be displaced by "held" in the sixteenth century. Shakespeare used "held" many times, and "holden" only once—in King Henry VI, Part II (II, 4, 71): "his majesty's parliament, holden at Bury."

Depending upon the Hebrew and the contexts, contemporary versions replace "holden" with "held" (CEV, NCV, NKJV, NRSV, RSV) or "kept" (NASB, NIV) in Isaiah 42:14; "hold" (CEV, NCV), "held" (NASB, NKJV, NRSV, RSV), and "keep its hold" (NIV) in Acts 2:24; "caught" (NASB, NRSV, RSV), "held" (NKJV), and "held fast" (NIV) in Job 36:8; and "caught" (CEV, NKJV, NRSV, RSV), "tie . . . up" (NCV), and "hold" (NLT; NIV, "hold . . . fast") in Proverbs 5:22.

"Holden up" (KJV) is now rendered as "supports" (CEV, NLT; NRSV and RSV, "supported"), "upholds" (NASB), "sustains" (NIV), and "held up" (NKJV) in Psalm 18:35; and as "made to stand" (NKJV) and "upheld" (NRSV, RSV) in Romans 14:4.

"By thee I have been holden up from the womb" (Psalm 71:6, KJV) is translated by the NRSV, "Upon you I have leaned from my birth." "Thou hast holden me by my right hand" (Psalm 73:23, KJV) reads in the NASB, "you have taken hold of my right hand"; the NRSV has "you hold my right hand." "Cyrus, whose right hand I have holden" (Isaiah 45:1, KJV) is rendered as "Cyrus, whose right hand I have grasped" (NRSV).

The earlier translations had "kept" or "celebrated" of the passover commanded by King Josiah (2 Kings 23:22, 23); the exception was the Geneva Bible, which used "holden" and was followed by the KJV. Luke 24:16, "Their eyes were holden that they should not know him" (KJV) now reads, "their eyes were prevented [NRSV, RSV, "were kept"] from recognizing" him (NASB, NRSV, RSV).

"And this is the cause that they are so holden with pride" is the rendering of Psalm 73:6a in the Book of Common Prayer. It comes from Coverdale, who probably took it from the Latin translation by Münster, which read, *tenet eos constrictos superbia.* The Geneva Bible had "Therefore pride is as a chaine unto them," and the KJV, "Therefore pride compasseth them about as a chain." The Hebrew here refers to an ornament, and the contemporary versions render "chain" (KJV) as "necklace."

HOLIER THAN THOU

People who are "holier than thou" behave toward others in a way that shows they think they are better, especially more moral or virtuous, than others. The origin of this phrase is Isaiah 65:5 (KJV), describing "a rebellious people" (v. 2) "Which say, Stand by thyself, come not near to me; for I am holier than thou. These are a smoke in my nose, a fire that burneth all the day."

The contemporary versions render the KJV expression "I am holier than thou" as "I am holier than you" (NASB, NKJV, NLT), "I am too holy for you" (NCV, NRSV), "I am too sacred for you" (NIV), and "I am set apart from you" (RSV). The adjective is now used to describe an attitude or person that is self-righteous.

HOLPEN

This is the old past participle of "help." From the fourteenth to the seventeenth century it was also spelled "holpe" or "holp," and it was gradually displaced by "helped." Shakespeare, according to the *Concordance,* used "holp" seventeen times and "helped" six times, as past tense and participle. Examples are:

"Would I had been by, to have helpt the nobleman!"
    —*The Winter's Tale* (III, 3, 110)

"By foul play, as thou say'st, were we heaved thence; But blessedly holp hither."
    —*The Tempest* (I, 2, 63)

The KJV uses "holpen" five times and "helped" six times, as past participle. "Holpen" appears in Psalms 83:8; 86:17; Isaiah 31:3; Daniel 11:34; and Luke 1:54. "Helped" appears as participle in 1 Samuel 7:12; 1 Chronicles 5:20; 2 Chronicles 26:15; Job 26:2; Psalm 28:7; and Isaiah 49:8.

The word "holpen" has been kept alive by liturgical use in the Magnificat—"He hath holpen his servant Israel." Its presence in the KJV version of the Magnificat is probably due to its use in the Book of Common Prayer. While "holpen" had appeared in Tyndale's first translation (1525) of Luke 1:54, he rejected it in his final edition (1534), and the word was not used at this point by any of the other English versions which preceded the KJV. The Great Bible and the Bishops' Bible had "He hath helped his servant Israel, in remembrance of his mercy."

The KJV translators retained "holpen" in Luke 1:54 in the interests of liturgical custom. Elsewhere the KJV uses "helped" (e.g., 1 Samuel 7:12; 2 Chronicles 26:15; Isaiah 49:8).

HOLY GRAIL

The "holy grail" is not an expression found in the Bible. According to medieval legend, the "Holy Grail" was the cup or platter used by Jesus at the Last Supper and in which Joseph of Arimathea received the blood of Christ at the cross.

The quest for the Holy Grail by medieval knights is described in Arthurian legends. According to one legend, Joseph of Arimathea brought the Holy Grail to Glastonbury in England. In extended use, a "holy grail" is something that people try very hard to obtain or achieve.

HOLY OF HOLIES

The "holy of holies" was "the most holy place," the innermost chamber of the tabernacle and temple, in which the ark of the covenant was kept and which was separated by a curtain from the outer chamber or the "holy place." In Exodus 26:34, the KJV has "And thou shalt put the mercy seat upon the ark of the testimony in the most holy place."

The expression "holy of holies" is a Hebraism, an example of the genitive superlative—an expression that renders the greatest example of a particular quality—that is reproduced literally in the Septuagint and Vulgate as *sanctum sanctorum*, then in Wycliffe, "holi of halowes."

At Exodus 26:34 the contemporary versions have "holy of holies" (NASB), "most holy place" (CEV; "most holy," RSV), and "Most Holy Place" (NCV, NIV, NLT; "Most Holy," NKJV). In a figurative sense in contemporary usage, the "holy of holies" is a place of special holiness, sometimes used humorously to refer to a place such as a room that is so special that only important people are allowed to enter.

HONEST

In modern usage, "honest" means "truthful," "sincere," or "having integrity." In the KJV New Testament, however, it always occurs in the older and wider sense of "honored," "honorable," or "worthy of honor."

In the parable of the sower, the CEV, NASB, NCV, NLT, NRSV, and RSV retain "honest" in their renderings of "honest and good heart" (Luke 8:15, KJV), the NIV and NKJV use the word "noble." Elsewhere the contemporary versions use the terms such as "honorable" (2 Corinthians 8:21, NASB, NKJV, NLT, NRSV, RSV), "right" (2 Corinthians 13:7, CEV, NASB, NCV, NIV, NLT, NRSV, RSV); "noble" (Phi-

lippians 4:8, NIV, NKJV); "pure" (Philippians 4:8, CEV); and "good" (Romans 12:17, NKJV).

"Having your conversation honest among the Gentiles" (1 Peter 2:12, KJV) is rendered in the NASB as "Keep your behavior excellent among the Gentiles." The seven "men of honest report" (Acts 6:3, KJV) who were to be chosen to care for the church's administrative needs were, in the NASB and NKJV, "men of good reputation"; the CEV and NLT have "men . . . respected" and "men well respected"; the NRSV, "men of good standing."

An example of the use of "honest" in its wider sense is found in Shakespeare's *Othello* (V, 1, 122), where Desdemona defends her virtuousness with the words:

"I am no strumpet; but of life as honest
As you that thus abuse me."

HONESTLY

The word "honestly" is used by the KJV to render two Greek adverbs. The first, which occurs in Hebrews 13:18 is rendered as "honorably" by the majority of contemporary versions; the second, in Romans 13:13, is rendered as "properly" (CEV, NASB, NKJV), "decently" (NIV), "in a right way" (NCV), "honorably" (NRSV), and "becomingly" (RSV).

The second of these adverbs occurs also in 1 Thessalonians 4:12, where the KJV reads, "That ye may walk honestly toward them that are without, and that ye may have lack of nothing." The CEV renders this verse as "Then you will be respected by people who are not followers of the Lord, and you won't have to depend on anyone."

HONESTY

This word appears once in the KJV (1 Timothy 2:2) as translation for the Greek noun which, as applied to God, means "holiness" and, as applied to men, means "reverence," "dignity," "respectfulness," "probity." "That we may lead a quiet and peaceable life in all godliness and honesty" (KJV) reads, in the NASB, "that we may lead a tranquil and quiet life in all godliness and dignity."

Other contemporary versions render "honesty" (KJV) in this verse as "respect" (NCV), "holiness" (NIV), and "reverence" (NKJV).

HONORABLE

Today, the word "honorable" may refer to a person's character, reputation or social status. The emphasis of the word in the KJV, however, is not upon inner principles, but upon an honored position among one's contemporaries.

"Honorable" is retained by the contemporary versions in some cases. In others it is replaced, according to context and varying Hebrew and Greek terms, by such expressions as "honored" (Genesis 34:19, NIV, NRSV, RSV; Isaiah 23:8, CEV, NASB, NRSV, RSV; Hebrews 13:4, NCV, NIV); "respected" (1 Samuel 22:14, NIV; 2 Kings 5:1, NASB); "powerful" (1 Corinthians 4:10, CEV); "distinguished" (1 Corinthians 4:10, NASB, NKJV; Luke 14:8, NASB, NIV, NRSV); "famous" (2 Samuel 23:19; 1 Chronicles 11:21, CEV, NLT); "renowned" (2 Samuel 23:19; 1 Chronicles 11:21, NRSV, RSV); "held in honor" (1 Samuel 9:6, 1 Corinthians 4:10, Hebrews 13:4, NRSV, RSV); "eminent" (Luke 14:8, RSV); "prominent" (Acts 17:12, NASB, NIV, NKJV, NLT); "of high standing" (Acts 13:50; 17:12, NRSV, RSV); "in high favor" (2 Kings 5:1, NRSV, RSV); "nobles" (Nahum 3:10, NIV, NRSV); and "man of rank" (Isaiah 3:3, NIV, RSV; "men of rank" Isaiah 5:13, NIV).

At Isaiah 42:21, the KJV reads: "The LORD is well pleased for his righteousness' sake; he will magnify the law, and make it honourable." The NASB reads:

"The LORD was pleased for His
   righteousness' sake
To make the law great and glorious."

HOPE DEFERRED MAKES THE HEART SICK

The expression "hope deferred makes the heart sick" is a saying sometimes used in contemporary English. It derives from Proverbs 13:12, KJV, "Hope deferred maketh the heart sick; but when the desire cometh, it is a tree of life."

This is rendered as follows by the contemporary translations: "hope deferred makes the heart sick" by the NASB, NIV, NKJV, NLT, NRSV, and RSV; the CEV has "Not getting what you want can make you feel sick" and the NCV, "It is sad not to get what you hoped for."

HOST

Except for the host of the inn in Jesus' parable of the good Samaritan (Luke 10:35, KJV) and Paul's reference to "Gaius mine host" (Romans 16:23, KJV) the word "host" in the KJV means "army." Derived from the Latin *hostis* ("enemy"), it translates three Hebrew words and one Greek word for "army." "The host of heaven" means (1) the multitude of angels that serve God, or (2) sun, moon, and stars, either as evidence of God's creative power or as themselves the objects of idolatrous worship. "The LORD of hosts" was used by the Hebrew prophets in the sense of God of the universe, signifying as no other title his supremacy and omnipotence.

The expression "Lord of Sabaoth," which the KJV has in Romans 9:29 and James 5:4, represents simply the fact that here the Hebrew word for "hosts" was left untranslated into Greek, and that Tyndale took it over untranslated into English. The Greek Septuagint had left "sabaoth" untranslated as part of this title in many passages, especially in Isaiah. It appears, to take the most notable example, in the Greek version of Isaiah 6:3, from which it was taken over by the Old Latin version, and consequently appears in the *Te Deum*:

Sanctus, Sanctus, Sanctus, Dominus
   Deus Sabaoth
"Holy, Holy, Holy, Lord God of
   Sabaoth."

The "of" was sometimes omitted, and the title was expressed in English as "the Lord Sabaoth." It so appears in the second verse of Hedge's translation of Martin Luther's great hymn, "A Mighty Fortress Is Our God":

"Did we in our own strength confide,
Our striving would be losing;
Were not the right man on our side,
The man of God's own choosing.
Dost ask who that may be?
Christ Jesus, it is he;
Lord Sabaoth his name,
From age to age the same,
And he must win the battle."

"The Lord of Sabaoth" (KJV) in Romans 9:29 and James 5:4 is retained by the NASB and NKJV; the NRSV and RSV render the title as "the Lord of hosts," while other versions have "the Lord All-Powerful" (CEV, NCV) and "the Lord Almighty" (NIV, NLT).

HOUGH

This word belongs to the "-ough" series of English words, which have such diverse pronunciations as "cough," "though," "through," "plough," "sough," "rough," "tough." When "slough" means "a stretch of mire," it rhymes with "how"; when it means "a river inlet," with "hue"; and when it means "to cast off," with "huff." "Hough" is pronounced "hock," and is generally so spelled. It is used in the KJV only as a verb, and means "to cut the tendons in the back of the foot of a horse or other animal."

In Joshua 11:6, Joshua is commanded to "hough their horses, and burn their chariots with fire" (KJV); in 2 Samuel 8:4, David likewise "houghed all the chariot horses, but reserved of them for an hundred chariots" (KJV). The synonym of "hough" or "hock" is "hamstring," and this is the verb used by the NASB, NIV, NKJV, NLT, and NRSV in these verses and in 1 Chronicles 18:4. The CEV, NCV, and NLT use "cripple."

HOUSE

The Hebrew *bayith* and the Greek *oikos*, like the English word "house," may mean (1) a building, (2) a household, (3) an immediate family of parents and children, or (4) a family of ancestors and descendants, distinguished by continuity of residence or by occupation, position, or renown. The context generally makes the meaning clear, even in chapters like 2 Samuel 7, where "make a house" (v. 11, KJV) and "build a house" (v. 27, KJV) refer to the dynasty of David, and "build a house" (v. 5, 13, KJV) refers to the future temple of Solomon.

The majority of the contemporary versions retain "house" in these verses, although "temple" is used by the CEV and NLT in verses 5 and 13, and "descendants" is used in verses 11 and 27 by the CEV. Verse 27 reads in the NLT, "O LORD Almighty, God of Israel, I have been bold enough to pray this prayer because you have revealed that you will build a house for me—an eternal dynasty!"

In the corresponding chapter, 1 Chronicles 17, the KJV uses the phrase "build a house" throughout, with reference to the dynasty in verses 10 and 25, and with reference to the temple in verses 4 and 12.

In Acts 16:31 comes Peter's promise to Cornelius, which reads in the KJV, "thou shalt be saved, and thy house." The NASB, NIV, NKJV, NRSV, and RSV render "thy house" (KJV) as "your household"; the NLT, "your entire household." The CEV has "everyone who lives in your home," and the NCV, "all the people in your house."

The comment concerning the Hebrew midwives, "because the midwives feared God, . . . he made them houses" (Exodus 1:21, KJV), now reads in the contemporary versions, "He established [NKJV, "He provided"] households for them" (NASB, NKJV), and "he gave them families of their own" (NCV, NIV, NLT). The NRSV and RSV read simply, "he gave them families."

HOUSE DIVIDED AGAINST ITSELF

The expression a "house divided against itself" is sometimes used to refer to an organization whose members quarrel with one another. Where there is such conflict, the organization will not survive.

The expression derives from Jesus' words recorded in Matthew 12:25, KJV, "Every kingdom divided against itself is brought to desolation; and every city or house divided against itself shall not stand." The context is the absurdity of the Pharisees' accusation that Jesus was casting out demons by Beelzebub, the prince of demons: if it were true, Satan would be opposing and destroying himself.

The contemporary versions render the KJV expression "every city or house divided against itself shall not stand" as "every city or house [NIV, "or household"] divided against itself will not stand" (NIV, NKJV), "any city or house divided against itself will not stand" (NASB), "no city or house divided against itself will stand" (NRSV, RSV), "any city or family that is divided against itself will not continue" (NCV), "a city or home divided against itself is doomed" (NLT), and "a town or family that fights will soon destroy itself" (CEV).

The parallels (Mark 3:25 and Luke 11:17) generally have similar wordings; of note are also: "A family that fights won't last long" (Mark 3:25, CEV), "A family that fights will break up" (Luke 11:17, CEV), and "A divided house is . . . doomed" (Luke 11:17, NLT).

HOUSE, TO

When the Levite from Ephraim, with his concubine and servant, turned aside to Gibeah to spend the night, "he sat him down in a street of the city; for there was no man that took them into his house to lodging" (Judges 19:15, KJV). When an old man, who was also an Ephraimite, asked him in friendly fashion where he was going and whence he had come, he answered in detail and ruefully added, "and there is no man that receiveth me to house" (19:18, KJV).

Except for the difference between "them" and "me" and the omission of the phrase "to lodging," the last clause of verse 18 and the last clause of verse 15 are identical in the Hebrew. The elliptical phrase "to house" first appeared in Matthew's Bible, 1537, which means that it was part of Tyndale's translation of the books from Joshua to Chronicles, first published in this volume edited by John Rogers under the pseudonym "Thomas Matthew." The clause "receiveth me to house" was kept by the Great Bible, the Geneva Bible, the Bishops' Bible, and the KJV.

Where did Tyndale get "to house"? Wright says that it "is probably due to the *zu Hause* of some German version." But Luther's German Bible, which Tyndale used, does not have *zu Hause*. Moreover, the German idiom *zu Hause* means "at home" rather than "into the house," and is not likely to be used here by any German version.

It is more probable that the phrase "to house" was Tyndale's own. There is no archaic English idiom "to house" corresponding to the German *zu Hause*. It is even possible that when Tyndale wrote "to house" as the closing words of verse 18 he meant them to be the infinitive of the verb "to house" rather than to be a preposition and a noun.

The NKJV renders the Levite's words in verse 18 as "there is no one who will take me into his house"; the CEV reads "no one here will let us spend the night in their home."

HOW, HOW THAT

The archaic combination "how that" appears frequently in the KJV. It usually simply means "that."

Examples are: "We will not hide it from my lord, how that our money is spent" (Genesis 47:18, KJV); the NASB, NRSV, and RSV read, "We will not hide from my lord that our money is all spent." "Ye may know how that I am the LORD" (Exodus 10:2, KJV); "you may know that I am the LORD" (NASB, NIV, NKJV, NRSV, RSV). "She had heard in the country of Moab how that the LORD had visited his people" (Ruth 1:6, KJV); "she had heard in the country of Moab that the LORD had visited his people" (NKJV, RSV). "Know ye not . . . how that the law hath dominion over a man as long as he liveth?" (Romans 7:1, KJV); "Do you not know . . . that the law has authority over a man only as long as he lives?" (NIV). "Ye see then how that by works a man is justified, and not by faith only" (James 2:24, KJV); "You can now see that we please God by what we do and not only by what we believe" (CEV).

Other cases are: Exodus 9:29; Joshua 9:24; 2 Samuel 18:19; 1 Kings 5:3; Acts 7:25; 13:32; 15:7; 23:30; 1 Corinthians 1:26; 10:1; 15:3; 2 Corinthians 12:4; 13:5; Ephesians 3:3; and Hebrews 12:17.

On seven occasions "how that" means "how." "Thou hast seen how that the LORD thy God bare thee" (Deuteronomy 1:31, KJV) reads, in the NASB, NIV, NKJV, and NRSV, "you saw how the LORD your God carried you." "How that beyond measure I persecuted the church of God, and wasted it" (Galatians 1:13, KJV) now reads, in the NIV, "how I intensely persecuted the church of God and tried to destroy it." The other cases are: Ruth 2:11; 1 Samuel 24:10, 18; 2 Kings 9:25; and Acts 10:28.

The word of the Lord in Jeremiah 9:7, "Behold, I will melt them, and try them; for how shall I do for the daughter of my people" (KJV) now reads in the NKJV, "Behold, I will refine them and try them; For how shall I deal with the daughter of My people?" The NASB, NIV, NLT, NRSV, and RSV render "how shall I do" (KJV) here as "what else can I do."

Protests or requests for explanation which begin with "How say ye?" or "How saidst thou?" and the like, now read, "How can you say?" or "How is it that you say?" and so on (Genesis 26:9; Psalm 11:1; Isaiah 19:11; Luke 20:41; John 8:33; 12:34; 14:9).

In the account of the birth of Tamar's twins (Genesis 38:27–30, KJV), the midwife's exclamation, "How hast thou broken forth? this breach be upon thee," reads in the NASB, NRSV, and RSV, "What a breach you have made for yourself!"

"How think ye?" (Matthew 18:12, KJV) is rendered as "What do you think?" by the NASB, NIV, NKJV, NRSV, and RSV, and is so translated by the KJV in Matthew 17:25 and 21:28. "How he would have him called" (Luke 1:62, KJV) is now rendered as "What he would have him called" (NKJV, RSV) and "what name he wanted to give him" (NRSV).

HOW ARE THE MIGHTY FALLEN
See MIGHTY FALLEN, HOW ARE THE.

HOWBEIT

This is an archaic word for "however," "nevertheless," "be that as it may." In the KJV it seems to serve as a general connective. It appears forty-one times in the Old Testament. In only five of these cases is there a corresponding word in the Hebrew, other than the ubiquitous conjunction *w* with which most sentences and clauses begin. It appears twenty-three times in the New Testament with a corresponding Greek word in ten of these cases.

The contemporary versions use other conjunctions in place of "howbeit" (KJV), such as "but" (Judges 18:29, NLT, NRSV, RSV), "only" (1 Samuel 8:9, NRSV, RSV), "nevertheless" (2 Samuel 12:14, NRSV, RSV), "however" (1 Kings 11:13, NASB, NKJV, NRSV, RSV), "yet" (1 Kings 11:13, NIV), "and so" (2 Chronicles 32:31, RSV), "so also" (NRSV), and "even" (CEV, NASB). Each of these passages has a different Hebrew conjunction.

In the New Testament, the contemporary versions use "however" (John 6:23, NKJV, RSV; 1 Corinthians 8:7, NASB, NKJV, NLT, NRSV, RSV; Acts 7:48, NASB, NIV, NKJV, NLT), "yet" (John 7:13, NASB, NRSV, RSV; Acts 7:48, NRSV, RSV), "but" (John 6:23, NCV; 7:13, CEV, NCV, NIV, NLT; 1 Corinthians 8:7, NCV, NIV; 1 Timothy

1:16, CEV, NCV, NIV, NLT, NRSV, RSV), and "rather" (1 Corinthians 14:20, NRSV).

The revised versions of 1881–1901 use "howbeit" in thirty-one cases where the KJV had used other terms. An interesting example is Philippians 4:14, where the KJV reads, "Notwithstanding ye have well done, that ye did communicate with my affliction." The RV and ASV have "Howbeit ye did well that ye had fellowship with my affliction." The NRSV has "In any case, it was kind of you to share my distress."

HUSBANDMAN

"Husbandman" is a word not used by Shakespeare, though he uses "husbandry." It appears twenty-six times in the KJV. In Genesis 9:20 we read that "Noah began to be an husbandman" (KJV), and that he went on to plant a vineyard. The NCV, NKJV, and NLT refer to him as "a farmer," and the NIV and NRSV as "a man of the soil." The RSV reads, "Noah was the first tiller of the soil."

Similarly the contemporary versions render the words "I am an husbandman" (KJV) in Zechariah 13:5 as "I am [NLT, "I'm"] a farmer" (NCV, NIV, NKJV, NLT) and "I am a tiller of the soil" [NASB, "the ground"] (NASB, NRSV, RSV). "O tillers of the soil" is the RSV's rendering of the poetic cadence in Joel 1:11.

The Hebrew word 'ikkar (KJV, "husbandman") is rendered in the plural as "farmers" by the CEV, NRSV, and RSV in 2 Chronicles 26:10, and by the majority of the contemporary versions in Jeremiah 14:4, 31:24, 51:23, and Amos 5:16. In 2 Kings 25:12 (and its parallel, Jeremiah 52:16) it is rendered as "plowmen" by the NASB and RSV, and as "tillers of the soil" by the NRSV. "Plowmen" is also used by the NASB in 2 Chronicles 26:10, and by the NKJV in Jeremiah 14:4.

Other versions translate "husbandmen" (KJV) in 2 Chronicles 26:10 with renderings such as "people who worked his fields" (NCV). The KJV, NKJV, and RSV render 'ikkar in Isaiah 61:5 as "plowmen."

For the Greek word georgos the general word "farmer" is used by contemporary versions in 2 Timothy 2:6 (NKJV, "The hardworking farmer must be first to partake of the crops" and in James 5:7 (NASB, "the farmer waits for the precious produce of the soil").

In Jesus' parable of the vineyard the "husbandmen" (KJV) are clearly tenants—the point of the parable turns upon that fact (Matthew 21:33–41; Mark 12:1–9; Luke 20:9–16). They are "renters" in the CEV, "tenants" in the NIV, NRSV, and RSV, and "tenant farmers" in the NLT. The NASB has "vine-growers"; the NKJV, "vinedressers"; the NCV, "farmers."

With Weymouth, Moffatt, Confraternity, and Phillips, the NASB, NKJV, and RSV translate georgos as "vinedresser" (NRSV, "vine-grower") in the quite different context of John 15:1–2. Goodspeed dissents in favor of "cultivator"; the CEV, NCV, NIV, and NLT have "gardener." The CEV reads, "I am the true vine, and my Father is the gardener. He cuts away every branch of mine that doesn't produce fruit. But he trims clean every branch that does produce fruit, so that it will produce even more fruit."

HUSBANDRY

The word "husbandry" in modern usage means "farming" ("animal husbandry") or, occasionally, "careful management of resources." In the KJV the word is used twice, in agricultural contexts. It is said of King Uzziah that "he loved husbandry" (2 Chronicles 26:10, KJV). The NASB's translation of the Hebrew in this verse reads, "He also had plowmen and vinedressers in the hill country and the fertile lands, for he loved soil."

Among the various meanings of "husbandry" in the sixteenth century was "land under cultivation," and in 1 Corinthians 3:9 the KJV translators probably used the word in that sense—a sense now obsolete. Paul's statement to the Corinthians, "ye are God's husbandry," now reads "you are God's field" in the NASB, NIV, NKJV, NLT, NRSV, and RSV. The CEV has "God's garden," and the NCV,

"God's farm." The Greek word here, *georgion,* means "cultivated land" or "field." The NRSV reads, "For we are God's servants, working together; you are God's field, God's building."

HUSKS

The word "husks" brings to mind the dry and worthless exterior of heads of grain. In Luke 15:76, however, the "husks" (KJV) that the swine ate were the pods of the carob tree, with a sweetish pulp containing seeds. They were used not only as fodder for animals, but as food by the poorer people, who ground and boiled them to extract their sugar, somewhat as molasses is extracted from sugar cane. The prodigal son could certainly have eaten them.

Wycliffe, Tyndale, Coverdale, the Great Bible, and the Bishops' Bible have "the coddes," because "cod" was the old word for "pod." The word "husk," which was introduced in the Geneva Bible, may not convey the full meaning, since it applies only to the outer covering and not to the whole fruit. While the rending "husks" certainly sharpens the point of the story, all the contemporary versions except the CEV use "pods."

The CEV paraphrases as "what the pigs were eating."

The Hebrew word represented by the KJV as "husk" in Numbers 6:4 probably refers to grapeskins. The law for one taking the vow of a Nazirite required strict abstinence: "He shall separate himself from wine and strong drink, and shall drink no vinegar of wine, or vinegar of strong drink, neither shall he drink any liquor of grapes, nor eat moist grapes, or dried. All the days of his separation shall he eat nothing that is made of the vine tree, from the kernels even to the husk" (vv. 3–4, KJV).

The NASB renders verse 4 as "All the days of his separation he shall not eat anything that is produced by the grape vine, from the seeds even to the skins."

In 2 Kings 4:42 we read that a man brought supplies to Elisha and his band, including "full ears of corn in the husk thereof" (KJV). The revised versions take the Hebrew word as referring not to the husk of the grain (which, incidentally, was not American corn), but to the sack in which the man carried it.

The NASB, NRSV, and RSV have "fresh ears of grain in his sack," and the NKJV has "newly ripened grain in his knapsack."

I

IF SO BE (THAT)

The OED describes this expression as a rhetorical equivalent of the simple "if." It occurs nine times in the KJV, where it represents six different terms—one Hebrew and five Greek. Contemporary versions do not use "if so be," but a variety of different expressions.

The passages are Joshua 14:12 (CEV, "maybe"; NASB, "perhaps"); Hosea 8:7 (NIV, "were . . . to"; NRSV, "if"); Matthew 18:13 (NASB, NKJV, NRSV, "if"); Romans 8:9, 17 (NASB, NKJV, "if indeed"); l Corinthians 15:15 (NASB, NIV, NKJV, "if in fact"; NRSV, RSV, "if it is true"); 2 Corinthians 5:3 (NASB, "inasmuch"; NCV, NIV, "because"); Ephesians 4:21 (NASB, NKJV,

"if indeed"; NIV, "surely"); 1 Peter 2:3 (NCV, "because"; RSV, "for"; NASB, "if").

IF THY RIGHT HAND OFFEND THEE
See HAND, RIGHT, OFFEND THEE.

ILLUMINATE

This word makes us think of light. At night we illuminate sharp bends on dangerous roads, window displays in shopping malls, and automobiles in showrooms. But we also use the word in the context of "understanding," and it occurs once in the KJV with this sense of "to enlighten": "after ye were illuminated" (Hebrews 10:32) The Greek verb used here occurs also in Hebrews 6:4 and

Ephesians 1:18, where it is rendered as "enlightened" by the KJV.

The NKJV retains "illuminated" in Hebrews 10:32, while other contemporary versions render the words "after ye were illuminated" (KJV) as "when you first received the light" (CEV), and "after being enlightened" (NASB). The NLT paraphrases as "when you first learned about Christ." The Rheims New Testament, translating from the Latin Vulgate, had "illuminated" in all three passages.

IMAGERY

"Imagery" is used by poets, writers, and artists to present something through the use of figures and images. When this word occurs in the KJV, however, it is used in its older sense as a collective term for "images" and "pictures." "Every man in the chambers of his imagery" (Ezekiel 8:12, KJV) refers to the scene that has just been described (vv. 10–11)—seventy elders of Israel gathered in secret worship of idols "portrayed upon the wall round about" (KJV).

"The chambers of his imagery" (KJV) is rendered by contemporary versions as "the room of his carved images" (NASB), "the shrine of his own idol" (NIV), "his room of images" (NRSV), and "the room of his idols" (NKJV). The elders' action transgressed the commandment, "Thou shalt not make unto thee any graven image, or any likeness of any thing that is in heaven above, or that is in the earth beneath, or that is in the water under the earth: Thou shalt not bow down thyself to them, nor serve them" (Exodus 20:4–5, KJV).

IMAGINATION

Imagination is the human ability to form mental images, used for example in artistic creations. In the KJV, however, "imagination" refers to an evil purpose, plan, scheme, device, or argument, rather than a mental faculty or activity. The key to the use of this word in the KJV is given in Genesis 6:5: "GOD saw that the wickedness of man was great in the earth, and that every imagina-

tion of the thoughts of his heart was only evil continually" (KJV). One Hebrew word, *sheriruth,* is translated "lust" by the KJV in Psalm 81:12, and "imagination" in Deuteronomy 29:19 and another eight passages in Jeremiah (3:17; 7:24; 9:14; 11:8; 13:10; 16:12; 18:12; 23:17).

The contemporary versions generally use "stubbornness," "stubborn," or "stubbornly" in these occurrences, although the NKJV renders *sheriruth* as "dictates." At Genesis 6:5, the NASB and NKJV have "intent"; the NIV and NRSV, "inclination." The RSV retains the KJV "imagination."

IMAGINE

When a little girl asks for a bandage for her teddy bear's knee, she imagines him to have scraped it as he slid down the banisters. In the KJV, however, the word "imagine" means to "purpose," "plan," or "contrive." Its object is action, and it is always directed to action that is evil or futile.

In Acts 4:25, "imagine" (KJV) translates a verb quoted from the Greek Septuagint; it is retained by the NRSV and RSV ("Why did the Gentiles rage, and the people imagine vain things?"), but other contemporary versions use "devise" (NASB), "plot" (NIV, NKJV), and the verb "make" (CEV, NCV).

Elsewhere, contemporary versions use words such as "think" (Job 6:26, NLT, NRSV, RSV) and "think up" (Psalm 38:12, NCV, NLT), "purpose" (Genesis 11:6, NASB), "meditate" (Psalm 38:12, NRSV, RSV), "propose" (Genesis 11:6, NKJV, NRSV, RSV), "plan" (Psalm 140:2, NKJV, NRSV, RSV), "plot" (Psalm 2:1, NIV, NKJV, NRSV, RSV), "conspire" (Nahum 1:9, NKJV), "intend" (Job 6:26, NASB, NKJV), and the verb "devise" (Psalm 10:2, NIV, NRSV, RSV; Zechariah 7:10 and 8:17, NASB, NRSV, RSV).

Hastings' *Dictionary of the Bible* quotes a sentence from Sir Thomas Elyot, *The Governour* (II, 74), which illustrates this obsolete use of "imagine": "It was reported to the noble emperour Octavius Augustus that Lucius Cinna, which was susters sonne to the great Pompei, had imagined his dethe."

IMITATE

See FOLLOW.

IMPART

To impart is to share. It is to give to others a part or share of something that we possess. Originally the word was used for the sharing of any sort of possession, but now we generally use it of non-material goods. We impart knowledge, news, secrets, happiness loyalty, friendship—such are possessions that we do not lose as we share them. The word "impart" is used four times in the KJV, as translation for a Hebrew verb and a Greek verb which mean "to share."

Contemporary versions read, "The man who has two tunics is to share with him who has none" (Luke 3:11, NASB); "we were delighted to share with you" (1 Thessalonians 2:8, NIV; the NASB and NKJV retain the KJV "impart"); "God has . . . given it no share in understanding" (Job 39:17, NRSV). Of the ostrich in Job 39:17, the NKJV says that "God . . . did not endow her with [KJV, "neither hath he imparted to her"] understanding." (See SHARE)

The NASB, NIV, NKJV, and RSV retain "impart" in Romans 1:11–12: "For I long to see you so that I may impart some spiritual gift to you, that you may be established; that is, that I may be encouraged together with you while among you, each of us by the other's faith, both yours and mine" (NASB).

IMPLEAD

This is an archaic word for "sue in a court of justice," "bring charges against." It occurs only in the KJV rendering of Acts 19:38, where the town clerk of Ephesus points out that if Demetrius and his fellow craftsmen have a complaint against anyone, the courts are open—"let them implead one another."

The Greek verb occurs in six other passages, where the KJV translates it as "accused" (Acts 23:28–29; 26:2, 7), "called in question" (Acts 19:40), and "lay to the charge of" (Romans 8:33). Prior translations had "let them accuse one another" and the revised versions returned to that.

At Acts 19:38, the NASB, NKJV, NRSV, and RSV have "let them bring charges [NRSV, "bring charges there"] against one another," and the NIV has "They can press charges."

IMPOTENT

The word "impotent" means "powerless," "unable," "helpless," "weak," "ineffective." It is used by the KJV in the New Testament passages. At the pool of Bethesda, we read, "lay a great multitude of impotent folk," one of whom "had an infirmity thirty and eight years" and is referred to as "the impotent man" (John 5:3, 5, 7, KJV). In each of these three verses, the Greek word means "ill" or "illness," without specifying the nature of the illness.

The "impotent man" healed by Peter and John at the gate of the temple had been "lame from his mother's womb" and had to be carried daily to the place where he sat for alms (Acts 4:9; 3:2, KJV). The man whom Paul healed at Lystra was "impotent in his feet, being a cripple from his mother's womb, who never had walked" (Acts 14:8, KJV).

In place of "the impotent man" (KJV) contemporary versions use "the sick man" (NASB, NCV, NKJV, NLT, NRSV, RSV) and "the invalid" (NIV) in John 5:7 and "crippled man" (CEV, NCV, NLT), "a helpless man" (NKJV), "someone who was sick" (NRSV), and "a cripple" (NIV, RSV) in Acts 4:9. The "impotent folk" (KJV) of John 5:3 are now referred to as "those who were sick" (NASB), "disabled people" (NIV), "sick people" (NCV, NLT), and "invalids" (NRSV, RSV).

IN

In the KJV, "in" is occasionally used with a verbal noun, while contemporary versions now adopt a more direct translation. "As her soul was in departing" (Genesis 35:18, KJV) is rendered "as her soul was departing" (NASB, NKJV, NRSV, RSV). "While the flesh was in seething" (1 Samuel 2:13, KJV) is now "while the meat was boiling" (NASB, NKJV, NRSV, RSV).

The phrase "in building" is retained only by the RSV in Ezra 5:16, where other versions have "under construction" (NASB, NIV, NKJV, NRSV, RSV), but not in 1 Kings 6:7 or John 2:20.

When the angel of God called to Hagar, "Arise, lift up the lad, and hold him in thine hand" (Genesis 21:18, KJV), the renderings offered by the NRSV and RSV suggest that the meaning is that she should hold him firmly and support him. The NRSV translates as "hold him fast with your hand; for I will make a great nation of him." The NASB and NKJV read, "lift up the lad, and hold him by the hand" [NKJV, "with your hand"]; the NLT reads, "Go to him and comfort him."

"They shall amerce him in an hundred shekels of silver" (Deuteronomy 22:19, KJV) is rendered in the NASB, NIV, NKJV, NRSV, and RSV as "they shall fine him a [NKJV, NRSV, "one"] hundred shekels of silver."

"The king of Egypt put him down at Jerusalem, and condemned the land in an hundred talents of silver and a talent of gold" (2 Chronicles 36:3, KJV) means that he deposed Jehoahaz in Jerusalem and "imposed on the land a tribute" (NKJV) of that amount.

In 1 Timothy 2:14–15, we read that "woman was deceived" (a reference to Eve), but that "she shall be saved in childbearing . . . if they continue in faith and charity and holiness" (KJV). This is a difficult passage, and the meaning of Paul's words is far from clear. Is he asserting that salvation will come to women as they submit to traditional roles like childbearing, or that women will be brought through childbirth safely—challenging the curse in Eden?

The NKJV retains the KJV rendering, while the NASB suggests that the sense is safety in delivery: "women will be preserved through the bearing of children." The renderings adopted by the NCV, NIV, NLT, NRSV, and RSV are more open-ended. They use "through" rather than "in" (KJV): "saved through child-bearing" (NIV, NLT, NRSV), "saved through bearing children" (RSV), "saved through having children" (NCV). The CEV reads, "women will be saved by having children."

IN ALL ITS GLORY
See GLORY, IN ALL ITS.

IN WORD AND DEED
See WORD AND DEED.

INCONTINENCY
This is an obsolete spelling for "incontinence," which means "lack of self-control," either in a general sense or, more often, with reference to sexual desire. It has the specific reference in 1 Corinthians 7:5, where "for your incontinency" (KJV) is now translated, "because of your lack of self-control" (CEV, NASB, NIV, NKJV, NRSV).

INCONTINENT
"Incontinent" is used by the KJV in a general sense in 2 Timothy 3:3, where the ASV, NASB, NIV, and NKJV translate the Greek adjective by "without self-control" and the NRSV and RSV by the noun "profligates."

INDITE
This word originally meant "to dictate a form of words to be repeated or written down by someone else," but it soon came to be used for the act of expressing one's thoughts in words, in any form of literary composition, without implication as to who wrote them down.

The original meaning appears in the preface to the King James Version, 1611, entitled "The Translators to the Reader," where the Scriptures are described as "a fountain of most pure water springing up unto everlasting life. And what marvel? The original thereof being from heaven, not from earth; the author being God, not man; the inditer, the Holy Spirit, not the wit of the Apostles or Prophets; the penmen, such as were sanctified from the womb, and endued with a principal portion of God's Spirit."

This original meaning is also implied in the one occurrence of the word in the text of the KJV, Psalm 45:1: "My heart is inditing a good matter: I speak of the things which I have made touching the king: my tongue is the pen of a ready writer." The Hebrew verb is vivid: it means to "bubble up," "seethe," "boil over." The old Greek and Latin translations use similarly strong words.

Of the contemporary versions, the NASB, NKJV, NLT, NRSV, and RSV use the verb "to overflow" ("My heart overflows" [NKJV, "is overflowing"]. The NIV has "My heart is stirred." The entire verse reads in the NASB,

"My heart overflows with a good
    theme;
I address my verses to the King;
My tongue is the pen of a ready writer."

INFIDEL

"Infidel" is a word which, in modern usage, has a rather offensive ring to it. Today, it denotes "a disbeliever in religion or divine revelation generally; especially one in a Christian land who professedly rejects or denies the divine origin and authority of Christianity" (OED). It appears twice in the KJV: "what part hath he that believeth with an infidel?" (2 Corinthians 6:15); "if any provide not for his own, and specially for those of his own house, he hath denied the faith, and is worse than an infidel" (1 Timothy 5:8).

The Greek word represented by "infidel" in these texts is *apistos*. It is applied to persons in twenty other contexts, where the KJV translates it by "faithless," "unbelieving," "unbeliever," "that believe not." The use of "infidel" in these two verses dates back to Tyndale, who meant by it one who is without the faith rather than one who denies or deliberately rejects it. In his *Prologe* to the five books of Moses, Tyndale wrote, "Behold how soberly and how circumspectly both Abraham and also Isaac behave themselves amonge the infideles." To the Crusaders the Saracens were "infidels."

In Shakespeare's *The Merchant of Venice*

(III, 2, 221; IV, 1, 334) the Jew Shylock and his daughter Jessica are referred to as "infidel." In this sense the word "infidel" is now obsolete or of only historical significance.

The word "infidel" today is loaded with specific applications and currents of feeling, and contemporary versions generally use "unbeliever" in its place; at 2 Corinthians 6:15 the NCV uses "nonbeliever," and at 1 Timothy 5:8 the CEV uses "someone who doesn't have faith in the Lord."

INFINITE

The word "infinite" makes us think of immeasurable qualities, great importance, or endlessness ("an infinite number of commuters; a meeting of infinite importance"). In the KJV it is used twice as a translation for the Hebrew words which mean "no end." This expression is translated thus by the KJV in Ecclesiastes 4:8, "yet is there no end of all his labour," and in Isaiah 9:7, "Of the increase of his government and peace there shall be no end."

But in Job 22:5 and Nahum 3:9, Job's iniquities and the strength of Egypt are described as "infinite," which is the language of hyperbole. Eliphaz the Temanite's rebuke to Job is translated as "Is not your wickedness great, and your iniquities [NKJV, "your infirmity"] without end?" by the NASB and NKJV; other versions render "infinite" (KJV) in this context as "endless" (NIV), "have no end" (NCV), and "has no limit!"(NLT).

In Nahum 3:9 contemporary versions use terms such as "without limit" (NLT, NRSV, RSV), "without limits" (NASB), and "boundless" (NIV, NKJV). The one other occurrence of the word "infinite" in the KJV is in reference to God: "his understanding is infinite" (Psalm 147:5). The Hebrew here means "innumerable" or "beyond measure." "Infinte" is here retained by the NASB and NKJV; the NCV and NIV render it as "no limit," the NLT as "beyond comprehension," and the NRSV and RSV as "beyond measure."

The use of the word "infinite" in Job and

Nahum was an innovation of the KJV translators, but the prior translations had used it in Psalm 147.

INFLUENCES

The "sweet influences" of the Pleiades (Job 38:31, KJV) have been cited often, from Milton's *Paradise Lost* (vii, 374) to Bartlett's *Familiar Quotations.* The question, "Canst thou bind the sweet influences of Pleiades, or loose the bands of Orion?" points to God's creative power and wisdom, as do the references to the Pleiades and Orion in Job 9:9 and Amos 5:8. The NASB, NRSV, and RSV read, "Can you bind the chains of the Pleiades" which is also the translation of the Septuagint and the Vulgate.

Martin Luther similarly had *Kanst du die Bande der sieben Sterne zusammen binden?* Of the sixteenth-century English versions, Coverdale, Matthew, and the first edition of the Bishops' Bible had similar renderings. The expression "sweet influences" was a product of Coverdale's later work on the Great Bible; it was taken into the Geneva Bible and into the second (revised) edition of the Bishops' Bible, from where it passed to the KJV.

Other contemporary versions render the question in Job 38:31 as "Can you tie up the stars of the Pleiades" (NCV), "Can you bind the beautiful Pleiades?" (NIV), "Can you bind the cluster of the Pleiades" (NKJV), and "Can you hold back the movements of the stars?" (NLT).

INFOLD

In Ezekiel's vision, Ezekiel saw "a whirlwind came out of the north, a great cloud, and a fire infolding itself, and a brightness was about it, and out of the midst thereof as the colour of amber, out of the midst of the fire" (Ezekiel 1:4, KJV). The verb translated "infold" is of uncertain meaning. It means literally "take hold of itself," and may suggest that one flame was igniting another and that the fire spread by itself without the need for fuel.

The contemporary versions render this expression as "fire flashing forth continually" (NASB, NRSV, RSV), "fire flashing out of it" (NCV), "raging fire engulfing itself" (NKJV), "flashing lightning" (NIV), "flashed with lightning" (NLT), and "lightning flashed" (CEV).

INJURIOUS

The word "injurious" is likely to make us think of the causing of harm or hurt ("an injurious habit"), but the word can also mean "insulting" or "abusive," and it is used with this sense by the KJV in 1 Timothy 1:13. The Greek adjective is *hubristes,* which means "wantonly insolent and insulting." Paul speaks of himself, before his conversion, as "a blasphemer, and a persecutor, and injurious" (KJV); contemporary versions render "injurious" (KJV) here as "a violent agressor" (NASB), "a violent man" (NIV), "a man of violence" (NRSV), and "an insolent man" (NKJV).

The same Greek adjective at Romans 1:30 is rendered as "despiteful" by the KJV and "insolent" (NASB, NIV, NLT, NRSV, RSV) and "violent" (NKJV) by contemporary versions. An example of sixteenth-century usage can be found in Shakespeare's play *Coriolanus* (III, 3, 69–74):

"Call me their traitor! Thou
    injurious tribune!
Within thine eyes sat twenty
    thousand deaths,
In thy hands clutch'd as many
    millions, in
Thy lying tongue both numbers, I
    would say
'Thou liest' unto thee with a voice as
    free
As I do pray the gods."

INN

While "inn" is likely to conjure up images of beautiful Bavarian taverns positioned by mountain waysides, originally the word referred to any place where a person could stay or lodge overnight. It is used by the KJV in Genesis 42:27, 43:21, and Exodus 4:24 as translation for the Hebrew *malon,* which the KJV elsewhere translates as "lodging," "lodging place," and "place where they lodged" (Joshua 4:3, 8; 2 Kings 19:23; Isaiah 10:29; Jeremiah 9:2). A building is nowhere implied, and the lodging may have been in the open air.

Contemporary versions use "lodging place" (NASB, NRSV, RSV) and "encampment" (NKJV) in Genesis 42:27 and 43:21, and "camp" (CEV), "encampment" (NKJV), "resting place" (NCV), and "lodging place" (RSV) in Exodus 4:24.

The "inn" (Luke 10:34), KJV) to which the good Samaritan took the wounded traveler, however, was probably a khan or caravanserai. It was a *pandocheion,* which means an "all receiving" place, open to all travelers; and it was under the management of a *pandocheus,* a host or innkeeper.

The inn at Bethlehem in which there was no place for Joseph and Mary (Luke 2:7) was a *kataluma,* a guest room. The KJV translates this word as "guestchamber" in Mark 14:14 and Luke 22:11, where it refers to a large upper room in a private house, which the owner afforded to Jesus for the celebration of the Passover with his disciples.

This was in accord with a custom which is described in Hastings' *Dictionary of the Bible* (vol. II, p. 474): "At the festivals of Passover, Pentecost, and Tabernacles the people were commanded to repair to Jerusalem; and it was a boast of the Rabbis, that, notwithstanding the enormous crowds, no man could truthfully say to his fellow, 'I have not found a fire where to roast my paschal lamb in Jerusalem,' or 'I have not found a bed in Jerusalem to lie in.' The vast numbers who came for the Passover from all parts were made free of the needed apartments, as far as the capacity of the houses permitted; and for this no payment was taken. It was, however, customary for the guests on departing to leave the skins of the paschal lambs, and the vessels which

had been employed in the ceremonies, in token of gratitude for their hospitable entertainment."

INNER MAN

In contemporary English "the inner man" (feminine, "the inner woman") is the soul or mind of a man/woman, or in jocular use, "the appetite." The phrase derives from Ephesians 3:16, KJV, "That he would grant you, according to the riches of his glory, to be strengthened with might by his Spirit in the inner man."

Of the contemporary versions, the NASB, NKJV, and RSV retain the KJV rendering "inner man"; the NIV and NRSV has "inner being"; the NLT has "inner" and NCV, "inwardly."

INNOCENT

The phrase "the blood of the souls of the poor innocents" (KJV) in Jeremiah 2:34 might seem ambiguous to contemporary readers, who, in the light of the fact that the word "innocents" is often applied to the children massacred by Herod (Matthew 2:16–18), might take "poor innocents" to mean children.

The KJV translators took this wording from the Geneva Bible, and substituted it for the translation used by Coverdale, Matthew's Bible, the Great Bible, and the Bishops' Bible, which read "the blood of poor and innocent people." The revised versions of 1885–1901 have "the blood of the souls of the innocent poor," and the NASB, NIV, and NRSV, "the lifeblood of the innocent poor." The reference is to the unjust oppression of the poor.

On the other hand, "the blood of innocents" appears in Coverdale, Matthew's Bible, The Great Bible, the Bishops' Bible, the NKJV ["the innocents"], and the RSV at Jeremiah 19:4, where the reference is to the sacrificing of children as burnt offerings to Baal. The NASB, NIV, and NRSV have "the blood of the innocent"; the NLT, "the blood of innocent children."

INQUISITION

The word "inquisition" gets its connotation of persecution and torture from the conduct, especially in Spain, of the Holy Office of the Inquisition organized in the thirteenth century under Pope Innocent III, for the suppression of heresy and the punishment of heretics. Basically, the word means "inquiry"; it is used particularly for judicial or official investigations. For "the judges shall make diligent inquisition" (Deuteronomy 19:18, KJV), the NKJV has "the judges shall make careful inquiry." For "when inquisition was made of the matter" (Esther 2:23, KJV), the NRSV and RSV have "when the affair was investigated."

The other occurrence of "inquisition" in the KJV may not be quite so clear to contemporary readers: "When he maketh inquisition for blood, he remembereth them" (Psalm 9:12a). "He" refers to the Lord, and the Hebrew verb for "maketh inquisition" is the one which is translated "require" by the KJV in a dozen similar contexts.

The basic passage is Genesis 9:5–6, which reads in the KJV: "And surely your blood of your lives will I require; at the hand of every beast will I require it, and at the hand of man; at the hand of every man's brother will I require the life of man. Whoso sheddeth man's blood, by man shall his blood be shed: for in the image of God made he man."

In the light of the word's usage in these other contexts, the contemporary versions read at Psalm 9:12a, "He who requires blood remembers them" (NASB), "he who avenges blood remembers" (NIV), and "he who avenges blood is mindful of them" (NRSV, RSV). Psalm 9:11–12 forms a strophe, which the NRSV translates:

> "Sing praises to the LORD, who dwells in Zion!
> Declare his deeds among the peoples.
> For he who avenges blood is mindful of them; he does not forget the cry of the afflicted."

INSTANT, INSTANTLY

The noun "instant" refers in the KJV, as in present English, to a moment or point of time. The prophet Isaiah likens the iniquity of Israel to "a breach ready to fall, swelling out in a high wall, whose breaking cometh suddenly at an instant" (Isaiah 30:13, KJV); the NASB reads "Whose collapse comes suddenly in an instant."

But our present-day use of the adjective "instant" and the adverb "instantly" is quite different from that of the KJV. In contemporary English, these words refer to time: we have instant coffee, and may well hear the waiter in a busy city café promise to "be with us in an instant." In the KJV, "instant" and "instantly" refer, not to time, but to the spirit or manner of an action.

For example, in Luke 7:4 we read that the elders of the Jews went to Jesus and "besought him instantly" to heal the servant of the centurion; contemporary versions say that they "earnestly implored Him" (NASB), "pleaded earnestly with him" (NIV), and "begged Him earnestly" (NKJV).

Paul's statement before King Agrippa reads in the KJV, "Now I stand and am judged for the hope of the promise made of God unto our fathers: Unto which promise our twelve tribes, instantly serving God day and night, hope to come" (Acts 26:6–7). The NRSV translates: "Now I stand here on trial on account of my hope in the promise made by God to our ancestors, a promise that our twelve tribes hope to attain, as they earnestly worship day and night."

"They were instant with loud voices, requiring that he might be crucified" (Luke 23:23) reads in the NKJV, "They were insistent, demanding with loud cries that He be crucified." The apostles' charge to Timothy, "be instant in season, out of season," (2 Timothy 4:2, KJV), is now rendered as "be ready" (NASB, NCV, NKJV), "be prepared" (NIV), "be persistent" (NLT, NRSV), and "be urgent" (RSV).

INTELLIGENCE

This word might turn our thoughts to spy novels and the information-gathering activities of the military or secret services. In Daniel 11:30, however, the expression "have intelligence with" simply means "have an understanding with." The Hebrew is the same as that which the KJV translates by the verb "regard" in Daniel 11:37.

It is translated as "show regard for" (NASB, NKJV), "show favor to" (NIV), "reward" (NLT), and "pay heed to" (NRSV) by contemporary versions at 11:30, and as "pay . . . respect to" by the NRSV at 11:37.

INTEND

To intend something today means to hold it in mind as a definite purpose or design. "Intend" is a verb that has had many meanings; the OED lists sixteen senses that are obsolete before it arrives at the current sense. Some of these are reflected in the KJV renderings which follow.

In Joshua 22:33 we read in the KJV, "The children of Israel blessed God, and did not intend to go up against them in battle." The contemporary versions render this as "There was no more talk about going to war" (CEV), "they did not speak of going up against them" (NASB), and they "spoke no more" of war against Reuben and Gad (NKJV, NLT, NRSV, RSV).

"Intending" is retained at Luke 14:28 by the NKJV and NRSV (KJV, "intending to build a tower"); the RSV has "desiring to build a tower." In Acts 5:35 Gamaliel says to the council, "Ye men of Israel, take heed to yourselves what ye intend to do as touching these men" (KJV); again, "intend" is retained in some contemporary versions (NIV, NKJV), and replaced in others with verbs such as "propose" (NASB, NRSV), "planning" (NCV, NLT). The RSV reads, "Men of Israel, take care what you do with these men."

The structure of Psalm 21 is not always recognized but is crucial if the psalm is to be understood. The first strophe (vv. 1–7) is addressed to the Lord, in grateful acknowledgment of the blessings he has bestowed upon the king; the second strophe (vv. 8–12) is addressed to the king, in confident promise of future victories; and the psalm ends with a final prayer to the Lord (v. 13). The word "intend" occurs in verse 11 with the sense of "plan" or "plot": "For they intended evil against thee: they imagined a mischievous device, which they are not able to perform" (KJV). The verb "intend" is retained by the NASB and NKJV; the other versions have "plot" (NIV, NLT) and "plan" (NRSV, RSV).

INTERMEDDLE

The word "intermeddle" might make us think of interfering friends meddling in matters which do not concern them. In the sixteenth century, however, "intermeddle" was an innocent word meaning to "mingle," "mix," or "take part in." "The heart knoweth his own bitterness; and a stranger doth not intermeddle with his joy" (Proverbs 14:10, KJV) now reads in the NASB as "The heart knows its own bitterness, And a stranger does not share its joy."

In Proverbs 18:1, however, "intermeddle" is used by the KJV as translation for a Hebrew verb which means "to break" or "burst out in contention": "Through desire a man, having separated himself, seeketh and intermeddleth with all wisdom." The verse reads in the NRSV as "The one who lives alone is self-indulgent, showing contempt for all who have sound judgment."

Other contemporary versions render "intermeddleth" (KJV) here as "quarrels" (NASB), "defies" (NIV), "rages" (NKJV), "snarling" (NLT), and "break out" (RSV). In Proverbs 17:14 and 20:3, the KJV uses the word "meddle" to translate the same Hebrew verb; the NASB has "abandon the quarrel before it breaks out" and "any fool will quarrel."

INTO

"Into" means "to point within a definite space or thing"; it implies entrance, the crossing of boundaries, or penetration of surfaces to reach the interior. In five passages in Acts, the word appears in the KJV in an obsolete sense. "Sailed . . . into Syria" (18:18, KJV) and "sail into Syria" (20:3, KJV) are now translated by the NASB, NCV, NIV, NKJV, NRSV (at 18:18 only), and RSV as "for Syria"; "sailed into Syria" (21:3) is generally rendered by the contemporary versions "to Syria"; "sail into Italy" and "sailing into Italy" (27:1, 6) are rendered as "to Italy" (NKJV), and "for Italy" (NASB, NIV, NRSV).

INTREAT

See ENTREAT.

INWARD

This is an adverb which we most commonly use to mean "toward the inside or interior of a place or space." Sometimes we also use it to mean "in the mind or soul" ("an inward feeling"). In the sixteenth and seventeenth centuries, however, the word "inward" was commonly used in the sense of "intimate," "close," "belonging to the inner circle of one's friends," and it occurs with this sense in the KJV rendering of Job 19:19: "All my inward friends abhorred me."

This sense is now obsolete, and the contemporary versions render "inward friends" (KJV) here as "best friends" (CEV), "associates" (NASB), "close friends" (NCV, NKJV, NLT), and "intimate friends" (NIV, NRSV, RSV). The obsolete sense appears in Shakespeare:

"Sir, I was an inward of his."
—*Measure for Measure* (III, 2, 132)

"Who is most inward with the royal duke?"
—*King Richard III* (III, 4, 8)

"For what is inward between us, let it pass."
—*Love's Labour's Lost* (V, 1, 89)

Shakespeare also uses the noun "inwardness" in a similar sense:

"You know my inwardness and love
Is very much unto the prince and
Claudio."
—*Much Ado About Nothing*
(IV, 1, 247–248)

INWARDS

As a noun, "inwards" is used twenty times by the KJV in Exodus and in Leviticus 1, 3—4, 7—9 to denote the entrails of an animal offered in sacrifice. The NASB, NKJV, NLT, and NRSV generally replace it with "entrails"; other versions use terms such as "inner organs" (NCV), "inner parts" (NIV), and "internal organs" (NLT).

ISHMAEL

An "Ishmael" is a social outcast. Ishmael was the son of Abraham and Hagar, the Egyptian maidservant of Sarah. According to Genesis 16, when Sarah realized that she could not conceive children, she gave her maidservant to Abraham so that she might conceive by proxy. When Hagar became pregnant, she began to despise her mistress, who then drove her out of her home. An angel of the Lord met Hagar and told her to return and submit to Sarah, saying that her descendants through Ishmael would be innumerable. God also assured Abraham that Ishmael would be the father of twelve rulers and ultimately of a great nation.

After Sarah bore a son, Isaac, by Abraham, she insisted that Ishmael and Hagar be expelled from their home. In the desert, the outcasts nearly died for lack of water, but God provided them with a well of water. Ishmael grew up to become an archer, and Hagar found a wife for him. He did indeed become the father of twelve sons.

Ishmael is important in Islam as the traditional ancestor of Muhammad and of the Arab peoples. Ishmael is also the name of the narrator in Herman Melville's *Moby Dick* (1851), which opens with the striking line, "Call me Ishmael."

IT

A neuter pronoun, "it" was originally spelled "hit." The masculine pronoun "he" and the neuter pronoun "hit" then had the same possessive form "his." In the sixteenth century a tendency arose to restrict "his" to males. "It" was used as a possessive, then "it's" began to be used, and finally "its" came into common use in the first half of the seventeenth century.

The Geneva Bible (1560), had "That which groweth of it owne accorde" in Leviticus 25:5, and "whiche opened to them by it owne accorde" in Acts 12:10. The KJV translators used "his owne accord" in Acts, but retained "it owne accord" in Leviticus 25:5.

This is, however, the only case in the KJV where "it" is used in the possessive case, and this was changed to "its" by later publishers. Except for this verse, the word "its" does not appear in the KJV. The translators used "his," "her," "of it," or "thereof" when they needed a neuter possessive. Examples are "the fruit tree yielding fruit after his kind" (Genesis 1:11–12), "the tree of life, which . . . yielded her fruit every month" (Revelation 22:2), "the sea ceased from her raging" (Jonah 1:15), "if the salt have lost his savour" (Matthew 5:13), "stamped the residue with the feet of it" (Daniel 7:7), "the fruit thereof" (Genesis 3:6), "the furrows thereof" (Psalm 65:10).

Longer passages that illustrate the expedients to which the translators resorted, because they did not use the new word "its," are Exodus 37:17–24 and Daniel 4:10–14. (See HIS)

J

JACOB'S LADDER

"Jacob's Ladder" is the name given to two things—a ladder used on a ship, and a plant. The former is made of rope or cable and has wooden or metal rungs. It is dropped over the side of the ship to allow people to ascend from or descend to small boats positioned alongside.

The plant known as Jacob's ladder (*Polemonium caeruleum*) has blue or white flowers and light green leaves which grow in a ladder-like arrangement.

The origin of the phrase "Jacob's ladder" is to be found in Genesis 28:12 (KJV): "And he [Jacob] dreamed, and behold a ladder set up on the earth, and the top of it reached to heaven: and behold the angels of God ascending and descending on it." All the contemporary versions except the NIV and the NLT have "ladder"; the NIV and NLT have "stairway."

JANGLING

This word is now used of noisy, quarrelsome, wrangling speech, but in the KJV it means "talk that is empty and useless." In 1 Timothy 1:6, Paul speaks of those who "have turned aside unto vain jangling" (KJV). The contemporary versions render "vain jangling" here as "empty talk" (CEV), "fruitless discussion" (NASB), and "meaningless talk" (NIV, NRSV). The same Greek word underlies the expression "vain talkers" (KJV) in Titus 1:10, where the NASB and RSV have "empty talkers."

It was in this now obsolete sense that King Henry VIII used "jangle" in his last appearance before Parliament, when he said that he was "very sorry to know and hear how irreverently that precious jewel, the Word of God, is disputed, rimed, sung, and jangled in every alehouse and tavern, contrary to the true meaning and doctrine of the same."

JEREMIAD; JEREMIAH

A "jeremiad" is a lengthy lamentation or complaint. The word comes via French with reference to the Old Testament books of the Lamentations (of Jeremiah) and the book of Jeremiah. The book of Jeremiah contains many prophecies of judgment, particularly against idolatry, immorality, and false prophets, and so Jeremiah is sometimes known as the "Prophet of Doom." Thus, the word "Jeremiah" has come to be used to refer to a pessimistic person who foresees a gloomy future or one who condemns the society he lives in.

JEROBOAM

A "jeroboam" (also known as a double magnum) is a very large wine bottle, holding the equivalent of four standard wine bottles, a standard bottle having a capacity of 0.7 liter or 0.75 liter. It seems that the name was first humorously given to such bottles in the nineteenth century, the allusion being to Jeroboam, the first king of the northern kingdom of Israel. The biblical text describes him as "a mighty man of valour" (1 Kings 11:28, KJV) and says that he "did sin, and . . . made Israel to sin" (1 Kings 14:16, KJV).

The bottle is without doubt "mighty" and the alcoholic drink contained in it could certainly cause sin. (See BALTHAZAR; METHUSELAH; NEBUCHADNEZZAR)

JEZEBEL

A "Jezebel" is a shameless, scheming, or immoral woman. The word comes from Jezebel, daughter of Ethbaal, king of Tyre and Sidon, who married Ahab, the king of Israel. Jezebel's notorious wickedness is described in 1 and 2 Kings. She worshiped the fertility god Baal and persuaded Ahab and his people to follow her idolatry. Under her orders, the Lord's prophets were killed, and were replaced by the prophets of Baal.

In answer to Elijah's prayer, the Lord defeated Baal at Mount Carmel. Jezebel then resolved to kill Elijah, who was forced to go into hiding. After the incident over Naboth's vineyard, Elijah predicted Jezebel's violent end, and some time later she

was thrown down from a high palace window.

The name is alluded to in literature, e.g., in Shakespeare's *Twelfth Night* (II, 5, 42), in Sir Andrew Aguecheek's reference to Malvolio, "Fie on him, Jezebel!"

JOB, PATIENCE OF

See PATIENCE OF JOB.

JOB'S COMFORTER

See COMFORTER, JOB'S.

JOINED TOGETHER, LET NO MAN PUT ASUNDER

When the Pharisees came to Jesus to test him on the matter of divorce, Jesus concluded, "Wherefore they [a husband and wife] are no more twain, but one flesh. What therefore God hath joined together, let not man put asunder" (Matthew 19:6). In the Prayer Book service, "The form of Solemnization of Matrimony," the rendering is "Those who God hath joined together let no man put asunder."

The contemporary versions translate the Scripture as: "Therefore what God [NASB, "What therefore God"] has joined together, let not man [NRSV, "let no one"] separate" (NASB, NIV, NKJV, NRSV); "And no one should separate a couple that God has joined together" (CEV); "God has joined the two together, so no one should separate them" (NCV); and "Let no one separate them, for God has joined them together" (NLT). The parallel, Mark 10:9, has the same texts.

JONAH

A "Jonah" is a person who is thought to bring bad luck. The expression derives from Jonah, the Hebrew prophet who was held responsible for the storm that struck the ship in which he was traveling (Jonah 1:4–7). Jonah had disobeyed God's command to go to Nineveh to denounce its people, had run away from the Lord, and had boarded the ship, which was bound for

Tarshish. When the sailors cast lots, "the lot fell upon Jonah" (Jonah 1:7, KJV). He acknowledged: "Pick me up and throw me into the sea; then the sea will quiet down for you; for I know it is because of me that this great storm has come upon you" (Jonah 1:12, NRSV).

The name is sometimes used allusively in literature, e.g., Kipling has *Captains Courageous* (1897), "A Jonah's anything that spoils the luck."

JORUM

A "jorum" is a large drinking bowl, named after Jorum, son of King Toi of Hamath. Joram brought to King David "vessels of silver, and vessels of gold, and vessels of brass" (2 Samuel 8:10, KJV) to congratulate him on his victory in battle over Hadadezer. The OED notes that the origin of jorum is uncertain, quoting the above reference, and adding, "it can scarcely be connected with WFlem. *djooren, djoorn,* half a pint."

JOT

"Jot" is what we do when we scribble down a brief note, and what we refer to when a matter is of very small significance ("I don't care a jot"). In the KJV, however, "jot" appears in Matthew 5:18 as translation of the Greek *iota,* where contemporary versions use "smallest letter" (NASB, NCV, NIV), "one letter" (NRSV), and "iota" (RSV). (The contemporary phrase "jot or tittle" derives from this verse.) In the CEV the verse reads: "Heaven and earth may disappear. But I promise you that not even a period or comma will ever disappear from the Law. Everything written in it must happen."

Tyndale translated the Greek *iota hen* in Matthew 5:18 as "one iott," and was followed by the other sixteenthth-century translators. In the 1611 KJV the word was spelled "iote," pronounced in one syllable, and this in time was changed to "jot." *Iota* is the smallest letter in the Greek alphabet;

and *yod,* the corresponding letter in Hebrew, is still smaller. In any case, whether Jesus referred to the Greek letter or to the Hebrew, "jot" means the smallest letter or least part of any writing, and so stands for the very least whit of anything.

Portia declares to Shylock, in Shakespeare's *Merchant of Venice* (IV, 1, 306): "This bond doth give thee here no jot of blood."

"Not an iota" is as clear an English idiom as "not a jot." Among OED's examples are a sentence from the correspondence of Edmund Burke, "Not an iota should be yielded of the principle of the bill" (1771), and a declaration by John Adams, "I would . . . demand, in a tone that could not be resisted, the punctual fulfilment of every iota of the treaty" (1786). (See TITTLE)

JUDAS

A "Judas" is a traitor, a person who betrays a friend. The word comes from the name of Jesus' betrayer, Judas Iscariot.

The name Judas occurs in a number of expressions that allude to betrayal or cunning. A "Judas kiss" is a pretense of affection that conceals treachery. A "Judas slit" is a peephole in a door through which guards can observe their prisoners. A "Judas tree" is an ornamental shrub or tree of the genus *Cercis,* with pinkish-purple flowers that bloom before the leaves appear. The genus is so called because it is traditionally thought that Judas hanged himself on such a tree.

JUDGE

As a verb, the word "judge" is used on one occasion in the KJV in the obsolete sense of "condemn" or "sentence to punishment." It is found in the nobleman's answer to his servant's excuse for having kept his pound hidden away in a napkin: "Out of thine own mouth will I judge thee, thou wicked servant" (Luke 19:22, KJV).

For the KJV "judge" the CEV, NCV, and

RSV use the verb "condemn"; the NASB, NIV, NKJV, and NRSV retain the KJV "judge." The RSV translates it, "I will condemn you out of your own mouth, you wicked servant!" The *Greek-English Lexicon of the New Testament*, edited by Arndt and Gingrich, states that the meaning is, "I will punish you on the basis of your own statement."

The KJV rendering of 2 Corinthians 5:14 is: "For the love of Christ constraineth us; because we thus judge, that if one died for all, then were all dead." "Judge" could be thought to be too weak a rendering of the Greek; of the contemporary versions for the KJV "we judge," the NIV, NRSV, and RSV have "we are convinced"; the CEV, "we are certain"; the NCV, "we know"; the NLT, "we believe"; and the NASB, "having concluded"; the NKJV retains the KJV rendering.

In James 4:12, the KJV omits the noun "judge" after "lawgiver," "There is one lawgiver, who is able to save and to destroy: who art thou that judgest another?" The NKJV also omits this (with the footnote: "NU-text adds *and Judge*"; the NASB, NCV, NIV have "Judge," the NRSV and RSV, "judge."

JUDGE NOT, THAT YE BE NOT JUDGED

The saying of Jesus, "judge not, that ye be not judged," comes in the Sermon on the Mount (Matthew 7:1, KJV). It is sometimes used by people to state that any kind of adverse or unfavorable opinions about others should not be expressed.

The contemporary versions render the saying as "Judge not, that you be not judged" (NKJV, RSV), "Do not judge, so that you may not be judged" (NRSV), "Do not judge so that you will not be judged" (NASB), "Do not judge, or you too will be judged" (NIV), "Don't judge other people, or you will be judged" (NCV), "Stop judging others, and you will not be judged" (NLT), and "Don't condemn others, and God won't condemn you" (CEV).

In his second inaugural address, Abraham Lincoln said that the two sides in the Civil War "read the same Bible, and pray to the same God . . . It may seem strange that any men should dare to ask a just God's assistance in wringing their bread from the sweat of other men's faces; but let us judge not, that we be not judged."

K

KEEP ONESELF UNSPOTTED FROM THE WORLD

To "keep oneself unspotted from the world" means to keep oneself pure from the corruptions of life in the world. The expression derives from James 1:27 (KJV): "Pure religion and undefiled before God and the Father is this, To visit the fatherless and widows in their affliction, and to keep himself unspotted from the world."

The contemporary versions render the KJV expression as "keep oneself unstained by the world" (NASB, NRSV, RSV), "keep oneself unspotted by the world" (NKJV), "keep oneself from being polluted by the world" (NIV), "not let this world make you evil" (NIV), "keeping yourself free from the world's evil influence" (NCV), and "refuse to let the world corrupt us" (NLT).

KERCHIEF

A kerchief is a cloth to cover the head. It is the word from which "neckerchief" and "handkerchief" have been derived. It appears only once in the KJV, in Ezekiel 13:17–23. This is an oracle of the Lord against women who pose as prophets, practicing magic and divination for their own profit. Verse 18a reads, "Woe to the women that sew pillows to all armholes, and make kerchiefs upon the head of every stature to hunt souls!" (KJV). The NRSV translates: "Woe to the women who sew bands on all wrists, and make veils for the heads of persons of every height, in the hunt for human lives!"

The "kerchiefs" were long veils thrown over the head and reaching down to the feet, covering the whole person, hence made in various sizes to fit "every height." Other contemporary versions render them as "scarves" (CEV), and "magic veils" (NLT); the NASB, NCV, NIV, NRSV, and NKJV have "veils."

Just what was the significance of the veils we do not know, or whether the veils were worn by the practitioner of divination or her clients. Probably they were worn by both. (See ARMHOLE; PILLOW)

KEYS OF THE KINGDOM

After Peter's confession at Caesarea Philippi of Jesus as the Christ, Jesus said to him, "And I say also unto thee, That thou art Peter, and upon this rock I will build my church; and the gates of hell shall not prevail against it. And I will give unto thee the keys of the kingdom of heaven; and whatsoever thou shalt bind on earth shall be bound in heaven: and whatsoever thou shalt loose on earth shall be loosed in heaven" (Matthew 16:18–19, KJV).

The KJV expression (v. 19) "I will give you the keys of the kingdom of heaven" [NLT, "the Kingdom of Heaven"] is retained by all the contemporary versions except the CEV which has "I will give you the keys to the kingdom of heaven."

The word "key" symbolizes the prominence given to Peter in the preaching of the gospel of Jesus Christ, i.e., the way into the kingdom of heaven.

In Milton's *Lycidas* (108–110), Peter is seen as a mourner:

"Last came, and last did go,
The Pilot of the Galilean lake,
Two massy Keyes he bore of metals
   twain,
(The Golden opes, the Iron shuts
   amain)."

See also Isaiah 22:22; Revelation 1:18; 3:7.

KICK AGAINST THE PRICKS

To "kick against the pricks" is, according to the OED, "to strike the foot against such sharp-pointed or piercing weapons" and figuratively, "to be recalcitrant to one's own hurt." The words come in the KJV in Acts 9:5 and 26:14, the words of Jesus to Saul on the Damascus road, "Saul, Saul, why persecutest thou me? it is hard for thee to kick against the pricks" (26:14).

In the contemporary versions the only translation that renders this expression in Acts 9:5 is the NKJV which has "It is hard for you to kick against the goads." This rendering is also adopted by the NASB, NIV, NKJV, and RSV at Acts 26:14. At that reference, the CEV has "It's foolish to fight against me!"; the NCV, "You are only hurting yourself by fighting me"; and the NLT, "It is hard for you to fight against my will."

The *NIV Study Bible* notes that "to kick against the goads" is "a Greek proverb for useless resistance—the ox succeeds only in hurting itself." As Jeffrey comments in *A Dictionary of Biblical Tradition in English Literature*, "The kicking against the goads or spurs is figurative for an unruly horse or beast of burden doomed to painfully unsuccessful rebellion."

At Numbers 33:55, KJV "pricks" are "barbs" (NIV, NRSV), "pointed sticks" (CEV), "sharp hooks" (NCV), "splinters" (NLT), and "irritants" (NKJV); the NASB and RSV retain the KJV "pricks."

KIDNEYS

The expression in Deuteronomy 32:14, "the fat of kidneys of wheat" (KJV) does not imply kidney-shaped grains of wheat. It refers to the kidney-fat, the best of the fat, "the best of the best," of the wheat. The Hebrews regarded the fat as the choicest and best part of the animal, not to be eaten but to be burned upon the altar as an offering by fire to the Lord. "The two kidneys, and the fat that is upon them, which is by the flanks" (Leviticus 3:15, KJV) are especially mentioned in the law of sacrifice recorded in Leviticus 3 and 7. Hence the best part of anything was called its "fat." "The fat of the land" which Joseph promised to his father and brothers meant the choicest products of the land (Genesis 45:18). (See FAT)

"All the best of the oil, and all the best of the wine, and of the wheat" (Numbers 18:12, KJV) and "the finest of the wheat" (Psalm 147:14, KJV, NASB, RSV) are phrases in which "best" and "finest" represent the Hebrew word for "fat." Contemporary versions render "the fat of kidneys of wheat" (Deuteronomy 32:14, KJV) as "the finest of the wheat" (NASB, RSV), "the best of the wheat" (NCV), and "the finest kernels of wheat" (NIV). (See REINS.)

KILL THE FATTED CALF

To "kill the fatted calf" is to give a lavish celebration in order to welcome someone, e.g., a returning member of one's family. The expression derives from Jesus' parable of the prodigal son, as the father prepares to welcome him home: "And bring hither the fatted calf, and kill it; and let us eat, and be merry: For this my son was dead, and is alive again; he was lost, and is found" (Luke 15:23–24, KJV).

The contemporary versions render the KJV expression "bring hither the fatted calf, and kill it" as: "bring the fattened [RSV, "fatted"] calf and kill it" (NASB, NIV, RSV), "bring the fatted calf here and kill it" (NKJV), "Get the fatted calf and kill it" (NRSV), "get the best calf and prepare it" (CEV), "get our fat calf and kill it" (NCV), and "kill the calf we have been fattening in the pen" (NLT).

Charles Lamb in his *Mackery End, in Hertfordshire* (1821) writes that he and his sister Bridget were given a generous welcome by their country cousins: "The fatted calf was made ready, or rather was already so, as if in anticipation of our coming."

KNOP

This is an archaic word for the bud of a flower or for an ornamental knob or boss. It is used in Exodus 25:31–36 and 37:17–22 (KJV) as part of the description of the "candlestick" or lampstand of pure gold which Bezalel made, under Moses' direction, for the tabernacle.

Contemporary versions render it as "bulb" (NASB), "bud" (NIV), "ornamental knob" or "knob" (NKJV), "calyx" (NRSV), and "capital" (RSV). It represents the Hebrew word *kaphtor*, which occurs also in Amos 9:1 and Zephaniah 2:14, where the KJV translates it as "lintel" with a marginal note, "or knops or chapiters." Other versions use "capitals" (Amos 9:1, NASB, NRSV, RSV; Zephaniah 2:14, NRSV, RSV), "top [NIV, "tops"] of the pillars" (Amos 9:1, NCV, NIV), "columns" (Amos 9:1, CEV; Zephaniah 2:14, NIV), and "doorposts" (Amos 9:1, NKJV).

These were most probably the rounded capitals of the pillars of the temple at Bethel, and of the columns in the ruins of Nineveh, and the rounded capitals in the framework of the golden lampstand and its branches.

In 1 Kings 6:18 and 7:24 the word "knops" (KJV) represents a quite different Hebrew word—*peqa'im*—which means "gourds." The reference is to the carved ornamentation of the cedar-lined walls of the house of the Lord, and similar ornamentation of the molten sea, which were cast together (1 Kings 7:24). This ornamentation may have been based upon the shape of the "wild gourds" mentioned in 2 Kings 4:39.

KNOW

The word "know" has as wide a range of meanings in Hebrew as in English, and its use in the KJV calls for little revision. The NKJV, NRSV, and RSV keep the word when it means to have sexual intercourse, for this idiom is natural not only to Hebrew but to many languages—Greek, Latin, French, German, for example. Passages are: Genesis 4:1, 17, 25; 19:8; 24:16; Numbers 31:17, 18, 35; Judges 11:39; 21:12; l Samuel 1:19; 1 Kings 1:4; Matthew 1:25. The word is also used in the sense of homosexual behavior (Genesis 19:5; Judges 19:22).

The contemporary translations generally render "know" in this sense as follows: "know" (NKJV, NRSV, RSV). "have relations with" (NASB), "have sexual relations with" (NCV), "lie with" (NIV) "have sex with" (CEV, NIV, NLT), "know intimately" (NASB, NKJV). In the account of the concubine at Gibeah (Judges 19:25), most of the contemporary translations render "knew" as "raped."

The Hebrew word for "know" may carry the connotation of "regard," "care for," "pay heed to," "approve." In Genesis 39:6–8, however, the statements concerning Potiphar are stated more clearly: "he knew not ought he had, save the bread which he did eat" (NKJV, "he did not know what he had"; NASB, NIV, "He did not concern himself"; NRSV and RSV, "he had no concern for anything").

A further example is Psalm 31:7: "Thou hast known my soul in adversities" (KJV) is rendered as "you [NASB, You] have seen my affliction" (NASB, NRSV), "you saw my afflic-tion" (NIV), "You saw all my suffering" (CEV), "You have considered my trouble" (NKJV).

KNOW NOT WHAT THEY DO

At his crucifixion Jesus said, "Father, forgive them; for they know not what they do" (Luke 23:24, KJV). This is one of Jesus' "seven words from the cross."

The contemporary versions render this: "Father, forgive them; [NIV. "forgive them,"] for they do not know what they are doing" (NASB, NRSV, RSV; the text is in double square brackets in the NRSV to show that "other ancient authorities lack [this] sentence"), "Father, forgive them, for they do not know what they do" (NKJV), "Father, forgive these people! They don't know what they're do-ing" (CEV), "Father, forgive these people, be-cause they don't know what they are doing" (NLT), and "Father, forgive them, because they don't know what they are doing" (NCV).

Shakespeare used the phrase in *King Henry VI, Part II* (IV, 4, 37), when the king hears of Jack Cade's rebellion: "O graceless men! they know not what they do."

KNOW THEM BY THEIR FRUITS

See FRUITS, KNOW THEM BY THEIR.

L

LABORER IS WORTHY OF HIS HIRE

The expression "the laborer is worthy of his hire" means that a person who works has the right to due payment for his or her work. The origin of the expression is in the instructions to the seventy (or seventy-two) disciples in Luke 10:7 (KJV), "And in the same house remain, eating and drinking such things as they give: for the labourer is wor-thy of his hire. Go not from house to house." The principle that Jesus declares here has its roots in the Old Testament: Deu-teronomy 25:4, quoted in 1 Corinthians 9:9–10 and 1 Timothy 5:18.

The contemporary versions render the KJV expression "the labourer is worthy of his hire" as: "the laborer is worthy of his wages" (NASB, NKJV), "the laborer deserves his wages" (RSV), "the laborer deserves to be paid" (NRSV), "the worker deserves his wages" (NIV), "a worker should be given his pay" (NCV), "workers are worth what they earn" (CEV), and "those who work deserve their pay" (NLT).

LADE

Except with reference to the lading of a ship, current English uses the verb "load" rather than "lade." But it retains the pas-sive participle "laden" as well as "loaded" or "loaden." In both respects it is following Shakespearean usage.

Contemporary versions use "loaded" (e.g., 1 Samuel 16:20, CEV, NASB, NCV, NIV, NKJV, NLT, NRSV), "laden" (e.g., Isaiah 1:4, NKJV, NRSV, RSV), and "weighed down" (Isaiah 1:4, NASB). "Laded" appears in the KJV rendering of Nehemiah 4:17: "They which builded on the wall, and they that bare burdens, with those that laded, every one with one of his hands wrought in the work, and with the other hand held a weapon" The NKJV translates as "Those who built on the wall, and those who carried burdens, loaded themselves so that with one hand they worked at construction, and with the other held a weapon."

Matthew 11:28, "all ye that labour and are heavy laden" (KJV), is now rendered "all of you who are tired and have heavy loads" (NCV), "all you who are weary and burdened" (NIV), and "all you that are weary and are carrying heavy burdens" (NRSV).

In Psalm 68:19, the KJV reads, "Blessed be the Lord, who daily loadeth us with benefits." The verb here means "to carry a load," rather than "to load." Contemporary versions have "who daily bears our burden" [NIV, "burdens"] (NASB, NIV), "who helps us every day" (NCV), and "who daily bears us up" (NRSV, RSV).

Habakkuk 2:6 reads in the KJV: "Shall not all these take up a parable against him, and a taunting proverb against him, and say, Woe to him that increaseth that which is not his! how long? and to him that ladeth himself with thick clay!"

The clause "ladeth himself with thick clay" is translated as "makes himself rich with loans" by the NASB, and as "loads himself with pledges" by the RSV. The whole verse reads in the NRSV: "Shall not everyone taunt such people and, with mocking riddles, say about them, 'Alas for you who heap up what is not your own!' How long will you load yourselves with goods taken in pledge?"

LAMB TO THE SLAUGHTER

The expression "like a lamb to the slaughter" means "quietly" and "without complaining." It is often used to refer to someone who is unwittingly about to go into a dangerous or difficult situation or to be the innocent and helpless victim of punishment. Sometimes the word "lamb" is replaced by "sheep."

The origin of the expression is Isaiah 53:7, describing the sacrifice of the suffering servant: "He was oppressed, and he was afflicted, yet he opened not his mouth: he is brought as a lamb to the slaughter, and as a sheep before her shearers is dumb, so he openeth not his mouth" (KJV).

The contemporary versions render the expression in Isaiah 53:7 as "like a lamb that is led to [NRSV, RSV, "to the"] slaughter" (NASB, NRSV, RSV), "he was led as [NIV, "led like"] a lamb to the slaughter" (NIV, NKJV, NLT), "He was like a lamb being led to be killed" (NCV), and "He was silent like a lamb being led to the butcher" (CEV).

In Acts 8:32 (KJV), "He was led as a sheep to the slaughter; and like a lamb dumb before his shearer, so opened he not his mouth," this prophecy is applied to Jesus Christ.

LANCET

The word "lancet" refers today to a small surgical instrument used for letting blood, opening abscesses, and so on. It has had this meaning since the fifteenth century, but may also, at one time, have referred to a small lance. If so, the meaning has long been obsolete. The KJV uses the word only once, in 1 Kings 18:28.

Coverdale's description of the behavior of the prophets of Baal at Mount Carmel includes: "And they hopped about the altar, as their use was to do . . . And they cried aloud, and provoked themselves with knives and botkins (as their manner was) till the blood flowed" (1 Kings 18:26–28). Subsequent sixteenth-century versions used "leapt" and "cut themselves," and instead of "bot-kins" had "lancers," with various forms of spelling. The KJV, as published in 1611, used "lancers" here, which was changed to "lancets" in 1762.

The Hebrew word here is *romah,* which means "a spear" or "lance." The KJV translates this word twelve times as "spear" and once as "javelin." It was the weapon with which Phinehas transfixed the bodies of the shameless man of Israel and his Midianite lover (Numbers 25:6–9). Its plural is the word used for the spears with which Nehemiah armed his men as they built the wall of Jerusalem (Nehemiah 4:13, 16, 21).

Contemporary versions render the "knives and lancets" (KJV) in 1 Kings 18:28 as "swords and knives" (CEV), "swords and lances" (NASB, NRSV, RSV), "swords and spears" (NCV, NIV), "knives and swords" (NLT).

LAND FLOWING WITH MILK AND HONEY

The expression "a land flowing with milk and honey" is used to refer to a place or state that promises to provide plentiful resources, great happiness and security, and abundant fulfillment of one's hopes. The expression occurs six times in the KJV: Exodus 3:8, 17; 13:5; 33:3; Jeremiah 11:5; 32:22.

Exodus 3:8 reads in the KJV: "And I am come down to deliver them out of the hand of the Egyptians, and to bring them up out of that land unto a good land and a large, unto a land flowing with milk and honey; unto the place of the Canaanites, and the Hittites, and the Amorites, and the Perizzites, and the Hivites, and the Jebusites."

All the contemporary versions except the CEV and the NCV retain the KJV expression "a land flowing with milk and honey"; the NCV has "a fertile land" and the CEV, "land, rich with milk and honey."

These renderings are followed at all the other instances, except the CEV at Jeremiah 11:5, which reads, "this wonderful land." The phrase "a land flowing with milk and

honey" has a similar meaning to the expression "the promised land," originally the land of Canaan promised by God to the Israelites. (See PROMISED LAND)

The phrase is found in literature, e.g., in Tennyson's *The Lover's Tale* in which the lovers look on the mountain view:

"A land of promise, land of memory,
A land of promise flowing with milk
And honey, of delicious memories"

and Byron's *Don Juan* (13.797–803) describing a great banquet:

"all human history attests
That happiness for man—the hungry
   sinner!—
Since Eve ate apples, much depends
   on dinner.

Witness the lands which 'flowed with
   milk and honey,'
Held out to the hungry Israelites:
To this we have added since the love
   of money,
The only sort of pleasure which
   requites."

LAND OF GIANTS

The expression "land of giants," sometimes used figuratively to refer to areas of great opportunity that contain apparently formidable difficulties, alludes to two references: Genesis 6:4 (KJV), "There were giants in the earth in those days; and also after that, when the sons of God came in unto the daughters of men, and they bare children to them, the same became mighty men which were of old, men of renown" and, in the report of those sent to explore the land of Canaan, Numbers 13:33 (KJV), "And there we saw the giants, the sons of Anak, which come of the giants: and we were in our own sight as grasshoppers, and so we were in their sight."

At both these verses, most of the contemporary versions render the KJV "giants" as "Nephilim" (CEV, NASB, NCV, NIV, NRSV, RSV); the NKJV and NLT retain the KJV "giants."

The Nephilim were traditionally regarded as giants, but were probably a group of people famed for their strength. They were also one of the pre-Israelite groups in Canaan who inspired fear in the Israelite spies.

LAND OF NOD

To be in "the land of Nod" (or "nod") is to be asleep. The phrase derives from Genesis 4:16, which refers to the region to which Cain was banished after he had killed Abel: "And Cain went out from the presence of the LORD, and dwelt in the land of Nod, on the east of Eden" (KJV). All the contemporary versions except the CEV have "the land of Nod." The Hebrew name means "wandering"; this is reflected in the CEV translation "the Land of Wandering." The expression "the land of Nod," suggesting the nodding of a drowsy head, is probably a pun.

LAND OF THE LIVING

To be "in the land of the living" is a Hebrew idiom used in poetry. It refers to all those who are alive, and is roughly equivalent to those who live on the earth. The expression occurs fifteen times in the KJV, e.g., Isaiah 53:8, "He was taken from prison and from judgment: and who shall declare his generation? for he was cut off out of the land of the living: for the transgression of my people was he stricken."

The NASB, NIV, NKJV, NRSV, and RSV retain the KJV expression; the CEV renders it "His life was taken away"; and the NCV, "He was put to death." Other renderings include: Job 28:13, "in the land of the living" (KJV); "among the living" (NLT); and "among those who are alive" (CEV); Psalm 142:5, "Thou art my refuge and my portion in the land of the living" (KJV); "You are my protection. You are all I want in this life" (NCV); and "You are my place of refuge. You are all I really want in life" (NLT).

LAODICEAN

The term "Laodicean" is used to describe someone who is lukewarm and indifferent, especially in religious or political matters. The origin of this term is the criticism expressed by Jesus toward the church at Laodicea (Revelation 3:14–22). The believers there were "lukewarm, and neither cold nor hot" (Revelation 3:16, KJV, with all the contemporary versions retaining these words): they showed a tepid, half-hearted commitment.

The first citation in the OED in this sense is dated 1633: "Worse . . . is profane New-tralitie, or Laodicean coldnesse."

LARGE

In the KJV we read that the chief priests "gave large money unto the soldiers" (Matthew 28:12) to get them to spread a false report concerning the resurrection of Jesus. The adjective "large" is used here in the obsolete sense of "ample" or "liberal." The word "largess" is still used for a liberal gift.

Contemporary versions render the Greek test as "a lot of money" (CEV), "a large amount of money" (NCV), and "a large sum of money" (NIV, NKJV, NRSV). The RSV has simply "a sum of money."

LASCIVIOUSNESS

In modern usage, this word means "an inclination to lust," "wantonness," or "lewdness." It is used six times by the KJV as translation for the Greek word *aselgeia* (Mark 7:22; 2 Corinthians 12:21; Galatians 5:19; Ephesians 4:19; 1 Peter 4:3; Jude 4), which it elsewhere translates as "wantonness" (Romans 13:13; 2 Peter 2:18), "pernicious ways" (2 Peter 2:2), and as the adjective "filthy" in the expression "filthy conversation" (2 Peter 2:7).

In all these cases the NRSV uses "licentiousness" or "licentious," as connoting a broad range of unbridled passions, including greed, drunkenness, and debauchery as well as sexual lust. The Greek word, however, also has a note of insolent pride. Those who "have abandoned themselves to *aselgeia*" are "greedy to practice every kind of impurity," (Ephesians 4:19, NRSV), and are proud of their emancipation from the restraints of personal conscience or public opinion. They have lost all sense of shame.

Other contemporary versions render the word with terms such as "indecency" (e.g., Mark 7:22, CEV), "sensuality" (2 Corinthians 12:21, NASB), "lewdness" (Mark 7:22, NIV, NKJV), "debauchery" (Galatians 5:19, NIV), "eagerness for lustful pleasure" (Mark 7:22, NLT), and "a license for immorality" (Jude 4, NIV).

LATCHET

This is an old word for "a shoelace," a thong used to fasten a shoe or sandal. In Genesis 14:23 Abraham tells the king of Sodom, "I will not take from a thread even to a shoelatchet, and . . . I will not take any thing that is thine" (KJV); the NASB reads, "I will not take a thread or a sandal thong or anything that is yours." Isaiah 5:27 describes the disciplined army that is coming to punish Israel: "None shall be weary nor stumble among them . . . neither shall the girdle of their loins be loosed, nor the latchet of their shoes be broken" (KJV).

The KJV rendering of John the Baptist's declaration reads in the KJV, "There cometh one mightier than I after me, the latchet of whose shoes I am not worthy to stoop down and unloose" Mark 1:7; Luke 3:16; John 1:27). Contemporary versions use "sandal thong" (NRSV, RSV, "sandal-thong") and "sandle strap."

LAW OF THE MEDES AND PERSIANS

The expression "the law of the Medes and Persians" refers to an unchangeable law that must be strictly followed. The expression comes from Daniel 6:8 (KJV): "Now, O king, establish the decree, and sign the writing, that it be not changed, according

to the law of the Medes and Persians, which altereth not."

The Medes were inhabitants of Media, northeast Mesopotamia, between the Black Sea and the Caspian Sea. In 550 B.C. the Persian King Cyrus the Great defeated his overlord and father-in-law Astyages to gain control of the Median Empire. Many Medes were then granted high positions in the Persian court and the Medes' customs and laws were amalgamated with those of the Persians—hence the expression "the law of the Medes and Persians." See also Daniel 6:25 and Esther 1:19.

The phrase "the law of the Medes and Persians" is retained by all the contemporary versions, except the NIV, NRSV, and RSV; the NIV has "laws of the Medes and Persians"; and the NRSV and RSV, "law of the Medes and the Persians."

LAW UNTO THEMSELVES

To be "a law unto oneself" refers to someone who does what he or she wants, acting in a headstrong manner, and setting his or her own guidelines about what is right and wrong, without considering the usual rules or conventions of society or the advice of others.

The expression derives from Romans 2:14 (KJV): "For when the Gentiles, which have not the law, do by nature the things contained in the law, these, having not the law, are a law unto themselves," but the contemporary application of this expression has developed from the meaning of the biblical text. Romans 2:14 shows that the moral nature of Gentiles served in place of the Law of Moses to show God's demands. In this sense, the Gentiles were "a law unto themselves."

The KJV phrase "law unto themselves" is rendered as follows by the contemporary versions: "a law to themselves" by the NASB, NKJV, NRSV, and RSV, and "a law for themselves" by the NCV and NIV. The KJV phrasing relating to the Gentiles doing "by nature" what the law requires is retained by the NIV,

NKJV, and RSV; the NASB, NLT, and NRSV have "instinctively," e.g., "Even when Gentiles, who do not have God's written law, instinctively follow what the law says, they show that in their hearts they know right from wrong" (NLT).

LAY

The word "lay" is part of many idioms, most of which are generally understood, but there are a few whose meanings in the KJV may not be clear. In modern usage, "lay at" means to "strike at," "attack," "assail." In the KJV, however, we find it used as translation for the Hebrew verb which means "reach" (Job 41:26) "The sword of him that layeth at him cannot hold" is now rendered in the NASB as "The sword that reaches him cannot avail."

"Lay away" (or "by" or "from"). "Lay away their robes" (Ezekiel 26:16, KJV) is now rendered as "remove their robes" (NASB, NRSV, RSV) and "lay aside their robes" (NIV, NKJV). So also "laid his robe from him" (Jonah 3:6, KJV) now reads "removed his robe" (NRSV, RSV), and "laid by her vail from her" (Genesis 38:19, KJV) is rendered "took off her veil" (NIV, NLT).

"Lay out" in the sense of "expend money" is still a current English idiom. But "they laid it out to the carpenters and builders" (2 Kings 12:11) is now expressed by "they paid it out to the carpenters and [NRSV, RSV, "and the"] builders" (NKJV, NRSV, RSV).

LAY NOT UP TREASURES UPON EARTH

See TREASURES UPON EARTH.

LEASING

The word "leasing" is likely to make us think of billboards advertising apartments or office space. In fact, "leasing" is an old English word for "lying" or "falsehood." Wycliffe's translation had "lesyngmongers" in 1 Timothy 1:10, but Tyndale and subsequent versions used "liars." Coverdale's version of 2 Esdras 14:18 reads, "The truth

is fled far away, and leasing is hard at hand," which was retained by the KJV. The RSV and NRSV have "falsehood." "Seek after leasing" appears in the KJV rendering of Psalm 4:2, and "them that speak leasing" in Psalm 5:6.

Contemporary versions use "deception" (NASB), "lies" (NCV, NLT, NRSV, RSV), "falsehood" (NKJV), and "false gods" (NIV) in Psalm 4:2, and "falsehood" (NASB, NKJV) and "lies" (NIV, NLT, NRSV, RSV; CEV, "liar")) in Psalm 5:6.

LEAVEN THE WHOLE LUMP

To "leaven the whole lump" refers to the baking of bread. Only a small quantity of leaven (yeast) is needed to leaven a large batch of dough—so the phrase has come to refer to something that is only a small element which has a transforming effect on a whole. The expression comes from 1 Corinthians 5:6: "Your glorying is not good. Know ye not that a little leaven leaveneth the whole lump?" (KJV).

Of the contemporary versions, the CEV, NCV, NIV and NRSV use the word "yeast"; with the NASB, NKJV, and RSV retaining the KJV "leaven." In Scripture, leaven (or yeast) usually represents evil or sin: in the NLT, the meaning is rendered as "Don't you realize that if even one person is allowed to go on sinning, soon all will be affected?", with the reference to leaven and dough in a footnote.

LEFT HAND DOES NOT KNOW WHAT ONE'S RIGHT HAND IS DOING

See HAND, LEFT.

LEOPARD CANNOT CHANGE ITS SPOTS

The saying "the leopard cannot change his spots" means that "the basic character or nature of a person cannot be changed." The expression derives from one of Jeremiah's warnings of judgment against Judah: "Can the Ethiopian change his skin, or the leopard his spots? then may ye also

do good, that are accustomed to do evil"
(Jeremiah 13:23, KJV).

The contemporary versions generally retain the verb "change" with the leopard's spots; for the whole verse the NLT has: "Can an Ethiopian change the color of his skin? Can a leopard take away its spots? Neither can you start doing good, for you always do evil," and the CEV: "Can you ever change and do what's right? Can people change the color of their skin, or can a leopard remove its spots? If so, then maybe you can change and learn to do right."

Shakespeare alludes to this phrase in *King Richard II* (I, 1, 175). When King Richard hears Bolingbroke accuse Thomas Mowbray, Duke of Norfolk, of treachery and murder, he tries to calm them by saying:

> "Rage must be withstood:—
> Give me his gage:—lions make
>   leopards tame."

The Duke of Norfolk replies:

> "Yea, but not change his spots: take
>   but my shame,
> And I resign my gage. My dear dear
>   lord,
> The purest treasure mortal times
>   afford
> Is spotless reputation."

LET

"Let" and "let" are two English verbs which are spelled and pronounced exactly alike, but which come from two distinct Old English roots. One verb means to "hinder," "impede," or "prevent"; the other means just the opposite, to "permit" or "allow." Both were in current use in 1611; both are used in the KJV and in Shakespeare. But only the second remains a part of living English today; the first survives only as a noun in the legal phrase "without let or hindrance" and in the game of tennis, where anything that interrupts or hinders the game and requires a point to be played again is called a "let."

In Shakespeare's *King Henry V* (V, 2, 64–67), the Duke of Burgundy, suing for peace with England, and speaking of the ruin that continued war entails, says:

> "my speech entreats
> That I may know the let, why gentle
>   Peace
> Should not expel these
>   inconveniences
> And bless us with her former
>   qualities."

In *Hamlet* (I, 4, 85), when friends seek to restrain Hamlet from following the beckoning ghost of his father, he cries:

> "Unhand me, gentlemen;
> By heaven, I'll make a ghost of him
>   that lets me."

This obsolete use of the verb "let" appears three times in the KJV. In Isaiah 43:13 God speaks through the prophet, "There is none that can deliver out of my hand: I will work, and who shall let it?" The contemporary versions have "who can [NKJV, "who will"] reverse it?" (NASB, NIV, NKJV) and "who can hinder it?" (NRSV, RSV). Paul, writing to the Romans, tells that he had "oftentimes purposed" to come to them, but that he "was let hitherto" (1:13, KJV); The CEV renders this, "I have often planned to come for a visit. But something has always kept me from doing it."

The other occurrence is in 2 Thessalonians 2:6–7, where the KJV reads: "And now ye know what withholdeth that he might be revealed in his time. For the mystery of iniquity doth already work: only he who now letteth will let, until he be taken out of the way." The KJV here uses the word "letteth" for the Greek word which it translates as "withholdeth" in verse 6. The NRSV reads: "And you know what is now restraining him, so that he may be revealed when his time comes. For the mystery of lawlessness is already at work, but only until the one who now restrains it is removed."

The proclamation of liberty, "Let my

people go," derives from the words of Moses and Aaron: "And afterward Moses and Aaron went in, and told Pharaoh, Thus saith the LORD God of Israel, Let my people go, that they may hold a feast unto me in the wilderness" (KJV). All the contemporary versions retain this expression (with the NASB and NKJV capitalizing "My").

LET THE DEAD BURY THEIR DEAD
See DEAD.

LETTER KILLETH; LETTER OF THE LAW

The two expressions "the letter killeth" and "the letter of the law" have their origins in 2 Corinthians 3:5–6 (KJV): "Not that we are sufficient of ourselves to think any thing as of ourselves; but our sufficiency is of God; Who also hath made us able ministers of the new testament; not of the letter, but of the spirit: for the letter killeth, but the spirit giveth life."

In contemporary English, the "letter of the law" is a literal, strict understanding of the law as it is expressed. This is often contrasted with "the spirit of the law," its general purpose, intent, or effect.

In the KJV, "the letter killeth" refers to the external standard of the law (originally written on tablets of stone) and the universal condemnation of death that it brings. In contrast, "the spirit giveth life" refers to the work of the Holy Spirit, who writes that law internally on the human heart and enables and invigorates believers to follow the law.

The contemporary versions render the KJV "the letter" as "written law" (NCV); "written Law . . . Law" (CEV); "written code" (RSV); with the other contemporary translations retaining the KJV wording. In the final clause "the spirit" (KJV) is "the Spirit" in all the contemporary versions. The NLT renders the whole verse as "He is the one who has enabled us to represent his new covenant. This is a covenant, not of written laws, but of the Spirit. The old way ends in

death; in the new way, the Holy Spirit gives life."

LEWD, LEWDNESS

These words are used in the KJV Old Testament with the reference to "lascivious behavior" that remains their modern meaning. But the word appears twice in the KJV New Testament with the obsolete sense of "base" or "vile." In Acts 17:5 "certain lewd fellows of the baser sort" (KJV) represents Greek which is now rendered as "some wicked men from the market place" (NASB), "some worthless fellows from the streets" (NLT), and "some ruffians in the marketplaces" (NRSV).

In Acts 18:14 "a matter of wrong or wicked lewdness" (KJV) is now translated as "a matter of wrong or of vicious crime" (NASB), and "a matter of crime or serious villainy" (NRSV).

LIBERTINES

This word is likely to remind us of people free from any kind of moral restraint. This is not the word's meaning, however, in Acts 6:9—its one occurrence in the KJV. Here we read that, in response to the "great wonders and miracles" (v. 8, KJV) which accompanied Stephen's ministry "there arose certain of the synagogue, which is called *the synagogue* of the Libertines . . . disputing with Stephen" (v. 9, KJV). These were not men of dissolute, licentious lives, but respectable freedmen. They were probably descendants of the Jews who had been taken as prisoners to Rome by Pompey in 63 B.C., and there sold as slaves.

Contemporary versions describe them as of the "Synagogue of the Freedmen" (NASB, NIV, NKJV; NRSV, RSV have lowercase "s"), of the "Synagogue of Freed Slaves" (NLT), and of the "synagogue of Free Men" (NCV). The CEV reads, "But some men from Cyrene and Alexandria were members of a group who called themselves 'Free Men.' They started arguing with Stephen."

LIEUTENANT

Today, a lieutenant is a person who is a junior officer in one of the armed forces, an officer below the rank of captain in the fire or police department, or the second-in-command in an organization. In the KJV, "lieutenant" stands for "a provincial ruler." The word occurs four times in the KJV, once in Ezra (8:36) and three times in Esther (3:12; 8:9; and 9:3).

Of the contemporary versions, the NASB, NIV, NKJV, NRSV, and RSV translate the KJV "lieutenants" as "satraps" in all these instances. Other translations adopted by the CEV, NCV, and NLT include "rulers," "governors," and "princes"; the NLT at Ezra 8:36 retains the KJV "lieutenants."

The Hebrew word actually comes from a Persian word meaning "satrap," that is, a governor of a province of the Persian Empire. In Daniel, the KJV translates the equivalent Aramaic term as "princes" (Daniel 3:2ff.; 6:1ff.).

LIGHT

Whether as noun, adjective, or verb, the word "light" is easily understood in the KJV. The adjective "light," however, is twice applied by the KJV to persons, in the obsolete sense which the OED defines as "not commanding respect by position or character; of small account." Abimelech is said to have "hired vain and light persons, which followed him" (Judges 9:4). The prophets of Jerusalem are condemned as "light and treacherous persons" (Zephaniah 3:4). In both cases the participle of the verb *pahaz*, which means to be "wanton" or "reckless," is used in the Hebrew.

The majority of contemporary versions render "light" (KJV) in Judges 9:4 as "reckless"; the NASB, NRSV, and RSV translate as "Abimelech hired worthless and reckless fellows." The prophets of Jerusalem are referred to as "reckless" (NASB, NRSV), "proud" (CEV, NCV), "arrogant" (NIV, NLT), "insolent" (NKJV), and "wanton" (RSV) by contemporary versions.

The Hebrew noun *pahaz*, which means "wantonness, recklessness, unbridled license" (BDB), appears in an adjectival phrase concerning Reuben, which the KJV translates "Unstable as water" (Genesis 49:4). This rendering is retained by the NRSV; the NIV has "Turbulent as the waters," and the NASB, "Uncontrolled as water."

In Numbers 21:5, "the people spake against God, and against Moses, Wherefore have ye brought us up out of Egypt to die in the wilderness? for there is no bread, neither is there any water; and our soul loatheth this light bread" (KJV). The "light bread" was the manna which the Lord rained from heaven (Exodus 16); in this context "light" means "contemptible" or "worthless." The NKJV translates the latter half of the verse, "For there is no food and no water, and our soul loathes this worthless bread." Other versions render "light" (KJV) here as "miserable" (NASB, NIV, NRSV), "awful" (CEV), and "wretched" (NLT).

LIGHTLY

"Lightly" is how we walk when our children have just been put to bed. We also use the word to mean "easily" ("lightly come, lightly go"), "cheerfully" ("he took the bad news lightly"), and "slightingly" ("she thinks lightly of herself, in spite of her skills"). When we meet the word in the KJV, however, the meaning is not always easy to gauge. It comes nearest to our modern meaning in Genesis 26:10, where the NASB, NRSV, and RSV use the word "easily."

In Mark 9:39 the Greek means "quickly" or "soon"; the NKJV has "soon afterward," as do the NASB and NRSV. In Jeremiah 4:24 we read in the KJV that "all the hills moved lightly" before the Lord's fierce anger. The NASB, NKJV, NRSV, and RSV say that "all the hills moved to and fro" [NKJV, "back and forth"]; the NCV, "all the hills were trembling."

"Lightly esteemed" (KJV) in Deuteronomy

32:15 is now rendered "scorned" (NASB), "rejected" (CEV, NCV, NIV), "made light of" (NLT), and "scornfully esteemed" (NKJV). The NRSV reads, "he abandoned God who made him, and scoffed at the Rock of his salvation."

Isaiah 9:1–7 contains a great messianic prophecy, referred to by both Matthew and Luke in their respective Gospels (Matthew 4:13–16; Luke 1:79). Verse 1 reads in the KJV: "Nevertheless the dimness shall not be such as was in her vexation, when at the first he lightly afflicted the land of Zebulun and the land of Naphtali, and afterward did more grievously afflict her by the way of the sea, beyond Jordan, in Galilee of the nations."

Contemporary translations of the Hebrew bring out a contrast between the contempt suffered in former times, and the glory to be revealed later; e.g., the NRSV reads: "But there will be no gloom for those who were in anguish. In the former time he brought into contempt the land of Zebulun and the land of Naphtali, but in the latter time he will make glorious the way of the sea, the land beyond the Jordan, Galilee of the nations."

This contrast was lost in the KJV by rendering the verbs "lightly afflict" and "grievously afflict" and regarding these as successive stages of "her vexation." Other contemporary versions render the change in the lands' fortunes with translations such as "once hated" and "greatly respected" (CEV), "treated with contempt" and "make it glorious" (NASB); "he humbled" and "he will honor" (NIV); and "humbled" and "filled with glory" (NLT).

LIGHTNESS

While the word "lightness" might remind us today of grandma's delicious cakes or the presence of light, in the KJV the word implies neither levity nor illumination. In Jeremiah 23:32 it is used as translation for the Hebrew word *pahazuth,* an abstract noun derived from the verb *pahaz.* The

Lord condemns the false prophets who "cause my people to err by their lies, and by their lightness" (KJV).

The NASB translates it as "led My people astray by their falsehoods and their reckless boasting." Other contemporary versions render "lightness" here as "reckless lies" (NIV) and "recklessness" (NKJV, NRSV, RSV). (See LIGHT)

Paul's question, "When I therefore was thus minded, did I use lightness?" (2 Corinthians 1:17, KJV) is now rendered as "When I planned this, did I do it lightly?" (NIV) and "Was I vacillating when I wanted to do this?" (NRSV, RSV).

LIKE

As a verb, "like" is used today to mean "to take pleasure in" or "to have a friendly feeling for someone." In the KJV, however, the word is used three times in the obsolete sense of "be pleasing to," "suit the tastes or wishes of someone." For "where it liketh him best" (Deuteronomy 23:16, KJV), the NKJV has "where it seems best to him" and the RSV has "where it pleases him best."

In Esther 8:8, "as it liketh you" (KJV) is now rendered "as you see fit" (NASB), and "as you please" (NKJV, NRSV, RSV). In Amos 4:5, "for this liketh you" (KJV), the Hebrew has the verb for "love"; the NCV translates as "because this is what you love to do." In *Two Gentlemen of Verona* (IV, 2, 56), Shakespeare wrote "the music likes you not."

The adjective "like" is twice used in the KJV in the archaic or colloquial sense of "likely." The first occurrence is in Ebedmelech's report to the king after Jeremiah has been cast into the dungeon, "he is like to die for hunger in the place where he is" (Jeremiah 38:9, KJV). The RSV translates it as "he will die there of hunger."

The second occurrence is in Jonah 1:4, "there was a mighty tempest in the sea, so that the ship was like to be broken." The NIV, NRSV, and RSV translate it as "the ship threatened to break up." In Shakespeare's *Romeo and Juliet* (I, 5, 137), when Juliet directs her nurse to ask the name of Romeo, she says,

"If he be married,
My grave is like to be my wedding bed."

LIKE UNTO

This phrase is an archaic equivalent of "like." The KJV renders Exodus 15:11 as "Who is like unto thee, O LORD, among the gods? who is like thee?" when, in fact, the Hebrew wording of the initial clauses of the two questions is the same.

"Like unto" occurs most frequently in the KJV in Matthew (6:8; 11:16; 13:33, 44–45, 47, 52; 20:1; 22:2, 39; 23:27) and in Revelation (1:13, 15; 2:18; 4:3, 6; 9:7, 10, 19; 11:1; 13:2, 4; 14:14; 18:18; 21:11, 18). Contemporary versions omit the "unto." (See UNTO)

"Like to" is another archaic expression which occurs less often. "Like to a bear" (Daniel 7:5, KJV) means "like a bear." Contemporary versions similarly omit the "to" in Song of Solomon 7:7 and 8:14. The KJV rendering of Psalm 144:4 is "Man is like to vanity: his days are as a shadow that passeth away." The NASB translates as "Man is like a mere breath, His days are like a passing shadow."

"Like as" is a redundant expression from which either "like" or "as" is omitted in the contemporary versions. (See AS, where examples are given.)

LIKING

Today "liking" refers to preference, inclination, or favor ("he's developed a liking for chocolate-coated coffee beans"). But the word was formerly used both as a noun and as an adjective to denote bodily condition. The chief of the eunuchs feared that, if he granted the request of Daniel and his friends, the king would "see your faces worse liking than the children which are of your sort" (Daniel 1:10, KJV).

The NKJV translates his reply: "I fear my lord the king, who has appointed your food and drink. For why should he see your faces looking worse than the young men who are your age?" Other contemporary versions render "worse liking" (KJV) here as "looking worse" (CEV, NIV), "looking more haggard" (NASB), and "in poorer condition" (NRSV, RSV).

Concerning the mountain goats and the hinds, the KJV reads in Job 39:4, "Their young ones are in good liking, they grow up with corn." Here there has been some confusion between the Hebrew words for "corn" and "open country," and the KJV uses "are in good liking" for the verb which means "be healthy and strong." The NASB reads, "Their offspring become strong, they grow up in the open field."

LIMIT

"They . . . limited the Holy One of Israel" (Psalm 78:41, KJV) is a rendering taken from the Geneva Bible, which adds the marginal note, "As thei all do that measure the power of God by their capacitie." The first edition of the Bishops' Bible had "prescribed boundes to," but the second edition returned to "moved," which was the translation of Coverdale and the Great Bible.

The contemporary versions have "provoked" (NRSV, RSV) or "pained" (NASB). This was the sense of the ancient Greek, Syriac, and Latin translations. The NIV has "vexed," and the NLT, "frustrated."

"He limiteth a certain day" (Hebrews 4:7) is a rendering which the KJV translators took from the Rheims New Testament. "Appointeth" or "appointed" had appeared in all translations from Tyndale to the Bishops' Bible. While the Greek verb may mean "limit" or "bound," it also means "determine," "define," "appoint," or "set," and the latter would appear to be the sense here.

Contemporary versions use verbs such as "fixes" (NASB), "planned" (NCV), "set" (NIV, NLT), "sets" (NRSV, RSV), and "designates" (NKJV). "Dost thou restrain wisdom to thyself?" (Job 15:8, KJV) now reads in the NIV,

NKJV, NRSV, and RSV, "do you limit wisdom to yourself?"

In Ezekiel 43:12 "the whole limit" (KJV) is now rendered "its entire area" (NASB), "the whole area" (NKJV), and "the whole territory" (NRSV, RSV).

LINEN YARN

This term occurs four times in the KJV, in the rendering of 1 Kings 10:28 and 2 Chronicles 1:16: "And Solomon had horses brought out of Egypt, and linen yarn: the king's merchants received the linen yarn at a price." The phrase "linen yarn" is a conjecture as to the meaning of the Hebrew word *miqweh*—a conjecture derived from the Geneva Bible (1560), which rendered it "fine linen."

The Great Bible (1539) had a quite different conjecture, "the collection of the wares." But Coverdale (1535) and the Matthew Bible (1537) had a geographical rendering, "from Keua." This means that Coverdale and Tyndale agreed, for the Matthew Bible contains Tyndale's translations from Genesis to 2 Chronicles.

Assyrian cuneiform records uncovered by archaeology have now shown that Tyndale and Coverdale were correct. All the contemporary versions except the NKJV and NLT refer to "Kue"; the NKJV refers to it as "Keveh"; the NLT has "Cilicia." The NASB has "And Solomon's import of horses was from Egypt and Kue, and the king's merchants procured them from Kue at a price."

Kue was the fertile coastal plain in the southeast portion of Asia Minor, known in the New Testament as Cilicia.

LION IN THE WAY

The phrase "a lion in the way [path or street]" is sometimes used to refer to an obstacle (either real or imaginary) that is given as an excuse for not doing something. The expression derives from Proverbs 26:13, "The slothful man saith, There is a lion in the way; a lion is in the streets" (KJV).

The NLT expands this to read, "The lazy person is full of excuses, saying, 'I can't go outside because there might be a lion on the road! Yes, I'm sure there's a lion out there!'"; the CEV has "Don't be lazy and keep saying, 'There's a lion outside!'"

LION SHALL LIE DOWN WITH THE LAMB

The expression "the lion shall lie down with the lamb" is sometimes used to describe a future age of peace and security when those who are hostile to each other will be reconciled. The expression is, in fact, a misquotation of Isaiah 11:6–7: "The wolf also shall dwell with the lamb, and the leopard shall lie down with the kid; and the calf and the young lion and the fatling together; and a little child shall lead them. And the cow and the bear shall feed; their young ones shall lie down together: and the lion shall eat straw like the ox" (KJV).

The expression is alluded to in literature, e.g., in Shelley's 1813 visionary poem *Queen Mab* (124–128):

> "The lion now forgets to thirst for
>   blood:
> There might you see him sporting
>   in the sun
> Beside the dreadless kid; his claws
>   are sheathed,
> His teeth are harmless, custom's
>   force had made
> His nature as the nature of a lamb."

LIONS' DEN

See DEN OF LIONS.

LIST

Most of us have to-do lists, grocery lists, and lists to make Santa's task a little easier. On the two final kinds of list, at least, we note the things which we would like, and on four occasions in the KJV the verb itself means "to desire" or "wish." "Whatsoever they listed" (Mark 9:13 and its parallel, Matthew 17:12) is now translated as "whatever they pleased" (NRSV, RSV) and "whatever they wished" (NASB, NKJV). For "the wind bloweth where it listeth" (John 3:8, KJV), we now have "the wind blows where it chooses" (NRSV) and "wherever it pleases" (NIV). In James 3:4 the Greek is different, and "whithersoever the governor listeth" (KJV) is now rendered as "wherever the will of the pilot directs" (NRSV). This sense of the word "list" is now archaic, though it survives in the word "listless."

LITTER

When we think of "litter" today, we call to mind highway cleanup campaigns, cuddly newborn puppies or kittens, or the dry substance that is put in a house cat's box. In the KJV a "litter" was "a light couch enclosed by curtains and carried on shoulders or by beasts of burden." Isaiah 66:20 in the KJV reads, "And they shall bring all your brethren for an offering unto the LORD out of all nations upon horses, and in chariots, and in litters, and upon mules, and upon swift beasts, to my holy mountain Jerusalem."

The NASB, NKJV, NRSV, and RSV render this "litters," except the CEV, NCV, NIV, and NLT, which have "wagons."

LIVE BY THE SWORD . . . PERISH BY THE SWORD

The expression "they that live by the sword shall perish [or: die] by the sword" is sometimes used to mean that people who live by perpetuating violence should themselves expect to suffer violent injury.

The origin of the phrase is the occasion when Simon Peter cut off the ear of Malchus, the high priest's servant: "Then said Jesus unto him, Put up again thy sword into his place: for all they that take the sword shall perish with the sword" (Matthew 26:52, KJV).

The contemporary versions render the KJV phrasing as: "all who take the sword will perish by the sword" (NKJV, NRSV, RSV), "for all those who take up the sword shall perish by the sword" (NASB), "all who draw

the sword will die by the sword" (NIV), "Those who use the sword will be killed by the sword" (NLT), "All who use swords will be killed with swords" (NCV), and "Anyone who lives by fighting will die by fighting" (CEV).

LIVE, MOVE, AND HAVE OUR BEING

When Paul gave his speech to the Athenians at the Areopagus, he quoted from Greek poets to show the relationship between human beings and God (Acts 17:28): "For in him we live, and move, and have our being; as certain also of your own poets have said, For we are also his offspring" (KJV). "In him we live, and move, and have our being" derives from the Cretan poet Epimenides (about 600 B.C.).

The contemporary versions render this quotation as "in him [NKJV, "Him"] we live and move and have our being" (NIV, NKJV, NRSV, RSV), "in him [NASB, "Him"] we live and move and exist" (NASB, NLT). The CEV has "he gives us the power to live, to move, and to be who we are"; the NCV, "We live in him. We walk in him. We are in him." The quotation "For we are also his offspring" derives from the Cilician poet Aratus (315–240 B.C.) in his *Phaenomena* and the *Hymn to Zeus* by Cleanthes (331–233 B.C.).

LIVELY

This word was just gaining its present meaning of "spirited" or "sprightly" when the KJV was issued. It appears in the KJV only in its earlier meaning of "living" or "vigorous." In Exodus 1:19 the meaning of the Hebrew is "vigorous"; the NASB translates: "the Hebrew women are not as the Egyptian women; for they are vigorous and give birth before the midwife can get to them."

Psalm 38:19 reads in the KJV, "But mine enemies are lively, and they are strong: and they that hate me wrongfully are multiplied." The NRSV and RSV read the Hebrew *hinnam,* "without cause," in place of *hay-yim,* "living." Their rendering of the verse is "Those who are my foes without cause are mighty, and many are those who hate me wrongfully." Other contemporary versions render *hayyim* instead, and have "vigorous" (NASB, NIV, NKJV), and "strong" (NCV).

In the New Testament "lively" represents the Greek participle which means "living." Moses received "lively oracles" (Acts 7:38, KJV) from God; the contemporary versions have "living oracles" (NASB, NKJV, NRSV, RSV), "living words" (NIV), and "life-giving words" (NLT). Peter writes that "we have been born anew to a lively hope by the resurrection of Jesus Christ from the dead" (1 Peter 1:3, KJV); the majority of contemporary versions have "living hope" here.

Later, Peter exhorts his readers as sharers in that hope: "To whom coming as unto a living stone, disallowed indeed of men, but chosen of God, and precious, Ye also, as lively stones, are built up a spiritual house, an holy priesthood, to offer up spiritual sacrifices, acceptable to God by Jesus Christ" (1 Peter 2:4–5).

The NRSV translates: "Come to him, a living stone, though rejected by mortals yet chosen and precious in God's sight, and like living stones, let yourselves be built into a spiritual house, to be a holy priesthood, to offer spiritual sacrifices acceptable to God through Jesus Christ."

LOATHE

This word appeared seven times in the 1611 edition of the KJV, and the older spelling "lothe" five times. For some reason not apparent, the spelling was changed to "lothe" in four passages: Exodus 7:18; Jeremiah 14:19; Ezekiel 6:9; Zechariah 11:8. The ASV and RSV use only "loathe." Other versions use other terms.

In Exodus 7:18, God announces to Moses his intention to smite the river so that "the Egyptians shall lothe to drink of the water" (KJV). The CEV, NCV, NIV, NLT, and NRSV say that the Egyptians will not "be able" [NRSV, "shall be unable"] to drink it. "Hath thy

soul lothed Zion?" (Jeremiah 14:19, KJV) is now rendered as "Do you [NLT, "Do you really"] hate Jerusalem?" by the CEV, NCV, and NLT, while the NASB, NKJV, NRSV, and RSV retain "loathed"/"loathe" here.

The NASB, NIV, NKJV, NRSV, and RSV have "loathe" (NRSV, "loathsome") in Ezekiel 6:9, where the KJV reads, "they shall lothe themselves for the evils which they have committed," while in Zechariah 11:8 many of the contemporary versions now render "lothed" (KJV) with the adjective "impatient." Passages which had "lothe" in the first edition of the KJV are Ezekiel 16:5, 45, 20:43, and 36:31.

On similar changes in spelling, the 1611 KJV had "flotes" in 1 Kings 5:9 and 2 Chronicles 2:16. This was changed to "floats" in Kings but not in Chronicles, and some current editions of the KJV retain the two spellings. A number also retain the obsolete spelling "sope" for "soap" (Jeremiah 2:22; Malachi 3:2).

LOFT

The word "loft" is likely to remind us of the cobwebs and memorabilia often found in the roof storage space of our homes. A loft today is an upper room or story, an attic, an upper floor without partitions, or even a hayloft, or organ loft. When Elijah carried the sick boy up "into a loft, where he abode" (1 Kings 17:19, KJV), it was "up to the upper room where he was staying" (NASB).

The Hebrew word signifies a roof chamber, such as the "roof chamber with walls" which the wealthy woman of Shunem made for Elisha (2 Kings 4:10, NRSV, CEV, "a small room on the flat roof of our house"). Such chambers, built upon the flat roofs of houses, were prized for their coolness and seclusion.

In Acts 20:9 "the third loft" (KJV) represents a Greek word which is now rendered as "the third story" (NIV, NKJV, RSV) and "the third floor" (NASB, NCV). The NRSV translates: "A young man named Eutychus, who was sitting in the window, began to sink off into a deep sleep while Paul talked still longer. Overcome by sleep, he fell down to the ground three floors below and was picked up dead."

LOG

In contemporary English a log is a thick piece of wood cut from a tree, or an official record, especially of a journey in a ship, airplane, etc. In the KJV the word "log" is used to refer to a measure of liquid capacity, approximately half a pint (a quarter of a quart) or 0.3 liter. It is always used as a measure of oil.

The word occurs five times in Leviticus 14 (vv. 10, 12, 15, 21, and 24) as part of the cleansing ritual for "leprosy" (Leviticus 14:3, KJV): "And on the eighth day he shall take two he lambs without blemish, and one ewe lamb of the first year without blemish, and three tenth deals of fine flour for a meat offering, mingled with oil, and one log of oil" (v. 10, KJV).

The NASB, NIV, NKJV, NRSV, and RSV retain the KJV "log"; the CEV has "a half pint"; the NCV, "two-thirds of a pint" the NLT, "three-fifths of a pint."

LONGSUFFERING

"Long-suffering" is what we would need to be if we were to wake up one winter morning and discover that the water pipes had frozen. The OED defines long-suffering as "patient endurance of provocation or trial" (OED). As noun and adjective, it appears seventeen times in the KJV. In the Old Testament the majority of contemporary versions replace it on three occasions by a literal translation of the Hebrew, "slow to anger." The proclamation in Exodus 34:6 reads in the KJV, "The LORD, The LORD God, merciful and gracious, longsuffering, and abundant in goodness and truth."

Contemporary versions render "longsuffering" (KJV) here as "slow to anger" (NASB, NIV, NLT, NRSV, RSV), "very patient" (CEV), and "doesn't become angry quickly" (NCV). The

proclamation reads, in the NRSV, "The LORD, the LORD, a God merciful and gracious, slow to anger, and abounding in steadfast love and faithfulness" (cf. Numbers 14:18 and Psalm 86:15).

In Jeremiah 15:15 "longsuffering" (KJV) is retained by the NIV ("You are long-suffering"), while other contemporary versions have "patience" (NASB), "enduring patience" (NKJV), and "forbearance" (NRSV).

In the Epistles, the Greek word *makrothumia* is rendered by contemporary versions as "patient" (e.g., 2 Peter 3:9, CEV, NASB, NCV, NIV, NLT, NRSV, RSV), "patience" (e.g., 2 Corinthians 6:6, NASB, NCV, NIV, NLT, NRSV), "forbearance" (e.g., 2 Peter 3:15, RSV), and "forbearing" (2 Peter 3:9, RSV). "Charity suffereth long, and is kind" (1 Corinthians 13:4, KJV) now reads in the NCV, NLT, and RSV, "Love is patient and kind." (See PATIENCE)

In Luke 18:7 Jesus, teaching the disciples about prayer, asks them, "shall not God avenge his own elect, which cry day and night unto him, though he bear long with them?" (KJV). Contemporary versions have "Will He [RSV, "will he"] delay long over them?" (NASB, RSV) and "Will he keep putting them off?" (NIV, NLT).

LOOK FOR

In the sense of "expect," or "watch for," this phrase is a well-established English idiom. The Greek verb *prosdokao* is translated by the KJV as "look for" (Matthew 11:3; Luke 7:19–20), "wait for" (Luke 1:21; 8:40), "were in expectation" (Luke 3:15), "expecting" (Acts 3:5); and the contemporary versions often retain these renderings. The question posed to Jesus by the disciples of John the Baptist, "do we look for another?" (Matthew 11:3, KJV), is rendered "should we wait for someone else?" (NCV) and "should we expect someone else?" (NIV).

In Matthew 24:50 (and its parallel, Luke 12:46), Jesus warns, in his parable, that "The lord of that servant shall come in a day when he looketh not for him" (KJV). "Looketh not for him" reads "does not expect him" in the NASB, NIV, NRSV, and RSV. "Cornelius waited for them" (Acts 10:24, KJV) now reads, "Cornelius was expecting them" (NIV, NRSV, RSV) and "Cornelius was waiting for them" (CEV, NASB, NCV, NKJV, NLT).

In the account of Paul's voyage and shipwreck this Greek verb occurs three times. The KJV represents it by "tarried" in Acts 27:33: "While the day was coming on, Paul besought them all to take meat, saying, This day is the fourteenth day that ye have tarried and continued fasting, having taken nothing." The NRSV translates: "Just before daybreak, Paul urged all of them to take some food, saying, 'Today is the fourteenth day that you have been in suspense and remaining without food, having eaten nothing.'"

The other two occurrences are in Acts 28:6, expressing the surprise of the people of Malta when Paul suffered no harm from the viper that fastened on his hand. Here the KJV has "looked." It reads, "Howbeit they looked when he should have swollen, or fallen down dead suddenly: but after they had looked a great while, and saw no harm come to him, they changed their minds, and said that he was a god."

The NASB translates as "But they were expecting that he was about to swell up or suddenly fall down dead. But after they had waited a long time and had seen nothing unusual happen to him, they changed their minds and began to say that he was a god."

The corresponding Hebrew verb, *qavah*, is usually translated as "look for" or "wait for." An exception is Isaiah 5:2, 4, "looked that it should bring forth grapes." Here "look" has the sense of expect, and is followed by a clause. This is an old English usage, now obsolete.

The NRSV translates as "expected it to yield grapes"; the NASB and NKJV also use "expected," while the NIV and RSV have "looked for" and the CEV and NCV have "hoped" (Isaiah 5:2, CEV, "He hoped they would be sweet, but bitter grapes were all it produced").

LOOK TO

When Jesse brought his youngest son before Samuel, the boy was "goodly to look to" according to the KJV (1 Samuel 16:12). This is an early usage in the sense of "to look at." The same usage appears in Ezekiel 23:15: "all of them princes to look to" (KJV). The NCV, NLT, NRSV, and RSV say that the young David was "handsome," the NIV has "handsome features," and the NASB, NRSV, and RSV describe the Chaldeans in Ezekiel 23:15 as "all of them looking like officers."

Nebuchadnezzar's command concerning Jeremiah was "Take him, and look well to him, and do him no harm; but do unto him even as he shall say unto thee" (Jeremiah 39:12, KJV). Contemporary versions render "look well to him" (KJV) as "keep him safe" (CEV), "take care of him" (NCV), and "look after him" (NIV, NKJV; NRSV, RSV, "look after him well"). The KJV, NKJV, and RSV translate the first clause of 2 John 8 alike as "Look to yourselves"; the NASB has "watch yourselves," the NIV, "Watch out," and the NRSV, "Be on your guard."

"Look unto" expresses trust and reliance in Micah 7:7 (KJV), which the NKJV translates as "Therefore I will look to the LORD; I will wait for the God of my salvation; My God will hear me."

LOVE

In the Greek New Testament, the noun *agape* occurs 114 times—far more frequently than the other Greek word which also appears and which primarily refers to personal friendship, *philia*. With its verb and adjective, *agapē* occurs over three hundred times. The KJV translates the verb *agapao* as "love" in 130 instances, and its participle as "beloved" in six. The adjective is translated as "beloved" fifty-nine times and "dear" three times.

But in the case of the noun, *agapē*, the KJV renders it—in twenty-six out of 112 instances—not as "love," but as "charity"

(Latin *caritas*). In one case a prepositional phrase is rendered by the adverb "charitably."

Thus, while we read in the KJV, "Beloved, let us love one another: for love is of God" (1 John 4:7) and "this is his commandment, That we should . . . love one another" (1 John 3:23), we also find renderings such as "the end of the commandment is charity" (1 Timothy 1:5) and "the charity of every one of you all toward each other aboundeth" (2 Thessalonians 1:3).

The word "charity" today conjures up images of fund-raising events and home-made cakes being sold at church bazaars. The idea is of generosity towards the less fortunate: we have charities devoted to aiding people in almost every part of the world and every area of need. However, we also use the word with other meanings.

The invitation to "show some charity" could just as well mean "stop being unkind" or "don't be judgmental" as "empty your purse." In the sixteenth century, as we will see in a moment, the word also had meanings such as these, and so the reasons for the KJV translators' decision to use this word in some instances, and "love" in others, has been the subject of some debate. A brief look at the background to the translation may help to shed light on the KJV usage.

Except in the one case when he also uses the adverb "charitably," Tyndale translated *agapē* by the word "love." When rebuked by Thomas More, who wished to retain the Latin-derived, ecclesiastically sanctioned word "charity," Tyndale argued that "charity is not known English, in that sense which *agapē* requireth," and that in common use it means either "almsgiving" or "patience and mercifulness in the judgment of others." He also called attention to the fact that "charity" is a noun that has no correlative verb or adjective, as *agapē* has. "I say not, charity God, or charity your neighbor; but, love God, and love your neighbor."

In his translation of *agapē* by "love,"

Tyndale was followed by all sixteenth-century versions up to 1568—Coverdale, Matthew, Taverner, the Great Bible, and the Geneva Bible. He was followed by the Bishops' Bible also, except for one verse, Romans 13:10, where the word "charity" was introduced.

The result is that the passage closes with a shift of language. Romans 13:8–10 reads in the Bishops' Bible: "Owe nothing to no man, but to love one another: For he that loveth another hath fulfilled the law. For this: Thou shalt not commit adultery, thou shalt not kill, thou shalt not steal, thou shalt not bear false witness, thou shalt not lust and if there be any other commandment it is comprehended in this saying: namely, thou shalt love thy neighbor as thyself. Charity worketh no ill to his neighbor, Therefore the fulfilling of the law is charity."

In 1572 came a real break. In the second edition of the Bishops' Bible, published in that year, the word "charity" is substituted for "love" in thirty-two cases. The word "love" remained in the other cases, and in the translation of the verb *agapao*.

When the committee appointed by King James revised the Bishops' Bible to make the Authorized Version of 1611, they restored the word "love" in six of the thirty-two cases, but they kept the word "charity" in twenty-six cases. Just why they did so is not clear.

Even an attempt to attribute the twenty-six divergent cases to differences in the Latin Vulgate does not explain them. There are three Latin words for "love"—*amor, dilectio,* and *caritas.* The first of these is never used to represent *agapē* in the Latin New Testament; *dilectio* is used in about one-fifth of the cases of its occurrence, and *caritas* is used in the rest.

The Rheims New Testament, which was made by translation from the Latin, reproduces this divergence. It always uses the English word "love" for *dilectio,* and "charity" for *caritas.* The result is translations such as: "My dearest, let us love one another, because charity is of God . . . He that loveth not, knoweth not God; because God is charity" (1 John 4:7–8).

However, the KJV translators do not follow this rendering or the Latin. Of the twenty-six cases where they use "charity," three have *dilectio* in the Latin and twenty-three have *caritas*. Of the eighty-five cases where they use "love," twenty have *dilectio* and sixty-five have *caritas*.

The Latin words *dilectio* and *caritas* were taken up, at various points in church history, in theological debates about whether there is a distinction to be made between the love of God for us, and the love which God makes possible between human beings. Jerome, in his translations of New Testament passages, used the word *dilectio* to represent *agape* in a few cases and *caritas* in the rest, but it is not clear whether he had a theological distinction in mind and, in any case, such a distinction is not present in the Greek. Nor, it would seem, was it maintained in the usage of the English Church in the 1570's.

The *Catechism* by Alexander Nowell, Dean of St. Paul's, sanctioned by the Convocation of Canterbury, written in Latin and then translated into English by Thomas Norton, was published in both languages in 1570. It appears to provide evidence that in Latin *caritas, dilectio,* and even *amor* were used interchangeably, and so were "charity" and "love" in English.

Take, for example, this clause from the answer to the question regarding our duty toward Christ: "That we with all our affection, love, esteem, and embrace Christ our Savior, which showed us such dear love while we were yet his enemies, as his most entire love toward us could not possibly be increased." In the Latin of this passage the verb for love was *amo,* and the verb for esteem *diligo;* while the first noun for love was *caritas,* and the second *amor.*

On the other hand, Bacon—writing some thirty years later—did see a distinction between the two words and hinted that "love"

had come to acquire meanings which did not taint the word "charity." In his *Certaine Considerations touching the Church of England* (1604) he wrote:

> "I did euer allow the discretion and tenderness of the Rhemish translation in this Poynt, that finding in the originall the Word *agapē* and never *eros,* doe euer translate *Charitie,* and neuer *Loue,* because of the indifferencie and œquiuocation of the word with impure Love."

However, even if the word "charity" was perceived, or was beginning to be perceived, as a more fitting rendering of the New Testament word for "love," this does not help us to explain the distribution of the twenty-six cases in which the KJV retains the word "charity."

There are no such cases of "charity" in the KJV before 1 Corinthians 8:1. Of the twenty-six cases, eleven are in 1 Corinthians, six in the Pastoral Epistles, four in the epistles of Peter, and one each in Colossians, 1 Thessalonians, 2 Thessalonians, 3 John, and Revelation. Eight of them are in 1 Corinthians 13. The First Letter of John, the epistle of love, contains none.

As to why these particular places should have been chosen for the change to "charity," we can only guess. Two guesses may not be wholly wrong. First Corinthians 13 was one of the most familiar parts of the New Testament; English versions of it had appeared in primers and aids to devotion; many people had probably committed it to memory, both in Latin and in English. Here the word "charity" was established in the public mind. And it was perhaps natural, too, to retain the Latin-derived word in the Pastoral Epistles.

The revised versions of 1881 and 1901 returned to the practice of the earlier sixteenth-century versions, and used "love" throughout. They have been followed in this by all contemporary translations based upon the original Greek including the New

Jerusalem Bible approved for liturgical use in the Roman Catholic Church. The Catholic translations from the Vulgate by Father Knox and the Confraternity of Christian Doctrine use "love" as the translation for *caritas* in the crucial passages contained in the epistles of John.

At 1 Corinthians 13:13 the KJV reads, "And now abideth faith, hope, charity, these three; but the greatest of these is charity." The CEV, NASB, NCV, NIV, NKJV, NLT, NRSV, and RSV all use "love" here and throughout the New Testament, ending Paul's great hymn with the words, "the greatest of these [CEV, "the greatest"] is love." Where the word "charity" occurs in contemporary versions, it always has the meaning of "almsgiving" (e.g., Luke 11:41, "give that which is within as charity," NASB; KJV, "give alms of such things as ye have"; Acts 9:36, NASB, RSV).

Philia and its verb *phileo* occurs only twenty-six times in the Greek New Testament, and the noun, *philos*, which means "friend," occurs twenty-nine times. The other Greek word for "love," *eros*, which refers primarily to sexual love, does not appear in the New Testament.

LOVE OF MONEY IS THE ROOT OF ALL EVIL

See MONEY IS THE ROOT OF ALL EVIL.

LOVE THY NEIGHBOUR

The command "love thy neighbour" is found eight times in the KJV, once in the Old Testament and seven times in the New Testament. In Leviticus 19:18, the command is: "Thou shalt not avenge, nor bear any grudge against the children of thy people, but thou shalt love thy neighbour as thyself: I am the LORD" (KJV). All the contemporary versions except the CEV render the KJV expression as "love your neighbor as [NCV, "as you love"] yourself"; the CEV has "love others as much as you love yourself."

This command is quoted by Jesus in the Sermon on the Mount (Matthew 5:43), to the rich young ruler (Matthew 19:19), and in describing the greatest commandment (Matthew 22:39 and its parallels Mark 12:31 and Luke 10:27, which reads in the KJV, "Love . . . thy neighbour as thyself"). It is quoted by Paul in Romans 13:9 and Galatians 5:14 and by James in James 2:8.

LOVER

This word is used occasionally in the KJV in its basic sense of one who loves. "Hiram was ever a lover of David" (1 Kings 5:1, KJV) is now rendered "Hiram had always loved David" (NKJV) and "Hiram had always been a friend of [NRSV, "friend to"] David" (NASB, NRSV). "My lovers and my friends stand aloof from my sore" (Psalm 38:11, KJV) now reads, "My friends and companions avoid me because of my wounds" (NIV), and "My loved ones and friends stay away, fearing my disease" (NLT).

Tyndale used the word "lover" often. "For the very sinners love their lovers" was his translation of Luke 6:32, and this was retained in successive versions up to and including the two editions of the Bishops' Bible. The Rheims New Testament changed to the rendering which the KJV adopted, "for sinners also love those that love them."

Other translations by Tyndale are: "When she hath found it she calleth her lovers and her neighbours" (Luke 15:9); "and yet thou gavest me never so much as a kid to make merry with my lovers" (Luke 15:29); "The lovers salute thee. Greet the lovers by name" (3 John 14). In the first and third of these passages, "lovers" was changed to "friends" by the Geneva Bible, and in the second, by the Great Bible; the KJV and contemporary translations have "friends" in all three passages.

The word "lover" (KJV) is used by the prophets Jeremiah, Ezekiel, and Hosea in the sense of the male party to an illicit sexual relation. It is an interesting fact that the word "lover" does not appear in the KJV Song of Solomon, where the young woman is referred to as "my love" and the man as "my beloved."

LOVINGKINDNESS

Although "loving" and "kindness" are words that go back to Old English, the term "lovingkindness" was introduced by Coverdale as translation for the Hebrew *hesed*. At first spelled as two words, in time it came to be printed as "loving-kindness" and later as "lovingkindness."

Tyndale, following the Greek Septuagint, took "mercy" as his translation for *hesed* when that denotes an attribute of God in his dealing with the human race. Coverdale made the combination "loving kindness," but he did not use it consistently: we can see this by comparing the Psalter in the Book of Common Prayer with the Psalms as printed in the ASV, where "lovingkindness" appears more than five times as often.

The KJV uses "mercy," "lovingkindness," and "kindness" to translate *hesed* as an attribute of God. The ASV uses "lovingkindness" in all cases where it denotes God's attitude toward human beings.

In recent years, the revival of interest in the Old Testament within biblical scholarship, and developments in Jewish-Christian dialogue, have resulted in fresh insights into the meaning of covenant in the literature of the Old Testament. These insights, in turn, have shed light on the meaning of *hesed* when it is asserted of God.

Hesed is a covenant word. Its original use was to denote that attitude of loyalty and faithfulness which both parties to a covenant should maintain toward each other. So says Professor Norman Snaith in *The Distinctive Ideas of the Old Testament* (Allenson, 1953, p. 99). However, the word occurs most frequently in the writings of the prophets—particularly Hosea, whose tender dealings with his wayward wife epitomized God's love for unfaithful Israel.

Professor Smith goes on to say: "When the word came to be used predominantly of the Covenant between Jehovah and Is-

rael, it was realized by the prophets that such a covenant could be maintained only by that persistent, determined steadfast love of God, which transcends every other love by its nature and depth . . . The most important of all the distinctive ideas of the Old Testament is God's steady and extraordinary persistence in continuing to love wayward Israel in spite of Israel's insistent waywardness."

This idea is expressed in Isaiah 54:8, 10, where the KJV reads, "In a little wrath I hid my face from thee for a moment; but with everlasting kindness will I have mercy on thee, saith the LORD thy Redeemer . . . For the mountains shall depart, and the hills be removed; but my kindness [Heb., *hesed*] shall not depart from thee, neither shall the covenant of my peace be removed, saith the LORD that hath mercy on thee."

Hosea 2:19 reads in the KJV, "And I will betroth thee unto me for ever; yea, I will betroth thee unto me in righteousness, and in judgment, and in lovingkindness, and in mercies."

Sir George Adam Smith once suggested "real love" as a translation for *hesed*. Others have suggested "sure love." The NASB generally uses "lovingkindness." "Kind" and "kindness" occur in other contemporary versions. The CEV's rendering of Psalm 103:17, for example, is "The LORD is always kind," and in Isaiah 63:7 the NCV uses "kind" and the NIV, "kindnesses."

Other terms used by contemporary versions are "love" (e.g., Isaiah 54:10, NCV; Hosea 2:19, NCV, NIV, CEV), "unfailing love" (e.g., Isaiah 54:10, NIV). The RSV translators adopted "steadfast love," and this rendering was taken up by the NRSV.

Professor Millar Burrows, in the *Introduction to the RSV Old Testament* (Thomas Nelson & Sons, 1952, p. 61), notes one important theological result of the new renderings: "the word 'love' now appears far more often in the Old Testament than it did in previous translations, counteracting the erroneous impression of many Christians that the God of the Old Testament was not a God of love." (See MERCY)

LUCRE

The word "lucre" is likely to make us think of money. In fact, there is no biblical warrant for the modern habit of jokingly referring to money as "filthy lucre." The word means "gain," and is used in the KJV only for gain which is unworthy or dishonest. It appears once in the Old Testament, where it is recorded that Samuel's sons, as judges, "walked not in his ways, but turned aside after lucre, and took bribes, and perverted judgment" (1 Samuel 8:3, KJV). The NASB, NIV, and NKJV use "dishonest gain" in this verse and the NRSV and RSV have simply "gain."

In 1 Peter 5:2, the elders are exhorted to "feed the flock of God which is among you, taking the oversight thereof, not by constraint, but willingly; not for filthy lucre, but of a ready mind." The NRSV reads: "tend the flock of God that is your charge, exercising the oversight, not under compulsion but willingly, as God would have you do it—not for sordid gain but eagerly."

The expression "filthy lucre" appears also in the KJV rendering of 1 Timothy 3:3, 8 and Titus 1:7, 11. In each case it stands for a combination in some form of the Greek words *aischron kerdos,* which mean "dishonest," "unworthy," or "shameful" gain. However, this sense is not always clear to readers, since a number of contemporary versions occasionally render "lucre" (KJV) simply as "money" (e.g., 1 Timothy 3:8, NKJV, NLT, NRSV).

"Greedy of filthy lucre" (1 Timothy 3:8, KJV) is rendered as "greedy for money" by the NRSV, but "given to filthy lucre" (Titus 1:7, KJV) is rendered by the NRSV as "greedy for gain."

LUNATICK

Some people brought to Jesus to be healed were described by the KJV as "lunatick" (Matthew 4:24; 17:15). The Greek means "moon-struck," for which the Latin was *lunaticus.* Intermittent nervous and mental disorders were formerly thought to be influenced by the changes of the moon. The contemporary versions generally read "epileptic," which fits the father's description of his son's malady (17:15). The first recorded use of "epilepsy" as an English word was in 1578; the first recorded use of "epileptic," in 1605.

The NIV refers to "those which were lunatick" in Matthew 4:24 as "those having seizures," and the CEV has "[those] thought to be crazy." The NASB retains the word "lunatic" in reference to the boy in 17:15; the NIV and NLT refer to him as having "seizures."

LUST

This word was used in the sixteenth century for any desire or wish for something pleasing, but it soon began to be limited, as it now is, to inordinate or lawless desires, and especially to those associated with sexual pleasure. The word appears fifty-three times in the KJV.

The "lust" of the children of Israel for meat is now described as a "craving" by the NIV, NKJV, NLT, NRSV, and RSV in Numbers 11:4, 34; Psalm 78:18 [NKJV, "fancy"]. "[They] lusted exceedingly in the wilderness" Psalm 106:14 (KJV) is now translated as "They became greedy for food in the desert" (NCV), "in the wilderness, their desires ran wild" (NLT), and "they had a wanton craving in the wilderness" (NRSV).

"Whatsoever thy soul lusteth after" (Deuteronomy 12:15, 20, 21, KJV) is rendered by the NASB and NKJV as "whatever you desire" (NASB) and "as much as your heart desires" (NKJV). On the other hand, "transgressors shall be taken in their own naughtiness" is now reworded as "the unfaithful will be caught by their lust" (Proverbs 11:6, NKJV).

The Greek noun *epithumia* is rendered by the KJV as "concupiscence" three times, "desire" three times, and "lust" thirty-two times. None of the contemporary versions use the word "concupiscence"; a number retain "lust" in some passages, and almost all use "desire(s)" or "passion(s)" in varying contexts.

Examples are Mark 4:19 ("the lusts of other things," KJV; "the desires for other things," NASB, NIV, NKJV); Galatians 5:17 ("the flesh lusteth against the Spirit, and the Spirit against the flesh," KJV; "what the flesh desires is opposed to the Spirit, and what the Spirit desires is opposed to the flesh," NRSV); 2 Timothy 2:22 ("flee youthful lusts," KJV; "Run from temptations that capture young people," CEV).

In Romans 7:7–8 the majority of the contemporary versions have "covet" and "covetousness" in place of "lust" and "concupiscence" (KJV).

A notable passage is James 1:13–15, which reads in the KJV: "Let no man say when he is tempted, I am tempted by God: for God cannot be tempted with evil, neither tempteth he any man: But every man is tempted, when he is drawn away of his own lust, and enticed. Then when lust hath conceived, it bringeth forth sin: and sin, when it is finished, bringeth forth death."

The word "lust" is retained by the NASB in these verses, but all other contemporary versions use the words "desire" (NRSV, RSV), "desires" (CEV), and "evil desire" (NCV, NIV; NLT, "evil desires").

"The spirit that dwelleth in us lusteth to envy" (James 4:5, KJV) is now rendered as "He jealously desires the Spirit which He has made to dwell in us" (NASB) and "God yearns jealously for the spirit that he has made to dwell in us" (NRSV). The entire verse reads in the NLT: "What do you think the Scriptures mean when they say that the Holy Spirit, whom God has placed within us, jealously longs for us to be faithful?"

In contemporary English "lusty" means "feeling or expressing strong sexual desires" and "strong, healthy, and energetic." It occurs in the KJV with this second meaning at Judges 3:29, "And they [the children of Israel] slew of Moab at that time about ten thousand men, all lusty, and all men of valour; and there escaped not a man."

The contemporary versions render "lusty" as "strong" (NCV, NRSV, RSV), "strongest" (NLT), "robust" (NASB), "stout" (NKJV); the KJV "all lusty, and all men of valour" is rendered by the NIV as "all vigorous and strong."

Shakespeare used "lusty" in this sense:

"Let me be your servant:
Though I look old, yet I am strong
 and lusty:
For in my youth I never did apply
Hot and rebellious liquors in my
 blood,
Nor did not with unbashful forehead
 woo
The means of weakness and debility;
Therefore my age is as a lusty winder,
Frosty, but kindly."
—*As You Like It* (II, 3, 47–54)

M

MAD

Today it is politically incorrect to apply this word to those who are mentally ill; its more common use in contemporary English is to describe great folly, extreme irritation, or explosive anger. "Mad" has traditionally been the normal word for "insane," "out of one's mind." It has a tinge of contempt or disgust and is also applied to cases of wild excitement, infatuation, uncontrolled anger, or extreme folly.

"Mad" in the sense of "insane" in the KJV is usually also translated in contemporary versions as "mad" or "insane," but sometimes as "crazy" (Acts 26:24 in the NCV, CEV, and NLT). In Acts 26:11, the KJV's "being exceedingly mad against them" becomes "so angry" (CEV, NCV), "furiously enraged"

(NASB, NRSV; NKJV, "exceedingly enraged"), "violently opposed" (NLT) and "in raging fury" (RSV); the NIV omits the sense of "furious anger" and translates the phrase as "in my obsession against them."

The KJV also uses "mad" in Ecclesiastes 7:7 ("Surely oppression maketh a wise man mad") and Isaiah 44:24–25 ("maketh diviners mad") to translate the Hebrew verb meaning "to make foolish" or "make a fool of." The contemporary translations retain the Hebrew sense of making fools of judges (Ecclesiastes 7:7) and diviners (Isaiah 44:25). In Job 12:17, the KJV also translates this Hebrew verb, speaking of the Lord, as "maketh the judges fools."

MAGNIFY

In contemporary English, "to magnify" is to enlarge a visual image, a problem, a situation, etc. We no longer use it in ordinary speech to celebrate the largeness, the greatness of God, but in this sense of "rendering praise or honor to God," the word "magnify" has become established in liturgical use through the translation of the Magnificat (Luke 1:46–55) in the Book of Common Prayer.

The KJV renders Luke 1:46 as "And Mary said, My soul doth magnify the Lord" and the word is retained in the NKJV and NRSV, although other contemporary translations prefer "My soul exalts" (NASB), "My soul praises" (NCV; NLT, "Oh, how I praise the Lord"), and "My soul glorifies" (NIV).

The NASB, NKJV, and NRSV also retain the word in David's prayer in 2 Samuel 7:26 and the parallel 1 Chronicles 17:24, Psalm 34:3, and Psalm 69:30. Other translations use words such as "honor" (Psalm 69:30, NCV), "glorify" (Psalm 34:3, NIV), "extol" (Job 36:24, NIV, NRSV), "Great is the LORD" (Malachi 1:5, NIV), and "God is great!" (Psalm 70:4, NLT, NRSV).

In the less liturgical context of Acts 10:46; 19:17 and Philippians 1:20, the contemporary translations use "exalt," "praise," "ex-

tol," and "honor" more or less interchangeably.

The KJV also uses "magnify" with reference to human beings (as when the apostles are magnified by the people in Acts 5:13) and in these cases the contemporary translations distinguish between the human and the divine by using less honorific language: the people "liked" the apostles (CEV), "held them in high esteem" (NASB, NRSV; NKJV, "esteemed them highly"), "respected them" (NCV), they were "highly regarded" (NIV).

Although the NASB, NKJV, and NRSV often retain "magnify" (e.g., NRSV in Isaiah 42:21), in the sense of "to make great," "to cause to be respected and honored," the word is more often translated with the verbs "exalt," "be respected," or "make great" (see, for example, Joshua 3:7; 4:14; 1 Chronicles 29:25; 2 Chronicles 1:1; 32:23; Job 7:17; Psalm 138:2).

In Genesis 19:19, the KJV has "thou hast magnified thy mercy, which thou hast shewed unto me in saving my life," which the NIV translates as "you have shown great kindness to me in sparing my life." The KJV's "the enemy hath magnified himself" (Lamentations 1:9) means that "the enemy has triumphed" (NIV, NLT, NRSV).

The KJV also uses "magnify" in the sense of "unwarranted pretension" or "aggressive action," as in the expression "magnifying (one)self" (Psalm 35:26; Job 19:5; Jeremiah 48:26, 42; Daniel 8:11, 25; 11:36–37). The contemporary translations render this expression as, for example, "become arrogant," "defied," "exalted himself," "rebelled" (Jeremiah 48:26, NASB, NIV, NKJV, NLT; the NRSV retains "magnified himself").

In a few contexts "magnify (one)self" is replaced by words which denote bragging or arrogant and aggressive behavior (Psalms 38:16; 55:12; Zephaniah 2:8).

MAKE

When the five explorers from the tribe of Dan recognized the voice of the young Levite in the house of Micah, and asked him, in the words of the KJV, "What makest thou in this place?", they did not imply that he was constructing or manufacturing anything. Their question was simply, "What are you doing in this place?", and this is the wording used by most of the contemporary versions.

Except for the difference between the singular and plural forms, the Hebrew verb used is the same as that in the Levite's later question to the Danites: "What are you doing?" (Judges 18:3, 18). The idiom "What make you here?" in the sense of "What are you doing here?" was common in the sixteenth and seventeenth centuries. Examples from Shakespeare are:

> "And what make you from
>   Wittenberg, Horatio?"
>   —*Hamlet* (I, 2, 164)

> "Thou frantic woman, what dost
>   thou make here?"
>   —*King Richard II* (V, 3, 89)

> "She was in his company at
>   Page's house; and what they
>   made there, I know not."
>   —*Merry Wives of Windsor*
>   (II, 1, 209)

MAKE FOR

This expression is used in contemporary English only in the sense of "going in a particular direction." "Make for high ground," we say as the flood waters rise. This meaning is there in a figurative sense in the older use of the word: "to be favorable to," "tend toward," "operate in aid of."

Tyndale's translation of Romans 14:19 was "Let us folowe tho thinges which make for peace," and this idiom, found in the KJV, is retained by the NASB, NKJV, and NRSV. Other contemporary translations render this expression as "live at peace" (CEV), "do what makes peace" (NCV), or "aim for harmony in the church" (NLT).

Applied to people, "make for" is awkward and ambiguous. "Neither shall Pharaoh with his mighty army and great company make for him in the war" (Ezekiel 17:17, KJV) is clarified in contemporary versions by the use of "help" (e.g., NRSV, "help him in war").

MALICIOUSNESS

Today "maliciousness" often has more to do with point-scoring than wickedness. In the sixteenth century, however, it was the equivalent of "malice," which has a more serious and evil aspect, often issuing in hurtful actions. The KJV uses the word in Romans 1:29, "Being filled with all unrighteousness . . . maliciousness"; the contemporary versions emphasize its seriousness, translating it as "evil" (NASB), "hatred" (NCV, NLT, "hate"), "depravity" (NIV), and "malice" (NRSV).

It also occurs in 1 Peter 2:16: "As free, and not using your liberty for a cloke of maliciousness, but as the servants of God" (KJV). Here the majority of contemporary translations have "evil."

MAN AFTER ONE'S OWN HEART

In contemporary English, if you say that a person is someone "after your own heart," it means that that person likes or appreciates something that you also like or appreciate very much ("so you're fond of Mozart; there's a man after my own heart"). The expression originally referred to David, as described in Samuel's rebuke of Saul in 1 Samuel 13:14: "But now thy kingdom shall not continue: the LORD hath sought him a man after his own heart, and the LORD hath commanded him to be captain over his people, because thou hast not kept that which the LORD commanded thee."

All the contemporary versions except the CEV and NCV retain the expression "after his own heart" (with the capitalized "H" in the NASB and NKJV); the NCV has "the kind of man he wants"; the CEV, "the one he wants." See also Acts 13:22. (See AFTER)

MAN CANNOT SERVE TWO MASTERS

The expression "no man can serve two masters" occurs in the Sermon on the

Mount (Matthew 6:24, KJV): "No man can serve two masters: for either he will hate the one, and love the other; or else he will hold to the one, and despise the other. Ye cannot serve God and mammon."

All the contemporary versions except the CEV render this as "No one can serve two masters"; the CEV has "You cannot be the slave of two masters!" The sense is brought out in the contemporary expression "be a slave to something," to be so devoted to something that it controls you completely" ("many people today are slaves to modern fashion"). At Luke 16:13, the KJV text has "No servant can serve two masters." (See also GOD AND MAMMON)

MANNA FROM HEAVEN

Manna was the food miraculously provided by God for the Israelites in the wilderness. It had the appearance of coriander seed and tasted like honey (Exodus 16:31). The word "manna" means "what is it?"—the question the Israelites posed when they saw the substance "because the people had never seen anything like this" (Exodus 16:15, CEV).

The word manna has a capital "M" at Exodus 16:31 in the KJV and NKJV and a lowercase "m" in all the other contemporary versions. It is known as "bread from heaven" (John 6:31, KJV, CEV, NCV, NKJV, NKJV, NLT, NRSV); the NASB has "bread out of heaven." So it is that the phrase "manna from heaven" (which is not actually found in the KJV text) is sometimes used in contemporary English to refer to a much-needed but unexpected gift.

MANNER

The word "manner" is used 234 times in the KJV, and in more than one-third of these cases it is unnecessary, that is, there is in these cases no corresponding Hebrew or Greek word to call for its use, and the meaning of the text can be conveyed more directly and simply without it.

This is partly because the KJV uses "manner" most often in the archaic sense of "kind"

or "sort," and partly because it forms part of periphrastic expressions such as "no manner of" for "no," and "all manner of" for "all." However, the KJV seems to feel that these phrases often have a slightly greater intensity than simply "no" or "all" and imply that several different kinds of object or activity are involved.

In Exodus 12:16, for example, the KJV's "no manner of work shall be done" is not simply rendered in most of the contemporary versions as "no work," but as "no work at all" (NASB, NIV), "not . . . any work" (NCV), "no work of any kind" (NLT); the NKJV retains "no manner of work," and the NRSV has simply "no work."

There are similar shades of translation in Leviticus 23:31: the majority of contemporary versions translate the KJV's "no manner of work" as "no work at all"; the NKJV retains "no manner of work"; and the NRSV has "no work." Likewise, the KJV "no manner of fat" (Leviticus 7:23) is "any fat" (NASB, NKJV, NRSV), and "no manner of blood" (7:26, KJV) or "any manner of blood" (7:27; 17:10, KJV) is "any blood" in some translations (e.g., NASB, NKJV), and the NRSV at 7:26 has "any blood whatever."

"All manner of beasts" (Numbers 31:30, KJV) is rendered simply as "cattle" by the contemporary versions, but "all manner of plague of leprosy" in the KJV's Leviticus 14:54 is translated as "any mark of leprosy" (NASB), "any kind of skin disease" (NCV), "any infectious skin disease" (NIV), "any leprous disease" [NKJV, "leprous sore"] (NKJV, NRSV). The same meaning of "all kinds," "various kinds," "every [different] kind" is found in 1 Chronicles 6:48; 12:37; 28:14; 29:5.

In the Gospels, "all manner of sickness [or: disease]" (Matthew 4:23; 10:1, KJV) is translated as "every kind of" sickness and disease in the contemporary versions; and the expression "all manner of sin" (Matthew 12:31) is rendered "every sin" by the NCV, NIV, NKJV, NLT, and NRSV.

In some cases, real differences of meaning may be inferred between the periphrastic "manner of" and the simple translation. "Two manner of people" (Genesis 25:23, KJV) means something quite different from "two peoples," which is how the majority of contemporary translations render the phrase. "No manner of similitude" in Deuteronomy 4:15 is translated "no form" by the NIV, NKJV, NRSV, and RSV.

The Jews' question concerning Jesus' meaning (John 7:36) and Jesus' question to the two disciples walking to Emmaus (Luke 24:17) are complicated by the KJV's insertion of the word "manner." In 1 Peter 1:15, "be holy in all manner of conversation" (KJV) falls short of the more direct translation, "be holy in all your conduct" (NKJV).

In Revelation 18:12 (KJV), "all manner vessels" occurs twice and is an archaism inherited from Tyndale, who spelled it "almanner vessels."

MANSIONS

Today, a mansion is a large and luxurious house with many rooms. But the word "mansion," as used by Tyndale and the KJV, had no reference to this kind of house. It meant simply "a place to stay," "a place of abode." The Greek word which it translates is *mone*, which comes from the verb *meno*, "to stay or abide." The Latin noun is *mansio*, from the verb *maneo*, which means "to stay or abide."

In John 14:2, Jesus simply promised to his disciples a place to dwell in his Father's house, "rooms" (CEV, NCV, NIV, NLT, RSV), or "dwelling places" (NASB, NRSV) rather than stately homes. The NKJV retains "mansions."

The word *mone* is also used in John 14:23, and here the KJV (and NASB) translate it "abode," and most of the other contemporary versions have "home": "My Father will love them, and we will come to them and make our home with them" (NRSV).

MANY ARE CALLED, BUT FEW ARE CHOSEN

The expression "many are called, but few are chosen" is sometimes used in con-

temporary English to mean that although there are a large number of people who want to have the qualifications to belong to a particular group, only a few actually have the good fortune to do so. The expression derives from Matthew 20:16, (KJV), the conclusion of the parable to the laborers in the vineyard, "So the last shall be first, and the first last: for many be called, but few chosen," and Matthew 22:14 (KJV), the conclusion of the parable of the wedding banquet, "For many are called, but few are chosen."

Of the contemporary versions, the NKJV is the only translation to include the phrase at Matthew 20:16: "For many are called, but few chosen" (the NRSV footnote has: "other ancient authorities add *for many are called but few are chosen*"). At Matthew 22:14 out of the contemporary versions, the NASB, NKJV, NLT, NRSV, and RSV retain the KJV rendering; the NIV has "For many are invited, but few are chosen"; the CEV, "Many are invited, but only a few are chosen" and the NCV, "Yes, many people are invited, but only a few are chosen." (See also CHOSEN FEW)

MAR

This is no longer a very common word in contemporary English, although the phrase "make or mar" is still in use, and celebrations and happiness can still be marred in the OED sense of "to spoil, injure, or harm." In the sixteenth to eighteenth centuries "mar" was a heavy, fatal word meaning "to damage beyond repair," "to ruin."

The only Old Testament occurrence where "mar" is retained in a number of contemporary translations is the description of the Suffering Servant in Isaiah 52:14. The KJV's "his visage was so marred" is translated as "marred" by the NASB, NKJV, NRSV, and RSV; the NIV has "his appearance was so disfigured," but retains "and his form marred" in the second half of the verse. The NLT also has "disfigured," while the CEV has "he no longer looked human" and NCV translates "marred" as "he did not look like a man."

The NRSV and the RSV retain "mar" in

Leviticus 19:27, where the KJV has "neither shalt thou mar the corners of thy beard"; other contemporary translations use more practical words for beard-trimming such as "cut" (NCV), "clip off" (NIV), although NKJV keeps closer to KJV with "disfigure."

The NIV and NKJV translate Jeremiah 18:4 as "the clay was marred," but the NASB, NRSV, and RSV use "spoiled" and the NCV has "something went wrong."

Elsewhere "mar" has to be replaced by more sombre terms which convey the ruinous connotation of the word "better" in contemporary English: in 1 Samuel 6:5, for the KJV "mar the land," most translations have "ravage the land" (the CEV has "wiping out," the NCV "ruining," and the NIV "destroying"). In 2 Kings 3:19, Nahum 2:2, Jeremiah 13:7, and Jeremiah 13:9, "mar" is translated as "ruin," "spoil," or "destroy" by almost all the contemporary versions.

The contemporary versions are closer to the Hebrew than the KJV when they translate Job 30:13 as "break up my path" (NASB, NKJV, NRSV, RSV; KJV, "mar my path"), and give Ruth 4:6 (KJV, "I mar mine own inheritance") a feeling of risk. The CEV has "make problems with the property"; the NASB, "jeopardize my own inheritance"; the NCV, "harm"; the NKJV, "ruin"; the NIV, "endanger"; the NRSV, "damaging"; and the RSV, "impair."

The KJV's translation of Mark 2:22 as "the wine is spilled, and the bottles will be marred" is altered by the contemporary versions in two broad groups (with minor stylistic variations): either (NASB, NRSV, RSV) as "the wine is lost and so are the skins" (NASB, "and the skins as well"), or "the wineskins will be (would be, are) ruined" (CEV, NCV, NIV, NKJV; the NLT has "spilling the wine and ruining the skins").

MARK/CURSE OF CAIN

These two expressions were derived from the judgment of God on Cain after he killed Abel. "The mark of Cain" is a stain on one's reputation caused by a crime which one has committed. The expression refers to the protective mark which God gave Cain to prevent him from being killed himself: "And the LORD set a mark upon Cain, lest any finding him should kill him" (Genesis 4:15, KJV).

The CEV, NCV, NIV, NKJV, NLT, and NRSV retain the expression "mark"; the NASB has "The LORD appointed a sign for Cain" (with "Or *set a mark on*" in a footnote).

"The curse of Cain" is the fate of someone who is forced to lead a fugitive life, wandering restlessly from place to place. This expression derives from the punishment mentioned in Genesis 4:11–12: "And now art thou cursed from the earth, which hath opened her mouth to receive thy brother's blood from thy hand; When thou tillest the ground, it shall not henceforth yield unto thee her strength; a fugitive and a vagabond shalt thou be in the earth" (KJV).

All the contemporary versions except the NLT use the word "curse" in verse 11, with the NASB, NCV, NKJV, NRSV, and RSV following the KJV with the verb "cursed" and the CEV and NIV using the phrase "under a curse." The NLT has for these verses, "You are hereby banished from the ground you have defiled with your brother's blood. No longer will it yield abundant crops for you, no matter how hard you work! From now on you will be a homeless fugitive on the earth, constantly wandering from place to place."

In literature, the protective mark of Cain is sometimes associated with the curse or brand of Cain and is thought of as a crimson brand on Cain's brow, e.g., Shelley in *Adonais*, the elegy on the death of Keats (1821), as a mourner, asked by Urania who he is:

> "He answered not, but with a sudden hand
> Made bare his branded and ensanguined brow,
> Which was like Cain's . . ."

MARTHA

The name "Martha" is sometimes used of a woman who is busily occupied with domestic matters, especially preparing meals, in contrast to a "Mary," a woman who leads a quieter, more contemplative life. Mary and Martha were two sisters who were friends of Jesus. On one occasion at Martha's home (Luke 10:38–42), Mary sat at Jesus' feet, listening to his words, while Martha was actively bustling away, preparing a meal.

The KJV has that "Martha was cumbered about much serving"; the contemporary versions render this as "Martha was distracted with much serving" (NKJV, RSV), "Martha was distracted with all her preparations" (NASB), "Martha was distracted by all the preparations that had to be made" (NIV), "Martha was distracted by her many tasks" (NRSV), "Martha was worried about all that had to be done" (CEV), "Martha was busy with all the work to be done" (NCV), and "Martha was worrying over the big dinner she was preparing" (NLT).

Martha's complaint about Mary's inactivity met with a gentle rebuke from Jesus: "Martha, Martha, thou art careful and troubled about many things: But one thing is needful: and Mary hath chosen that good part, which shall not be taken away from her" (KJV), "You are worried and upset about many [CEV, "so many"] things" (CEV, NCV, NIV); "but only one thing is necessary" (CEV, NASB); Mary has chosen what is "better" (NCV, NIV, NRSV).

For Martha's complaint and Jesus' reply, the NLT has "She [Martha] came to Jesus and said, 'Lord, doesn't it seem unfair to you that my sister just sits here while I do all the work? Tell her to come and help me.' But the Lord said to her, 'My dear Martha, you are so upset over all these details! There is really only one thing worth being concerned about. Mary has discovered it—and I won't take it away from her' " (Luke 10:40–42).

MASTER

In the Old Testament, the Hebrew word 'adon is translated one hundred times in the KJV by "master" and 215 times by "lord." There is general agreement on these two renderings between the KJV and contemporary translations. Two difficult texts call for mention.

In the KJV, Ecclesiastes 12:11 reads, "The words of the wise are as goads, and as nails fastened by the masters of assemblies, which are given from one shepherd." Most contemporary translations, including that of the Jewish Publication Society, abandon the rabbinical rendering "masters of assemblies." Several, however, keep the general idea of "assembly" by the use of the phrase "collected sayings" (NIV, NLT, NRSV); with the phrase "masters of these collections are like well-driven nails"; the NASB includes the senses of both "masters" and "assemblies."

Malachi 2:12 reads in the KJV: "The LORD will cut off the man that doeth this, the master and the scholar, out of the tabernacles of Jacob, and him that offereth an offering unto the LORD of hosts." Here most modern translations reject the rendering "the master and the scholar," but include its general meaning of "inclusiveness" with words or phrases such as "everyone" (NASB), "whoever he may be" (NIV), "every last man" (NLT), and "any to witness or answer" (NRSV).

In the Gospels the word "Master," as applied to Jesus, stands for the Greek word *epistates* (seven times), "rabbi" (eight times), and *didaskalos* (forty-one times). All the contemporary versions remove ambiguity by translating *didaskalos* as "teacher." In John 13:13–14, the KJV's "Master and Lord" is rendered "Teacher and Lord," and in Matthew 10:24, "The disciple is not above his master, nor the servant above his lord" (KJV) is generally translated "not above [his] teacher, nor . . . above [his] master." (See TEACHER)

MATTER

The noun "matter" is used today mainly to refer to a subject, task, situation, or event. It occurs less frequently to indicate a literal substance ("printed matter," i.e., books, newspapers, etc.; "particles of matter"; "vegetable matter"). In the KJV the word occurs mostly in the sense of "subject," "task," "situation," or "event."

It occurs once in the literal sense of "the substance of which a thing is made," in James 3:5, to indicate forest, timber, or fuel: "Even so the tongue is a little member, and boasteth great things. Behold, how great a matter a little fire kindleth!" All the contemporary versions render the KJV "matter" as "forest," e.g., NKJV, "See how great a forest a little fire kindles!"

Chaucer used the word in this sense in *Parson's Tale:*

"But for youre synne ye be woxe thral, and foul, and membres of the feend, hate of aungels, sclaunder of holy chirche, and food of the fals serpent, perpetuel matier of the fuyr of helle."

MAUL

"Maul" is now used mainly as a verb, the noun having only a technical meaning as a heavy wooden hammer used in industry. The noun occurs only once in the KJV, in Proverbs 25:18: "A man that beareth false witness against his neighbour is a maul, and a sword, and a sharp arrow." Here, "maul" means the same as "mace," which is defined by the OED as "a heavy staff or club, either entirely of metal or having a metal head, often spiked; formerly a regular weapon of war."

Giant Maul, in Bunyan's *Pilgrim's Progress,* was armed with a club, which is the word used by the contemporary versions in Proverbs 25:18. With "maul" now confined to industrial use and "mace" associated with the pageantry of public office and academic processions, neither word is now a suitable translation of the Hebrew.

The Hebrew word *mephits* also appears in Nahum 2:1, where the KJV translates it

as "he that dasheth in pieces." Several contemporary translations have minor variations on "the one who scatters" (CEV, NASB, NKJV), and others have "destroyer" (NCV), "attacker" (NIV), and "shatterer" (NRSV). With different pointing, it can may be read as *mappets,* which appears in the KJV of Jeremiah 51:20 as "battle axe" and in most contemporary translations as "war club," the definition given in the Hebrew dictionary.

MAUNDY THURSDAY

Maundy Thursday is the name given to the Thursday before Easter, which commemorates Christ's Last Supper with His disciples. The name comes from the Old French word *mandé,* meaning "commanded"; this word in turn comes from the Latin *mandatum,* or "commandment," which occurs in the Latin translation of Christ's words in John 13:34: *"Mandatum novum do vobis"*— "A new commandment I give unto you." This new commandment was "that ye love one another as I have loved you," and had been shown by Jesus' washing of his disciples' feet.

Tradition has it that on Maundy Thursday the reigning British monarch presents specially minted coins to a number of elderly people (one man and one woman for each year of his or her life) in a chosen cathedral city. Originally the monarch washed the feet of a few poor people and then distributed food and clothes, but the former custom was discontinued and the latter was replaced by the giving of money.

MAW

In current formal or literary English, the word "maw" is used to refer to an animal's mouth or throat or something that seems to swallow things up completely. The word occurs once in the KJV, in Deuteronomy 18:3, in the sense of "an animal's stomach": "And this shall be the priest's due from the people, from them that offer a sacrifice, whether it be ox or sheep; and they shall give unto the priest the shoulder, and the two cheeks, and the maw."

All the contemporary versions except the NCV and NIV render the KJV "maw" as "stomach"; the NCV translates the word as "inner organs," the NIV, "inner parts."

The OED dates the word in the sense of "stomach" from about 725; e.g., Chaucer in *Man of Law's Tale:*

> "Who kepte Jonas in the fisches
>   mawe,
> Til he was spouted up at Nineve?"

MEAN

In contemporary English, the most common use of "mean" is in the accusation of someone being nasty and small-minded, or penny-pinching. The seventeenth-century adjective was nearer to today's less common use of "mean" as something average, halfway between two extremes, and so "common," "ordinary," "undistinguished." "Greenwich Mean Time" is the standard, ordinary time in England, based on the particular longitude line on which Greenwich is situated.

The "mean man" of Isaiah 2:9, 5:15, and 31:8 means simply "man"—man in general, the ordinary, common man. The Hebrew text of these verses has no such adjective; the word for "man" is simply *'adam,* the generic word for "mankind." The more specific word for "a man" is *'ish,* which is related to *'adam* in much the same way as the Latin *vir* is related to *homo.*

The prior English translations did not use the adjective "mean" in these verses; that was an addition made by the KJV translators, who meant by it simply "common"; for them "the mean man" was not nasty or penny-pinching. In each of these three verses of Isaiah both *'adam* and *'ish* are used in parallel constructions, and the KJV makes a distinction which is not there in the Hebrew, by using "mean man" for *'adam,* and "great man" (2:9) or "mighty man" (5:15; 31:8) for *ish.*

Most contemporary versions of these

three verses have simply "man" (NIV) or "people" (NRSV), although the NASB echoes the KJV with its use of "the common man" in Isaiah 2:9 and 5:15.

None of the contemporary translations preserves the KJV's use of "mean" in Proverbs 22:29: "Seest thou a man diligent in his business? he shall stand before kings; he shall not stand before mean men." The Hebrew text has an adjective which means "obscure," which the contemporary versions translate as "obscure" (NASB, NIV, RSV), "ordinary" (NCV, NLT), "unknown" (NKJV), or "common" (NRSV).

One of the happy innovations of the KJV is Paul's claim to be a citizen of "no mean city" (Acts 21:39). This is an admirable translation of the Greek, which means literally "a not unknown city." Tyndale, the Great Bible, and the Bishops' Bible had "of no vyle citie"; the NKJV and RSV retain "of no mean city," the NASB has "no insignificant city," and the NIV, "no ordinary city." The other contemporary translations (CEV, NCV, NLT, NRSV) make the phrase positive and call Tarsus an "important city."

MEASURE FOR MEASURE

The expression "measure for measure" is the title of Shakespeare's tragi-comedy, printed in 1623. The title alludes to Matthew 7:2, "For with what judgment ye judge, ye shall be judged: and with what measure ye mete, it shall be measured to you again" (KJV).

The noun "measure" in this verse in the contemporary versions is generally retained (NIV, NKJV, NLT, NRSV) or rendered as "standard of measure" (NASB); the verb "measure" is used by the NIV and NKJV. Variants include, "God will be as hard on you as you are on others! He will treat you exactly as you treat them" (CEV)

As noted in *A Dictionary of Biblical Tradition in English Literature,* "By Shakespeare's day the phrase 'measure for measure' (or 'meed for meed') had acquired proverbial status and was applied in a variety of contexts with different meanings . . . 'measure for measure' often carried the sense of a violent, exactly matching revenge: in *3 Henry 6* (II, 6, 55), 'measure for measure must be answered' refers to an order that Clifford's head be set up on the gates of York in reprisal for Clifford's having placed the Duke of York's head there.

"Similarly, at the end of *Titus Andronicus,* Lucio cries out, 'Can the son's eye behold his father bleed? / There's meed for meed, death for a deadly deed,' as he kills Saturninus, who has just killed Titus (V, 3, 65–66). In *Measure for Measure* (5.1.405–409) the words of the title occur in the dialogue during the last act, at a point where the Duke is pronouncing judgment on his corrupted deputy, Angelo:

> The very mercy of the law cries out
> Most audible, even from his
>   proper tongue:
> 'An Angelo for Claudio; death for
>   death.
> Haste still pays haste, and leisure
>   answers leisure;
> Like doth quit like, and Measure
>   still for Measure.'

"The Duke's comment at this climactic moment has two functions: first, to emphasize the exact justice which he apparently intends to exercise in the punishment of his deputy, an expected letter-of-the-law justice, which Angelo, now completely exposed, willingly embraces; and second, to provide a trial or test for the attitudes of Mariana and Isabella: Is this the kind of justice they desire?

"Earlier in the play Shakespeare has Isabella remind Angelo of each individual's need for something more than mere judgment—indeed, for mercy: 'How would you be, if He, which is the top of judgment, should but judge you as you are?' (II, 2, 77). It is this larger and more merciful concept of justice, dependent not upon equally weighted retribution but upon recognition, self-awareness, and forgiveness, which

prevails in the conclusion of the play." (See METEYARD, METE)

MEAT

Today the word "meat" is limited to the flesh of animals used for food. Only our Christmas mincemeat preserves the KJV use of the word for food in general, "anything used as nourishment." It is applied especially to solid food, to what people eat in contrast to what they drink. The clause in Habakkuk 3:17, "the fields shall yield no meat," means that the fields yield no food. Meat is also generally translated as "food" in Psalm 145:15; Ezekiel 47:12; and Matthew 6:25.

When Jesus is described in Mark 7:19 as "purging all meats," it means that he "declared all foods clean" (NASB, NIV, NRSV, RSV; CEV has "all foods were fit to eat;" NCV, "no longer was any food unclean"; and NLT, "every kind of food is acceptable"). The disciples left Jesus at Jacob's well and went into Samaria "to buy meat" (John 4:8, KJV), that is, food; and when they returned he told them, "I have food [KJV, "meat"] to eat that you do not know about" (John 4:32, NRSV).

When Jesus revealed himself to his disciples at the Sea of Tiberias, the food in his question in the KJV, "Have ye any meat?" is better translated by the contemporary versions as "fish" (John 21:5). The sixteenth-century translators apparently did not know that the Greek noun in this question was constantly used for fish, the chief delicacy of the Athenians.

The meat offering which is mentioned more than one hundred times in the KJV Old Testament actually contained no flesh; it was meat in the sense of "food" and consisted of fine flour or meal, and oil. In most contemporary versions, it is a grain offering (see, for example, Leviticus 2:1 in NASB, NCV, NIV, NKJV, NLT, and NRSV); the RSV has "cereal offering."

The prostitution of this offering to the worship of idols is the burden of God's accusation of Jerusalem in Ezekiel 16:19, KJV:

"My meat also which I gave thee, fine flour, and oil, and honey, wherewith I fed thee, thou hast even set it before them for a sweet savour." This is variously translated as "food" (NIV, NKJV) or "bread" (NASB, NCV, NRSV, RSV); the CEV and NLT omit it altogether.

MEET

The word "meet" is most commonly used in contemporary English as a verb meaning "to come face to face with"; "to come together"; "to join"; "to settle or fulfill." In contemporary English the word occurs only as an adjective meaning "suitable or right."

In the KJV the word occurs as a verb in the sense that we are familiar with. There are several examples of its use as an adjective, of which perhaps the most well-known is Genesis 2:18: "And the LORD God said, It is not good that the man should be alone; I will make him an help meet for him." (See HELPMEET)

Some other examples are: "If any man therefore purge himself from these, he shall be a vessel unto honour, sanctified, and meet for the master's use, and prepared unto every good work" (2 Timothy 2:21, KJV), rendered as "useful to the Master" (NASB, NCV, NIV, NKJV), "useful to the owner of the house" (CEV), and "ready for the Master to use" (NLT);

"Even as it is meet for me to think this of you all, because I have you in my heart; inasmuch as both in my bonds, and in the defence and confirmation of the gospel, ye all are partakers of my grace" (Philippians 1:7, KJV), where the KJV "meet" is "right" (NASB, NCV, NIV, NKJV, NLT, NRSV) and "only natural" (CEV): "You have a special place in my heart. So it is only natural for me to feel the way I do";

"But Jesus said unto her, Let the children first be filled: for it is not meet to take the children's bread, and to cast it unto the dogs" (Mark 7:27, KJV) where the KJV "meet" is rendered "right" (CEV, NCV, NIV, NLT),

"fair" (NRSV), "good" (NASB, NKJV), and "proper" (NASB, footnote);

"It was meet that we should make merry, and be glad: for this thy brother was dead, and is alive again; and was lost, and is found" (Luke 15:32, KJV), rendered as "But we had to celebrate" (NASB, NCV, NIV, NLT, NRSV), "We should be glad and celebrate!" (CEV), and "It was right that we should make merry" (NKJV);

"Bring forth therefore fruits meet for repentance" (Matthew 3:8, KJV), where the KJV "meet for" is rendered "in keeping with" (NASB, NIV) and "worthy of" (NKJV, NRSV); the CEV has "Do something to show that you have really given up your sins" and the NLT, "Prove by the way you live that you have really turned from your sins and turned to God";

"Giving thanks unto the Father, which hath made us meet to be partakers of the inheritance of the saints in light" (Colossians 1:12, KJV), where the KJV is rendered "qualified . . . to share" (NASB, NIV, NLT, NRSV, RSV) and "qualified to be partakers" (NKJV); the CEV has "I pray that you will be grateful to God for letting you have part in what he has promised his people in the kingdom of light" and the NCV, "And you will joyfully give thanks to the Father who has made you able to have a share in all that he has prepared for his people in the kingdom of light";

"Look even out the best and meetest of your master's sons, and set him on his father's throne, and fight for your master's house" (2 Kings 10:3) where the KJV "best and meetest" is rendered "best and most worthy" (NCV, NIV), "best qualified" (NKJV, NLT, NRSV), "best and fittest" (NASB), and simply "best" (CEV).

MEMORIAL

In contemporary English, the word "memorial" is used almost exclusively for an activity that remembers or honors the dead, for example, a memorial service, a memorial garden, or a war memorial. In the seventeenth century the noun was used not only in this way, to preserve the memory of a person, thing or event, but also for an act of commemoration, and even for memory itself.

God's word to the people of Israel through Moses (Exodus 3:15), "this is my name for ever, and this is my memorial unto all generations" (KJV), tells them that this is how God is to be remembered throughout all generations. The NRSV has "this [is] my title;" the NASB has "memorial-name," and the NIV, "the name by which I am to be remembered."

"The LORD is his memorial" (Hosea 12:5, KJV) reminds the Israelites to remember the name of the Lord and his power. In the NIV this is translated as "name of renown" and in the NKJV as "memorable name."

The censers used by the rebellious Korah and his company were hammered out into plates as a covering for the altar, not as a "memorial" (KJV) to the sinners but as an ever-present "reminder" (thus NASB and NRSV; NCV and NIV "to remind"; the CEV has "warning") that no person who is not a priest should burn incense before the Lord (Numbers 16:40). In place of "memorial" in Esther 9:28 (KJV), the NRSV has "commemoration," while most other contemporary translations have "memory." In Psalm 135:13, the NIV, NRSV, and RSV translate the KJV's "memorial" as "renown," while the CEV has "he will be famous," the NASB, "remembrance," the NCV, "you will be remembered," and the NKJV and NLT, "fame." "Their memorial" in Psalm 9:6 (KJV) becomes "the very memory" in the NASB and RSV, and in the NIV, NKJV, and NLT, "even the [NKJV, "their"] memory."

In the KJV, Jesus' comment on the action of the woman who poured costly ointment on his head closes with the words: "Wheresoever this gospel shall be preached throughout the whole world, this also that she hath done shall be spoken of for a memorial of her." The NRSV translates it "wherever the good news is proclaimed in the whole world, what she has done will be told in remembrance of her" (Mark 14:9 and its parallel, Matthew 26:13). The NASB, NIV, and RSV have "in memory of her"; NKJV has "as a memorial"; and NLT, "in her memory."

MERCHANTMEN

This is a word used today only for the old cargo sailing ships, rather than for the men who sailed in them. It is an archaic word for "merchants," which occurs in the KJV in Genesis 37:28 for the Midianites who bought Joseph, and in 1 Kings 10:15 for the traders who provided revenue for King Solomon and are called "chapmen" in 2 Chronicles 9:14. (See CHAPMEN)

The Hebrew terms translated "merchantmen" denote men who travel for the purpose of buying and selling; the word used for the traders of Solomon's empire carries the further connotation of "seeking," "spying out," "exploring for profitable ventures." This use of "merchantmen" is in line with the early restriction of the word "merchant" to wholesale traders, especially those dealing with foreign countries. The contemporary versions render both "merchantmen" and "chapmen" interchangeably as "merchants" and "traders."

In Matthew 13.45 the KJV's "merchant man, seeking goodly pearls" represents two words in the reverse order—"man merchant"—in the Greek text used by the KJV translators. But the best ancient Greek manuscripts do not have the word for "man," and the majority of contemporary versions translate simply as "merchant."

MERCY, MERCIES, MERCIFUL

These words appear 355 times in the KJV. The Hebrew and Greek terms thus translated emphasize the compassion, pity, forbearance, forgiveness, or kindness shown by the merciful rather than the guilt or lack of deserving on the part of those to whom mercy is extended. Characteristic texts are Jesus' injunction, "Be ye therefore merciful, as your Father also is merciful" (Luke

6:36, KJV) and the lawyer's description of the good "Samaritan as He that shewed mercy on him" (Luke 10:37, KJV).

In many instances, the contemporary translations do not use the word "mercy" when it appears in the KJV. This is because the original Hebrew word being translated is *ḥesed*. The KJV uses "mercy" for this word 178 times, but in 163 of these cases *ḥesed* denotes a basic attribute of God in relation to his chosen people, for which "mercy" is a partial but inadequate term.

In Exodus 20:6 (paralleled in Deuteronomy 5:10), the contemporary versions use "kind" (CEV), "lovingkindness" (NASB), "kindness" (NCV), "love" (NIV, NLT), and "steadfast love" (NRSV); the NKJV retains "mercy." In Psalm 23, perhaps influenced by the familiarity of the version in the Book of Common Prayer, the NKJV and NRSV retain "mercy" in the phrase "Surely goodness and mercy shall follow me"; however, other contemporary translations replace "mercy" with "lovingkindness" and "[unfailing] love." (See LOVINGKINDNESS)

Where *ḥesed* is used to denote human attitudes and behavior, it is best translated by "kindness," "loyalty," or "faithfulness." Jonah 2:8 (KJV) has "They that observe lying vanities forsake their own mercy"; the contemporary versions translate this as "forsake their faithfulness" (NASB), "give up their loyalty" (NCV), "forfeit the grace" (NIV), "turn their backs on all God's mercies" (NLT), and "forsake their true loyalty" (NRSV).

The translations are divided when they deal with the great summary of human duty in Micah 6:8, which in the KJV reads, "He hath shewed thee, O man, what is good; and what doth the LORD require of thee, but to do justly, and to love mercy, and to walk humbly with thy God?" The CEV, NIV, NKJV, and NLT retain "mercy"; the other contemporary versions have "kindness."

In Deuteronomy 21:8 and 32:43 the KJV has "be merciful unto" for the Hebrew verb which means "forgive," "atone for." The contemporary versions translate this with words relating to atonement, absolution, and forgiveness.

Three other Hebrew verbs and three groups of Greek words are translated by "mercy" or "be merciful" both in the KJV and the majority of the contemporary versions (though in Exodus 33:19, the NASB and NKJV use "compassion" instead).

MESS

We may be accustomed to thinking of a mess only as extreme untidiness or disorder in homes and lives, but the archaic term for "a portion, or serving, of food" is still in colloquial use. When the KJV says in Genesis 43:34 that Joseph "sent messes" to his brothers, these were portions from his own table which he sent to his brothers, who could not sit with him at Pharaoh's table. When David in 2 Samuel 11:8 told Uriah to go to his home, he sent a present after him. The KJV describes this gift as "a mess of meat," but there is no indication in the Hebrew that the gift was a portion of food, although the NKJV translates it as "a gift of food" and CEV has "dinner."

The other contemporary versions translate the word simply as "gift" or "present," and "gifts" is the translation given by the KJV and all the versions when the same Hebrew word appears in Esther 2:18: King Ahasuerus, celebrating Queen Esther's coronation, "made a release to the provinces, and gave gifts" (KJV).

Interestingly, the well-worn phrase "a mess of pottage" does not, in fact, appear in the biblical account of Esau's sale of his birthright (Genesis 25:29–34) or in the reference to it in Hebrews 12:16. (See SELL HIS BIRTHRIGHT)

METEYARD, METE

"Meteyard" appears once in the KJV, in Leviticus 19:35: "Ye shall do no unrighteousness in judgment, in meteyard, in weight, or in measure." At first sight, this may seem a totally unfamiliar and obsolete word, but the still-familiar phrase "mete out punishment" comes from the same verb, meaning "to measure." So "mete-yard" and its associated word "metewand" both refer to a rod used to measure length, and that is how "meteyard" is translated in the contemporary versions: as "measuring length" (NIV, NLT, NRSV) and "in measurement of length" (NKJV). The KJV rendering of this verse goes back to Tyndale. In the preface to the KJV, the translators used the word "meteyard" in the section on "The unwillingness of our chief Adversaries, that the Scriptures should be divulged in the mother tongue." They said: "This seemeth to argue a bad cause, or a bad conscience, or both. Sure we are, that it is not he that hath good gold, that is afraid to bring it to the touchstone, but he that hath the counterfeit; neither is it the true man that shunneth the light, but the malefactor, lest his deeds should be reproved: neither is it the plaindealing Merchant that is unwilling to have the weights or the meteyard brought in place, but he that useth deceit."

The now archaic verb "mete" meaning "to measure" is generally translated with the verb "measure" in the contemporary versions, e.g., Exodus 16:8, "And when they did mete it [manna] with an omer, he that gathered much had nothing over, and he that gathered little had no lack; they gathered every man according to his eating," where the NASB, NCV, NIV, NKJV, and NRSV have "measured" for the KJV "did mete."

In Isaiah 40:12, "Who hath measured the waters in the hollow of his hand, and meted out heaven with the span, and comprehended the dust of the earth in a measure, and weighed the mountains in scales, and the hills in a balance?" the contemporary versions render the KJV "meted out" as "marked off" (NASB, NIV, NRSV), "measured" (NKJV), "measured off" (NLT), "measure" (NCV), and "stretch out" (CEV).

It occurs three times in the New Testament, "with what measure ye mete" (Matthew 7:2; Mark 4:24) and "with the same measure that ye mete" (Luke 6:28). The

contemporary versions render these, e.g., "with the measure [NLT, "whatever measure"] you use" (Matthew 7:2, NIV, NKJV, NLT), and "the measure you give" (Matthew 7:2, NRSV, RSV). (See MEASURE FOR MEASURE)

METHUSELAH

A "methuselah" is a size of bottle equivalent to eight standard wine bottles, about six liters, named in allusion to Methuselah, son of Enoch and grandfather of Noah, who lived to a great age of 969 years (Genesis 5:27). The expression, "as old as Methuselah," meaning "extremely old," refers to the age of this Old Testament patriarch. (See BALTHAZAR; JEROBOAM; NEBUCHADNEZZAR)

MIGHTY FALLEN, HOW ARE THE

The phrase "how are the mighty fallen" is sometimes used in contemporary English to refer to a great decline in importance or wealth or a serious lapse into sin by someone powerful and influential. The origin of the phrase is in David's lament over the deaths of Saul and Jonathan in battle. The expression occurs three times in 2 Samuel 1, in verses 19, 25, and 27.

The contemporary versions generally use the adjective "mighty" (the CEV has "warriors," the NLT "mighty heroes") and all use the verb "fallen"; e.g., verse 25, NKJV, "How the mighty have fallen in the midst of the battle!"

MILLSTONE AROUND ONE'S NECK

In contemporary English the expression to have "a millstone around your neck" is used to refer to something that is a great burden, causing a lot of problems, and from which you cannot escape.

This figurative application is suggested by the usage in Matthew 18:6: "But whoso shall offend one of these little ones which believe in me, it were better for him that a millstone were hanged about his neck, and that he were drowned in the depth of the sea" (KJV). The millstone referred to here is the heavy top stone of two stones between which grain is crushed, and which is drawn by a donkey. (This is in contrast with the much smaller hand-mill referred to in Matthew 24:41.) See also Mark 9:42 and Luke 17:2.

At Matthew 18:6, the contemporary versions render the KJV "millstone" (retained by the NKJV) as: "a large millstone" (NIV, NLT), "a great millstone" (NRSV, RSV), "a heavy millstone" (NASB), "a heavy stone" (CEV), "a large stone" (NCV).

In the middle of the heavy millstone was a hole through which the grain was poured, to be crushed between the two stones. The hole could therefore be used to hang the millstone around someone's neck—and so drown someone beyond any hope of escape. So grave is the sin of causing one of God's children to sin that it would be better for such a person to have the large heavy millstone hung around his or her neck and to be thrown into the sea.

MINISH

This is an archaic word meaning "to make or become less." When Pharaoh commands in Exodus 5:6–19 that the Hebrew people should be given no straw for the making of bricks, but should still make and deliver the same number of bricks, the KJV reads in verse 8, "ye shall not diminish ought thereof"; and in verse 19, "Ye shall not minish ought from your bricks of your daily task." The Hebrew verb is the same in these two verses.

The NASB, NIV, and NKJV translate the verb as "reduce," as does the NLT in verse 8 (although it omits the phrase altogether in v. 19). The NRSV retains "diminish" in verse 8, but uses "lessen" in verse 19; the RSV has "lessen" in both verses. The CEV and NCV make Pharaoh's command positive: "make the same number of bricks" (NCV, v. 19, "make just as many . . . as you did before").

In Psalm 107:39 the KJV uses "minish" intransitively for the Hebrew verb which means "to become small or few." The meaning of the passage is obscured by the KJV translation of verses 39, 40, and 41 as though each were an independent sentence: "they are minished and brought low through oppression, affliction, and sorrow" (v. 39).

The majority of contemporary translations regard verses 39–43 as a strophe and translate verses 39–41 as a single sentence. Some of them (NASB, NKJV, NRSV) retain "diminished" as the verb in verse 39; others translate it as "decreased" (NIV, NLT; NCV, "grew smaller and weaker"; CEV, "only a few . . . are left to survive").

MITE

A "mite" is a copper coin of very small value. The two mites which the poor widow contributed to the temple treasury in Mark 12:42 were two *lepta*, "which make a *kodrantes*" (KJV). This is simply the Greek spelling of the Latin *quadrans*, which was a quarter of an *as*. The *as* had suffered successive devaluations throughout Roman history, and was then worth about two-thirds of a cent. A *lepton* was therefore worth about one twelfth of a cent.

The word "mite" in this context goes back to Tyndale; it is retained by the NKJV ("two mites, which make a quadrans"). The majority of other contemporary translations have "two small [NIV, "two very small"] copper coins," "worth only a few pennies" (CEV), "which amount to a cent" (NASB), "only worth a few cents" (NCV), "worth only a fraction of a penny" (NIV), "worth a penny" (NRSV). In the NLT, the widow simply "dropped in two pennies." The parallel passage at Luke 21:2 has similar translations.

The phrase "widow's mite" has come to refer to the small sum of money that is as much as, or more than, one can afford. The phrase is used in literature, e.g., in *Don Juan* (6.41), Byron speaks of Antony, who gave all for love, and of himself who, when younger, and "had no great plenty," gave all he had—his heart:

"'T was the boy's 'mite,' and, like the
   'widow's', may
Perhaps be weigh'd hereafter, if not
   now."

MOCK

"Mock" means to "deride," "jeer at," "tantalize," or "ridicule" by imitating the speech or action of another. In the sixteenth century it also had a lighter meaning, "to jest, trifle, play, or make sport," without implying that it is at the expense of another." This meaning is now obsolete. The latest example of its use in the sense "to jest, trifle; to make sport" given by the OED is from the KJV, Genesis 19:14, where Lot warned his sons-in-law that Sodom would be destroyed, but "he seemed as one that mocked unto his sons in law." The Hebrew verb is *tsahaq*, which means "to laugh, jest, or play." The contemporary versions translate this sentence as "he appeared [NKJV, "seemed"] . . . to be jesting" [NKJV, "joking"] (NASB, NKJV), they "thought he [NCV, "Lot"] was joking" (NCV, NIV).

From *tsahaq* Abraham derived the name for his son, "Isaac," which means "laughter." It is the verb involved in all that is said about laughing in the accounts of God's promise and its fulfillment in the birth of this son (Genesis 18:9–15; 21:1–7). But in the account of the feast to celebrate the weaning of the young Isaac, this same verb is represented by "mocking"—it is said "that Sarah saw the son of Hagar the Egyptian, which she had born unto Abraham, mocking" (Genesis 21:9).

The KJV translators may have used the term in the innocent sense which is now obsolete, but "playing" would have been a less ambiguous word. In fact, a phrase seems to have been lost from the Hebrew text here, for the Septuagint and the Vulgate have "playing with her son Isaac." Some contemporary translations (CEV, NRSV, RSV) accept this reading, but others (e.g., NASB, NIV, NKJV) retain the sense of "scoffing" or "mocking."

A quite different Hebrew verb is used in Jeremiah 38:19, for which the KJV's translation "mock" is not strong enough: "I am afraid of the Jews that are fallen to the Chaldeans, lest they deliver me into their hand, and they mock me." The contemporary versions translate it as "torture" (CEV), "abuse" (NASB, NKJV, NRSV), "treat badly" (NCV), "mistreat" (NIV).

The KJV also uses "mock" to translate yet another Hebrew verb, which appears in Job 13:9 with reference to God: "Is it good that he should search you out? or as one man mocketh another, do ye so mock him?" The contemporary translations render this "deceive" or "fool," as in "will you deceive Him as one deceives a man?" (NASB).

MODERATION

Today, moderation is particularly connected with eating, drinking, and smoking in quantities which will not be physically harmful. In Paul's exhortation in Philippians 4:5, "Let your moderation be known unto all men," "moderation" is a mistranslation by the KJV of the Greek adjective *epieikeia* which is used here as a noun. The Greek means "gentle," "gracious," "kind," "forbearing," and it is as "gentle" or "gentleness" that it is translated in the contemporary versions.

As a noun it also appears in Acts 24:4, where the KJV translates it as "clemency" and other versions as "kind," "kindness," "courtesy," or "graciousness," and in 2 Corinthians 10:1, where the versions have "gentleness."

As an adjective, the word is found in 1 Timothy 3:3 (KJV, "patient"; contemporary versions, "gentle"), Titus 3:2 and James 2:17 (KJV and the majority of versions, "gentle"; NIV, "considerate"), and 1 Peter 2:18 (KJV, NASB, NKJV, NRSV, "gentle"; CEV, "thoughtful"; NIV, "considerate"; NLT, "reasonable").

MONEY IS THE ROOT OF ALL EVIL

The saying "money is the root of all evil" is a popular misquotation of 1 Timothy

6:10, "For the love of money is the root of all evil: which while some coveted after, they have erred from the faith, and pierced themselves through with many sorrows" (KJV). It is not money itself, but the love of money that is condemned by Paul.

The contemporary versions render this part of 1 Timothy 6:10 as "the love of money is a root of all kinds [NASB, "all sorts"] of evil" (NASB, NIV, NKJV, NRSV); "the love of money causes all kinds of trouble" [NCV, "of evil"] (CEV, NCV); and "For the love of money is at the root of all kinds of evil" (NLT).

MORE

This word is used occasionally by the KJV in the sense of "larger" or "greater." "To the more ye shall give the more inheritance" (Numbers 33:54, KJV) means that the larger (tribe) should have a larger inheritance (thus the contemporary versions). The nations in Deuteronomy 7:17 (KJV) which are "more than I" are the nations which are "greater" (NASB, NKJV), "more powerful" (CEV, NLT), "stronger" (NCV, NIV), and "more numerous" (NRSV). And "A people more than thou" (Deuteronomy 20:1, KJV) is an army larger than your own.

In the New Testament, in the confused assembly in the theater at Ephesus, "the more part" (Acts 19:32, KJV) did not know why they had come together—a group which the majority of contemporary translations render as "most of them." Later in Acts (27:12) the captain and owner of the ship taking Paul to Rome rejected his advice and took the advice of "the more part," meaning the majority.

MORTIFY

"I was totally mortified," wails the anguished and humiliated teenager whose mother has worn the wrong clothes to her daughter's school play. But the original meaning, now obsolete, is "to put to death." Wycliffe's translation of 1 Samuel 2:6 was "The LORD mortifieth, and quykeneth," for which the KJV has "The LORD killeth, and

maketh alive." The KJV has retained "mortify" in Romans 8:13, "if ye through the Spirit do mortify the deeds of the body, ye shall live," which the NASB, NIV, NKJV, and NRSV translate as "put [NASB, "putting"] to death," and other contemporary versions have "say 'No' to your desires" (CEV), "stop doing . . . wrong things" (NCV), and "turn from [the flesh]" (NLT).

At Colossians 3:5, the KJV reads, "Mortify therefore your members which are upon the earth; fornication"; for KJV "mortify" the NIV, NKJV, NLT, NRSV, and RSV have "put to death"; the CEV has "Don't be controlled by your body. Kill every desire for the wrong kind of sex"; the NASB, "Therefore consider the members of your earthly body as dead to . . . immorality"; the NCV, "So put all evil things out of your life: sexual sinning."

MOSES BASKET

A portable, shallow, wickerwork cradle for a baby is sometimes known as a "Moses basket." This expression alludes to the papyrus cradle into which the infant Moses was placed, among the reeds by the River Nile (Exodus 2:3): "And when she could no longer hide him, she took for him an ark of bulrushes, and daubed it with slime and with pitch, and put the child therein; and she laid it in the flags by the river's brink" (KJV).

For the KJV "ark of bulrushes" (retained by the NKJV) the contemporary versions have "a papyrus basket" (NIV, NRSV), "a basket [made] out of reeds" (CEV), "a wicker basket" (NASB), and "a little basket made of papyrus reeds" (NLT).

MOTE

See BEAM IN ONE'S OWN EYE.

MOTIONS

At a formal meeting, motions are the proposals and plans which may be put into action if carried by the voting. In this sense, the word "motions" is clearly related to the verb "move," which occurs often in the

Bible. The nouns "move" or "movement," however, do not appear at all, and the noun "motion" occurs only once, in the plural, and then only in the obsolete sense of "an inward impulse, passion, or emotion."

This solitary appearance is in Romans 7:5, which the KJV translates as: "For when we were in the flesh, the motions of sins, which were by the law, did work in our members to bring forth fruit unto death." The NASB, NIV, NKJV, and NRSV translate "motions of sins" as "sinful passions"; the CEV and NLT have "sinful desires"; and the NCV, "to do sinful things."

In Shakespeare's *Othello* (I, 3, 326), Iago says:

> "If the balance of our lives had not one scale of reason to poise another of sensuality, the blood and baseness of our natures would conduct us to most preposterous conclusions. But we have reason to cool our raging motions, our carnal stings, our unbitted lusts."

In *Cymbeline* (II, 5, 20), Posthumus rails at women:

> "For there's no motion
> That tends to vice in men but I affirm
> It is the woman's part."

MOUNT

The word "mount" occurs nine times in the KJV in the sense of "a military earthwork," an embankment or heaped-up mound of earth or other material, by which the besiegers fought on a level with the besieged. In the contemporary versions the word used in, for example, Jeremiah 6:6 is "mound" (NKJV), "ramp(s)" (CEV, NLT), "attack ramp" (NCV), or "siege ramps" (NIV), and similar translations are found in Ezekiel 4:2; 17:17; 21:22; 26:8; Daniel 11:15. The NASB goes behind the object to its purpose and translates Jeremiah 6:6 as "cast up a siege."

In Jeremiah 32:24; 33:4, the contemporary translations are evenly divided between "siege ramps" and "siege mounds." The KJV also uses "mount" to translate a different Hebrew word in Isaiah 29:3, for which the majority of contemporary translations use the more accurate "towers." The same Hebrew word for "a siege mound" is three times translated in the KJV as "bank" and now rendered "siege mound" or "siege ramp" (2 Samuel 20:15; 2 Kings 19:32; Isaiah 37:33).

The word "mound" does not appear in the KJV. The use of "mount" in this military sense is illustrated by a passage in Bunyan's *Holy War*: "Besides, there were Mounts cast up against it. The Mount *Gracious* was on the one side, and Mount *Justice* was on the other. Further, there were several small banks and advance-grounds, as *Plain-Truth-Hill* and *No-Sin-Banks*, where many of the Slings were placed against the Town."

MOUTHS OF BABES AND SUCKLINGS

The comment "out of the mouths of babes and sucklings" is sometimes made when a young child or uneducated person utters a wise and perceptive remark which adults or supposedly wiser people have not comprehended or which they are not frank enough to express. The source of this quotation is Psalm 8:2: "Out of the mouth of babes and sucklings has thou ordained strength because of thine enemies, that thou mightest still the enemy and the avenger" (KJV).

The contemporary versions render the KJV expression as "Out of the mouth [NRSV, "mouths"] of babes and infants" [NKJV, "nursing infants"] (NKJV, NRSV); "From the mouth of infants and nursing babes" (NASB); "From the lips of children and infants" (NIV); "You have taught children and babies" [NLT, "and nursing infants"] (NCV, NLT); and "With praises from children and from tiny infants" (CEV). See also Matthew 11:25.

MUCH

"Much" is a word that is applied today as an adverb to indicate great extent or intensity ("laugh too much"; "it doesn't matter much"). The same meaning of "a great deal," "a lot of," was also once applied as an adjective to "people," and it is the phrase "much people" (obsolete, according to the OED, since the seventeenth century) which appears twenty-five times in the KJV.

Contemporary versions use a variety of words to describe "much people." In Joshua 11:4 the KJV's wording, "And they went out, they and all their hosts with them, much people, even as the sand that is upon the sea shore in multitude," is rendered "as many people as the sand that is on the seashore" (NKJV, NASB), "a huge army, as numerous as the sand" (NIV), "a great army [RSV, "host"], in number like the sand" (NRSV, RSV), "as many soldiers as grains of sand" (NCV).

In the Gospels, "much people" is generally replaced with "a large crowd" (a literal translation of the Greek), although the NKJV has "a great multitude" in, for example, Mark 5:21.

In Acts 5:37, the contemporary translations differ in their choice of words and do not always convey the sense of "large numbers" contained in the KJV's "much people" in the sentence: "After this a man rose up Judas of Galilee in the days of the taxing, and drew away much people after him." The NKJV retains "many people," and CEV has "a lot of people"; but the NASB and NLT have simply "some people"; NCV has "a group of followers"; NIV, "a band of people"; RSV, "some of the people"; and NRSV, "people."

Other instances in Acts (11:24, 26; 18:10; 19:26) remain closer to the KJV "much people," with phrases such as "many people," "a great many people," "large numbers," "a considerable number." "The great voice of much people in heaven" (Revelation 19:1, KJV) becomes, in the majority of contemporary translations, "a great multitude."

In Paul's letter to Philemon, verse 8, the KJV has "though I might be much bold in Christ to enjoin thee that which is conve-

nient." This is rendered "very bold" by the NKJV, as "bold enough" by the NRSV, and simply as "bold" in other versions.

MUNITION

The word "munition" is a rather dated word used today in the plural for "war-time munitions factories" and virtually replaced by "armaments." In the KJV it is used in the obsolete sense of "a fortification or fortress for the purpose of defense." In Isaiah 33:16, the KJV's "his place of defence shall be the munitions of rocks" becomes in contemporary translations "the fortress [NRSV, "fortresses"] of rocks" (NKJV, NRSV), "the mountain fortress" (NIV), "the impregnable rock" (NASB), "fortress of safety" (NLT), "a high, walled city" (NCV), and "a fortress high on a rocky cliff" (CEV).

In Isaiah 29:7, the KJV "munition" is generally rendered in the contemporary versions as "fortress" or "stronghold." "Keep the munition" in Nahum 2:1 is translated "Guard the ramparts" (NRSV) or "Man the fort!" (NKJV).

MUSE

This word is used by the KJV in the current sense of "meditate" in Psalms 39:3 and 143:5, and the word is retained in Psalm 39:3 by the NASB, NKJV, and NRSV. The NIV uses the verb "meditate"; and in Psalm 143:5, "think about" (NCV, NLT) is also used.

It is used in the now rare sense of "asking oneself some question," "wondering whether or how or what," in Luke 3:15, "all men mused in their hearts of John, whether he were the Christ, or not" (KJV). The contemporary versions generally translate this usage with the verbs "wonder" or "question." Shakespeare uses it in this sense in *King John* (III, 1, 317):

> "I muse your majesty doth seem so cold,
> When such profound respects do pull you on."

NABOTH'S VINEYARD

A "Naboth's vineyard" is a possession that is greatly coveted by someone who has no scruples about obtaining it for himself or herself. The expression alludes to the incident related in 1 Kings 21.

A vineyard (the word adopted by the KJV and all the contemporary translations) belonging to Naboth the Jezreelite lay close to King Ahab's palace. Ahab coveted the vineyard, but Naboth refused to sell it. So Ahab's wife Jezebel undertook to obtain it for him by having Naboth falsely accused of blasphemy and then stoned to death. When Ahab went to take possession of the vineyard, the prophet Elijah met him and pronounced judgment on him and his descendants.

NAME IN VAIN

The phrase "to take someone's name in vain" is sometimes used humorously to refer to mentioning someone's name in an improper or disrespectful way. The expression derives from the third of the Ten Commandments, "Thou shalt not take the name of the LORD thy God in vain; for the LORD will not hold him guiltless that taketh his name in vain" (Exodus 20:7, KJV), to use God's name without due reverence, especially by blaspheming.

Of the contemporary versions, the NASB, NKJV, and RSV have "take the name of the LORD your God in vain"; the NIV and NLT have "not misuse the name of the LORD your God"; the CEV, "Do not misuse my name"; the NRSV, "You shall not make wrongful use of the name of the LORD your God, for the LORD will not acquit anyone who misuses his name"; the NCV, "You must not use the name of the LORD your God thoughtlessly; the LORD will punish anyone who misuses his name."

NAUGHT

This word appears twice in the KJV. It is not a synonym for "nought," which appears thirty-six times. "Nought" is a noun meaning "nothing"; "naught" appears only as an adjective, translating the Hebrew adjective *ra'*, which means "bad" or "evil." When the men of Jericho told Elisha, "the situation of this city is pleasant . . . but the water is naught" (2 Kings 2:19–22), they were not complaining that the city lacked water, but that the water was "bad," which is the translation used in all the contemporary versions.

The second example of "naught" in the KJV is found in Proverbs 20:14: "It is naught, it is naught, saith the buyer." This is variously translated in the contemporary versions: the NASB, NCV, and NRSV have "bad" or "it is bad"; the NKJV has "good for nothing"; the NCV and NIV, "no good"; and NLT, "It's worthless."

The OED cites Pepys' *Diary* (29 October 1661): "We . . . should have been merry, but their wine was so naught . . . that we were not so." Shakespeare uses "naught" in the sense of morally bad in such passages as:

"Beloved Regan, Thy sister's naught."
—*King Lear* (II, 4, 128)

"Theres no trust,
No faith, no honesty in men; all
    perjured,
All forsworn, all naught, all
    dissemblers."
—*Romeo and Juliet* (III, 2, 87)

(See also NOUGHT, SET AT)

NAUGHTINESS, NAUGHTY

Naughtiness today is associated with the minor—though often deliberate—misdeeds of children or, playfully, of adults who behave in a childish way. In the seventeenth century, however, it meant downright "wickedness." The KJV's injunction in James 1:21 to "lay apart all filthiness and superfluity of naughtiness" becomes, in the contemporary versions, getting rid of, or putting aside "wickedness" (NASB, NKJV, NRSV) or "evil" (CEV, NIV, NLT). The "very naughty figs" that

Jeremiah saw in his vision (24:2) were simply very bad, or rotten, figs, "so bad [NIV, "so bad that"] they could not be eaten" (NRSV, NIV).

Shakespeare uses "naughty" frequently; perhaps the best-known example occurs in *The Merchant of Venice* (V, i, 91):

"How far that little candle throws
his beams!
So shines a good deed in a naughty
world."

NEBUCHADNEZZAR

A "nebuchadnezzar" is a size of bottle equivalent to twenty standard wine bottles, about fifteen liters, named in allusion to King Nebuchadnezzar of Babylon (Nebuchadnezzar II, 605–562 B.C.), who took the people of Judah into exile in Babylonia, established the New Babylonian Empire, and built the Hanging Gardens of Babylon. The OED lists citations referring to the bottle size dating from 1913. (See BALTHAZAR; JEROBOAM; METHUSELAH)

NECESSITY

The KJV's rendering of Hebrews 8:3, "For every high priest is ordained to offer gifts and sacrifices: wherefore it is of necessity that this man have somewhat also to offer," reads awkwardly. There are three difficulties:

(1) "Of necessity" is a confusing circumlocution for the simple Greek adjective which means "necessary." (2) The translators of the KJV inserted the word "man" but did not mark it by italics; the Greek has simply the masculine demonstrative pronoun "this," which links "every high priest" at the beginning of the sentence with "this particular high priest," i.e., Jesus, the Son of God, our "great high priest" (4:14; 5:5, 10; 6:20; 7:15—8:2). The inserted word "man" is therefore unnecessary. (3) The Greek word for "also" belongs with "this [high priest]" rather than with "somewhat."

The contemporary versions clarify all three points. The majority of them translate "it is

of necessity" as "it is necessary." "This man" becomes "this one" (NIV; "this One," NKJV) or "this priest" (NRSV; NASB, "this high priest"; NCV, "our high priest," NLT, "our High Priest"). And "also" is clearly attached to "this man" and its variations.

NEEDS

This is an adverb which means "necessarily" or "of necessity"; it was originally the genitive case of the word "need." The expression "must needs" or "needs must" was common speech in the late sixteenth and early seventeenth centuries; it is cited eighty-five times in the *Concordance to Shakespeare*. It survives today in the proverbial expression "Needs must when the devil drives," meaning "There is no way of avoiding something unpleasant." "Must needs" appears fourteen times in the KJV, and in the contemporary versions is generally translated simply as "must" or "it is (was) necessary," as in Genesis 17:13: "He that is born in thy house . . . must needs be circumcised" (KJV) becomes "must be circumcised" in the majority of contemporary versions.

However, the NASB several times prefers to translate "must needs" by a different expression such as "surely" (e.g., in 2 Samuel 14:14, the KJV has "For we must needs die" and the NASB (and also the NKJV) has "For we will surely die") and "it is inevitable" (Matthew 18:7).

Other examples of the use of "must needs" in the KJV include Genesis 24:5; Jeremiah 10:5; Mark 13:7; Luke 14:18; John 4:4; Acts 1:16; 17:3; 21:22; 1 Corinthians 5:10; and 2 Corinthians 11:30. Contemporary renderings include "had to" (e.g., CEV, NASB, NCV, NIV, NLT, NRSV, and RSV for John 4:4; KJV, "he must needs go through Samaria"; CEV, NASB, NIV, and NKJV for Acts 17:3; KJV, "that Christ must needs have suffered"), "must" (Acts 17:3, NCV), "necessary for" (Acts 17:3, NRSV and RSV).

Although no longer common, the adverb "needs" is still used in an ironic sense, implying "foolish or perverse insistence." Such irony is found in Genesis 19:9; the KJV has "he [Lot] will needs be a judge," and this is variously translated in the contemporary versions as "already he is acting like a judge" (NASB; NKJV, "he keeps acting as a judge"), or "he wants to play the judge" (NIV; NRSV, "he would play the judge"). The irony contained in Genesis 31:30 (KJV), "thou wouldest needs be gone," with its overtones of insistence, is not carried over into the contemporary versions, where it is translated simply as "you have indeed gone away" (NASB), "you have gone off" (NIV), "you have surely gone" (NKJV), or "you had to go" (NRSV).

NEESING, NEESED

These are old words for "sneezing" or "to sneeze." "Fnese," "nese," "neese," "neeze," "sneeze" constitute an interesting chapter in the history of words. The OED tells us that "fnese" went out of use in the early fifteenth century. Its place was taken by "nese," a word formed by dropping the initial "f," which was itself later replaced by "snese," a word which may have been felt to represent better the sound of sneezing, or which was formed by misreading or misprinting the initial "f" as a long "s." The Hebrew word is 'atishah, which, like the remarkably similar English "atishoo," is an almost perfect example of matching sound and sense.

As published in 1611 and for 150 years after, the KJV translation of 2 Kings 4:35 was that, when Elisha miraculously restored to life the young son of the woman of Shunem, "the child neesed seven times." This was changed to "sneezed" in 1762, according to Dr. Scrivener. He restored "neesed" in the Cambridge Paragraph Bible of 1873, but the restoration served no useful purpose and has not been followed by other editions. All the contemporary versions have "sneezed."

The plural "neesings" continues to appear in the KJV in the chapter about Leviathan in the book of Job (Job 41:18): "By his neesings a light doth shine." In the majority of the contemporary versions this is given as "sneezings" or "sneezes," or as the verb "sneezes." The NCV and NIV prefer "When it snorts" and "His snorting," respectively.

NEITHER

The word "neither" is familiar in today's English as a determiner or pronoun referring to two nouns, and (perhaps more formally) as an adverb with "nor." In the KJV it is also used as part of a double negative, "not . . . neither . . . neither." An example is 2 Samuel 14:7: "they . . . shall not leave to my husband neither name nor remainder upon the earth." Most of the contemporary versions make this sentence more accessible to today's readers by simply omitting "not"; thus, the NRSV has "they would . . . leave to my husband neither name nor remnant on the face of the earth." Similarly, the rather complex syntax of Genesis 21:26 (KJV: "I wot not who hath done this thing; neither didst thou tell me, neither yet heard I of it, but to day") is simplified in the contemporary versions by replacing "neither" with "not"; for example, "you did not tell me, and I have not heard of it" (NRSV).

Matthew 12:32 in the KJV has a similar sequence of "not . . . neither . . . neither": "whosoever speaketh against the Holy Ghost, it shall not be forgiven him, neither in this world, neither in the world to come," which the majority of contemporary versions translate as "not [CEV, NLT: "never"] . . . either . . . or."

Romans 4:19 in the KJV is based on a Greek text which says that Abraham did not consider the state of his own body or that of Sarah: "And being not weak in faith, he considered not his own body . . . neither yet the deadness of Sara's womb." The contemporary versions are generally based on the more ancient manuscripts, which say that he did. The NRSV, for example, reads: "He did not weaken in faith when he considered his own body . . . or when he considered the barrenness of Sarah's womb."

In two places in the New Testament the

KJV has more complex constructions using "neither": "if thou be not that Christ, nor Elias, neither that prophet" (John 1:25), and "call not thy friends, nor thy brethren, neither thy kinsmen, nor thy rich neighbours" (Luke 14:12). In the first, the majority of the contemporary versions translate "not . . . nor . . . nor" (although the NRSV retains "neither" in "neither the Messiah"); in the second, most of them have "do not invite your friends, [or] your brothers," etc.

NEPHEW

In modern English, at least in the West, the word "nephew" is always restricted to the son of a brother or sister. In the KJV it is used in a wider sense, common in the seventeenth century but now obsolete, meaning "a descendant" and particularly "a grandson." In Judges 12:14, for example, Abdon "had forty sons and thirty nephews" (KJV), which the contemporary versions translate according to the Hebrew, which means "sons of sons," that is, "thirty grandsons."

"If any widow have children or nephews" (1 Timothy 5:4, KJV) means, in the Greek, "If a widow has children or grandchildren," and this is how it is translated in the contemporary versions.

In the wider sense of a descendant, "He shall neither have son nor nephew among his people" (Job 18:19, KJV) is translated as "He has neither son nor posterity among his people" (NKJV; NASB, "no offspring or posterity"); or "no offspring or descendant(s)" (NRSV, NIV). The NLT retains the more restricted meaning of "children and grandchildren."

Similarly, in Isaiah 14:22 (KJV), "nephew" in "name, and remnant, and son, and nephew" becomes "posterity" or "descendants" in the contemporary versions. "Posterity" or "descendants" are also used in Genesis 21:23, where the KJV translates the Hebrew terms specifically: "Now therefore swear unto me here by God that thou wilt not deal falsely with me, nor with my son, nor with my son's son."

NEW JERUSALEM

The expression "the new Jerusalem" is used to refer to heaven or paradise. The phrase derives from Revelation 21:2, "And I John saw the holy city, new Jerusalem, coming down from God out of heaven, prepared as a bride adorned for her husband" (KJV).

The contemporary versions render the expression as the KJV "new Jerusalem" (retained exactly by the NASB and RSV), with stylistic variants: "New Jerusalem" (CEV, NKJV), "the new Jerusalem" (NCV, NIV, NLT, NRSV). The subject is alluded to on many occasions in literature. For example, William Blake's short poem which appears at the beginning of *Milton* and begins:

> "And did those feet in ancient time
> Walk upon England's mountains
>   green?"

and ends:

> "I will not cease from Mental
>   Fight,
> Nor shall my Sword sleep in my
>   hand,
> Till we have built Jerusalem,
> In England's green and pleasant
>   Land."

NEW WINE INTO OLD BOTTLES

The phrase "new wine into old bottles" derives from Matthew 9:17: "Neither do men put new wine into old bottles: else the bottles break, and the wine runneth out, and the bottles perish: but they put new wine into new bottles, and both are preserved."

The contemporary versions all retain "new wine" but the KJV "old bottles" is "old wineskins" in all the contemporary versions, except the NCV, which has "old leather bags." (The parallels at Mark 2:22 and Luke 5:37 have the same wording.) The meaning is that the new order of things that Jesus ushered in does not fit into the old molds or forms.

As William Hendriksen comments: "The

wine-skin was usually made of the skin of a goat or a sheep. After being removed from the animal it was tanned, and after the hair had been cut close the skin was turned inside out. The neck opening became the mouth of the 'bottle.' The other openings, at the feet and the tail, were closed with cords. Naturally an old wine-skin is no match for new, still fermenting wine, for such wine tends to stretch the container. A new wine-skin would be sufficiently elastic to stand the pressure, but under similar conditions an old one, stiff and rigid, would crack. The wine would spill out and the skin would be of no further use" (*New Testament Commentary: The Gospel of Matthew*, Banner of Truth, 1974).

NITRE

"Nitre" is the modern name for saltpeter, i.e., potassium nitrate or sodium nitrate. In the KJV, however, the word refers to natron, i.e., sodium carbonate, which was used in ancient times in embalming, ceramic pastes, and as a means of cleansing.

The word occurs twice in the KJV. In Proverbs 25:20, "As he that taketh away a garment in cold weather, and as vinegar upon nitre, so is he that singeth songs to an heavy heart" (KJV): the effect of songs on someone with a heavy heart is likened to the working of vinegar on nitre ("soda" NASB, NCV, NIV, NKJV); the CEV, NRSV, and RSV render the comparison as being like vinegar on a "wound" (NRSV, RSV) or "open cut" (CEV); the NLT paraphrases the whole verse as "Singing cheerful songs to a person whose heart is heavy is as bad as stealing someone's jacket in cold weather or rubbing salt in a wound."

Jeremiah 2:22 reads, "For though thou wash thee with nitre, and take thee much soap, yet thine iniquity is marked before me, saith the Lord GOD" (KJV); the contemporary versions render the KJV "nitre" as "lye" (NASB, NKJV, NLT, NRSV, RSV), "soda" (NIV), "bleach" (CEV), and "cleanser" (NCV). The *Illustrated Bible Dictionary* notes, "In

Jeremiah 2:22 nitre ('lye') is used in a purificatory sense; mixed with oil it formed a kind of soap."

NO MAN, ANY MAN

Indefinite pronouns, referring to any person, use the masculine form in the Greek, just as in English we often use the pronoun "he" in a general statement which includes both men and women—although this is becoming less common with the modern concern for inclusive language. The KJV takes this masculine usage to extremes by using "no man" and "any man" where the meaning is "no one" or "any one." This practice unduly limits many statements, results in occasional infelicities, and can jar on modern ears.

For example, in Matthew 11:27 the KJV says that "no man knoweth the Son, but the Father." The word "but" is ambiguous here, for it could mean that men do not know the Son but do know the Father, which is absurd. But if the sentence means that no man knows the Son except the Father, this implies that the Father is a man (i.e., a human being). The Greek is perfectly clear, and the contemporary versions translate it clearly by using the expression "no one": "no one knows the Son except the Father" (NKJV).

The translation "no one" immediately enlarges the scope of the sayings of Jesus such as "No one can serve two masters" (Matthew 6:24, NKJV); "No one sews a piece of unshrunk cloth on an old cloak" (Matthew 9:16, NRSV); "No one lights a lamp and hides it in a jar" (Luke 8:16, NIV).

It was not merely to any man but to any one, male or female, that Jesus extended the invitation to eat of the bread of life (John 6:51), to drink of the water of life (John 7:37), to enter the door of the good shepherd (John 10:9), and to serve Him and follow him (John 12:26), and the contemporary versions make this clear by their use of "anyone" or "whoever."

"But if any man love God, the same is

known of him" (1 Corinthians 8:3, KJV) is translated in a variety of ways by the contemporary versions: the NKJV has "But if anyone loves God, this one is known by Him"; the NRSV translates it as "but anyone who loves God is known by him"; the NLT expands the sentence to, "But the person who loves God is the one God knows and cares for"; and the CEV turns the sentence around, "But God has no doubts about who loves him." The NIV, however, retains "man": "But the man who loves God is known by God."

The message of Revelation 3:20 (KJV): "Behold, I stand at the door, and knock; if any man hear my voice, and open the door, I will come in to him, and will sup with him, and he with me," is enlarged to include all people by the use of "you" in the NRSV, CEV, NCV, and NLT. However, although other contemporary versions replace "any man" with "anyone," they retain the masculine pronoun "him" in the rest of the verse (NASB, NIV, NKJV).

NO MAN CAN SERVE TWO MASTERS

See MAN CANNOT SERVE TWO MASTERS.

NO PEACE FOR THE WICKED

See PEACE FOR THE WICKED.

NO ROOM IN THE INN

See ROOM IN THE INN.

NOISOME

This word may appear to modern eyes to be connected with "noise," but in fact, according to the OED, it shares a common origin with the word "annoying." In the sixteenth century, "noisome" meant "hurtful" or "noxious"; however, its meaning began to change from the sixteenth century to its modern meaning of "causing disgust," especially through the sense of smell. The KJV was written during this period of transition and shows evidence of both meanings of "noisome."

The versions of the New Testament from Tyndale to the Bishops' Bible translated 1 Timothy 6:9 as "They that will be rich fall into temptations and snares, and into many foolish and noisome lusts." In view of the change in meaning taking place, the KJV substituted "hurtful" for "noisome," since "disgusting, especially bad-smelling" was not an appropriate adjective for "lusts."

All the contemporary versions except the RSV translate this as "harmful"; the RSV retains the KJV "hurtful." However, the KJV retains "noisome" in its old meaning in Psalm 91:3 ("the noisome pestilence") and Ezekiel 14:15, 21 ("noisome beasts"). The contemporary versions translate Psalm 91:3 as "deadly" diseases or pestilence (NKJV, "perilous pestilence"; NLT, "fatal plague"), and Ezekiel 14:15, 21 as "wild animals."

NONE EFFECT

This expression is obsolete in contemporary English, except in legal jargon, where agreements can still be rendered "void" and of "none effect." The KJV uses the expression eight times, and its related expressions, "no effect" and "without effect" once each. The contemporary versions use several different verbs to translate "make of none effect" in different contexts.

In Numbers 30:8, where the KJV has "he shall make her vow . . . of none effect," the NKJV translates this as "he shall make void her vow"; other versions have "he shall nullify [NIV, "he nullifies"] the vow" (NRSV, NIV); "he shall annul her vow" (NASB); "he cancels her pledge" (NCV); and "he nullifies her commitments" (NLT).

Similarly, in Romans 4:14 the KJV's "the promise [is] made of none effect" is translated in the contemporary versions by words such as "is nullified"; "is worthless"; "is meaningless"; and "is void"; closest to the KJV in this and other examples is the NKJV, with "made of no effect." The verbs "nullify," "frustrate," "fail," and "lose its power" are the expressions used by the contemporary versions in Romans 3:3; 9:6; Galatians

3:17; 5:4; Psalm 33:10; 1 Corinthians 1:17; Matthew 15:6; and Mark 7:13.

NOTABLE

The word "notable" can mean (1) "capable of being noted," (2) "easily noted," or (3) "worth noting as of outstanding importance or worth." The third is the most common meaning today; the second was in common use in the sixteenth and seventeenth centuries, but is now obsolete. There is an obvious link between these two meanings: "what is easily noted or conspicuous" may well stand out because it is important or of great worth.

In Daniel 8:5–8, the "notable horn[s]" of the goat in verses 5 and 8 (KJV) are generally "conspicuous" and "powerful" in the contemporary versions.

Barabbas (Matthew 27:16) was "a notorious prisoner" (according to the majority of the contemporary versions) rather than "a notable prisoner" (KJV). The NKJV and NRSV retain "notable" in Acts 4:16 to refer to the miraculous healer of the crippled beggar; but Paul's reference in the KJV to Andronicus and Junias as "men of note among the apostles" (Romans 16:7), although retained almost unchanged in the NKJV ["who are of note"], becomes "outstanding" (NASB, NIV), "highly respected" (CEV; NLT has simply "respected"), "very important" (NCV), and "prominent" (NRSV).

In his address to the people on the day of Pentecost, Peter cited the prophecy of Joel (Acts 2:16–21, quoting Joel 2:28–32). In verse 20 (KJV) his quotation reads, "before that great and notable day of the Lord come," but in Joel 2:31 in the KJV the prophecy has "before the great and the terrible day of the LORD come."

The difference is due to the fact that Peter quoted the Septuagint, the Greek translation of the Old Testament. Because they confused the Hebrew words for "fear" and "see," the translators of the Septuagint used the Greek word *epiphanes* in Joel 2:31, Habakkuk 1:7, and Malachi 1:14. This word

described "the day of the Lord" not as "fearful," "inspiring fear," but as "appearing to the sight," "coming into open view," "manifest," "illustrious"—i.e., notable in its second meaning.

The KJV translation in Acts 2:20, "before that great and notable day of the Lord come," goes back to Tyndale and was used by subsequent sixteenth-century versions made from the Greek. The Latin Vulgate had *dies Domini magnus et manifestus,* so the Rheims New Testament translated the clause as "before the great and manifest day of our Lord doth come." None of the contemporary versions (except the RSV) agree with Rheims; for their translation they generally go behind the Greek of the Septuagint, with its *epiphanes,* to the original Hebrew and translate "notable" as "glorious" (NASB, NCV, NIV, NLT, NRSV)—its third meaning; the NKJV has "awesome"; the CEV has "wonderful"; the NASB has "manifest."

The noun *epiphaneia* is used six times to denote our Lord's appearing (2 Thessalonians 2:8; 1 Timothy 6:14; 2 Timothy 1:10; 4:1, 8; Titus 2:13). The noun has become part of the English language as the name of "Epiphany," the festival commemorating the manifestation of Christ to the Gentiles in the person of the "wise men from the East," and as the common noun "epiphany," which the OED defines as "a manifestation or appearance of some divine or superhuman being."

The title of Antiochus Epiphanes, king of Syria, meant more than "Antiochus the Notable." It meant "Antiochus the Manifest God," for he claimed to be divine. His title was parodied as *Epimanes,* "Antiochus the Mad." Accounts of his attempt to abolish Judaism are found in 1 Maccabees 1:10—6:16 and 2 Maccabees 4:7—9:29.

NOTHING

The word "nothing" is used occasionally in the KJV as an adverb, meaning "not at all," "in no way," although in modern English it is used almost solely as a noun. In Mark 5:26, the woman with a hemorrhage had spent all her money on doctors but "was nothing bettered." Most of the contemporary versions translate this simply as "was no better" or "instead of getting better," although the NASB has "she . . . was not helped at all."

"When Pilate saw that he could prevail nothing" (Matthew 27:24, KJV) is translated by the NKJV as "that he could not prevail at all"; other contemporary versions have "that he was accomplishing nothing" (NASB); "that he was getting nowhere" (NIV); "that he could do nothing" (NRSV); "that he wasn't getting anywhere" (NLT); or "there was nothing he could do" (CEV).

Similar translations are used for "prevail nothing" in John 12:19, with the NIV again favoring "getting us nowhere." In Acts 4:21 (KJV) the Jewish leaders express their frustration at "finding nothing how they might punish" Peter and John; in the NKJV and NRSV this is translated as "finding no way to punish [NKJV, "of punishing"] them"; the NASB has "finding no basis on which to punish them."

When the Spirit tells Peter to go with the three men sent by Cornelius, "nothing doubting" (Acts 11:12, KJV), the NKJV simply reverses the two words to make them sound more contemporary—an arrangement which the KJV itself uses in Acts 10:20. Other contemporary versions simply translate "nothing doubting" as "without misgivings" (NASB); "without doubting" (NCV); or "to have no hesitation" (NIV); the NRSV changes it to, "not to make a distinction between them and us."

In instances such as "the heir . . . differeth nothing from a servant" (Galatians 4:1, KJV), the contemporary versions render as "does not differ" and "is [or, "are"] no different," although the NRSV again differs slightly, with "are no better than slaves."

In John 6:63 and 1 Corinthians 13:3, the KJV's "nothing" in "profiteth nothing" is retained by the contemporary versions, while in Galatians 5:2 "nothing" is simply translated as an adjectival "no," e.g., NASB,

"Behold, I, Paul, say to you that if you receive circumcision, Christ will be of no benefit to you."

This adverbial use of "nothing" points to the origin of "not," which is simply the contracted form of "nought."

NOTHING NEW UNDER THE SUN

The expression "nothing new under the sun" means that "there is nothing in the world that has not been already thought of, seen, experienced." It is sometimes used to refer to something that looks original and novel but in reality is not.

The expression derives from Ecclesiastes 1:9: "The thing that hath been, it is that which shall be; and that which is done is that which shall be done: and there is no new thing under the sun" (KJV). The contemporary versions render the KJV expression as "there is nothing new under the sun" (NASB, NIV, NKJV, NRSV, RSV); "Nothing under the sun is truly new" (NLT); "there is nothing new here on earth" (NCV); and "nothing is new, nothing under the sun" (CEV).

NOUGHT, SET AT

To "set at nought" is "to value at nothing," "to regard as good for nothing or worthless," and hence "to despise" or "to reject."

As an obsolete expression in today's English, the contemporary versions invariably change it to expressions such as "ignored" (Proverbs 1:25; NKJV, "disdained"); "rejected" (Acts 4:11, NASB, NCV, NIV, NKJV, NLT, NRSV, RSV); "treated with contempt" (Mark 9:12, NKJV, NRSV, RSV; NLT, "treated with utter contempt"; NIV, CEV, "rejected"); or, in Romans 14:10, "look down on" (CEV, NIV, NLT); "regard with (NKJV, "show") contempt" (NKJV, NASB); or "despise" (NRSV).

When Herod and his soldiers mock Jesus and "set him at nought" (Luke 23:11, KJV), the contemporary versions translate this as "treated him [NKJV, NASB, "Him"] with contempt" (NKJV, NASB, NRSV); "ridiculed" him (NIV, NLT); or "made fun of Jesus" (NCV).

A different group of Greek words and a

quite different Greek construction underlie the speech of Demetrius to his fellow craftsmen and their workmen, in Acts 19:27. Here, the KJV has "our craft is in danger to be set at nought," using "set at nought" to translate Greek which literally means "come into disrepute." Most of the contemporary versions translate this as "come (or, fall) into disrepute," although the NIV and NCV have our business "will lose its good name." (See also NAUGHT)

NOURISH

This is a word which in today's English is almost entirely connected with food, although it is sometimes used in the metaphorical sense of "nourishing a gift or talent." In the KJV it usually means to "rear," "raise," "bring up," "care for," "nurture," "provide for," rather than "to feed." "Nourish" in the sense of "rear" is usually translated in the contemporary versions as "rear," "raise," or occasionally "bring up"; see Isaiah 1:2; 23:4; Ezekiel 19:2. In 2 Samuel 12:3, the NKJV and NASB retain "nourished."

In Acts 7:20, 21, most of the contemporary versions again use the verbs "bring up" or "raise" to describe the action of Pharaoh's daughter in adopting Moses, where the KJV has "nourish," but to describe the care given to Moses by his natural parents (for which the KJV also uses "nourish"), the NCV, NIV, and NLT have "cared for," and the NASB has "nurtured."

A similar use of "nourish" can be found in Genesis 45:11; 47:12; 50:21, where the word in the KJV, describing Joseph's provision for his family, is translated in most of the contemporary versions as "I will provide for you," which has a wider meaning than simply putting food on the table.

Daniel and his friends were not merely fed at Nebuchadnezzar's court (Daniel 1:5); the provision of food was "nourishing them" (KJV), in the sense of "educating" or "training" them to serve the king—the translations of "nourishing" used by the contemporary versions. "Nourished" in the basic sense of

"fed" does occur in the KJV, however; Tyre and Sidon asked for peace with Herod, because their country "was nourished by the king's country," i.e., it depended on it for food (Acts 12:20).

Colossians 2:18–19 in the KJV provides an example of how the English language has changed in the last 350 years. Not only the words but also the syntax makes these verses very difficult for today's readers to understand: "Let no man beguile you of your reward in a voluntary humility and worshipping of angels, intruding into those things which he hath not seen, vainly puffed up by his fleshly mind. And not holding the Head, from which all the body by joints and bands having nourishment ministered, and knit together, increaseth with the increase of God."

The contemporary versions translate the passage in a variety of ways. The NKJV makes minimal changes to the KJV which nevertheless adds considerable clarity: "Let no one cheat you of your reward, taking delight in false humility and worship of angels, intruding into those things which he has not seen, vainly puffed up by his fleshly mind, and not holding fast to the Head, from whom all the body, nourished and knit together by joints and ligaments, grows with the increase that is from God."

Other versions translate "having nourishment ministered" as "being supplied" (NASB), "supported" (NIV), and "nourished" (NRSV).

NOVICE

Today, a "novice" is "a learner in any field," and, in a religious context, "someone who is in the first stages of becoming a monk or nun." The Greek word translated by the KJV as "novice" in the list of qualifications for the office of bishop given in 1 Timothy 3:6 ("Not a novice, lest being lifted up with pride he fall into the condemnation of the devil") is *neophutos*, which means "newly planted." It appears in Latin as *neophytus*, and has passed into English as "neophyte."

The emphasis in 1 Timothy is on the

bishop not being a recent convert to Christianity. The NKJV retains the word "novice," but other contemporary versions express this idea as "not . . . new followers of the Lord" (CEV); "not a new convert" (NASB); "not . . . a new believer" (NCV); "not . . . a recent convert" (NIV, NRSV); "not . . . a new Christian" (NLT); "He must not be a beginner in the faith" (Phillips).

In using the word "novice" here, the KJV moved away from earlier translations. Wycliffe (like our contemporary versions) had "not newe conuertid to the feith." Tyndale, followed by the other Protestant versions of the sixteenth century, had "He maye not be a yonge skoler." The Rheims translators used "neophyte," and stoutly defended it in their Preface to the Reader: "If Proselyte be a received word in the English bibles, . . . why may we not be bold to say, Neophyte?"

NURTURE

In modern English, "nurture" is a word with connotations of "loving care and attention to the bringing up of children," of "providing the right environment for good growth." In its only appearance in the KJV (Ephesians 6:4), "nurture" translates a Greek word *paideia,* meaning "education," "training," "discipline," which is elsewhere in the KJV translated as "chastening," "chasten," "chastisement," "chastise" in Hebrews 12:5–11; Luke 23:16, 22; 1 Corinthians 11:32; 2 Corinthians 6:9; Revelation 3:19.

The admonition to fathers in Ephesians 6:4 (KJV) to "bring [your children] up in the nurture and admonition of the Lord" is an encouragement to train them through correction and discipline. The contemporary versions express this meaning of *paedeia* by translating it as "training" or "discipline."

O

OBSERVE

When Herod seized John the Baptist and put him in prison because of the enmity of Herodias, we are told in Mark 6:20 (KJV), "Herod feared John, knowing that he was a just man, and an holy, and observed him; and when he heard him, he did many things, and heard him gladly." Reading this today, we would probably conclude that Herod watched John carefully, since this is the most common use of the word.

However, in the seventeenth century "observe" also had the meaning of "treat with ceremonious respect or reverence," a meaning which survives today in the title of The Lord's Day Observance Society, an organization which campaigns for Sunday to be treated with reverence and respect, and in the "observance" of national occasions such as Remembrance Day or Independence Day. It is used in this sense by Shakespeare in, for example, *King Henry IV, Part II* (IV, 4, 30). The king advises his son Thomas to ob-

serve his older brother, who is heir to the throne:

"Blunt not his love,
Nor lose the good advantage of his
    grace
By seeming cold or careless of his will:
For he is gracious, if he be observed."

In *Julius Caesar* (IV, 3, 45), Brutus quarrels with Cassius:

"Must I budge?
Must I observe you? Must I stand and
    crouch
Under your testy humour?"

In place of "observed him" (Mark 6:20), Tyndale, the Great Bible, the Geneva Bible, and the Bishops' Bible had "gave him reverence." But the original Greek word means "keep safe," "watch over," "protect"; and this is the meaning given by the Latin Vulgate, Martin Luther's German Bible, Wycliffe, Coverdale, Rheims, and the contemporary versions.

OCCUPY

Today, the word "occupy" is used only with the meaning of "take up," "fill," "be in." We occupy a house and our time; invading soldiers occupy a country. The Greek verb which the KJV translates as "occupy" is *pragmateuomai,* which means "do business," "trade with."

Luke 19:13, for example, reads in the KJV, "He called his ten servants, and delivered them ten pounds, and said unto them, Occupy till I come." Tyndale and the Geneva Bible translated it, "Buy and sell till I come." But the KJV translators followed Coverdale, the Bishops' Bible, and the Rheims translation in using the word "occupy."

The contemporary versions are divided between "do business" (NASB, NCV, NKJV, NRSV) and phrases like NIV's "Put this money to work."

The version of Psalm 107:23 in the Book of Common Prayer, "They that go down to the sea in ships, and occupy their business in great waters," goes back to Coverdale. The KJV changes this to a literal rendering, "do business in great waters," a translation followed by the majority of the contemporary versions. "Occupy," meaning "do business," "trade," covers all but two of the occurrences of the word in the KJV, many of which are found in Ezekiel 27.

Another meaning of "occupy" occurs in Judges 16:11, where Samson explains to Delilah: "If they bind me fast with new ropes that never were occupied, then shall I be weak, and be as another man." Here, and also in Exodus 38:24, "occupy" means "used," and this is the translation generally given in the contemporary versions.

In his warning against "tongues," and urging the use of the understanding, Paul wrote in 1 Corinthians 14:16 (KJV): "Else when thou shalt bless with the spirit, how shall he that occupieth the room of the unlearned say Amen at thy giving of thanks, seeing he understandeth not what thou sayest?" This is the translation of Tyndale

and the sixteenth-century versions generally. "Room" means "place," and here the KJV uses "occupy" in its modern sense of "be in."

The contemporary versions express this in a variety of ways: "occupies the place of the uninformed" (NKJV); "fills the place of the ungifted" (NASB); "finds himself among those who do not understand" (NIV); "in the position of an outsider" (NRSV).

In Hebrews 13:9, the KJV reads: "For it is a good thing that the heart be established with grace; not with meats, which have not profited them that have been occupied therein." Here, "have been occupied" represents the Greek verb which means "walk" or "live." This is a difficult verse to translate without resorting to paraphrase. Of the contemporary versions, NKJV and NASB retain "occupied"; NRSV translates "those who observe them" (i.e., regulations about food); the NCV has "those who obey them."

OCCURRENT

As a noun, "occurrent" means "an occurrence," "something that happens," "an incident." The word was in common use in the sixteenth and seventeenth centuries, although it is now obsolete. It appears once in the Bible, in 1 Kings 5:4. In his message to Hiram, king of Tyre, Solomon says (KJV), "But now the LORD my God hath given me rest on every side, so that there is neither adversary nor evil occurrent." The Hebrew word here translated as "occurrent" means "occurrence" or "happening."

"Occurrent" appears in one other passage in the Hebrew Bible, in Ecclesiastes 9:11, where both the KJV and the contemporary versions translate it as "chance": "time and chance happen to them all" (NKJV).

ODD

This word appears just once in the KJV, in Numbers 3:48, where it has the meaning of "surplus," "excess," "that which is over and above a certain number." This corresponds to modern English, which still uses expressions such as "the odd day or two," "the odd pound [in money or weight]."

The Lord accepted the service of the Levites instead of requiring such service from all the first-born sons of Israel. There were 22,000 Levites and 22,273 first-born sons, and the odd number (the difference, 273) had to be redeemed by the payment of five shekels apiece—1,365 shekels. Many of the contemporary versions use "in excess" or "excess number."

The Hebrew word appears in seven other verses, but there the KJV translates it as "more than" (Numbers 3:46); "over and above" (Numbers 3:49); "over" (Exodus 16:18, 23); "that remaineth" (Exodus 12:12, 13); "the overplus" (Leviticus 25:27). The contemporary versions use similar terms such as "over and above," "in excess of," "additional," "the balance."

OF

This is the most versatile and ambiguous of the prepositions in the KJV. It is used in many situations where we would now use other prepositions such as "by," "about," "from," "for," "with," "over," "on," or "to." The contemporary versions generally replace the KJV's "of" with the appropriate alternative preposition.

In Mark 1:9, 13, Jesus is baptized "of John" and afterwards tempted "of Satan" in the wilderness; "Do not your alms before men, to be seen of them . . . do not sound a trumpet before thee, as the hypocrites do . . . that they may have glory of men" (Matthew 6:1–2, KJV); "When thou art bidden of any man to a wedding" (Luke 14:8). For all these instances the contemporary translations generally use "by."

A further example of the KJV's use of "of" in constructions where modern English would use "by" can be found in Matthew 2:15: "that it might be fulfilled which was spoken of the Lord by the prophet." Here, the majority of the contemporary versions change "of the Lord" to "by the Lord," and "by the prophet" to "through the prophet."

In John 8:40 (KJV), "the truth, which I have heard of God" is generally translated by the contemporary versions as the truth that Jesus heard "from God." In the same way, "for" replaces the KJV's "of" in John 2:17 ("The zeal of thine house"); Acts 8:11 ("Of long time"); Acts 21:20 ("zealous of the law"); and Romans 10:2 ("a zeal of God").

The KJV sometimes uses "of" where we would now use "with," and this change of use is reflected in the contemporary versions. Examples can be found in Judges 8:3 ("in comparison of you") and 2 Samuel 19:32 ("provided the king of sustenance"). The expression "I am sick of love" (Song of Solomon 2:5, KJV) now implies surfeit and distaste; the better translation of the Hebrew is "I am sick with love," although the majority of the contemporary versions avoid the use of the word "sick," preferring "lovesick" (NKJV, NASB, NLT); "faint with love" (NIV NRSV, NCV, "weak"); or "hungry for love" (CEV).

Other instances of changes of preposition between the KJV and the contemporary translations include Matthew 18:13 ("he rejoiceth more of that sheep, than of the ninety and nine which went not astray," translated as "he rejoices over"); 1 Corinthians 7:4 ("The wife hath no power of her own body," translated in various ways by the contemporary versions, but generally using "over" instead of "of"); and 1 Timothy 4:12 ("be thou an example of the believers" does not urge Timothy to be an exemplary believer, but an example "to" or "for" others).

Hebrews 10:34 presents more of a puzzle to the translators, because it is not simply a matter of replacing the KJV's "ye had compassion of me" with "compassion for me," but in most cases (CEV, NASB, NCV, NIV, NLT, NRSV) the object of the sentence (and of the compassion) is changed from the singular "me," i.e., Paul, to the plural "prisoners" or "those in prison." Only the NKJV retains the singular as a reference to Paul.

Occasionally "of" is redundant and can simply be dropped, as, for example, in 2 Samuel 2:21 ("Asahel would not turn aside from following of him"); John 11:13 ("they thought that he had spoken of taking of rest in sleep"); and Acts 21:32 ("they left beating of Paul," which in all the contemporary versions becomes "they stopped beating Paul").

The redundant "of" is found frequently in Shakespeare; for example, in *As You Like It* (IV, 3, 10), when Silvius delivers Phoebe's letter to the disguised Rosalind, he says:

"I know not the contents; but, as I
     guess
By the stern brow and waspish action
Which she did use as she was writing
     of it,
It bears an angry tenour."

OFFEND

In addition to its usual meanings, the verb "offend" is used in the KJV New Testament in a peculiar sense, to translate the Greek verb *skandalizo*. The noun *skandalon* meant a "trap" or "snare," and the verb meant "to place something in another's way which would cause him or her to stumble, fall, or sin."

In the KJV, Matthew 5:29–30 reads, "If thy right eye offend thee, pluck it out . . . And if hand offend thee, cut it off." The majority of contemporary versions translate "offend thee" as "causes you to sin" (NKJV, CEV, NCV, NIV, NLT, NRSV; NASB has "makes [or, "causes"] you [to] stumble." There is some variation between the translations in the parallel texts Matthew 18:8–9 and Mark 9:43, 45, 47.

Similarly, "Whoso shall offend one of these little ones which believe in me" (Matthew 18:6 and parallels in Mark 9:42 and Luke 17:2, KJV) becomes in the majority of the contemporary translations, "causes one of these little ones . . . to sin" [or, "to stumble"].

The noun occurs in the KJV of Luke 17:1, with a parallel in Matthew 18:7: "It is impossible but that offences will come: but woe unto him, through whom they come!" The NKJV retains the word "offenses," but the other contemporary versions show wide variation in their translation of "offences": "stumbling blocks" (NASB); "things that cause people to sin" (CEV; NCV; NIV); "temptations to sin" (NLT; Matthew 18:7: "temptation to do wrong"); "stumbling blocks," "occasions for stumbling" (NRSV). In Matthew 13:41 (KJV), "all things that offend" has a similar variety of translations in the contemporary versions.

Jesus' statement to his disciples as they went together to Gethsemane, "All ye shall be offended because of me this night" (Matthew 26:31, 33 and Mark 14:27, 29, KJV), is translated by the contemporary versions as "you will all fall away" (NASB, NIV); "you will all stumble in your faith" (NCV; NKJV, "All of you will be made to stumble"); "You will all become deserters" (NRSV; NLT, "all of you will desert me").

"Stumble" and "fall away" are also contemporary translations of John 16:1 in the KJV: "that ye should not be offended," although CEV has "to keep you from being afraid"; NCV has "to keep you from giving up"; and NIV has "so that you will not go astray."

"Offend" in Paul's declaration in 1 Corinthians 8:13 (KJV): "Wherefore, if meat make my brother to offend, I will eat no flesh while the world standeth, lest I make my brother to offend," is translated in the contemporary versions as "stumble," "fall," "fall into sin."

Paul's climactic question in his spirited defense of himself in 2 Corinthians 11:29 (KJV), "Who is offended, and I burn not?" becomes "Who is made to stumble" in the NKJV and NRSV and in the NASB and NIV, "Who is led into sin?"

OFTEN

The word "often" is used today solely as an adverb, but in 1 Timothy 5:23 the KJV uses it as an adjective: "Drink no longer water, but use a little wine for thy stomachs sake and thine often infirmities." The majority of contemporary versions translate it as "frequent." The use of "often" as an adjective was common in the sixteenth and seventeenth centuries. The KJV rendering of this verse comes from Tyndale and was used by all the sixteenth-century English versions.

OLD ADAM

The expression "old Adam" is sometimes used to refer to "the unregenerate condition or character" (OED). The OED considers that this refers to the " 'old man' of St. Paul (Romans 6:6, etc.)." Romans 6:6 in the KJV reads: "Knowing this, that our old man is crucified with him, that the body of sin might be destroyed, that henceforth we should not serve sin"; for the KJV "old man" (retained by the NKJV) the contemporary versions have: "old self" (NASB, NIV, NRSV), "sinful selves" (NLT), and "old life" (NCV).

As John Murray comments in *Epistle to the Romans* (Eerdmans, 1960): " 'Our old man' is the old self or ego, the unregenerate man in his entirety in contrast with the new man as the regenerate man in his entirety. It is a mistake to think of the believer as both an old man and new man or as having in him both the old man and the new man, the latter in view of regeneration and the former because of remaining corruption. That this is not Paul's concept is made apparent here by the fact that the 'old man' is represented as having been crucified with Christ and the tense indicates a once-for-all definitive act after the pattern of Christ's crucifixion. The 'old man' can no more be regarded as in the process of being crucified than Christ in his sphere could he thus regarded.

"Furthermore, as was noted already, Paul is insisting in this context upon the definitive breach with sin which occurs through union with Christ in his death, and the appeal to the crucifixion of the old man is coordinate with this insistence and particularly illustrative or probative of it."

OLD AS METHUSELAH

See METHUSELAH.

OLD WIVES' FABLES

"Old wives' tales" is an expression which appears once in the KJV, in 1 Timothy 4:7, "refuse profane and old wives' fables." The OED defines "old wives' fable, story, tale" as "a foolish story such as is told by garrulous old women." Closer to the contemporary application is the definition of the *Oxford Dictionary of Current Idiomatic English* (vol. 2): "a legend, myth, account of historical, or supernatural, events such as old women handed on to rising generations; an unsupported piece of information, recommended practice, etc."

The expression goes back to Tyndale and beyond and has passed into literature. In today's climate of feminism and political correctness, it might be considered unsuitable for a contemporary translation, but it is in fact retained by the NKJV, NIV, NLT and NRSV. The NASB has "worldly fables fit only for old women"; CEV, "worthless, senseless stories"; RSV, "godless and silly myths"; and NCV, "foolish stories." (See FABLE; PROFANE; REFUSE)

OLDNESS

This word appears in Romans 7:6 (KJV): "But now we are delivered from the law, that being dead wherein we were held; that we should serve in newness of spirit, and not in the oldness of the letter." This is a misleading translation, which could have been avoided if the translators had given sufficient weight to the prior versions of Tyndale and his successors.

The Geneva Bible, for example, reads: "But now we are delivered from the Lawe, being dead unto that wherein we were in bondage, that we should serve in a newe conversation of the Spirit, and not in the olde conversation of the letter" (remembering that the word "conversation" in the sixteenth century meant "behavior" or "manner of life"). This sound translation appeared in all the versions based upon the Greek, from Tyndale to the Bishops' Bible.

However, the KJV followed in principle the translation of the Rheims New Testament, which was based on the Latin Vulgate, and in the process acquired three difficulties: (1) it says that the law is dead, while Paul said that we are dead to the law; (2) it contrasts "newness of spirit" and "the oldness of the letter" as though "newness" was the principal good; (3) it thus fails to convey to the reader the fact that what is new is the Spirit, the law of the Spirit of life in Christ Jesus which Paul goes on to describe in the matchless words of Romans 8.

The contemporary versions return to the Greek text and make it clear that we are dead to the law and that we now serve God in the new way of the Spirit; for example, the NRSV reads, "But now we are discharged from the law, dead to that which held us captive, so that we are slaves not under the old written code but in the new life of the Spirit."

OLIVE BRANCH

In contemporary English an "olive branch" is a symbol of peace. To offer an olive branch to someone is to do something to show that you want to end a disagreement. The expression alludes to the olive branch brought back by the dove to Noah in the ark: "And the dove came in to him in the evening; and, lo, in her mouth was an olive leaf pluckt off: so Noah knew that the waters were abated from off the earth" (Genesis 8:11, KJV).

The KJV has "an olive leaf pluckt off"; the NIV, NKJV, NRSV, and RSV have: "a freshly plucked olive leaf"; the NASB, "a freshly picked olive leaf"; the NCV and NLT, "a fresh olive leaf"; and the CEV, "a green leaf from an olive tree."

Shakespeare used the phrase in this sense:

"No, Warwick, thou art worthy of
    the sway,

To whom the heavens, in thy nativity,
Adjudged an olive-branch and
    laurel-crown,
As likely to be blest in peace and
    war;
And therefore I yield thee my free
    consent."
            —*King Henry VI* (III, 4, 6, 33)

The OED also notes the "now humorous" use of "olive-branch" to be children, in allusion to Psalm 128:3, from Coverdale's translation, "Thy children like the olyue braunches rounde aboute thy table." The KJV, NASB, and NKJV have "olive plants"; the NIV and NRSV, "olive shoots"; the NCV, "olive branches"; and the NLT, "young olive trees."

ONCE

"Woe unto thee, O Jerusalem! wilt thou not be made clean? When shall it once be?" cries Jeremiah in the KJV translation of Jeremiah 13:27. "Once" is used here in the sense of "ever."

The majority of the contemporary versions conflate the last two sentences, to give a translation such as "Will you still not be made clean?" (NKJV); "How long will you remain [NIV, "be"; NCV, "continue being"] unclean?" (NASB, NIV, NCV); the NRSV and NLT have "How long will it be before you are made clean [NLT, "before you are pure"]?"; the CEV has "Will you ever be worthy to worship me again?"

The Preface to the KJV, entitled "The Translators to the Reader," in the first sentence of the second paragraph, uses the word "once" in this same sense of "ever": "in some Commonweals it was made a capital crime, once to motion the making of a new law for the abrogating of an old, though the same were most pernicious."

ONE AND OTHER

This expression is clearly the forerunner of the modern "one another," "each other."

Its interest in the KJV is that its one appearance occurs as part of an inaccurate translation of the Hebrew of Jeremiah 36:16, taken over from the Geneva Bible. The KJV has "they were afraid both one and other." Other sixteenth-century translations, from Coverdale to the Bishops' Bible, had "they were abashed one upon another."

The Hebrew idiom is more accurately understood by the contemporary versions as "they looked in fear from one to another" (NKJV; NASB, "they turned in fear one to another"); "they looked at each other in fear" (NIV; NCV, "they became afraid and looked at each other"); "they turned to one another in alarm" (NRSV).

OPEN

The verb "open" is used twice in the KJV (in Luke 24:32 and Acts 17:3) in the archaic sense of "expound" or "explain." In the contemporary translations of Luke 24:32 (where the KJV has "Did not our heart burn within us . . . while he opened to us the scriptures?"), the NKJV, NIV, and NRSV retain "opened the Scriptures," while the NASB, CEV, NCV, and NLT have "explained."

In the second occurrence, in Acts 17:3, where Paul's use of the Scriptures at Thessalonica is described as (KJV) "Opening and alleging, that Christ must needs have suffered," the contemporary versions generally replace "opening" with "explaining," which is a more accurate rendering of the Greek text. (See ALLEGE)

OR EVER

This is now an obsolete expression, but it occurs three times in the KJV in the sense of "before." This is the more literal translation in the majority of the contemporary versions of Proverbs 8:23, which reads in the KJV, "I was set up from everlasting, from the beginning, or ever the earth was." "Or ever" also occurs in the sense of "before" in Song of Solomon 6:12 (KJV: "Or ever I was aware") and in the story of the lions' den in Daniel

6:24 (KJV: "or ever they came at the bottom of the pit; NRSV: "Before they reached the bottom of the den").

Tyndale had used "or ever" in John 4:49, "Syr come awaye or ever that my chylde dye," and this was retained by some of the subsequent versions. The KJV, however, changed to "Sir, come down ere my child die," and the contemporary versions all use "before."

Shakespeare used "or ere" nine times in this sense of "before," and used "or ever" in *Hamlet* (I, 2, 183):

> "Would I had met my
> dearest foe in heaven
> Or ever I had seen that day!"

ORDAIN

The word "ordain" is used today almost entirely in connection to someone being appointed by God to office within the church, usually as a deacon, priest, or minister. It is also used (often rather flippantly) in a phrase such as "It must be ordained," meaning that what has happened seems to have been organized by some outside force such as God, the government, fate, the planets, or nature.

In the KJV, "ordain" has a much wider range of meanings. The OED lists sixteen meanings, thirteen of which are obsolete or archaic; the KJV uses the word to mean "to arrange, prepare, set up, or establish something"; "to appoint a person to some duty or office"; "to make an authoritative decision"; "to decree that some practice or day be observed."

The verb "ordain" is used forty-one times in the KJV, and represents ten different Hebrew verbs and twelve different Greek verbs. A few of the contemporary versions sometimes retain "ordain" (as NKJV, NASB, and NRSV do in Numbers 28:6 and 2 Kings 23:5; see also Acts 10:42; Galatians 3:19), but at other times the contemporary versions use words such as "appointed," "instituted," "establish."

In Esther 9:27–28, none of the contemporary versions retain the KJV's "ordained" ("The Jews ordained . . . that they should keep these two days . . . according to their appointed time every year"). The NKJV, NASB, NIV, and NRSV have "the Jews established"; the NCV uses "set up"; NLT has "inaugurate." A similar variation in the contemporary translations, where the KJV has "ordain," occurs in Isaiah 26:12; Habakkuk 1:12; Acts 13:48.

An interesting case is Acts 1:21–22 (KJV): "Wherefore of these men which have companied with us all the time that the Lord Jesus went in and out among us . . . must one be ordained to be a witness with us of his resurrection." Tyndale had used "ordeyned" in this passage, and was followed by the other sixteenth-century translations made from the Greek. Wycliffe and Rheims, which translated the Latin Vulgate, had "be made a witness."

But the Greek verb means "become," and the contemporary versions translate it literally, as, for example, "one of these must become a witness with us of His resurrection" (NKJV).

Sometimes the contemporary versions use "ordain" where the KJV has another word—often "consecrate." This occurs in, for example, eight references to the ordination of Aaron and his sons as priests (Exodus 28:41; 29:9, 29, 33, 35; 32:29; Leviticus 8:33; Numbers 3:3). In 1 Chronicles 15:13, the NASB translates the KJV's "we sought him not after the due order" as "we did not seek Him according to the ordinance," but other contemporary versions use words such as "in the prescribed way" (NIV); "about the proper order" (NKJV).

"Ordinance" in the KJV's 2 Chronicles 2:4, meaning "a rule for worship," is retained by the NIV and NKJV; NRSV has "as ordained forever for Israel." Alone among the contemporary versions, the NRSV and RSV use "ordained" in 2 Samuel 17:14; Lamentations 2:17; and Lamentations 3:37, where the KJV has, respectively, "The LORD had appointed"; "he had commanded"; and "the Lord commandeth."

ORDER

The fact that this is a word still in common use today makes it the more confusing when the KJV uses it with a meaning which is now obsolete—or rather, as a verb where we would now only use it as a noun. To have "order" in one's life is to live according to a plan, according to certain principles and rules; things are properly arranged, whether it is the way we do our work, or the tidiness of our cupboards. But we more rarely use the related verb "to order," with the meaning of "setting straight," "organizing according to a plan."

However, this is what the KJV means when it describes Manoah asking the angel for guidance about his son-to-be, Samson: "How shall we order the child?" (Judges 13:12).

The contemporary translations generally bring out the idea of "rules": "What will be [NRSV, "is to be"] the boy's rule of life?" (NKJV, NRSV); "what is to be the rule for the boy's life?" (NIV); "what rules must he obey?" (CEV); "what shall be the boy's mode of life?" (NASB).

There is something of the same meaning of organizing according to plans and rules in the KJV's use of "order" in Psalm 37:23 ("The steps of a good man are ordered by the LORD"); here, and in Psalm 119:133 and Isaiah 9:7, "order" is used for the Hebrew verb which means "establish" and "direct," and this (together with "made firm," "guide," "keep") is the range of meanings used in the contemporary versions, with the exception of the NKJV, which retains "ordered."

When Ahab asked the prophet (in 1 Kings 20:14, KJV), "Who shall order the battle?", he wished to know whether to take the initiative and attack the enemy or to remain in positions of defense; the simple translation of the Hebrew (followed by most of the contemporary versions) is "Who shall begin the battle?"

The KJV's rendering of Psalm 40:5, "They cannot be reckoned up in order unto thee," is now translated in a variety of ways: the NKJV joins the clause to the preceding one, to give "Your thoughts toward us cannot be recounted to You in order"; the NIV does the same, with "The things you have planned for us no one can recount to you"; the NASB has "There is none to compare with You" (NRSV, "none can compare with you"). The KJV itself translates the same Hebrew verb in Isaiah 40:18 as "what likeness will ye compare unto him?"

Detailed instructions concerning the pattern of the tabernacle are recorded in Exodus 25—27, and most of these details are repeated in Exodus 36—38, which describe its construction by Bezalel and Oholiab. Each board or frame for the walls of the tabernacle had two tenons, which are described by identical Hebrew clauses in 26:17 and 36:22. Yet in 26:17 the KJV reads, "Two tenons shall there be in one board, set in order one against another," and in 36:22 it reads, "One board had two tenons, equally distant one from another."

All the contemporary versions translate the Hebrew meaning of "fitting or joining together" (e.g., at 26:17 the NRSV has "There shall be two pegs in each frame to fit the frames together").

OUCHES

This is the plural of an old word which was already becoming obsolete in 1611. Tyndale had used it in his translation of Exodus, published in 1530, with a note explaining its meaning: "ouches, ornaments fit to display jewels or precious stones." Tyndale applied the term to the gold settings of the two jewels on the shoulders of the high priest's ephod, and to the gold settings of the twelve jewels of his "brestlappe" (KJV,

NKJV, "breastplate"; NASB, NIV, NRSV, "breast-piece").

These settings were not solid bars or capsules of gold. Instead of "ouches of gold" in Exodus 28:11, 13–14, 25; 39:6, 13, 16, 18, the contemporary versions have expressions such as "gold filigree settings" (NASB, NIV), "settings of gold," or "settings of filigree" (NKJV, NRSV). Such filigree work had been done by Egyptian goldsmiths from early times. The method is described in Exodus 39:3.

The Hebrew term also appears in Psalm 45:13, where the KJV says of the king's daughter that "her clothing is of wrought gold," and the contemporary versions describe her robes as "woven with gold," "interwoven with gold," or "gold-woven."

The word "ouche" was originally "nouche," but before Tyndale's time "a nouche" had become "an ouche," just as "a nadder" became "an adder" and "a napron" became "an apron." "Ouches" appears once in Shakespeare's *King Henry IV, Part II* (II, 4, 49) where Falstaff teases Doll Tearsheet about "Your brooches, pearls, and ouches."

OUT OF COURSE

This is an obsolete expression with much the same range of meaning as "out of order" has today. In Psalm 82:5 (KJV) it is said that "all the foundations of the earth are out of course." This is an inaccurate rendering of the Hebrew, which means "are shaken," the translation used by most of the contemporary versions (NKJV, "All the foundations of the earth are unstable").

OUT OF HAND

See HAND.

OUT OF THE EATER CAME FORTH MEAT; OUT OF THE STRONG CAME FORTH SWEETNESS

See STRONG, OUT OF THE, CAME FORTH SWEETNESS.

OUT OF THE MOUTHS OF BABES

See MOUTHS OF BABES.

OUTER DARKNESS

See DARKNESS, OUTER.

OUTGOINGS

Today we use the singular form "outgoing" as an adjective to describe a friendly, lively person, and the plural "outgoings" for items of expenditure in domestic or business accounts. The KJV uses the plural of "outgoing" in the obsolete sense of "extremity," "utmost limit," "end," in the allotment of the land of Canaan to the tribes of Israel described in Joshua 17—19.

"The outgoings of it were at the sea" (17:9) is translated in most of the contemporary versions as "it ended [NRSV, "ends"] at the sea"; and "The outgoings of it shall be thine" (17:18, KJV) promises the tribe of Joseph "its farthest borders" (NASB, NRSV); "its farthest limits" (NIV); "its farthest extent" (NKJV).

A different Hebrew word is used in Psalm 65:8, which the KJV translates as "thou makest the outgoings of the morning and evening to rejoice"; the original denotes the act or place of going forth, the source of a spring, the start of a journey. The NKJV and RSV retain the KJV "outgoings"; the NRSV has "gateways."

OUTLANDISH

The word "outlandish" is used in modern English to describe an object or behavior which looks or sounds foreign or bizarre. The KJV uses "outlandish" once, in Nehemiah 13:26, to represent the Hebrew word which it translates elsewhere by "alien," "foreigner," "strange," or "stranger." The passage refers to Solomon: "among many nations was there no king like him, who was beloved of his God, and God made him king over all Israel: nevertheless even him did outlandish women cause to sin."

All the contemporary versions except the NKJV translate "outlandish women" as "foreign" wives; the NKJV has "pagan wives." For the same Hebrew phrase the KJV has "strange women" in 1 Kings 11:1, and "strange wives" in 1 Kings 11:8 and Nehemiah 13:27, usually rendered now as "foreign wives" or "foreign women." Coverdale had the word "outlandish" in all these passages, meaning by it "from a foreign land."

OUTWENT

The word "outwent" is obsolete today but has obvious connections with words such as "outran" or "outgrew" which are still in use. "Outwent" means "went faster than." In its one occurrence in the KJV (Mark 6:33), "outwent" is a loose translation of the Greek. Wycliffe had "camen bifor hem"; Tyndale and subsequent translations, "came thither before them"; Rheims, "prevented them." (See PREVENT)

The contemporary versions generally use the phrase "got there ahead of them" (NASB, NIV; NKJV, "arrived before them"; NRSV, "arrived ahead of them"). The final phrase in the KJV "and came together unto him" does not appear in some ancient manuscripts; it is retained only in the NKJV.

OVER

In Luke 19:41 the KJV altered the earlier translations from Wycliffe to the Bishops' Bible, which stated that when Jesus saw Jerusalem, he "wept on it." The KJV translated this verse: "he beheld the city, and wept over it," and the contemporary versions follow this translation.

In 1 Thessalonians 3:7, however, the KJV follows the innovation of the Bishops' Bible in rendering it as "we were comforted over you," rather than the earlier versions, "we had consolation in you." "Comforted over you" reads awkwardly in today's English, so the contemporary translations replace "over you" with "about you" (NKJV: "concerning you").

Coverdale had used "over" in the sense of "about" or "concerning" in 1 Chronicles

19:2 ("to comfort him over his father"). The Great Bible and the Bishops' Bible expanded this to "over the death of his father"; the Geneva Bible said "for his father"; and the KJV used "concerning his father," which has been retained by most of the contemporary versions.

OVERCHARGE

The word "overcharge" today means "to ask too much money for some product or service." In the KJV it occurs once in the sense of "overburden," and once in the obsolete sense of "accuse too strongly." Luke 21:34 reads: "Take heed to yourselves, lest at any time your hearts be overcharged with surfeiting, and drunkenness, and cares of this life, and *so* that day come upon you unawares." Here "overcharged" is rendered by most of the contemporary versions as "weighed down"; the NASB has "weighted down."

In 2 Corinthians 2:5 the KJV reads, "But if any have caused grief, he hath not grieved me, but in part: that I may not overcharge you all." Here mistaken punctuation has attached "but in part" to "me," when it should belong to "you all."

The contemporary versions follow the amended punctuation and translate "that I may not overcharge" as "not to be too severe" (NKJV; NIV and RSV, "not to put it too severely"); "not to exaggerate it" (NRSV); "in order not to say too much" (NASB).

OVERLIVE

This word means to "live longer than" or "after the death of," "to survive," "to outlive." The same Hebrew words which mean "prolonged [their] days after Joshua" are translated "overlived Joshua" in the KJV of Joshua 24:31, and "outlived Joshua" in Judges 2:7. This difference in rendering goes back to Tyndale.

The majority of the contemporary versions have "outlived Joshua" in both passages, except for the NASB, which has "survived Joshua." Shakespeare uses "outlive" in eighteen passages and "overlive" just once, in *King Henry IV, Part II* (IV, 1, 15).

OVERPASS

We are generally familiar with a highway or railroad overpass. The word "overpass" is used as a verb once by the KJV in the obsolete sense of "go too far," "go beyond limit or restriction," "transgress." The passage is Jeremiah 5:28: "They are waxen fat, they shine: yea, they overpass the deeds of the wicked: they judge not the cause, the cause of the fatherless, yet they prosper; and the right of the needy do they not judge." The Hebrew of the second line of this verse means "they overflow with wicked things."

This is variously translated by the contemporary versions as: "they surpass the deeds of the wicked" (NKJV; "They also excel in deeds of wickedness" (NASB); "They know no limits in deeds of wickedness" (NRSV); "Their evil deeds have no limit" (NIV).

OVERPAST, BE

The expression "be overpast" is used twice in the sense of "be ended," "be past," "be over and gone." "Until these calamities be overpast" (Psalm 57:1, KJV) is now translated as "Until these calamities have passed by" (NKJV); "Until destruction passes by" (NASB); "until the destroying storms pass by" (NRSV); "until the disaster has passed" (NIV).

The other example in the KJV is Isaiah 26:20: "Come, my people, enter thou into thy chambers, and shut thy doors about thee: hide thyself as it were for a little moment, until the indignation be overpast." Here the NKJV and NRSV have "is past"; the NASB has "runs its course"; the NIV, "has passed by."

OVERRUN

In modern English, a place which is overrun—whether it be a house with mice or a country with soldiers—is invaded by an overwhelming swarm or horde. A play which overruns exceeds its allotted performance time. In the KJV, however, "overrun" means literally to "outrun," "run faster than someone else." Thus, "Ahimaaz ran by way of the plain, and overran Cushi" (2 Samuel 18:23, KJV) is generally translated by the contemporary versions as "outran the Cushite" (the NASB has "passed up the Cushite").

The only other occurrence of the word in the KJV is in Nahum 1:8 ("with an overrunning flood he will make an utter end of the place thereof") and here its participle is closer to modern usage and means "overflowing." The contemporary versions translate this as "an overflowing flood" (NKJV, NASB); "a roaring flood" (CEV); "an overwhelming flood" (NIV, NLT); "a rushing flood" (NRSV, NCV).

P

PADDLE

In today's English "paddle" at once brings to mind canoes or other boats which are propelled by what the OED describes as "a small spade-like implement with a long handle" or "a sort of short oar used without a rowlock, having a broad blade." The word occurs once in the KJV, in Deuteronomy 23:13: "Thou shalt have a paddle upon thy weapon; and it shall be, when thou wilt ease thyself abroad, thou shalt dig therewith, and shalt turn back and cover that which cometh from thee."

Tyndale's version was more intelligible: "thou shalt have a sharpe poynt at the ende of thy wepon." The Geneva Bible was the first to use "paddle," translating this passage as "thou shalt have a paddle among thy weapons." In adopting the word, the KJV further strained the reader's imagination by putting the paddle upon the weapon, when the more accurate translation is the Geneva Bible's "among thy weapons." In the fifteenth and sixteenth centuries, the spadelike implement described by the OED was "used for cleaning a ploughshare of earth or clods, digging up thistles, etc."

In Deuteronomy, the KJV's "paddle" is a sixteenth-century modernization, similar to the use of the word "candlestick" for a lampstand. The Hebrew word *yathed* means a "tent peg" or "stake." The KJV translates it as "stake" in Isaiah 33:20 and 54:2, and "pin" in the story of Samson and Delilah

(Judges 16:13–14). Elsewhere, the KJV uses "nail" or "pin."

In Deuteronomy 23:13, the contemporary versions translate the KJV's "paddle" as "a spade" (NASB; NLT); "an implement" (NKJV); "a trowel" (NRSV); "a small shovel" (CEV); the NIV has simply "something to dig with."

PAINED

As a verb, "pained" is now obsolete, but it appears in the KJV in Revelation 12:1–2: "There appeared a great wonder in heaven; a woman clothed with the sun, and the moon under her feet, and upon her head a crown of twelve stars: And she being with child cried, travailing in birth, and pained to be delivered."

The word "pained" has two possible meanings here, for it can be understood in the obsolete sense of "took pains," "endeavored," "strove." But the Greek here is the passive participle of the verb which the KJV usually translates as "torment." This woman was in anguish.

The contemporary versions replace the verb with a phrase such as "she cried out . . . in pain to give birth" (NKJV); "was crying out . . . in the agony of giving birth" (NRSV), the NIV has "cried out in pain," the CEV, "she was crying because of the great pain," and the NLT, "she cried out in the pain of labor."

PALMERWORM

A palmer was someone who had returned from a visit to the Holy Land as a crusader or pilgrim, in token of which he carried a leaf of palm. The term was also applied to itinerant monks who went from shrine to shrine, under a perpetual vow of poverty. In the sixteenth century "palmer" and "palmerworm" appear in English literature as names for a migratory caterpillar which swarms in great numbers, devouring vegetation.

The OED quotes from Edward Topsell's *The historie of serpents* (1658): "There is another sort of these Caterpillers, who have no certain place of abode, nor yet cannot tell where to finde their food, but like unto superstitious Pilgrims, do wander and stray hither and thither, . . . these have purchased a very apt name among us Englishmen, to be called Palmer-worms, by reason of their wandering and roguish life, (for they never stay in one place, but are ever wandering)."

"Palmerworm" is used in the KJV translation of Joel 1:4; 2:25; Amos 4:9 for the Hebrew *gazam*, which means a cutting, destructive locust. The theme of the book of Joel is an unparalleled plague of locusts, which the prophet takes as a judgment of God, and a warning of the "great and terrible day of the LORD."

There are nine Old Testament Hebrew words for "locust." Four of these appear in Joel 1:4, which reads in the KJV, "That which the palmerworm hath left hath the locust eaten; and that which the locust hath left hath the cankerworm eaten; and that which the cankerworm hath left hath the caterpiller eaten." "Palmerworm" is now translated "the chewing locust" (NKJV; NASB, "the gnawing locust"); "the cutting locust" (NRSV, NCV, NLT, RSV); the NIV has simply "the locust swarm."

In the judgment of some scholars, the four names in this verse (in the KJV, the palmerworm, locust, cankerworm, and caterpillar), denote four stages in the life and development of the locust. There is a brief but clear discussion in *The Interpreters Bible* (vol. 6, p. 737). For a vivid description of the devastations of locusts in Bible lands, see Hastings' *Dictionary of the Bible* (vol. III, pp. 130–131).

PALSY

The word "palsy," which is used today mainly in connection with diseases which cause a muscular tremor, is a contraction of the older English "paralysie," derived from the French and meaning "paralysis." In the sixteenth century "paralysie" was passing out of use, and "paralysis" was coming in; in the period of transition, "palsy" was the common term.

The contemporary versions use "paralytic" and "paralyzed" where the KJV has "palsy" in Matthew 4:24; 8:6; 9:2, 6; Mark 2:3–10; Luke 5:18, 24; Acts 8:7; 9:33. Some scholars have suggested from these references that there may have been polio epidemics in Palestine in New Testament times.

PAPS

"Paps is an old word for "breasts" or "nipples," which is now an archaic or dialect word. It was used by Tyndale in three passages of the New Testament (Luke 11:27; 23:29; Revelation 1:13), where it was retained by the KJV. Where the context is feminine (in Luke, and especially at 23:29), the contemporary versions use "breasts"; where the context is masculine (in Revelation), they use "chest."

"Paps" also occurs in the KJV's translation of Ezekiel 23:21, but this reflects a probable error in the transmission of the Hebrew text, which most of the contemporary translations emend to a phrase such as "your young breasts" (NIV, NCV, NRSV; NKJV, "your youthful breasts").

PART

Among other usages in the KJV, "part" is used in the now archaic senses of "divide among recipients" and "participate in a division into shares." As a transitive verb, "part" is used nine times by the KJV in the archaic sense of "divide among a number of recipients," "distribute." The outstanding example occurs at the crucifixion of Jesus: "And when they had crucified him, they parted his garments, casting lots upon them, what every man should take" (Mark 15:24).

The majority of the contemporary versions translate "parted his garments" as "divided his garments [or "clothes"]." Other examples of the KJV's "part" now being translated as "divide" occur in Psalm 22:18; Job 41:6 (NKJV, "apportion"); Joel 3:2. The verb also occurs in Acts 2:45 (KJV): "[They] sold their possessions and goods, and parted them to all men, as every man had need." In the contemporary versions this becomes "divided them among all" (NKJV); "sharing them with all" (NASB); "they would . . . distribute the proceeds to all" (NRSV); "they gave to anyone" (NIV); "give the money to whoever needed it" (CEV).

As an intransitive verb, "part" is used once in the KJV (in 1 Samuel 30:24) in the obsolete sense of "participating in a division into shares." Here, "part" is used twice as a noun and in the final clause as a verb. The KJV reads: "But as his part is that goeth down to the battle, so shall his part be that tarrieth by the stuff: they shall part alike."

The NKJV retains "part" as a noun ("But as his part is who goes down to the battle, so shall his part be who stays by the supplies"), but replaces the verb with "share" ("they shall share alike"). All the other contemporary versions except the CEV replace all three instances of "part" with "share"; the CEV has "Soldiers who stay behind to guard the camp get as much as those who go into battle."

PARTAKER

The word "partaker" means "one who takes a part or share," hence a "partner" or "participator." The word is used thirty times in the KJV New Testament, and presents no real difficulty; the contemporary versions often translate it as "share," although the NKJV (and occasionally the NASB,

e.g., at Hebrews 3:1, and other versions) several times retain "partake" and "partaker."

For example 2 Peter 1:4, KJV: "Whereby are given unto us exceeding great and precious promises: that by these ye might be partakers of the divine nature, having escaped the corruption that is in the word through lust." The NASB and NKJV retain the KJV "partakers"; the NCV and NLT use the verb "share"; the NIV has "participate in"; and the NRSV, "participants"; the CEV has "God made great and marvelous promises, so that his nature would become part of us." At 1 Corinthians 10:17 (KJV), "For we being many are one bread, and one body: for we are all partakers of that one bread," the CEV and NCV use the verb "share"; and the NASB, NIV, and NKJV use the verb "partake."

The one occurrence in the KJV Old Testament, Psalm 50:18, is not entirely clear: "When thou sawest a thief, then thou consentedst with him, and hast been partaker with adulterers." A literal translation of the Hebrew of the last clause is "and with adulterers is your portion," that is, your chosen, habitual companionship and way of life. The NKJV retains "partaker"; other contemporary translations have "associate with" (NASB); "take part in" (NCV); "throw in your lot with" (NIV); "spend your time with" (NLT); "keep company with" (NRSV).

An example of Shakespeare's use of the term is found in *King Henry VI, Part I* (II, 4, 100):

"For your partaker Pole, and you
    yourself,
I'll note you in my book of memory,
To scourge you for this
    apprehension."

PARTICULAR

The phrase "in particular" appears twice in the KJV in the sense of "individually," "each," "one by one." For the KJV's "ye are the body of Christ, and members in particular" (1 Corinthians 12:27), the NKJV, NASB, and NRSV have "members individually" or "individually members"; the CEV, NCV, and NIV have "each one of you."

"Let every one of you in particular so love his wife even as himself" (Ephesians 5:33, KJV) is similarly translated in the contemporary versions by "each one of you" (NKJV, NIV, NCV; NRSV, "each of you"); "each individual" (NASB); "each husband" (CEV); "each man" (NLT). The adverb "particularly" has this same older, almost obsolete sense on the two occasions in which it occurs in the KJV.

Paul's report to James and the elders at Jerusalem is described in Acts 21:19: "And when he had saluted them, he declared particularly what things God had wrought among the Gentiles by his ministry."

Contemporary translations have "he told in detail" (NKJV; NIV, "reported in detail"; NLT, "gave a detailed account"); "relate [NRSV, "related"] one by one" (NASB, NRSV); "told them everything" (NCV). In Hebrews 9:5, the KJV's "speak particularly" is generally now reworded as "speak in detail."

PASS ALL UNDERSTANDING

If something "passes all understanding," it is extremely difficult for someone to grasp with the mind or to accept. The phrase comes from Philippians 4:17 (KJV), "And the peace of God, which passeth all understanding shall keep your hearts and minds through Christ Jesus."

The contemporary versions render this as: "surpasses all understanding" (NKJV), "transcends all understanding" (NIV), "surpasses all comprehension" (NASB), "peace that no one can completely understand" (CEV), "peace, which is so great we cannot understand it" (NCV), and "peace, which is far more wonderful than the human mind can understand" (NLT).

PASS BY ON THE OTHER SIDE

The expression "pass by on the other side," meaning to give no help or sympathy to someone in need, derives from the ac-

tions of the priest and the Levite in the parable of the good Samaritan: "And by chance there came down a certain priest that way: and when he saw him, he passed by on the other side. And likewise a Levite, when he was at the place, came and looked on him, and passed by on the other side" (Luke 10:31–32, KJV).

The contemporary versions generally (NASB, NIV, NKJV, NRSV, and RSV) retain the KJV wording for this phrase; the CEV has "walked by on the other side" and "went by on the other side"; the NCV, "walked by on the other side"; the NLT, "crossed to the other side of the road and passed him by" (v. 31). (See also GOOD SAMARITAN)

PASSAGE

The word "passage" in the KJV has the same two main meanings as it still has today: "the act of passing" (as in "a bird of passage" or the novel *A Passage to India*) and "the place which allows passing to take place." The first meaning occurs in the KJV only in Numbers 20:21: "Edom refused to give Israel passage through his territory." The NKJV and NRSV retain "passage" here; other contemporary versions have "refused to allow Israel to pass through" or a similar wording.

As a place of passage, it is used by the KJV in 1 Samuel 13:23; 14:4 to denote the pass of Michmash, the scene of the exploit of Jonathan and his armor-bearer and, three centuries later, a stage in the advance of an invading army from the north (Isaiah 10:29); in all these instances, the contemporary versions simply use "pass."

In Judges 12:5–6 the KJV uses "passages" for the fords of the Jordan where the men of Gilead tested the Ephraimites by making them pronounce "Shibboleth"; and the same word is used for the fords, far to the east, seized by the enemies of Babylon (Jeremiah 51:32). The contemporary versions generally use "fords."

In Jeremiah 22:20 the Hebrew word represented in the KJV by "passages" is "Abarim," the proper name of the mountain in Moab where Moses died, and this name is used in all the contemporary versions.

PASSENGER

The word "passenger" is used in the KJV in the old sense of "a passer-by," "a traveler or wayfarer," not in the more modern sense of "one who is carried by a vehicle or vessel." In Proverbs 9:15 (KJV), the foolish woman who sits at the door of her house "to call passengers" is "calling to those who pass by," the translation used (with variations in the tense of the verb) by all the contemporary versions.

In the Gog and Magog oracles (Ezekiel 38—39), the KJV's "valley of the passengers" (Ezekiel 39:11) is "the valley of those who pass by" (NKJV, NASB; NIV, "of those who travel"); "the Valley of the Travelers" (NCV, NLT; CEV, "Travelers' Valley"). In the same verse, the KJV speaks of the burial ground of Gog which "shall stop the noses of the passengers"; in the contemporary versions there is no mention of noses, simply a phrase such as "block the path of the travelers" (NRSV) or similar wording.

"Passengers" in Ezekiel 39:14 is more difficult. Referring to the clean-up operation after the defeat of Gog and his army, the KJV has "passing through the land to bury with the passengers those that remain upon the face of the earth." The NASB retains the idea of "passengers" with the translation, "burying those who were passing through" (i.e., the invaders); the NRSV has "bury any invaders"; but the other contemporary versions do not have a special reference to "passengers" or "travelers." (See PASSAGE)

PASTOR

The word "pastors" appears once in the KJV New Testament, in Ephesians 4:11, where it means "a shepherd of souls," "a Christian minister." Tyndale and Coverdale used "shepherd" at this point; the Geneva Bible was the first to use "pastor,"

which the majority of all subsequent versions have retained.

In the KJV Old Testament, "pastor" appears eight times, all in Jeremiah, as a translation of the Hebrew word which elsewhere is translated "shepherd" sixty-two times and "herdman" seven times. These eight passages are Jeremiah 2:8; 3:15; 10:21; 12:10; 17:16; 22:22; 23:1–2, which all refer to those who care or should care, for the people.

Here, again, the Geneva Bible took the initiative. But the word "shepherd" also appears in twelve other passages of Jeremiah, and in ten of these the shepherds care for people rather than for animals. So there is no real basis for the Geneva Bible and the KJV to use "pastor" as if for a special, different group of people, and this is reflected in contemporary translations, which replace "pastors" with "shepherds" (although the NKJV uses "rulers" in Jeremiah 12:10; 22:22).

The KJV translation of Jeremiah 17:16, "I have not hastened from being a pastor to follow thee," is based on a Hebrew word which can have two very different meanings, depending on the accent in the middle. *Ra'ah* is the participle of the verb "to shepherd"; *ra'ah* is a noun meaning "evil." Both readings are possible; some scholars hold that the latter is more natural and fits the context better, and the RSV translated the verse as "I have not pressed thee to send evil."

However, the majority of the more recent translations retain the word "shepherd"; for example, "I have not hurried away from being a shepherd who follows You" (NKJV; NASB, "from being a shepherd after You"); "I have not run away from being your shepherd" (NIV; NRSV, "from being a shepherd in your service").

PATIENCE

The Greek New Testament has two words for "patient endurance." The KJV usually translates *makrothumia* by "longsuffering" and *hupomone* by "patience." The NKJV retains "longsuffering" in, for example, 2 Corinthians 6:6, but the majority of the contemporary versions translate *makrothumia* as "patience" (see LONGSUF-FERING) and *hupomone* as "endurance," "patient endurance," "perseverance," "patience," and "standing firm."

"In your patience possess ye your souls" (Luke 21:19, KJV) seems to advise resignation, but it is far more positive than that, and this aspect is brought out in the contemporary versions. "By your endurance you will gain your lives" (NASB; NRSV, "you will gain your souls"); "By standing firm you will gain life" (NIV; NLT, "you will win your souls"). The NKJV remains close to the KJV, with "By your patience possess your souls."

"Perseverance" and "endurance" are the translations used by the majority of the contemporary versions where the KJV has "patience" (in, e.g., Romans 5:3; Hebrews 12:1; Revelation 1:9; 2:2–3, 19; 3:10; 13:10; 14:12), although the NIV has a frequent liking for "patient endurance" (e.g., at Revelation 1:9; 13:10; 14:12) which is shared by the NRSV in Revelation 1:9.

The KJV translation of Hebrews 10:36 ("For ye have need of patience, that, after ye have done the will of God, ye might receive the promise") seems to imply that patience is needed because of delay on the part of God. But that is not what the text means.

The NKJV and NASB translate "ye have need of patience" as "you have need of endurance" (NRSV, "you need endurance"; NIV, "you need to persevere"). The CEV retains a link with the KJV, with "Learn to be patient."

William Barclay, in *A New Testament Wordbook*, has admirable chapters on "*Makrothumia*, the divine patience" and "*Hupomone*, the manly virtue."

PATIENCE OF JOB

"The patience of Job" has become proverbial: how this man of upright character lost his wealth, his ten children, and his health. Satan brought these disasters on him, with God's permission. The book of Job tells how he kept his faith in God in the midst of all his afflictions. So to have "the patience of Job" has come to mean "to endure difficulties, misfortunes, or laborious tasks with supreme patience, courage, and tolerance."

James 5:11 reads in the KJV: "Behold, we count them happy which endure. Ye have heard of the patience of Job, and have seen the end of the Lord; that the Lord is very pitiful, and of tender mercy." This rendering fails to indicate that the verb for "endure" and the noun for "patience" (*hupomeno* and *hupomone*) have the same meaning. The NKJV follows the KJV in using two different words, although neither of them are "patience" ("Indeed we count them blessed who endure. You have heard of the perseverance of Job").

The majority of the contemporary versions, however, make the meaning of the Greek clear by using the same word for both verb and noun: "We count those blessed who endured. You have heard of the endurance of Job" (NASB; the NLT and NRSV also use variations on "endure/endurance"; NIV has "persevered/perseverance").

PATTERN

A pattern is something to be copied. In the sixteenth and seventeenth centuries the word was also used for "a copy." This obsolete sense appears twice in the KJV. In Joshua 22 the men of the tribes of Reuben, Gad, and Manasseh protest that the altar which they had built by the Jordan was not for burnt offering or sacrifice, but was simply a copy of the altar of the Lord, to serve as a reminder and a witness: "Behold the pattern of the altar of the LORD, which our fathers made, not for burnt offerings, nor for sacrifices; but it is a witness between us and you" (v. 28, KJV). The NRSV, NASB, and NLT translate "pattern" as "copy"; the NKJV and NIV have "replica."

In Hebrews 9:23, the KJV has: "It was therefore necessary that the patterns of the things in the heavens should be purified with these [i.e., sacrifices]; but the heavenly things themselves with better sacrifices than these."

The majority of the contemporary versions render "patterns" as "copies," except for the NRSV, which has "the sketches of the heavenly things," which means something slightly different. A copy is a more or less exact reproduction of something else; a sketch is a preliminary representation of a finished product.

In Hebrews 8:5 the KJV translates the same Greek word as "example": "Who serve unto the example and shadow of heavenly things." In the same way, the majority of the contemporary versions have "copy," whereas the NRSV has "sketch." (See EXAMPLE)

PEACE FOR THE WICKED

The saying "there is no peace for the wicked" is often used ironically as a mild comment when one is under pressure. The expression comes originally from Isaiah 57:21 (KJV), "There is no peace, saith my God, to the wicked." (See also Isaiah 48:22.)

The contemporary versions (NASB, NIV, NKJV, NLT, NRSV, RSV) generally have "there is no peace for the wicked," (NLT) with stylistic variations of "says my God"; the NCV has "There is no peace for evil people" and the CEV, "But I, the LORD, have promised that none who are evil will live in peace."

PEACE, GOOD WILL TOWARD MEN

The phrase "peace, good will toward men" is sometimes used at Christmas to refer to harmonious and kind relationships among everyone. The expression derives from the words of the heavenly host that appeared to the shepherds after the birth of Jesus, "Glory to God in the highest, and on earth peace, good will toward men" (Luke 2:14, KJV). Most of the contemporary versions take the expression to refer to the "'peace' or well-being which Christ's incarnation brings to persons 'of [God's] goodwill,' i.e., those who are the objects of his favor" (David Lyle Jeffrey, *A Dictionary of Biblical Tradition in English Literature*). Some of the contemporary versions (NIV, NLT, NRSV) use the word "favor," e.g., NIV, "and on earth peace to men on whom his favor rests," NRSV, "and on earth peace among those whom he favors"; others (CEV, NASB, NCV, RSV) use the verb "please," e.g., NASB, "And on earth peace among men with whom He is pleased" and CEV, "Peace on earth to everyone who pleases God." The NKJV retains the KJV translation: "And on earth peace, goodwill toward men!"

PEACEMAKERS

"Blessed are the peacemakers: for they shall be called the children of God," are the words of one of the Beatitudes in Jesus' Sermon on the Mount (Matthew 5:9, KJV). According to the OED, a "peacemaker" is "one who makes or brings about peace; one who allays strife or reconciles opponents." Tyndale's New Testament (1534) had "peacemakers," but, according to the OED, his earlier (1526) translation had "Blessed are the maynteyners of peace."

Of the contemporary versions, the NASB, NIV, NKJV, NRSV, and RSV retain the word "peacemakers"; other renderings are: "those people who make peace" (CEV), "those who work to bring peace" (NCV), and "those who work for peace" (NLT).

PEARL OF GREAT PRICE

The phrase "a pearl of great price" refers to something or someone that is extremely valuable. The expression derives from Jesus' parable in Matthew 13:45–46: "Again, the kingdom of heaven is like unto a merchant man, seeking goodly pearls: Who, when he had found one pearl of great price, went and sold all that he had, and bought it" (KJV).

The contemporary versions have: "one [NLT, "a"] pearl of great value" (NASB, NLT, NRSV, RSV); and "a very valuable" pearl (CEV, NCV); the NKJV retains the KJV expression, "one pearl of great price."

PEARLS BEFORE SWINE, TO CAST

To "cast pearls before swine" is to offer something valuable to someone who is not able to appreciate it. The first citation of this phrase in the OED is 1362, William Langland's *Piers Plowman*, "Noli mittere Margeri—perles Among hogges." The expression has gained currency from Matthew 7:6 (KJV): "Give not that which is holy unto the dogs, neither cast ye your pearls before swine, lest they trample them under their feet, and turn again and rend you."

The other contemporary versions have: "Do not throw your pearls before swine" (NASB, NRSV, RSV), "nor cast your pearls before swine" (NKJV), "Do not [NCV, "Don't"] throw your pearls to [NCV, "before"] pigs" (NCV, NIV), "Don't throw pearls down in front of pigs" (CEV), and "Don't give pearls to swine!" (NLT).

The phrase is alluded to in literature, e.g., in "Sonnet 12" Milton, writing about the hostile reactions to his liberal views on divorce, noted that "This is got by casting Pearls to Hoggs." In *The Dulham Ladies* by the American writer Sarah Orne Jewett (1849–1909), Miss Dobbin prides herself on trying always "to elevate people's thoughts and direct them into higher channels. But as for the Woolden woman, there is no use in casting pearls before swine."

PECULIAR

Today, "peculiar" almost always has a slightly disparaging tone: to describe a person, thing, or event as "peculiar" means that they are "strange," "eccentric," and "odd." It therefore sounds strange when the KJV calls God's chosen people of both the Old and New Testaments "a peculiar people" (Deuteronomy 14:2; 26:18; Titus 2:14; 1 Peter 2:9), or, in the words of the well-known hymn by Isaac Watts, "Jesus shall reign where'er the sun," all God's creatures are exhorted to "rise and bring peculiar honours to our King." What is odd about the Israelites, and why should God want strange presents?

The confusion arises because when the KJV was published in 1611 the word had not yet acquired its modern meaning of "strange" or "odd." It still meant "belonging to the individual," "one's very own," meanings which today are rarely used. In the seventeenth and eighteenth centuries, "peculiar" was applied to private personal property as distinguished from what is owned in common.

So the contemporary versions render "a peculiar people" in Deuteronomy 14:2 as "a people for His own possession" (NASB); "his treasured possession" (NRSV, NIV); "a special treasure" (NKJV); Titus 2:14 uses phrases such as "his very own" (NIV, NLT); "His own special people" (NKJV); and 1 Peter 2:9, "a people for God's own possession" (NASB, NCV).

The same Hebrew word, *segullah*, which the KJV translates as "peculiar" in Deuteronomy 14:2 and 26:18 is translated "special" in Deuteronomy 7:6, which reads: "For thou art an holy people unto the LORD thy God: the LORD thy God hath chosen thee to be a special people unto himself, above all people that are upon the face of the earth." Elsewhere, the KJV translates *segullah* as "peculiar treasure" (Exodus 19:5; Psalm 135:4; Ecclesiastes 2:8), "own proper good" (1 Chronicles 29:3), and "jewels" (Malachi 3:17).

More recent translations have given up the use of the word "peculiar" in these passages, and use instead phrases such as "treasured possession," "special treasure," as they do in Deuteronomy. In Ecclesiastes 2:8, the majority of them simply omit the word which the KJV translates as "peculiar," except for the NKJV which renders it "special treasures" and the CEV which has "precious treasures."

PEELED

The word "peeled" is used in the KJV as passive participle for the Hebrew verb which means "to make smooth, bare, or bald"; "to scour, polish." In Ezekiel 29:18 it is used of the overworked soldiers of Nebuchadnezzar: "every shoulder was peeled," which is generally rendered by the contemporary versions as "every shoulder was rubbed raw" or "rubbed bare."

The same Hebrew participle is applied to a sword in Ezekiel 21:9–11, 28, where the KJV translates it "furbished" and the majority of the contemporary versions have "polished" (the NRSV has "honed" in v. 10). It is also used for the temple utensils, which the KJV says were of "bright [i.e., polished] brass," and the contemporary versions of "burnished bronze" (1 Kings 7:45; NASB and NCV have "polished bronze").

In Isaiah 18:2, 7, the KJV's description of the Ethiopians as "a nation scattered and peeled" is now translated as "smooth" or "smooth-skinned" in the contemporary versions.

PEEP

The most common use of "peep" today refers to sly or prying glances, looking through a narrow opening, or coming slowly or partly into view. However, in the phrase "I don't want to hear a peep out of you," modern English retains the earlier meaning of the word, which imitated the sound of young birds, mice, etc., and meant a "cheep" or "faint squeak." The KJV's "wizards that peep, and that mutter" in Isaiah 8:19 is now rendered "whisper" by the NKJV, NASB, NCV, NIV, and NLT; the NRSV and CEV remain closer to "peep" with "chirp" and "make soft chirping sounds," respectively. In Isaiah 10:14, where the KJV has "there was none that moved the wing, or opened the mouth, or peeped," the NKJV, NLT, and CEV retain "peep"; the NASB, NIV, and NRSV have "chirp."

For the same Hebrew word in Isaiah 29:4, the KJV uses "whisper" ("thy speech shall whisper out of the dust") and is followed by all the contemporary versions.

PERADVENTURE

This is is a word that pleases purists because it is wholly Latin in origin, even though it came into English from medieval French. "Perhaps," on the other hand, which has replaced "peradventure" in modern English, couples Latin "per" with Old English "hap." English acquired "peradventure," "percase," and "perchance" through the Norman Conquest; "perhaps" appeared later, but has outlived all three. The KJV does not use "perchance" at all and has "perhaps" only three times, but uses "peradventure" thirty-two times.

"Peradventure" as an adverb meaning "by chance" is obsolete; in the sense of "perhaps," it is archaic. Contemporary translations usually replace "peradventure" with "perhaps," although, depending on the context and whether the sentence is a question, they may also use "suppose," "maybe," or "what if." (See, e.g., Genesis 24:5; 1 Kings 18:27; Romans 5:7; 2 Timothy 2:25.) They vary in their translations where the KJV has "Lest peradventure."

In Exodus 13:17 ("Lest peradventure the people repent," KJV), they alter the syntax to read, "The people [or: they] might change their minds" (although the NKJV retains "Lest perhaps the people change their minds"). In 2 Kings 2:16, on the other hand, where the KJV has "lest peradventure the Spirit of the LORD hath taken him up," the contemporary versions simply use "perhaps" or "maybe."

PERSECUTE

The word "persecute" meant originally "to pursue," literally "to follow after," but is now obsolete in this sense. The OED well defines its current usage as "To pursue with malignancy or enmity or injurious action; esp. to oppress with pains and penalties for holding a belief or opinion held to be injurious or heretical; To harass, trouble, vex, worry." It is ill-will which characterizes "persecute" today.

In the Old Testament the word "persecute" is used by the KJV in the older sense of "pursue," and the majority of the contemporary versions replace it with "pursue" in, for example, Psalms 7:1, 5; 35:3, 6; 71:11; 83:15; Jeremiah 29:18; Lamentations 3:66, although the NKJV retains "persecute" in Psalm 7:1, and the CEV and NCV usually translate "persecute" as "chase."

The KJV's use of "persecute" and "persecutors" in Psalms 10:2 and 7:13 represents a Hebrew verb which means "burn" or "hotly pursue" (it translates the same word as "hotly pursue" in Genesis 31:36). The contemporary versions try to convey the greater intensity of the Hebrew by using stronger words than simply "pursue": Psalm 10:2, "the wicked hotly pursue the afflicted" (NASB); "the wicked chase down those who suffer" (NCV); "the wicked man hunts down the weak" (NIV); "wicked people viciously oppress the poor" (NLT); the NKJV and NRSV retain "persecute," intending it to be understood in its modern meaning.

The KJV translates the Hebrew of Psalm 7:13 as "he [God] ordaineth his arrows against the persecutors." The contemporary versions, however, refer to the other meaning of the Hebrew word ("burn") and omit any reference to human persecutors; God has made ready his "fiery shafts" (NKJV, NASB, NRSV) or "flaming arrows" (NIV, NCV, NLT).

In the New Testament "persecute," "persecution," and "persecutor" are generally used by the KJV in the sense which these words have today, and the contemporary versions usually retain this wording. There are two exceptions: in 1 Thessalonians 2:15 the majority of the contemporary translations have "drove us out" (the NKJV retains "persecuted"), and in Revelation 12:13 the woman is "pursued" according to the NIV, NRSV and RSV, but "persecuted" in the NKJV and NASB.

PERSON

Today we think of a person as an individual human being with his or her own character, history, and consciousness. "Respect for persons" is regarded as a basic principle of sound democracy and true religion. But we then read in the KJV that "God is no respecter of persons" (Acts 10:34), and this idea is repeated in one form or another in a dozen passages of the Old and New Testaments. The Greek word which the KJV translates as "respecter of persons" means "one who accepts the face"; the Latin equivalent is *acceptor personae*, that is, "one who accepts the mask worn by an actor or the character he assumed."

When the KJV was published, the English word "person" was still close to this primary meaning of the Latin word *persona*, mask. It referred to people's outward appearance or circumstances—physical presence, dress, wealth, position—rather than to their intrinsic worth or inner springs of conscious, self-determining being. "God is no respecter of persons" or similar wording in Acts 10:34 and elsewhere means that God does not regard mere externals.

Indeed, the expression "no respecter of persons" has come to describe an attitude that treats all the people involved in the same way, regardless of their wealth, fame, class, etc. In the contemporary translations, God "shows no partiality" (Acts 10:34, NKJV, NRSV, RSV; NASB, "God is not one to show partiality"); he "treats all people alike" (CEV); he "does not show favoritism" (NIV); "to God every person is the same" (NCV).

In Moses' instructions to the men whom he appointed as judges, the meaning of the expression "respect persons" in the KJV is stated clearly: "Ye shall not respect persons in judgment; but ye shall hear the small as well as the great; ye shall not be afraid of the face of man; for the judgment is God's" (Deuteronomy 1:17).

The contemporary versions generally translate this phrase as an admonition not to "show partiality" or "be partial." A pointed exposition of the meaning of the phrase for the life of the early Christians is found in James 2:1–9, where "respect of persons" in verse 1 (KJV) is translated by the contemporary versions as "partiality" or "favoritism."

PERSUADE

The word "persuade" now implies success; we speak of persuading people only if our arguments and pleas are successful in getting them to accept the judgment or make the decision we are advocating. Yet in the KJV's translation of Acts 19:8–9 we read of Paul "disputing and persuading" at Corinth, with the result that some "were hardened, and believed not, but spake evil of that way."

In Acts 28:23 the KJV tells us that at Rome "there came many to him into his lodging; to whom he expounded and testified the kingdom of God, persuading them concerning Jesus, both out of the law of Moses, and out of the prophets, from morning till evening"; but the next verse records that some believed and some did not, so his persuasion was obviously not entirely successful.

In the Corinthian example, some of the contemporary versions (NASB, NCV, NKJV) retain "persuading," while others (NIV, NLT, NRSV) have "arguing persuasively." In their account of Paul in Rome, the majority of the contemporary versions acknowledge Paul's partial lack of success by adding the verb "try": "trying [NCV, "tried"] to persuade them" (NASB, NCV); NIV and NRSV, "tried [NRSV, "trying"] to convince them"; the NKJV retains "persuading."

In *The Merchant of Venice* (III, 2, 281) Salerio describes the unyielding attitude of Shylock:

"Twenty merchants,
The Duke himself, and the
   magnificoes
Of greatest port have all persuaded
   with him,
But none can drive him from the
   envious plea
Of forfeiture, of justice, and his bond."

The KJV uses "persuade" in its modern sense of "successful argument" in such passages as Matthew 27:20; Acts 14:19; 19:26; the majority of contemporary versions retain the word, although the NASB, NIV, and NRSV have "won over" in Acts 14:19, and the NIV and NCV have "convinced" in Acts 19:26.

The passive form of the Greek verb is used in some passages, but the KJV's translation ("I am persuaded, "they be persuaded") does not always adequately convey the conviction of the original. The famous "I am persuaded" of the KJV's Romans 8:38–39 ("For I am persuaded, that neither death, nor life, nor angels, nor principalities . . . shall be able to separate us from the love of God, which is in Christ Jesus our Lord") is rendered as "I am convinced" (NASB, NIV, NLT, NRSV) or "I am sure" (CEV, NCV).

"Convinced" is the most general contemporary translation of the passive "persuaded" in, for example, Luke 16:31; 20:6; Romans 4:21; 14:5; 2 Timothy 1:5, 12; Hebrews 6:9 (for this final reference, the NKJV, NRSV, and NIV have "we are confident" for the KJV's "we are persuaded"). The NKJV generally, and the NIV occasionally, retain "persuaded" in all these examples.

In the Old Testament, the word "persuade" usually has a bad sense, being used as the equivalent of "entice," "mislead," or "deceive." Compare 1 Kings 22:20–22, where the KJV uses "persuade" for the same Hebrew verb which it translates "entice" in 2 Chronicles 18:19–21. The majority of contemporary versions have "entice" in all these examples, although the NKJV retains "persuade." In the accounts of Hezekiah in 2 Kings 18 and 19, 2 Chronicles 32, and Isaiah 36 and 37, the KJV's "persuade" is now generally translated "mislead" (though the NKJV is again the exception).

PHYSICIAN, HEAL THYSELF

The expression "physician, heal thyself" is sometimes used to mean "doctors, lawyers, ministers of religion, teachers etc sometimes cannot do for themselves what they profess to be able to do for others" (*Oxford Dictionary of Current Idiomatic English*, vol. 2). The saying derives from Luke 4:23: "And he [Jesus] said unto them, Ye will surely say unto me this proverb, Physician, heal thyself: whatsoever we have heard done in Capernaum, do also here in thy country" (KJV). Evidently, among the ancients this proverb was well known.

The contemporary versions render the proverb as "Physician, heal yourself" (NASB, NIV, NKJV, NLT, RSV), "Doctor, heal yourself" (NCV), "Doctor, cure yourself" (NRSV), and "Doctor, first make yourself well" (CEV).

PILL

Today we no longer use "pill" as a verb, but in the KJV it means "to peel, strip off the skin, rind, or bark." "And Jacob took him rods of green poplar, and of the hazel and chestnut tree; and pilled white strakes in them . . . And he set the rods which he had pilled before the flocks in the gutters in the watering troughs when the flocks came to drink" (Genesis 30:37–38, KJV).

"Pilled" was the word used in these verses by Tyndale, Coverdale, and the other sixteenth-century translations made from the Hebrew. It was the word used by Shylock in Shakespeare's *The Merchant of Venice* (I, 3, 80), when he recounted the story of Jacob:

"The skilful shepheard pild me certaine wands,
And . . . stucke them up before the fulsome Ewes."

Later editions of Shakespeare's play, and the contemporary versions of the Bible, have changed the word to "peeled."

The KJV also uses "pilled" in one of the books of the Apocrypha, Tobit 11:13. When Tobias returned from his journey, he anointed his blinded father's eyes with gall and when he rubbed them, "the whiteness pilled away from the corners of his eyes." The NRSV has "peeled off."

Tyndale used the verb "to pill" in quite another sense, meaning "to rob, plunder, pillage, extort from." He translated Paul's question in 2 Corinthians 12:17, "Did I pill you by any of them which I sent unto you?" The KJV renders this as "Did I make a gain of you by any of them whom I sent unto you?" and the majority of the contemporary versions (NASB, NKJV, NLT, NRSV, RSV) use "take advantage" (NIV, "Did I exploit you?"; CEV, "Were you cheated?"; NCV, "Did I cheat you?").

PILLAR OF SALT

When Lot was fleeing from Sodom, the angel said to him, his wife and two daughters, "Escape for thy life; look not behind thee, neither stay thou in all the plain; escape to the mountain, lest thou be consumed" (Genesis 19:17, KJV). But Lot's wife "looked back from behind him, and she became a pillar of salt" (v. 26, KJV). The phrase "a pillar of salt" is adopted by all the contemporary versions except the CEV, which has for the whole verse: "On the way, Lot's wife looked back and was turned into a block of salt."

Jesus warns, "Remember Lot's wife" (Luke 17:32); ("Remember what happened to Lot's wife," CEV). She disobeyed and continued to long for the earthly pleasures that she was leaving behind, rejecting the way of salvation and refusing to break with the world.

PILLOW

The word "pillow" may be applied to whatever is used to support the head in sleeping or reclining, although today the noun usually refers to a (relatively) soft, stuffed cushion for a bed, or something which resembles it, such as a lap. The word is appropriate, therefore, in three of the four KJV passages in which it appears, although in Genesis 28:11, 18 the contemporary versions generally omit "pillow" and simply use a phrase such as "the stone he [Jacob] had put under his head" rather than the KJV's "the stone that he had put for his pillows" (v. 18).

In Mark 4:38, however, the contemporary versions retain the KJV's idea of a pillow, although most of them describe Jesus as sleeping on a "cushion" (the NKJV and CEV retain "pillow"). In 1 Samuel 19:13, 16 the KJV describes Michal covering David's escape by putting "a pillow of goats' hair for his bolster"; the contemporary versions all omit "pillow" and use a variety of words to describe Michal's construction: "quilt of goats' hair" (NASB); "a cover of goats' hair" (NKJV); "a net [and "the covering"] of goats' hair" (NRSV); other translations simply have "goats' hair."

The fourth occurrence of "pillow" in the KJV is in an obscure passage in Ezekiel (13:17–23) concerning women who prophesy lies as they hunt souls. "Women that sew pillows to all armholes" is an inaccurate translation of the Hebrew, which is now rendered as "sew magic bands on all wrists" (NASB; NRSV omits "magic"); "sew magic charms on [NIV, "on all"] their wrists" (NCV, NIV; NKJV: "on their sleeves"); "wear magic charms on their wrists" (CEV); "tie magic charms on their wrists" (NLT). (See ARMHOLE; KERCHIEF)

PITIFUL

In contemporary English "pitiful" means "arousing or deserving pity" ("the animals in the zoo were a pitiful sight") or "so inadequate that it arouses contempt" ("a pitiful offer of a one percent pay increase"). In the KJV, however, the word, which occurs three times, has the meaning "full of pity; compassionate." In one instance "pitiful" is used to describe the Lord's character: "The Lord is very pitiful, and of tender mercy" (James 5:11, KJV), where "very pitiful" is rendered in the contemporary versions as "full of compassion" (NASB, NIV), "very compassionate" (NKJV), "compassionate" (NRSV, RSV), "full of mercy" (NCV), "so merciful" (CEV), and "full of tenderness" (NLT).

In two instances "pitiful" is used to refer to human behavior: Lamentations 4:10, "The hands of the pitiful women have sodden their own children" (KJV), rendered by the contemporary versions as "compassionate" by the NASB, NIV, NKJV, NRSV, and RSV, "loving" (CEV), "kind" (NCV), and "tenderhearted" (NLT); and 1 Peter 3:8, "Finally, be ye all of one mind, having compassion one of another, love as brethren, be pitiful, be courteous" (KJV); rendered by the contemporary versions as "kind" (CEV, NCV), "kindhearted" (NASB), "tenderhearted" (NKJV), "a tender heart" (NRSV, RSV), "tender hearts" (NLT), and "compassionate" (NIV).

PLAIN

Today, to call someone "plain" usually refers to his (or more often her) looks, and "plain speaking" is telling the truth in a downright (and often tactless) manner. Then we read in the KJV that "Esau was a cunning hunter, a man of the field; and Jacob was a plain man, dwelling in tents" (Genesis 25:27) and may well wonder what it means. The first clause means that Esau was a skillful hunter, a man of the open country. "Dwelling in tents" implies that Jacob stayed home and attended to his cattle. But in what sense was he a "plain" man?

The Hebrew adjective is *tam,* which means "complete," "perfect." It is the adjective applied to Job, when the Lord calls him "a perfect and an upright man" (Job 1:8; 2:3, KJV). It is the adjective used in Psalm 37:37 (KJV), "Mark the perfect man, and behold the upright." The majority of the contemporary versions read "blameless" instead of "perfect" in these verses.

The Great Bible and the Bishops' Bible did not hesitate to call Jacob "a perfect man" in this contrast with Esau. Martin Luther's translation was *ein frommer Mann,* which means "pious" but may also mean "gentle," "quiet," "steady." The Greek Septuagint had *aplastos,* "natural," "unaffected"; and the Latin Vulgate, *simplex,* "simple,"

P

"plain." Coverdale used "simple"; the Geneva Bible took "plain" and the KJV followed it.

It seems clear that Genesis 25:27 is to be taken as a quite objective statement. The writer is not concerned here with the moral character of either of the twins; he is not apportioning praise or blame. He is simply stating the basic difference between their respective interests and ways of life. In contrast with Esau's special craving and skill, Jacob was an *'ish tam,* "a complete man," in the sense that he took life's ordinary duties seriously.

The contemporary translations all convey this sense of quiet solidarity, although they use several different adjectives to do so: "Jacob was a quiet man" (NIV, NCV, NRSV); "a peaceful man" (NASB); "a mild man" (NKJV). The NLT paraphrases as "Jacob was the kind of person who liked to stay at home."

PLAY

In contemporary English the word "play" has many meanings, including "amuse oneself," "take part in a game," and "perform on a musical instrument." These meanings also occur in the KJV, but in a few instances, there is a more specific meaning that is no longer current in contemporary English.

In 2 Samuel 2:14, the KJV has "And Abner said to Joab, Let the young men now arise, and play before us. And Joab said, Let them arise." According to William Wright (*The Bible Word-Book*), here "the word is used in the technical sense of playing at fence, fencing." The marginal note in the Geneva version is, "Let us see how they can handle their weapons."

The contemporary versions render the KJV (also retained by the RSV) as: "have [NRSV, "hold"] a contest" (NASB, NRSV), "fight hand to hand" (NIV), "have a contest" (NCV), "put on an exhibition of hand-to-hand combat" (NLT), "compete" (NKJV), and "fight each other" (CEV).

In Exodus 32:6, the KJV reads, "And they rose up early on the morrow, and offered burnt offerings, and brought peace offerings, and the people sat down to eat and to drink and rose up to play." The NASB and NKJV retain the KJV "play"; the other contemporary versions render this as: "revel" (NRSV), "indulge in pagan revelry" (NLT), "indulge in revelry" (NIV), "began to carry on like wild people" (CEV), and "sinned sexually" (NCV).

This verse is quoted in 1 Corinthians 10:7, with similar translations, except the CEV, which has "dance around," and the NRSV, which has "play."

PLAY THE FOOL

When Saul was searching for David, David found him inside his camp with his army encamped around him. David could have killed Saul, but he would not "raise his hand against the LORD's anointed" (1 Samuel 26:9, NRSV). Later Saul realized his folly: "Then said Saul, I have sinned: return, my son David: for I will no more do thee harm, because my soul was precious in thine eyes this day: behold, I have played the fool, and have erred exceedingly" (v. 21, KJV).

The KJV expression "I have played the fool" is retained by the NASB, NKJV, and RSV; the CEV and NIV have "I have [CEV, "I've"] acted like a fool"; the NLT and NRSV, "I have been a fool"; and the NCV, "I have been very stupid."

PLEAD

The word "plead" in the KJV does not have the modern meaning of "to pray, supplicate, beg, or implore." It always has the sense of "seeking a judgment," and means "to argue for or against a cause," "to urge a person's claim or state their case." This usage survives today in legal terminology. "If ye plead against me my reproach" (Job 19:5, KJV) is now translated as "plead my disgrace against me" (NKJV); "prove my disgrace against me" (NASB); "use my humiliation against me" (NIV); "make my humiliation an argument against me" (NRSV).

In Jeremiah 30:13, the NASB, NIV, and NKJV retain the KJV's use of "plead" ("There is none to plead thy cause"); the NRSV has "There is no one to uphold your cause," and the NCV has "no one to argue your case." In Job 16:21, the majority of the contemporary versions retain the KJV's "plead" ("O that one might plead for a man with God"), although the NRSV renders it "that he would maintain the right of a mortal with God." The verb here is translated "reason" by the KJV in Job 13:3 and Isaiah 1:18.

The four Hebrew verbs which are represented by "plead" in the KJV have the basic meanings of "to contend, prove, judge"; and each can imply action as well as words. These and similar words are quite often used by the contemporary translations to replace the KJV's use of "plead." See, e.g., Judges 6:31; Job 19:5; and Proverbs 31:9.

The word "plead" does not appear in the KJV New Testament.

POINT OUT

In modern English, "to point out" means "to draw attention to an object or a piece of information." In the KJV it is used in the archaic sense of "to mark out an area." This is its meaning in Numbers 34:7–8, 10, in the description of the boundaries of the land of Canaan which the Lord is granting to Israel: "Ye shall point out your east border from Hazarenan to Shepham" (v. 10). The NKJV and NRSV translate these verses as "mark out your border" (NRSV, "boundary"); the NASB, "draw a line"and the NIV, "run a line."

POLL

The basic meaning of the noun "poll," and its only meaning in the KJV, is "the human head." A "poll tax" is "a head tax," and "to take a poll" is "to count heads." The book of Numbers records the census of the people of Israel which was taken by

Moses at the command of the Lord, every male "by their polls" (Numbers 1:2, 18, 20, 22, KJV). The NKJV and NRSV render this as "individually"; other contemporary versions have "head by head" (NASB); "one by one" (NIV).

In Numbers 3:47 the price of redeeming the firstborn is fixed at "five shekels apiece by the poll" (KJV); "by the poll" is now translated as "apiece" (NRSV); "apiece, per head" (NASB); "for each one" (NIV, CEV); "for each one individually" (NKJV).

When David made a census of the Levites who were thirty years old and upward, "their number by their polls, man by man, was thirty and eight thousand" (1 Chronicles 23:3, KJV). The contemporary versions simply omit any reference to "polls" or "heads." In verse 24 of the same chapter, the KJV's "they were counted by number of names by their polls" is now translated as "they were enrolled according to the number of the names of the individuals" (NRSV); "they were counted individually" (NKJV, NIV); "[they] were counted, in the number of names by their census" (NASB).

As a verb, "to poll" means "to cut off the hair of the head," which survives in modern English in the related verb "to pollard," to cut trees such as willows back to their main trunk to encourage young growth. The classic passage is the description of Absalom in 2 Samuel 14:26 (KJV): "And when he polled his head, (for it was at every year's end that he polled it: because the hair was heavy on him, therefore he polled it)."

The majority of the contemporary versions have "cut the hair of his head" for the KJV's "polled his head" and simply "cut" for the other two instances of "polled."

Similarly in Micah 1:16 the KJV's "poll thee" is now translated as "cut off your hair" (NIV, "shave your heads"). In Ezekiel 44:20 (KJV), "they shall only poll their heads" is translated in the contemporary versions as "trimming hair." The Hebrew verb used here cannot mean "shave"; it is a contrast to the verb at the beginning of the verse, which all versions translate as "shave their heads." This emphasis is brought out in the KJV by the use of "only" with "poll their heads," and is retained by the NRSV and NASB.

POMMEL

In modern English, the word "pommel" is used for the rounded front of a saddle or the rounded knob which terminates the hilt of a sword. The word is used for a similar object in the KJV, which speaks in 2 Chronicles 4:12–13 of "the two pommels of the chapiters which were on the top of the pillars." Here "pommel" refers to a spherical or bowl-like ornament on the capital ("chapiter") of a pillar. The same Hebrew text is found in 1 Kings 7:41–42, but here the KJV has "the two bowls of the chapiters."

In both places the contemporary versions generally use "bowls" or "bowl-shaped capitals." The Hebrew word, *gullah,* is also found in Ecclesiastes 12:6 and Zechariah 4:3, where all versions translate it as "bowl."

POOR ARE ALWAYS WITH US

The expression "the poor are always with us" means that there will always be people who live in poverty and so need assistance from others.

The saying is found in Matthew 26:11, and its parallels Mark 14:7 and John 12:8, when at Bethany a woman (John's Gospel identifies the woman as Mary) anointed Jesus with a very expensive ointment. The disciples rebuked the woman, saying that the ointment could have been sold and the money given to the poor. Jesus said, "Why trouble ye the woman? for she hath wrought a good work upon me. For ye have the poor always with you; but me ye have not always. For in that she hath poured this ointment on my body, she did it for my burial. Verily I say unto you, Wheresoever this gospel shall be preached in the whole world, there shall also this, that this woman hath done, be told for a memorial of her" (Matthew 26:10–13, KJV).

For the KJV expression, all the contemporary versions have wordings that are similar, e.g., "For you always have the poor with you" (Matthew 26:11, NASB, NRSV), "You will always have the poor among you" (NLT).

The expression is found in literature, e.g., in Longfellow's *Evangeline* (1847) the walls of the almshouse, surrounded by the city:

> "seem to echo
> Softly the words of the Lord:—'The
> poor ye have always with you.' "

PORT

The word "port" is generally used today to mean "a harbor," or "a place or town where ships (and nowadays aircraft) arrive and depart." But the older meaning of the word as "an entrance or gate," used once by the KJV, could be behind the new use of the word "port" in connection with computers.

The one occurrence of "port" in the KJV is in Nehemiah 2:13, where Nehemiah is said to have gone to the "dung port" in his nocturnal inspection of the walls of Jerusalem. In three other cases, however, this is called the "dung gate" (3:13–14; 12:31), and "Gate" is how all the contemporary versions translate all four references. The Hebrew word *sha'ar* means "gate," and this is how the KJV translates 361 out of 370 occurrences. The contemporary versions correct the few inconsistencies.

PORTER

Today the word "porter" has two distinctive meanings, reflecting the two French words from which it derives: the verb *porter,* "to carry," and the noun *porte,* "a door." A porter is someone who carries things (a station, hotel or market porter) and someone who guards a door, to attend those entering a block of offices or apartments.

The Hebrew word *sho'er* means "gate-keeper," and is almost always represented in the KJV by "porter" (i.e., "doorkeeper").

The contemporary versions avoid the word "porter" because of the ambiguity of its two distinct meanings; instead they use "gatekeeper" or "doorkeeper," depending on which is most appropriate to the context. It is possible that the OED is mistaken when it lists "porter" in Wycliffe's translation of 1 Chronicles 16:42 as the first example of the word's use for a luggage porter. The duties of the men at the gate, in this context, were those of gatekeepers.

PORTION

This word is used in the KJV not only in the modern sense of "a part, share, or allowance of something," but also in the now archaic sense of "one's lot, destiny or rightful heritage."

Job and his friends speak of "the wicked man's portion from God, the heritage decreed for him by God" (20:29; see also 27:13); and Job speaks of "my portion from God above, and my heritage from the Almighty on high" (31:2). Moses declares that "the LORD's portion is his people, Jacob his allotted heritage" (Deuteronomy 32:9), and the psalmist sings, "The LORD is my portion" (119:57); "God is the strength of my heart and my portion for ever" (73:26).

The contemporary versions are consistent in their translation of these and other verses. The NASB, NKJV, and NRSV generally retain "portion" (though the NKJV has "allotment" in Job 31:2); the NIV has "fate" and "lot" in addition to retaining "portion"; and the CEV, NCV, and NLT generally use a phrase such as "what God plans," "what God has decided," "how God treats those who are wicked."

POSSESS

The word "possess" is used by the KJV fifty-four times in the book of Deuteronomy, and nearly a hundred times more in the rest of the Bible. In almost all these

cases it has the now archaic sense of "seize," "acquire," "gain," or "take possession of," rather than its more usual modern meaning of "to own." The key to the book of Deuteronomy is found in 1:8 (KJV), "Go in and possess the land," which is translated in the NIV and NRSV as "go in and take possession of the land."

Shakespeare also used the word in this sense. In *King Henry VI, Part III* (I, 1, 26), the Earl of Warwick encourages the ambition of Richard Plantagenet, Duke of York, to gain Henry's throne:

> "Possess it, York;
> For this is thine, and not King Henry's heirs'."

In *The Tempest* (III, 2, 89), Caliban tells Stephano how to oust Prospero from control of the island:

> "Remember
> First to possess his books; for without them
> He's but a sot, as I am, nor hath not
> One spirit to command."

The Greek verb which the KJV translates by "purchased" in Acts 1:18 and 8:20, and by "obtained" in Acts 22:28, is rendered as "possess" in three other New Testament passages (Luke 18:12; 21:19; 1 Thessalonians 4:4), with the result that the English reader is not aware of their true meaning.

The Pharisee's statement in Luke 18:12 (KJV), "I give tithes of all that I possess," sounds as if he tithes his capital, whereas the Greek actually says that he tithes his income, translated in the contemporary versions as "all [that] I get" (NASB, NIV); "all I earn" (CEV); "all my income" (NRSV); the NKJV retains "all that I possess."

"In your patience possess ye your souls" (Luke 21:19, KJV) is correctly translated as "By your endurance you will gain your lives" (NASB; NRSV, "you will gain your souls"); "By standing firm you will gain life" (NIV); "You will be saved by being faithful to me" (CEV); "By continuing to have faith you will save your lives" (NCV); again, the NKJV retains "possess your souls."

In the KJV, Paul's counsel to the Thessalonians that each of them should "know how to possess his vessel" (1 Thessalonians 4:4) is not easy to understand. The contemporary versions are divided on the meaning: the NKJV and NASB follow the KJV in retaining "possess his own vessel"; the NCV, NIV, and NRSV have "should learn how to control your [NIV, "his"] own body"; and the CEV and RSV translate "vessel" as "wife," making the sentence into advice for treating one's wife with holiness and honor. (See VESSEL)

POST

The word "post" is used eight times in the KJV as a translation of the Hebrew participle which means "running" or "a runner." The word survives in "posthaste," which means with all possible speed.

The contemporary translations are consistent in their choice of words: in 2 Chronicles 30:6, 10 and Esther 3:13, 15; 8:10, 14, the CEV, NCV, and NLT use "messengers"; the NASB, NIV, and NRSV have "couriers"; and the NKJV has "couriers" in Esther, where the context indicates that these were royal messengers, mounted, according to Esther 8:14, on swift horses, but "runners" in 2 Chronicles.

"My days are swifter than a post" (Job 9:25, KJV) sounds strange to modern ears, since a (wooden) post is quite the opposite of swift. The majority of contemporary versions here translate "post" as "runner." The KJV's "One post shall run to meet another" in Jeremiah 51:31 suffers from similar ambiguity, and is now translated as "messenger" (CEV, NCV, NLT); "courier" (NASB, NIV); or "runner" (NKJV, NRSV).

Shakespeare used the word in this sense:

"came there a reeking post,
Stew'd in his haste, half breathless,
   panting forth."
                    —*King Lear* (II, 4, 29)

"Our posts shall be swift and
   intelligent betwixt us."
                    —*King Lear* (III, 7, 11)

POWER

This word is used by the KJV in the archaic sense of "an army" in 2 Chronicles 32:9: "Sennacherib . . . laid siege against Lachish, and all his power with him." The contemporary versions translate this as "forces" (NASB, NIV, NKJV, NRSV); "troops" (CEV); or "army" (NCV). Shakespeare used the word frequently in this sense. For example, *King Lear* has "Are my brother's powers set forth?" (IV, 5, 1); "draw up your powers" (V, 1, 51); "He led our powers" (V, 3, 63).

A difficult use of the word "power" is found in the KJV of Genesis 32:28: "Thy name shall be called no more Jacob, but Israel: for as a prince hast thou power with God and with men, and hast prevailed." The contemporary versions have gotten rid of the misleading "prince" and "power" and provide a more accurate translation of the Hebrew, which has to do with wrestling or struggling with God: the CEV and NCV have "you have wrestled with God"; the NASB and NRSV have "you have striven with God"; and the NIV, NKJV, and NLT have "you have struggled with God."

POWERS THAT BE

"The powers that be" are "the controlling authorities," "the government," or "the establishment" ("Are the powers that be really aware of the effects of the cutbacks in finance?"). The expression derives from Romans 13:1: "Let every soul be subject unto the higher powers. For there is no power but of God: the powers that be are ordained of God" (KJV).

The contemporary versions render the KJV expression "the powers that be" as "the [NRSV, "those"] authorities that exist" (NIV, NKJV, NRSV). The NASB and RSV are similar: "For there is no authority except from God, and those which [RSV, "that"] exist are established [RSV, "have been instituted"] by God"; the CEV has "he [God] puts these rulers in their places of power"; and the NLT, "All governments have been placed in power by God."

PRANSING

The word "pransing" is a survival of 1611 spelling in the present editions of the KJV which is not even listed in the OED, which only has the more familiar spelling of "prance." It is the wrong word in the Song of Deborah (Judges 5:22) and Nahum's prophecy of the downfall of Nineveh (Nahum 3:2). A prancing horse, dancing about and needing skilled control, would be of no use in a cavalry charge, and the Hebrew verb in these two passages means to "rush," "dash," "gallop."

The KJV's translation of Judges 5:22 is inaccurate: "Then were the horsehoofs broken by the means of the pransings, the pransings of their mighty ones" appears in the contemporary versions as, for example, "Then the horses' hooves pounded, The galloping, galloping of his steeds" (NKJV).

Again, the vivid, staccato Hebrew of Nahum's picture of battle is inaccurately represented by the KJV's "The noise of a whip, and the noise of the rattling of the wheels, and of the pransing horses, and of the jumping chariots" (Nahum 3:2). The NRSV, for example, translates this verse: "The crack of whip and rumble of wheel, galloping horse and bounding chariot!"

PREFER

The word "prefer" now generally denotes an attitude of mind. We prefer something when we like it better or esteem it more highly than something else. The KJV's one example of "prefer" in this sense is found in Psalm 137:6: "if I prefer not Jerusalem above my chief joy."

For the KJV "prefer" the contemporary versions have "exalt" (NASB, NKJV), "think about" (CEV, NCV), "consider" (NIV), and "set" (NRSV, RSV). Elsewhere the word is used in the older sense of "advancement" or "promotion," a meaning which survives in the modern use of "preferment."

The officer in charge of the harem of King Ahasuerus took a liking to Esther and "preferred her and her maids unto the best place" (Esther 2:9); the contemporary versions describe how this was done: Esther and her maids were "advanced" or "moved" into the best place in the harem. "Daniel was preferred above the presidents and princes" (Daniel 6:3, KJV); he "distinguished himself" (NASB, NIV, NKJV, NRSV); he "did his work so much better" (CEV, NCV).

John the Baptist pointed to Jesus as "a man which is preferred before me" (John 1:30, KJV); in the words of the contemporary versions, "he is greater than I am" (CEV, NCV); he "has a higher rank" (NASB); he "has surpassed me" (NIV); "he ranks ahead of me" (NRSV); the NKJV retains "preferred."

Paul counseled the Romans to act "in honour preferring one another" (Romans 12:10, KJV). In the contemporary versions this is translated as "giving preference" (NASB, NKJV); "outdoing one another" in showing honor (NRSV); "honoring one another" above yourselves (NIV).

Timothy is solemnly charged in the KJV to "observe these things without preferring one before another, doing nothing from partiality" (1 Timothy 5:21). This does not mean that he is not to prefer some rules to others, but that he should administer them "without prejudice" (NKJV, NRSV); "without bias" (NASB); "without showing favour" (NCV); "without partiality" (NIV).

PRESENTLY

The word "presently" is used in the KJV in the sense of "at once," "immediately," "without delay." This meaning is now archaic, and "presently" is used most often today in the sense of "soon," "shortly," "in a little while." When Jesus said to the barren fig tree, "May no fruit ever come from you again!" (Matthew 21:19, NRSV), the

Greek records that the fig tree withered at once; the KJV statement that "presently the fig tree withered away" was an accurate translation in 1611, but is not so today; the contemporary versions generally use "immediately" or "at once."

When Jesus rebuked one of his followers for drawing a sword and striking out in defense of his Master in the Garden of Gethsemane (Matthew 26:52–53), he said that if he needed defending, his Father could "presently" (v. 53, KJV) send twelve legions of angels. Jesus uses a clear, strong word which means "right now" or "at once," the translation generally given in the contemporary versions.

Similarly, when the KJV states in Proverbs 12:16 that "A fool's wrath is presently known: but a prudent man covereth shame," it is not saying that the anger will emerge eventually, but that it will be known "at once," which is how the word is generally translated by the contemporary versions.

In 1 Samuel 2:16, the KJV's injunction to "burn the fat presently" becomes "burn the fat first" (or similar wording) in all the contemporary versions. The use of "presently" by the KJV in Philippians 2:23 ("Him therefore I hope to send presently, so soon as I shall see how it will go with me") is omitted by the majority of the contemporary translations as superfluous; "send him as soon as" (CEV, NASB, NIV, NRSV) conveys the sense adequately, and only the NKJV has "I hope to send him at once, as soon as I see how it goes with me."

PRESS

As a noun in contemporary English, "press" usually refers to the act of pushing ("at the press of a button"), newspapers or journalists, or a printing press. In the KJV, the word "press" occurs as a noun five times with the meaning "a crowd" (Mark 2:4; 5:7, 30; Luke 8:19; 19:3). For example, Mark 2:4, "And when they could not come nigh unto him for the press, they uncovered the roof where he was: and when they had broken

it up, they let down the bed wherein the sick of the palsy lay" (KJV), where the KJV "the press" is rendered as "the crowd" by all the contemporary versions.

At all the other references, the word is translated in the contemporary versions by "crowd," except for the NLT at Luke 8:19 and 19:3 which has the "crowds," e.g., of Zacchaeus Luke 19:3, "And he sought to see Jesus who he was; and could not for the press, because he was little of stature" (KJV), "He tried to get a look at Jesus, but he was too short to see over the crowds" (NLT).

In the 1611 edition of the KJV, the word was spelled "preasse" at Mark 2:4 and 5:30 and "prease" at the other passages.

The word occurs in literature, e.g., Chaucer, *House of Fame* (I, 167):

> "And how he fled, and how that he
> Escaped from all the prees"

and Shakespeare, *Julius Caesar* (I, 2, 15):

> "Who is it in the press that calls
> on me?"

PREVENT

In contemporary English, "to prevent something" is to make sure that it does not happen or to make it impossible for someone to do something. In the KJV "prevent" means "to go before," "to anticipate," "to precede," from the Latin *prae* (before) + *venire* (to come).

When the psalmist says (Psalm 119:147), "I prevented the dawning of the morning," the modern reader of the KJV is mystified. The NASB, NIV, RSV, and NKJV express the meaning as "I rise before (the) dawn(ing)," the CEV as "before sunrise." This is a part of the description of the devotional habits of a pious Hebrew who rises before the dawn to begin the day with meditation and prayer.

In Psalm 119:148, "Mine eyes prevent the night watches" is translated in the RSV as "My eyes are awake before the watches of the night." The NASB translates, "My eyes anticipate the night watches," the NRSV, "My eyes are awakened before each watch of the night." The NIV, NKJV, and NLT render "before" as "through" (the watches of) the night; the CEV, "I lie awake at night."

When Peter came to Jesus to report that they were asked to pay the half-shekel tax (Matthew 17:25), the KJV says that Jesus "prevented him." That does not mean that he kept Peter from speaking; it means simply that Jesus "spoke to him first" (NASB, RSV). The NKJV has "Jesus anticipated him"; the NRSV "Jesus spoke of it first"; and the NIV, "Jesus was the first to speak." The CEV has simply, "Jesus went up to Peter and asked him."

When Paul tells the Thessalonians, anxious to know what will happen on the last great day, that "we which are alive and remain unto the coming of the Lord shall not prevent them which are asleep" (1 Thessalonians 4:15), he is not thinking of a possible attempt to keep the dead in their tombs; he is saying simply that those who are alive will not precede the dead to the triumphant meeting with the Lord.

"Precede" is generally used in the contemporary versions; the CEV has "We won't go up to meet him ahead of his followers who have already died." In other cases "prevent" is translated in many different ways. In 2 Samuel 22:6 (paralleled in Psalm 18:5) as "confronted" (NASB, NIV, NKJV, NRSV, RSV) or, with paraphrases, as "were before" (NCV), "stared me in the face" (NLT), "had set a trap in my path" (CEV). Psalm 21:3 has "meet" (NASB, NKJV, NRSV, RSV), "put before" (NCV), "welcomed" (NIV, NLT), and "truly blessed" (CEV). Psalm 88:13 has "come before" (NASB, NIV, NKJV, NRSV, RSV) and, with paraphrases, "pray" (CEV, NCV) or "keep on pleading" (NLT).

PREY

In many passages, especially in Numbers, Joshua, Judges, and Esther, the noun "prey" means booty, spoil, or plunder, and this is how it is translated in the contempo-

rary versions. For example, in Esther 3:13, the KJV has "Take the spoil of them for a prey"; the contemporary versions render this as "plunder their goods" (NIV, NRSV; NKJV, "plunder their possessions"); "seize their possessions as plunder" (NASB).

In the Song of Deborah (Judges 5:30, KJV) the mother of Sisera is depicted as eagerly awaiting his return, and answering her own question why he is so long in coming: "Have they not sped? have they not divided the prey?" The NASB translates this: "Are they not finding, are they not dividing the spoil?" The NIV, NKJV, and NRSV have "Are they not finding and dividing the spoil?" (NIV, "spoils"). Other examples of this use of "prey" can be found in Joshua 8:2 and Esther 9:15.

A further meaning of the noun "prey," recorded by the OED as "In Scriptural use," is "That which one brings away or saves from any contest." Jeremiah 21:9b reads in the KJV: "he that goeth out, and falleth to the Chaldeans that besiege you, he shall live, and his life shall be unto him for a prey."

Here the NKJV has "he who goes out and defects to the Chaldeans who besiege you, he shall live, and his life shall be as a prize to him"; the NASB translates the last clause as "he will have his own life as booty"; the NIV has "he will escape with his life"; and the NRSV makes the sentence plural: "those who go out . . . shall have their lives as a prize of war." The idiom also occurs in Jeremiah 38:2; 39:18; 45:5.

Zephaniah 3:8 (KJV) reads, "Therefore wait ye upon me, saith the LORD, until the day that I rise up to the prey." The Hebrew word for "prey" is 'ad, and the word for witness is 'ed; the consonants are the same, the only difference is in the vowel points, where a short underline means "a" and two underlined dots mean "e."

In view of the context, and in view of the fact that the Greek Septuagint and the Syriac read "to witness," the majority of the contemporary versions translates the word as "witness"; the NKJV, however, follows the

KJV in reading "Until the day I rise up for plunder." The KJV depicts the Lord as a witness elsewhere, in Jeremiah 29:23; Micah 1:2; Malachi 3:5.

PRIDE GOES BEFORE A FALL

The proverb "pride goes before a fall" means that a person who behaves in an over-confident and vain manner is soon likely to suffer misfortune. The expression is a shortened rendering of Proverbs 16:18: "Pride goeth before destruction, and an haughty spirit before a fall" (KJV).

The contemporary versions have mainly updated the wording: "Pride goes before destruction, And [the NIV omits "and"] a haughty spirit [NLT, "and haughtiness"] before a fall" [NASB, "before stumbling"] (NASB, NIV, NKJV, NLT, NRSV, RSV); the CEV has "Too much pride will destroy you"; and the NCV, "Pride will destroy a person; a proud attitude leads to ruin."

PRINT

"Oh that my words were now written! oh that they were printed in a book! That they were graven with an iron pen and lead in the rock for ever!" (Job 19:23–24, KJV). The modern reader gets a vivid picture of three stages of desire: a written record, a printed and permanently bound volume, a memorial cut into rock.

Unfortunately, the second of these stages is an inaccurate rendering of the Hebrew by the KJV writers, because the word does not mean "printed" but "cut," "engraved," or "inscribed." The Greek Septuagint translated it by the word for "put," the Latin Vulgate by another word for "written." Martin Luther, Coverdale, the Great Bible, and the Bishops' Bible followed the Greek, and the Geneva Bible followed the Latin.

The majority of the contemporary translations (NASB, NKJV, NLT, NRSV) have "inscribed"; the CEV, NCV, and NIV have "written." It is an anachronism to depict Job as speaking of a printed book, but from the literary point of view it is an inspired anachronism.

The KJV rendering of Job 13:27 ("thou settest a print upon the heels of my feet") is translated by the NASB, NKJV, and NRSV as "You set a limit for [NRSV, "a bound to"] the soles of my feet"; the NIV is closer to the KJV with "you keep close watch on all my paths by putting marks on the soles of my feet," as is the NCV, which has "You even mark the soles of my feet." The meaning of all the contemporary versions is that God fixes limits beyond which Job's feet may not tread.

PRIVILY

The word "privily" is an archaic word used by the KJV for "secretly" (Psalm 101:5; Matthew 2:7; Acts 16:37; 2 Peter 2:1), which is how the contemporary versions generally translate these verses. "Privily" in 1 Samuel 24:4 is now variously translated "secretly" (NASB, NKJV); "quietly" (NCV); "unnoticed" (NIV); "stealthily" (NRSV). In Psalm 11:2, the KJV uses "privily" to translate a Hebrew word meaning "in the dark": "For lo, the wicked bend their bow, they make ready their arrow upon the string, that they may privily shoot at the upright in heart."

The NKJV retains the KJV's use of "privily" to mean "secretly" ("that they may shoot secretly"), but the other contemporary versions translate the Hebrew in a variety of ways: "standing in the shadows, aiming at good people" (CEV); "To shoot in darkness at the upright in heart" (NASB; NRSV, "to shoot in the dark"); "They shoot from dark places" (NCV; NIV, NLT, "from the shadows").

Translations also vary for Judges 9:31, where the KJV speaks of messengers being sent "privily" to Abimelech. The majority of the contemporary versions follow this interpretation of the Hebrew with words such as "deceitfully," "under cover," "secretly." However, the NRSV, the RSV, and the NLT describe the messengers as sent to Abimelech "at Arumah." Though this is a correction to the Hebrew, it is consistent with Judges 9:41 and makes good sense of an otherwise unknown word.

When Joseph discovered that Mary was pregnant, he "was minded to put her away privily" (Matthew 1:19, KJV), divorcing her "quietly" or "secretly," according to the contemporary translations.

PRIVY

To be privy to is to share in the knowledge of something private or secret. Sapphira was "privy to" the attempted deception of Ananias (Acts 5:2, KJV); the NASB, NIV, and NRSV say that it was "with his wife's full knowledge" (the NRSV omits "full"); the NKJV says "his wife also being aware of it."

King Solomon's words to Shimei, as he condemned him to death, were "Thou knowest all the wickedness which thine heart is privy to, that thou didst to David my father" (1 Kings 2:44, KJV). In the contemporary versions this becomes an acknowledgment by Shimei of what he had done; the NKJV, for example, translates it, "You know, as your heart acknowledges, all the wickedness that you did to my father David."

A man's "privy member" (Deuteronomy 23:1, KJV) is his penis (NLT, NRSV) or male organ (NASB). The KJV's translation of Ezekiel 21:14 as "It is the sword of the great men that are slain, which entereth into their privy chambers" is generally regarded now as an inaccurate rendering; the majority of the contemporary versions translate the phrase as "the sword for the great one slain, which surrounds them" (NASB) or similar wording; only the NKJV follows the KJV with "The sword that slays the great men, That enters their private chambers."

PRODIGAL SON

The word "prodigal" does not mean "wandering or wayward," as is sometimes thought, but "extravagant or wasteful." The expression "prodigal son" derives from Jesus' parable in Luke 15:11–32, the well-known story of the younger of the two sons who took his share of his father's estate and wasted it in "a far country, and there wasted his substance with riotous living" (v. 13, KJV). Having spent everything, he came to his senses and, realizing his sin against God and his earthly father, returned home in repentance to receive the conditional welcome of his father. (See KILL THE FATTED CALF)

The expression "prodigal son" does not occur in the Bible text itself but only in the heading of some editions of the (KJV) Bible; the OED quotes the marginal note in 1523 of the Vulgate and the Thomas Matthew Bible (1551) among its citations. The headings of this section in the contemporary versions are: "The Prodigal Son" (NASB); "The Parable of the Prodigal and His Brother" (NRSV); "The Parable of the Lost Son" (NIV); "Story of the Lost Son" (NLT); "The Son Who Left Home" (NCV); and "Two Sons" (CEV).

Shakespeare alludes to this parable more often than to any other, e.g., in *As You Like It* (I, 1, 38–42) Orlando arguing with his elder brother Oliver: "Shall I keep your hogs, and eat husks with them? What prodigal portion have I spent, that I should come to such penury?" and in *King Henry IV, Part I* (IV, 2, 36–38) Sir John Falstaff describes soldiers: "you would think that I had a hundred and fifty tatter'd prodigals lately come from swine-keeping, from eating draff and husks."

PROFANE

The OED lists three major meanings of the adjective "profane," which may be summarized as (1) secular, lay, common; (2) unholy, unhallowed, ritually unclean or polluted; (3) irreverent, blasphemous, irreligious. Each of these meanings is found in the KJV, and are distinguished in the contemporary versions.

The difference between "the holy and profane" in Ezekiel 22:26; 44:23 (KJV) is between "the holy and the common" (NIV, NRSV); "between holy and unholy things" (NCV; NKJV: "the holy and unholy"); the NASB retains "the holy and the profane." The KJV's "profane place" in Ezekiel 42:20; 48:15 is the common area of the temple—a place for ordinary, common use—and this is brought out clearly in the majority of the contemporary versions.

The command not to marry a woman who is "profane" (Leviticus 21:7, 14, KJV) translates a Hebrew word that means "has been defiled"; the NKJV renders this "a defiled woman"; the NRSV has "a woman who has been defiled"; other contemporary translations combine the KJV's two phrases, "a wife that is a whore, or profane" and speak of "a woman who is profaned by harlotry" (NASB); "an unclean prostitute" (NCV); "women defiled by prostitution" (NIV, NLT).

The epithet "profane" applied to King Zedekiah by the KJV in Ezekiel 21:25 receives various translations in the contemporary versions: "evil" (CEV); "unclean" (NCV); "vile" (NRSV); the NIV and NKJV retain "profane"; while the NASB refers to Zedekiah as "O slain, wicked one."

In the letters to Timothy, the KJV's "profane" in 1 Timothy 1:9 is retained by the NASB, NKJV, and NRSV; the NIV has "irreligious." Elsewhere, in 1 Timothy 4:7; 6:20; 2 Timothy 2:16, "profane" is kept by some of the contemporary versions (usually the NKJV and NRSV) and replaced in others by words such as "godless," "foolish," and "worldly."

Esau is called "a profane person" by the KJV in Hebrews 12:16, but is referred to by most of the contemporary versions as "godless"; the CEV has "ungodly"; and the NKJV retains the KJV "profane."

PROFIT

As noun and verb, "profit" and the adjective "profitable" are now almost entirely confined in meaning to "making money." This is probably why, although the KJV uses the words seventy times, many of the contemporary versions avoid them, using instead terms such as "gain," "use," "interest," "success," or "benefit." The NKJV often retains "profit," and the NASB and NRSV use it

occasionally, but other contemporary translations always use alternative wording.

In Genesis 37:26, for example, where the KJV has "What profit is it if we slay our brother?", the contemporary versions are divided between "What profit" (NASB, NKJV, NRSV), and "What will we gain" (CEV, NCV, NIV); in Mark 8:36 (KJV: "For what shall it profit a man, if he shall gain the whole world, and lose his own soul?"), the NASB, NKJV, and NRSV retain "profit"; the CEV has "What will you gain?"; the NCV, "It is worth nothing for them"; NIV, "What good is it?"

There is greater variation in the contemporary versions of Esther 3:8, and none of them retain "profit": the KJV has "it is not for the king's profit to suffer them [i.e., the Jews]"; the NASB has "not in the king's interest to let them remain"; the NIV, "not in the king's best interest to tolerate them"; the NKJV, "it is not fitting for the king to let them remain"; the NRSV, "it is not appropriate for the king to tolerate them"; the NCV, "it is not right for you to allow them to continue living in your kingdom."

Similar variety is found in the contemporary translations of Job 33:27–28, where the KJV has "it profited me not": "it is not proper for me" (NASB); "I did not receive the punishment I should have received" (NCV); "I did not get what I deserved" (NIV); "it was not paid back to me" (NRSV); the NKJV retains "it did not profit me." In 2 Timothy 3:16 "All scripture is given by inspiration of God, and is profitable for doctrine, for reproof, for correction, for instruction in righteousness" (KJV) the contemporary versions are divided between "profit"/"profitable" (NASB, NKJV) and "useful" (CEV, NCV, NIV, NRSV).

In Job 35:8, where the KJV has "Thy wickedness may hurt a man as thou art; and thy righteousness may profit the son of man," the majority of the contemporary versions follow the Hebrew and omit "profit," and using "affects" to translate the KJV's verb "may hurt," make both clauses of the sentence dependent on the one verb (as, for example, in the NKJV: "Your wickedness affects a man such as you, and your righteousness a son of man").

The KJV translates Ecclesiastes 10:10 as "wisdom is profitable to direct," but the contemporary versions stay closer to the Hebrew, and declare that wisdom brings "success" (NASB, NIV, NKJV), helps one "to succeed" (NRSV), or makes it "easier" (NCV).

The verb "to profit" is twice used by the KJV in the obsolete sense of "advance," "go forward," "improve," "make progress." Paul's statement that he had "profited in the Jew's religion above many my equals in mine own nation" (Galatians 1:14, KJV) represents Greek which the majority of the contemporary versions translate by "advanced" (as in the NKJV, "I advanced in Judaism beyond many of my contemporaries").

Again, in the KJV's exhortation to Timothy (1 Timothy 4:15), "Meditate upon these things; give thyself wholly to them; that thy profiting may appear to all," "thy profiting" is translated by most of the contemporary versions as "your progress." Only the NKJV retains "meditate on these things." The other translations, following the Greek, have "Take pains" (NASB); "Be diligent" (NIV); "Put these things into practice" (NRSV).

This returns to Tyndale's understanding of the verse, which began "These things exercise" which was followed by the other sixteenth-century translations made from the Greek. The KJV got "meditate" from the Rheims New Testament, which took it from the Latin Vulgate *Haec meditare*, without regard for the fact that *meditare* means "exercise," "practice," "rehearse" as well as "think about" and "meditate upon."

Today the adjective "profitable" is not usually applied to people, but two examples of this usage can be found in the KJV. In 2 Timothy 4:11 it has "Take Mark, and bring him with thee: for he is profitable to me for the ministry"; in the contemporary versions, Mark is "helpful" (CEV, NIV, NCV, "can help") or "useful" (NASB, NKJV, NRSV). Paul, writing to Philemon, describes Onesimus as one

"which in time past was to thee unprofitable, but now profitable to thee and to me" (v. 11). The NKJV retains the "unprofitable/profitable" contrast; the other contemporary versions all have "useless/useful."

Shakespeare also uses "profit" in the sense of "advance" or "progress":

> "Sir Hugh, my husband says my son profits nothing in the world at his book."
> —*The Merry Wives of Windsor*
> (IV, 1, 11)

> "My brother Jaques he keeps at school, and report speaks goldenly of his profit."
> —*As You Like I* (I, 1, 6)

PROFOUND

This word appears once in the KJV, in Hosea 5:2; in the clause, "the revolters are profound to make slaughter." The word is thought by the OED to mean "deep or subtle in contrivance," "crafty," "cunning."

The contemporary versions translate this verse as "The revolters have gone deep in depravity" (NASB); "The rebels are deep in slaughter" (NIV); "The revolters are deeply involved in slaughter" (NKJV). The NRSV accepts an emendation to the Hebrew text and links this verse to the one before: "you have been a snare at Mizpah, and a net spread upon Tabor, and a pit dug at Shittim; but I will punish all of them." The snare at Mizpah, the net upon Tabor, and the pit of Shittim were centers of seductive Baal worship against which judgment is declared.

PROLONGED

In modern usage "prolonged" generally means "drawn out," "lengthened." It is used twice by the KJV in the obsolete sense of "delayed," "postponed," "put off." These instances occur in Ezekiel 12:25, 28. In verse 25 the KJV has "the word that I shall speak . . . shall be no more prolonged," and verse 28 reads, "There shall none of my words be prolonged any more, but the word which I have spoken shall be done, saith the Lord GOD." The contemporary versions generally translate "prolonged" in both these verses as "delayed" or (NKJV) "postponed."

Among the examples cited by OED are this sentence from a sermon by Bishop Thomas Watson (1558): "Wee saye with the wicked seruaunt, my Lord prolongeth his commynge," and this from William Lisle (1623): "Prolong not to turne unto God, lest the time passe away through thy slow tarrying."

PROMISED LAND

According to *Merriam-Webster's Collegiate Dictionary* (tenth edition) the "promised land" is "something and esp. a place or condition believed to promise final satisfaction or realization of hopes." It is "the land of Canaan, as promised to Abraham and to his posterity (Genesis 12:7; 13:15, etc.); hence allusively applied to heaven, or to any place of expected felicity" (OED).

In the KJV Genesis 12:7 reads, "And the LORD appeared unto Abram, and said, Unto thy seed will I give this land." The expression "the promised land" does not itself appear in the KJV; though in the contemporary versions references to it include: Deuteronomy 11:11 (CEV): "But the hills and valleys in the promised land are watered by rain from heaven"; Hebrews 11:9 (CEV, "Because Abraham had faith, he lived as a stranger in the promised land" and NIV, "By faith he made his home in the promised land like a stranger in a foreign country"; the KJV has "the land of promise"), and ten times in the NLT, e.g., Exodus 13:17: "When Pharaoh finally let the people go, God did not lead them on the road that runs through Philistine territory, even though that was the shortest way from Egypt to the Promised Land." (See LAND FLOWING WITH MILK AND HONEY)

PROPER GOOD

In 1 Chronicles 29:3–5, when King David announced to the assembly of Israel his plans for the building of the temple, and entrusted these plans to Solomon together with the store of materials he had provided, he also made a personal gift of three thousand talents of gold and seven thousand talents of silver. He referred to this, according to the KJV, as "mine own proper good."

The word "proper" is use here in the archaic sense of "owned as property," and "good" is archaic for "goods." The Hebrew is simply, "I have a *segullah* of gold and silver," which the contemporary versions translate as "my own gold and silver" (CEV); "the treasure I have of gold and silver" (NASB); "my own treasures" (NCV); "my personal treasures" (NIV); "my own special treasure" (NKJV); "a treasure of my own" (NRSV). (For the meaning of *segullah* in various contexts, see PECULIAR.)

"Proper" is used by the KJV in the sense of "one's own" in Acts 1:19 ("their proper tongue" becomes in the contemporary versions "their [own] language") and 1 Corinthians 7:7 (where "his proper gift" is now translated "his own gift" or, in the NRSV, "a particular gift"). Modern English still uses "proper" in this sense in, for example, proper nouns, which are names used to designate a particular individual person, animal, place, or thing, a name which is uniquely its own.

In Hebrews 11:23 the KJV uses "proper" in the archaic sense of "beautiful," which is how the contemporary versions generally translate it; the NIV has, "no ordinary" and the NLT, "unusual." In Shakespeare's *As You Like It* (III, 5, 114), the shepherdess Phebe, smitten with the disguised Rosalind, says that "he" will make "a proper man," a handsome man with a good complexion and fine eyes.

PROPHET IS WITHOUT HONOR IN HIS OWN COUNTRY

In contemporary usage, the expression "a prophet is without honor in his own country" is applied to anyone who is generally recognized as great, except by his own family, compatriots, etc. The saying is based on Jesus' words, after he had been rejected in his hometown of Nazareth, "A prophet is not without honour, save in his own country, and in his own house" (Matthew 13:57, KJV).

The NASB, NKJV, NRSV, and RSV retain the KJV expression "not without hono[u]r"; "except in his hometown and in his household" (NASB), "except in his own country and in his own house" (NKJV, RSV), "except in their own country and in their own house" (NRSV). The NCV and NLT have "A prophet is honored everywhere except in his own hometown and in his own home" [NLT, "and among his own family"]; the CEV has "Prophets are honored by everyone, except the people of their hometown and their own family"; and the NIV, "Only in his hometown and in his own house is a prophet without honor."

See also Mark 6:4; Luke 4:24; John 4:44. In the KJV Luke 4:24 reads, "No prophet is accepted in his own home country"; the NCV, NIV, NKJV, NLT, and NRSV retain the verb "accepted"; the NASB has "no prophet is welcome in his hometown"; the CEV, "But you can be sure that no prophets are liked by the people of their own hometown."

PROVE

In contemporary English, "to prove" means "to show that something is true by argument or evidence," "to turn out that something has a particular quality" ("the experience proved to be useful"), and "to test" ("the exception proves the rule"). In the KJV, the word is often used in this third sense of "test," or "put to the proof" on several occasions. This sense comes from the Latin *probare*, "to test something according to its goodness."

Examples are: Psalm 17:3, "Thou hast proved mine heart; thou hast visited me in the night; thou hast tried me, and shalt find nothing; I am purposed that my mouth shall not transgress" (KJV). The contemporary versions render the KJV "proved" as

"tested" (NKJV, NLT), "tried" (NASB), "try" (NRSV), "probe" (NIV), "examined" (NCV), and "know" (CEV).

Exodus 16:4, "Then said the LORD unto Moses, Behold, I will rain bread from heaven for you; and the people shall go out and gather a certain rate every day, that I may prove them, whether they will walk in my law, or no" (KJV); the contemporary versions render the KJV "prove" (retained by the RSV) as "test" (NASB, NIV, NKJV, NLT, NRSV); the CEV renders the KJV clause "that I may prove them, whether they will walk in my law, or no" as "That's how I will see if they obey me."

First Samuel 17:39, "And David girded his sword upon his armour, and he assayed to go; for he had not proved it. And David said unto Saul, I cannot go with these; for I have not proved them. And David put them off him" (KJV). Here the two occurrences of "proved" are rendered "tested" (NASB, NKJV) and "not used to" (CEV, NCV, NIV, NLT, NRSV).

Malachi 3:10, "Bring ye all the tithes into the storehouse, that there may be meat in mine house, and prove me now herewith, saith the LORD of hosts, if I will not open you the windows of heaven, and pour you out a blessing, that there shall not be room enough to receive it" (KJV); the contemporary versions render the KJV "prove" as "test" (NASB, NCV, NIV), "put me to the test" (CEV, NRSV), "try" (NKJV), and "Try it! Let me prove it to you!" (NLT).

Luke 14:19, "And another said, I have bought five yoke of oxen, and I go to prove them: I pray thee have me excused" (KJV); here "prove them" is rendered as "try them out" (CEV, NASB, NIV, NLT, NRSV), "try them" (NCV), and "test" (NKJV).

John 6:6, "And this he [Jesus] said to prove him [Philip]: for he himself knew what he would do" (KJV); the contemporary versions render the KJV "prove" with the verb "test" (CEV, NASB, NCV, NIV, NKJV, NLT, NRSV).

1 Thessalonians 5:21, "Prove all things;

hold fast that which is good" (KJV); the contemporary versions render the KJV "prove" as "test" (NCV, NIV, NKJV, NLT, NRSV), "put everything to the test" (CEV), and "examine" (NASB).

1 Timothy 3:10, "And let these also first be proved; then let them use the office of a deacon, being found blameless" (KJV); here the KJV "let . . . proved" is rendered by the contemporary versions as "let . . . be tested" (NKJV, NRSV, RSV), "must . . . be tested" (NASB, NIV), "test them" (NCV), "must . . . prove themselves" (CEV); the NLT expands to "they should be given other responsibilities in the church as a test of their character and ability."

In Romans 3:9, the KJV verb "prove" means "charge": "What then? are we better than they? No, in no wise: for we have before proved both Jews and Gentiles, that they are all under sin" (KJV). The KJV "proved" is rendered by the contemporary versions as "charged" (NASB, NKJV, NRSV), "made the charge" (NIV), "said" (CEV, NCV), and "shown" (NLT).

PROVIDE

The word "provide" meant originally "to foresee," then "to exercise foresight in making provision for the future"; but today the idea of foresight has waned, and "provide" now commonly means simply "to furnish or supply." As the word is used in the KJV, the element of prudent foresight is usually present or implied; the contemporary versions often use an alternative to "provide," to make clear the specific meaning of various Hebrew and Greek terms.

Thus, the KJV's "provide out of all the people able men" in Exodus 18:21 is rendered "select" (NASB, NIV, NKJV); "choose" (NCV); "appoint" (CEV); "look for" (NRSV). "He provided the first part for himself" (Deuteronomy 33:21, KJV), is rendered "chose" in the CEV, NCV, NIV, and NRSV; the NASB and NKJV retain "he provided." The KJV translates Luke 12:20 as "Then whose shall those things be, which thou hast pro-

vided?"; the NKJV has "which you have provided," but the other contemporary versions generally use "what you have prepared."

"Provide things honest in the sight of all men" (Romans 12:17, KJV) has a greater variety of contemporary translations: "Have regard for good things" (NKJV); "Respect what is right" (NASB); "Be careful to do what is right" (NIV); "take thought for what is noble" (NRSV); "try to earn the respect of others" (CEV); "Try to do what everyone thinks is right" (NCV). There is similar variation in 2 Corinthians 8:21: "Providing for honest things" (KJV); "providing honorable things" (NKJV); "we have regard for what is honorable" (NASB); "We are trying hard to do what the Lord accepts as right" (NCV); "we are taking pains to do what is right" (NIV); "we intend to do what is right" (NRSV).

More of the contemporary versions (NASB, NKJV, NRSV) retain "provided" in Hebrews 11:40, where the KJV has "God having provided some better thing for us." The NCV and NIV have "planned"; the CEV renders it as "God had something better in store for us."

PROVIDENCE

Today, the use of the word "providence" is generally applied to God's provision for His world, His church, and His people. In the sixteenth century, however, it could also refer to anyone's provision, particularly provision made with (usually prudent) foresight. (See PROVIDE)

The only appearance of "provide" in the KJV is in Acts 24:2, where the orator employed by the high priest to present the accusation against Paul began: "Seeing that by thee we enjoy great quietness, and that very worthy deeds are done unto this nation by thy providence, We accept it always, and in all places, most noble Felix, with all thankfulness." The NKJV, NRSV, and NIV render "thy providence" as "your foresight"; the CEV has "your concern"; the NCV has "your wise help"; only the NASB retains "your providence."

The question here centers on the translation of the Greek word *pronoia*. It occurs in one other passage, Romans 13:14, where it is translated by the KJV as "make not provision for the flesh, to fulfil the lusts thereof." The NKJV, NASB, and NRSV also translate it as "provision"; the CEV and NCV both use "satisfy" ("you won't try to satisfy" and "forget about satisfying," respectively); and the NIV has "do not think about how to gratify the desires of the sinful nature."

"Provision" could, in fact, be regarded as a more accurate translation of Acts 24:2 than "foresight," which does not express the full meaning of the Greek *pronoia* or the parallel Latin *providentia*. They stand for the kind of foresight which issues in sound provision for the future, in "prudent or wise management, government, or guidance" (OED). From the first, both "providence" and "provision" have meant this; but "providence" has come to be the more general term, now more or less confined to God, whereas "provision" usually refers to specific needs or materials and to human forethought, planning, and care.

For both of these reasons, the RSV's use of "provision" in Acts 24:2 could be the better translation. Had he been addressing the emperor, the spokesman for the Jews would doubtless have included a discreet reference to his divine providence, but he would hardly risk that in presenting a case to the governor of a Roman province.

PROVOKE

This verb and the noun "provocation" occur some sixty times in the KJV in the sense of "inciting to anger." But it also uses "provocation" for "blasphemies" (Nehemiah 9:18, 26) and "rebellion" (Hebrews 3:8, 15), words used by the majority of the contemporary versions in these passages. The KJV also uses "to provoke" for the Hebrew words which mean "to despise" (Numbers 14:11, 23; 16:30; Deuteronomy 31:20; Isaiah 1:4) and "to rebel" (Exodus 23:21; Psalms 78:40, 56; 106:7, 43).

In all these instances, the contemporary versions translate the Hebrew literally, or use related words for "despise" such as "reject," "treat with contempt," "spurn"; occasionally the NKJV retains "provoke." In Isaiah 3:8, the KJV's "To provoke the eyes of his glory" is now translated "defying his glorious presence" (NRSV, NIV); "To rebel against His glorious presence" (NASB); "they turn against him" (NCV); the NKJV retains the KJV translation.

The KJV states in 2 Samuel 24:1 that the Lord "moved" David to number Israel, and in 1 Chronicles 21:1 that Satan "provoked" David to number Israel; but the Hebrew verb is the same in both cases, and means "to move or incite." The KJV translators may not have though it acceptable to use the same verb for the Lord and for Satan.

In 2 Corinthians 9:2 and Hebrews 10:24 "provoke" is used by the KJV in the simple sense of "to stir up or call forth." "Your zeal hath provoked very many" seems to be saying that their zeal is very irritating to others, but this is misleading; Paul is saying to the Corinthians that their zeal has (in the word used by the majority of the contemporary versions) "stirred up" similar zeal on the part of the people of Macedonia.

In Hebrews, "Let us consider one another to provoke unto love and to good works" (10:24, KJV) is now translated as "encouraging each other" (CEV); "stimulate one another" (NASB); "help each other" (NCV); "spur one another" (NIV); "stir up" (NKJV); the NRSV uses "provoke one another."

PSALTERY

The Greek verb *psallo* means "to pluck, pull, twitch." Applied first to the string of a bow, drawn to propel the arrow, it came to be used for the strings of a musical instrument, played by plucking with the fingers rather than by striking with a plectrum. So a *psalma* became a tune played on a harp, *psalmos* a song or psalm sung to the accompaniment of a harp, *psaltes* a harper, and *psalterion* a harp. The word passed into Latin as *psalterium* and into English as *psaltery.*

In the KJV the word occurs only in the Old Testament, where it is used to translate the Hebrew *nebel,* while "harp" is used for the Hebrew *kinnor.* In general, scholars now translate *kinnor* as "lyre" or "zither" and *nebel* as "harp," but several variations from this practice can be found. The NIV, for example, usually has "harp" for *kinnor* and "lyre" for *nebel,* as sometimes does the RSV, while the NKJV prefers "lute" to "lyre."

"Psaltery" does not appear in the New Testament, but the noun *psalmos* and the verb *psallo* do. The Psalms of the Old Testament are referred to, and songs of praise and thanksgiving are encouraged in such passages as Ephesians 5:18–19 (KJV): "Be filled with the Spirit; Speaking to yourselves in psalms and hymns and spiritual songs, singing and making melody in your heart to the Lord."

The Greek word in the New Testament which corresponds to "psaltery" in the Old Testament is *kithara,* translated "harp." It appears in 1 Corinthians 14:7, where the KJV reads: "And even things without life giving sound, whether pipe or harp, except they give a distinction in the sounds, how shall it be known what is piped or harped?" The contemporary versions translate the noun as "harp," but use "played" for the verb.

Harps accompany the song of the redeemed before the throne of God in the vision of John recorded in the book of Revelation (5:8; 14:2; 15:2). The KJV's translation of 14:2 ("I heard the voice of harpers harping with their harps") is not as pleasing in English as the corresponding words in Greek; the majority of the contemporary versions replace "harpers" with "harpists" and the verb "harping" with "playing," as in the NKJV: "I heard the sound of harpists playing their harps."

PUBLICAN

The word "publican" is used today solely for the licensee of a public house. In the Roman Empire, however, a *publicanus* was a man who farmed the public revenue, that is, who leased the right to collect the taxes and customs in a particular district, with the understanding that he might retain the revenue in excess of a fixed annual sum but would make good any deficiency. The Greek term for such a man was *telones,* a word which appears in the Synoptic Gospels and is translated "publican" from the Latin.

The status of these publicans is described clearly by Arndt and Gingrich in *A Greek-English Lexicon of the New Testament* (p. 820): "The *telonai* in the synoptics are not the holders of the tax-farming contracts themselves, but subordinates hired by them; the higher officials were usually foreigners, but their underlings were taken from the native population as a rule. The prevailing system of tax collection afforded the collector many opportunities to exercise his greed and unfairness. Hence they were particularly hated and despised as a class. The strict Jew was further offended by the fact that the tax-collector had to maintain continual contact with Gentiles in the course of his work; this rendered a Jewish tax-collector ceremonially unclean."

Zacchaeus is described in Luke 19:2 (KJV) as "the chief among the publicans, and he was rich." He was probably the head of the tax and customs organization for Jericho, an important center of trade. But that does not mean that he was himself the *publicanus,* the man who held the contract with the Roman government. The contemporary versions generally refer to Zacchaeus as "a chief tax collector" (CEV, "in charge of collecting taxes"; NCV, "a very important tax collector").

PULSE

This word is a collective noun for "the edible seeds of leguminous plants culti-

vated for food, as peas, beans, lentils, etc."
(OED). The word has become much more
common in modern English with the recent increased interest in vegetarianism
and healthy eating. It is not an accurate
rendering in the one passage where it is
used in the KJV, Daniel 1:12, 16.

Daniel did not ask for his diet to be restricted to beans and other legumes ("let
them give us pulse to eat"), but that he and
his friends should be allowed to refrain
from meat and eat only vegetables. The
word which the KJV translates "pulse" is a
much wider term which means vegetables,
which is how the contemporary versions
translate it.

Daniel's reason for requesting a vegetar-
ian diet was to avoid defiling himself (that
is, incurring ceremonial uncleanness) by
eating non-kosher food. The Jewish dietary
law is stated in Leviticus 20:24–26. Daniel's
strict conscience in this matter was not exceptional for a pious Jew.

PURCHASE

"To purchase" now means "to buy." It
involves the payment of a price, usually of
money. But in 1611 it was still a general
word that meant "to acquire, obtain, or
gain." In Shakespeare's *The Tempest* (IV,
1, 14) Prospero agrees to the marriage of
Ferdinand and Miranda in these words:

> "Then, as my gift, and thine
> own acquisition
> Worthily purchased, take my
> daughter."

The contemporary versions of the Bible
retain the word "purchase" only where the
context implies the payment of a price,
which may be money or may be work, effort or suffering.

In Psalm 74:2, for example, the KJV has
"Remember thy congregation, which thou
hast purchased of old." The majority of the
contemporary versions also translate this
by words related to buying for a price: the
NASB, NIV, and NKJV have "purchased"; the

NCV has "bought"; the NRSV has "acquired";
the CEV and NLT have "rescued" and
"chose" respectively.

In Acts 20:28 both the KJV and the majority of the contemporary versions have
"purchased" or a related word such as
"bought" in the context of the price paid
by Jesus Christ for the salvation of the
church of God, "which he hath purchased
with his own blood" (KJV). The NRSV and
RSV translate the KJV "purchased" as "obtained." "Buy" is also used in some of the
contemporary translations of Acts 8:20
(CEV, NCV, NIV, NLT), where the KJV has "thou
hast thought that the gift of God may be
purchased with money."

Elsewhere, where the context has nothing to do with payment, the contemporary
versions translate "purchased" by "taken,"
"gained," "acquired," or "won" (see, for
example, Psalm 78:54). In Ephesians 1:14,
the KJV's "purchased possession" is an ex-
pansion of the Greek word for "possession" retained as such only by the NKJV.

The KJV's translation of 1 Timothy 3:13
("They that have used the office of a deacon
well purchase to themselves a good degree") does not refer to men who use an
office for their own profit or try to buy
honorary degrees. In the contemporary
versions it is translated as "obtain for
themselves a good [NASB, "high"] standing"
(NKJV; NRSV, "gain a good standing for themselves"; NIV, "gain an excellent standing");
"are making an honorable place for themselves" (NCV); "will earn a good reputation"
(CEV).

PURE ALL THINGS ARE PURE

The expression "to the pure all things
are pure" means that "pure-minded people are less likely than others to be aware
of evil, obscenity, coarseness, etc" (*Oxford
Dictionary of Current Idiomatic English*, vol.
2). The expression comes from the first part
of Titus 1:15 (KJV): "Unto the pure all things
are pure: but unto them that are defiled

and unbelieving is nothing pure; but even their mind and conscience is defiled."

The contemporary versions have: "to the pure all things are pure" (NASB, NIV, NKJV, NRSV, RSV; the NASB and NIV insert a comma after the first "pure"); the CEV has "Everything is pure for someone whose heart is pure"; the NCV, "To those who are pure, all things are pure"; and the NLT, "Everything is pure to those whose hearts are pure."

PURGE

As a verb, "purge" is still used today for "the act of making physically clean or pure," especially of "ridding the body of impurities." However, it is perhaps used more frequently today in its figurative and political sense of "cleaning out the body politic"—the state—as presidents may do to their governments.

The verb is used thirty-one times by the KJV, representing seven different Hebrew words and five different Greek words. It is retained by the majority of the contemporary translations in the three cases where it has its figurative and political meaning: Josiah purged the land of idolatry (2 Chronicles 34:3, 8), and the word of the Lord to Ezekiel was that he would purge out the rebels (Ezekiel 20:38). In the great penitential Psalm 51, where the KJV has "Purge me with hyssop, and I shall be clean; wash me, and I shall be whiter than snow" (v. 7), the NKJV and NRSV retain "purge," but the NASB has "purify"; the NIV, "cleanse"; the CEV, "wash"; and the NCV, "take away."

In nearly all other cases in the KJV, "purge" has a moral sense or refers to a ceremonial ritual of moral significance. Nine times it represents the Hebrew word for "forgive," "atone for," or "expiate" (1 Samuel 3:14; Psalms 65:3; 79:9; Proverbs 16:6; Isaiah 6:7; 22:14; 27:9; Ezekiel 43:20, 26). Twelve times it means "cleanse" or "purify."

Generally, the contemporary translations render the KJV "purge" by using these words. Twice the underlying Hebrew terms are figures of speech drawn from the

refining of metals (Isaiah 1:25; Malachi 3:3). In the Isaiah passage, where the KJV has "I will turn my hand upon thee, and purely purge away thy dross," the NKJV and NIV retain "purge away your dross"; the NASB and NRSV have "smelt away your dross"; the CEV and NCV both adjust the image to "burn away everything that makes you unfit" (CEV) and "clean away all your wrongs" (NCV).

In the Malachi passage, where the KJV has "he shall . . . purge them as gold and silver," the majority of the contemporary versions have "refine them as [or, "like"] gold and silver"; the NKJV retains "purge them."

"Throughly purge his floor" (Matthew 3:12; Luke 3:17, KJV) contains the old spelling "throughly" for "thoroughly" and is misleading because it can be taken to mean that the floor is in need of physical cleansing or ceremonial purification. The more ancient manuscripts of Luke 3:17 read: "His winnowing fork is in his hand, and he will clear his threshing floor and gather his wheat into the granary, but the chaff he will burn with unquenchable fire." The cleaning up of the threshing floor is not a preliminary to the threshing, but part of the process, and "clean up," "clean out," or "clear" are used by the majority of the contemporary versions.

In John 15:2 (KJV), "to purge" means "to prune"; in the sixteenth century people spoke either of "purging" or of "pruning a tree or vine," and except for this one verse the KJV translates the Greek as "prune" and "pruning hooks." The contemporary versions generally use "prune" here.

The KJV's translation of Mark 7:18–19 is "Do you not perceive, that whatsoever thing from without entereth into the man, it cannot defile him; Because it entereth not into his heart, but into the belly, and goeth out into the draught, purging all meats?" The final "purging all meats" is effectively a subordinate clause to the introductory words of verse 18 (in the KJV, "And he saith unto them," [thereby purging all meats]).

Most of the contemporary versions create a new sentence after the question, with wording such as "(Thus he declared all foods clean.)" (NRSV; NASB, "He"). The NKJV retains the KJV's arrangement of verse 19 with "because it does not enter his heart but his stomach, and is eliminated, thus purifying all foods?" Neither in this verse nor anywhere else in the KJV does the word "purge" refer to the purging of the intestines.

PURTENANCE

This word is a shortened form of "appurtenance," which today is used only in a legal context; it means "whatever pertains or belongs to something larger" or of "more consequence." Its earlier meaning was the "inwards" (or in today's pronunciation, the "innards") of an animal. Tyndale used "purtenance" in this sense in his translation of Exodus 12:9 to refer to the inner parts of the Passover lamb, and the KJV follows him in its only use of the word.

The contemporary versions use "entrails" (NASB, NKJV); "inner organs" (NCV, NRSV); "inner parts" (NIV); "insides" (CEV).

PUSH

In the law concerning fatal injuries inflicted by cattle (Exodus 21:28–32, 35–36), the KJV uses the word "gore" in verses 28 and 31, "push with his horn" in verse 29, and "push" in verses 32 and 36. The Hebrew verb is the same in all these cases, and the majority of the contemporary versions use "gore" throughout; the CEV and NCV use "kill" and the NKJV has "thrust with its horn" in verse 29. Tyndale and Coverdale were responsible for some of the inconsistent renderings; the Bishops' Bible introduced "push with his horn."

Q

QUARREL

As a noun, "quarrel" appears four times in the KJV. It is used in 2 Kings 5:7: "see how he seeketh a quarrel against me"; the contemporary versions generally retain "quarrel," for example in the NKJV, "see how he seeks a quarrel with me." "Quarrel" is used in the obsolete sense of "complaint" in Colossians 3:13, where the KJV reads, "Forbearing one another, and forgiving one another, if any man have a quarrel against any."

The contemporary versions translate this as "complaint," "grievance," or "wrong": "if anyone has a complaint against another" (NKJV, NRSV; NASB, "whoever has a complaint against anyone"); "forgive whatever grievances you may have" (NIV); "forgive anyone who does you wrong" (CEV). The statement in Mark 6:19 (KJV) that "Herodias had a quarrel against him [John the Baptist]" is translated in the majority of the contemporary versions as "having a grudge"; the NKJV has "Herodias held it against him."

The Greek says literally that she "had it in for him."

In Leviticus 26:25 (KJV), "avenge the quarrel of my covenant" is an awkward attempt to put into English a cognate accusative, "avenge the vengeance." The NASB, NKJV, NRSV, and RSV have "execute [NRSV, "executing"] vengeance"; the NIV, "avenge the breaking of the covenant."

On a number of occasions, the contemporary versions use "quarrel," as both noun and verb, to replace the KJV's use of such words as "strive," "strife," "contention," "debate," and "meddling." In Isaiah 58:4, for example, "Behold, ye fast for strife and debate, and to smite with the fist of wickedness" (KJV) becomes "you fast only to quarrel and fight" (NRSV) or "Your fasting ends in quarreling and strife" (NIV).

QUATERNION

The word "quaternion" means "a group" or "set of four." The word is still used in

English in the realm of mathematics, and in the field of publishing, where it means "a quire of four sheets, doubled so as to make sixteen pages." The Latin word *quaternio* was applied to the number four on dice; the Greek *tetradion* refers to four days in one of the ancient papyri discovered within the last seventy years, and to quires of four sheets of parchment in another.

When Herod put Peter in prison, he assigned four quaternions of soldiers to guard him (Acts 12:4). The word "quaternion" was taken by Wycliffe, and later by Tyndale, directly from the Latin Vulgate; however, the majority of the contemporary versions lose the idea of four groups of four by replacing "quaternions" with "squads" (although the NCV keeps the literal meaning by specifying "sixteen soldiers").

The significant fact is not that each squad was made up of four men, but that there were four squads, each to be on duty during one of the four three-hour watches of the night. The squad of soldiers which was detailed to crucify Jesus (John 19:23) seems to have consisted of four men, since they divided Jesus' clothes into four parts.

QUESTION

As noun or verb, "question" raises no difficulty as used by the KJV in the Old Testament. In more than half its occurrences in the KJV New Testament, however, it does not clearly convey the meaning of the Greek. In Mark 8:11, for example, the KJV uses "to question with him" in a sense which is now obsolete; the NASB and NRSV replace it with "to argue with him" (NKJV, "to dispute"); the NCV and NIV retain "to ask him questions" and "to question Jesus," respectively.

The disciples of John the Baptist and the Jews in John 3:25 get involved in "a question between them," now rendered as "an argument" (CEV, NCV, NIV); "a discussion" (NASB, NRSV); "a dispute" (NKJV). In Mark 9:14, 16 the KJV's idiom, "questioning with them," is translated as "arguing" by the majority of the contemporary versions, although the NKJV prefers "disputing with them" in verse 14 and "discussing with them" in verse 16.

The words of the town clerk at Ephesus (Acts 19:40, KJV), "For we are in danger to be called in question for this day's uproar," are more exactly translated, "We are in danger of being charged with rioting" (NRSV, NIV), or "accused of a riot" (NASB; CEV, "of starting a riot"); the NKJV stays closest to the KJV, with "we are in danger of being called in question for today's uproar."

In Acts 23:6; 24:21 (KJV), Paul cried out in the council, "I am called in question"; in the majority of the contemporary versions this becomes "I am on trial"; the NKJV has "I am being judged."

Festus says in Acts 25:19 (KJV) that Paul's accusers "had certain questions against him"; the NKJV retains "questions" but other contemporary versions have "points of disagreement" (NASB, NRSV; NIV, RSV, "points of dispute"). Paul stated that he was glad to appear before King Agrippa, because Agrippa was "expert in all customs and questions which are among the Jews" (Acts 26:3, KJV); in two contemporary versions (NIV, NRSV) these become "customs and controversies"; the NKJV and NASB keep "customs and questions."

In 2 Timothy 2:23 the KJV reads, "But foolish and unlearned questions avoid, knowing that they do gender strifes." "Questions" here is now translated "arguments" (CEV, NCV, NIV); "disputes" (NKJV); "controversies" (NRSV); the NASB translates the sentence, "But refuse foolish and ignorant speculations, knowing that they produce quarrels." Similar translations of the KJV's "questions" occur in 1 Timothy 6:4 and Titus 3:9.

In 1 Timothy 1:4 the KJV has "Neither give heed to fables and endless genealogies, which minister questions, rather than godly edifying which is in faith: so do." The contemporary versions render "minister questions" as "cause disputes" (NKJV); "promote speculations" (NRSV; NIV, "controversies"); "give rise to mere speculation" (NASB);

"bring arguments" (NCV). The whole verse reads in the NRSV: "and not to occupy themselves with myths and endless genealogies that promote speculations rather than the divine training that is known by faith."

QUICK, QUICKEN

A person or thing that is quick moves or acts with great speed. In the KJV, however, "quick" means "alive" or "living." The word "quick" is not retained by the contemporary versions. In these the "quick and the dead" (the KJV AT Acts 10:42; 2 Timthy 4:1; 1 Peter 4:5) is replaced by "the living and the dead," except the CEV for 2 Timothy 4:1 which has "living or dead."

In Hebrews 4:12 instead of "the word of God is quick, and powerful" (KJV), we now read, "the word of God is living and active"; the CEV has "What God has said isn't only alive and active!"; the NLT has "the word of God is full of living power."

When Korah and his company went down quick into the mouth of the earth, and it swallowed them up, the KJV "quick" refers not to the immediacy of the catastrophe or the speed of their descent, but to the fact that they were buried alive (Numbers 16:23–33). It is interesting to note that verse 30 uses "quick" and verse 33 "alive." A similar use of "quick" is found in Psalms 55:15 and 124:3. The word "alive" is now used in all these cases in all the contemporary versions, except the CEV at Psalm 124:3 where the word is left untranslated.

The word "quick" is retained by the NASB, NRSV, and the RSV in one passage, Leviticus 13:10 (KJV), where it refers to the "quick raw flesh" of leprosy. The word is left untranslated in the NCV, NIV, CEV, and NKJV; the NLT paraphrases it as "an open sore."

In modern English, if something "quickens," it becomes faster ("her pulse quickened"); in the KJV, the word means "to make alive." It appears fourteen times in the Psalms, twelve of which are in Psalm 119, and eleven times in the New Testament; it is replaced in the contemporary versions

by such terms as "revive," "give life," "preserve life," "make alive," and "life-giving."

For example, in Psalm 119:107 (KJV), "Quicken me" becomes in the NASB and NKJV, "Revive me"; in the NCV, NRSV, and the RSV, "Give me life." The NIV has "Preserve my life"; and the NLT, "Restore again." "It is the spirit that quickeneth" (John 6:63) in the KJV is rendered in the NASB and NKJV as "the Spirit who [NCV, "that"] gives life"; the NIV as "the Spirit gives life"; the CEV, "The Spirit is the one who gives life!"; while the NLT has "who gives eternal life." The NRSV has "the spirit that [RSV, "who"] gives life."

"That which thou sawest is not quickened, except it die" (1 Corinthians 15:36) in the KJV is rendered in the NASB, NIV, NRSV, and RSV as "does not come to life"; in the NKJV, "is not made alive"; in the NCV, "before it can live and grow"; the CEV paraphrases as "before it can sprout from the ground" and the NLT paraphrases it as "doesn't grow into a plant."

"The last Adam was made a quickening spirit" (1 Corinthians 15:45) in the KJV is rendered in the CEV, NASB, NIV, NKJV, NLT, NRSV, and RSV as "a life-giving spirit"; and in the NCV as "a spirit that gives life." "Hath quickened us together with Christ" (Ephesians 2:5) in the KJV is rendered in the NASB, NKJV, NRSV, and RSV as "made us alive together with Christ"; in the NLT, "he gave us life when he raised Christ from the dead," in the NCV, "he gave us new life with Christ," and in the CEV as "God had Christ choose us to live with him."

QUIT

The main meaning of "quit" in contemporary English is "to leave" or "to give up" ("to quit smoking"; "to quit a job"). In the KJV the word occurs as both a verb, in the sense of "to conduct or acquit oneself," and as an adjective meaning "acquitted or set free," uses that are now chiefly archaic in English.

As a verb, "quit" occurs three times in the KJV, twice in 1 Samuel 4:9: "Be strong, and quit yourselves like men, O ye Philistines, that ye be not servants unto the Hebrews, as they have been to you: quit yourselves like men, and fight." The contemporary versions render the phrases "quit yourselves like men" as "conduct yourselves like men" (NKJV), "acquit yourselves like men" (RSV), "be men" (NASB, NIV, NRSV), "fight like men" (NCV), and "don't be afraid" (CEV).

At 1 Corinthians 16:13, the KJV reads, "Watch ye, stand fast in the faith, quit you like men, be strong." The contemporary versions render the expression "quit you like men" as "be courageous" (NLT, NRSV, RSV), "Have courage" (NCV), "be men of courage" (NIV), "stay brave" (CEV), "be brave" (NKJV), and "act like men" (NASB).

Shakespeare used the word in this sense:

> "Seem to defend yourself; now
> quit you well."
> —*King Lear* (II, 1, 32)

As an adjective in the KJV, "quit" means "acquitted" or "set free." It occurs in three instances:

Exodus 21:19, "If he rise again, and walk abroad upon his staff, then shall he that smote him be quit: only he shall pay for the loss of his time, and shall cause him to be thoroughly healed." Here "quit" is rendered as follows in the contemporary versions: "unpunished" (NASB), "acquitted" (NKJV), "not be held responsible" (NIV), "free of liability" (NRSV), "innocent" (NLT), and "not to be punished" (NCV).

Exodus 21:28, "If an ox gore a man or a woman, that they die: then the ox shall be surely stoned, and his flesh shall not be eaten; but the owner of the ox shall be quit." The renderings in the contemporary versions are as at Exodus 21:19, except "shall not be liable" (NRSV), "will not be liable" (NLT), and "not guilty" (NCV).

Joshua 2:20, "And if thou utter this our business, then we will be quit of thine oath which thou has made us to swear." The contemporary versions' renderings of "quit of" are "free from" (NASB, NCV, NKJV), "released from" (NIV, NRSV), and "not bound by" (NLT).

Again, this usage is found in Shakespeare:

> "He that dies this year is quit for the
> next."
> —*King Henry IV, Part II* (III, 2, 246)

R

RAIN FALLS ON THE JUST AND THE UNJUST

The saying the "rain falls on the just and the unjust" means, according to the *Oxford Dictionary of Current Idiomatic English* (vol. 2), "virtue does not ensure all benefits or protect against all hazards." The phrase derives from Jesus' Sermon on the Mount (Matthew 5:45): "That ye may be the children of your Father which is in heaven: for he maketh his sun to rise on the evil and on the good, and sendeth rain on the just and on the unjust" (KJV).

Of the contemporary versions, the NKJV, NLT, and RSV have "sends rain on the just and on the unjust"; the NASB, NIV, and NRSV have "sends rain on the righteous and [NRSV, "and on"] the unrighteous"; the CEV and NCV have "sends rain for the ones [NCV, "to those"] who do right and for the ones [NCV, "to those"] who do wrong."

RANGE

The word "range" today has a wide variety of meanings, including "a row of mountains," "a cooking stove," "a place for practicing rifle shooting or golf shots," and "an extent or limit." Some of these meanings have changed over the years, and confusion can be caused when the KJV uses "range" with a now unfamiliar meaning.

In Job 39:8, for example, "The range of

the mountains is his pasture" does not refer to a range of mountains but the area over which animals range or move about in search of food, in the sense in which "range" is used in the song, "Home, Home on the Range."

The Bishops' Bible had "seek their pasture about the mountains," and the Geneva Bible, "seeketh out the mountain for his pasture." The majority of the contemporary versions convey the sense of space by using verbs such as "ranges" (NIV, NRSV); "roam" (CEV, NCV); "explores" (NASB); the NKJV retains the KJV "The range of the mountains."

"Range" in the sense of a row or line of things does occur in the KJV. In 2 Kings 11:15, Jehoiada commands the captains of the guard to seize Queen Athaliah and "Have her forth without the ranges." Here the ranges, lines, or rows are ranks of soldiers.

The contemporary translations of the word vary according to their interpretation of the KJV's "without." The NASB, NIV, and NRSV have "between the ranks"; the CEV, "out in front of the troops"; the NCV, "surround her with soldiers."

"A ranging bear" (Proverbs 28:15, KJV) could be thought to be too quiet for the Hebrew verb, which means "run" or "rush." The sixteenth-century English versions had "a hungry bear"; the majority of today's translations have "a charging bear"; the NASB has "a rushing bear."

In the command to break everything upon which any part of the carcass of an unclean animal falls, "whether it be oven, or ranges for pots" (Leviticus 11:35, KJV), the Hebrew term means "a very simple stove for cooking food in pots."

The renderings in the contemporary versions refer to the pot itself or the stove on which it is placed: the NASB, CEV, and NRSV have "stove"; the NKJV has "cooking stove"; the NIV has "cooking pot"; and the NCV has "clay baking pan."

READY

The word "ready" is used ambiguously in a few cases in the KJV. "Ready to die" (Luke 7:2, KJV) does not mean that the centurion's servant was prepared to die, but that he was "at the point of death." The contemporary versions render this "about to die" (CEV, NASB, NIV); "ready to die" (NKJV); "close to death" (NRSV). Similarly, the KJV's expression "ready to perish" in Job 29:13 and Isaiah 27:13 is generally rendered in the contemporary versions as "about to perish," "dying," or the people concerned already "were perishing."

Paul's statement in 2 Timothy 4:6 (KJV), "I am now ready to be offered," translates a Greek original which means literally "I am already being poured out as a libation" (NRSV) and this sense of something already happening is brought out in the contemporary versions. The same Greek phrase occurs in Philippians 2:17 and is translated in similar terms, generally in the contemporary versions as "poured out as a [NIV, NLT, "poured out like"] a drink offering" (NASB, NIV, NKJV, NLT) although the KJV does not use "ready."

In Deuteronomy 26:5, the NKJV retains the sense of the KJV's "A Syrian ready to perish was my father," with "My father was a Syrian, about to perish," but the other contemporary versions have: "My father was a wandering Aramean" (NASB, NCV, NIV); "A wandering Aramean was my ancestor" (NRSV).

REAP WHERE ONE HAS NOT SOWN

The expression "reap where one has not sown" means to receive the rewards or punishment that are not in accordance with what one has done. The saying comes from Matthew 25:24, Jesus' parable of the talents, in which the person who received one talent said to the master, "Lord, I knew thee that thou art an hard man, reaping where thou hast not sown, and gathering where thou hast not strawed" (KJV).

Of the contemporary versions, the NASB, NKJV, NRSV, and RSV have "reaping where you did not sow" [NKJV, "you have not sown"]; the NIV, "harvesting where you have not sown"; the NLT, "harvesting crops you didn't plant"; and the CEV, "You harvest what you don't plant." See also Luke 19:21; 2 Corinthians 9:6; and Galatians 6:7, which affirms the general rule that "whatever a man sows, that he will also reap"—in other words, "we reap what we sow." (See also SOWING AND REAPING)

REASON *(noun)*

As a noun, "reason" occurs once in the KJV where it seems to be used as an adjective (Acts 6:2): "It is not reason that we should leave the word of God, and serve tables." The Greek has an adjective here which means "acceptable," "satisfactory"; the Latin Vulgate has an adjective which means "fair," "equitable," "just," "right." Tyndale and his successors translated the Greek by "mete"; Wycliffe translated the Latin by "right," and Rheims by "reason," which was adopted by the KJV.

The idiom used by the KJV here, "it is reason" or "it is not reason," meaning that it is or is not an act or proceeding agreeable to reason, was common from about 1400 to 1650, according to OED, but is now rare. Of the contemporary translations, the NCV, NIV, and NRSV have "right"; the NASB and NKJV have "desirable."

REASON *(verb)*

As a verb, "reason" appears twenty-three times in the KJV. Today, "to reason" with someone implies (at least at the start) a calm and rational discussion which puts forward the facts of a case. But in the sense in which the KJV translators used "reason," the word was sharper and more confrontational, and closer to the original Greek of the New Testament.

Because "reason" no longer conveys this meaning today, the contemporary versions often use other verbs to translate it: "ar-gue," "discuss," "question," "dispute." Some of the translations, however, stay closer to the modern understanding of "reason" and use blander words such as "debate," "talk it over," or "wonder."

Where the context seems to require it, some of the contemporary versions retain "reason," as in Isaiah 1:18, where the KJV has "Come now, and let us reason together, saith the LORD." Sometimes, as in Job 23:7, the same Hebrew verb is translated by the KJV itself as "dispute" rather than "reason," and it is some of the contemporary versions which translate the verb as "reason" (NASB, NKJV, NRSV, NCV, NIV, "present his case").

In the New Testament, a pattern can be observed in the contemporary versions' translation of the KJV's "reason." The NKJV almost always retains "reason"; the NIV sometimes uses "reason," but also uses other words such as "discuss"; the NASB often retains "reason" but also uses "discuss"; the CEV tends to use words such as "thought it over," "talked it over," "started wondering"; the NCV occasionally has "discussed" but also uses "argued"; the NRSV has words such as "argued" and "questioned."

In Mark 12:28, the majority of the contemporary versions use the sharper "argue" or (NRSV) "dispute"; the NKJV alone has "reason." The passages where the KJV translates the Greek verbs by "reason" are: Matthew 16:7–8; 21:25; Mark 2:6, 8; 8:16–17; 11:31; 12:28; Luke 5:21–22; 20:5, 14; 24:15; Acts 17:2; 18:4, 19; 24:25. In Mark 9:33–34; Acts 6:9; 9:29; 17:17; 19:8–9; 24:12, the KJV translates the same verbs by "dispute."

REASONING

As a noun, "reasoning" occurs three times in the KJV. It is the correct word in Job 13:6 ("Hear now my reasoning"), and is retained by the NKJV and NRSV; the CEV, NASB, NCV, and NIV have "argument." But it is not the right word in Luke 9:46, where the KJV reads, "there arose a reasoning among them," and the majority of the contemporary versions have "argument" (NKJV, "dispute").

In Acts 28:29 (KJV), "the Jews departed, and had great reasoning among themselves." The majority of the contemporary versions include this verse only as a footnote; the NASB and NKJV include it in the text, translating it as having "a great dispute," and drawing attention to its provenance in a footnote. The Arndt and Gingrich *Greek-English Lexicon of the New Testament* suggests the translation, "disputing vigorously among themselves."

RECEIPT OF CUSTOM

See CUSTOM.

RECORD

As noun and verb, "record" appears thirty-four times in the KJV. In twenty-seven of these instances it carries the obsolete meaning of "a witness," "to witness," "a testimony," or "to testify." "I call heaven and earth to record this day against you" (Deuteronomy 30:19, KJV; compare 31:28) is translated in the contemporary versions as "I call heaven and earth as witnesses against you" (NKJV, NIV); "to witness against you" (NASB, NRSV); "to be witnesses" (CEV, NCV).

The KJV translates 2 Corinthians 1:23 as "I call God for a record upon my soul"; the contemporary versions have the more accurate rendering, which calls upon God as witness "against my soul" (NKJV), or "to my soul" (NASB). Another example of "record" in the KJV being sometimes translated as "witness" in the contemporary versions can be found in Philippians 1:8. "My record is on high" (Job 16:19, KJV) is now translated as "my evidence is on high" (NKJV); "my advocate is on high" (NASB, NIV); "he that vouches for me is on high" (NRSV).

"Faithful witnesses to record" (Isaiah 8:2, KJV) is retained in the NKJV, and the NASB has "faithful witnesses for testimony," but other contemporary translations omit "to record" and have simply "reliable witnesses" (NCV, NIV, NRSV). Shakespeare uses "record" in this obsolete sense in *King Richard II* (I,

1, 30): "First, heaven be the record of my speech!"

The noun "record" is used seven times in the KJV (in John 1:19; 8:13–14; 19:35; 1 John 5:10–11; 3 John 12) as a translation for the Greek noun meaning "testimony," which is the rendering of the majority of the contemporary versions. The KJV uses the phrase "bear record" twelve times to translate the Greek verb which means "to bear witness" or "to testify" (John 1:32, 34; 8:13–14; 12:17; 19:35; Romans 10:2; 2 Corinthians 8:3; Galatians 4:15; Colossians 4:13; 3 John 12; Revelation 1:2).

John 8:13–14 contains both "bear record" and "record" (KJV, "The Pharisees therefore said unto him, Thou bearest record of thyself; thy record is not true. Jesus answered and said unto them, Though I bear record of myself, yet my record is true"), and the distinction is preserved in the contemporary versions with translations such as "So the Pharisees said to Him, 'You are testifying about Yourself; Your testimony is not true.' Jesus answered and said to them, 'Even if I testify about Myself, My testimony is true'" (NASB).

"I take you to record" (Acts 20:26, KJV) is an obsolete phrase which means "I call you to witness." In this case, however, it is an erroneous translation dating back to Tyndale. The contemporary translations have the rendering: "I testify to you" (NASB, NKJV); "I declare to you" (NIV, NRSV); "I tell you" (CEV, NCV).

The KJV's "In all places where I record my name" (Exodus 20:24) is variously translated in the contemporary versions. The NKJV remains close to the KJV, with "In every place where I record My name." The NASB and NRSV have "in every place where I cause my [NASB, "My"] name to be remembered." The CEV ("Wherever I choose to be worshiped,") and the NCV ("Worship me in every place that I choose") focus on choice, and the place where God chooses to be worshiped; and the NIV has "Wherever I cause my name to be honored."

R

The duty of certain Levites, as ministers before the ark of the Lord, was "to record, and to thank and praise the LORD God of Israel" (1 Chronicles 16:4, KJV). Here "to record" is translated in the contemporary versions as "to celebrate" (NASB); "to make petition" (NIV); "to commemorate" (NKJV); "to invoke" (NRSV).

When King Ahasuerus could not sleep (Esther 6:1), he ordered his attendants to read to him from "the book of the records of the chronicles" (KJV, NKJV; NIV, "the book of the chronicles, the record of his reign"; NRSV, "the book of records").

RECOVER

In the story of Naaman (2 Kings 5), the KJV uses the following expressions: "the prophet . . . would recover him of his leprosy" (v. 3); "that thou mayest recover him of his leprosy" (v. 6); "this man doth send unto me to recover a man of his leprosy" (v. 7); "recover the leper" (v. 11).

Although the OED does not record this usage as obsolete or archaic, it is no longer in regular use. Today we do not say that the doctor will "recover" the patient, but that the patient, as a result of the doctor's ministrations, "will recover." Accordingly, in these verses the majority of the contemporary versions have "cure" or "heal."

"Recover" is used by the KJV to translate eleven different Hebrew verbs, each of which has a distinct meaning. In the following passages, the contemporary versions express the sense of the Hebrew more literally.

Isaiah 38:16 (KJV), "so wilt thou recover me, and make me to live"; now, "You will restore me" (NKJV); "O restore me to health" (NASB, NRSV; NIV, "You restored me to health").

Psalm 39:13 (KJV), "that I may recover strength"; now, "that I may smile again" (NASB, NRSV); "that I may rejoice again" (NIV); the NKJV has "that I may regain strength."

Hosea 2:9 (KJV), "recover my wool and my flax"; now, "take back my [NASB, NKJV, "My"] wool and my [NASB, NKJV, "My"] flax"

[or: "linen"] (CEV, NASB, NCV, NIV, NKJV; NRSV, "take away").

Second Samuel 8:3 (KJV), "recover his border"; now, "recover his territory" (NKJV); "restore his rule" (NASB; NIV, "his control"); the NRSV has "restore his monument."

Second Chronicles 14:13 (KJV), "the Ethiopians were overthrown, that they could not recover themselves"; the NKJV, NASB, and NIV retain "they could not recover"; the NRSV has "until no one remained alive."

REFRAIN

The word "refrain," as a transitive verb meaning to "bridle," "restrain," or "check a person or thing," is obsolete or archaic. The word is now used intransitively, in the sense of "abstain," "forbear," "keep oneself from doing some act or yielding to some feeling." "Refrain" occurs seventeen times in the KJV, and fourteen of these instances are in the obsolete transitive sense.

In these fourteen cases (Genesis 43:31; 45:1; Esther 5:10; Job 7:11; Psalm 40:9; Proverbs 10:19; Isaiah 42:14; 64:12; Jeremiah 14:10; Psalm 119:101; Proverbs 1:15; Jeremiah 31:16; 1 Peter 3:10), the majority of the contemporary versions generally use "control" or "restrain."

In Job 7:11, where the KJV has "I will not refrain my mouth," the NIV has "I will not keep silent" and the NCV, "I will not stay quiet." "I have refrained my feet" in Psalm 119:101 (KJV) becomes "I have kept my feet" in the NIV, and "I hold back my feet" in the NRSV.

In Proverbs 1:15, the KJV's "refrain thy foot" is rendered "keep your foot" (NKJV, NRSV; NASB, "your feet"); "do not set foot" (NIV). The NKJV retains "refrain" in Jeremiah 31:16, where the KJV has "refrain thy voice from weeping," and in 1 Peter 3:10, where the KJV has "let him refrain his tongue from evil"; here, the majority of the other contemporary versions use "keep from."

In Job 29:9 (KJV), "the princes refrained talking"; the majority of the contemporary versions simply insert "from": "the princes refrained from talking." The NKJV and NRSV keep the KJV wording in Ecclesiastes 3:5, "a time to embrace, and a time to refrain from embracing." The NIV has simply "a time to embrace and a time to refrain"; the NASB uses "a time to shun embracing."

REFUSE

"To refuse" now means "to decline a request, suggestion, or offer." It is a simple objective term. If the refusal is made under emotional stress or with more than ordinary vigor, that fact must be expressed in accompanying adverbs such as "flatly," "deliberately." But in Elizabethan English the word was applied to persons, and had a variety of meanings, often with emotional implication, which are now obsolete. These meanings included, among others, to "reject," "renounce," "abandon," "forsake," "cast off a person," "divorce a wife."

For example, Isaiah 54:6 (KJV) reads: "For the LORD hath called thee as a woman forsaken and grieved in spirit, and a wife of youth, when thou wast refused, saith thy God." To a modern reader, the verb "refuse" here suggests no more than a woman not getting something she wanted, but in fact the Hebrew verb here is a strong one. Its basic meaning is "to reject," and elsewhere (in sixty instances) the KJV translates it by "abhor," "despise," "loathe," "reject," "cast away," "cast off."

On ten occasions, the verb is translated as "refuse." So the woman in Isaiah 54:6 has been rejected and cast off, and although the NKJV retains "refused," the majority of the contemporary versions use stronger verbs such as "divorced" (CEV); "rejected" (NASB, NIV); "cast off" (NRSV).

This same strong verb is used in Psalm 118:22, which the KJV renders as "The stone which the builders refused is become the head stone of the corner." The contemporary versions all translate it as "rejected," which the KJV itself uses when this verse is quoted in the New Testament (Matthew 21:42; Mark 12:10; Luke 20:17). In other references to it, the KJV uses "was set at nought" (Acts 4:11) and "disallowed" (1 Peter 2:7). The contemporary versions generally use "rejected" in these passages.

"Refuse profane and old wives' fables" (1 Timothy 4:7, KJV) is an example of the use of "refuse" in an obsolete sense. The Greek verb here means to "shun," "avoid." The majority of the contemporary versions translate it as "Have nothing to do with" (for example, the NIV has "Have nothing to do with godless myths and old wives' tales"); the NKJV has "reject." (See DISALLOW; OLD WIVES' FABLES)

REHEARSE

The word "rehearse" is generally used today in the sense of "practice a play or performance," "go over words or an argument"; it is seldom used in the sense of "describe" or "narrate." In the sixteenth century, however, the word was still used in its now obsolete sense of "say," "state," "declare." "Rehearse" appears six times in the KJV.

In Judges 5:11, "rehearse the righteous acts of the LORD" is replaced in the contemporary translations with: "recount the righteous acts" [NASB, "deeds"] (NKJV, NASB); "recite the righteous acts" (NIV); "repeat the triumphs" (NRSV). In 1 Samuel 8:21, the majority of the contemporary versions have "repeated"; the range of translations is wider in 1 Samuel 17:31, where the KJV's "rehearsed" is replaced by "reported" (NIV, NKJV); "repeated" (NRSV); and "told" (NASB, NCV).

There is a similar variety of translations in Exodus 17:14: "recite" (NASB, NRSV, RSV); "recount" (NKJV); "announce" (NLT); "make sure . . . hears" (NIV). "They rehearsed all that God had done with them" (Acts 14:27, KJV) is now translated as "reported," "related," or "told."

In Acts 11:4 the KJV has an inaccurate translation, "But Peter rehearsed the matter from the beginning, and expounded it by order unto them." This was taken from

R

the Great Bible and the Bishops' Bible, in spite of the fact that Wycliffe, Tyndale, Coverdale, the Geneva Bible, and the Rheims New Testament had translated the verse correctly. In this case Coverdale's later judgment was unsound, for as editor of the Great Bible he misconstrued a clause which he had translated properly in his earlier work. The contemporary versions have restored the correct rendering. The NKJV, for example, has "But Peter explained it to them in order from the beginning."

REINS

Today we associate the word "reins" only with strips of leather for controlling horses; this meaning of the word came into English via Old French from the Latin *retinere*, "to restrain." The plural "reins" may look and sound the same, and is also a Norman French contribution to the English language, but it is derived from an entirely different Latin word, *renes*, which means "kidneys." It is a name for "the kidneys" or "the loins," the region of the kidneys, and is now obsolete, although another word derived from the same Latin source, "renal," is still used as an adjective, "to do with the kidneys."

The corresponding Hebrew word is *kelayoth*, which the KJV translates as "kidneys" eighteen times and "reins" thirteen times. The former group of passages is concerned with the ritual of animal sacrifice, in which the two kidneys and their surrounding fat had an important part (Exodus 29:13, 22; Leviticus 3:4, 10, 15; 4:9; etc.).

In eleven of the passages which use "reins," the word has the figurative meaning for which we now use "heart," as the seat of the feelings and affections. Thus, "my reins also instruct me in the night seasons" (Psalm 16:7, KJV) is translated in the majority of the contemporary versions as "my heart instructs me." The NASB has "my mind instructs me."

"I was pricked in my reins" (Psalm 73:21, KJV) is now variously translated: "I was pricked in heart" (NRSV); "I was vexed in

my mind" (NKJV); "I was pierced within" (NASB); "my spirit [was] embittered" (NIV); "I was angry" (NCV).

In his plea to the Lord concerning the prosperity of the wicked, Jeremiah says (Jeremiah 12:2, KJV), "thou art near in their mouth, and far from their reins"; here, the contemporary translations are divided between "hearts" (NRSV, NIV, NCV) and "mind" (NASB, NKJV).

In Jeremiah 17:10 (KJV, "I the LORD search the heart, I try the reins"), "reins" is translated as "mind" in the majority of the contemporary versions. This combination of "heart and reins," where the meaning is either "hearts and minds," "minds and hearts," "the mind and the heart," or "the heart and the mind" (the order and singular or plural seem to be used with no particular pattern in the contemporary versions), occurs in five other passages: Psalms 7:9; 26:2; Jeremiah 11:20; 20:12; Revelation 2:23.

In the one New Testament passage, the Greek *nephros* replaces *kelayoth*, but the thought is familiar from the Old Testament: "I am He who searches the minds and hearts" (NKJV).

Job's answer to his "miserable comforters" is in the language of deep distress and extravagant metaphor. "He cleaveth my reins asunder" (Job 16:13, KJV) is translated in the contemporary versions as "he slashes open my kidneys" (NRSV; NCV, "he stabs my kidneys"; NASB, "He splits my kidneys open"; NIV, "he pierces my kidneys"); the NKJV has "He pierces my heart."

The KJV's "For thou hast possessed my reins: thou hast covered me in my mother's womb" (Psalm 139:13) is now translated "you [NASB, NKJV, "You"] formed my inward parts" (NASB, NKJV, NRSV); "You . . . put me together" (CEV); "You made my whole being" (NCV); "you created my inmost being" (NIV).

REMEMBRANCE

This is a lovely word, more likely to be used of memories that are cherished than of those that are bitter. The Lord's "book of remembrance" (Malachi 3:16, KJV and the majority of the contemporary versions [NIV, NLT, "a scroll of"]) was "for them that feared the LORD, and that thought upon his name" (KJV).

"This do in remembrance of me," said Jesus when he instituted the Lord's Supper (1 Corinthians 11:23–26, KJV); in verse 24 the NASB, NIV, NKJV, and NRSV retain "in remembrance of me" (NASB, NKJV, "Me"); the CEV has "Eat this and remember me"; and the NCV, "Do this to remember me."

When Paul writes to the Philippians in the KJV that "I thank my God upon every remembrance of you" (Philippians 1:3), the contemporary versions have "I thank my God every time I remember you" (NCV, NIV, NRSV); "I thank my God upon every remembrance of you" (NKJV; NASB, "in all my remembrance of you"); "Every time I think of you, I thank my God" (CEV).

The word is used in an ironic or disparaging sense, however, in Job's answer to his comforters. The KJV renders Job 13:12 as "Your remembrances are like unto ashes, your bodies to bodies of clay." Here the word "remembrances" represents "memorable sayings" in the Hebrew, translated in the contemporary versions as "maxims" (NIV, NRSV); "platitudes" (NKJV); "memorable sayings" (NASB); "wise sayings" (NCV). In the second half of the verse, "bodies" is now generally translated as "defenses." Job is telling his friends that the old saws which they have dredged up from their memories are dusty answers to his problem.

In Isaiah 57:8 "remembrance" is used by the KJV in the sense of a symbol of phallic worship. The contemporary versions translate it as "symbol" (NRSV); "pagan symbols" (CEV, NIV); "sign" (NASB); "idols" (NCV); the NKJV retains "remembrance."

REMOVE

The word "remove" means "to take something away from its place," either by transfer to another place or by destruction. In Elizabethan English it was used more widely,

in various senses of the verb "to move" (such as "to shake," "change") without implying change of place. Since the KJV used "to remove" as a rendering for twenty-four different Hebrew verbs and seven Greek verbs, it inevitably included some of these now obsolete senses.

For example, in Psalm 104:5, where the KJV has "Who laid the foundations of the earth, that it should not be removed for ever," the contemporary versions have "it can never be moved" (NCV, NIV); "it should not be moved forever" (NKJV); "it shall [CEV, "will"] never be shaken" (CEV, NRSV); "it will not totter" (NASB).

In Psalm 125:1, the KJV's description of Mount Zion as that "which cannot be removed but abideth for ever" becomes in the contemporary versions either "cannot be moved" (NASB, NKJV, NRSV, NCV, "sits unmoved") or "cannot be shaken" (CEV, NIV). Psalm 46:2 (KJV, "Therefore will not we fear, though the earth be removed") becomes "though the earth should change" (NASB, NRSV); "even if the earth shakes" (NCV); "though the earth give way" (NIV); the NKJV retains "though the earth be removed."

In other passages, the contemporary versions replace the KJV's "removed" with words such as "will move," "will be shaken" (Isaiah 13:13); "moved" (Exodus 14:19); "trembled" (Exodus 20:18).

In Lamentations 3:17 (KJV), "thou hast removed my soul far off from peace" becomes in the contemporary versions: "You have moved my soul far from peace" (NKJV); "my soul is bereft of peace" (NRSV); "my soul has been rejected from peace" (NASB).

In Jeremiah 15:4, the KJV appears to mistranslate the Hebrew as "I will cause them to be removed into all kingdoms of the earth," which seems to imply sending into exile; all the contemporary versions translate this verse as having something to do with horror and trouble: "I will hand them over to trouble, to all kingdoms of the earth" (NKJV); "I will make them an object of horror among all the kingdoms of the earth"

R

(NASB); "I will make the people of Judah hated by everyone" (NCV); "you will be disgusting to all nations" (CEV); "I will make them abhorrent" (NIV); "I will make them a horror" (NRSV). A similar expression also appears in Deuteronomy 28:25 and Jeremiah 24:9; 29:18; 34:17.

RENDER

The word "render" in its modern meaning of "pay," "show," "give," and "submit" is clearly understandable in such texts as "Render to Caesar the things that are Caesar's, and to God the things that are God's" (Mark 12:17, KJV; and its parallels Matthew 20:21 and Luke 20:25), where in the contemporary versions the KJV "render" is generally translated as "give"; the NASB and NKJV retain "render," and "For he will render to every man according to his works" (Romans 2:6, KJV).

In other texts, however, "render" fails to convey the idea of "requite," "recompense," "repay," or "return" which is present in the Hebrew word it seeks to translate. At the close of the bloody adventure of Abimelech, the KJV has the comment: "Thus God rendered the wickedness of Abimelech, which he did unto his father, in slaying his seventy brethren: And all the evil of the men of Shechem did God render upon their heads" (Judges 9:56–57). The majority of the contemporary versions translate "render" in verse 56 as "repaid" (NASB, NIV, NKJV, NRSV); the CEV, NCV, and NLT have "punished."

In verse 57 the contemporary translations become rather more complicated (although the CEV, NCV, and NLT simply repeat "punished"): "all the evil of the men of Shechem God returned on their own heads" (NKJV); "God also made all the wickedness of the people of Shechem fall back on their heads" (NRSV); "God returned all the wickedness of the men of Shechem on their heads" (NASB); "God also made the men of Shechem pay for all their wickedness" (NIV).

For other examples see 1 Samuel 26:23 (where the contemporary versions have "rewards" or "repays"); Job 34:11 ("pays"/"repays"); Jeremiah 51:24 (generally "repay"); Zechariah 9:12 (generally "restore").

REPENT

"Repent" is a characteristically biblical word. The verb appears eighty-four times in the KJV, almost equally divided between the Old Testament and the New Testament; and the noun "repentance" occurs twenty-six times, all but once in the New Testament.

"Repent" was originally a reflexive verb, but it began early to be used without the reflexive pronoun. Out of sixty-five occurrences in Shakespeare's plays, only eight are reflexive, all in the first person: "I repent me."

Examples from the KJV are: "the children of Israel repented them for Benjamin" (Judges 21:6, compare 21:15); "The LORD shall . . . repent himself for his servants" (Deuteronomy 32:36, compare Psalm 135:14); "The LORD repented him of the evil" (2 Samuel 24:16; 1 Chronicles 21:15); "no man repented him of his wickedness" (Jeremiah 8:6); "I may repent me" (Jeremiah 26:3); "the LORD will repent him" (Jeremiah 26:13); "the LORD repented him" (Jeremiah 26:19); "I repent me" (Jeremiah 42:10); "repenteth him of evil" (Joel 2:13); "repentest thee of the evil" (Jonah 4:2); "Judas repented himself" (Matthew 27:3).

In all these cases the contemporary versions omit the reflexive pronoun, and, especially when referring to a change in God's intention, use a variety of words to translate "repent."

In Judges 21:6, for example, the Israelites "grieved for Benjamin their brother" (NKJV); "had compassion for Benjamin their kin" (NRSV); "were sorry for their brother Benjamin" (NASB); "the LORD will . . . have compassion" is also used by the majority of the contemporary versions in Deuteronomy 32:36.

In 2 Samuel 24:16 the majority translation is "relented"; "repent" is retained for the human repentance in Jeremiah 8:6, but replaced by "relent" (NIV, NKJV) and "change my mind" (CEV, NCV, NRSV) in Jeremiah 26:3; Jonah 4:2 has "relent" as its majority translation; in Matthew 27:3, Judas "was remorseful" (NKJV); "was seized with remorse" (NIV); the CEV and NCV have the weaker "was [NCV, "very"] sorry," and the NRSV retains "repented."

The verb "to repent" is also used impersonally in the KJV. "And it repented the LORD that he had made man on the earth . . . And the LORD said . . . it repenteth me that I have made them" (Genesis 6:6–7). The majority of the contemporary versions make the verb personal and translate this as "The LORD was sorry . . . I am sorry."

Other examples are: "it repented the LORD because of their groanings" (Judges 2:18, KJV); in the contemporary versions the Lord was "moved to pity by their groanings" (NASB, NKJV, NRSV); the CEV and NCV have the Lord feeling "sorry" for Israel; and in the NIV he "had compassion on them."

In 1 Samuel 15:11, the KJV's "It repenteth me that I have set up Saul to be king" now becomes "I regret" (NASB, NRSV, NKJV, "greatly regret"); "I am grieved" (NIV); "I am sorry" (CEV, NCV). "Let it repent thee concerning thy servants" (Psalm 90:13, KJV) is now "Have compassion on your servants" (NIV, NKJV, NRSV); "be sorry for Your servants" (NASB); "show kindness to your servants" (NCV); "Pity your servants" (CEV); "Have pity on thy servants" (RSV).

REPLENISH

The word "replenish" today means "to fill up again," "to restore to a former condition of being full or complete." But this meaning did not develop until after the work on the KJV had been done. The first example cited by the OED could be thought to be ambiguous and is dated 1612. The second example, which more clearly carries the new meaning, is dated 1666.

In the fifteenth and sixteenth centuries, however, "replenish" meant "to fill," "to make full," "to occupy the whole of." It is in this sense that the word is used in Genesis 1:28 (KJV), "Be fruitful, and multiply, and replenish the earth," a blessing and injunction to Adam and Eve which is later repeated, in the same words, to Noah (Genesis 9:1). In both cases, the Hebrew is translated by all the contemporary versions as "fill the earth."

REPORT

Apart from its use for the sound of a gunshot, "report" today refers mainly to a factual account of something that has happened or been done. This contrasts with its earlier meaning of "rumor," "common talk," "something generally said or believed, which might have no basis in fact at all." With this meaning it appears in the KJV in such passages as Eli's remonstrance with his sons (1 Samuel 2:24), and the Queen of Sheba's conversation with Solomon (1 Kings 10:6); in both these passages the majority of the contemporary versions also use "report."

The KJV's use of "report" in Deuteronomy 2:25; Isaiah 23:5 (shared by most of the contemporary translations) comes somewhere between the older and more modern meanings, since the reports of military prowess or disaster may or may not be rumor or truth. In Isaiah 53:1, "who hath believed our report?" in the KJV is now variously translated as "Who has believed our message?" (NASB, NIV); "Who has believed what we heard?" (NRSV; NCV, "Who would have believed what we heard?"); the NKJV retains "Who has believed our report?"

In Exodus 23:1 (KJV), "Thou shalt not raise a false report" means not only not starting a false report, but also not passing it on; the majority of the contemporary versions retain "false reports" but the NIV and NRSV translate "raise" as "spread," and the NKJV has "You shall not circulate a false report."

In the sixteenth century, "report" also meant reputation. Tyndale had "men of

honest reporte" (Acts 6:3) and "in evyll reporte and good reporte" (2 Corinthians 6:8),
and these phrases passed on to the KJV
"look ye out among you seven men of honest report, full of the Holy Ghost and wisdom"; in the first passage, the NASB and
NKJV have "men of good reputation" (NRSV,
"of good standing"); the NIV has "men who
are known to be full of the Spirit"; and the
CEV and NCV have "men who are respected"
(NCV, "are good").

In 2 Corinthians 6:8 the NASB, NIV, and
NKJV retain "report," and the NRSV has "ill
repute and good repute." From Tyndale
also comes the description of Cornelius as
"of good report among all the people (KJV,
"nation") of the Jews" (Acts 10:22); in this
passage and Acts 22:12; 1 Timothy 3:7, the
contemporary versions use phrases such
as "well spoken of," "(well) respected,"
"having a good reputation," "well thought
of."

The eleventh chapter of Hebrews, beginning in the KJV as "Now faith is the substance of things hoped for, the evidence of
things not seen" goes on in verse 2: "For by
it the elders obtained a good report." This
translation comes from the Great Bible and
the Bishops' Bible. Tyndale had "By it the
elders were well reported of," and was followed by Coverdale and the Geneva Bible.

The contemporary versions, which use
"obtained a good testimony" (NKJV); "gained
approval" (NASB; NRSV, "received approval");
"were commended for" (NIV), do not always
make clear whether the approval comes
from God or human beings. The tenor of
the whole chapter, especially verses 4 and
5, makes it clear that it was the approval
of God that these men of old sought and
obtained.

A thousand years ago, Oecumenius suggested that this be made more explicit; and
among today's translations it is the CEV ("It
was their faith that made our ancestors
pleasing to God"), the RSV ("For by it the
men of old received divine approval"), and

the NLT ("God gave his approval to people
in days of old") which emphasize this.

REPROBATE

As an adjective, "reprobate" today means,
according to the OED, "Depraved, morally
corrupt . . . unprincipled" and "Rejected
by God; lost or hardened in sin." Although
this latter meaning is noted as sixteenth
century, the KJV also uses "reprobate" in
its earlier meaning (noted by the OED as
"Now rare") of "rejected as . . . worthless,
inferior, or impure." "Reprobate silver" is a
term applied in Jeremiah 6:30 to the people
whom the Lord has rejected; the contemporary versions generally translate it as
"rejected silver."

In the New Testament the Greek word
translated by the KJV as "reprobate" is *adokimos,* which means "failed to meet the test,"
hence "unfit," "disqualified," "worthless,"
"base." It is the word which Paul uses when
he writes of his own self-discipline, "lest
that by any means, when I have preached
to others, I myself should be a castaway"
(1 Corinthians 9:27, KJV); the contemporary
versions generally have "disqualified."

The KJV's use of "reprobate mind" in
Romans 1:28 is now translated as "a debased mind" (NKJV, NRSV); "a depraved mind"
(NASB, NIV); "worthless thinking" (NCV); "useless minds" (CEV). In 2 Corinthians 13:5–7,
the KJV's "except ye be reprobates" in
verse 5 is translated in the majority of the
contemporary versions as "unless you fail
the test," and the idea of failing a test, being
a failure, is behind the various translations
of the KJV's "reprobate" in all these verses.

In 2 Timothy 3:8, where the KJV has "men
of corrupt minds, reprobate concerning the
faith," the contemporary versions have "dis-
approved concerning the faith" (NKJV); "they
have failed in trying to follow the faith"
(NCV); "men . . . rejected in regard to the
faith" (NASB); "men . . . who, as far as the
faith is concerned, are rejected" (NIV); and
"people, of corrupt mind and counterfeit
faith" (NRSV).

REQUIRE

The word "require," which today has overtones of ordering or demanding, of something which is essential and imperative, once meant simply "to ask." It is used in that sense in Ezra 8:22, where the KJV has "For I was ashamed to require of the king a band of soldiers and horsemen" and the contemporary versions translate "require" as "ask" (CEV, NCV, NIV, NRSV) or "request" (NASB, NKJV). Shakespeare uses the word in the request that the defeated Mark Antony sends to Caesar:

"Lord of his fortunes he salutes
    thee, and
Requires to live in Egypt: which
    not granted,
He lessens his requests; and to
    thee sues
To let him breathe between the
    heavens and earth,
A private man in Athens."
—*Antony and Cleopatra* (III, 12, 12)

"Required" translated by the contemporary versions as "asked" or "requested" also occurs in 2 Samuel 12:20, where the KJV has "when he [David] required, they set bread before him." In Nehemiah 5:18, the KJV uses "require": "yet for all this required not I the bread of the governor, because the bondage was heavy upon this people." The contemporary versions bring out the stronger emphasis of the Hebrew by the use here of "demanded." A stronger word than "required" is also needed in Luke 23:23, where the KJV has "they were instant with loud voices, requiring that he might be crucified," and the contemporary versions generally have "demanded," as in the NKJV: "they were insistent, demanding with loud voices that He be crucified."

RESEMBLE

This word appears twice in the KJV. In Judges 8:18 it has its normal meaning and is retained by some of the contemporary

versions: they "resembled [NASB, "resembling"] the son [NRSV, "sons"] of a king" (NASB, NKJV, NRSV); "Each one of them looked like a prince" (NCV), or had "the bearing of a prince" (NIV). But in Luke 13:18, "Unto what is the kingdom of God like? and whereunto shall I resemble it?" the KJV translators used "resemble" in the sense of "compare," although Tyndale and his successors had "wherto shall I compare it?" The same Greek is used in verse 20, where the KJV has "liken."

All the contemporary versions except the NLT use "compare" in both verse 18 and verse 20, although the NKJV retains "liken" in verse 20, and the NLT has "How can I illustrate it" (v. 18) and "What else is the Kingdom of God like?" (v. 20).

RESPECTER OF PERSONS
See PERSON.

REVERENCE

When Mephibosheth (in 2 Samuel 9:6) and Bathsheba (in 1 Kings 1:31) "did reverence" (KJV) to King David, it was a gesture of respect and gratitude, an obeisance. When Haman was promoted by King Ahasuerus to a seat above all the princes who were with him, all the king's servants "reverenced" him, with the exception of Mordecai (Esther 3:2, 5); according to the contemporary versions, they "paid homage" to Haman (NASB, NKJV, NIV, "paid honor"); "did obeisance" (NRSV).

When the owner of the vineyard, in Jesus' parable, sent his son to secure the rental due from his wicked tenants, his thought was: "They will reverence my son" (Matthew 21:37; Mark 12:6; Luke 20:13, KJV); "reverence" is now replaced by "respect." The contemporary versions' "respect" rather than the KJV's "reverence" is the natural translation for the attitude of sons to fathers (Hebrews 12:9), and of the wife to her husband (Ephesians 5:33).

On the other hand, the KJV's "reverence" is a sound translation of the Hebrew and

Greek terms used with reference to God and his sanctuary (Leviticus 19:30; 26:2). Hebrews 12:28 reads in the KJV: "Wherefore we receiving a kingdom which cannot be moved, let us have grace, whereby we may serve God acceptably with reverence and godly fear." The majority of the contemporary versions retain "reverence" here, as being an appropriate term for respect shown to God; the NCV translates as "respect" and the NLT has "holy fear."

In Psalm 89:7, the KJV's rendering, "God is . . . to be had in reverence of all them that are about him," means that God inspires and deserves reverence in all around him. Some of the contemporary versions (NASB, NIV, NRSV) translate this as "awesome"; another has "more frightening" (NCV); and the NKJV retains "to be held in reverence." (See REVEREND)

REVEREND

The word "reverend" means worthy of deep respect or reverence. As such, it fits naturally into a psalm of praise to the Lord: "holy and reverend is his name" (Psalm 111:9, KJV). But it is not strong enough to express the Hebrew word used here, and its use as a title for the clergy has tended to blur its significance. The Hebrew word means "inspiring fear," which is better conveyed by the majority of the contemporary translations of this psalm, which have "Holy and awesome is his name."

The same Hebrew word appears frequently in the Old Testament, but elsewhere the KJV does not translate it by "reverend." For example, in three other passages concerning the name of the Lord, the KJV translates it as "glorious and fearful name" (Deuteronomy 28:58); "great and terrible name" (Psalm 99:3); "my name is dreadful among the heathen" (Malachi 1:14). It appears in the KJV of Psalm 96:4 (paralleled in 1 Chronicles 16:25), "he is to be feared above all gods"; and in Psalm 130:4, "there is forgiveness with thee, that thou mayest be feared." Joined to "great" and/or "mighty," the He-

brew word is translated by the KJV as "terrible," and affirmed as an attribute of God, in Deuteronomy 7:21: 10:17; Nehemiah 1:5; 4:14; 9:32.

Daniel prays to "the great and dreadful God" (Daniel 9:4); Jacob exclaims, "How dreadful is this place!" (Genesis 28:17); Manoah's wife reports that the countenance of the man who spoke to her was "like the countenance of an angel of God, very terrible" (Judges 13:6); Joel speaks of "the great and the terrible day of the Lord" (Joel 2:31), and Malachi of "the great and dreadful day of the Lord" (Malachi 4:5).

In all these passages the Hebrew word is the one which the KJV represents by "reverend" in Psalm 111:9. The rendering comes from Coverdale, and was picked up by the revision of the Bishops' Bible, whence it passed to the KJV. The Geneva Bible had "holie and fearful," and the first edition of the Bishops' Bible, "holy and terrible." The contemporary versions render it as "awesome," e.g., Nehemiah 1:5 (NASB, NIV, NKJV, NLT, NRSV) and Psalm 130:4, "feared" (KJV, NASB, NIV, NKJV, RSV), "revered" (NRSV).

RID

The word "rid" today means to free a person or place of something or someone; we "get rid of trash," we "rid the house of mice," or "rid myself of this cold." The use of "rid" in the sense of rescue, save, or deliver someone from some threat or predicament is regarded as rare in the OED. So "Rid me, and deliver me . . . from the hand of strange children" (Psalm 144:7, 11) sounds strange to modern ears, and the contemporary versions translate it as "rescue me" (NASB, NKJV); "set me free" (CEV, NRSV); "deliver me" (NIV).

"Rid" occurs in three other contexts in the KJV. Reuben advised his brothers to cast Joseph into a pit, "that he might rid him out of their hands" (Genesis 37:22, KJV); the contemporary versions have "rescue" (CEV, NASB, NIV, NRSV); "save" (NCV); "deliver" (NKJV). In the promise of the Lord to the people of

Israel, "I will rid you out of their bondage" is parallel to "I will bring you out" and "I will redeem you" (Exodus 6:6); the NASB and NRSV both translate this as "I will deliver you"; the NIV has "free you"; the NKJV, "rescue."

The prayer of Psalm 82:4 (KJV), "Deliver the poor and needy: rid them out of the hand of the wicked," is now translated "free" (NCV, NKJV); "deliver" (NASB, NIV, NLT, NRSV).

The verb "rid" occurs in a quite different sense in Leviticus 26:6 (KJV): "I will rid evil beasts out of the land." The contemporary translations use a variety of words: "remove" (NIV, NRSV); "eliminate" (NASB); "keep . . . out" (NCV); "wipe out" (CEV).

RIDDANCE

This word is scarcely heard today, except in the contemptuous "good riddance!" In the sixteenth century, however, it meant a "removal," "clearance," "scouring out."

The command in Leviticus 23:22 (KJV), "thou shalt not make clean riddance of the corners of thy field when thou reapest," forbids gathering in every scrap of the crop, in order to leave some for the poor to glean; the NKJV translates the command as "you shall not wholly reap the corners of your field"; other contemporary versions make it clear with phrases such as "to the very corners" (NASB); "all the way to the corners" (NCV); "to the very edges" (NIV, NRSV).

Zephaniah's prophecy of the day of the wrath of the Lord, "for he shall make even a speedy riddance of all them that dwell in the land" (1:18, KJV), is retained almost unchanged in the NKJV ("For He will make speedy riddance Of all those who dwell in the land"), while other contemporary versions have "He will make a complete end" (NASB; NIV, "a sudden end"); "for a full, a terrible end he will make" (NRSV).

RINGSTRAKED

The adjective "ringstraked" referring to animals and meaning "having bands of colour round the body" (OED) is now archaic.

It appears in the KJV's account of Jacob's dealings with Laban and his flocks (Genesis 30:35, 39–40; 31:8, 10, 12), e.g., "And he [Laban] removed that day the he goats that were ringstraked and spotted, and all the she goats that were speckled and spotted, and every one that had some white in it, and all the brown among the sheep, and gave them into the hand of his sons" (Genesis 30:35) and "If he [Jacob] said thus, The speckled shall be thy wages; then all the cattle bare speckled: and if he said thus, The ringstraked shall be thy hire; then bare all the cattle ringstraked" (Genesis 31:8).

The word seems to have originated with the English Bible. Tyndale had "straked" in Genesis, and was followed by subsequent versions, until the Bishops' Bible used "ringstraked," which was adopted by the KJV. For all the occurrences of this word, the contemporary versions generally render "ringstraked" as follows: "streaked" (NCV, NIV, NKJV, NLT), "striped" (NASB, NRSV, RSV), and "spotted" (CEV).

RIOT, RIOTOUS

These words stand in the KJV for "revelry," "extravagance" (especially in eating or drinking), "loose living," or "debauchery" rather than their current meanings relating to scenes of public violence and lawless disorder. "Be not among winebibbers; among riotous eaters of flesh" (Proverbs 23:20, KJV) is translated in the contemporary versions as "Do not mix with winebibbers, or with gluttonous eaters of meat" (NKJV); the NASB and NRSV also have "gluttonous eaters of meat"; the NIV has "gorge themselves on meat"; and the NCV, "eat too much food" (CEV: "stuff yourself with food").

The KJV's use of "riotous men" in Proverbs 28:7 represents a Hebrew word meaning "glutton," which the KJV itself uses in Proverbs 23:21 and Deuteronomy 21:20 and is the translation often used by the contemporary versions.

The "riotous living" of the prodigal son (Luke 15:13, KJV) is now "prodigal living"

(NKJV); "loose living" (NASB); "foolish living" (NCV); "dissolute living" (NRSV); "wild living" (CEV, NIV, NLT). Paul's counsel against "rioting" in Romans 13:13 is now "revelry" (NKJV, NRSV, "reveling"); "carousing" (NASB); "orgies" (NIV); "wild parties" (CEV, NCV, NLT).

The contemporary versions use similar words (particularly "dissipation") in 2 Peter 2:13; Titus 1:6, where the KJV has "riot." The KJV itself translates the same Greek word as "excess" in Ephesians 5:18.

RISING

As a noun, "rising" is used in Leviticus 13:2, 10, 19, 28, 43; 14:56 in the sense of a body swelling which is a symptom of disease. The contemporary versions generally use "swelling"; for example, in Leviticus 13:28 the KJV reads, "it is a rising of the burning"; the majority of the contemporary versions have "it is the/a swelling from the burn."

ROAD

In contemporary English, a "road" is "a way for vehicles"; "a highway." In the KJV, however, in its one occurrence, the word is used in the now obsolete sense of "raid." It is found at 1 Samuel 27:10: "And Achish said, Whither have ye made a road to day? And David said, Against the south of Judah, and against the south of the Jerahmeelites, and against the south of the Kenites" (KJV).

The contemporary versions generally render the KJV "road" as "raid" (NASB, NKJV, NLT, NRSV, RSV); the other contemporary translations render the KJV "made a road" as "go raiding" (NCV, NIV) and "attack" (CEV).

The OED notes that in the sense of "the act of riding with hostile intent against a person ... a foray, raid" was "very common c. 1500–1650." The word "inroad" is used in a similar sense in contemporary English: "a sudden hostile incursion" and "an advance or penetration often at the expense of someone or something" (*Merriam-Webster's Collegiate Dictionary*, tenth edition).

ROAD TO DAMASCUS EXPERIENCE

To have a "road-to-Damascus experience" or a "Damascus-road experience" is to have a sudden conversion in one's beliefs. Hence, someone's conversion is sometimes referred to as his or her "road to Damascus."

The expressions allude to the experience of Saul of Tarsus, who, on his way to persecute the Christians in the city of Damascus, encountered the risen Jesus Christ. Suddenly a light from heaven shone around him, hence the phrase "see the light," meaning suddenly to come to agree with or understand something, especially after a long period when that person has not agreed with or understood it. Saul fell to the ground and heard Christ speak to him (Acts 9:1–9; 22:3–10; 26:12–19). So he became a disciple of Jesus Christ and an apostle.

ROLL

Where the KJV has "roll of a book," "roll," or "book" throughout Jeremiah 36, Ezekiel 2 and 3, and Zechariah 5, the contemporary versions generally use "scroll," although the NKJV sometimes retains "scroll of a book." The contemporary translations also use "scroll" in Ezra 6:2 for the KJV's "roll" for the record of the decree of Cyrus, king of Babylon, which was revealed by the search ordered by King Darius.

In 6:1, however, the KJV's "house of the rolls, where the treasures were laid up" is now translated as "the archives, where the treasures were stored" (NASB, NKJV; NRSV: "where the documents were stored"); "the archives stored in the treasury" (NIV); "the old records" (CEV); "the records kept in the treasury" (NCV). The KJV's "great roll" in Isaiah 8:1 is a "large scroll" (NCV, NIV, NKJV); a "large tablet" (NASB, NRSV); the CEV has simply "something to write on." (See BOOK; VOLUME)

ROOM

The rooms in Noah's ark (Genesis 6:14, KJV) and the "upper room" where the apostles gathered in Jerusalem were rooms with a floor and walls. Elsewhere in the KJV "room" refers to space or place. "Thou hast set my feet in a large room" translates the Hebrew word for "a broad place" (Psalm 31:8, KJV); all the contemporary versions translate "room" as "place," but their translations of the accompanying adjective vary greatly: "a broad place" (NRSV); "a wide place" (NKJV); "a spacious place" (NIV); "a large place" (NASB); "a safe place" (NCV). In the KJV, "uppermost room," "chief room," and "highest room" translate the same Greek word *protoklisia*, which means "the place of honor." "Room" occurs in the singular (Matthew 23:6; Luke 14:8) and in the plural (Mark 12:39; Luke 14:7). "The lowest room" (Luke 14:9–10) is now "the lowest place" (NKJV, NRSV); "the last place" (NASB, NCV); "the least important place" (NIV).

"In the room of Joab" (2 Samuel 19:13, KJV) is, according to most of the contemporary versions, "in place of Joab." "Dwelt in their rooms" (1 Chronicles 4:41) means that the invading Israelites "settled in their place" (NRSV). "In the room of his father Herod" (Matthew 2:22) represents the Greek preposition *anti*, which means "instead of," "in place of," which is how the construction is translated in the contemporary versions. "Porcius Festus came into Felix' room" (Acts 24:27, KJV) represents the Greek which means literally, "Felix received a successor Porcius Festus." The contemporary translations generally have either "Felix was succeeded by Porcius Festus" or "Porcius Festus succeeded Felix."

In Genesis 24:23, 25; 26:22; Luke 14:22 both the KJV and the contemporary versions generally use "room" in the sense of "space" or "place." Proverbs 18:16 in the KJV reads: "A man's gift maketh room for him," and although some of the contemporary versions retain "makes room" (NASB, NKJV), others translate the whole idiom and have "A gift will get you in" (CEV); "A gift opens the way for the giver" (NIV); "Giving a gift works wonders" (NLT); "A gift opens doors"

(NRSV). (For a note on 1 Corinthians 14:16, see OCCUPY.)

ROOM IN THE INN

"No room for them in the inn" (Luke 2:7) is in the Greek "no place for them in the inn." The expression "no room in the inn" is sometimes used in contemporary English to mean that there is no suitable accommodation or shelter for people either because there is none or because it has been denied. All the contemporary versions retain a similar wording to the KJV, e.g., NCV, "Because there were no rooms left in the inn"; NLT, "because there was no room for them in the village inn"; and NRSV, "because there was no place for them in the inn."

RUDE

When Paul admitted, according to the KJV, that he was "rude in speech" (2 Corinthians 11:6), it did not mean that he was coarse, unrefined, boorish, or discourteous. The word "rude" here goes back to Tyndale, and has the now rare and archaic meaning of "inexpert," "unskilled." It translates the Greek term *idiotes*. (See UNLEARNED)

What Paul grants is that he is not a professional orator. The contemporary versions translate the *idiotes* phrase as "untrained in speech" (NKJV, NRSV; NASB, "unskilled"); "not . . . a trained speaker" (NCV, NIV); the CEV has "I may not speak as well as they do."

RULE WITH A ROD OF IRON

To rule with a rod of iron is to exercise authority and control in a severe way. The expression "rule with a rod of iron" occurs three times in the KJV: Revelation 2:27 (quoting Psalm 2:9 (KJV), "break them with a rod of iron"); 12:5; and 19:15. At the references in Revelation all the contemporary versions use the word "rule" and all except the NIV have "a rod of iron" or "an iron rod"; the NIV has "He will rule them with an iron scepter" (2:27).

In 2:27 the words form part of the letter

to the church in Thyatira: "Christ will rule as Shepherd in the interest of his flock by smiting their enemies with a staff of iron and smashing them to pieces like pottery" (Geoffrey B. Wilson, *Revelation*, Evangelical Press, 1985).

S

SACKBUT

A sackbut was a bass trumpet, an early form of the slide trombone. In the KJV the word appears only in the stylized list of musical instruments sounded at the dedication of the golden image which King Nebuchadnezzar had set up (Daniel 3:5, 7, 10, 15).

The Aramaic word in this list is *sabbeka'*, which means a "trigon," a triangular lyre or harp with four strings. The Greek word for this instrument was *sambuke*, which appears in both Latin and English as "sambuca." Coverdale thought that a sambuca was a wind instrument, and "the Geneva translators, accepting this view, seem to have chosen the rendering "sackbut" on account of its resemblance in sound to the Aramaic word" (OED). The NASB, NRSV, and RSV have "trigon"; the NIV and NKJV, "lyre."

SACKCLOTH AND ASHES

The phrase "sackcloth and ashes" refers to the custom of wearing a garment of rough woven cloth and of scattering ashes over one's head and body as a sign of mourning or repentance. The phrase occurs five times in the KJV: Esther 4:3; Isaiah 58:5; Daniel 9:3; Matthew 11:21; and Luke 10:13.

Esther 4:3 (KJV) reads, "And in every province, whithersoever the king's commandment [to kill all the Jews] and his decree came, there was great mourning among the Jews, and fasting, and weeping, and wailing; and many lay in sackcloth and ashes." The KJV translation "many lay in sackcloth and ashes" is rendered by the contemporary versions as: "Many of them even put on sackcloth and sat in ashes" (CEV) and "many of them lay down on rough cloth and ashes to show how sad they were" (NCV); the NASB, NIV, NKJV retain the KJV expression and the NRSV and RSV have "most of them lay in sackcloth and ashes."

Other contemporary renderings include "I wore rough sackcloth and sprinkled myself with ashes" (Daniel 9:3, NLT). At Matthew 11:21 (and its parallel Luke 10:13 has similar wording) the KJV reads, "Woe unto thee, Chorazin! woe unto thee, Bethsaida! for if the mighty works, which were done in you, had been done in Tyre and Sidon, they would have repented long ago in sackcloth and ashes."

The NASB, NIV, NKJV, and NRSV retain the KJV expression "repented long ago in sackcloth and ashes"; other contemporary translations render the phrase: "They would have dressed in sackcloth and put ashes on their heads" (CEV), "They would have worn rough cloth and put ashes on themselves to show they had changed" (NCV), and "their people would have sat in deep repentance long ago, cloth in sackcloth and throwing ashes on their heads to show their remorse" (NLT).

In Shakespeare's *King Henry IV, Part II* (I, 2, 197–200), Falstaff tells the Lord Chief Justice that Prince Hal has given him a box on the ear. Falstaff says, "I have checkt him for it; and the young lion repents,—marry, not in ashes and sackcloth, but in new silk and old sack."

SAFEGUARD

The noun "safeguard" in modern usage is likely to make us think of credit card protection schemes and plugs which protect little fingers from electric shocks. In 1 Samuel 22:23 the KJV uses it in its obsolete sense to mean "safekeeping." David assures Abiathar, "with me thou shalt be in safeguard." Contemporary versions render the assurance as "You will be safe with me" (NCV, NIV, NRSV), and the RSV reads, "with me you shall be in safekeeping."

SALT OF THE EARTH

People who are described as being the "salt of the earth" are thought to have a fine, kind character and are regarded as being of great value. The expression comes from the words of Jesus in the Sermon on the Mount, Matthew 5:13: "Ye are the salt of the earth: but if the salt have lost his savour, wherewith shall it be salted? it is thenceforth good for nothing, but to be cast out, and to be trodden under foot of men" (KJV).

All the contemporary versions except the CEV retain the KJV expression "the salt of the earth"; the CEV has "You are like salt for everyone on earth." The expression refers to the preservative, purifying, and seasoning qualities of salt.

SAMSON

A man of great strength is sometimes known as a "Samson." The allusion here is to the judge of Israel. His outstanding feats of strength included tearing a lion apart with his bare hands, fighting single-handedly against the Philistines, catching three hundred foxes and then tying them tail to tail in pairs, and striking down one thousand men with the jawbone of a donkey.

The secret of Samson's strength lay in his hair, and when Delilah discovered this fact, she had it all shaved off so that his strength left him. Samson's final act was to entertain the Philistines at the temple of Dagon. His hair had by now grown again, and so, calling upon God, he braced himself against the two central pillars that supported the temple. Above him were about three thousand people. He pushed with all his strength, so destroying the temple.

Thus, in his death he killed more Philistines than he had killed during his whole life.

SARDINE

We may be familiar with the small fish preserved in cans known as sardines. The word "sardine" occurs once in the KJV, but this is, in fact, a historically different word and is used to refer to a kind of "red precious stone." The one occurrence in the KJV is at Revelation 4:3: "And he that sat was to look upon like a jasper and a sardine stone: and there was a rainbow round about the throne, in sight like unto an emerald"; the contemporary versions render "a sardine stone" as "a sardius" (NASB), "a sardius stone" (NKJV), and "carnelian" (CEV, NCV, NIV, NLT, NRSV, RSV).

The OED quotes various translations of Revelation 4:3: Wycliffe, "sardyn"; Tyndale (1526), "a sardyne stone"; the RV had "a sardius."

SAY ME (THEE) NAY

This phrase means "to say no to me (thee)," "to refuse." The expression appears in 1 Kings 2:16–20 (KJV) as a translation of a Hebrew idiom which means literally "turn back my (thy) face." This Hebrew idiom is employed twice by Adonijah in making a request of Bathsheba (vv. 16–17), and twice by Bathsheba in making this request of Solomon (v. 20). The KJV translates it as "deny" in verse 16 and "say nay" in the other three cases.

The revised versions of 1885–1901 use "deny" in verses 16 and 20, and "say nay" in verse 17. The NASB, NCV, NIV, NRSV, and RSV use "refuse" in each case. The NKJV has "deny" in verse 16, and "refuse" in verses 17 and 20.

SAY THE WORD

The expression "say the word," to state one's intentions to someone who is willing to fulfill them immediately, has its basis in Matthew 8:8: "The centurion answered and said, Lord, I am not worthy that thou shouldest come under my roof: but speak the word only, and my servant shall be healed" (KJV).

The contemporary versions render this as "just say the word" (NASB, NIV, NLT), "only say the word" (RSV), "only speak the [NKJV, "speak a"] word" (NKJV, NRSV), "just give the order" (CEV), and "you only need to command it" (NCV).

SCALES FELL FROM ONE'S EYES

The expression "scales fell from one's eyes" is sometimes used to refer to a state of physical or moral blindness being removed. The expression alludes to Acts 9:18: "And immediately there fell from his eyes as it had been scales: and he received sight forthwith, and arose, and was baptized" (KJV).

The contemporary versions generally have "something like scales" (NASB, NIV, NKJV, NLT, NRSV, RSV) fell from Saul's eyes; the CEV and NCV have "something like [NCV, "something that looked like"] fish scales."

The OED quotes two earlier citations than the KJV for their expression: the "Cursor Mundi" from the early part of the fourteenth century and Wycliffe's translation of Acts 9:18.

SCALL

The word "scall" was formerly used for various scalp diseases. In the KJV it occurs only in Leviticus 13:30–37 and 14:54 as translation for the Hebrew word *netheq*, which means "a scab," "an eruption of skin on the head or in the beard." Literally, it means "a tearing off," that is, something which one wants to scratch or tear away. The NCV, NIV, NRSV, and RSV translate it as "itch," and for "the plague of the scall" (KJV), the NRSV and RSV have "the itching disease." The NASB has "scale" and "the infection of the scale." The OED says that "dry scall" is "psoriasis" and that "humid scall" is "eczema."

SCAPEGOAT

A "scapegoat" is someone who is made to take the blame for the actions of others. It occurs in the description of the Day of Atonement in Leviticus 16:8, 10 (twice), 26: "And Aaron shall cast lots upon the two goats; one lot for the LORD, and the other lot for the scapegoat. But the goat, on which the lot fell to be the scapegoat, shall be presented alive before the LORD, to make an atonement with him, and to let him go for a scapegoat into the wilderness" (Leviticus 16: 8, 10, KJV).

The word was coined by Tyndale from the words "escape" and "goat," intended to translate the meaning of Hebrew *'azazel* (which was possibly the name of a demon) which was confused with *'ez ozel*, "goat which escapes." The scapegoat and the goat that was sacrificed on the altar symbolized together the removal of all Israel's sins. The sending of the scapegoat into the wilderness never to return probably represented the idea that their sins were taken away forever.

The NASB, NIV, NKJV, and NLT retain the KJV "scapegoat"; other contemporary versions have "goat . . . sent into the desert to the demon Azazel" (CEV), "goat that removes sin" (NCV), and "Azazel" (RV, NRSV).

SCARCE

The word "scarce" is used three times in the KJV as an adverb. In two cases a number of contemporary versions now use "scarcely": Genesis 27:30 (NKJV, NRSV, RSV; NIV, "Jacob had scarcely left his father's presence"), and Acts 14:18 (NKJV, NLT, RSV; NRSV, "Even with these words, they scarcely restrained the crowd from offering sacrifice to them").

In Acts 27:7 "scarce" has the rare or obsolete meaning "with difficulty." The RSV reads, "We sailed slowly for a number of days, and arrived with difficulty off Cnidus." The same Greek adverb occurs in the following verse, where it is translated "hardly" by the KJV and "with difficulty" by the NASB, NKJV, NRSV, and RSV.

SCARLET WOMAN

The phrase "a scarlet woman" is sometimes used to refer to a prostitute or seductress. The expression alludes to Revelation 17:1–5: "And there came one of the seven angels which had the seven vials, and talked with me, saying unto me, Come hither; I will shew unto thee the judgment of the great whore that sitteth upon many waters: With whom the kings of the earth have committed fornication, and the inhabitants of the earth have been made drunk with the wine of her fornication. So he carried me away in the spirit into the wilderness: and I saw a woman sit upon a scarlet coloured beast, full of names of blasphemy, having seven heads and ten horns. And the woman was arrayed in purple and scarlet colour, and decked with gold and precious stones and pearls, having a golden cup in her hand full of abominations and filthiness of her fornication: And upon her forehead was a name written, MYSTERY, BABYLON THE GREAT, THE MOTHER OF HARLOTS AND ABOMINATIONS OF THE EARTH" (KJV).

All the contemporary versions except the NCV refer to the woman being dressed in "purple and scarlet"; the NCV has "purple and red."

Different interpretations of the representation of the prostitute had been made; in verse 5 of the Bible text she is named as "Babylon the Great" (KJV, NASB, NIV, NKJV, NLT, NRSV, RSV, with various conventions on capitalization for the different translations); "the Great City of Babylon" (CEV); and "The Great Babylon" (NCV).

SCRIP

"Scrip" is defined by the OED as "a small bag, wallet, or satchel, esp. one carried by a pilgrim, a shepherd, or a beggar." The word, in this sense, is quite lost to us today, and *Merriam-Webster* marks it as archaic.

The KJV uses it for the receptacle in which the young David carried the stones for his sling (1 Samuel 17:40) and for the traveling bags which Jesus forbade his disciples to carry (Matthew 10:10, Mark 6:8, Luke 9:3; 10:4; 22:35–36). The RV retained "scrip" in the account of David's exploit, but changed to "wallet" in the New Testament; the ASV in 1901 used "wallet" in the Old Testament story as well.

However, the use of the word "wallet" in this sense was already on the decline. The OED records N. P. Willis, 1845, as the first to use "wallet" for a pocketbook for holding paper money without folding, or documents. Since the publication of the RV and ASV, this meaning has replaced all others in common speech.

In the New Testament passages, the contemporary versions generally have simply "bag," a word which fits the traveling bags of today as well as those of the first century. First Samuel 17:40 reads in the KJV: "He . . . chose him five smooth stones out of the brook, and put them in a shepherd's bag which he had, even in a scrip." The Hebrew word for "scrip" is *yalqut*, which occurs only here. Many scholars regard "in the shepherd's bag which he had" as a gloss to explain *yalqut* and "even" as simply the sign of apposition. (See EVEN)

The majority of contemporary versions translate *yalqut* as "pouch"; the NKJV reads "put them in a shepherd's bag, in a pouch which he had," and the RSV reads "to put them in his shepherd's bag or wallet."

Shakespeare has a fancy use of "scrip" in *As You Like It* (III, 2, 163): "Come, shepherd, let us make an honourable retreat; though not with bag and baggage, yet with scrip and scrippage."

SEA MONSTER

This expression appears once in the KJV: "Even the sea monsters draw out the breast, they give suck to their young ones" (Lamentations 4:3). Its appearance is due to the presence of two Hebrew words

S

which are spelled alike, one meaning "dragon" or "sea monster," and the other meaning "jackal." The revised versions and other contemporary translations use "jackals" here, except the NCV which has "wild dogs." The NASB has "Even jackals offer the breast, They nurse their young."

The mix-up has a long history, for the Greek Septuagint here used the word for "dragons" and the Latin Vulgate used *lamiae*. A *lamia*, in Latin, was a witch who was supposed to suck children's blood; and the same word in Greek means a fabulous she-monster who feeds on human flesh, a bugbear to frighten children, or a man-eating shark.

The word "lamia" came into English from the Greek and Latin by the way of French and was used in this text by Coverdale and Matthew: "The Lamyes geue their young ones suck with bare brestes." The Great Bible changed to "dragons," which was retained by the Geneva Bible and the Bishops' Bible.

The KJV stands alone in the use of "sea monsters" here. "Jackals" was a new word in 1611, and recognition of its place in this text had to await the increasing knowledge of Bible lands and languages which the nineteenth century began to bring.

A number of the contemporary versions use "sea monster" instead of "whale" (KJV) in Genesis 1:21 and Job 7:12 and instead of "dragon" (KJV) in Psalm 148:7.

SEASON, TO EVERY THING THERE IS A

See TIME AND A PLACE FOR EVERYTHING.

SECONDARILY

The word "secondarily" is used in an obsolete sense in the KJV translation of 1 Corinthians 12:28: "first apostles, secondarily prophets." The Greek simply means "second" or "secondly," without the connotation of subordinate importance which "secondarily" now conveys. The NRSV translates, "And God has appointed in the church first apostles, second prophets, third teachers; then deeds of power, then gifts of healing, forms of assistance, forms of leadership, various kinds of tongues."

Shakespeare's *Much Ado About Nothing* (V, 1, 211), has an example of the use of "secondarily" in this obsolete sense: "they have spoken untruths; secondarily, they are slanders; . . . thirdly, they have verified unjust things; and, to conclude, they are lying knaves."

SECURE

As used in the KJV, "secure" means "without care or anxiety," "confident," "free from apprehension or distrust." It describes a state of mind, which may or may not be justified by the objective facts. This sense of the word is archaic; when we now use the word "secure," it means more than feeling safe; it means "being safe," insofar as we can judge safety today.

In Judges 8:11 the KJV says that "the host was secure," and the NASB now says that "the camp was unsuspecting." The people of Laish, "quiet and secure" (Judges 18:7, KJV; see also vv. 10, 27), are described as "quiet and unsuspecting" by the NRSV and RSV; the NASB and NKJV retain the KJV reading, however, and the NIV has "unsuspecting and secure."

"Thou shalt be secure, because there is hope" (Job 11:18, KJV) reads "you will have confidence, because there is hope" (NRSV) and "You will feel safe" (NCV). "Devise not evil against thy neighbour, seeing he dwelleth securely by thee" (Proverbs 3:29, KJV) reads in the NIV, "Do not plot harm against your neighbor, who lives trustfully near you."

In Micah 2:8, "them that pass by securely as men averse from war" (KJV) now reads "those who pass by trustingly with no thought of war" (NRSV) and "unsuspecting passers-by . . . those returned from war" (NASB).

SEE THE LIGHT

See ROAD TO DAMASCUS EXPERIENCE.

SEE THROUGH A GLASS, DARKLY

See GLASS, DARKLY.

SEE TO

The expression "see to" means "attend to," "provide for," "take care of." But it does not have this meaning in Joshua 22:10, where the altar erected by the tribes of Israel which settled in Gilead is described: "when they came unto the borders of Jordan, . . . [they] built there an altar by Jordan, a great altar to see to" (KJV). The Hebrew means that it was great to look at, great in appearance, great to the sight.

Contemporary versions render it as "a huge altar" (CEV), "a large altar in appearance" (NASB), "an imposing altar" (NIV), and "a great, impressive altar" (NKJV); the NRSV and RSV have "an altar of great size." The same Hebrew phrase occurs in Genesis 2:9, where the KJV, NASB, NKJV, NRSV, and RSV read, "every tree that is pleasant [NASB, "pleasing"] to the sight."

SEEING

When used as a conjunction, "seeing" means "in view of the fact that," "inasmuch as," "since," "because." In the fifteenth and sixteenth centuries "seen" was also used as a conjunction, in the same sense. The two words were late additions to a group of conjunctions, having the same meaning, which date from Old English—"sen," "sene," "sin," "syne," "sith," "sithen," "sithence," "since."

"Seeing" appears 112 times in the KJV. The conjunction "seeing" represents corresponding conjunctions in the Hebrew or Greek in twenty-three cases. Some contemporary versions occasionally retain it—for example in Judges 19:23 (NKJV, RSV), 1 Samuel 17:36 (NKJV, RSV), and Ezra 9:13 (NRSV, RSV). Elsewhere the contemporary versions use other terms, such as "because" (e.g., Eze-

kiel 21:4, NASB, NCV, NIV, NRSV, RSV), "for" (e.g., Daniel 2:47, NIV, NLT, NRSV, RSV), and "since" (e.g., Judges 21:16, NASB, NKJV, NLT, NRSV, RSV).

"Since" is used by the majority of contemporary versions in Luke 1:34, which reads in the KJV, "Then said Mary unto the angel, How shall this be, seeing I know not a man?" Other New Testament examples are Luke 23:40; Acts 2:15; 13:46; Romans 3:30; 2 Corinthians 11:18; 2 Thessalonians 1:6; Hebrews 4:6; 5:11.

Simpler translations are sometimes offered, for example at 1 Corinthians 14:16 where the KJV reads, "how shall he that occupieth the room of the unlearned say Amen at thy giving of thanks, seeing he understandeth not what thou sayest?" and the RSV now reads, "how can any one in the position of an outsider say the 'Amen' to your thanksgiving when he does not know what you are saying?"

Similarly at Ecclesiastes 6:11 the KJV has "Seeing there be many things that increase vanity, what is man the better?" and the NRSV, "The more words, the more vanity, and how is one the better?"

In fifty-six cases the conjunction "seeing" does not represent a corresponding conjunction in the Hebrew or Greek. The list is too long to reproduce here; it can be found in Strong's *Concordance*. "Seeing" is in these cases usually an interpretation of the ubiquitous Hebrew connective *w* or of the causal use of a Greek participle. The RSV retains "seeing" in sixteen of these cases, and in others replaces it chiefly by "since."

Occasionally contemporary versions delete "seeing" without replacement. Examples are: Job 21:34 (CEV, NCV, NIV, NLT, NRSV, RSV); Job 28:21 (CEV, NCV, NIV, NKJV, NRSV, RSV); Isaiah 49:21 (CEV, NCV, NIV, NRSV, RSV); Acts 17:24 (CEV, NCV, NIV, NRSV, RSV); 2 Corinthians 4:1 (CEV, NCV, RSV); 2 Corinthians 11:19 (NASB, NRSV, RSV); 2 Peter 3:17 (CEV, NASB, RSV).

First Peter 1:22 reads in the KJV: "Seeing ye have purified your souls in obeying the truth through the Spirit unto unfeigned love of the brethren, *see that ye* love one another with a pure heart fervently." The NRSV reads: "Now that you have purified your souls by your obedience to the truth so that you have genuine mutual love, love one another deeply from the heart."

The Shakespeare *Concordance* cites fifty-three occurrences of "seeing" in his plays and poems. In eleven of these it is a conjunction. Examples are:

"Seeing gentle words will not
    prevail,
Assail them with the army."
    —*King Henry VI, Part II* (IV, 2, 184)

"Seeing thou hast proved so
    unnatural a father."
    —*King Henry VI, Part III* (I, 1, 218)

"Seeing that death, a necessary end,
Will come when it will come."
    —*Julius Caesar* (II, 2, 36)

Shakespeare uses "sith" twenty-two times, "sithence" twice, and "since" eighty-six times.

SEEK AND YE SHALL FIND

In the Sermon on the Mount, Jesus told his disciples: "Ask, and it shall be given you; seek, and ye shall find; knock, and it shall be opened unto you: For every one that asketh receiveth; and he that seeketh findeth; and to him that knocketh it shall be opened." (Matthew 7:7–8, KJV, with similar wording at the parallel Luke 11:9–10).

The contemporary versions render the active endeavor of the KJV expression "seek, and ye shall find" as: "seek, [NIV, "seek"] and you will find" (NASB, NIV, NKJV, RSV); "search, and you will find" (CEV, NCV, NRSV); and "keep on looking, and you will find" (NLT).

SEETHE, SOD, SODDEN

The word "seethe" today makes us think of fits of anger or frustration; "sod" we sometimes hear as a term of abuse; and

"sodden" is what we might be after a journey home in the pouring rain. In the KJV, however, these terms are always used in an obsolete sense. "Seethe" is used as a transitive verb meaning "to cook food by boiling or stewing"; "sod" is used as the past tense of this verb, and "sodden" as its past participle.

In eight cases these words refer to the boiling of sacrificial meat that it may be eaten. A typical passage is the account of the behavior of the sons of Eli (1 Samuel 2:12–17). It was specifically stated, however, that the passover lamb should not be boiled: "Eat not of it raw, nor sodden at all with water, but roast with fire" (Exodus 12:9, KJV); The NKJV reads, "Do not eat it raw, or boiled at all with water, but roasted in fire."

This distinction was observed at the great Passover commanded by King Josiah at Jerusalem: "they roasted the passover with fire according to the ordinance: but the other holy offerings sod they in pots, and in caldrons, and in pans, and divided them speedily among all the people" (2 Chronicles 35:13). The contemporary versions say that they "boiled" the holy offerings in pots.

"Thou shalt not seethe a kid in his mother's milk" (Exodus 23:19; 34:26; Deuteronomy 14:21, KJV) commands the rejection of a Canaanite pagan practice of preparing a sacrifice by cooking it in milk.

"Jacob sod pottage" (Genesis 25:29, KJV), now reads "Jacob was boiling a pot of vegetable soup" (NCV), "Jacob was cooking some stew" (NIV, NLT), and "Jacob was boiling pottage" (RSV). "The hands of the pitiful women have sodden their own children" (Lamentations 4:10, KJV) now reads "The hands of compassionate women boiled their own children" (NASB).

"Seethe," "sod," and "sodden" began early to acquire the physical and figurative meanings which they have today. Theseus, one of Shakespeare's characters, says:

"Lovers and madmen have such
   seething brains."
      —*A Midsummer Night's Dream*
                              (V, 1, 4)

Shakespeare also has this play on words:

   "*Pandarus:* I will make a complimental
   assault upon him, for my business
   seethes.
   Servant: Sodden business! there's a
   stewed phrase indeed!"
         —*Troilus and Cressida* (III, 1, 44)

But none of these other meanings appear
in the KJV, where "seethe" always means
"boil," and "sod" and "sodden" mean
"boiled."

SELFSAME

This word means "the very same." The
word is not used by contemporary versions, which have expressions such as "On
the very same day" (Genesis 7:13, NASB,
NKJV, NRSV, RSV), "that very day" (Deuteronomy 32:48, NRSV, RSV), "that very moment"
(Matthew 8:13, NASB, RSV; NCV, NKJV, NLT,
"that same hour").

First Corinthians 12:11 reads in the KJV,
"But all these worketh that one and the
selfsame Spirit, dividing to every man severally as he will." The NRSV has "All these
are activated by one and the same Spirit,
who allots to each one individually just as
the Spirit chooses."

Second Corinthians 7:11 reads in the KJV,
"For behold this selfsame thing, that ye sor-
rowed after a godly sort, what carefulness
it wrought in you, yea, what clearing of
yourselves, yea, what indignation, yea, what
fear, yea, what vehement desire, yea, what
zeal, yea, what revenge! In all things ye have
approved yourselves to be clear in this matter." The CEV has, "Just look what God has
done by making you feel sorry! You sin-
cerely want to prove that you are innocent.
You are angry. You are shocked. Your are
eager to see that justice is done. You have

proved that you were completely right in
this matter."

SELL HIS BIRTHRIGHT

The expression "Esau sold his birthright
for a mess of pottage" alludes to the biblical
account of Esau's sale of his birthright to
his twin brother Jacob (Genesis 25:29–34
and Hebrews 12:16).

Genesis 25:29–34 reads in the KJV, "And
Jacob sod pottage: and Esau came from the
field, and he was faint: and Esau said to
Jacob, Feed me, I pray thee, with that same
red pottage; for I am faint: therefore was
his name called Edom. And Jacob said, Sell
me this day thy birthright. And Esau said,
Behold, I am at the point to die: and what
profit shall this birthright do to me? And
Jacob said, Swear to me this day; and he
sware unto him: and he sold his birthright
unto Jacob. Then Jacob gave Esau bread
and pottage of lentils; and he did eat and
drink, and rose up, and went his way: thus
Esau despised his birthright."

Hebrews 12:16 (KJV) says, "Lest there be
any fornicator, or profane person, as Esau,
who for one morsel of meat sold his birthright." As can be seen, the actual wording
"Esau sold his birthright for a mess of pottage" does not appear in the Bible text.

The KJV "pottage of lentils" is rendered
in the contemporary versions as "pottage
of lentils" (RSV); "lentil stew" (NASB, NIV, NLT,
NRSV); "stew of lentils" (NKJV); "bean stew"
(CEV); and "vegetable soup" (NCV).

SEPARATE THE SHEEP FROM THE
   GOATS

The phrase "separate the sheep from the
goats" is sometimes used in contemporary
English to refer to a separation of people
who are good or useful from those who
are not. The expression derives from Jesus'
description of judgment as found in Matthew 25:32–33: "And before him shall be
gathered all nations: and he shall separate
them one from another, as a shepherd di-
videth his sheep from the goats: And he

shall set the sheep on his right hand, but the goats on the left" (KJV).

All the contemporary versions except the NKJV use the verb "separate"; the NKJV retains the KJV's use of the verb "divide."

SEPARATE THE WHEAT FROM THE CHAFF

To "separate the wheat from the chaff" is used in contemporary English to mean "to separate what is valuable from what is worthless." The expression alludes to Matthew 3:12: "Whose [Jesus'] fan is in his hand, and he will throughly purge his floor, and gather his wheat into the garner; but he will burn up the chaff with unquenchable fire" (KJV, and its parallel Luke 3:17), where John the Baptist declares Jesus' imminent judgment. The chaff is the term for the husks (the kernels' outer covering) of corn or other grain separated by threshing or winnowing to leave the grain.

Of the contemporary versions, the CEV, NCV, and NLT explicitly mention the separation of the wheat and the chaff: "he is ready to separate the wheat from the husks" (CEV); "separating the good grain from the chaff" (NCV); and "He is ready to separate the chaff from the grain" (NLT). All the contemporary versions except the NCV and the NLT refer to "wheat"; the NCV has "the good part of the grain" and the NLT, "grain." All the contemporary versions except the CEV refer to "chaff"; the CEV has "husks."

SERVE

An obsolete idiom appears in Jeremiah 25:14, prophesying punishment for Babylon and the Chaldeans: "Many nations and great kings shall serve themselves of them also" (KJV). Contemporary versions have "make slaves of them" (NASB, NRSV) and "be enslaved" (NIV), while the NKJV reads, "Many nations and great kings shall be served by them also."

This idiom is described, and examples given, in paragraph 39 of the OED's treatment of the verb "serve." Its first appearance was in the Geneva Bible. Other occurrences in the KJV are Jeremiah 27:7; 30:8; 34:9, 10; Ezekiel 34:27.

In Jeremiah 34:9 the KJV reads, "that none should serve himself of them, to wit, of a Jew his brother," and the contemporary versions replace "serve himself of them" with "keep them . . . in bondage" (NASB), "hold a fellow Jew in bondage" (NIV), and "hold another Judean in slavery" (NRSV).

SET AT NOUGHT

See NOUGHT, SET AT.

SETTLE

A "settle" is something to sit on. In the KJV the word was applied to either of the two ledges of the altar in the temple described in Ezekiel 43:13–17. These ledges were part of the structure of the altar, each a cubit wide, surrounding the altar. The lower ledge was at the height of two cubits, and the upper ledge six cubits, above the base of the altar. The altar hearth was four cubits above the upper ledge, and the four horns of the altar projected one cubit above the hearth. "Ledge" generally replaces the word "settle" in the contemporary renderings of the passage.

SEVEN STARS, THE

This is the term used in the KJV in Amos 5:8 for the Pleiades: "Seek him that maketh the seven stars and Orion, and turneth the shadow of death into the morning, and maketh the day dark with night: that calleth for the waters of the sea, and poureth them out upon the face of the earth: The LORD is his name" (KJV). The same Hebrew word is translated "Pleiades" by the KJV in Job 9:9 and 38:31. In all three passages the Pleiades and Orion are cited as evidence of God's creative power and control. (See INFLUENCES)

SEVER

This word today might make us think of the action of pruning, cutting, or breaking apart ("we've decided to sever links with that organization"). In the KJV, however, the idea is more of "separation." In the seven passages where the word appears, contemporary versions use other terms such as "separate" or "set apart."

"Moses severed three cities" (Deuteronomy 4:41, KJV) is now rendered as "Moses set apart three cities" (NASB, NKJV, NLT, NRSV, RSV) and "Moses set aside three cities" (NIV) to be cities of refuge east of the Jordan. "They shall sever out men of continual employment, passing through the land" (Ezekiel 39:14, KJV) now reads, "They will set apart men who will continually pass through the land" (NASB). These are examples of the use of "sever" in an obsolete sense which the OED describes as "Biblical language."

In Leviticus 20:26, "I . . . have severed you from other people" (KJV) now reads "I have set you apart" (NASB, NCV, NIV, NLT) and "I . . . have separated you" (NKJV, NRSV, RSV). "Heber . . . had severed himself from the Kenites" (Judges 4:11, KJV) is rendered as "Heber . . . had left the other Kenites" (NCV, NIV), "had moved away from the other members of his tribe" (NLT), and "had separated himself from the Kenites" (NKJV).

In Matthew 13:49, Jesus tells how, at the end of the age, "angels shall come forth, and sever the wicked from among the just" (KJV). All the contemporary versions, with the exception of the NASB, which has "take out," use the term "separate" here.

An identical Hebrew verb is used in Exodus 8:22, "I will sever in that day the land of Goshen" (KJV); in Exodus 9:4, "the LORD shall sever between the cattle of Israel and the cattle of Egypt" (KJV); and in Exodus 11:7, "the LORD doth put a difference between the Egyptians and Israel" (KJV). The NASB, NKJV, NRSV, and RSV use "set apart" in the first of these passages; the NASB, NIV, NRSV, and RSV, "make a distinction" in the other two.

SEVERAL

This word makes us think of a number or quality ("several packets of muffin mix").

In the KJV, however, the meaning is not always clear to contemporary readers. For example, in 2 Kings 15:5 (and its parallel, 2 Chronicles 26:21) we read that King Azariah "dwelt in a several house" because he was a leper.

This is the word's obsolete sense, and contemporary versions use "separate" instead (NASB, NCV, NIV, NRSV, RSV). The NKJV says he dwelt in "an isolated house"; the NLT, "in a house by himself."

"A several tenth deal of flour" (KJV) is prescribed in Numbers 28:13, to accompany the burnt offering of a lamb. It means the tenth of an ephah of flour, according to verse 5 of the same chapter. Verse 12 prescribes that three-tenths of an ephah of flour be offered with a bullock, and two-tenths with a ram; verse 13 requires simply "a tenth" with a lamb.

The Hebrew does not have the numeral one, nor any adjective. The word "several" was inserted by the KJV translators, and was employed in the obsolete sense of "single," "one and only one." This prescription of "a several tenth deal" is repeated in 28:21, 29; 29:10, 15 in a code of sacrificial law. Contemporary versions take out "several" in these chapters.

In Revelation 21:21, "every several gate was of one pearl" (KJV) is part of the description of the new Jerusalem. The versions prior to the KJV had "every gate," and contemporary versions have "each [NASB, "each one"] of the gates" (NASB, NRSV, RSV) and "each individual gate" (NKJV).

"To every man according to his several ability" (Matthew 25:15, KJV) is now translated as "to each according to his ability" (NRSV, RSV). (For "severally," 1 Corinthians 12:11, see SELFSAME.)

SHADE, SHADOW

The KJV uses "shade" only once, in Psalm 121:5: "The LORD is thy keeper: the LORD is thy shade upon thy right hand." All the contemporary versions also have "shade" in this verse. We usually use "shade" today when we mean "protection from the light and heat of the sun," and so contemporary versions use this word, rather than "shadow" as in the KJV.

Examples are: Isaiah 4:6, "a shadow in the daytime from the heat" (KJV) reads, "a shade by day from the heat" (NRSV). Jonah 4:5, "Sat under it in the shadow" (KJV) reads "sat under it in the shade" (NASB, NRSV).

SHAKE THE DUST OFF ONE'S FEET

The expression, "shake the dust off one's feet" is sometimes used to mean "to depart from a place angrily because one has not been well treated there." The quotation derives from Matthew 10:14: "And whosoever shall not receive you, nor hear your words, when ye depart out of that house or city, shake off the dust of your feet" (KJV).

The contemporary versions retain the expression "shake off the dust from your feet" (NKJV, NRSV, RSV), "shake the dust off your feet" (NASB, NIV), "shake the dust from your feet at them" (CEV), and "shake off the dust of that place from your feet" (NLT). The footnotes explain the meaning: NCV: "A warning. It showed that they had rejected these people," CEV: "This was a way of showing rejection." The parallels of Matthew 10:14, Mark 6:11 and Luke 9:5 have similar wordings.

An example of this is seen in the actions of Paul and Barnabas (Acts 13:51), who "shook off the dust of their feet against [NIV, NRSV, "in protest against"] them," and went to Iconium.

SHAMBLES

This word might make us think of our teenager's room, or the chaotic state a kitchen can get into during a child's birthday party. We use the word today to describe "disorder in a room" or "a scene of wreckage," but its meaning in the Middle Ages was "a table or stall for the sale of meat," then "a slaughterhouse." First Corinthians 10:25 reads in the KJV: "Whatsoever is sold in the shambles, that eat, asking

no question for conscience sake." Contemporary versions generally read "meat market."

When King Henry disclaims any thought "to make a shambles of the parliament-house" in *King Henry VI, Part III* (I, 1, 71), he means to refrain from making it a scene of bloodshed and carnage.

SHAMEFACEDNESS

In 1 Timothy 2:9 the KJV translators wrote "that women adorne themselves in modest apparell, with shamefastnesse and sobrietie." This is how the text appeared in 1611 and for sixty years thereafter. Then, as one of various printer's changes, the word "shamefac'dness" appeared. Its spelling was changed to "shamefacedness" in 1743, and this has been kept to the present day.

The change is a little unfair to the KJV translators, because the word which they used, "shamefastness," referred to character, while "shamefacedness" refers to appearance. The revised versions of 1881 and 1901 restored "shamefastness," but the word is no longer current; "modesty" could clarify the meaning.

"Modesty" is used by the NASB, NRSV, and RSV here, while the NIV renders the KJV "with shamefacedness and sobriety" as "with decency and propriety," and the NKJV has "with propriety and moderation."

SHAPEN

The word "shapen" might make us think of a sculptor at work, or of aerobic exercises aimed at getting us back into shape. But in the KJV, where it appears only once, the word means "to create" or "to form." The Old English word is *scieppan*. Psalm 51:5, "I was shapen in iniquity" (KJV), now reads "I was brought forth in iniquity" (NASB, NKJV, RSV), "I was sinful at birth" (NIV), and "I was born guilty" (NRSV). The KJV translates the same Hebrew word as "brought forth" in Proverbs 8:24, 25.

SHARE

This word appears only once in the KJV (1 Samuel 13:20), where it means "a plowshare," "the blade of a plow." As a verb meaning "to divide a possession with others" and as a noun denoting the portions thus allotted, the word was still new in 1611. Shakespeare used it freely, but the KJV translators not at all. They used the nouns "portion" and "part," and the verbs "communicate," "impart," and "partake" or "be partaker of." In the great chapter concerning fasting, they use the verb "deal": "Is it not to deal thy bread to the hungry?" (Isaiah 58:7, KJV).

The NASB, NIV, NKJV, NRSV, and RSV read, "Is it not to share [NASB, "to divide"] your bread with the hungry?" (See COMMUNICATE)

SHEEP TO THE SLAUGHTER

See LAMB TO THE SLAUGHTER.

SHEEPMASTER

This is an old word for a sheep owner. In the KJV it is applied to Mesha, king of Moab, with the statement that he "rendered unto the king of Israel an hundred thousand lambs, and an hundred thousand rams, with the wool" (2 Kings 3:4). The Hebrew word used here means "a sheep breeder, dealer, or tender." It is the word in Amos 1:1, where Amos is described as "among the sheepbreeders of Tekoa" (NKJV). King Mesha was in the business on a large scale.

The Hebrew for "rendered" means "used to pay," and the Targum adds "annually." The NASB translates as "Mesha king of Moab was a sheep breeder, and used to pay the king of Israel 100,000 lambs and the wool of 100,000 rams."

SHEW

This is a variant spelling of "show," which is now obsolete except in legal language and in the KJV. The OED states that it represents an obsolete pronunciation, rhyming with words like "view" and "true." Where they retain it, the ASV and contemporary versions use the spelling "show."

In some contexts, contemporary versions use other terms. "Surely every man walketh in a vain shew" (Psalm 39:6, KJV) is now translated, "Surely every man walks about like a shadow" (NKJV) and "Man is a mere phantom as he goes to and fro" (NIV). Where it is said that the scribes "for a shew make long prayers" (Luke 20:47, KJV), the Greek word is used which the KJV, NKJV, and RSV translate as "in pretense" in Philippians 1:18. The NIV renders "for a shew" (KJV) in Luke 20:47 as "for a show," and the NRSV has "for the sake of appearance."

In Colossians 2:15, "made a shew of them openly" (KJV) is now "made a public spectacle of them" (NIV, NKJV), and in 2:23 "a shew of wisdom" (KJV) is "an appearance of wisdom" (NASB, NIV, NKJV, NRSV, RSV).

The verb "shew" is used in the KJV for eighteen different Hebrew verbs and for twenty-five Greek verbs, each of which has its own meaning. "Shew" appears nearly four hundred times in the KJV, and "show" appears almost three hundred times in the RSV.

In the following examples, "shew" is replaced by "proclaim" or "declare" in the NASB, NRSV, and RSV: Psalms 19:1, "the firmament sheweth his handywork"; 71:18, "I have shewed thy strength unto this generation"; Matthew 12:18, "he shall shew judgment to the Gentiles"; Acts 16:17, "shew unto us the way of salvation"; 26:23, "shew light unto the people, and to the Gentiles."

A well-loved passage which uses the verb "shew" is 1 Corinthians 11:26: "For as often as ye eat this bread, and drink this cup, ye do shew the Lord's death till he come." The NRSV translates as "For as often as you eat this bread and drink the cup, you proclaim the Lord's death until he comes."

The KJV rendering of Job 36:32–33 may prove difficult for contemporary readers to follow. It reads, "With clouds he covereth the light; and commandeth it not to shine

S

by the cloud that cometh betwixt. The noise thereof sheweth concerning it, the cattle also concerning the vapour." The NRSV translation is:

> "He covers his hands with the
>   lightning,
> and commands it to strike the
>   mark.
> Its crashing tells about him;
> he is jealous with anger
>   against iniquity."

SHINING LIGHT

Someone who is described as a "shining light" is notable and outstanding in a particular area of achievements. The expression derives from the description of John the Baptist: "He was a burning and a shining light: and ye were willing for a season to rejoice in his light" (John 5:35, KJV).

The contemporary versions render the KJV phrase "a burning and a shining light" as: "He was a [NKJV, "the"] burning and shining lamp" (NKJV, NRSV, RSV), "He was like a burning and shining lamp" (NCV), "He was the lamp that was burning and shining" (NASB), "John was a lamp that burned and gave light" (NIV), "John was a lamp that gave a lot of light" (CEV), and "John shone brightly for a while" (NLT).

The phrase "shining light" also occurs in Proverbs 4:18: "But the path of the just *is* as the shining light, that shineth more and more unto the perfect day" (KJV).

SHIPPING

To "take shipping" is an archaic phrase which means "to embark." It appears in the KJV rendering of John 6:24, "they also took shipping," and "Took shipping" was used by Tyndale and other sixteenth-century translations which also had "ship" and "ships" in verses 22 and 23. The KJV followed the Rheims New Testament in rendering the Greek words as "boat" and "boats" in verses 22 and 23, but did not follow it in verse 24.

The contemporary versions generally have "they themselves got into the [NASB, "the small"] boats" (NASB, NRSV, RSV). The passage reads in the NRSV: "The next day the crowd that had stayed on the other side of the sea saw that there had been only one boat there. They also saw that Jesus had not got into the boat with his disciples, but that his disciples had gone away alone. Then some boats from Tiberias came near the place where they had eaten the bread after the Lord had given thanks. So when the crowd saw that neither Jesus nor his disciples were there, they themselves got into the boats and went to Capernaum looking for Jesus."

SHROUD

A shroud is a garment or piece of cloth used to wrap the dead. We often use the word figuratively today ("shrouded in mist"), or to mean "encased" or "enveloped." In the KJV, however, the word has the archaic meaning of "shade" or "protection."

The expression "with a shadowing shroud" occurs in the KJV rendering of Ezekiel 31:3, a text depicting a cedar in Lebanon which was the greatest and most beautiful of trees. In fact it is a double translation, because one of the two Hebrew words which it represents means "shade" and the other is elsewhere translated by the KJV as "bough" (Isaiah 17:9), "forests" (2 Chronicles 27:4), and "a (the) wood" (1 Samuel 23:15–16, 18–19). The revised versions of 1881–1901 have "a forest-like shade"; the NASB, NLT, NRSV, and RSV have "forest shade." In Shakespeare's *Antony and Cleopatra* (III, 13, 71), the messenger from Caesar to Cleopatra invited her to put herself "under his shrowd."

SIGN OF THE TIMES

A "sign of the times" is a representative aspect of a particular period ("we must recognize the signs of the times and realize that families are not as close as they once were"). The expression has its origins in Matthew 16:3: "And in the morning, It will be foul weather to day: for the sky is red and lowring. O ye hypocrites, ye can discern the face of the sky; but can ye not discern the signs of the times?" (KJV).

The contemporary versions render the KJV "can ye not discern the signs of the times" as "cannot discern [NIV, NRSV, RSV, "cannot interpret"] the signs of the times" (NASB, NIV, NKJV, NRSV, RSV), "you can't read the obvious signs of the times" (NLT), "you don't understand what is happening now" (CEV); the NCV has "you see the things that I am doing now, but you don't know their meaning."

SILVERLING

A "silverling" is "a piece of silver," "a silver coin," "a shekel." Tyndale used the word in Acts 19:19: "Many of them which used curious craftes, brought their bokes and burned them before all men and they counted the price of them and founde it fifty thousande silverlynges." He added the marginal note: "These syluerlinges which we now and then call pence the Jues call sicles, and are worth a x. pence sterlynge."

Coverdale and Rheims used "pence" here; the Great Bible and the Geneva Bible, "siluerlynges"; the Bishops' Bible, the KJV, the revised versions, and the NASB, NKJV, and NRSV, "pieces of silver." In the Old Testament, Coverdale used "silverlings" in Judges 9:4; 16:5; 17:2–4, 10 and Isaiah 7:23. The Geneva Bible used "pieces of silver" or "shekels of silver" in these passages.

The KJV followed Geneva except in Isaiah 7:23, where it followed the Bishops' Bible in the retention of "silverlings." In all likelihood Tyndale and Coverdale got the word from Martin Luther's German Bible which has *Silberlinge* in all the Old Testament passages.

Contemporary versions have "shekels of silver" (NASB, NKJV, NRSV, RSV) and "pieces of silver" (CEV, NLT) at Isaiah 7:23, which reads in the KJV: "And it shall come to pass in that day, that every place shall be, where there were a thousand vines at a thousand sil-

verlings, it shall even be for briers and thorns."

SIMILITUDE

The word "similitude" means the form, likeness, or image of a person or thing. The word appears twelve times in the KJV, six times in the RV, once in the ASV, and only once in the contemporary versions. The word concerning Moses, "the similitude of the LORD shall he behold" (Numbers 12:8, KJV) is now rendered "he beholds [NIV, NKJV, "he sees"] the form of the LORD" (NASB, NIV, NKJV, NRSV, RSV).

"Form" is the also the majority rendering in Deuteronomy 4:12, 15–16. The NRSV has "one in human form" (Daniel 10:16), "resembling Melchizedek" (Hebrews 7:15), "made in the likeness of God" (James 3:9). The NKJV retains the KJV "similitude" at James 3:9: "made in [KJV, "after"] the similitude of God."

The description of the ornamentation of the molten sea which is given in 2 Chronicles 4:3 differs from that in 1 Kings 7:24. The NRSV harmonizes these, and uses "figures" rather than "the similitude." (See KNOP)

"They changed their glory into the similitude of an ox" (Psalm 106:20, KJV) refers to the Israelites' worship of the molten calf. The NCV translates as "They exchanged their glorious God for a statue of a bull that eats grass."

Psalm 144:12 begins an individual's prayer for the welfare of the community. It reads in the KJV: "That our sons may be as plants grown up in their youth; that our daughters may be as corner stones, polished after the similitude of a palace." The second sentence reads in the NKJV, "That our daughters may be as pillars, Sculptured in palace style," and in the NLT, "May our daughters be like graceful pillars, carved to beautify a palace." The NRSV has "our daughters like corner pillars, cut for the building of a palace."

In Romans 5:14, Paul's reference to "them

S

that had not sinned after the similitude of Adam's transgression" (KJV) now reads "those whose sins were not like the transgression of Adam" (NRSV, RSV).

Because the Latin Vulgate sometimes translated the Greek word for "parable" by *similitudo*, the word "similitude" was occasionally used in the sense of "parable" by Wycliffe, Tyndale, and their successors. The KJV retains the word only once in this sense, "I have multiplied visions, and used similitudes, by the ministry of the prophets" (Hosea 12:10). The NASB has "I gave numerous visions, and through the prophets I gave parables."

SIMONY

The term "simony" is used to refer to the practice of buying and selling church or spiritual benefits or offices. It alludes to Simon Magus, a sorcerer referred to in Acts 8. After becoming a believer, Simon tried to buy the gift of spiritual power from the apostles, but was strongly rebuked (Acts 8:9–24).

SIMPLE

The word "simple" today means "uncomplicated and straightforward," "unassuming," "unimportant," and "unlearned." Used of a person, it now often connotes that he or she is ignorant or lacking in mental astuteness. In the KJV, however, "simple" is used with its oldest meaning, which the OED gives as "free from duplicity, dissimulation, or guile"; "innocent and harmless"; "honest," "open," "straightforward." Paul says that he wants the Romans to be "wise unto that which is good, and simple concerning evil" (Romans 16:19, KJV).

The Greek adjective it represents appears also in Jesus' counsel to the Twelve as He sent them out to preach and to heal, "be wise as serpents, and harmless as doves" (Matthew 10:16 KJV), which contemporary versions render as "innocent" (CEV, NASB, NCV, NIV, NRSV, RSV). And Paul used it in urging the Philippians to be "blameless and

innocent, children of God without blemish in the midst of a crooked and perverse generation" (2:15, NRSV).

The NRSV translates his word to the Romans, "I want you to be wise in what is good and guileless in what is evil."

SIMPLICITY

The word "simplicity" today means "freedom from complexity," "plainness," "unpretentiousness" ("the simplicity of the furnishings"; "there was a simplicity about her which was very appealing"). When we read in the KJV, "he that giveth, let him do it with simplicity" (Romans 12:8), we might imagine that Paul is encouraging us to give without fuss. In fact, the Greek noun here translated as "simplicity" means "liberality," which is how the KJV itself translates it in 2 Corinthians 8:2, along with the terms "bountifulness" in 9:11 and "liberal distribution" in 9:13.

Contemporary versions translate "simplicity" (KJV) in Romans 12:8 as "generosity" (NRSV), and "liberality" (NASB, NKJV, RSV).

The primary meaning of this Greek noun is "singleness of mind and heart," "sincerity." It comes in 2 Corinthians 11:3, where the KJV reads, "I fear lest . . . your minds should be corrupted from the simplicity that is in Christ." The best ancient manuscripts have also the word for "purity," and the NASB translates: "I am afraid that . . . your minds will be led astray from the simplicity and purity of devotion to Christ." The NIV, NRSV, and RSV have "sincere and pure devotion to Christ."

SIN WILL FIND YOU OUT

The expression "your sin will find you out" is used in contemporary English to mean that a person's misdemeanor or deception will be discovered. The phrase derives from Numbers 32:23 (KJV), when the Reubenites and the Gadites were discouraged about crossing over the River Jordan. Moses told them to arm themselves and go over the Jordan until the Lord had driven out his enemies and then they may return: "But if ye will not do so, behold, ye have sinned against the LORD: and be sure your sin will find you out."

Of the contemporary versions, the expression "your sin will find you out" is retained by the NASB, NIV, NKJV, NLT, NRSV, and RSV; the NCV has "you will be punished for your sin," and the CEV, "be punished."

SINCERE

This was a new word in the sixteenth century, and was applied to things as well as to persons and motives. "As newborn babes, desire the sincere milk of the word, that ye may grow thereby" is the KJV rendering of 1 Peter 2:2. The verb "to desire" (KJV) has a correlative adjective which the KJV translates as "to long for" in Philippians 4:1: "my brethren dearly beloved and longed for."

The NASB, NRSV, and RSV use "long for" in their translations of 1 Peter 2:2, and the NIV has "crave." And the aim is not simply to grow, but to "grow up to salvation." The last phrase appears in the ancient Greek manuscripts, but had been lost from the medieval manuscripts upon which the KJV was based.

The adjective *adolos,* which the KJV renders as "sincere," means "without deceit," "unadulterated," "pure," and frequently occurs in the last of these senses in the Greek papyri. Most contemporary versions render it as "pure." The NRSV translation of Peter's words is, "Like newborn infants, long for the pure, spiritual milk, so that by it you may grow into salvation."

In his second epistle Peter says, "I stir up your pure minds by way of remembrance" (3:1, KJV). The adjective for "pure" here is *eilikrines,* which the KJV translates as "sincere," and the CEV, NIV, NLT, NRSV, and RSV as "pure" in Philippians 1:10. The NASB, NIV, NKJV, NRSV, and RSV translate *eilikrineia* as "sincerity" (1 Corinthians 5:8; 2 Corinthians 1:12; 2:17). The NRSV has in 2 Peter 3:1, "This is now, beloved, the second letter I am writing to you in which I am stirring up your sincere mind by way of reminder."

SINGULAR

The word "singular" today usually has the sense of "something which stands alone," or "something which is eccentric or peculiar." In Leviticus 27:2, however, the adjective "singular" (KJV) means "above the ordinary," "especially good or great" ("a singular vow"). It is a sense in which the word was commonly used from about 1500 to 1650, the OED records, but is now more rare.

This chapter of Leviticus deals with the rates and procedures whereby vows and tithes may be commuted by the payment of money. Verse 2 introduces the section dealing with the dedication of persons to the Lord, as Jephthah's daughter or Samuel had been dedicated, and providing a scale of redemption.

The NIV, NLT, and RSV read "a special vow"; the NASB has "a difficult vow," and the NRSV has "an explicit vow." The same Hebrew expression appears in Numbers 6:2, where the NASB reads, "When a man or a woman makes a special vow, the vow of a Nazirite."

SINS OF THE FATHERS

The phrase "the sins of the fathers" is sometimes used to refer to the misdemeanors, crimes, and errors of one generation. When the words "are visited upon the children" are added, this means that the misdemeanors, etc., of one generation have an effect upon that descendant's generation. The expression derives from the second of the Ten Commandments: "Thou shalt not bow down thyself to them, nor serve them: for I the LORD thy God am a jealous God, visiting the iniquity of the fathers upon the children unto the third and fourth generation of them that hate me" (Exodus 20:5, KJV).

The contemporary versions have: "visiting the iniquity of the fathers on [RSV, "upon"] the children" (NASB, NKJV, RSV), "punishing the children for the sin of the fathers" (NIV), "punish the children for the sins of their parents" (NLT), "punishing children for the iniquity of parents" (NRSV), and "punish your families" (CEV). See also Deuteronomy 5:9; the rendering of the second commandment in the Book of Common Prayer is "visit the sins of the fathers upon the children." See also Exodus 34:7; Numbers 14:18; Jeremiah 32:18; and Ezekiel 18:2. (See TEETH SET ON EDGE)

SITH

"Sith" is an old word for "since," sharing its several meanings. "Sith" appears once in the KJV, and "since" sixty-nine times. (See SEEING)

The one occurrence of "sith" in the KJV is Ezekiel 35:6: "sith thou hast not hated blood, even blood shall pursue thee." The NRSV, with the aid of the Septuagint, translates as "since you did not hate bloodshed, bloodshed shall pursue you."

Shakespeare uses "sith" twenty-two times. Examples are:

> "Talk not of France, sith thou
>   hast lost it all."
> —*King Henry VI, Part III* (I, 1, 110)

> "sith there's no justice in earth
>   nor hell,
> We will solicit heaven."
>   —*Titus Andronicus* (IV, 3, 49)

> "sith I am enter'd in this cause
>   so far, . . . I will go on."
>   —*Othello* (III, 3, 411)

SKILL

The obsolete phrase "can skill" meant to have "knowledge, competence, or skill, in some specified field." It is used three times with a following infinitive, in Solomon's message to Hiram, king of Tyre. "There is not among us any that can skill to hew timber like unto the Sidonians" (1 Kings 5:6, KJV) now reads, "there is no one among us who knows how to cut timber like the Sidonians" (NASB, RSV). So also "can skill to cut timber in Lebanon" (2 Chronicles 2:8,

KJV) now reads, "know how to cut timber of Lebanon" (NASB).

The preceding verse (2:7) reads in the KJV, "Send me now therefore a man cunning to work in gold, and in silver, and in brass, and in iron, and in purple, and crimson, and blue, and that can skill to grave with the cunning men that are with me in Judah and in Jerusalem, whom David my father did provide." The CEV has: "Send me a worker who can not only carve, but who can work with gold, silver, bronze, and iron, as well as make brightly colored cloth. The person you send will work here in Judah and Jerusalem with the skilled workers that my father has already hired."

In 2 Chronicles 34:12 the phrase "can skill of" occurs: "all that could skill of instruments of musick" (KJV). The OED states that this usage with "of" was common in the period 1525 to 1640. The NRSV translates, "all skillful with instruments of music."

The KJV description of Chenaniah in 1 Chronicles 15:22 reads, "Chenaniah, chief of the Levites, was for song: he instructed about the song, because he was skilful." The NRSV translates as "Chenaniah, leader of the Levites in music, was to direct the music, for he understood it."

The word "skill" and its derivatives are used sixteen times in the KJV and many more times in contemporary versions. This is largely because of the frequent use in the KJV Old Testament of "cunning" and "curious" in the sense of "skilful" or "skilfully done." (See CUNNING; CURIOUS)

The word "wise" appears in the KJV occasionally where contemporary versions use "skilled;" see Jeremiah 4:22; Ezekiel 27:8–9; 1 Corinthians 3:10. The first of these passages reads in the KJV: "For my people is foolish, they have not known me; they are sottish children, and they have none understanding: they are wise to do evil, but to do good they have no knowledge." The NRSV translates:

"For my people are foolish,
they do not know me;
they are stupid children,
they have no understanding.
They are skilled in doing evil,
but do not know how to do good."

SKIN OF ONE'S TEETH

If you do something "by the skin of your teeth," you only just manage to do it ("they escaped by the skin of their teeth"). This expression derives from Job 19:20: "My bone cleaveth to my skin and to my flesh, and I am escaped with the skin of my teeth" (KJV).

The contemporary versions have "I have escaped by [NASB, "only by"] the skin of my teeth" (NASB, NCV, NKJV, NRSV, RSV), "have escaped death by the skin of my teeth" (NLT), "I have escaped with only the skin of my teeth" (NIV), and "just barely alive" (CEV).

SLEIGHT

The primary meaning of "sleight" is defined by the OED as "craft or cunning employed so as to deceive." The word was common in the sixteenth and seventeenth centuries, but is now rare or obsolete except in connection with feats of juggling or tricks of legerdemain. "Sleight of hand" is a familiar expression, but "sleight of man" is not.

The Greek word translated "sleight" by the KJV in Ephesians 4:14 means "dice playing," "gambling," "cheating," "trickery." The KJV has "by the sleight of men, and cunning craftiness, whereby they lie in wait to deceive." The NASB and NKJV have "by the trickery of men." The NRSV reads, "by people's trickery, by their craftiness in deceitful scheming."

SLIME

The word "slime" is likely to conjure up images of used engine oil or the glutinous mud which abounds in horror movies. In the KJV, however, it means "bitumen," or "asphalt," and was used by Tyndale as a translation for the Hebrew word *chemar.*

The word was kept by the KJV: "slime had they for morter" (Genesis 11:3); "the vale of Siddim was full of slimepits" (Genesis 14:10); "she took for him an ark of bulrushes, and daubed it with slime and with pitch" (Exodus 2:3).

In the prologue to his translation of the five books of Moses (1530), Tyndale wrote: "That slyme was a fatnesse that issued out of the earth, like unto tarre; and thou mayest call it cement if thou wilt." The Greek Septuagint has *asphaltos,* and the Latin Vulgate, *bitumen,* in these three texts. The revised versions of 1885 and 1901 kept "slime" with a marginal note, "That is, bitumen."

Contemporary versions use "tar" (NASB, NCV, NIV), "asphalt" (NKJV, NLT), and "bitumen" (NRSV, RSV).

SMELL, SAVOUR

The nouns and verb which are translated "smell" in the KJV only refer to what is pleasing; the Hebrew had other words for bad odors. The RSV retains "smell" for the verb, and in a few cases for the noun. But it generally uses "fragrance," "scent," "perfume," or "pleasing odor" for the noun, depending upon the context.

"Sweet smelling myrrh" is the KJV rendering for "liquid myrrh" (NASB, NRSV, RSV) and "the smell of thy nose" is now translated as "the scent of your breath" by the NLT, NRSV, and RSV (Song of Solomon 5:5, 13; 7:8). The "perfume" which Moses was commanded to make was "incense" holy to the Lord; the commandment not to make any like it "to smell thereto" (Exodus 30:38, KJV) means that none of it should be made "to use as perfume" (CEV, NASB, NCV, NRSV, RSV).

The term "sweet savour" in the KJV refers to God's pleasure in the odor of burnt offerings, and is now translated as "soothing aroma" (NASB, NKJV), "pleasing aroma" (NIV), and "pleasing odor" (NRSV, RSV: Genesis 8:21 and many other occurrences). The word of the Lord through the prophet Amos, "I will not smell in your solemn assemblies" (Amos 5:21, KJV) means that the Lord

S

will not take pleasure in the burnt offerings of their solemn assemblies. The NRSV and RSV translate the clause, "I take no delight in your solemn assemblies."

The noun "savour" refers to "taste" in the well-known text about salt (Matthew 5:13; Luke 14:34). The verb "savour" which appears in Jesus' rebuke at Caesarea Philippi means "to have a taste for," "to relish," "to like," or "to care for": "Get thee behind me, Satan: thou art an offence unto me: for thou savourest not the things that be of God, but those that be of men" (Matthew 16:23 and its parallel, Mark 8:33, KJV). The Greek verb means "to think," "to set the mind on," "to purpose"; it is the verb which is translated, "Let this mind be in you, which was also in Christ Jesus" (Philippians 2:5, KJV).

The NASB renders Jesus' words as "you are not setting your mind on God's interests, but man's"; the NCV reads, "You don't care about the things of God, but only about the things people think are important."

SNORTING

See GLORY.

SNUFF

The word "snuff" is a sixteenth-century verb for purposeful and audible inhaling the breath. It is probably imitative in origin, like "sniff," "sniffle," "snuffle," "sneeze," and "snort." To "snuff at" something or some person was to express disdain or contempt. This expression is now obsolete, as its place began to be taken in the eighteenth century by "sniff at," which differs only in being sharper and more audible.

Malachi 1:6–14 accuses the priests of neglect of duty and of showing contempt for the altar and the table of the Lord. Verse 13 reads in the KJV, "Ye said also, Behold, what a weariness is it! and ye have snuffed at it" is replaced in contemporary versions by "disdainfully sniff at it" (NASB), "sniff at it in disgust" (NCV), "sniff at it contemptuously" (NIV), and "sneer at it" (NKJV).

The NLT paraphrases, "you turn up your noses at his commands." The NRSV and RSV have "sniff at me," a reading "based upon a Jewish tradition that the original reading was changed to at it in order to avoid the appearance of irreverence (Professor Robert Dentan, *The Interpreter's Bible,* vol. 6, p. 1129).

"Snuff up the wind" occurs twice in the KJV, in translation of a different Hebrew verb. The NASB reads, "A wild donkey accustomed to the wilderness, that sniffs the wind in her passion" (Jeremiah 2:24), and "the wild donkeys stand on the bare heights; they pant for air like jackals" (Jeremiah 14:6).

SO THAT

This expression occurs three times in the KJV in a limiting sense which is now rarely used, meaning "on condition that," "provided that," "if only." Examples of this usage are cited in the OED under "So," paragraph 2b. The occurrences in the KJV are in connection with God's promise to David: "There shall not fail thee a man in my sight to sit on the throne of Israel; so that thy children take heed to their way, that they walk before me as thou hast walked before me" (1 Kings 8:25). This is repeated in 2 Chronicles 6:16, with the addition of "yet," resulting in the expression "yet so that."

In 2 Chronicles 33:8, another promise to David is cited, "Neither will I any more remove the foot of Israel from out of the land which I have appointed for your fathers; so that they will take heed to do all that I have commanded them." This appears with slightly different wording in 2 Kings 21:8, where "only if" is used rather than "so that." In Deuteronomy 15:4–5 God's blessing is promised, "Only if thou carefully hearken unto the voice of the LORD thy God."

In all five of these cases the Hebrew has the same adverb and conditional conjunction, *raq im,* which mean "only if." The meaning is expressed in contemporary English by "if only," which the revised versions and twentieth-century translations generally use in these passages.

SODOM AND GOMORRAH

Sodom and Gomorrah were two cities that were notorious for their wickedness and sexual depravity and were destroyed by God (Genesis 18:16—19:29): "Then the LORD rained upon Sodom and Gomorrah brimstone and fire from the LORD out of heaven; And he overthrew those cities, and all the plain, and all the inhabitants of the cities, and that which grew upon the ground" (Genesis 19:24, KJV).

All the contemporary versions retain the names of Sodom and Gomorrah as in the KJV. The cities are repeatedly mentioned in the Bible with reference to God's judgment.

Isaiah 1:9–10, "Unless the LORD of hosts Had left to us a very small remnant, We would have become like Sodom, We would have been made like Gomorrah" (NKJV);

Amos 4:11, "'I destroyed some of your cities, as I destroyed Sodom and Gomorrah. Those of you who survived were like half-burned sticks snatched from a fire. But still you wouldn't return to me,' says the LORD" (NLT);

Luke 17:29, "But the day Lot left Sodom, fire and sulfur rained down from the sky and killed them all" (NIV);

2 Peter 2:6, "And God also destroyed the evil cities of Sodom and Gomorrah by burning them until they were ashes. He made those cities an example of what will happen to those who are against God" (NCV);

Jude 7, "We should also be warned by what happened to the cities of Sodom and Gomorrah and the nearby towns. Their people became immoral and did all sorts of sexual sins. Then God made an example of them and punished them with eternal fire" (CEV). (See FIRE AND BRIMSTONE)

SODOMY

The word alludes to the homosexual desires of the men of Sodom (Genesis 19:1–11). Genesis 19:5 in the KJV reads, "And they called unto Lot, and said unto him, Where are the men which came in to thee this night? bring them out unto us, that we may know them."

Of the contemporary versions, the NRSV and RSV retain the KJV "that they may know them"; the NKJV has "know them carnally"; the CEV, NIV, and NLT have "have sex with them"; the NASB, "have relations with them," and the NCV, "have sexual relations with them."

SOFT ANSWER TURNETH AWAY WRATH

The saying "a soft answer turneth away wrath" means that a gentle reply to an accusing or insulting remark lessens the anger and sense of enmity. The expression derives from Proverbs 15:1: "A soft answer turneth away wrath: but grievous words stir up anger" (KJV).

The contemporary versions render this as "A soft [NASB, NIV, NLT, "gentle"] answer turns away wrath" (NASB, NIV, NKJV, NLT, NRSV, RSV), "A gentle answer will calm a person's anger" (NCV), and "A kind answer soothes angry feelings" (CEV).

SOME

The word "some" is in the singular number in the KJV of Romans 5:7. It means "one," "someone"—a now obsolete usage. The verse reads, "For scarcely for a righteous man will one die: yet peradventure for a good man some would even dare to die" (KJV). There seems to be a contrast here between "one" in the first clause and "some" in the second clause, but in the Greek the subject of each clause is the same singular indefinite pronoun.

The NKJV translates, "For scarcely for a righteous man will one die; yet perhaps for a good man someone would even dare to die."

SOMETIME, SOMETIMES, SOME TIME

For us today, "sometime" refers to a particular period, "sometimes" means "occasionally," and "some time" can refer to a period of duration. In the KJV, however, all three forms refer to a time in the past. They have the same obsolete meaning, and translate the same Greek adverb.

We might be forgiven for thinking that when Paul writes "ye who sometimes were far off" (Ephesians 2:13, KJV), "ye were sometimes darkness" (Ephesians 5:8, KJV), and "we ourselves also were sometimes foolish" (Titus 3:3, KJV), he is referring to merely occasional remoteness or darkness or folly. And we might think that "In the which ye also walked some time, when ye lived in them" (Colossians 3:7, KJV) means "for some time," that is, for a considerable duration.

In fact, the Greek adverb, which in these passages and in the two where the KJV has "sometime" (Colossians 1:21; 1 Peter 3:20), simply means "once," "at one time," or "formerly" and is so generally translated by contemporary versions.

SORE (adjective, adverb)

While "sore" might make us think of a grazed knee or a tearful toddler holding up a bruised finger, in the KJV "sore," as adjective and adverb, appears nearly a hundred times in the archaic sense of "severe(ly)," "intense(ly)," "very great(ly)."

"The famine was sore" (Genesis: 43:1, KJV) is now rendered as "the famine was [NIV, "was still"] severe" (NASB, NIV, NKJV, NRSV, RSV), (cf. Genesis 41:56, 57; 47:4, 13; 1 Kings 18:2; Jeremiah 52:6). "Because thou sore longedst after thy father's house" (Genesis 31:30, KJV) now reads "because you longed greatly for your father's house" (NASB, NRSV, RSV).

Thirty different Hebrew and Greek words are listed in Young's *Concordance* for "sore" as adjective and adverb. Twenty of these are verbs, with which "sore" is used to intensify their meaning. For example, "wept (weep) sore" occurs ten times. In four of these cases "sore" represents the cognate accusative with the adjective for "great." A literal translation would be

"wept a (very) great weeping" (Judges 21:2; 2 Samuel 13:36; 2 Kings 20:3; Isaiah 38:3).

In Ezra 10:1 the cognate accusative appears without the adjective. In four cases "sore" represents the Hebrew idiom which expresses intensity of meaning by repetition, using the absolute infinitive as well as the finite verb (1 Samuel 1:10; Jeremiah 13:17; 22:10; Lamentations 1:2). (See GENERALLY; SURELY)

The majority of contemporary versions use renderings such as "wept (weep) bitterly" and "cried (crying) bitterly" in these nine cases. The other occurrence of "wept sore" (KJV) is Acts 20:37, which the NRSV translates as "There was much weeping among them all; they embraced Paul and kissed him."

"Sore war" (1 Samuel 14:52, KJV) is now "hard fighting" (NRSV, RSV); "the battle was sore" (Judges 20:34, KJV) is now "the battle became fierce" (NASB); "there was a very sore battle" (2 Samuel 2:17, KJV) is now "the battle was very severe" (NASB). "Sore wounded" (1 Samuel 31:3; 2 Chronicles 35:23, KJV) is rendered as "badly wounded" (NASB, NRSV, RSV). "Sore pained" (Psalm 55:4, KJV) is now translated as "in anguish" (NASB, NIV, NLT, NRSV, RSV), and "he died of sore diseases" (2 Chronicles 21:19, KJV) as "he died in great pain" (NIV).

In the story of Samson's wedding (Judges 14:17), "lay sore upon him" (KJV) means "pressed him hard." The NCV has "kept bothering him," the NRSV, "nagged him." The context is the woman of Timnath's attempt to solve the riddle with which Samson was taunting her people. "Lay sore upon him" (KJV) stands for the same Hebrew verb which the KJV translates, in the case of the woman of Timnath, by "pressed him" in Judges 16:16: "she pressed him daily with her words, and urged him, so that his soul was vexed unto death." The KJV, NASB, NRSV, and RSV all translate this verb as "constrain" in Job 32:18.

The complaint of the inhabitants of Ashdod, "his hand is sore upon us" (1 Samuel

5:7, KJV), is now rendered as "his hand is heavy upon us" (NIV, RSV). "Sore broken" (Psalm 44:19, KJV) is now simply "broken" (NRSV, RSV) or "crushed" (CEV, NASB, NCV, NIV, NLT), and "I am feeble and sore broken" (Psalm 38:8, KJV) is now translated as "I am benumbed and badly crushed" (NASB), "I am feeble and severely broken" (NKJV), and "I am utterly spent and crushed" (NRSV, RSV).

The expression "sore afraid" appears a dozen times in the KJV, and is rephrased by contemporary versions. Examples are: "very frightened" (Exodus 14:10, NASB, NCV); "in dread" (Numbers 22:3, NASB); "feared greatly for our lives" (Joshua 9:24, NASB, NRSV); "very much afraid" (1 Samuel 17:24, NCV, NRSV); "terrified" (1 Samuel 28:20, CEV; Luke 2:9, NIV, NRSV); "horribly afraid" (Ezekiel 27:35, NRSV, RSV); "overcome by fear" (Matthew 17:6, NRSV).

"It grieved me sore" (Nehemiah 13:8, KJV) reads "I was very angry" in the NRSV and RSV and "it grieved me bitterly" in the NKJV. "We roar all like bears, and mourn sore like doves" (Isaiah 59:11, KJV) is rendered in the NRSV as "We all growl like bears; like doves we moan mournfully."

Psalm 38:2 reads in the KJV, "For thine arrows stick fast in me, and thy hand presseth me sore." The NKJV translates, "For Your arrows pierce me deeply, And Your hand presses me down."

Contemporary versions do not use "sore" as an adverb. The RSV replaces "sore" by "sorely" in half a dozen cases (e.g., Judges 10:9; 1 Samuel 1:6; Psalms 6:3, 10; 118:18; Isaiah 64:12); other versions use words such as "greatly" and "severely." Genesis 49:23 reads in the KJV: "The archers have sorely grieved him, and shot at him, and hated him." The NRSV translates it as "The archers fiercely attacked him; they shot at him and pressed him hard."

SORE (noun)

As a noun, "sore" appears eleven times in the KJV. It is retained by contemporary versions in Isaiah 1:6, Luke 16:20–21, and Revelation 16:2, 11. For "a boil breaking forth with blains" (Exodus 9:9, 10), the NASB and RSV have "boils breaking out in sores" and the NIV has "festering boils." For Job's "sore boils" (Job 2:7, KJV), contemporary versions have "painful sores" (NCV, NIV) and "painful boils" (NKJV), and "loathsome sores" (NRSV, RSV).

At two points in the Psalms the KJV's use of "sore" might cause confusion. "My lovers and my friends stand aloof from my sore" (Psalm 38:11, KJV) is rendered by the RSV as "My friends and companions stand aloof from my plague"; the NASB and NKJV also render "sore" (KJV) here as "plague," while the other contemporary versions have "wounds" (NCV, NIV), "disease" (NLT), and "affliction" (NRSV).

"My sore ran in the night, and ceased not" (Psalm 77:2) is the KJV rendering for a Hebrew line which the RV and ASV translate as, "My hand was stretched out in the night, and slacked not." The NRSV translates the verse, "In the day of my trouble I seek the Lord; in the night my hand is stretched out without wearying; my soul refuses to be comforted."

SOTTISH

Until about the seventeenth century a "sot" was "a foolish or stupid person," "sotie" was "folly," and "sottish" was "foolish" or "stupid." Then "sot," "sottish," and "besotted" began to be restricted to drunkards, and the older meanings became obsolete. The KJV uses "sottish" once, in translation of the Hebrew word which it everywhere else translates by "fool," "foolish," "foolishly."

The passage is Jeremiah 4:22, which reads in the KJV: "For my people is foolish, they have not known me; they are sottish children, and they have none understanding: they are wise to do evil, but to do good they have no knowledge." The NRSV reads:

"For my people are foolish,
they do not know me;
they are stupid children,

they have no understanding.
They are skilled in doing evil,
but do not know how to do good."

The CEV renders "sottish" (KJV) here as "foolish"; the NIV and NLT have "senseless," and the NKJV, "silly."

"Stupid" was a new word in 1611, and does not appear in the KJV. Shakespeare used "stupid" once, "sottish" once, and "sot" seven times. In *The Tempest* (III, 2, 100), when Caliban advises Stephano to seize Prospero's books, "for without them he's but a sot," the meaning is that without their aid Prospero is as stupid or foolish as Caliban himself.

SOUNDING BRASS

The phrase "sounding brass" is sometimes used to refer to the noise produced from a brass musical instrument. The expression derives from 1 Corinthians 13:1: "Though I speak with the tongues of men and of angels, and have not charity, I am become as sounding brass, or a tinkling cymbal" (KJV).

The contemporary versions render the KJV "sounding brass" as "noisy gong" (CEV, NASB, NRSV, RSV), "resounding gong" (NIV), and "noisy bell" (NCV); the NKJV retains the KJV expression and the NLT renders the whole verse as "If I could speak in any language in heaven or on earth but didn't love others, I would only be making meaningless noise like a loud gong or a clanging cymbal."

The phrase occurs in Bunyan's *Pilgrim's Progress*, when Christian describes Talkative's conversation: "Paul calleth some men, yea and those great Talkers too, sounding Brass and tinckling Cymbals."

SOW THE WIND AND REAP THE WHIRLWIND

The expression "sow the wind and reap the whirlwind" means to do something that appears harmless but leads to the suffering of disastrous unforeseen consequences. The source of this expression lies

in Hosea's prophecy in Hosea 8:7: "For they have sown the wind, and they shall reap the whirlwind: it hath no stalk: the bud shall yield no meal: if so be it yield, the strangers shall swallow it up" (KJV).

The phrasing "sow the wind and [NASB, NRSV, RSV, "and they"] reap the whirlwind" is found in the NASB, NIV, NKJV, NRSV and RSV; the NLT has "They have planted the wind and will harvest the whirlwind," the CEV, "If you scatter wind instead of wheat, you will harvest a whirlwind," and the NCV, "Israel's foolish plans are like planting the wind, but they will harvest a storm."

SOWING AND REAPING

The expression "whatsoever a man sows that he shall reap" refers to the fact that people will receive a due reward or punishment for what they have done. The source of this expression is Galatians 6:7: "Be not deceived; God is not mocked: for whatsoever a man soweth, that shall he also reap" (KJV).

The contemporary versions render this "whatever a man sows, that [NASB, "this"] he will also reap" (NASB, NKJV, RSV); "A man reaps what he sows" (NIV); "you reap whatever you sow" (NRSV); "You will always reap what you sow!" (NLT); "You will harvest what you plant" (CEV); "People harvest only what they plant" (NCV). (See REAP WHERE ONE HAS NOT SOWN)

SPACE

The word "space" in modern usage conjures up images of astronauts and space stations. In the KJV, however, "space" usually refers to a period of time. "The space in which we came from Kadesh-barnea, until we were come over the brook Zered, was thirty and eight years" (Deuteronomy 2:14, KJV) is rendered in the NASB as "the time that it took for us to come from Kadesh-barnea until we crossed over the brook Zered was thirty-eight years."

"Space to repent" (Revelation 2:21, KJV) is "time to repent" in most of the contemporary versions. "A little space" (Ezra 9:8, KJV) is translated by the NASB, NIV, NLT, NRSV, and RSV as "a brief moment." When Gamaliel "commanded to put the apostles forth a little space" (Act 5:34, KJV), his order was that they "be put outside for a little while" (NIV, NKJV).

"After they had tarried there a space" (Acts 15:33, KJV) now reads "after they had spent time there" (NASB). "About the space of three hours after" is rendered in the NRSV as "After an interval of about three hours" (Acts 5:7; cf. Luke 22:59). "There was silence in heaven about the space of half an hour" (Revelation 8:1, KJV) now reads "there was silence in heaven for about half an hour" (CEV, NASB, NCV, NIV, NKJV, NRSV, RSV).

Other examples are Genesis 29:14; Leviticus 25:8, 30; and Acts 19:8, 10, 34.

SPARE THE ROD

The expression "spare the rod and spoil the child" is sometimes used to support physical punishment so that a child will learn to behave properly and know the difference between right and wrong. The expression derives from Proverbs 13:24, "He that spareth his rod hateth his son: but he that loveth him chasteneth him betimes."

The contemporary versions render this as "He who spares the [NKJV, "spares his"] rod hates his son" (NIV, NKJV, RSV), "He who withholds his rod hates his son" (NASB), "Those who spare the rod hate their children" (NRSV), "If you do not punish your children, you don't love them" (NCV), "If you refuse to discipline your children, it proves you don't love them" (NLT), and "If you love your children, you will correct them" (CEV).

The form of the contemporary expression that derives from the saying in Proverbs, "Spare the rod and spoil the child," is found in Samuel Butler's *Hudibras,* Part II (published 1663; 1, 843).

SPECIAL

"Special" is a word that we use today to mean "exceptional," "cherished," "above the ordinary," or "fit for a particular use." We have special friends, special folders for important documents, and find special offers on supermarket shelves. The word appears twice in the KJV, with meanings close to our present ones. In Deuteronomy 7:6 it translates the Hebrew word *segullah,* for which the KJV usually has "peculiar." The KJV reads, "the LORD thy God hath chosen thee to be a special people unto himself, above all people that are upon the face of the earth."

Contemporary versions render this verse in various ways. The NIV and NRSV say that God has chosen Israel "to be his people, his treasured possession"; the NKJV has "a people for Himself, a special treasure above all the peoples on the face of the earth," and the NLT, "his own special treasure." The NASB reads, "the LORD your God has chosen you to be a people for His own possession out of all the peoples who are on the face of the earth." (See PECULIAR)

In Acts 19:11 "special" (KJV) translates a Greek phrase which means "not happening as usual," "out of the ordinary run of events." The NRSV renders the verse as "God did extraordinary miracles through Paul," and the NASB and NIV also use "extraordinary." The NLT has "unusual," and the NCV says that "God used Paul to do some very special miracles."

SPECIALLY

This word appears five times in the KJV, always as translation of the Greek adverb which means "most of all," "above all," "especially." Contemporary versions generally use "especially" in these cases: Acts 25:26; 1 Timothy 4:10; 5:8; Titus 1:10; Philemon 16.

SPED

"Sped" is the past participle of the verb "speed." It occurs once in the KJV, in the Song of Deborah (Judges 5:30). The mother of Sisera is pictured as reassuring herself, when her son does not return, by the thought that he and his army have won a great victory and are occupied with the division of the spoil. "Have they not sped?" she says, "have they not divided the prey?" "Sped" is here used in the oldest sense of the verb "speed"—"to succeed," "to attain one's purpose." "Have they not sped?" means "Have they not won?"

The Hebrew in this verse, however, means "to find." Contemporary versions have "Are they not finding" (NASB, NIV, NKJV, NRSV, RSV). The NKJV translates: "Are they not finding and dividing the spoil?" (See PREY; SPEED)

SPEED

While today we think of fast cars and electric food mixers, in Old and Middle English "speed"—as a noun—meant "success," "prosperity," "good fortune" (though it could denote the opposite if preceded by such adjectives as "evil" or "ill"). In the KJV the word is used in its primary sense in Genesis 24:12, where Abraham's servant, having arrived at the city where his master's brother lived, prayed, "O LORD God of my master Abraham, I pray thee, send me good speed this day, and shew kindness unto my master Abraham."

Contemporary versions render "send me good speed" (KJV) here as "grant me success" (NASB, NRSV, RSV) and "give me success" (NIV, NKJV, NLT). The NRSV has "O LORD, God of my master Abraham, please grant me success today and show steadfast love to my master Abraham." (See LOVINGKIND-NESS)

SPIRIT IS WILLING

The saying "the spirit is willing but the flesh is weak" is used to show that someone lacks the ability, energy, or willpower to put his or her good intentions into practice. The expression is sometimes used as an explanation of someone's failure to do something.

The phrase derives from the warning by Jesus to His disciples in the Garden of Gethsemane to remain alert and not to yield to temptation: "Watch and pray, that ye enter not into temptation: the spirit indeed is willing, but the flesh is weak" (Matthew 26:41, KJV).

Of the contemporary versions, the NASB, NKJV, NRSV, and RSV have "the spirit indeed is willing but the flesh is weak"; the NIV has "the spirit is willing, but the body is weak"; the NLT has "For though the spirit is willing enough, the body is weak!"; the NCV, "The spirit wants to do what is right, but the body is weak"; and the CEV, "You want to do what is right, but you are weak."

In the parallel verse at Mark 14:38, the KJV has "The spirit truly is ready, but the flesh is weak," but the contemporary versions retain their phrasing (mainly with "willing") as in the Matthew passage.

SPITEFULLY

The word "spitefully" is synonymous today with "maliciously": a person who behaves spitefully is deliberately trying to humiliate or offend. In the KJV, however, "spitefully" is used in the obsolete sense of "disgracefully," "shamefully." In Matthew 22:6 and Luke 18:32 the KJV has "entreated them spitefully" and "be spitefully entreated." The same Greek verb is translated "were shamefully entreated" by the KJV in 1 Thessalonians 2:2.

In Matthew, the parable of the marriage feast, the NKJV retains the word, but other contemporary versions read "treated them shamefully" (NKJV, RSV) or simply "mistreated them" (NASB, NIV, NRSV). In Luke, for Jesus' prophecy of his death, the CEV and NASB use the verb "mistreat," the NCV, NIV, NKJV, and NRSV use the verb "insult," and the NLT has that he will be "treated shamefully."

In Paul's reminiscence of his treatment at Philippi, he remembers how he and his companions had been "insulted" (CEV, NCV, NIV), "spitefully treated" (NKJV), and "shamefully mistreated" (NRSV). (See ENTREAT)

SPOIL

The verb "to spoil" in modern usage makes us think of accidents which lead to destruction. But in the KJV it has the archaic meaning of "to despoil or plunder." "Ye shall spoil the Egyptians" (Exodus 3:22, KJV) now reads in the NKJV and NRSV, "you shall plunder the Egyptians." "All that pass by the way spoil him" (Psalm 89:41, KJV) is "All who pass by plunder [RSV, "despoil"] him" (NRSV, RSV).

"For the LORD will plead their cause, and spoil the soul of those that spoiled them" (Proverbs 22:23, KJV) might seem a little ambiguous to readers. The NASB translates as "For the LORD will plead their case And take the life those who rob them." The NKJV has "For the LORD will plead their cause, And plunder the soul of those who plunder them."

"They spoiled all the cities; for there was exceeding much spoil in them" (2 Chronicles 14:14, KJV) is worded in the NRSV, "They plundered all the cities; for there was much plunder in them." Haman's edict against the Jews, so dramatically reversed by Esther, included the command "to take the spoil of them for a prey" (Esther 3:13; 8:11, KJV); the NASB translates "to seize their possessions as plunder" (3:13) and "to plunder their spoil" (8:11).

"Because thou hast spoiled many nations, all the remnant of the people shall spoil thee" (Habakkuk 2:8, KJV) reads in the NLT, "You have plundered many nations; now they will plunder you." In Jesus' saying about the strong man (Matthew 12:29; Mark 3:27), "spoil his goods" and "spoil his house" (KJV) are rendered as "plunder his goods" and "plunder his house" in the NKJV.

In 2 Samuel 23:10 the Hebrew verb rendered "to spoil" means "to strip"; the NASB translates, "and the people returned after him only to strip the slain." In 1 Samuel 31:8 (and its parallel, 1 Chronicles 10:8) the same Hebrew verb appears and the KJV also has "to strip the slain."

In Nahum 3:16 this verb is used for locusts stripping off the sheaths of their wings; the KJV reads, "the cankerworm spoileth, and fleeth away" and the NRSV reads, "The locust sheds its skin and flies away." Other contemporary versions use the verbs "strip" and "plunder": "The creeping locust strips and flies away" (NASB), "like locusts, they strip the land and then fly away" (NCV), "the locust plunders and flies away" (NKJV).

In Isaiah and Jeremiah the word "spoil" is often used for the Hebrew verb which means "destroy," "devastate," "ruin." An example is "the spoiler spoileth" (Isaiah 21:2, KJV) where contemporary versions have "the looter takes loot" (NIV), "the plunderer plunders" (NKJV), and "the destroyer destroys" (NRSV, RSV). The same verb occurs in Micah 2:4, where the KJV has "We be utterly spoiled" and the NKJV has "We are utterly destroyed."

Similarly in Jeremiah 4:13 the KJV reads, "Woe unto us! for we are spoiled" and the NASB, NRSV, and RSV read, "woe to us, for we are ruined!"

In Colossians 2:8, "Beware lest any man spoil you" (KJV), the Greek verb means "to carry off as booty or as a captive." The NRSV translates the verse, "See to it that no one takes you captive through philosophy and empty deceit, according to human tradition, according to the elemental spirits of the universe, and not according to Christ." In verse 15, "having spoiled principalities and powers" (KJV), the Greek verb means "to strip."

Contemporary versions render it as "defeated" (CEV), "stripped" (NCV), and "disarmed" (NASB, NIV, NKJV, NLT, NRSV, RSV): "Having disarmed principalities and powers, He made a public spectacle of them, triumphing over them in it" (NKJV).

The verb "spoil" occurs with its modern meaning in Song of Solomon 2:15. The Hebrew verb means "to ruin," and the NLT paraphrases as "Quick! Catch all the little foxes before they ruin the vineyard of your love, for the grapevines are all in blossom."

"Spoiled" is used by the RSV where the KJV has "marred" in Jeremiah's acted parable of the "girdle" (Jeremiah 13:7). The Hebrew verb means "to be ruined," and other contemporary versions have "rotted" (CEV), "mildewed" (NLT), and "ruined" (NASB, NCV,

NIV, NKJV, NRSV, RSV). The RSV has "the waist-cloth was spoiled; it was good for nothing."

SPREAD ONE'S NET

The expression "to spread one's net" is sometimes used to mean "to get ready to catch or trap someone." The expression derives from Proverbs 29:5, "A man that flattereth his neighbour spreadeth a net for his feet" (KJV).

Of the contemporary versions' rendering of this phrase, the NASB, NIV, NKJV, NRSV, and RSV use the verbal phrase "spread a net"; the CEV and NCV use "set a trap" (e.g., "Those who give false praise to their neighbors are setting a trap for them," NCV); and the NLT, "lay a trap."

SPRING

As a noun, "spring" has a variety of meanings today. We are most likely to think of a spring of water, or the season of the year which begins with the vernal equinox. In the KJV the word is used with the first of these meanings (e.g., Hosea 13:15), but not with the second—though the month Nisan (corresponding to part of March and part of April) was regarded as the first month of the year.

Contemporary versions use "spring" when the Hebrew refers to that season. In some cases the Hebrew expression means "at the return of the year." It is so translated by the KJV in 1 Kings 20:22, 26, but is rendered "after (when) the year was expired" in 2 Samuel 11:1; 1 Chronicles 20:1; 2 Chronicles 36:10.

In 2 Kings 13:20 the Hebrew means "at the coming in of the year." In the promises to Sarah and the woman of Shunem, the Hebrew means "when the time revives" (Genesis 18:10, 14; 2 Kings 4:16–17).

"The latter rain" means "the spring rain," and is so rendered by the majority of contemporary versions (Job 29:23; Proverbs 16:15; Jeremiah 3:3; 5:24; Hosea 6:3; Zechariah 10:1). Exceptions are Deuteronomy 11:14 and Joel 2:23, concerning the Lord's gift of "the early rain" and "the later [NKJV, "the latter"] rain" (NKJV, NRSV, RSV).

On one occasion the noun "spring" is used in the KJV as a collective term for the fresh green shoots of trees or plants: "it shall wither in all the leaves of her spring" (Ezekiel 17:9). In this rendering the KJV stands alone. Coverdale, Matthew, and the Great Bible had "his green branches"; Geneva and the Bishops' Bible, "her bud."

The revised versions of 1885–1901 have "that all its fresh springing leaves may wither." Contemporary versions render "the leaves of her spring" (KJV) as "its sprouting leaves" (NASB), "its fresh sprouting leaves" (NRSV, RSV), "its new growth" (NIV), and "its spring growth" (NKJV).

In the sixteenth century a person spoke as naturally of "the spring of the day" as "the break of day." Both expressions appear in the KJV. First Samuel 9:26 has "it came to pass about the spring of the day," and Judges 19:25 has "when the day began to spring." But the KJV also has "until the breaking of the day" (Genesis 32:24), "the day breaketh" (Genesis 32:26), "at break of day" (2 Samuel 2:32), "until the day break, and the shadows flee away" (Song of Solomon 2:17; 4:6), "even till break of day" (Acts 20:11). It uses "the dawning of the day" (Joshua 6:15; Judges 19:26; Job 3:9; 7:4) and "the dawning of the morning" (Psalm 119:147).

Contemporary versions use such terms as "dawn" and "break," "sunrise" and "daybreak." The Hebrew figures of speech are literally translated by the NRSV and RSV in Job 3:9, "the eyelids of the morning," and in Song of Solomon 2:17 and 4:6, "until day breathes."

Tyndale had an interesting rendering of Jonah 4:7: "The lorde ordeyned a worme agenst the springe of ye morow morninge." Coverdale began the verse with "But upon the nexte morow agaynst the springe of the daye," and this was kept in Matthew's Bible and the Great Bible. The KJV rendering, "when the morning rose the next day," follows the Geneva Bible and the Bishops' Bible.

In the KJV the verb "spring" is used with vegetation, in the sense of "sprout," "shoot," "grow," "be green." For example, Isaiah 44:4 reads in the KJV, "they shall spring up as among the grass, as willows by the water courses." "The pastures of the wilderness do spring" (Joel 2:22) is now rendered as "the pastures of the wilderness have turned green" (NASB), "the open pastures have grown grass" (NCV), and "the open pastures are springing up" (NKJV).

SPY OUT THE LAND

According to the OED, the expression "spy out the land" means "to make stealthy observations in (a country or place) from hostile motives."

The expression occurs five times in the KJV. Numbers 13:16–17 in the KJV reads, "Those are the names of the men which Moses sent to spy out the land. And Moses called Oshea the son of Nun Jehoshua. And Moses sent them to spy out the land of Canaan, and said unto them, Get you up this way southward, and go up into the mountain."

The NASB, NKJV, and NRSV retain the KJV expression "spy out the land"; the NCV, NIV, and NLT have "explore the land."

For the Danites' "spy out the land and search it" (Judges 8:2), the NLT has "scout out a land for them to settle in." See also Numbers 21:32, Judges 18:17, and 1 Chronicles 19:3.

As the OED notes, the expression is frequently used figuratively as in Agatha Christie's *ABC Murders* (1936), xv, 112: "This man must have been spying out the land beforehand and discovered your brother's habit of taking an evening stroll."

STABLISH

The word "stablish" appears eighteen times in the KJV and "establish" 121 times, as translation for the same group of Hebrew and Greek verbs. There seems to be no distinction in the KJV's use of the two terms.

Contemporary versions use "establish," but other terms also appear. Among these are "found" (NRSV) and "founds" (NASB, RSV), in Habakkuk 2:12 ("Woe to him who builds a city with bloodshed And founds a town with violence!", NASB); "make . . . strong" (CEV, NCV, NLT) in Romans 16:25 ("He can make you strong," CEV); and "strengthen" (NASB, NIV, NRSV, RSV) in 2 Thessalonians 3:3 ("he will strengthen you," NRSV, RSV).

STAGGER

This word is used four times in the KJV Old Testament, always with reference to drunkenness, and is generally retained by the contemporary versions (Job 12:25; Psalm 107:27; Isaiah 19:14; 29:9). The NRSV and RSV also use it to translate the same Hebrew words in passages in Isaiah where the KJV uses "err" (19:14), "reel to and fro" (24:20), and "out of the way" (28:7).

In Romans 4:20, the KJV says of Abraham that "he staggered not at the promise of God through unbelief; but was strong in faith, giving glory to God." To stagger at a promise, opinion, or proposal meant to begin to doubt, waver, or hesitate concerning it—an idiom which we still use today.

The revised versions of 1881–1901 give a literal translation, following the order of the Greek words: "looking unto the promise of God, he wavered not through unbelief, but waxed strong through faith, giving glory to God." The NRSV reads: "No distrust made him waver concerning the promise of God, but he grew strong in his faith as he gave glory to God."

STAND UPON

This expression might give contemporary readers the wrong impression in 2 Samuel 1, where a young Amalekite relates the dying Saul's last words: "Stand, I pray thee, upon me, and slay me . . . So I stood upon him" (vv. 9–10). This is not archaic English; the translators had not recognized that "upon" is not the only meaning of the preposition 'al.

In this context "stand over" (NIV, NKJV, NRSV), and "stand by" and "stand beside" (NASB, RSV) are also appropriate translations of the Hebrew.

STAY

As noun and verb, "stay" is used sixty-seven times in the KJV Old Testament, and represents twenty-three different Hebrew words, each with its own meaning. In general, the meanings of "stay," as used in the KJV, cluster about the ideas of "stop," "remain," "support," "sustain."

The RSV retains it in many passages, such as: "the moon stayed" (Joshua 10:13), "stay your hand" (2 Samuel 24:16), "stayed until now" (Genesis 32:4), "stayed on the mountain" (Deuteronomy 10:10), "the LORD was my stay" (Psalm 18:18), "stay and staff, the whole stay of bread, and the whole stay of water" (Isaiah 3:1), and the great text from the song of Judah (Isaiah 26:3): "Thou dost keep him in perfect peace, whose mind is stayed on thee, because he trusts in thee."

Other contemporary versions use other terms: "the moon stopped" (Joshua 10:13, NASB, NCV, NIV, NKJV, NRSV), "relax your hand" (2 Samuel 24:16, NASB), "remained . . . till now" (Genesis 32:4, NIV), "the LORD was my support" (Psalm 18:18, NIV, NKJV, NRSV). Isaiah 26:3 reads in the NRSV, "Those of steadfast mind you keep in peace—in peace because they trust in you."

In many other passages, the RSV uses terms closer to the meaning of the Hebrew, such as "waited another seven days" (Genesis 8:10, 12); "refrain from marrying" (Ruth 1:13); "restrain the lightnings" (Job 37:4); "withheld the dew" (Haggai 1:10).

Aaron and Hur "held up" (NCV, NRSV, RSV) Moses' hands at the battle with Amalek (Exodus 17:12); the wounded King Jehoshaphat was "propped up" (CEV, NASB, NIV, NKJV, NLT, NRSV, RSV) in his chariot (1 Kings 22:35); the woe to those who "stay on horses" (Isa-

iah 31:1, KJV) is meant for those who "rely on horses" (NASB, NIV, NKJV, NRSV, RSV).

The "stays on each side of the sitting place" (KJV) of King Solomon's throne are now rendered as "armrests" by the NCV, NIV, NKJV, NLT; NRSV "arm rests" (2 Chronicles 9:18; cf., 1 Kings 10:19). "Stay me with flagons" (Song of Solomon 2:5, KJV) is now "Sustain me with raisins" (NRSV, RSV). (See FLAGON)

Isaiah 27:8 is a difficult text, because the meaning of its first word is uncertain. It reads in the KJV: "In measure, when it shooteth forth, thou wilt debate with it: he stayeth his rough wind in the day of the east wind." The NRSV reads:

> "By expulsion, by exile you struggled against them;
> with his fierce blast he removed them in the day of the east wind."

Another verse which is rendered quite differently by the contemporary versions is Isaiah 29:9: "Stay yourselves, and wonder; cry ye out, and cry: they are drunken, but not with wine; they stagger, but not with strong drink" (KJV). For "Stay yourselves" (KJV) they have "Be shocked" (CEV), "Be delayed" (NASB), "Pause" (NKJV), "Be surprised" (NCV), "Be stunned" (NIV), and "Stupefy yourselves" (NRSV, RSV). The whole verse reads in the NRSV:

> "Stupefy yourselves and be in a stupor, blind yourselves and be blind!
> Be drunk, but not from wine;
> stagger, but not from strong drink!"

STEAD

"Stead" is an archaic word for "place," which may denote locality, position, situation, or function. Except for its share in such words as "farmstead" and "homestead," it is now used chiefly in phrases referring to one who is in the place of another, whether as successor, substitute, representative, or agent. "Reigned in his stead" is a phrase which appears seven times in the list of the successive kings of Edom, "before there reigned any king over the children of Israel" (Genesis 36:31–39, KJV), and it recurs like a refrain throughout the books of Kings and Chronicles.

"Dwelt in their stead" (KJV) is used in Deuteronomy 2:12, 21–23 to express what the descendants of Esau and Lot did to the older peoples whom they dispossessed. In another context (1 Chronicles 5:22) the KJV has "dwelt in their steads," although the Hebrew in all these cases has a preposition meaning "instead of." For the same Hebrew expression the KJV has "dwelt in their rooms" in 1 Chronicles 4:41.

Jacob's impatient reply to Rachel, "Am I in God's stead?" (Genesis 30:2, KJV) is now rendered as "Am I in the place of God?" (NASB, NIV, NKJV, NRSV, RSV). "If your soul were in my soul's stead" (Job 16:4, KJV) means simply "if you were in my place" (thus NCV, NIV, NLT, NRSV, RSV).

Elihu was a bold and brash young man, but perhaps not as brash as the words the KJV attributes to him in Job 33:6: "Behold, I am according to thy wish in God's stead." The NRSV translates the verse, "See, before God, I am as you are; I too was formed from a piece of clay."

"Stead" occurs only twice in the KJV New Testament (2 Corinthians 5:20 and Philemon 13). In both cases it renders the preposition which means "on behalf of." "We pray you in Christ's stead" (KJV) is translated by the NASB as "we beg you on behalf of Christ"; and in Paul's letter to Philemon "in thy stead" is "on your behalf" (NASB, NKJV, NLT, RSV).

STILL

As an adverb, "still" is often used today with a sense of "waiting" or "delay" ("are you still waiting to hear about your pay raise?"; "the street light still hasn't been fixed"). In Psalm 84:4, however, the KJV uses the word in the old sense of "continually," "constantly," "habitually," "always": "Blessed are they that dwell in thy house: they will

be still praising thee." The NRSV translates: "Happy are those who live in your house, ever singing your praise." Other contemporary versions have "ever praising You" [NIV, "you"] (NASB, NIV) and "always praising you" (NCV).

Coverdale translated Isaiah 60:11 as "Thy gates shal stonde open still both day and night." The KJV has "thy gates shall be open continually; they shall not be shut day nor night." The NASB reads:

"Your gates will be open continually;
They will not be closed day and night."

Examples from Shakespeare of this sense of "still" are:

"Thou still hast been the father of
  good news."
                  —*Hamlet* (II, 2, 42)

"And then my soul shall wait on thee
  to heaven,
As it on earth hath been thy servant
  still."
               —*King John* (V, 7, 73)

STILL SMALL VOICE

The phrase "a still small voice" is sometimes used in contemporary English to stand for the quiet "voice" of one's conscience, one's inner sense of right and wrong.

The phrase comes from the quiet gentle means with which the Lord spoke to the fearful and discouraged Elijah after he had fled to Horeb following his victory over the false prophets on Mount Carmel. The Lord told Elijah to "Go out, and stand on the mountain before the LORD" (1 Kings 19:11, NKJV). Verse 11 continues, "And behold, the LORD passed by, and a great and strong wind tore into the mountains and broke the rocks in pieces before the LORD, but the LORD was not in the wind; and after the wind an earthquake, but the LORD was not in the earthquake" (NKJV). First Kings 19:12 reads, "And after the earthquake a fire; but the LORD was not in the fire: and after the fire a still small voice" (KJV).

The contemporary versions render the KJV expression "a still small voice" as: "a gentle whisper" (NIV; NLT, "the sound of a gentle whisper"), "a gentle breeze" (CEV), "a sound of a gentle blowing" (NASB), "a quiet, gentle sound" (NCV), and "a sound of sheer silence" (NRSV); the NKJV and RSV retain the KJV expression.

The phrase and passage is alluded to in the hymn by John Greenleaf Whittier (1807–92):

"Breathe through the heats of our
  desire
Thy coolness and Thy balm;
Let sense be dumb—let flesh retire;
Speak through the earthquake,
  wind, and fire,
O still small voice of calm!"

STOMACHER

The word "stomacher" might inspire pictures of thermal body belts or items of figure-shaping lingerie such as girdles and corselets. We would not be completely off-track, however, because a "stomacher" is, in fact, an ornamental covering for the stomach and chest, formerly worn by both men and women, but especially by women under the lacing of a bodice. The term was first used in this sense, and in Isaiah 3:24, by Coverdale. It was a modernization derived from sixteenth-century fashions in women's dress.

The Hebrew word means "a rich robe," and the Greek means "a purple robe." The NKJV, NRSV, and RSV read, "instead of a rich robe, a girding [NRSV, "a binding"] of sackcloth."

STORE

The word "store" in the sense of "an abundant supply" is still current English and is used in contemporary versions of the Bible as well as in the KJV. But it no longer applies naturally to persons, and the statement that Isaac had "great store of servants" (Genesis 26:14, KJV) and reads in the NKJV, "a great

number of servants." The NASB, NRSV, and RSV have "a great household."

Joseph's counsel to Pharaoh, "that food shall be for store to the land" (Genesis 41:36, KJV), is now translated, "that food shall be a reserve for the land" (NRSV, RSV). The promise in Deuteronomy 28:5, "Blessed shall be thy basket and thy store," reads in the NASB, NKJV, and NRSV, "Blessed shall be your basket and your kneading bowl" (cf. 28:17). The Hebrew word which the KJV here renders as "store" appears as "kneadingtrough" in Exodus 8:3 and 12:34. Referring to the downfall of Nineveh, Nahum 2:9 reads in the KJV, "there is none end of the store and glory out of all the pleasant furniture." The NKJV reads:

"There is no end of treasure,
Or wealth of every desirable prize."

STRAIGHT AND NARROW

The phrase "the straight and narrow" is used in contemporary English to refer to a way of righteousness and virtue or a conformity to right behavior.

The phrase derives from Jesus' statement in the Sermon on the Mount: "Enter ye in at the strait gate: for wide is the gate, and broad is the way, that leadeth to destruction, and many there be which go in thereat: Because strait is the gate, and narrow is the way, which leadeth unto life, and few there be that find it" (Matthew 7:13–14, KJV). The contemporary phrase "straight and narrow" derives from verse 14.

The contemporary versions render the KJV "strait" as: "small" (NASB, NCV, NIV, NLT), "narrow" (NKJV, NRSV, RSV), "very narrow" (CEV), and the KJV "narrow" (retained by the NASB, NCV, NIV, and NLT) as "difficult" (NKJV), "hard" (NRSV, RSV), and "hard to follow" (CEV). (See STRAIT)

STRAIN AT A GNAT

The expression in the KJV rendering of Matthew 23:24, "strain at a gnat," has caused some confusion. As an English idiom, "strain at" may mean "to balk or scruple at," "to have scruples," or it may mean "to strive hard for." Tyndale, all other sixteenth-century English versions, and the NASB, NIV, NKJV, and NRSV among contemporary revised versions have "strain out a gnat."

The reason for the KJV rendering is not clear. Bishop Lightfoot and Archbishop Trench were convinced that the "at" was a printer's error, and not the fault of the translators. "We have here," wrote Trench, "an unnoticed, and thus uncorrected, error of the press; which yet, having been once allowed to pass, yielded, or seemed to yield, some sort of sense, and thus did not provoke and challenge correction, as one making sheer nonsense would have done."

On the other hand, the OED gives evidence, from quotations dated 1583 and 1594, that the translators in 1611 may have adopted a phrase that was already current. Its meaning would be "strain (a liquid) at (the sight of) a gnat." If so, the phrase "strain at a gnat" probably was first used colloquially, in oral speech. It did not come from the Bible translations current from 1580 to 1611—the Bishops' Bible, the Geneva Bible, or the Rheims New Testament.

The NLT paraphrases the verse: "Blind guides! You strain your water so you won't accidentally swallow a gnat; then you swallow a camel!" See the OED, under the verb *Strain* (sections 14e, 19, and 21); also Webster's *New International Dictionary*.

STRAIT, STRAITNESS

"Strait" as an adjective means "tight" or "narrow," and as a noun means "a tight or narrow place." Geographically, the noun is applied to any narrow waterway connecting two large bodies of water. Biographically, it may be applied to any tight place or difficult human predicament. The plural noun is often used in a singular sense, as "the Straits of Gibraltar" or "he was in dire straits." As a waterway, "strait" does not appear in the KJV; the nouns "strait" and "straitness" always refer in the KJV to human predicaments.

In 1 Samuel 13:6 the NASB retains the KJV reading "they were in a strait"; the RSV has the Israelites "in straits," while other versions say that they were "in trouble" (NCV), "in danger" (NKJV), "in distress" (NRSV).

Similarly in Job 20:22 "he shall be in straits" is now rendered "he will be cramped" (NASB), and "he will be in distress" (NKJV, NRSV). "Even so would he have removed thee out of the strait into a broad place, where there is no straitness" (Job 36:16, KJV) now reads in the NRSV, "He also allured you out of distress into a broad place where there was no constraint."

Lamentations 1:3, "all her persecutors overtook her between the straits" (KJV), is now translated as "All her pursuers have overtaken her in the midst of distress" (NASB). Other versions render "between the straits" (KJV) as "when she was in trouble" (NIV) and "in dire straits" (NKJV). David's reply to the prophet Gad, "I am in a great strait" (KJV) is now "I am in great distress" (2 Samuel 24:14 and its parallel 1 Chronicles 21:13, NASB, NKJV, NRSV, RSV).

In the Deuteronomic chapter of blessings and curses, the formula "in the siege and in the straitness" (28:53, 55, 57, KJV) is rendered in the RSV as "in the siege and in the distress," while the NKJV and NRSV have "[NKJV, "in the siege and"] in the desperate straits."

Paul's dilemma in Philippians 1:23, "I am in a strait betwixt two" (KJV) is now translated, "I am hard pressed between the two" (NKJV, NRSV, RSV), and "I am hard-pressed from both directions" (NASB); "I am torn between the two" (NIV).

"The strait gate" in Matthew 7:13 (KJV) is translated by the NRSV and RSV as "the narrow gate." In Luke 13:24, the most ancient manuscripts have the Greek words which mean "narrow door." (See STRAIGHT AND NARROW)

The double superlative in Acts 26:5, "the most straitest sect of our religion," is one of Tyndale's special touches. The NASB, NIV, NKJV, NLT, and NRSV read "the strictest sect of our religion." The use of double superlatives was not uncommon in the sixteenth century. Shakespeare wrote:

"With the most boldest and best hearts of Rome."
—Julius Caesar (III, 1, 121)

"This was the most unkindest cut of all."
—Julius Caesar (III, 2, 187)

In *King Lear* (I, 1, 219) Cordelia is spoken of as

"she, that even but now was your best object,
The argument of your praise, balm of your age,
Most best, most dearest."

The editors of *The Folger Library General Reader's Shakespeare* have revised the last line to read: "The best, the dearest."

STRAITEN

The word "straiten" means "to narrow, restrict, hamper, or distress." In Jeremiah 19:9 "shall straiten them" is used for the Hebrew verb which the KJV translates as "shall distress thee" in Deuteronomy 28:53, 55, 57. In Job 12:23 "straiteneth them again" is rendered as "leads them away" by the NASB, NRSV, and RSV.

The passive participle "straitened" appears eight times in the KJV, to represent six different Hebrew and Greek verbs. For "The steps of his strength shall be straitened" (Job 18:7, KJV), the NKJV reads, "The steps of his strength are shortened," and for "When thou goest, thy steps shall not be straitened" (Proverbs 4:12, KJV) it has "When you walk, your steps will not be hindered."

In Ezekiel 42:6, where the KJV has "the building was straitened," the NASB and NRSV read, "the upper chambers were set

back from the ground [NASB, "from the ground upward"]."

In Job 37:1–13, majestic poetry portrays the acts of God as the Lord of winter. Verses 10 and 11 read in the KJV: "By the breath of God frost is given: and the breadth of the waters is straitened. Also by watering he wearieth the thick cloud: he scattereth his bright cloud." The NRSV translates:

"By the breath of God ice is given,
and the broad waters are frozen fast.
He loads the thick cloud with moisture;
the clouds scatter his lightning."

In the other contexts, contemporary versions render the KJV "straitened" with other terms: e.g., "impatient" (NASB, RSV), "angry" (NIV), "restricted" (NKJV), "exhausted" (NRSV) in Micah 2:7 (KJV, "is the spirit of the LORD straitened?"); "distressed" (NASB, NIV, NKJV) and "constrained" (RSV) in Luke 12:50 (KJV, "how I am straitened till it be accomplished"); "restricted" (NKJV, RSV) and "restrained" (NASB) in 2 Corinthians 6:12 (KJV, "Ye are not straitened in us, but ye are straitened in your own bowels").

STRAITLY

The word "straitly" is used in the obsolete sense of "tightly" in the KJV rendering of Joshua 6:1, "Jericho was straitly shut up because of the children of Israel." The NKJV has "securely shut up" and the NASB, NIV, and NLT have "tightly shut [NIV, "tightly shut up"]." In ten other contexts the KJV uses the word in the archaic sense of "strictly." Here it is used in connection with questions, commands, obligations, or warnings.

Contemporary versions have: "questioned us carefully" (Genesis 43:7, NCV, NRSV, RSV); "solemnly sworn" (Exodus 13:19, RSV); "strictly charged" (1 Samuel 14:28, NKJV, NRSV, RSV); "gave strict orders" (Mark 5:43; Acts 5:28, NASB, NCV, NIV); "sternly warned" (Matthew 9:30; Mark 1:43, NASB, NKJV); "strictly ordered" (Mark 3:12, NRSV, RSV).

STRANGE, STRANGER

These are words which we connect today with what is unfamiliar and even questionable. We call a thing "strange" when we mean that it is "odd," "out of the ordinary," or "baffling," and a "stranger" is someone unknown and so likely to put us on our guard. In the KJV, however, the words are used to translate Hebrew words which mean "foreign," "sojourner," "foreigner," "alien," "an outsider." The KJV uses "strange" and "stranger" 301 times, "foreign" and "foreigner" four times; "alien" eight times and "sojourner" eleven times. The contemporary versions make much more frequent use of these latter terms. The RSV, for example, uses "foreigner" eighty-six times and "sojourner" sixty-three times.

Moses' reason for naming his son Gershom, "I have been a stranger in a strange land" (Exodus 2:22, KJV), is translated by the NASB and RSV as "I have been a sojourner (*ger*) in a foreign (*nokri*) land." The NCV, NKJV, and NLT retain "stranger," but have "foreign land" rather than "strange land" (KJV). In the context of the Sabbath commandment, "thy stranger that is within thy gates" (Exodus 20:10; Deuteronomy 5:14, KJV) now reads in the NRSV, "the alien resident in your towns."

"Ye shall have one manner of law, as well for the stranger, as for one of your own country" (Leviticus 24:22, KJV) now reads "You shall have one law for the alien and for the citizen" (NRSV) (cf. Numbers 9:14). The transience of human life is beautifully expressed in the KJV in Psalm 39:12, where two different Hebrew words for "sojourner" are used:

> "Hear my prayer, O LORD, and give
> ear unto my cry; hold not thy peace at
> my tears: for I am a stranger with thee,
> and a sojourner, as all my fathers were.

Contemporary versions render "a stranger . . . and a sojourner" (KJV) as "an alien, a stranger" (NIV), "your guest—a traveler" (NLT), and "your passing guest, an alien" (NRSV).

Ruth's reply to Boaz, "Why have I found grace in thine eyes, that thou shouldest take knowledge of me, seeing I am a stranger?" (Ruth 2:10, KJV) reads in the NRSV, "Why have I found favor in your sight, that you should take notice of me, when I am a foreigner?" Similarly, "foreigner" helps to bring out the full meaning of David's words to Ittai and Ittai's reply in 2 Samuel 15:19–21.

The "strange wives" (Ezra 10) whom Ezra required the men of Judah and Benjamin to put away were "foreign wives" (NASB, NRSV, RSV; CEV, NIV, "foreign women"; "pagan wives").

The Hebrew adjective for "strange" is used in the first line, and that for "foreign" in the second line, of Proverbs 2:16. Here, and in other passages in Proverbs (5:3, 20; 6:24; 7:5; 22:14; 23:27) where both or one appear, the reference is to women of loose sexual behavior. The NKJV translates:

> "To deliver you from the
>   immoral woman,
> From the seductress who flatters
>   with her words."

"Strange incense" (Exodus 30:9, KJV) is rendered as "unholy incense" by the NLT, NRSV, and RSV, and "strange fire" is now rendered as "unauthorized fire" (NIV), "profane fire" (NKJV), and "unholy fire" (NRSV, RSV).

In the part of the law reserving to Aaron and his sons the rights and duties of the priesthood, "a stranger shall not eat thereof" is now rendered as "a layman shall not eat them" (NASB), "no one else may eat them" (NIV), "an outsider shall not eat them" (NKJV, RSV), and "ordinary people may not eat them" (NLT). See also Exodus 30:33 and Leviticus 22:10, 13.

"The stranger that cometh nigh shall be put to death" (Numbers 1:51, KJV) is part of the law defining the rights and duties of the Levites; the NKJV and NRSV have "The [NRSV, "any"] outsider who comes near, shall be put to death." See also Numbers 3:10, 38; 18:4, 7.

The testimony of the woman before Solomon, "there was no stranger with us in the house" (1 Kings 3:18, KJV) means simply "there was no one else with us in the house" (NRSV, RSV).

In two verses of Job 19, the word "strange" (KJV) is a mistaken rendering of the Hebrew. In place of "ye are not ashamed that ye make yourselves strange to me" (19:3), the NRSV and RSV translate with a question, "are you not ashamed to wrong me?" In place of "My breath is strange to my wife, though I intreated for the children's sake of mine own body" (19:17, KJV), the NKJV translates as "My breath is offensive to my wife, and I am repulsive to the children of my own body."

The Hebrew in Deuteronomy 32:27, rendered as "lest their adversaries should behave themselves strangely" by the KJV, is now translated as "Lest their adversaries should misunderstand" (NKJV) and "that their adversaries would misjudge" (NASB).

The comment upon Paul at Athens, "He seemeth to be a setter forth of strange gods" (Acts 17:18, KJV) is now translated as "He seems to be a proclaimer of foreign divinities" (NRSV). In verse 21, "strangers which were there" (KJV) refers to "the foreigners who lived there" (NIV, RSV).

STRANGLED

The letter sent to the Gentiles by "the apostles and elders, with the whole church" in Jerusalem laid upon them "no greater burden than these necessary things: That ye abstain from meats offered to idols, and from blood, and from things strangled, and from fornication" (Acts 15:29, KJV). The same list is stated, in slightly different words, in James's statement of his judgment (15:20) and in the account of Paul's final conference, seven years later, with James and the elders at Jerusalem (21:25).

In all three of these statements, Tyndale has the elliptic expression "from strangled." He was followed by the subsequent sixteenth-century versions except Rheims. The KJV changed to "from things strangled" in the first two statements, but retained Tyndale's phrase in 21:25. Rheims had "from the immolated to idols, and bloud, and suffocateds and fornication."

The NASB reads, "abstain from meat sacrificed to idols and from blood and from what is strangled and from fornication."

STRAWED

"Strawed" is the past tense and past participle of the verb "straw." "Straw" and "strow" are obsolete or archaic verbs which mean the same as "strew." The KJV reports that Moses in anger burnt the golden calf which Aaron had made, "and ground it to powder, and strawed it upon the water, and made the children of Israel drink of it" (Exodus 32:20).

In 2 Chronicles 34:4 Josiah, king of Judah, "brake in pieces" the images his people had been worshiping, "and made dust of them, and strowed it upon the graves of them that had sacrificed unto them" (KJV). Most contemporary versions use "scattered" in the two readings.

When the multitudes welcomed Jesus to Jerusalem, those who "spread their garments in the way" and those who "cut down branches from the trees and strawed them in the way" (KJV) acted alike. The same Greek verb is used for "spread" and "strawed" (Matthew 21:8 and its parallel, Mark 11:8).

A different Greek verb is used in the parable of the talents (Matthew 25:24, 26). "An hard man, reaping where thou hast not sown, and gathering where thou hast not strawed" is translated by the NRSV as "a harsh man, reaping where you did not sow, and gathering where you did not scatter seed."

Shakespeare does not use the verb "straw" or the participle "strawed." He has "strown" once, in *Twelfth Night* (II, 4, 61). "Strew" and "strewed" appear twenty-five times in his plays.

STREETS OF GOLD

The expression "streets of gold" is sometimes used in contemporary English to refer to a city which offers many favorable opportunities to prosper and become wealthy. In Revelation, the vision of the New Jerusalem is that "the street of the city was pure gold" (21:21, KJV).

The NASB, NKJV, and RSV retain the exact wording of the KJV; the other contemporary versions refer to "the great street" (NIV), "the main street" (NLT), "the streets" (CEV).

The expression is alluded to in literature, e.g., Bunyan's *Pilgrim's Progress:* As Christian came near to the heavenly city, he could see that "It was builded of Pearls and Precious Stones, also the Street thereof was paved with Gold"; and George Colman the Younger's *The Heir At Law* has "Oh, London is a fine town, A very famous city, Where all the streets are paved with gold."

STRENGTH

"Strength" means "vigor," "power," or "effective force." The word makes us think of bodybuilding, weight lifting, and the ability to endure under pressure. It is used in these senses many times in the KJV. In Isaiah 40, for example, we read: "He giveth power to the faint: and to them that have no might he increaseth strength . . . they that wait upon the LORD shall renew their strength" (vv. 29, 31).

But on other occasions, the KJV uses the word as translation for the Hebrew noun which means "a place or means of safety," "protection," "refuge"—and so, derivatively, "a stronghold or fortress." In Psalm 28:8 the KJV has "The LORD is their strength, and he is the saving strength of his anointed."

"Saving strength" (KJV) is translated by contemporary versions as "saving defense" (NASB), "fortress of salvation" (NIV), and "saving refuge" (NKJV, NRSV, RSV).

Contemporary versions use terms such

as "strong fortress" (CEV, NASB, NLT) in 2 Samuel 22:33; "refuge" (NIV, NRSV, RSV) in Psalm 31:4 and Nahum 3:11; "stronghold" (NASB, NRSV, RSV) in Proverbs 10:29, Ezekiel 24:25, 30:15, and Joel 3:16; "safe haven" (NLT) in Psalm 43:2; "safety" (NCV) in Isaiah 17:10; and "protection" (NRSV, RSV) in Isaiah 27:5. These versions also generally substitute "helmet" for "strength of mine head" (Psalms 60:7; 108:8, KJV).

The verse in Daniel (11:31) which is cited by Jesus in Matthew 24:15 reads in the KJV: "And arms shall stand on his part, and they shall pollute the sanctuary of strength, and shall take away the daily sacrifice, and they shall place the abomination that maketh desolate."

The NRSV translates it as "Forces sent by him shall occupy and profane the temple and fortress. They shall abolish the regular burnt offering and set up the abomination that makes desolate."

STRIKE HANDS

The expression "strike hands with someone" is used to indicate the giving of a pledge, to become surety for someone. The expression is a Hebraism; the ceremony of striking hands with someone indicated the conclusion of an agreement (cf. our present shaking hands with someone to confirm a promise, deal, etc.).

For example, Job 17:3, "Lay down now, put me in a surety with thee; who is he that will strike hands with me?" (KJV). This is rendered in the contemporary versions as "Lay down, now, a pledge for me with Yourself; Who is there that will be my guarantor?" (NASB), "Now put down a pledge for me with Yourself. Who is he who will shake hands with me?" (NKJV), "Lay down a pledge for me with yourself; who is there that will give surety for me?" (NRSV), "Give me, O God, the pledge you demand. Who else will put up security for me?" (NIV), and "God, make me a promise. No one will make a pledge for me" (NCV).

The expression also occurs in Proverbs,

S

e.g., at 6:1, 17:18; 22:26: "Be not thou one of them that strike hands, or of them that are sureties for debts" (KJV); "Do not be one of those who shakes hands in a pledge, One of those who is surety for debts" (NKJV); "Don't guarantee to pay someone else's debt" (CEV); and "Don't promise to pay what someone else owes, and don't guarantee anyone's loan" (NCV).

STRONG, OUT OF THE, CAME FORTH SWEETNESS

The expression "out of the strong came forth sweetness" is the second half of the riddle posed by Samson, after he passed by the remains of a lion which he had killed with his bare hands (Judges 14:6) and later saw "a swarm of bees and honey in the carcase of the lion" (v. 8, KJV).

At his wedding feast he posed a riddle: "Out of the eater came forth meat, and out of the strong came forth sweetness" (v. 14, KJV). His Philistine listeners could not understand the riddle, but persuaded Samson's wife to trick Samson into telling her its answer. He eventually told her and she went straight to the young men with the answer: "What is sweeter than honey? and what is stronger than a lion?" (v. 18, KJV).

The riddle is rendered by the NRSV as:

> "Out of the eater came something
> to eat.
> Out of the strong came something
> sweet."

The other contemporary versions except the CEV are similar; the CEV has:

> "Once so strong and mighty—
> now so sweet and tasty!"

The answer to the riddle is again similar in all the contemporary versions, except the CEV: "What is sweeter than honey? And what is stronger than a lion?" (NASB); "A lion is the strongest—honey is the sweetest!" (CEV).

John Bunyan wrote in *Grace Abounding to the Chief of Sinners:* "Temptations, when we meet them at first, are as the lion that roared upon Samson; but if we overcome them, the next time we see them, we shall find a nest of honey within them."

STRONG MEAT

If something is "strong meat," it is thought not to be suitable for people who are easily distressed or upset. The expression derives from Hebrews 5:12 (KJV): "For when for the time ye ought to be teachers, ye have need that one teach you again which be the first principles of the oracles of God; and are become such as have need of milk, and not of strong meat."

The Hebrews needed someone to teach them again the "milk" of the elementary truths of God's word. They were not yet ready for the "solid food" (the rendering adopted by all the contemporary versions) of more advanced teaching.

The OED quotes Thomas Carlyle in *Misc., Mirabeau* (1840; V. 139), "But then his style! . . . Strong meat, too tough for babes."

STUDY

The word "study" makes us think of examinations, textbooks, and the discipline necessary for all kinds of academic achievement. But in the KJV the word is not always used in this sense. It can also mean "to endeavor," or "to make it one's aim."

In Ecclesiastes 12:12 the word is used in a familiar sense: contemporary readers are likely to agree that "much study is a weariness of the flesh" (KJV). "Too much study will wear you out" says the CEV, while the NASB reads, "excessive devotion to books is wearying to the body." The KJV uses the verb "study" twice in Proverbs where other contemporary versions have "ponder" (15:28, NASB, NRSV, RSV) and "devise" (24:2, NASB, NKJV, NRSV, RSV). The first of these passages reads in the NRSV:

> "The mind of the righteous ponders
> how to answer,
> but the mouth of the wicked pours
> out evil."

In 2 Timothy 2:15 Paul counsels his young friend: "Study to shew thyself approved unto God, a workman that needeth not to be ashamed, rightly dividing the word of truth" (KJV). The NRSV translates as "Do your best to present yourself to God as one approved by him, a worker who has no need to be ashamed, rightly explaining the word of truth." "Study" is used here by the KJV in the archaic sense of "endeavor" or "set oneself deliberately to do something" (OED).

The Greek verb *spoudazo* is now translated as "Do your best" (NCV, NIV, NRSV, RSV) and "Make every effort" (NASB; KJV "Do thy diligence") in 2 Timothy 4:9; "Try as hard as you can" (NCV; KJV, "Do thy diligence") in 2 Timothy 4:21; "Be diligent" (NKJV; KJV, "Be diligent") in Titus 3:12; "be all the more eager" (NIV, NRSV; KJV, "give diligence") in 2 Peter 1:10; "strive" (NRSV; KJV, "be diligent") in 2 Peter 3:14; "eager" (CEV, NASB, NIV, NKJV, NLT, NRSV, RSV; KJV, "forward") in Galatians 2:10; "making every effort" (NRSV; KJV, "Endeavouring") in Ephesians 4:3; and "do our best" (NLT; KJV, "labour") in Hebrews 4:11.

"Study" (KJV) in 1 Thessalonians 4:11 ("study to be quiet, and to do your own business") represents a different Greek verb *philotimeomai*, which means "to have as one's ambition," "consider it an honor," "aspire." The NASB and NIV have "make it your ambition" and the NKJV, NRSV, and RSV translate it as "aspire." This verb occurs also in Romans 15:20, "I strived" (KJV), and 2 Corinthians 5:9, "we labour" (KJV). (See FORWARD)

STUFF

Today we often use the word "stuff" to refer to belongings, and especially clutter or things of little value ("a loft full of kids' old stuff"; "when are you going to get rid of this stuff?"). But the word's primary meaning is "the material of which something is made" ("cushions filled with soft stuff"). In

the KJV the word occurs most often in the sense of "movable property."

In Joshua 7:11, Israel is said to have taken some of the things to be devoted to destruction, "and put [them] even among their own stuff." The contemporary versions render "stuff" (KJV) here as "belongings" (NRSV), "possessions" (NIV), and "things" (NASB).

Other terms used elsewhere are "goods" (Genesis 31:37, Exodus 22:7, NASB, NIV, NRSV, RSV), "valuables" (Exodus 22:7, CEV), "baggage" (1 Samuel 10:22, CEV, NASB, NCV, NIV, NLT, NRSV, RSV), "supplies" (1 Samuel 25:13, NCV, NIV, NKJV), "equipment" (1 Samuel 30:24, NLT), and "pack" (Ezekiel 12:7, NLT).

"Household stuff" in Nehemiah 13:8 is now rendered as "household goods" (NASB, NIV, NKJV) and "household furniture" (NRSV, RSV).

In the KJV "stuff" appears once in the sense of "the material out of which something is or may be made" (Exodus 36:7). Only the RSV retains it as "the stuff they had was sufficient to do all the work, and more." The NASB and NKJV have "material" instead.

STUMBLING BLOCK

A stumbling block is, literally, a rock or other impediment that is in someone's way and against which if people strike their feet they will stumble or fall. It is in more common use figuratively, and is used to indicate something that is an obstacle, a problem that prevents you from doing something, or something that causes anger, opposition, or sin.

The OED notes that the word was introduced by Tyndale as a rendering of *proskomma*, quoting Romans 14:13. In the KJV this reads: "Let us not therefore judge one another any more: but judge this rather, that no man put a stumblingblock or an occasion to fall in his brother's way."

The contemporary versions render "a stumblingblock or an occasion to fall" as "a stumbling block or hindrance" (NRSV, RSV), "a stumbling block or a cause to fall" (NKJV), "any stumbling block or obstacle"

S

(NIV), and "an obstacle or a stumbling block" (NASB).

The CEV, NCV, and NLT paraphrase the last part of Romans 14:13 as "We must also make up our minds not to upset anyone's faith" (CEV), "We must make up our minds not to do anything that will make another Christian sin" (NCV), and "Decide instead to live in such a way that you will not put an obstacle in another Christian's path" (NLT).

The word "stumbling block" is also used to translate *skandalon,* originally referring to the bait-stick in a trap or snare, e.g., in 1 Corinthians 1:23, "But we preach Christ crucified, unto the Jews a stumblingblock, and unto the Greeks foolishness" (KJV); the NASB, NIV, NKJV, NRSV, and RSV have "stumbling block"; for this phrase the CEV has "Most Jews have problems with this"; the NCV, "This is a big problem to the Jews," and the NLT, "the Jews are offended."

In the Old Testament the word is used in a literal sense in Leviticus 19:14, "Thou shalt not curse the deaf, nor put a stumblingblock before the blind, but shalt fear thy God: I am the LORD" (KJV); the NASB, NIV, NKJV, NRSV, and RSV have "stumbling block"; the CEV has "not . . . to cause a blind person to stumble"; the NCV, "not . . . put something in front of a blind person to make him fall"; the NLT, "not taking advantage of the blind."

This word is used figuratively in Isaiah 57:14, "And shall say, Cast ye up, cast ye up, prepare the way, take up the stumblingblock out of the way of my people" (KJV). The KJV "stumblingblock" is rendered "obstacle" (NASB), "obstacles" (NIV), "obstruction" (NRSV, RSV), "stumbling block" (NKJV), "Make the way clear" (NCV), and "Clear away the rocks and stones" (NLT). See also Ezekiel 14:3–4.

SUBSCRIBE

Today to "subscribe" means "to give one's support or agreement to an opinion or belief"; "to promise to contribute money" (e.g., to a charity); "to pay to receive a periodical regularly" ("subscribe to a magazine"). In

the KJV the word is used in the older sense of "write," or "sign in agreement with a document" (e.g., a deed of purchase).

For example, Jeremiah 32:10, "And I subscribed the evidence, and sealed it, and took witnesses, and weighed him the money in the balances." For the KJV "subscribe" all the contemporary versions have "signed," e.g., "And I signed the deed and sealed it, took witnesses, and weighed the money on the scales" (NKJV). See also Isaiah 44:5; Jeremiah 32:12, 44.

SUBURBS

The word "suburbs" speaks to us of the outer areas of our cities. In the KJV, however, the word "suburbs" is used as translation for the Hebrew word *migrash,* which contemporary versions render with terms such as "pasture fields" (Leviticus 25:34, NASB) and "pasture lands" (Numbers 35:7, NASB, NIV, NRSV).

In Ezekiel 27:28, (KJV, "the suburbs shall shake at the sound of the cry of thy pilots"), "suburbs" is rendered as "shorelands" (NIV), "the shore" (CEV, NCV), and "the cities by the sea" (NLT); the NKJV has "the common-land," the NASB, "pasture lands," and the NRSV and RSV, "the countryside."

In Ezekiel, "suburbs" (KJV) is used for the open country about the holy city and the open space which was to be left around the sanctuary (45:2; 48:15, 17). Contemporary versions generally refer to it by such phrases as "open space," "pastureland," or "commonland."

"Suburbs" is used once by the KJV to represent another Hebrew word, *parwar,* the exact meaning of which is uncertain (2 Kings 23:11). The KJV reads "at the entering in of the house of the LORD, by the chamber of Nathan-melech the chamberlain, which was in the suburbs." The chamber of Nathan-melech could not be at the entrance to the house of the Lord and in the suburbs at the same time and the contemporary versions use "precincts"

(NASB, NRSV, RSV). This chamber was in the precincts of the house of the Lord.

SUCCOUR

This word is derived through French from the Latin verb *succurro,* "run to the aid of," and means "help," "aid," "assist." It is used in 2 Samuel in military contexts, and contemporary versions replace it with "help" (8:5), "send us help" (18:3, NRSV, RSV; NIV, "give us support"), "came to his aid" (21:17, NKJV, NRSV, RSV).

"Succour" is used in the sense of "moral and spiritual help" in Hebrews 2:18 ("Because he himself was tested by what he suffered, he is able to help those who are being tested," NRSV) and in 2 Corinthians 6:2 ("on the day of salvation I helped you," NASB, NCV). The latter clause is a quotation from Isaiah 49:8; the KJV uses "succoured" in Hebrews but "helped" in Isaiah.

Romans 16:1–2 reads in the KJV: "I commend unto you Phebe our sister, which is a servant of the church which is at Cenchrea: that ye receive her in the Lord, as becometh saints, and that ye assist her in whatsoever business she hath need of you: for she hath been a succourer of many, and of myself also."

The NASB and NKJV refer to Phoebe as "a helper of many"; the NRSV, as "a benefactor of many." Contemporary versions render "servant" here as "leader" (CEV), "helper" (NCV), and "deacon" [RSV, "deaconess"] (NRSV, RSV).

We know nothing about Phoebe except what these verses imply. She must have been a person of some wealth and position, a resident of the eastern seaport of Corinth, where she could afford aid and hospitality to Paul and others as they made the journey by sea between Corinth and Ephesus. The Geneva Bible, indeed, translates the last clause, "for she hath gyuen hospitalitie unto many, and to me also." Tyndale had "she hath suckered many," and this was retained in the Great Bible and the Bishops' Bible.

The KJV translators followed the Greek more closely, which states that "she has been a *prostatis* of many and of myself." The word is the feminine form of *prostates,* which means "leader," "protector," "guardian," "patron," even "ruler" or "administrator." Arndt and Gingrich translate as "she has been of great assistance to many, including myself."

SUCH A ONE

This expression appears three times and "such an one" ten times in the KJV. Except for the inconsistent use of "a" and "an," the phrase causes no trouble when it refers to a person or thing just mentioned or when it is defined by a subsequent clause.

Contemporary versions' use of the phrase includes Job 14:3 (NIV, NKJV, NRSV, RSV) and 1 Corinthians 5:11 (NASB, NRSV, RSV). For "thou thoughtest that I was altogether such an one as thyself," the NASB has "you thought that I was just like you" (Psalm 50:21).

For "Let such an one think this, that, such as we are in word by letters when we are absent, such will we be also in deed when we are present," The NRSV has "Let such people understand that what we say by letter when absent, we will also do when present" (2 Corinthians 10:11).

The phrase "such a one" can be used without qualification, as an archaic equivalent of "so-and-so," to designate someone whose name is not mentioned. It is so used by the RSV in Matthew 26:18 ("a certain one").

But it is not an appropriate form of direct address, as seems to be implied when Boaz called to his fellow kinsman of Ruth, "Ho, such a one! turn aside, sit down here" (Ruth 4:1, KJV). There is no word for "Ho" in the Hebrew, which has two words to express the fact that Boaz definitely indicated whom he was addressing, but did not use his name. It was a friendly greeting, not a challenge.

The NASB and RSV translate his words as "Turn aside, friend; sit down here"; the NKJV has "Come aside, friend," the NIV, "Come over here, my friend," and the NLT, Come over here, friend."

SUCHLIKE

Printed as one word, "suchlike" is recognized as old but still living English by the OED and Webster. The OED quotes its use in the eleventh edition of the *Encyclopedia Britannica,* and *Webster* its use by Henry James. In the KJV it is printed as two words. The word of the Lord by the prophet Ezekiel assures freedom from a father's iniquity to a son "that seeth all his father's sins which he hath done, and considereth, and doeth not such like" (Ezekiel 18:14, KJV). The NASB, NKJV, NRSV, and RSV have "does not do likewise."

The second half of Mark 7:8 is not in the ancient manuscripts, but the last clause of 7:13 reads in the KJV, "and many such like things do ye," which the NKJV rewords, "and many other such things you do." In Galatians 5:21, for "and such like" the NIV, NKJV, and NRSV have "and the like."

SUDDENLY

This word is likely to make us think of a surprise or unexpected development: a water pipe might suddenly burst or a boyfriend might suddenly propose. On one occasion in the KJV, however, "suddenly" is used in the obsolete sense of "hastily." "Lay hands suddenly on no man" (1 Timothy 5:22) warns Paul.

The "laying on of hands" referred to here was the gesture of ordination (see 1 Timothy 4:14; 2 Timothy 1:6), and Paul's advice is now rendered as "Do not be hasty" (NIV), "Don't be too quick" (CEV), "Never be in a hurry" (NLT); the NRSV reads, "Do not ordain anyone hastily."

SUFFER

The word "suffer" is used by the KJV in two quite distinct senses. It is used, of course, to translate the Hebrew and Greek verbs which mean "to endure hardship, pain, affliction, insult, penalty," and so on. There are sixty-nine cases of this use, which is the primary sense of the word. But it is also used sixty times to translate Hebrew and Greek verbs which mean "to let, allow, or permit."

Contemporary versions do not use the word "suffer" in the sense of "let" or "permit," and retain it only when it is used in the sense of "undergo" or "endure." Matthew 19:14 reads in the KJV, "But Jesus said, Suffer little children, and forbid them not, to come unto me: for of such is the kingdom of heaven." The CEV translates Jesus' words as "Let the children come to me, and don't try to stop them! People who are like these children belong to God's kingdom."

Jesus' rebuke in Mark 9:19, "O faithless generation, how long shall I be with you? how long shall I suffer you?" (KJV) is now rendered as "how long shall [NCV, "must"] I put up with you?" (NASB, NCV, NIV) and "How long shall I bear with you" (NKJV). (See LET)

SUFFER FOOLS GLADLY

A person who "does not suffer fools gladly" is impatient and unsympathetic toward foolish people. The expression derives from 2 Corinthians 11:19: "For ye suffer fools gladly, seeing ye yourselves are wise" (KJV). The Corinthians thought themselves to be wise and so respected and submitted themselves naively to false teachers.

The contemporary versions render this verse as "you gladly put up with fools" (NIV, NRSV), "you put up with fools gladly" (NKJV), "you will gladly put up with a fool" (CEV), "you gladly bear with fools" (RSV), "you . . . tolerate the foolish gladly" (NASB), "you will gladly be patient with fools!" (NCV), and "you . . . enjoy listening to fools!" (NLT).

SUFFICIENT UNTO THE DAY IS THE EVIL THEREOF

The saying "sufficient unto the day is the evil thereof," sometimes shortened to "sufficient unto the day," means that "anything unpleasant will be quite difficult enough to bear when it happens without worrying about it beforehand" (*Oxford Dictionary of Current Idiomatic English,* vol. 2).

The expression derives from Jesus' statement in the Sermon on the Mount: "Take therefore no thought for the morrow: for the morrow shall take thought for the things of itself. Sufficient unto the day is the evil thereof" (Matthew 6:34, KJV).

This is rendered by the contemporary versions as "Each day has enough trouble of its own" (NASB, NCV, NIV); "Today's trouble is enough for today" (NLT, NRSV), "Let the day's own trouble be sufficient for the day" (RSV); "You have enough to worry about today"; (CEV); and "Sufficient for the day is its own trouble" (NKJV).

The expression is alluded to in literature. For example, in Trollope's *Barchester Towers,* Charlotte Stanhope says to her brother Bertie, "I look forward to the time when the governor must go. Mother, and Madeline, and I,—we shall be poor enough, but you will have absolutely nothing." "Sufficient for the day is the evil thereof," said Bertie. Galsworthy in *To Let* (1921) has "He never looks happy—not really happy. I don't want to make him worse, but of course I shall have to, when Jon comes back. Oh! well, sufficient unto the night!" (See also TOMORROW WILL TAKE CARE OF ITSELF)

SUN GO DOWN ON ONE'S ANGER

The expression "do not let the sun go down on your anger (or: wrath)" means that you should not carry your anger over from one day to the next. The expression comes from Ephesians 4:26: "Be ye angry, and sin not: let not the sun go down upon your wrath" (KJV).

The contemporary versions render this as "do not let the sun go down on your anger" [NKJV, "your wrath"] (NASB, NKJV, NRSV, RSV), "Do not [NLT, "Don't"] let the sun go down while you are still angry" (NIV, NLT), "Don't go to bed angry" (CEV; Phillips has "Never go to bed angry"), and "be sure to stop being angry before the end of the day" (NCV).

SUPPLE

The word "supple" makes us think of hand creams and pliable dough mixture. We only rarely use the word as a verb, and this form appears only once in the KJV. Ezekiel 16:4 reads, "in the day thou wast born thy navel was not cut, neither wast thou washed in water to supple thee." Only the KJV adopted this rendering. All but one of the sixteenth-century English versions had "to make thee clean." The Geneva Bible had "to soften thee," which the KJV changed to "supple."

The meaning of the Hebrew word is uncertain, and so is its authenticity. There is nothing corresponding to it in the Vaticanus Codex of the Septuagint, or in the Syriac. It may be an explanatory gloss that got into the text. German translations from Luther down and most contemporary translations agree that the idea is "for cleansing" or "to cleanse you."

SURELY

This word appears 266 times in the Old Testament, and in 140 of these cases there is no corresponding Hebrew word. The KJV translators commonly used "surely" to express the emphasis or intensity of meaning that is expressed in the Hebrew by repetition, which in the case of verbs consists of the absolute infinitive plus a finite form. (See GENERALLY)

Some contemporary versions omit the "surely" in these cases, since in modern English it can weaken rather than strengthen the statement. The NRSV and RSV, for example, have "you shall die" (Genesis 2:17); "You will not die" (Genesis 3:4); "Abraham shall become a great and mighty nation" (Genesis 18:18); "shall be put to death" (Exodus 21:12, 15, 16–17).

On the other hand, they retain "surely" in some contexts, as in Joseph's reception of his brothers, "surely you are spies" (Genesis 42:16), and in the Lord's answer to David, "you shall surely overtake and shall surely rescue" (1 Samuel 30:8).

In the injunction to give to the poor, "Thou shalt surely give him" (Deuteronomy 15:10, KJV), most contemporary versions replace "surely" by "freely" (NCV, NLT, RSV), "generously" (NASB, NIV), and "liberally" (NRSV).

David's answer to Nathan's parable of the rich man who caught and killed the poor man's single ewe lamb was "As the LORD lives, the man who has done this thing shall surely die," which the CEV, NASB, NIV, NLT, NRSV, and RSV translate as "deserves to die" (2 Samuel 12:5). The Hebrew idiom is the same as in 1 Samuel 26:16, which the KJV translates as "ye are worthy to die" and the NIV, NKJV, NLT, NRSV, and RSV, "you deserve to die." Contemporary versions begin Job 13:3 with a strong adversative "But" rather than "Surely" (KJV).

Instead of "those things which are most surely believed among us" (Luke 1:1, KJV), the NIV and NRSV translate the Greek, in accordance with evidence in the papyri, "the things that have been fulfilled among us." Other contemporary versions offer similar renderings.

SURFEITING

A surfeit of anything is too much of it. In the sixteenth century the word was often used as an intransitive verb meaning "to overindulge in something." The word was applied particularly to excessive eating or drinking, to the consequent sickness or nausea, and to the resulting disgust or loathing. It was a natural translation for the Greek *kraipale*, which stands for "carousing," "intoxication," and the subsequent headache and hangover. It appears in Luke 21:34: "Take heed to yourselves lest at any time your hearts be overcharged with surfeiting, and drunkenness, and cares of this life" (KJV).

Because "surfeiting" is now obsolete in this sense, the NASB, NIV, NRSV, and RSV use "dissipation" and the NKJV has "carousing." The primary reference of *kraipale* is to excessive drinking and its effects, but some contemporary versions draw on the idea of

"gluttony" and use "eating" (CEV) and "feasting" (NCV) in their translations.

Shakespeare used the word "surfeiting." The opening lines of Shakespeare's *Twelfth Night* are:

"If music be the food of love, play on;
Give me excess of it, that, surfeiting,
The appetite may sicken, and so die."

The Archbishop of York, in *King Henry IV, Part II* (IV, 1, 55), says:

"we are all diseased,
And with our surfeiting and wanton hours
Have brought ourselves into a burning fever."

SWEAT OF THY BROW

The expression "sweat of thy brow" is used to refer to wearisome toil that was a consequence of the fall. The expression derives from the KJV expression "the sweat of thy face" from Genesis 3:19, "In the sweat of thy face shalt thou eat bread" (KJV).

The contemporary versions render this as "By [NKJV, "In"] the sweat of your face [NIV, "brow"] you shall eat bread" (NIV, NKJV, NRSV), "You will have to sweat to earn a living" (CEV), "You will sweat and work hard for your food" (NCV), and "All your life you will sweat to produce food" (NLT).

The expression is alluded to in literature, e.g., Robert Southey *Essays* (1832): "When he receives his daily wages for the sweat of his brow" and John Ruskin, *Sesame and Lilies* (1865, 1871): "No true workmen will ever tell you, that they have found the law of heaven an unkind one—that in the sweat of their face they should eat their bread, till they return to the ground."

SWELL, SWELLING

These words, in reference to bodily ills, are retained by contemporary versions. But in "a breach ready to fall, swelling out in a high wall" (Isaiah 30:13, KJV), they generally use "bulge" and "bulging."

"The swelling of Jordan" (Jeremiah 12:5; 49:19; 50:44, KJV) represents a Hebrew phrase which the KJV elsewhere translates "the pride of Jordan" (Zechariah 11:3). It does not refer to a swelling flood of water in the Jordan river, but to the lush, rank vegetation on its banks. This was the habitat of lions. It is now known as the jungle of the Jordan, and contemporary versions refer to it as "the forest" (CEV), "the thicket" and "the thickets" (NASB, NIV, NLT, NRSV), "the floodplain" (NKJV), and "the jungle" (RSV).

Jeremiah 12:5 reads in the KJV: "If thou hast run with the footmen, and they have wearied thee, then how canst thou contend with horses? and if in the land of peace, wherein thou trustedst, they wearied thee, then how wilt thou do in the swelling of Jordan?" In the NRSV it reads:

"If you have raced with foot-runners
    and they have wearied you,
how will you compete with horses?

And if in a safe land you fall down,
    how will you fare in the thickets of
        the Jordan?"

In 2 Peter 2:18, "when they speak great swelling words of vanity" (KJV), contemporary versions have "arrogant words of vanity" (NASB), "empty, boastful words" (NIV), and "bombastic nonsense" (NRSV). In Jude 16 "and their mouth speaketh great swelling words" now reads, "they boast about themselves" (NIV) and "they are bombastic in speech" (NRSV).

In 2 Corinthians 12:20 we find a list of faults which Paul frankly says that he fears he may find in the church at Corinth. Most of the words in this list are used in an archaic sense. The KJV has "debates, envyings, wraths, strifes, backbitings, whisperings, swellings, tumults."

The NRSV and RSV have "quarreling, jealousy, anger, selfishness, slander, gossip, conceit, and disorder."

T

TABERING

"Taber" was the old name for "a drum," and the verb "taber" means "to beat as upon a drum." It occurs once in the KJV, in Nahum 2:6–7: "The gates of the rivers shall be opened, and the palace shall be dissolved. And Huzzab shall be led away captive, she shall be brought up, and her maids shall lead her as with the voice of doves, tabering upon their breasts." Contemporary versions render "tabering" here as "beat" and "beating." The NRSV translates:

"The river gates are opened,
    the palace trembles.
It is decreed that the city be exiled,
    its slave women led away,
moaning like doves
    and beating their breasts."

There is uncertainty at some points in this passage, but the last line is not one of them. The lamenting women, beating their breasts, are a natural part of the picture.

TABLE

The word "table" is likely to remind us of Thanksgiving dinners and the heavy, carved table in grandma's kitchen. As an item of furniture, the word appears several times in the KJV—for example in Psalm 23:5, "Thou preparest a table before me in the presence of mine enemies." But the KJV also uses the word for the two "tables of stone" (KJV) given to Moses on Mount Sinai.

Contemporary versions generally use "tablets," except for the RSV and on occasion the NASB which retain "tables" (Exodus 24, 31–32, 34; Deuteronomy 4, 5, 9, 10; 1 Kings 8:9; 2 Chronicles 5:10; Hebrews 9:4). (The CEV has "stones" or "flat stones" for KJV "tables of stone.") The KJV also uses "table" to refer to a portable tablet, of whatever material, upon which to write.

Zechariah, unable to speak, asked for "a writing table" (Luke 1:63, KJV). The word to Habakkuk is, "Write the vision; make it plain upon tables, that he may run that readeth it" (2:2, KJV). The injunction concerning the commandments and teachings of Proverbs is to "write them upon the table of thine heart" (3:3; 7:3, KJV). The sin of Judah, says Jeremiah, "is graven upon the table of their heart" (17:1, KJV). In all these instances, the contemporary versions generally have "tablets."

Paul, in 2 Corinthians 3:2–3, tells the Corinthians that he needs no recommendation to them. The NRSV translates as "You yourselves are our letter, written on our hearts, to be known and read by all; and you show that you are a letter of Christ, prepared by us, written not with ink but with the Spirit of the living God, not on tablets of stone but on tablets of human hearts."

In Mark 7:4, the evangelist explains to his non-Jewish readers the reasons for the Pharisees' scruples over eating with unwashed hands: "They . . . follow a lot of other teachings, such as washing cups, pitchers, and bowls" (CEV). Some Greek manuscripts add "dining couches" to this list. The KJV reads "cups, and pots, brasen vessels, and . . . tables"; the NKJV, "cups, pitchers, copper vessels, and couches."

TABLET

In contemporary English, a "tablet" has a number of meanings, including "a pill," "a small flat piece of something," and "a small flat plate on which to write, paint, etc." In the KJV, however, the word is used to refer to a necklace, locket, or a box of perfume. The word occurs twice with the meaning "necklace": at Exodus 35:22 and Numbers 31:50 and once with the meaning of "box of perfume," at Isaiah 3:20.

At the first two references, the contemporary versions render the KJV "tablets" as "necklaces" (both references in the NKJV,

NLT; CEV at Exodus 35:22; NASB, NCV, and NIV at Numbers 31:50); "pendants" (NRSV at both references); "bracelets" (NASB, NCV at Exodus 35:22); "ornaments" (NIV at Exodus 35:22); "armlets" (RSV at Exodus 35:22); and "beads" (RSV at Numbers 31:50).

In Isaiah 3:20, the KJV "tablets" is rendered in the contemporary versions as follows: "perfume boxes" (NASB, NKJV, NRSV, RSV), "perfume bottles" (NIV), "bottles of perfume" (NCV), "perfumes" (NLT), and "perfume" (CEV), though the precise meaning of the Hebrew phrase remains uncertain.

TABRET

This is the diminutive of "taber," thus "a small drum," "timbrel," or "tambourine." The KJV uses "tabret" and "timbrel" as translations of the Hebrew *toph;* the contemporary versions use "tambourine" and "timbrel." "Tabrets" and "pipes" (KJV) in Ezekiel 28:13 are rendered as "settings and sockets" by the NASB, and as "settings and . . . engravings" by the NRSV and RSV.

In Job 17:6, "I was as a tabret" (KJV) is now "I am one before whom people spit" (NRSV). (See AFORETIME, where this reading is explained)

TACHE

"Tache" is an obsolete word for "a means of fastening two parts together," such as a clasp, a buckle, a hook and eye. The word "tack" originally had the same meaning, and both are related to "attach" and "detach." "Tache" (KJV) is used in Exodus for the clasps of gold that fitted into loops on the curtains of the tabernacle to join them together, and for the clasps of bronze that joined together the curtains of its tent. The arrangement is described in chapters 26 and 36.

"Taches of gold" (Exodus 26:6, KJV) are now rendered as "clasps of gold" (NASB, NKJV, NRSV, RSV) and "gold hooks" (NCV).

TACKLING

This is an obsolete term for "the rigging or tackle of a ship." It appears in Luke's account of Paul's shipwreck (Acts 27:18–19), where the NASB reads, "as we were being violently storm-tossed, they began to jettison the cargo; and on the third day they threw the ship's tackle overboard with their own hands." A more obscure passage is Isaiah 33:23, which reads in the NRSV:

"Your rigging [KJV, "Thy tacklings"] hangs loose;
it cannot hold the mast firm in its place,
or keep the sail spread out."

TAKE SOMEONE'S NAME IN VAIN

See NAME IN VAIN.

TAKEN WITH THE MANNER

This expression means, in the KJV, "taken in the act." The "law of jealousies" recorded in Numbers 5:11–31 begins with the hypothetical case of a wife's infidelity, if "there be no witness against her, neither she be taken with the manner." The phrase "taken with the manner" goes back to Tyndale, and was passed on through the other sixteenth-century translations to the KJV.

The word here is "mainour," an Anglo-French term which as early as Tyndale's day had begun to be spelled "maner" or "manner." The phrase "taken with the mainour" meant, in the case of a thief, "taken with the stolen property in his possession"; and in the case of others, "taken in the act of doing something unlawful."

In Shakespeare's *King Henry IV, Part I* (II, 4, 322), Prince Hal says to Bardolph: "O villain, thou stolest a cup of sack eighteen years ago, and wert taken with the manner." In *Love's Labour's Lost* (I, 1, 205), Costard admits his approach to Jaquenetta: "The matter of it is, I was taken with the manner . . . I was seen with her in the manor-house, sitting with her upon the form, and taken following her into the park."

"Mainour" is related to "manoeuvre," and the question whether it originally meant a stolen thing or an unlawful act is still open.

There is an interesting discussion, with plenty of illustrative material, in the OED. Both there and in Webster, the reader should look up "mainour" rather than "manner."

TALE

In the numerical sense, the word "tale" means "the complete number or amount." It has this meaning in two notable occurrences in the KJV: "the tale of bricks" which Pharaoh daily required the people of Israel to make (Exodus 5:8, 18), and the two hundred Philistine foreskins which David presented "in full tale" to King Saul, that he might marry the king's daughter (1 Samuel 18:27).

Contemporary versions have "number" (CEV, NCV, NIV, RSV), "quota" (NASB, NKJV, NLT), and "quantity" (NRSV) in Exodus 5:8, and "number" (NASB, NIV, NRSV, RSV) and "count" (NKJV) in 1 Samuel 18:27. The KJV says that certain of the Levites "had the charge of the ministering vessels" of the house of God, "that they should bring them in and out by tale" (1 Chronicles 9:28). The NRSV translates as "Some of them had charge of the utensils of service, for they were required to count them when they were brought in and taken out."

In the sense of a story or narrative, "tale" appears in the KJV only as part of the word "talebearer." This is retained by the NASB, NKJV, and RSV in Proverbs 11:13, but elsewhere is replaced by "whisperer" (Proverbs 18:8; 26:20, 22, NASB, NRSV, RSV), "gossip" (Proverbs 11:13, CEV, NCV, NIV, NLT, NRSV), and "slanderer" (Leviticus 19:16, NASB, NRSV, RSV).

Coverdale's rendering of Psalm 90:9 is retained in the Book of Common Prayer: "we bring our years to an end, as it were a tale that is told." The KJV has "we spend our years as a tale that is told." Just what Coverdale meant by the last five words is uncertain; he may have meant a sum that is counted, or a story that is told. The Hebrew means "we bring our years to an end like a sigh."

The Greek Septuagint and Latin Vulgate have the equivalent of "our years are spent like a cobweb." Martin Luther's rendering was *wir bringen unsere Jahre zu wie ein Geschwätz*—"we bring our years to an end like empty talk." It may be that Coverdale got from Luther the idea for "a tale that is told."

Most contemporary versions have "as a sigh" or "like a sigh" (CEV, NASB, NKJV, NRSV, RSV); the NIV has "with a moan" and the NLT has "with a groan."

Knox had "swift as a breath our lives pass away," and J. M. P. Smith, "our years are like a cobweb wiped away."

TALENT

In contemporary English a "talent" is "a special ability, gift, or skill." In the KJV, however, a "talent" was "a measure of weight, equal to 3,000 shekels" (about 34 kilograms, 75 pounds). It was used to weigh gold, silver, and bronze and was also employed as a form of currency. Of the contemporary versions, the NASB, NIV, NKJV, NRSV, and RSV retain the name of the weight as in the KJV; the CEV, NCV, and NLT render the amount in modern weights in the main Bible text.

For example, gifts toward work on the temple (1 Chronicles 29:7): "of gold five thousand talents and ten thousand drams, and of silver ten thousand talents, and of brass eighteen thousand talents, and one hundred thousand talents of iron" (KJV) is rendered as "5,000 talents and 10,000 darics of gold, and 10,000 talents of silver, and 18,000 talents of brass, and 100,000 talents of iron" by the NASB and "five thousand talents and ten thousand darics of gold, ten thousand talents of silver, eighteen thousand talents of bronze, and one hundred thousand talents of iron" by the NKJV; similarly the NIV and NRSV have the numbers spelled out in words rather than as numerals.

The CEV has "almost two hundred tons of gold, three hundred eighty tons of silver, almost seven hundred tons of bronze, and three thousand seven hundred fifty tons of iron"; the NCV, "about three hundred eighty thousand pounds of gold, about seven hundred fifty thousand pounds of silver, about one million three hundred fifty thousand pounds of bronze, and about seven million five hundred thousand pounds of iron to the Temple of God"; and the NLT, "almost 188 tons of gold, 10,000 gold coins, about 375 tons of silver, about 675 tons of bronze, and about 3,750 tons of iron."

By the time of the New Testament the talent was adopted as the name of a coin. In Matthew 28:24 in Jesus' parable of the unmerciful servant, the servant owes "ten thousand talents" (KJV) to the king. The NASB, NIV, NKJV, NRSV, and RSV retain the KJV amount; the NCV has "several million dollars," the NLT, "millions of dollars," and the CEV, "fifty million silver coins."

In Jesus' parable of the talents (Matthew 25:14–30), the three servants are given "five talents," "three talents," and "one talent" (v. 15, KJV, NASB, NKJV, NRSV, RSV; the NIV has "five talents of money"); the NCV and NLT have "bags of gold" (five, two, and one) and the CEV, "five thousand coins . . . two thousand . . . and one thousand."

In Revelation 16:21 the KJV has "And there fell upon men a great hail out of heaven, every stone about the weight of a talent: and men blasphemed God because of the plague of the hail; for the plague thereof was exceeding great." For the KJV "about the weight of a talent" (retained by the NKJV), the contemporary versions have "about a [NASB, "about one"] hundred pounds" (CEV, NASB, NCV, NIV, NRSV), "weighing seventy-five pounds" (NLT), and "heavy as a hundredweight" (RSV).

TARGET

While "target" makes us think today of aims and objectives ("a sales target") and missile attacks, in the KJV "target" refers to a light shield or buckler: "King Solomon made two hundred targets of beaten gold: six hundred shekels of gold went to one target" (1 Kings 10:16 and its parallel, 2 Chronicles 9:15); "Asa had an army of men that bare targets and spears" (2 Chronicles 14:8).

The Hebrew word is *tsinnah*. With the exception of the RSV, contemporary versions use "shields" in both passages. The RSV uses "shields" for Solomon's display and "bucklers" for the men of Asa's army. (See BUCKLER)

The KJV uses "target" once as translation for the Hebrew word *kidon*. It says that Goliath had "a target of brass between his shoulders" (1 Samuel 17:6). The contemporary versions generally have "javelin"; the NCV has "spear" and the CEV, "sword."

The target of concentric circles for shooting and the figurative use of the word are fairly recent developments in English. They were not common before the nineteenth century. Robin Hood's men shot at a "butt," and we still use this term in referring to a person who is a target for ridicule.

Contemporary versions use "target" in Job 16:12, which reads in the KJV, "he hath . . . set me up for his mark." The NRSV has "He set me up as his target."

TEACH, TEACHER, TEACHING

The verb *didasko* appears ninety-seven times in the Greek New Testament and is always translated as "teach." It is used more often than any other verb to describe what Jesus did throughout his ministry.

The four Gospels all portray Jesus as a teacher (*didaskalos*). People spoke of him as such, and they addressed him as "Teacher." The KJV, however, represents the Gospels as applying the word "teacher" to Jesus only once. This is because it used the English word "master" as a translation for the Greek word for "teacher" in forty-one other cases where this word is applied to Jesus.

This overwhelming preference of the KJV for the word "master" simply reflects the usage in schools in Britain, where teachers were called "masters." (See MASTER)

The word "doctor" originally meant "teacher," and it is so used three times in the KJV. When Jesus' parents "found him in the temple, sitting in the midst of the doctors" (Luke 2:46, KJV), he was "sitting among the teachers" (NIV, NRSV, RSV). The expression "doctor of the law" (Luke 5:17; Acts 5:34, KJV) stands for the Greek word *nomodidaskalos*, which means "teacher of the law." In 1 Timothy 1:7 the KJV itself translates the plural of *nomodidaskalos* as "teachers of the law."

In 1611, the word "doctrine" denoted the act of teaching as well as the content of teaching. "He said unto them in his doctrine" (Mark 4:2; 12:38, KJV) means "He said to them in His teaching" (NKJV). This sense of the word is now obsolete, and the revised versions use "teaching" more often than "doctrine."

In Proverbs 6:13, "teach" is used by the KJV in the sense of "to show or point out." "He speaketh with his feet, he teacheth with his fingers" is part of the quaint description of "a naughty person" (vv. 12–13). The second of these verbs means to "throw," "shoot," "direct," "point out," "show," and hence "teach"; contemporary versions render it as "points" (NASB, NKJV, RSV. NRSV, "pointing"), "making signs" (NCV, NLT), and "motions" (NIV).

The KJV rendering of the description is: "A naughty person, a wicked man, walketh with a froward mouth. He winketh with his eyes, he speaketh with his feet, he teacheth with his fingers; Frowardness is in his heart, he deviseth mischief continually; he soweth discord." The NRSV translates verses 12–14 as:

> "A scoundrel and a villain
> goes around with crooked speech,
> winking the eyes, shuffling the feet,
> pointing the finger,
> with perverted mind devising evil,
> continually sowing discord."

(See NAUGHTINESS, NAUGHTY)

T

TEETH SET ON EDGE

The proverb "The fathers have eaten a sour grape, and the children's teeth are set on edge" (Jeremiah 31:29–30, KJV) and also Ezekiel 18:2 (except in Ezekiel the KJV has "eaten sour grapes") was a proverb that expressed the fact that God's judgment was not imposed on Judah because of their own sins but rather was a consequence of their father's sins.

The CEV renders Jeremiah 31:29 as "Sour grapes eaten by parents leave a sour taste in the mouths of their children," the NCV as "The parents have eaten sour grapes, and that caused the children to grind their teeth from the sour taste," and the NLT as "The parents eat sour grapes, but their children's mouths pucker at the taste"; the other contemporary versions retain the expression "sour grapes" and "set on edge."

The prophets Jeremiah and Ezekiel emphasized individual responsibility: Jeremiah 31:30, "But every one shall die for his own iniquity: every man that eateth the sour grape, his teeth shall be set on edge" (KJV); rendered by the NCV as "Instead each person will die for his own sin; the person who eats sour grapes will grind his own teeth." See also Ezekiel 18:20; 33:7–18. (See SINS OF THE FATHERS)

TELL

Today, the word "tell" can mean to "narrate" or "judge." "Tell me a story" a child might ask, but not be able to tell that her granddad is too sleepy for the task. In the KJV the expression "cannot tell," meaning "do not know," occurs nine times. We also find "tell" used eight times in the archaic sense of "number" or "count."

In the word of the Lord to Abram, "Look now toward heaven, and tell the stars, if thou be able to number them" (KJV), the same Hebrew verb is translated "tell" and "number," and in both cases it means "count" (Genesis 15:5). "They told the money" (2 Kings 12:10, KJV) is in most of the contemporary versions translated as "[they] counted the money."

"I may tell all my bones" (Psalm 22:17, KJV) is now "I can count all my bones." "Walk about Zion, and go round about her: tell the towers thereof" (Psalm 48:12, KJV) now reads, "count her towers" (NASB, NIV, NKJV) and "number her towers" (RSV). Other occurrences are in 2 Chronicles 2:2; Psalms 56:8; 147:4; Jeremiah 33:13.

An example of Shakespeare's use of "tell" for "count" is in *Hamlet* (I, 2, 238), where Hamlet asks concerning the ghost, "Stay'd it long?" and Horatio answers, "While one with moderate haste might tell a hundred."

In Milton's *L'Allegro*, the picture of dawn and early morning in the country includes:

"While the ploughman, near at hand,
Whistles o'er the furrowed land,
And the milkmaid singeth blithe,
And the mower whets his scythe,
And every shepherd tells his tale
Under the hawthorn in the dale."

The last lines do not mean that the shepherd is an idle storyteller, but that he is counting his sheep as they come from the fold.

On nine occasions in the KJV we find the verbal expression "cannot [or "could not" or "canst not"] tell," meaning "do not know." The KJV New Testament translates the Greek verb *oida* by the English verb "know" 280 times. But in these cases it translates *oida*, used with a negative, by "cannot tell."

Three of the passages are Matthew 21:27 (and its parallels, Mark 11:33 and Luke 20:7), the answer of the Pharisees to Jesus' question concerning the baptism of John. Three are in the Gospel of John: 3:8, addressed to Nicodemus; 8:14, addressed to the Pharisees; 16:18, the puzzled comment of the disciples, "We cannot tell what he saith." Three are in 2 Corinthians 12:2–3, Paul's statement concerning his visions and revelations.

These nine cases of "cannot tell" come from the translation by William Tyndale, and appear also in Coverdale, Thomas Matthew, the Great Bible, the Geneva Bible, and the Bishops' Bible. They are examples of Tyndale's lively and occasionally wayward style. He uses the expression elsewhere— three times in the account of the man born blind (John 9:21, 25), who answers: "Whether he be a sinner or no, I cannot tell; one thing I am sure of, that I was blind, and now I see."

Tyndale's version of Mary Magdalene's excited words to Peter and John is, "They have taken away the Lord out of the tomb, and we cannot tell where they have laid him" (John 20:2). In 1 John 2:11 Tyndale had "cannot tell whither he goeth."

So out of fourteen cases where Tyndale and the other sixteenth-century translators from the Greek used "cannot tell" for "do not know," the KJV translators kept nine and rejected five.

Contemporary translators, beginning with the English Revised Version of 1881, have generally rejected "cannot tell" in all these cases (except for J. B. Phillips, who uses "I couldn't tell" in John 9:25). The reason is not so much that the expression is wrong, as that it could be ambiguous. "Do not know" is clearer.

TEMPER

In modern English, the word "temper" means "to soften," "to moisten," or "to bring to a proper state of blending or mixing" ("to temper justice with mercy"; "to temper criticism with encouragement"). It is an archaic word for "mix," which is its meaning in the KJV. "Cakes unleavened tempered with oil" (Exodus 29:2, KJV) is now translated as "unleavened cakes mixed with oil" (NASB, NKJV, NRSV, RSV). "The third part of a hin of oil, to temper with the fine flour" (Ezekiel 46:14, KJV) is "a third of a hin of oil to moisten the fine flour" (NKJV).

In the instructions given to Moses for making the incense to be used in the worship of the Lord (Exodus 30:34–38), the expression "tempered together" (KJV) renders the Hebrew participle which means "seasoned with salt." The KJV translates the verb thus in Leviticus 2:13, "every oblation of thy meat offering shalt thou season with salt."

The archaic meaning of "render as to combine in due proportions" explains the KJV reading of 1 Corinthians 12:24–25: "God hath tempered the body together, having given more abundant honour to that part which lacked: That there should be no schism in the body." Contemporary versions use the terms "composed" (NASB, NKJV, RSV), "combined" (NIV), "arranged" (NRSV), and "put together" (CEV, NCV, NLT).

TEMPERANCE

In the KJV "temperance" means "self-control," although today it can also mean "moderation in the drinking of alcohol," or "total abstinence" from it. Because of these contemporary meanings, translations now replace "temperance" with "self-control."

Wisdom, courage, temperance, and justice were the four cardinal virtues of Greek philosophy. Paul spoke before Felix of justice and self-control and judgment to come (Acts 24:25). Self-control is part of "the fruit of the Spirit" described in Galatians 5:22–23 (cf. 2 Peter 1:3–8). "Every man that striveth for the mastery is temperate in all things" (1 Corinthians 9:25, KJV) is rendered by the NLT as "All athletes practice strict self-control."

"A bishop," says Titus 1:7–8, must be "a lover of hospitality, a lover of good men, sober, just, holy, temperate" (KJV). The NASB says that he must be "hospitable, loving what is good, sensible, just, devout, self-controlled."

TEMPT, TEMPTATION

These words today lead us to think of enticements to evil, or to what is unwise or inappropriate. But in the KJV "tempt" is also used in the sense of "test," "make trial of," "put to the proof."

Examples are: "And it came to pass after these things, that God did tempt Abraham"

(Genesis 22:1, KJV), rendered in the NIV as "Some time later God tested Abraham"; "Why tempt ye me, ye hypocrites?" (Matthew 22:18, KJV), which the NRSV translates as "Why are you putting me to the test, you hypocrites?"; and "one of them, which was a lawyer, asked him a question, tempting him" (Matthew 22:35, KJV), now rendered as "One of them, a lawyer, asked Him a question, testing Him" (NASB).

"Temptations" is used in the sense of trials in Deuteronomy 4:34; 7:19; 29:3, where the word is linked with signs and wonders in a recurring formula of reminder. It is now rendered as "trials" (4:34, NASB, NKJV, NLT, NRSV, RSV), "testings" (4:34, NIV), "troubles" (7:19, NCV), and "tests of strength" (29:3, NLT).

The NRSV translates the first of these verses: "Or has any god ever attempted to go and take a nation for himself from the midst of another nation, by trials, by signs, by wonders, by war, by a mighty hand and an outstretched arm, and by terrifying displays of power, as the LORD your God did for you in Egypt before your very eyes?"

TENDER EYED

Jacob's preference for Rachel over Leah is explained simply: "Leah was tender eyed; but Rachel was beautiful and well favoured" (Genesis 29:17, KJV). Many a reader has given Leah credit for melting, doelike eyes. The expression comes from Tyndale, and was adopted by Coverdale and succeeding versions. The meaning of the Hebrew is unclear. The Greek Septuagint says, "The eyes of Leah were weak" and the idea is followed by the majority of contemporary translations.

The NLT, however, has "Leah had pretty eyes," and the NRSV similarly reads, "Leah's eyes were lovely."

THANK

As a noun in the singular number, "thank" was still used in the sixteenth century in the sense of "a grateful thought," "a

feeling of gratitude." It had begun to be replaced, however, by the plural form "thanks." The plural is used in the KJV, except for one passage, Luke 6:32–34. Instead of "what thank have ye?" the NASB, NIV, NKJV, NRSV, and RSV here translate the Greek, "what credit is that to you?"

THANKWORTHY

This word means "worthy of thanks," "deserving gratitude or credit," "meritorious," "creditable." While not in common speech, like "blameworthy" and "praiseworthy," it is still considered by some as living English. The adjective is usually applied to action and the results of action, rather than to the person who acts.

"Thankworthy" appears once in the KJV, in a passage addressed to servants (1 Peter 2:18–25). Verses 19–20 read: "For this is thankworthy, if a man for conscience toward God endure grief, suffering wrongfully. For what glory is it, if, when ye be buffeted for your faults, ye shall take it patiently? but if, when ye do well, and suffer for it, ye take it patiently, this is acceptable with God."

"Conscience" and "grief" are used here in obsolete senses, and the same Greek word is rendered as "thankworthy" in the beginning and as "acceptable" at the end. The NRSV translates: "For it is a credit to you if, being aware of God, you endure pain while suffering unjustly. If you endure when you are beaten for doing wrong, what credit is that? But if you endure when you do right and suffer for it, you have God's approval."

Other contemporary translations agree, with minor differences of wording, that it is the approval of God that is meant at both points. The NASB translates the Greek as "this finds favor" in verse 19 and "this finds favor with God" in verse 20; the NIV has "it is commendable" and "This is commendable before God." The RSV has "one is approved" and "you have God's approval."

THAT

"That," by ellipsis, may sometimes stand alone in the sense of "that (thing) that," or "that (person) that." The OED says that the usage as applied to things was common down to the sixteenth century.

Examples in the KJV are: "beat out that she had gleaned" (Ruth 2:17, KJV; NASB, NKJV, NRSV, RSV, "beat out what she had gleaned"). "I uttered that I understood not" (Job 42:3, KJV; NKJV, NRSV, RSV, "I have uttered what I did not understand"). "Take that thine is, and go thy way" (Matthew 20:14, KJV; NRSV, RSV, "Take what belongs to you, and go").

The convenient word "what" is not available when this elliptic construction is applied to persons, as in Proverbs 11:24: "There is that scattereth, and yet increaseth; and there is that withholdeth more than is meet, but it tendeth to poverty." The NRSV translates this:

> "Some give freely, yet grow all the
> richer;
> Others withhold what is due and
> only suffer want."

The supreme example of this terse idiom is the name of God: "I AM THAT I AM (Exodus 3:14, KJV). Contemporary versions translate the Hebrew as "I AM WHO I AM" (NASB, NKJV) and "I AM WHO I AM" (NCV, NIV, NRSV, RSV); there are also alternative renderings in footnotes. The NLT paraphrases as "I AM THE ONE WHO ALWAYS IS."

THEREUNTO

This is an archaic adverb which the KJV uses nine times in the sense of "to it" or "for it." "Sacrificed thereunto" (Exodus 32:8, KJV) is now "sacrificed to it" (NASB, NIV, NKJV, NLT, NRSV, RSV), and "made thereunto" (Exodus 36:36, KJV) is "made for it" (NASB, NCV, NIV, NKJV, RSV). Exodus 37:11–12, "unto all the places nigh thereunto" (Deuteronomy 1:7, KJV), is now translated as "to all their neighbors" (NASB, RSV) and "to all the neighboring places" (NKJV).

In Ephesians 6:18, "watching thereunto with all perseverance and supplications for all saints" (KJV), contemporary versions have "with this in view" (NASB), "With this in mind" (NIV), and "To that end" (NRSV, RSV).

In 1 Thessalonians, Paul counsels his converts not to be unsettled by their trials and persecutions: "you yourselves know," he says, "that we are appointed thereunto" (3:3, KJV). The NKJV has "we are appointed to this," the NRSV, "this is what we are destined for."

In 1 Peter 3:9, Christians are told to repay abuse with a blessing, "knowing that ye are thereunto called, that ye should inherit a blessing." The NKJV has "you were called to this, that you may inherit a blessing." See also Hebrews 10:1.

THIEF IN THE NIGHT

If something happens "like a thief in the night," it comes unexpectedly. The expression derives from 1 Thessalonians 5:2–3, "For yourselves know perfectly that the day of the Lord so cometh as a thief in the night. For when they shall say, Peace and safety; then sudden destruction cometh upon them, as travail upon a woman with child; and they shall not escape" (KJV).

The NCV renders verse 2 as "You know very well that the day the Lord comes again will be a surprise, like a thief that comes in the night" and the NLT, "For you know quite well that the day of the Lord will come unexpectedly, like a thief in the night."

The same figure of speech also occurs at 2 Peter 3:10, CEV, "The day of the Lord's return will surprise us like a thief." See also Matthew 24:43; Luke 12:39; Revelation 3:3; 16:15.

THINGS IN COMMON

The expression "all things in common," referring to joint possession, derives from Acts 2:44, "And all that believed were together, and had all things common; And sold their possessions and goods, and parted them to all men, as every man had need" (KJV). The first Christians sold their property and possessions and gave to anyone who had need. The OED quotes manuscripts "Q" and "X" of Wycliffe's translation of this verse: "Alle men that bileuyden . . . hadden alle thingis in comoun."

The contemporary versions render this "had all things [NIV, "everything"] in common" (NASB, NIV, NKJV, NRSV, RSV); "shared everything they had" (CEV, NLT); and "shared everything" (NCV). See also Acts 4:32–35 (v. 33 "in common," NKJV, NRSV, RSV).

THINGS TO ALL MEN

People who are "all things to all men" try to please everyone, modifying their behavior to adapt to those with whom they are associate. Sometimes the efforts are genuine, but sometimes the attempt is simply to ingratiate oneself in a somewhat calculating manner. The expression has its source in 1 Corinthians 9:22, "To the weak became I as weak, that I might gain the weak: I am made all things to all men, that I might by all means save some" (KJV). Paul was willing to be completely versatile to fit in with different groups of people in an attempt to bring about their salvation.

The NASB NIV, NKJV, and RSV have "I have become all things to all men"; the NCV and NRSV have "I have become all things to all people"; the NLT has "Yes, I try to find common ground with everyone," and for the whole verse the CEV simply has "When I am with people whose faith is weak, I live as they do to win them. I do everything I can to win everyone I possibly can."

THIRTY PIECES OF SILVER

The expression "thirty pieces of silver" is sometimes used in contemporary English to refer to money given as the price paid for a person's betrayal. The expression derives from Judas's betrayal of Jesus: "And [Judas] said unto them [the chief priests], What will ye give me, and I will deliver him unto you? And they covenanted with him for thirty pieces of silver." The expression "thirty pieces

of silver" is retained by the NASB, NKJV, NLT, NRSV, and RSV; the CEV, NCV, and NIV have "thirty silver coins."

After Jesus had been led away and handed over to Pilate, Judas repented and brought back the money and "cast down the pieces of silver in the temple, and departed, and went and hanged himself" (Matthew 27:5, KJV). The priests refused to put the money back into the treasury, calling it "blood money" (NIV, NRSV). Rather, the money was used to buy the "potter's field" (KJV, NIV, NKJV, NLT, NRSV; NASB and NCV, capitals P and F) as a place to bury foreigners (called "field of blood" v. 8, KJV), capitals F and B in all the contemporary versions (Matthew 27:7–8).

In Matthew, "And they took the thirty pieces of silver, the price of him that was valued, whom they of the children of Israel did value; And gave them for the potter's field, as the Lord appointed me" at 27:9–11 quotes from Zechariah 11:12–13: "And I said unto them, If ye think good give me my price; and if not, forbear. So they weighed for my price thirty pieces of silver. And the LORD said unto me, Cast it unto the potter: a goodly price that I was prised all of them. And I took the thirty pieces of silver, and cast them to the potter in the house of the LORD."

Allusions to "thirty pieces of silver" are found in literature, e.g., Shakespeare's *King Henry IV, Part II* (II, 1, 102): "And didst thou not kiss me, and bid me fetch thee thirty shillings?" and in Robert Browning's *The Lost Leader* (1–2, 5–6), a poem attacking Wordsworth for his supposed desertion of the liberal cause:

"Just for a handful of silver he left us,
Just for a riband to stick on his
    coat—. . .
They, with the gold to give, doled him
    out silver
So much was their who so little
    allowed."

THITHERWARD

This word means "toward that place," "in that direction." "They shall ask the way to Zion with their faces thitherward" (Jeremiah 50:5, KJV) is reworded in the NASB as "They will ask for the way to Zion, turning their faces in its direction." "They turned thitherward" (Judges 18:15, KJV) is rendered as "they turned aside there" by the NASB and NKJV, and as "they turned in that direction" by the NRSV.

In Romans 15:24, Paul says that he hopes to see the Roman community on his way to Spain, "and to be brought on my way thitherward by you" (KJV). The NASB has "to be helped on my way there by you"; the RSV, "to be sped on my journey there by you."

THORN IN THE FLESH

A "thorn in the flesh (or side)" is "a source of constant annoyance." The expression derives from Paul's description in 2 Corinthians 12:7 of his own experience of such a problem: "And lest I should be exalted above measure through the abundance of the revelations, there was given to me a thorn in the flesh, the messenger of Satan to buffet me, lest I should be exalted above measure" (KJV).

The exact nature of Paul's affliction is unknown (suggestions include blindness, stammering, malaria, and epilepsy) but whatever the infirmity was, Paul pleaded with the Lord three times to remove it, but was given the answer that in his human weakness he should depend on divine grace and power (2 Corinthians 12:8–9).

The contemporary versions render the KJV "thorn in the flesh" (retained by the NASB and NKJV) as "a thorn in my flesh" (NIV, NLT), "a painful physical problem" (NCV); the NRSV and RSV have "a thorn was given me in the flesh"; the CEV has "One of Satan's angels was sent to make me suffer terribly, so that I would not feel too proud."

THOUGHT

"Thought" is "a product or act of thinking," "an idea or notion." In the KJV, however, it means "anxiety." When the word appears in the expression "take thought," it means "to be anxious." "Take no thought for the morrow" (Matthew 6:34, KJV) means "do not worry about tomorrow" (NASB, NIV, NKJV, NRSV). "Take no thought how or what ye shall speak" (Matthew 10:19, KJV) means "Do not be anxious how you are to speak or what you are to say" (RSV).

Other occurrences in the Gospels are Matthew 6:25, 27–28, 31; Mark 13:11; Luke 12:11, 22, 25–26. The same Greek verb, which means "to be anxious or worried," is used in all these cases.

This use of "take thought" occurs once in the Old Testament, where the young Saul, failing to find his father's donkeys, says to his servant, "Come, and let us return; lest my father leave caring for the asses, and take thought for us" (1 Samuel 9:5, KJV). In 1 Samuel 10:2, Samuel informs Saul that the donkeys are found, "and lo, thy father hath left the care of the asses, and sorroweth for you." The same Hebrew verb is translated "take thought" and "sorroweth" by the KJV.

As an illustration of this now obsolete use of the word "thought" in the sense of "anxiety" or "trouble," the OED cites a sentence from Samuel Purchas's *Pilgrimage* (1613) which informs the reader that "Soto died of thought in Florida." Instances found in Shakespeare are:

> "Thus conscience does make
>   cowards of us all,
> And thus the native hue of
>   resolution
> Is sicklied o'er with the pale
>   cast of thought."
>   —*Hamlet* (III, 1, 83–85)

> "and there is pansies, that's
>   for thoughts."
>   —*Hamlet* (IV, 5, 177)

T

THREE SCORE YEARS AND TEN

Three score years and ten is seventy years, the period of time that people may generally be expected to live. The expression comes from Psalm 90:10: "The days of our years are threescore years and ten; and if by reason of strength they be fourscore years, yet is their strength labour and sorrow; for it is soon cut off, and we fly away" (KJV). Four score is eighty years. The contemporary versions have: "seventy years . . . eighty years" (NASB, NCV, NKJV) and "seventy years . . . eighty" (CEV, NIV, NLT, NRSV).

The biblical expression "three score years and ten" still lingers in the English language. It is interesting to note, however, that the original Hebrew had just simply "seventy" . . . "eighty."

TIME AND A PLACE FOR EVERYTHING

The expression "there is a time and a place for everything" means that there are certain circumstances when a particular action is appropriate. It is often used with the implication that a particular action may not be done at any time or in any place.

The origin of the expression lies in the Preacher's statement of the varying seasons of human existence in Ecclesiastes 3:1–8: "To every thing there is a season, and a time to every purpose under the heaven: A time to be born, and a time to die; a time to plant, and a time to pluck up that which is planted; A time to kill, and a time to heal; a time to break down, and a time to build up; A time to weep, and a time to laugh; a time to mourn, and a time to dance; A time to cast away stones, and a time to gather stones together; a time to embrace, and a time to refrain from embracing; A time to get, and a time to lose; a time to keep, and a time to cast away; A time to rend, and a time to sew; a time to keep silence, and a time to speak; A time to love, and a time to hate; a time of war, and a time of peace" (KJV).

Phrasing of the introductory section (v. 1)

varies in the contemporary versions. The NASB begins, "There is an appointed time for everything. And there is a time for every event under heaven"; the NCV, "There is a time for everything, and everything on earth has its special season"; the NIV and NLT, "There is a time for everything, a season [NIV, "and a season"] for every activity under heaven"; the NKJV, "To everything there is a season, A time for every purpose under heaven"; the NRSV, "For everything there is a season, and a time for every matter under heaven."

Chaucer alludes to this passage, e.g., in the Prologue to *The Clerk's Tale*,

> "I trowe ye studie about som
>   sophyme;
> But Salomon seith, 'every thyng
>   hath tyme.'
> For Goddes sake, as beth of bettre
>   cheere!
> It is no tyme for to studien heere."

TIRE

The word "tire" is likely to remind us of fatigue or the rims of wheels. In the KJV, however, it is a shortened form of "attire." As a noun, it means "a headdress" or "an ornament"; as a verb it means "adorn." "Bind the tire of thine head upon thee" (Ezekiel 24:17, KJV) is translated in the NASB, NRSV, and RSV as "Bind on your turban" (see also Ezekiel 24:23).

The Hebrew noun here translated as "tire" by the KJV is rendered as "bonnet" in Isaiah 3:20 and Ezekiel 44:18, "beauty" in Isaiah 61:3, and "ornaments" in Isaiah 61:10. When Jezebel "painted her face, and tired her head, and looked out at a window" (2 Kings 9:30, KJV), the Hebrew verb for "tired" has the general meaning "adorned." According to the NCV, she "put on her eye makeup and fixed her hair."

The "round tires like the moon" (Isaiah 3:18, KJV) were crescent-shaped ornaments, here included in a list of feminine finery. The KJV translates the Hebrew word simply as "ornaments" in Judges 8:21, 26. That they were items of luxury, probably of gold, may be inferred from the fact that they were worn by the kings of Midian and were hung on the necks of their camels.

The NKJV, NRSV, and RSV use "crescents" in Isaiah, where the NIV and NLT have "crescent necklaces."

TITLE

The word "title" will make us think of headings and captions, sports and championships, and ranks or offices. In the KJV rendering of 2 Kings 23:17, however, it has the obsolete sense of "an inscribed monument or tomb." King Josiah's question, "What title is that that I see?" reads in the NKJV, "What gravestone is this that I see?" The account of the man of God, whose tombstone or monument it was, appears in 1 Kings 13.

The inscription over the head of Jesus upon the cross is described with general agreement, but different wording, in the four Gospels. Matthew 27:37 reads in the NRSV: "Over his head they put the charge against him, which read, 'This is Jesus, the King of the Jews.'" Mark 15:26 (NRSV) has "The inscription of the charge against him read, 'The King of the Jews.'" Luke 23:38 (NRSV) says, "There was also an inscription over him, 'This is the King of the Jews.'"

John 19:19–22 has the fullest account: "Pilate also had an inscription written and put it on the cross. It read, 'Jesus of Nazareth, the King of the Jews.' Many of the Jews read this inscription, because the place where Jesus was crucified was near the city; and it was written in Hebrew, in Latin, and in Greek. Then the chief priests of the Jews said to Pilate, 'Do not write, "The King of the Jews," but, "This man said, I am King of the Jews."' Pilate answered 'What I have written I have written'" (NRSV).

John's Gospel is the only one which used the customary term for such an inscription. In Greek, it was *titlos;* in Latin, *titulus.* From Wycliffe on to the KJV, all the early

versions used "title" here, and it is retained by the NKJV and RSV. Other versions have "sign" (NCV, NLT), "notice" (NIV), and "inscription" (NASB, NRSV).

TITTLE

This word was used by Tyndale to translate the Greek *keraia* in Matthew 5:18 and Luke 16:17. Meaning "horn," this word, like the Latin *apex,* was applied to any projection, extremity, hook, or serif of a written letter, then to vowel-points, accents, dots, diacritical marks—in short, to any small stroke or point in writing.

In Jesus' use of the term, it stands for the smallest possible part of the written law; contemporary versions therefore translate it as "comma" (CEV), "stroke" (NASB; NIV, "the least stroke of a pen"; NRSV, "one stroke of a letter"), and "dot" (RSV). Luke 16:17 reads in the NRSV, "But it is easier for heaven and earth to pass away, than for one stroke of a letter in the law to be dropped." (See JOT)

TO

An uncommon use of the preposition "to" occurs in the KJV rendering of Judges 17:13, "I have a Levite to my priest," and in Matthew 3:9 (and its parallel, Luke 3:8), "We have Abraham to our father." The NRSV translates as "I have a Levite as priest," and "We have Abraham as our father." The OED describes this use of "to" as obsolete or archaic, meaning "for, as, by way of, in the capacity of" (*To,* A, 11b).

The Latin Vulgate translated the Greek of John the Baptist's words simply and exactly, *Patrem habemus Abraham.* The Anglo-Saxon Gospels, about A.D. 1000, complicated this by inserting a double dative, "us" and "to faeder," reading, "We habbao us to faeder abraham." Wycliffe read in Matthew "we han abraham to fadir," and in Luke "we han a fadir abraham." Tyndale translated it as "we have Abraham to oure father," which was accepted by the other sixteenth-century versions and by the KJV.

Examples of this idiom are found in

Spenser's *The Faerie Queene* (I, 1, 28): "So forward on his way (with God to frend) He passed forth," and in Shakespeare's *King Richard II* (IV, 1, 308): "I have a king here to my flatterer."

TO HIM THAT HATH SHALL BE GIVEN
See HATH SHALL BE GIVEN.

TO OUT-HEROD HEROD
See HEROD, TO OUT-HEROD.

TO THE PURE ALL THINGS ARE PURE
See PURE ALL THINGS ARE PURE.

TOMORROW WILL TAKE CARE OF ITSELF

The expression "tomorrow will take care of (or: look after) itself" means that "the future will take its own shape, will bring problems and solutions that can't be predicted and pre-arranged" (*Oxford Dictionary of Current Idiomatic English*, vol. 2). The saying derives from Matthew 6:34, "Take therefore no thought for the morrow: for the morrow shall take thought for the things of itself" (KJV).

The KJV "the morrow shall take thought for the things of itself" is rendered by the contemporary versions as "tomorrow will worry about itself" (NIV), "tomorrow will worry about its own things" (NKJV), "tomorrow will bring its own worries" (NLT), "tomorrow will bring worries of its own" (NRSV), "tomorrow will have its own worries" (NCV), "tomorrow will care for itself" (NASB), "tomorrow . . . will take care of itself" (CEV), and "tomorrow will be anxious for itself" (RSV). (See also SUFFICIENT UNTO THE DAY IS THE EVIL THEREOF)

TOUCH THE HEM OF HIS GARMENT
See HEM OF HIS GARMENT.

TOUCHING

The present participle of the verb "touch" is used thirty times in the KJV as a preposition. The use is now rather archaic. In half of the occurrences it appears in the form "as touching."

Contemporary versions replace "touching" with "concerning" (e.g., the NRSV in Isaiah 5:1; Jeremiah 22:11; Colossians 4:10; 1 Thessalonians 4:9) or "about" (e.g., the NASB in Matthew 18:19; 2 Corinthians 9:1), and replace "as touching" with terms such as "as for," "regarding," "about," "concerning" (1 Samuel 20:23; Matthew 22:31; Mark 12:26; Acts 21:25; 1 Corinthians 16:12).

"Behold, thy brother Esau, as touching thee, doth comfort himself, purposing to kill thee" (Genesis 27:42, KJV) is reworded in the NASB as "Behold your brother Esau is consoling himself concerning you by planning to kill you." "Touching the Almighty, we cannot find him out" (Job 37:23, KJV) reads in the NCV, "The Almighty is too high for us to reach."

Paul's statement, "as touching things offered unto idols" (1 Corinthians 8:1, KJV), represents the Greek preposition *peri*, which appears also in 1 Corinthians 12:1 and is there translated by the KJV as "concerning."

In Philippians 3:5–6 the Greek preposition *kata*, in three parallel clauses, is translated in three different ways: "as touching the law, a Pharisee; Concerning zeal, persecuting the church; touching the righteousness which is in the law, blameless." The NRSV maintains the parallelism: "as to the law, a Pharisee; as to zeal, a persecutor of the church; as to righteousness under the law, blameless."

TOWER OF BABEL
See BABEL.

TRANSLATE, TRANSLATION

These words make us think of languages. But in the KJV the verb "translate" means "to transfer," "to move from one place to another." In Hebrews 11:5 we read, "By faith Enoch was translated that he should not see death; and was not found, because God had translated him: for before his translation he had this testimony, that he pleased God" (KJV).

The NASB, NLT, and RSV say that he was "taken up"; the NIV has him "taken from this life." The Greek noun here used, *metathesis*, has passed directly into the English language and is fairly common in English grammar and in chemistry, for the transposition of letters or ions.

For "translate the kingdom" (2 Samuel 3:10, KJV), the NASB, NIV, NKJV, NRSV, and RSV have "transfer the kingdom." For "translated us into the kingdom of his dear Son" (Colossians 1:13, KJV), the NRSV and RSV have "transferred us to the kingdom of his beloved Son"; the NKJV reads "conveyed *us* into the kingdom of the Son of His love."

TREASURE UPON EARTH

The expression "lay not up treasure upon earth," meaning "do not live merely in order to gain wealth or other material possessions," derives from Jesus' saying in the Sermon on the Mount (Matthew 6:19–20), "Lay not up for yourselves treasures upon earth, where moth and rust doth corrupt, and where thieves break through and steal: But lay up for yourselves treasures in heaven, where neither moth nor rust doth corrupt, and where thieves do not break through nor steal" (KJV).

The contemporary versions have "Do not store up [NKJV, RSV, "Do not lay up"] for yourselves treasures on earth" (NASB, NIV, NKJV, NRSV, RSV), "Don't store up treasures on earth!" (CEV), "Don't store up treasures here on earth" (NLT), and "Don't store treasures for yourselves here on earth" (NCV).

Instead, Jesus enjoins his followers to "lay up for yourselves treasures in heaven" (v. 20), again most of the contemporary versions except the NKJV and RSV have "store up"; the NKJV and RSV retain the KJV "lay up."

TREATISE

The word "treatise" now means "a book or essay which deals with the principles of a subject." The term was formerly applied also to "a story" or "a narrative." When Luke refers to his Gospel as "the former treatise" (Acts 1:1, KJV), the word is used in this obsolete sense. Contemporary versions have "the first account" (NASB), "The former account" (NKJV), "[T]he first book" (NCV, NRSV, RSV), and "my former book" (NIV).

TREE OF LIFE

The "tree of life," symbolizing life and salvation, is mentioned several times in Scripture: in the Garden of Eden (Genesis 2:9; 3:22, 24), and in Revelation (2:7; 22:2, 14). The expression is also used metaphorically in Proverbs (3:18; 11:30; 13:12; 15:4).

In Genesis 2:9 the expression "the tree of life" is retained by the NASB, NIV, NKJV, NLT, NRSV, and RSV; the CEV has "one of the trees gave life" and the NCV, "the tree that gives life." At Genesis 3:22, the CEV has "the tree that lets them live forever" and at 3:24, "the life-giving tree." In Revelation, the contemporary versions retain the KJV expression, except the CEV which has "the life-giving tree" (2:7) and "the tree that gives life" (22:14).

The "tree of life" is referred to in literature, e.g., by Milton in *Paradise Lost* (4.219–222):

> "High, eminent, blooming
>   Ambrosial Fruit
> Of vegetable Gold; and next to Life
> Out Death the Tree of Knowledge
>   grew fast by,
> Knowledge of Good bought dear
>   by knowing ill."

TREE OF THE KNOWLEDGE OF GOOD AND EVIL

The "tree of the knowledge of good and evil" and "the tree of life" were in the middle of the Garden of Eden: "And out of the ground made the LORD God to grow every tree that is pleasant to the sight, and good for food; the tree of life also in the midst of the garden, and the tree of knowledge of good and evil" (Genesis 2:9, KJV).

God forbade Adam and Eve from eating from the tree of the knowledge of good and evil (v. 17), "for in the day that thou eatest thereof thou shalt surely die" (KJV). Genesis 3 records Adam and Eve disobeying God and eating the fruit of the tree of the knowledge of good and evil (See FALL; FORBIDDEN FRUIT) and so the coming of death into the world (3:3, 5–6, 22).

The contemporary versions render the KJV "the tree of knowledge of good and evil" (v. 9) and "the tree of the knowledge of good and evil" (v. 17) both as: "the tree of the knowledge of good and evil" (NASB, NIV, NKJV, NLT, NRSV, and RSV); the NCV has "the tree that gives [v. 17, "which gives"] the knowledge of good and evil"; and the CEV at verse 9, the tree that "gave the power to know the difference between right and wrong" and at verse 17, "the one that has the power to let you know the difference between right and wrong."

The "tree of the knowledge of good and evil" is referred to often in literature, e.g., in Milton's *Paradise Lost* (8.321–330):

"Of every Tree that in the Garden growes
Eate freely with glad heart; fear here no dearth:
But of the Tree whose operation brings
Knowledge of good and ill, which I have set
The Pledge of thy Obedience and thy Faith,
Amid the Garden by the Tree of Life,
Remember what I warne thee, shun to taste,
And shun the bitter consequence: for know,
The day thou eat'st thereof, my sole command
Transgrest, inevitably thou shalt dye."

and Byron's poetic drama *Manfred* (1.1.9–12),

"grief should be the instructor of the wise
Sorrow is knowledge: they who know the most
Must mourn the deepest o'er the fatal truth
The Tree of Knowledge is not that of Life."

TRIBUTE

The word "tribute" refers to the tax paid by a subject state or vassal in token of submission or as the price of peace and security. The KJV does not use the word in the derived sense of "compliment" or "praise." Almost half the occurrences of the word "tribute," however, are due to the KJV's use of it for the Hebrew *mas*, which means "forced labor." The revisers in the 1870s were aware of this, and chose the term "taskwork." This term, however, is a little too weak for the grim reality.

For "a servant unto tribute" (Genesis 49:15, KJV) the NASB, NRSV, and RSV have "a slave at forced labor"; for "put the Canaanites to tribute" (Joshua 17:13; Judges 1:28, KJV), they have "put the Canaanites to forced labor." "Adoram was over the tribute" (2 Samuel 20:24, KJV) reads in the NIV, NRSV, and RSV as "Adoram was in charge of [NRSV, RSV, "of the"] forced labor" (cf. 1 Kings 4:6).

"And this is the reason of the levy which king Solomon raised" is rendered by the NASB as "Now this is the account of the forced labor which King Solomon levied." The passage which begins with these words, 1 Kings 9:15–22, is a summary list of Solomon's vast building operations and of the human material he employed.

"Upon those did Solomon levy a tribute of bondservice unto this day" in verse 21 reads in the NRSV, "these Solomon conscripted for slave labor, and so they are to this day."

TRIM

In contemporary English the word "trim" has several meanings, including "to clip the edges or ends of," "to arrange sails," and "to decorate something" (e.g., a hat). In the KJV the word is used in the first sense (2 Samuel 19:24) describing Mephibosheth who had not "trimmed his beard" (KJV), with most of the contemporary versions retaining the KJV "trimmed" and in the sense "to put (a lamp, fire, etc.) into proper order, by removing any deposit or ash, and adding fresh fuel" (OED). In Matthew 25:7, "the virgins trimmed their lamps" (KJV), most of the contemporary versions retain the KJV "trimmed"; the CEV and NCV have "getting [NCV, "got"] their lamps ready."

It is also used in the sense "to arrange carefully," at Jeremiah 2:33: "Why trimmest thou thy way to seek love? therefore hast thou also taught the wicked ones thy ways" (KJV). The contemporary versions render the KJV "trimmest . . . thy way" as: "prepare your way" (NASB), "beautify your way" (NKJV), "direct your course" (NRSV, RSV), and "plot and scheme" (NLT); the NIV has "How skilled you are at pursuing love!"; the NCV, "You really know how to chase after love"; and the CEV, "You are so clever at finding lovers."

TROW

This is an archaic word for "think," "believe," "be of the opinion that." It appears in the KJV rendering of Luke 17:9, "Doth he thank that servant because he did the things that were commanded him? I trow not." The last three words do not appear in the most ancient Greek manuscripts.

The *ou doko*, "I do not think," which they represent, were probably a marginal comment or gloss by a copyist who felt it incumbent upon him to answer the Lord's rhetorical question. Among contemporary versions, only the NKJV renders them.

TRUE

In current usage, the word "true" means "real" or "genuine," not false. In Genesis 42, however, the KJV employs it in the archaic sense of "honest." It survives today perhaps in the phrase for a jury, "twelve

good men and true." In Genesis 42:11, Joseph's brothers attempt to reassure him of their integrity: "We are all sons of one man; we are honest men; your servants have never been spies" (NRSV).

John 19:35 contains the archaism "saith true," and an obsolete use of "record." It reads in the KJV, "And he that saw it bare record, and his record is true: and he knoweth that he saith true, that ye might believe." The NKJV has "He who has seen has testified, and his testimony is true; and he knows that he is telling the truth, so that you may believe." (See RECORD)

TRUTH, WHAT IS?

When Jesus was put on trial before Pilate, Jesus said, "To this end was I born, and for this cause came I into the world, that I should bear witness unto the truth. Every one that is of the truth heareth my voice," to which Pilate responded, "What is truth?" (John 18:38, KJV). The phrasing of this question is followed by all the contemporary versions. Pilate did not realize that the answer to his question stood before him: "I am the way, the truth, and the life: no man cometh unto the Father, but by me" (John 14:6, KJV).

Francis Bacon, in his essay *Of Truth*, wrote, "'What is truth,' said jesting Pilate; and would not stay for an answer."

TURN THE OTHER CHEEK

To "turn the other cheek" means to respond to unkindness or harm with patience; not to retaliate when one is provoked, but even to be prepared to accept further unkindness, etc. The expression is derived from the words of Jesus in the Sermon on the Mount recorded in Matthew 5:39: "But I say unto you, That ye resist not evil: but whosoever shall smite thee on thy right cheek, turn to him the other also" (KJV).

Instead of the KJV verb "smite," the CEV, NASB, NCV, NKJV, and NLT use the verb "slap" and the NIV, NRSV, and RSV use the verb "strike." All the contemporary versions retain the KJV

T

"turn" and "other" for the responding action. At the parallel Luke 6:29, for the KJV "smite" the CEV, NCV, and NLT use the verb "slap"; the NIV, NKJV, NRSV, and RSV use the verb "strike"; while the NASB uses the verb "hit."

TURTLE

This word makes us think of the endearing, slow-moving reptiles sometimes kept as family pets. But in the KJV it is used five times for the Hebrew and Greek terms which mean "turtledove." The revised versions use "turtledove" or "dove" throughout, except the RV which retains "turtle" in Song of Solomon 2:12 and Jeremiah 8:7.

"The voice of the turtle is heard in our land" (Song of Solomon 2:12) is a text that has passed into general literature. The OED cites more examples of turtle as a term of endearment than it does for "turtledove," and as many as for "dove." One of these is from E. W. Benson (1865): "I am a solitary Turtle (Dove, not Reptile) just now, my wife being at Rugby."

TUTOR

While a "tutor" in modern terminology is "a teacher" or "a personal instructor," in the one place where "tutor" appears in the KJV it means "guardian." The context is Paul's teaching on the role of the Law in Galatians 3 and 4. Galatians 4:1–2 reads in the KJV: "the heir, as long as he is a child, differeth nothing from a servant, though he be lord of all but is under tutors and governors until the time appointed of the father."

In Roman law, the Latin word *tutor* was used for the guardian and administrator of the estate, of a youth not yet of legal age to manage his own affairs. The word "tutor" passed into English with the same meaning. This meaning is now obsolete except in the language of law. The Greek word here is *epitropos*, which the KJV translates as "steward" in its other two occurrences (Matthew 20:8; Luke 8:3).

"Tutor" was a correct translation in this passage, both in Latin and in English, but the word's meaning has changed. Contemporary versions generally use the word "guardian" instead.

TWAIN

"Twain" is an archaic word for "two." The OED says that "its use in the Bible of 1611 and in the Marriage Service, and its value as a rime-word, have contributed to its retention as an archaic and poetic synonym of *two*." It appears seventeen times in the KJV.

"Wherefore Saul said to David, Thou shalt this day be my son in law in the one of the twain" (1 Samuel 18:21) is now translated as "Therefore Saul said to David a second time, 'You shall now be my son-in-law'" (NRSV). For "shut the door upon them twain" (2 Kings 4:33, KJV) the NKJV has "shut the door behind the two of them."

"They twain shall be one flesh" (Matthew 19:5–6; Mark 10:8, KJV) is now rendered as "the two shall [NIV, "will"] become one flesh" (NASB, NIV NKJV, NRSV, RSV). In the Matthean account of Jesus' trial, Pilate's words to the crowd, "Whether of the twain will ye that I release unto you?", are rendered by the NASB, NIV, NKJV, NRSV, and RSV as "Which of the two do you want me to release for [NIV, NKJV, "release to"] you?" (Matthew 27:21).

In Ephesians 2:15, "for to make in himself of twain one new man" is translated by the NRSV as "that he might create in himself one new humanity in place of the two."

TWINKLING OF AN EYE

The expression "in the twinkling of an eye" means "instantaneously" or "very quickly." The OED lists ten quotations of this expression before 1600. It also occurs in 1 Corinthians 15:51–52, "Behold, I show you a mystery; We shall not all sleep, but we shall all be changed, In a moment, in the twinkling of an eye, at the last trump: for the trumpet shall sound, and the dead shall be raised incorruptible, and we shall be changed" (KJV), describing the resurrection of the dead at the return of Jesus Christ.

The KJV expression is retained by the NASB, NIV, NKJV, NRSV, and RSV; the CEV has "quicker than the blink of an eye," the NLT, "in the blinking of an eye," and the NCV, "as quickly as an eye blinks."

TWO OR THREE ARE GATHERED TOGETHER

The expression "where two or three are gathered together" is sometimes used in contemporary English to refer to a group of people, however few in number, that are one in purpose. The expression derives from Jesus' words in Matthew 18:19–20: "That if two of you shall agree on earth as touching any thing that they shall ask, it shall be done for them of my Father which is in heaven. For where two or three are gathered together in my name, there am I in the midst of them" (KJV).

The contemporary versions retain a similar wording to the KJV, except the CEV, NCV, and NIV use the verb "come" instead of the KJV "gather" and for the KJV "in the midst of them" the NLT and NRSV have "among them"; the NCV and NIV have "with them"; and the CEV, "with you."

U

UNAWARES

This word today means "unknowingly" or "unexpectedly." We often use it to convey an element of surprise ("he came upon me unawares, just as I was choosing his Christmas present"). In the KJV, the word appears three times in the phrase "at unawares." Numbers 35:11 reads: "Then ye shall appoint you cities to be cities of refuge for you; that the slayer may flee thither, which killeth any person at unawares."

This leaves some doubt as to who was unaware, and contemporary versions clarify the situation with renderings such as "accidentally" (CEV, NCV, NIV, NKJV, NLT), "unintentionally" (NASB), and "without intent" (NRSV). There is a similar passage in Joshua 20:9. In Psalm 35:8 (KJV, "Let destruction come upon him at unawares"), the NASB, NRSV, and RSV retain the word "unawares," without the "at," while other versions have "suddenly" (NCV), "by surprise" (NIV), and "unexpectedly" (NKJV).

In the account of Jacob's flight from Laban, the expression "stole away unawares to" (KJV) appears twice (Genesis 31:20, 26). The Hebrew literally means "stole the mind of." Contemporary versions translates it as "outwitted" (RSV) in verse 20 and as "deceived" (NIV, NRSV; NASB, "deceiving") and "cheated" (NCV, RSV) in verse 26.

In Luke 21:34 "come upon you unawares" (KJV) is now translated as "come on [RSV, "come upon"] you suddenly" (NASB, NCV, RSV), "close on you unexpectedly" (NIV), and "catch you unexpectedly" (NRSV). In 1 Thessalonians 5:3, the only other occurrence of this Greek word in the Bible, the KJV, NKJV, NRSV, and RSV have "sudden destruction."

Paul's description of the Judaizers as "false brethren unawares brought in" (Galatians 2:4, KJV) now reads, "false brethren secretly brought in" (NASB, NKJV). Similarly, in Jude 4 "crept in unawares" (KJV) is now rendered as "crept in unnoticed" (NASB, NKJV), "secretly slipped in" (NIV), and "stolen in" (NRSV).

UNCOMELY *(adjective)*

As an adjective, "uncomely" is used in the KJV rendering of 1 Corinthians 12:23 in the archaic sense of "unseemly" or "improper." It refers to the *aschemona*, the unpresentable, indecent parts of the body, which it contrasts with the *euschemona*, the presentable, decent parts. In 1611 "comely" and "uncomely" still had a moral meaning, and so expressed the contrast well. Today the words have practically become synonyms of "pretty" and "ugly."

Contemporary versions translate "uncomely parts" (KJV) in 1 Corinthians 12:23 as "less presentable members" (NASB), "less respectable members" (NRSV), "unpresentable parts" (NKJV, RSV), and "the parts we want to hide" (NCV).

UNCOMELY *(adverb)*

As an adverb, "uncomely" is an obsolete word for "unbecomingly," "unsuitably," "improperly." It occurs in 1 Corinthians 7:36: "But if any man think that he behaveth himself uncomely toward his virgin" (KJV). The KJV and NASB renderings of 7:36–38 assume that the man is a father and the virgin his daughter, and that the man's problem is whether or not to give her in marriage to someone else who is not mentioned. The NASB renders "behaveth himself uncomely" here as "acting unbecomingly."

The majority of contemporary translations, on the other hand, assume that Paul is discussing the problem of a couple who are engaged, but are in doubt whether their Christian faith requires them to remain unmarried. The man is described in these versions as "not doing the right thing" (NCV), "acting [NKJV, "behaving"] improperly" (NIV, NKJV), "not behaving properly" (NRSV, RSV), and as having "trouble controlling his passions" (NLT).

UNCORRUPTNESS

This word occurs once in the KJV, as translation for a Greek word which means "incorruptibility," "soundness," "integrity." The KJV renders Titus 2:7–8 as an incomplete sentence, substituting "shewing thyself" for the imperative "shew thyself" which had been used by Tyndale and his sixteenth-century successors. The verses read: "In all things shewing thyself a pattern of good works: in doctrine shewing uncorruptness, gravity, sincerity, Sound speech, that cannot be condemned; that he that is of the contrary part may be ashamed, having no evil thing to say of you."

With the exception of the NKJV, contemporary versions return to the construction of Tyndale. The NRSV reads: "Show yourself in all respects a model of good works, and in your teaching show integrity, gravity, and sound speech that cannot be censured; then any opponent will be put to shame, having nothing evil to say of us."

UNCTION

"Unction" may make us think of the anointing of the sick, or of the oil used for this purpose. But in 1 John 2 the KJV uses "unction" as translation for the Greek word *chrisma*—rendered as "unction" in verse 20 and "anointing" in verse 27. The revised versions, and contemporary translations generally, use "anointing" or "anointed" in both verses. The first reads in the KJV, "But ye have an unction from the Holy One, and ye know all things." Relying on the more ancient manuscripts for the last clause, the NRSV reads, "But you have been anointed by the Holy One, and all of you have knowledge."

The text refers to the gift of the Holy Spirit, and the NCV and NLT bring this out in their paraphrases: "You have the gift that the Holy One gave you" (NCV); "the Holy Spirit has come upon you" (NLT). Other references for comparison are 3:24; 4:2, 13; 5:7–8.

UNDERTAKE

In modern usage, "undertake" means "to take in hand or attempt" ("she's decided to undertake a course of study"), or "to take something on by formal agreement." In the KJV the word is used in the archaic sense of "become surety or security for," "assume responsibility for," which is the meaning of the Hebrew verb that it translates.

Isaiah 38:9–20 is a psalm of thanksgiving which bears the title, "A writing of Hezekiah king of Judah, when he had been sick, and was recovered of his sickness" (KJV). In verse 14 appears the line: "O LORD I am oppressed; undertake for me" (KJV). The revised versions of 1885–1901 have "be thou my surety"; contemporary versions, "be my security" (NASB, NRSV), "Please help me" (NCV), "come to my aid" (NIV).

UNICORN

A unicorn is a mythical, legendary animal often depicted in heraldry, with the head and body of a horse, the legs of a deer, the tail of a lion, and one long horn projecting straight from the center of its forehead. The word appears nine times in the KJV, to represent the Hebrew *re'em*, which the revised versions translate as "wild ox" (Numbers 23:22; 24:8; Job 39:9–10; Psalms 22:21; 29:6; 92:10; Isaiah 34:7).

In Deuteronomy 33:17 it is clear that a *re'em* has more than one horn, and the KJV resorts to the plural, "the horns of unicorns." For KJV "unicorns" here, all the contemporary versions have "wild ox."

The KJV rendering began with the Greek Septuagint, which used *monokeros,* and the Latin Vulgate, which used *unicornis* or *rhinoceros.* The animal referred to was probably *bos primigenius,* which the Old Germans called *Auerochs.* Caesar mentioned it in his *Gallic Wars,* and it is pictured on Assyrian monuments as one of the animals hunted by the kings. The *Auerochs* was noted for its size and strength and for the prodigious length of its horns.

UNJUST

While "unjust" today makes us think of what is unfair or not in keeping with justice ("an unjust sentence"), in the KJV the word is sometimes used in a broad sense which includes all sorts of wrongdoing. A number of contemporary versions retain the word where it implies injustice or unfair dealing, and in statements like "he . . . sends rain on the just and the unjust" (Matthew 5:45, NKJV, NLT, RSV).

Elsewhere contemporary versions use more specific terms. The "unjust men" of Proverbs 11:7 (KJV) are "the godless" in the NRSV and RSV and "strong men" in the NASB. "Unjust gain" (Proverbs 28:8, KJV) is "usury" (NASB), "extortion" (NKJV), and "increase" (RSV). The "unjust steward" (Luke 16:8, 10, KJV) is rendered as the "dishonest manager" by the NIV, NCV, CEV, and NRSV.

No one would ever "go to law before the unjust" (1 Corinthians 6:1, KJV), and the NRSV now reads, "When any of you has a grievance against another, do you dare to take it to court before the unrighteous, instead of . . . before the saints?" "He that is unjust, let him be unjust still" (Revelation 22:11, KJV) is now rendered as "Let the evildoer still do evil" (NRSV, RSV).

UNLEARNED

This word occurs six times in the KJV, and represents four distinct Greek words. When Peter and John are termed "unlearned and ignorant" (Acts 4:13, KJV), the first of these adjectives means "illiterate," "uneducated." The NRSV reads, "that they were uneducated and ordinary men." In 2 Peter 3:16 Paul is said to have written "some things hard to understand, which the untaught and unstable distort" (NASB).

Here the Greek word for "unlearned" is rendered as "ignorant" by the CEV, NCV, NIV, NLT, NRSV, and RSV. "Foolish and unlearned questions avoid" (2 Timothy 2:23, KJV) is worded by the NRSV and RSV as "Have nothing to do with stupid, senseless controversies."

In 1 Corinthians 14:16, 23–24, "unlearned" (KJV) represents the Greek noun *idiotes,* which does not mean what the English word "idiot" has come to mean. The Greek *idiotes* was the ordinary, common person, as contrasted with the person of rank or official position, or with the expert or specialist of any sort. Such people were unskilled, uninitiated, outsiders, ones who do

U

not belong to the social or professional group which at the moment occupies the stage.

The context is Paul's advice on the use of spiritual gifts. The church, he says, must be sensitive to those who do not possess these gifts. "He that occupieth the room of the unlearned" (KJV) is "those who don't understand" (14:16, NLT). In verse 23, "those that are unlearned" (KJV) is rendered in contemporary versions as "outsiders" (CEV, NRSV, RSV), "ungifted men" (NASB), "some who do not understand" (NIV), and "those who are uninformed" (NKJV).

UNPERFECT

This is an old word, now rarely used, which has the same general meanings as "imperfect." It occurs once in the KJV, in Psalm 139:16: "Thine eyes did see my substance, yet being unperfect." These nine words stand for three Hebrew words, one meaning "thine eyes," one meaning "saw," and one meaning "my embryo." The ASV, NASB, RSV and NRSV read "my unformed substance." The NKJV has "my substance, being yet unformed."

UNSAVOURY

The word "unsavoury" is likely to make us think of tasteless or unappetizing food. The use of the word in 2 Samuel 22:27 will seem strange to contemporary readers. In a song of praise to God, David says, "With the pure thou wilt shew thyself pure; and with the froward thou wilt shew thyself unsavoury" (KJV). The word's presence here results from the dropping out of a consonant from the Hebrew text, which thus became the word for "unsavoury" instead of the word for "perverse."

Fortunately, 2 Samuel 22 and Psalm 18 are almost identical. Except for this slip, the Hebrew text of verse 27 is identical with that of Psalm 18:26, which in the KJV reads, "with the froward thou wilt show thyself

froward." Contemporary versions render the Hebrew in both texts as "astute" (NASB), "shrewd" (NIV, NKJV), "hostile" (NLT), and "perverse" (NRSV, RSV).

UNSPEAKABLE

In modern English the word "unspeakable" tends to be applied to bad or objectionable things rather than to good ("unspeakable behavior"). In the KJV it always means "unutterable," "inexpressible," "exceeding the power of speech." At 2 Corinthians 9:15 (KJV, "Thanks be unto God for his unspeakable gift"), contemporary versions render "unspeakable" as "indescribable" (NASB, NIV, NKJV, NRSV), "inexpressible" (RSV), and "too wonderful for words" (CEV, NCV).

"He . . . heard unspeakable words, which it is not lawful for a man to utter" (2 Corinthians 12:4, KJV) is rendered by the NRSV as "[he] heard things that are not to be told, that no mortal is permitted to repeat." The NASB, NIV, and NKJV render "unspeakable words" (KJV) as "inexpressible words [NIV, "inexpressible things"]."

UNTO

Since the end of the seventeenth century "unto" has been "employed chiefly in poetry, or in formal, dignified, or archaic style, or after Biblical use" (OED). Samuel Johnson's *Dictionary*, in the eighteenth century, noted it as "now obsolete."

Noah Webster omitted it entirely from his revision of the English Bible, published in 1833, entitled *The Holy Bible, containing the Old and New Testaments, in the Common Version, with Amendments of the language.* In the introductory notes he wrote: "*To* is used for *unto.* The first syllable *un* adds nothing to the signification or force of *to;* but by increasing the number of unimportant syllables, rather impairs the strength of the whole clause or sentence in which it occurs. It has been rejected by almost every writer, for more than a century."

In the KJV "unto" stands for fourteen different Hebrew or Greek prepositions. Examples of contemporary translations from the Old Testament are: "into one place" (Genesis 1:9, NASB, NKJV, NLT, NRSV, RSV); "for Adam and his wife" (Genesis 3:21, NASB, NIV, NKJV, NLT, NRSV); "I have sworn to the LORD" (Genesis 14:22, NASB, NRSV, RSV); "until the morning" (Exodus 29:34, NKJV, NLT, NRSV, RSV); "until the second year" (Ezra 4:24, NASB, NCV, NIV, NKJV, NLT, NRSV, RSV); "up to a hundred talents of silver" (Ezra 7:22, NIV, RSV); "her house sinks down to death" (Proverbs 2:18, NASB, NRSV).

From Matthew: "no one puts a patch of unshrunk cloth on an old garment" (9:16, NASB); "Come to me, all of you who are tired and have heavy loads" (11:28, NCV); "the kingdom of God has come upon you" (12:28, NASB, NIV, NKJV, RSV); "Let the children come to me, and don't try to stop them" (19:14, CEV); "the chief priests and the Pharisees gathered before Pilate" (27:62, NRSV, RSV).

From Acts: "as far as Paphos" (13:6, NASB, NRSV, RSV); "Up to this point they listened to him" (22:22, NRSV).

From the epistles: "accustomed to idols until now" (1 Corinthians 8:7, NRSV); "you were called to freedom" (Galatians 5:13, NASB, NRSV, RSV); "created in Christ Jesus for good works" (Ephesians 2:10, NASB, NKJV, NRSV, RSV); "you have not yet resisted to the point of shedding your blood" (Hebrews 12:4, NRSV, RSV).

In Romans 9:29 and Hebrews 2:17 "like unto" (KJV) simply means "like." In Hebrews 8:5 "serve unto" (KJV) means "serve." In 1 John 5:16–17, "sin unto death" (KJV) is now rendered as "sin . . . leading to death" (NASB) and "mortal sin" (NRSV, RSV).

The word "unto" is redundant in the expression "shall be forgiven unto men" (Matthew 12:31, KJV), as is shown by the next verse in the KJV, which has "it shall be forgiven him." It is similarly redundant in Matthew 6:12 (KJV, "forgive unto us our debts"), and Luke 5:20 (KJV, "thy sins are forgiven unto thee").

UNTOWARD

Applied to persons or animals, "untoward" means "difficult to manage, restrain, or control"; "intractable," "unruly," "perverse." The OED, from which this definition is taken, states that the word was in frequent use, in this sense, from about 1580 to about 1700. The Greek adjective *skolios*, for which it stands in the KJV rendering of Acts 2:40, means "crooked," "unscrupulous," "dishonest." It is the first of the two adjectives in the phrase which the KJV translates as "in the midst of a crooked and perverse generation" (Philippians 2:15).

The NIV and NRSV translate Peter's exhortation on the day of Pentecost, "Save yourselves from this corrupt generation"; other versions have "perverse" (NASB, NKJV) and "crooked" (RSV).

UPHOLDEN

This is the old past participle of "uphold." Contemporary versions replace it with "upheld" (NKJV, RSV), "supported" (NIV, NRSV), and "helped" (NASB) in Job 4:4, and with "upheld" (NRSV, RSV) and "made secure" (NIV, NLT) in Proverbs 20:28. The first of these passages reads in the NKJV:

> "Your words have upheld him
>   who was stumbling,
> And you have strengthened
>   the feeble knees."

USURY

U

While today we think of "usury" as "exorbitant interest rates," in the KJV "usury" simply means "the practice of lending money or goods at interest." The word is also used to denote the interest which is charged and paid, but is not employed in the modern sense of "excessive or illegal interest." Consequently, the word "usury" appears less often in contemporary versions than in the KJV. They use the word "interest" instead—a word which does not appear in the KJV.

The Jewish law with respect to lending reads in the NRSV: "If you lend money to my people, to the poor among you, you shall not deal with them as a creditor; you shall not exact interest from them" (Exodus 22:25); (KJV) "neither shalt thou lay upon him usury."

"You shall not charge interest on loans to another Israelite, interest on money, interest on provisions, interest on anything that is lent. On loans to a foreigner you may charge interest, but on loans to another Israelite you may not charge interest, so that the LORD your God may bless you in all your undertakings in the land that you are about to enter and possess" (Deuteronomy 23:19–20); (KJV) "Thou shalt not lend upon usury to thy brother; usury of money, usury of victuals, usury of any thing that is lent upon usury: Unto a stranger thou mayest lend upon usury; but unto thy brother thou shalt not lend upon usury."

Nehemiah's condemnation of the "usury" that was practiced among the remnant of the Jews at Jerusalem (5:1–13) was based upon the principle that interest should not be exacted of a fellow Israelite. The KJV rendering of "usury" is retained occasionally in certain of the contemporary versions, e.g., at Nehemiah 5:7 (NASB, NIV, NKJV). The New Testament reflects the commercial practices of the Roman Empire, and assumes the legitimacy of banking, credit, and interest: "Thou oughtest therefore to have put my money to the exchangers, and then at my coming I should have received mine own with usury" (Matthew 25:27, KJV). The NKJV reads, "So you ought to have deposited my money with the bankers, and at my coming I would have received back my own with interest."

UTTER

As a verb, "utter" means "to speak or express." In the sixteenth century, however, it was frequently used in the sense of "to disclose or reveal something," or "to make known the character or identity of a person." It has this meaning in Joshua 2:14, 20, where the spies instruct Rahab not to "utter" (KJV) their business.

The NRSV translates as "The men said to her, 'Our life for yours! If you do not tell this business of ours, then we will deal kindly and faithfully with you when the LORD gives us the land . . . But if you tell this business of ours, then we shall be released from this oath that you made us swear to you.'"

In Leviticus 5:1 it is declared to be a sin if one is a witness and does not "utter" what he knows. The Hebrew verb is *nagad,* which has a similar meaning in Proverbs 29:24 (KJV, "bewray"; NKJV, "reveal"; NRSV, "disclose") and Jeremiah 20:10 (KJV, "report"; NASB, NRSV, "denounce").

Tyndale's translation of Mark 3:12 was, "And he straygtly charged them that they should not utter him." In Genesis 45:1 Tyndale had, "Joseph commaunded . . . that there shuld be no man with him, whyle he uttred him selfe unto his brethern."

Examples of Shakespeare's use of "utter" in this sense are:

> "My duty pricks me on to utter that
> Which else no worldly good should
>   draw from me."
>   —*The Two Gentlemen of Verona*
>   (III, 1, 8–9)

> "I will, like a true drunkard, utter
>   all to thee."
>   —*Much Ado About Nothing*
>   (III, 3, 112)
> "I am glad to be constrain'd to
>   utter that
> Which torments me to conceal."
>   —*Cymbeline* (V, 5, 141)

VAIN

For "vanity" the meaning of "undue self-esteem" is as old as the fourteenth century, but the adjective "vain" was not used in this sense until the late seventeenth century. In the KJV "vain" is used one hundred times and always has its original meaning of "empty," "worthless," "futile," "foolish."

"Vain" is used by the KJV as the translation for a dozen Hebrew words, each of which has its distinct meaning. "Thy vain thoughts" (Jeremiah 4:14, KJV) is now rendered as "your wicked thoughts" (NASB) and "your evil schemes" (NRSV). "Vain knowledge" (Job 15:2, KJV) is rendered as "windy knowledge" by the NASB, NRSV, and RSV, and "vain words" (Job 16:3, KJV) as "windy words."

"For vain man would be wise, though man be born like a wild ass's colt" (Job 11:12, KJV) has no word for "like" in the Hebrew, and is translated by the NASB, "An idiot will become intelligent when the foal of a wild donkey is born a man." The Hebrew word for which the KJV has "vain" literally means "hollow" or "empty-headed" (thus NKJV, NLT).

In Isaiah 45:18–19 the KJV has "in vain" for the Hebrew word which means "chaos"; in Jeremiah 3:23 and 8:8 it has "in vain" for the word which means "a delusion," "false," "a lie."

The KJV rendering of Lamentations 2:14 is a little obscure. It reads, "Thy prophets have seen vain and foolish things for thee: and they have not discovered thine iniquity, to turn away thy captivity; but have seen for thee false burdens and causes of banishment." The NASB translates:

"Your prophets have seen for you
False and foolish visions;
And they have not exposed your
iniquity
So as to restore you from captivity,
But they have seen for you false
and misleading oracles."

Zechariah 10:2 is also a little awkward: "For the idols have spoken vanity, and the diviners have seen a lie, and have told false dreams; they comfort in vain: therefore they went their way as a flock, they were troubled, because there was no shepherd" (KJV). In the NRSV this verse reads:

"For the teraphim utter nonsense,
and the diviners see lies;
the dreamers tell false dreams,
and give empty consolation.
Therefore the people wander like
sheep;
they suffer for lack of a shepherd."

In the New Testament, the contemporary versions convey the meaning represented by "vain" in the KJV with translations such as "empty words" (Ephesians 5:6, NASB, NIV, NKJV, NRSV, RSV); "empty deceit" (Colossians 2:8, NKJV, NRSV, RSV); "foolish person" (James 2:20, NCV); "senseless person" (NRSV); "futile" (1 Corinthians 3:20; 15:17, NIV, NKJV, NRSV, RSV), "useless" (Titus 3:9, CEV, NIV, NKJV, NLT), and "empty" (1 Peter 1:18, NIV, NLT). "Profane and vain babblings" (1 Timothy 6:20; 2 Timothy 2:16, KJV) is now translated as "empty [NIV, RSV, "godless"] chatter" (NASB, NIV, RSV).

VAINGLORY

This is an old word for "empty conceit" or "idle boasting." It appears as one word in Philippians 2:3, "Let nothing be done through strife or vainglory" (KJV) and as two words in Galatians 5:26, "Let us not be desirous of vain glory" (KJV). The Greek has the noun *kenodoxia* in Philippians and the adjective *kenodoxos* in Galatians. The NRSV translates as "Do nothing from selfish ambition or conceit"; "Let us not become conceited."

VALLEY OF THE SHADOW OF DEATH

The expression "the valley of the shadow of death" is used to refer to the dark circumstances in which one finds oneself facing death. It is in English versions of Psalm 23:4 from Coverdale; the earlier versions followed the Vulgate and Septuagint which had "midst" instead of "valley." In the KJV the verse reads: "Yea, though I walk through the valley of the shadow of death, I will fear no evil: for thou art with me; thy rod and thy staff they comfort me."

The KJV expression is retained by the NASB, NIV, NKJV, and the RSV; the other contemporary translations have: "the darkest valley" (NRSV), "the dark valley of death" (NLT), "a very dark valley" (NCV), and "valleys as dark as death" (CEV).

There are several other instances in the KJV of the expression "the shadow of death," e.g., Job 3:5, Psalm 107:10, Isaiah 9:2, and Jeremiah 2:6. The expression occurs in Bunyan's *Pilgrim's Progress* (Part 2): "The Valley it self . . . is as dark as pitch: we also saw there Hobgoblins, Satyrs, and Dragons of the Pit: We heard also in that Valley a continual howling and yelling, as of a People under unutterable misery; who there sat bound in affliction and Irons: and over that Valley hangs the discouraging cloud of confusion, death also doth always spread his wings over it: in a word, it is every wit dreadful, being utterly without Order."

VANITY

The word "vanity" now means "the quality of being personally vain." We usually apply the word to an excessive pride in one's own appearance. In the KJV, however, the word is never used in this sense. In the KJV, it means "emptiness," "worthlessness," "futility," or is applied to things that are empty, worthless, or futile. The KJV also uses the word "vanity" for "idolatry" and "idols," and occasionally for "sin" and "evil."

The word appears thirty-seven times in the Book of Ecclesiastes, where it is retained by the NASB, NKJV, NRSV, and RSV. The keynote of the book is set in the opening verses (1:2–3, KJV):

"Vanity of vanities, saith the Preacher, vanity of vanities; all is vanity.

What profit hath a man of all his labour which he taketh under the sun?"

Renderings in the other contemporary versions include: " 'Meaningless! Meaningless!' says the Teacher. 'Utterly meaningless! Everything is meaningless' " (NIV), " 'Everything is meaningless,' says the Teacher, 'utterly meaningless!' " (NLT), "Nothing makes sense! Everything is nonsense. I have seen it all—nothing makes sense!" (CEV), and "The Teacher says, 'Useless! Useless! Completely useless! Everything is useless' " (NCV). The Preacher's refrain, "all is vanity and vexation of spirit" (1:14, KJV) is translated by the NRSV as "all is vanity and a chasing after wind."

Outside the book of Ecclesiastes, the contemporary versions generally use terms that are closer to the primary meaning of the several Hebrew and Greek words for which the KJV uses "vanity." "Man is like to vanity" (Psalm 144:4, KJV) is now rendered by the NIV, NKJV, and RSV as "Man is like a breath." "Vanity shall take them" (Isaiah 57:13, KJV) is now "a breath will take them away" (NASB, NRSV, RSV).

"They are altogether lighter than vanity" (Psalm 62:9, KJV) reads in the NLT, "they are lighter than a puff of air." "Therefore their days did he consume in vanity" (Psalm 78:33, KJV) reads in the NRSV and RSV, "So he made their days vanish like a breath."

For "vanity," contemporary versions also use the following: "empty" and "emptiness" (Job 7:3, NCV, NRSV, RSV; Job 15:31, NRSV, RSV; Job 35:13, NASB, NIV, NKJV, NRSV, RSV; Psalm 41:6, NRSV, RSV; Isaiah 40:17, NRSV, RSV; Isaiah 59:4, NIV, NKJV, NRSV, RSV);

"worthless" and "worthlessness" (Job 15:31, NIV; Jeremiah 2:5, CEV, NIV, NRSV, RSV; Jeremiah 10:15, NASB, NIV, NLT, NRSV, RSV; Jeremiah 16:19, NKJV, NLT, NRSV, RSV; Jeremiah 51:18, NASB, NIV, NLT, NRSV, RSV);

"false" (Psalm 24:4, NIV, NRSV, RSV);

"falsehood" (Job 31:5, NASB, NIV, NKJV, NRSV, RSV; Psalm 12:2, NASB; Psalm 24:4, NASB; Isaiah 5:18, NASB, NLT, NRSV, RSV);

"lies" (Psalm 12:2, CEV, NCV, NIV, NLT, NRSV, RSV; Psalm 144:8, NIV, NLT, NRSV, RSV);

"deceit" (Psalm 144:8, NASB; Isaiah 5:18, NIV);

"false visions" (Ezekiel 13:6, NCV; Ezekiel 21:29, NASB, NCV, NIV, NKJV, NRSV, RSV; Ezekiel 22:28, CEV, NASB, NCV, NIV, NKJV, NRSV, RSV).

Agur's prayer is translated by the NRSV as "Remove far from me falsehood and lying; give me neither poverty nor riches; feed me with the food that I need" (Proverbs 30:8).

The word "vanity" is used in the KJV for "idolatry" and "idols." "Are there any among the vanities of the Gentiles that can cause rain?" (Jeremiah 14:22, KJV) now reads "Can any idols of the nations bring rain?" (NRSV). "Strange vanities" (Jeremiah 8:19, KJV) are now "foreign idols" (NASB, NCV, NIV, NKJV, NRSV, RSV), "useless idols" (CEV), and "worthless gods" (NLT).

"Lying vanities" (Psalm 31:6; Jonah 2:8, KJV) are "vain idols" (NASB). "They have provoked me to anger with their vanities" (Deuteronomy 32:21, KJV) reads in the NRSV, "they... provoked me with their idols"; so also 1 Kings 16:13, 26. "The stock is a doctrine of vanities" (Jeremiah 10:8, KJV) is rendered by contemporary versions as "Their teachings come from worthless wooden idols" (NASB), "A wooden idol is a worthless doctrine" (NKJV), and "the instruction given by idols is no better than wood!" (NRSV).

The KJV uses "vanity" occasionally for one of the Hebrew words which means "iniquity." "They conceive mischief, and bring forth vanity" (Job 15:35, KJV) now reads, "they conceive mischief and bring forth evil" [NASB, "bring forth iniquity"] (NASB, NRSV, RSV). "Under his tongue is mischief and vanity" (Psalm 10:7, KJV) is translated by the NKJV as "under his tongue is trouble and iniquity."

"He that soweth iniquity shall reap vanity" (Proverbs 22:8, KJV) is now rendered as "He who sows wickedness reaps trouble" (NIV), "He who sows iniquity will reap sorrow" (NKJV), "Those who plant seeds of injustice will harvest disaster" (NLT), and

"Whoever sows injustice will reap calamity" (NRSV). The NASB retains the KJV rendering.

In the New Testament, contemporary versions use the words "futility" (NASB, NKJV, NRSV, RSV) and "frustration" (NIV) in Romans 8:20 (KJV, "For the creature was made subject to vanity"); the CEV has "creation is confused." "Confused" is also used by the NLT in its rendering of Ephesians 4:17, which reads in the KJV: "This I say therefore, and testify in the Lord, that ye henceforth walk not as other Gentiles walk, in the vanity of their mind."

The NASB, NKJV, NRSV, and RSV have "in the futility of their mind" [NRSV, RSV, "minds"]; the NCV has "Their thoughts are worth nothing," and the NLT, "they are hopelessly confused." In 2 Peter 2:18 contemporary versions have "emptiness" (NKJV) and "folly" (RSV).

VENTURE, AT A

The word "venture" is used in contemporary English to refer to an undertaking that includes some risk. It is used in the KJV in the expression "at a venture" to mean "at random." It occurs twice in this sense, at 1 Kings 22:34 and its parallel 2 Chronicles 18:33, referring to the death of Ahab, king of Israel.

First Kings 22:34 reads in the KJV, "And a certain man drew a bow at a venture, and smote the king of Israel between the joint of the harness: wherefore he said unto the driver of his chariot, Turn thine hand, and carry me out of the host; for I am wounded." The contemporary versions render the KJV "at a venture" (retained by the RSV) in this verse and its parallel as: "at random" (NASB, NIV, NKJV), "randomly" (NLT), "unknowingly" (NRSV), "without even aiming" (CEV), and "by chance" (NCV).

The phrase was originally "at aventure," or "at adventure":

> "He was some hilding fellow that had stolen

The horse he rode on, and, upon my
life,
Spoke at a venture."
—*King Henry IV, Part II* (I, 1, 59)

According to the OED, "the correct 'Speake
at aduenture' is printed in the *Globe* ed.
'Speak *at a venture.'* "

VESSEL

The Hebrew word *keli* can stand for any
material thing or object, any tool, implement, or weapon, any vessel or receptacle
that can be handled and carried. The KJV
translates it 146 times by "vessel," and 136
times by other terms including "armour,"
"artillery," "bag," "carriage," "furniture,"
"instrument," "jewel," "pot," "sack," "stuff,"
"thing," "wares," "weapon."

In Hosea 13:15, "he shall spoil the treasure of all pleasant vessels" (KJV) is rendered by contemporary versions as: "It will
plunder his treasury of every precious article" (NASB), "His storehouse will be plundered of all its treasures" (NCV), and "It
shall strip his treasury of every precious
thing" (NRSV, RSV).

The Greek word *skeuos* likewise stands
for any thing or object which may be used
for any purpose. "And would not suffer that
any man should carry any vessel through
the temple" (Mark 11:16, KJV) unduly limits
Jesus' prohibition, which the NRSV translates as "he would not allow anyone to
carry anything through the temple."

Other versions have "merchandise" (NASB,
NIV, NLT), "goods" (NCV), and "wares" (NKJV).
"Something" is the translation adopted by
most contemporary versions for "a certain
vessel" (KJV) in the case of Peter's vision
(Acts 10:11, 16; 11:5).

The plural of *skeuos* is rendered as "his
stuff" (KJV) in Luke 17:31, but as "his goods"
(KJV) in Matthew 12:29 and Mark 3:27—the
Greek is the same. The Greek word is used
for a ship's "anchor" (NASB, NIV, NLT, NRSV)
in Acts 27:17, and for "the vessels used in
worship" (NRSV, RSV) in Hebrews 9:21.

The NASB, NKJV, and RSV retain the word
"vessel" in the notable passages Romans
9:20–24 and 2 Timothy 2:20–21, where the
term is applied to people. Key verses to
Paul's thought are Acts 9:15, which the
NASB translates as "he is a chosen instrument of Mine," and 2 Corinthians 4:7, "we
have this treasure in earthen vessels" (NASB,
NKJV, RSV).

The relevance of the term *skeuos* is not
so much that the body is a vessel containing
the mind or spirit, as that the body is the
instrument of the person, and the person
an instrument of God's will.

The expression "the weaker vessel" (1 Peter
3:7, KJV) shares with "filthy lucre" the
doubtful distinction of descent from biblical associations to jocular slang. This verse
reads in the KJV: "Likewise, ye husbands,
dwell with them according to knowledge,
giving honour unto the wife, as unto the
weaker vessel, and as being heirs together
of the grace of life; that your prayers be not
hindered."

The NKJV retains "the weaker vessel";
other contemporary versions have "someone weaker" (NASB), "the weaker partner"
(NIV), and "the weaker sex" (NRSV, RSV). (See
WEAKER VESSEL)

In 1 Thessalonians 4:4 "know how to
possess his vessel" (KJV) is an expression
about which there has been a good deal of
debate. Does "vessel" here mean "body"—
one's own body, or does it mean "wife"—
one's own wife? Chrysostom, Tertullian,
and Calvin are the most notable of those
who have taken it to mean "body." Au-
gustine, Thomas Aquinas, and Zwingli took
it to mean "wife."

Of the contemporary versions, the NCV,
NIV, NLT, and NRSV take *skeuos* here to mean
"body," and the CEV and RSV translate it as
"wife." The NASB and NKJV retain the KJV
wording. Verses 3 and 4 read in the NKJV:
"For this is the will of God, your sanctification, that you should abstain from sexual
immorality: that each of you should know

how to possess his own vessel in sanctification and honor." (See POSSESS)

VEX

"Vex" was a popular Elizabethan word which had far more force than it has today. It stood for "physical aggression or affliction" as well as for "irritation." In the KJV "vex" usually means to "hurt," "harass," "oppress," "afflict," "torment," "distress." It only occasionally refers to the feeling of the victims of such aggression or affliction.

"Vex" appears thirty-seven times in the KJV as translation for twenty-three different Hebrew or Greek verbs, which contemporary versions render more literally. To "vex a stranger" (Exodus 22:21; Leviticus 19:33, KJV) is now rendered as to "wrong a stranger" (NASB, RSV), to "mistreat an alien" (NIV), to "oppress" or "exploit" foreigners (NLT). "Vex the Midianites" (Numbers 25:17, 18; cf. Isaiah 11:13, KJV) is "harass the Midianites" (NKJV, NRSV, RSV). "The Egyptians vexed us, and our fathers" (Numbers 20:15, KJV) reads in the NRSV, "oppressed us and our ancestors."

"Vex" is used for the Hebrew verb rendered as "crush" by the NRSV and RSV (Judges 10:8), and for Hebrew verbs rendered as "terrify" by most contemporary versions in Psalm 2:5.

Elisha's word to his servant concerning the Shunammite woman, "Let her alone; for her soul is vexed within her" (2 Kings 4:27, KJV), is translated by the NRSV as "Let her alone, for she is in bitter distress." The same Hebrew verb occurs in Job 27:2, where "the Almighty, who hath vexed my soul" (KJV) is rendered as "the Almighty, who has made my soul bitter" (NKJV, NRSV, RSV).

The reluctance of David's servants to tell him that Bathsheba's child had died may be a little understated in the KJV, "how will he then vex himself?" (2 Samuel 12:18). Contemporary versions have "He may do something desperate" (NIV) and "He may do himself some harm" (NRSV, RSV).

A woman of Canaan cried out to Jesus that her daughter was "grievously vexed with a devil" (Matthew 15:22, KJV); contemporary versions have "cruelly demon-possessed" (NASB), "suffering very much" (NCV), and "is tormented by a demon" (NRSV).

The son who was a "lunatick, and sore vexed" (Matthew 17:15, KJV) was "an epileptic" who "suffers severely" (NKJV). The "vexed with unclean spirits" (Acts 5:16, KJV) were "tormented by with unclean spirits" (NRSV).

In 2 Peter 2:8 Lot is said to have been "vexed in his righteous soul" (KJV) day after day by the wickedness of Sodom; contemporary versions say he was "tormented" (NASB, NIV, NKJV, NRSV), "distressed" (NLT), and, with the KJV, "vexed" (RSV).

VEXATION

In the KJV "vexation" means more than annoyance or irritation. Like "vex" it was a strong term in the sixteenth and seventeenth centuries. (See VEX) Even with the stronger connotation that it had in 1611, "vexation" may be too weak a translation in Isaiah 28:19, "it shall be a vexation only to understand the report."

The revised versions of 1885–1901 have "it shall be naught but terror to understand the message"; the NASB, NIV, NRSV, RSV, it will be "sheer terror." In Isaiah 9:1 the KJV reads, "Nevertheless the dimness shall not be such as was in her vexation"; following the revised versions, the NRSV has "But there will be no gloom for those who were in anguish."

Similarly, "ye . . . shall howl for vexation of spirit" (Isaiah 65:14, KJV) is now rendered by the NKJV as "you shall . . . wail for grief of spirit," and by the NRSV as "you . . . shall wail for anguish of spirit." In Ecclesiastes the often repeated "vexation of spirit" (1:14, etc.) is the KJV rendering for a different Hebrew phrase—translated by contemporary versions as "striving after wind" (NASB, RSV), "chasing after the wind" (NIV), and "grasping for the wind" (NKJV). (See VANITY)

VILE

Today we use the word "vile" to mean "disgusting" or "despicable" ("vile soup";

"a vile play"). Along with these senses, and like the Latin *vilis*, "vile" has meant also "cheap," "paltry," or "worthless." The KJV translators were fond of the word. They used it eighteen times to translate nine different Hebrew words, each of which had a distinct meaning—"despised," "worthless," "a fool," "disgusting," "stupid," "trifling," "dishonored," "defiled," "whipped"—and three times to translate three quite distinct Greek words.

"Vile" is retained by the NKJV, NRSV, and RSV in Judges 19:24, as an appropriate word for the behavior of the men of Sodom; other versions have "horrible" (CEV), "terrible" (NCV), "disgraceful" (NIV), and "shameful" (NLT).

"Vilest men" (KJV) in Psalm 12:8 is now rendered as "vileness" (NASB, NKJV, NRSV, RSV) and "what is vile" (NIV), and in Jeremiah 29:17 "vile figs, that cannot be eaten" is rendered as "split-open figs" (NASB), "poor figs" (NIV), and as "rotten figs" (NRSV).

"Thou art vile" (KJV), God's rebuke to Nineveh (Nahum 1:14), is rendered as "you are vile" by the NIV, NKJV, and RSV, while other versions render "vile" here as "worthless" (CEV, NRSV), "contemptible" (NASB), and "wicked" (NCV).

In Isaiah 32:5 "vile person" represents the Hebrew word for "fool" (so rendered by the majority of the contemporary versions). "I am vile" (Job 40:4; Lamentations 1:11) now reads "I am insignificant" (Job 40:4, NASB), "I am of small account" (Job 40:4, NRSV, RSV), and "I am despised" (Lamentations 1:11, NASB, NIV, NLT, RSV).

Bildad's question, "Wherefore are we . . . reputed vile in your sight?" (Job 18:3, KJV), is now translated by the NRSV and RSV as "Why are we stupid in your sight?" "They were viler than the earth" (Job 30:8) is the KJV translation for the Hebrew text which is now rendered as "They were scourged from the land" (NASB, NKJV) and "they have been whipped out of the land" (NRSV, RSV).

In Philippians 3:21 Paul discusses the transformation of believers' physical bod-

ies at the Lord's coming. The verse reads in the KJV: "Who shall change our vile body, that it may be fashioned like unto his glorious body, according to the working whereby he is able even to subdue all things unto himself."

Contemporary versions render "vile bodies" here as "poor bodies" (CEV), "the body of our humble state" (NASB), "our simple bodies" (NCV), "our lowly bodies" [NKJV, RSV, "body"] (NIV, NKJV, RSV), "these weak mortal bodies" (NLT). The study of Greek papyri in recent years has made it clear that the "vile raiment" (KJV) of James 2:2 is shabby or ill-kept clothing (NASB, NCV, NRSV, "dirty clothes"; NKJV, "filthy clothes"; CEV, "worn-out clothes").

"Vile affections" (Romans 1:26, KJV) is now rendered as "evil desires" (CEV), "degrading [RSV, "dishonorable"] passions" (NASB, NRSV, RSV), and "shameful lusts" (NIV).

VIRTUE

In two contexts of the KJV New Testament the word "virtue" does not refer to "moral character," as it does today, but to "power." It occurs in the statement made by Jesus when a woman touched him in the hope of being healed: "Somebody hath touched me: for I perceive that virtue is gone out of me" (Luke 8:46, KJV; cf. Mark 5:30).

"Virtue" here, and in Luke 6:19, renders the Greek term *dynamis*. It is translated as "[NLT, "healing"] power" by all contemporary versions.

VISAGE

The word "visage" means "face," and in the story of Nebuchadnezzar's anger against Shadrach, Meshach, and Abednego "the form of his visage was changed" (Daniel 3:19, KJV) is now rendered as "his facial expression was altered" (NASB) and "his face was distorted" (NRSV). In Isaiah 52:14, however, the word "visage" is used in the more general sense of appearance.

"His visage was so marred" (KJV) is now rendered as "His appearance was marred"

(NASB), and "his appearance was so disfigured" (NIV).

VOICE CRYING IN THE WILDERNESS

The expression "a voice crying in the wilderness" is sometimes used in contemporary English to refer to someone who is proclaiming a warning or other message that generally goes unheeded by listeners.

The expression derives from the references to John the Baptist, at Matthew 3:3, "For this is he that was spoken of by the prophet Esaias, saying, The voice of one crying in the wilderness, Prepare ye the way of the Lord, make his paths straight" and with its parallels Mark 1:3, Luke 3:4 as a quotation from Isaiah 40:3.

At Matthew 3:3 the contemporary versions read as the KJV, "the voice of one crying in the wilderness" (NASB, NKJV), "the voice of one crying out in the wilderness" (NRSV), "a voice of one shouting in the wilderness" (NLT), "a voice of one calling in the desert" (NIV), "a voice of one who calls out in the desert" (NCV), and "in the desert someone is shouting" (CEV), with similar translations at the parallels and John 1:23, including John 1:23 (CEV): "John answered in the words of the prophet Isaiah, 'I am only someone shouting in the desert, "Get the road ready for the Lord!" ' "

In the source of the New Testament quotation, in Isaiah 40:3, the KJV (and only the NKJV among the contemporary versions) has the expression "in the wilderness" immediately after the verb "cry," i.e., describing where the prophet was crying; in all the other contemporary versions, the expression "in the wilderness" (or its contemporary renderings such as "in the desert") is part of what the prophet is crying, e.g., NASB, "A voice is calling, 'Clear the way for the LORD in the wilderness.' "

VOLUME

The English word "volume" is an adaptation of the Latin *volumen,* from *volvere,* which means "to roll." It originally meant a roll of manuscript, such as constituted a book or part of a book in ancient times. The expression "the volume of the book," which appears twice in the KJV, is rendered as "the scroll of the book," "the scroll," "the roll of the book," or simply, "the book" by the revised versions.

The KJV translated the Hebrew word *megillah* as "roll" twenty-one times and as "volume" once (Psalm 40:7). In Hebrews 10:7 this verse from the Psalms is quoted and "volume" appears as a translation for the Greek word which the Septuagint had used for *megillah.*

W

WAGES OF SIN IS DEATH

The expression "the wages of sin is death" is sometimes used in contemporary English to mean "the inevitable consequence of wrong-doing is punishment and suffering" (*Oxford Dictionary of Current Idiomatic English,* vol. 2). The phrase derives from Romans 6:23: "For the wages of sin is death; but the gift of God is eternal life through Jesus Christ our Lord" (KJV).

Of the contemporary versions, the NASB, NIV, NKJV, NLT, NRSV, and RSV retain the KJV expression; the CEV has "Sin pays off with

death" and the NCV, "When people sin, they earn what sin pays—death."

In Bunyan's *Pilgrim's Progress,* Apollyon meets Christian in the Valley of Humiliation and claims him as one of his subjects. Christian answers, "I was born indeed in your dominions, but your service was hard, and your wages such as a man could not live on, for the Wages of Sin is death."

In his poem *Wages,* Tennyson wrote:

"The wages of sin is death: if the wages of Virtue be dust,

Would she have the heart to endure
for the life of the worm and the fly?
... Give her the wages of going on,
and not to die."

WAIT ON, WAIT UPON

Today the expression "wait upon" makes us think of service and the task of attending to people's needs. A waiter waits upon tables; a mother might complain that she does nothing but wait upon her family. In the KJV, "wait on" is sometimes used in this sense of "attend" or "serve," but it often means "to place one's hope in (God)." In the KJV of 1611 the phrase renders several Hebrew verbs of identical meaning.

The NASB, NRSV, and RSV usually replace it by "wait for" (Psalms 25:3, 5, 21; 27:14; 37:9, 34; 62:1, 5; Proverbs 20:22; Isaiah 8:17; 40:31; 51:5; Hosea 12:6; Zephaniah 3:8), but in some contexts the NRSV and RSV express more clearly the implied attitude of hope: "We set our hope on you" (Jeremiah 14:22, NRSV); "Do not let those who hope in you be put to shame through me" (Psalm 69:6, NRSV).

Other versions use "hope in" and "trust" or "trust in" more often. "On thee do I wait all the day" (Psalm 25:5, KJV) reads in the NCV, "I trust you all day long" and in the NLT, "All day long I put my hope in you." "Those who wait upon the LORD" (Psalm 37:9, KJV) are "those who trust [NLT, "who trust in"] the LORD" (NCV, NLT) and "those who hope in the LORD" (NIV).

In Psalms 104:27 and 145:15 "Look to" is used by the NIV, NRSV, and RSV in Psalm 104:27; this expression is chosen by the majority of contemporary versions in Psalm 145:15. The second of these verses reads in the NRSV:

"The eyes of all look to you,
and you give them their food in
due season."

Psalm 123:2 reads in the NASB:

"Behold, as the eyes of servants look
to the hand of their master,
As the eyes of a maid to the hand of
her mistress,
So our eyes look to the Lord our God,
Until He is gracious to us."

"Wait on" is also used by the KJV in the sense of "attend" or "serve." "They waited on their office" (1 Chronicles 6:32, KJV) reads in the NIV, "they performed their duties"; and "to wait on the sons of Aaron" (1 Chronicles 23:28, KJV) reads, "to assist the sons of Aaron" (NASB, RSV). "The priests waited on their offices" (2 Chronicles 7:6, KJV) is rendered as "The priests took their assigned positions" (NLT).

"These waited on the king" (2 Chronicles 17:19, KJV) now reads, "These were in the service of the king" (NRSV, RSV). To "wait at the altar" (1 Corinthians 9:13, KJV) is now rendered as to "serve at the altar" (NCV, NIV, NKJV, NLT, NRSV, RSV).

WAKE

While most people know that a "wake" is "a watch over the dead," the verb in this sense has gone out of standard speech. It originally meant "to remain awake" and, so, "to watch over something." Psalm 127:1 is a much quoted verse, but the second half of it is frequently omitted: "Except the LORD build the house, they labour in vain that build it; except the LORD keep the city, the watchman waketh but in vain."

Contemporary versions have "stays awake" (NKJV, RSV), "stand guard" (NIV), "keeps watch" (NRSV). Examples of this use of the word in literature are:

"Watch thou and wake when others
be asleep."
—*King Henry VI, Part II* (I, 1, 249)

"Thus must we do though, that
wake for the public good; and

> thus hath the wise magistrate
> done in all ages."
> —Ben Jonson,
> *Bartholomew Fair* (II, 1)

WANT

This is a favorite word with children, whose demands often seem incessant. In the KJV, however, "want" is always used in the older sense of "lack," and not in the sense of "desire."

In John's account of the marriage at Cana (John 2:1–11), the KJV reads, "And when they wanted wine, the mother of Jesus saith unto him, They have no wine." The seventeenth-century reader understood the clause "And when they wanted wine" (John 2:3, KJV) to mean "when they lacked wine" just as naturally as we would understand it to mean "when they desired wine."

Tyndale translated the clause as "And when the wine failed." His rendering was used in the successive versions of Coverdale, Thomas Matthew, the Great Bible, the Geneva Bible, and the first edition of the Bishops' Bible. The Greek text implies that the bridegroom had supplied wine, according to Jewish custom, but that he had miscalculated and did not supply enough.

Contemporary versions say that the wine "ran out" (NASB, NLT), "gave out" (NRSV, Goodspeed, Phillips, Verkuyl), and "ran short" (Moffatt, Weymouth, Twentieth Century, Ballantine, Rieu).

Contemporary versions do occasionally use "want" in the older sense, retaining such renderings as "The LORD is my shepherd, I shall not want" (Psalm 23:1, NASB, NKJV, NRSV, RSV; NIV, "I shall not be in want"; NCV, NLT, "I have everything I need"); "those who fear him have no want" (Psalm 34:9, NRSV, RSV; NIV, "lack nothing"); "he began to be in want" (Luke 15:14, NKJV, RSV; NASB, "impoverished"; NRSV, "in need"); "Not that I complain of want" (Philippians 4:11, RSV; NRSV, "being in need").

"When I was present with you, and wanted" (2 Corinthians 11:9, KJV) now reads in the NIV, "when I was with you and needed something."

In other passages, the contemporary versions replace "want" with another word, usually "lack." Examples are: "Fools die for want of wisdom" (Proverbs 10:21, KJV); NIV, "fools die for lack of judgment." "A prince that wanteth understanding" (Proverbs 28:16, KJV); NKJV, NRSV, RSV, "a ruler who lacks understanding." "He wanteth nothing for his soul of all that he desireth" (Ecclesiastes 6:2, KJV); NRSV, "they lack nothing of all that they desire"; "him that wanteth understanding" (Proverbs 9:4, KJV); NRSV, "without sense."

A familiar verse is Psalm 34:10, which reads in the KJV, "The young lions do lack, and suffer hunger: but they that seek the LORD shall not want any good thing." The NRSV translates:

> "The young lions suffer want and
>   hunger,
> but those who seek the LORD
>   lack no good thing."

A slightly obscure rendering is found in Proverbs 13:23, which reads in the KJV: "Much food is in the tillage of the poor: but there is that is destroyed for want of judgment." The NASB translates:

> "Abundant food is in the fallow
>   ground of the poor,
> But it is swept away by injustice."

The verb "want" did not begin to be used in the sense of "desire" until almost one hundred years after the publication of the KJV. This is now, however, its more common meaning. In the New Testament, contemporary versions now use the word "want" to translate Greek verbs which mean to "wish," "desire," or "will." These verbs are usually represented in the KJV by "would," "will," or "wilt," which may easily be mistaken for auxiliary verbs denoting a future tense.

Examples are: "What wilt thou?" (Matthew 20:21, KJV); NCV, NRSV, RSV, "What do you

W

want?" "He would not reject her" (Mark 6:26, KJV); NIV, NKJV, NRSV, RSV, "he did not want to refuse her." "Wilt thou be made whole?" (John 5:6, KJV); CEV, RSV, "Do you want to be healed?" "Wherefore would ye hear it again? will ye also be his disciples?" (John 9:27, KJV); NRSV, "Why do you want to hear it again? Do you also want to become his disciples?" "Wilt thou kill me?" (Acts 7:28, KJV); NCV, NIV, NRSV, RSV, "Do you want to kill me?" "Would pervert the gospel of Christ" (Galatians 1:7, KJV); NKJV, NRSV, RSV, "want to pervert the gospel of Christ."

The outstanding example is Romans 7:15–21, Paul's account of his sinful plight. In these verses "I would" (KJV) serves as translation of the present tense of the Greek verb *thelo*, which means to "wish," "desire," "want."

WARD

In modern usage, a "ward" might be "a district," "a division of a hospital," or "a minor." But in the KJV the word stands for "custody," "a place of custody," "a body of guards or watchmen" or "the duties of such men." The NIV, NKJV, NRSV, and RSV use "custody" in the story of Joseph's imprisonment (Genesis 40:3, 4, 7; also 41:10, NKJV, NRSV, RSV) and in two incidents leading to the death penalty while the people of Israel were in the wilderness (Leviticus 24:12; Numbers 15:34; also NASB, NIV, NLT).

Contemporary versions use "prison" (NASB, NCV, NKJV, NRSV, RSV) and "custody" (NIV) in Genesis 42:17. When David returned to Jerusalem after the collapse of Absalom's rebellion, and put his ten concubines "in ward" (KJV), the NRSV says that he "put them in a house under guard, and provided for them, but did not go in to them" (2 Samuel 20:3).

In 1 Chronicles 9:23; 25:8; 26:12, 16 and Nehemiah 12:24–25, 45; 13:30, the term "ward" (KJV) refers to guards and their duties. The statement concerning the tribe of Benjamin, that "hitherto the greatest part of them had kept the ward of the house of

Saul" (1 Chronicles 12:29, KJV) means that "until now the greatest part of them had kept their allegiance to the house of Saul" (NASB).

"In my ward" (Isaiah 21:8, KJV) is now rendered as "at my post" (NIV, NKJV, NLT, NRSV, RSV). "A captain of the ward" (Jeremiah 37:13, KJV) is rendered as "sentry" (NLT, RSV), "sentinel" (NRSV), "captain of the guard" (NASB, NIV, NKJV). "The first and the second ward" (KJV) of the prison in which Peter was confined means "the first and second [NRSV, "the second"] guard" (Acts 12:10, NASB, NRSV).

-WARD

The suffix "-ward" means "in the direction of." It appears in such words as "upward," "downward," "inward," "outward," "earthward," "heavenward," and "skyward." In the sixteenth century it was still a matter of taste or mood whether to write "toward you" or "to youward," "toward us" or "to us-ward," and the like. The KJV uses "toward" 320 times, but has eleven instances of the archaic usage. Numbered for subsequent reference, these are:

(1) "Be thou for the people to God-ward" (Exodus 18:19); NKJV, "Stand before God for the people"; NLT, "be the people's representative before God."

(2) "And such trust have we . . . to God-ward" (2 Corinthians 3:4); NASB, "Such confidence we have . . . toward God."

(3) "your faith to God-ward" (1 Thessalonians 1:8); CEV, NCV, NIV, NLT, NRSV, RSV, "your faith in God."

(4) "to the mercy seatward" (Exodus 37:9); NASB, NKJV, NRSV, RSV, "toward the mercy seat."

(5) "his works have been to thee-ward very good" (1 Samuel 19:4); NASB, "his deeds have been very beneficial to you."

(6) "thy thoughts which are to us-ward" (Psalm 40:5); NASB, NKJV, NRSV, "Your [RSV, "thy"] thoughts toward us."

(7) "his power to us-ward who believe" (Ephesians 1:19); NLT, NRSV, "his power for us."

(8) "is longsuffering to us-ward" (2 Peter 3:9); NASB, "is patient toward you."

(9) "more abundantly to you-ward" (2 Corinthians 1:12); NASB, "especially toward you"; NRSV, "all the more toward you."

(10) "which to you-ward is not weak" (2 Corinthians 13:3); NRSV, "is not weak in dealing with you."

(11) "the grace of God which is given me to you-ward" (Ephesians 3:2); NIV, NRSV, RSV, "God's grace that was given to me for you."

Of these instances, the archaic expressions were derived: (6) from the second edition of the Bishops' Bible; (3), (4), (5), (10) from the first edition of the Bishops' Bible; and (1), (2), (7), (8), (9), (11) from Tyndale. Tyndale uses "to Godwarde" (Acts 22:3; 1 John 3:21); "to me warde" (2 Corinthians 7:7); "to manwarde" (Titus 3:4); "to us warde" (Ephesians 2:7; 1 John 4:9); "to Jewrye warde" (2 Corinthians 1:16); and "to his buryinge warde" (Mark 14:8). All but the last of these also appear in the Geneva Bible, but were rejected by the KJV.

Strangely, the revisers in 1881 and 1901 inserted the archaic expression in four passages where the KJV did not use it: "to us-ward" (Romans 8:18), and "to you-ward" (Galatians 5:10; Colossians 1:25; 1 Thessalonians 5:18).

WARE

As an adjective, "ware" is now obsolete. We use "aware" and "wary" instead. When an attempt was made at Iconium to organize a gang to stone Paul and Barnabas, the KJV says that "they were ware of it, and fled unto Lystra and Derbe" (Acts 14:6). The RV and ASV have "they became aware of it"; the NLT, NRSV, and RSV, the apostles "learned of it."

Paul did not forget Alexander the coppersmith, saying that he "did me much evil" and warning Timothy, "Of whom be thou ware also" (2 Timothy 4:14–15). Contemporary versions translate Paul's advice as "Be on guard against him yourself" (NASB), "You also must beware of him" (NKJV), "Be careful of him" (NLT).

WASH ONE'S HANDS OF

To "wash one's hands of" something means to say or show that one no longer wants to be responsible for or involved in an action; one disclaims all responsibility for it. This idiomatic phrase has its origins in Matthew 27:24: "When Pilate saw that he could prevail nothing, but that rather a tumult was made, he took water, and washed his hands before the multitude, saying, I am innocent of the blood of this just person: see ye to it" (KJV).

Pilate refused to assume responsibility for Jesus' death, washing his hands, so symbolizing his dissociation from the desire of the people to crucify Jesus. Wording referring to the action of Pilate's taking some water and washing his hands in front of the crowd is retained by all the contemporary versions.

The expression is often referred to in literature, e.g., by Shakespeare in *King Richard II* (IV, 1, 237–242) where, in the abdication scene, King Richard condemns his accusers:

"Nay, all of you that stand and look upon me
Whilst that my wretchedness doth bait myself,
Though some of you with Pilate wash your hands
Showing an outward pity; yet you Pilates
Have here deliver'd me to my sour cross,
And water cannot wash away your sin."

WASTENESS

The word "wasteness" occurs just once in the KJV, in Zephaniah 1:15, "a day of wasteness and desolation." The Hebrew has "a day of *sho'ah* and *mesho'ah*." The interchangeability of these Hebrew words is attested by the fact that in the KJV *sho'ah* is usually translated by "desolation," and *mesho'ah* by "waste." The OED calls this sense of the word "chiefly Biblical" and marks it as obsolete.

In Zephaniah 1:15 contemporary versions have "destruction and desolation" (NASB), "trouble and ruin" (NIV), and "ruin and devastation" (NRSV, RSV).

WASTER

"He also that is slothful in his work is brother to him that is a great waster" (Proverbs 18:9, KJV) seems to link the man who wastes time with the man who wastes money. In fact, the Hebrew word here rendered "waster" does not mean a spendthrift, but one who lays waste, ravages, destroys.

The NASB and RSV translate as "He who is slack in his work is brother [RSV, "is a brother"] to him who destroys." Other versions render "a great waster" (KJV) as "someone who destroys things" (NCV), "a great destroyer" (NKJV), and "a vandal" (NRSV).

The only other occurrence of "waster" (KJV) is in Isaiah 54:16, which reads: "Behold, I have created the smith that bloweth the coals in the fire, and that bringeth forth an instrument for his work; and I have created the waster to destroy." Here contemporary versions have "armies" (CEV, NLT), "destroyer" (NASB, NCV, NIV), "spoiler" (NKJV), and "ravager" (NRSV, RSV).

WATCH AND PRAY

The expression "watch and pray" means "to be alert" and at the same time "to be prayerful." It occurs three times in the KJV at Matthew 26:41; Mark 13:33; and Mark 14:38 ("Watch ye and pray," KJV). The first

and last references are Jesus' words in Gethsemane.

The contemporary versions render these as "Watch and pray" (NIV, NKJV, RSV), "Stay awake and pray" (CEV, NCV, NRSV at Matthew 26:41; the NRSV at Mark 14:38 is "Keep awake and pray"); "Keep alert and pray" (NLT), and "Keep watching and praying" (NASB).

The expression "watch and pray" also occurs at Mark 13:33 (KJV and NKJV) when Jesus is talking about the day of the Lord's appearance.

WAX

This is a common verb in the KJV, where it means "to grow." We use it now only for the phases of the moon and in the idiom "wax and wane." Otherwise, as the OED remarks, the word is obsolete or literary "with a somewhat archaic flavor." Of the contemporary versions the RSV retains it in only one verse (Deuteronomy 32:15):

"But Jeshurun waxed fat, and kicked;
you waxed fat, you grew thick, you
    became sleek."

The second line of this verse, in the Hebrew, consists of only three words. If put as tersely into English, it would read: "you fattened, you thickened, you sleekened." "Waxed," "grew," and "became" have a merely auxiliary status here, equivalent to the suffix "-en"; moreover, these three auxiliary verbs are synonyms.

This status is characteristic of the KJV's use of the verb "to wax." It carries no connotation of increase in magnitude or strength. It is only equivalent to "grow" in the sense that both "wax" and "grow" are equivalent to "become." See OED, *Grow,* 12; *Wax,* 9(b).

"Wax old" (2 Chronicles 24:15; Job 14:8; Hebrews 8:13, KJV) means "grow old." "Is the LORD's hand waxed short?" (Numbers 11:23, KJV) is now rendered as "Is the LORD's power limited" (NASB, NRSV), "Is the LORD's arm too short?" (NIV), and "Is the LORD's hand shortened?" (RSV).

In the parable of the grain of mustard seed the KJV has "it grew, and waxed a great tree" (Luke 13:19). The Greek word here represented by "waxed" means "became." Similarly in Hebrews 11:34, "waxed valiant" represents Greek words which contemporary versions render as "became mighty" (NASB, NRSV, RSV), "became powerful" (NIV), and "became valiant" (NKJV). In Luke's statements concerning the child John (1:80) and the child Jesus (2:40), "waxed strong" is now "became strong" (NASB, NCV, NIV, NKJV, NLT, NRSV, RSV).

WEAKER VESSEL

The phrase "weaker vessel" is sometimes used in contemporary English to refer to "a person less able to withstand physical or mental strain, temptation or exploitation, than others" (*Oxford Dictionary of Current Idiomatic English,* vol. 2). The phrase derives from 1 Peter 3:7, describing the wife of a husband: "Likewise, ye husbands, dwell with them according to knowledge, giving honour unto the wife, as unto the weaker vessel, and as being heirs together of the grace of life; that your prayers be not hindered" (KJV).

The contemporary versions render this expression as follows: "the weaker partner" (NIV), "the weaker sex" (NRSV, RSV), "someone weaker" (NASB), "she isn't as strong as you are" (CEV), "[of wives] they are weaker than you" (NCV), and "she may be weaker than you are" (NLT).

In contemporary language, the phrase is not usually applied to women, as it is considered by some people to be sexist.

Shakespeare used this phrase, for example, in *Love's Labour's Lost* (I, 1, 266–268). Don Adriano de Armado reported in a letter to the king that one Costard, " 'a shallow vassal,' unlawfully 'sorted and consorted' with 'Jaquenetta, so is the weaker vessel called which I apprehended with the aforesaid swain,—I keep her as a vessel of the law's fury.' " (See VESSEL)

WEALTH

The word "wealth" today causes us to think of bulging pocketbooks and luxuriant lifestyles, but in the sixteenth century the word was also used in the sense of "well-being" or "welfare." Unless we remember this, Paul's counsel in 1 Corinthians 10:24 looks like encouragement to theft: "Let no man seek his own, but every man another's wealth." The NASB translates as "Let no one seek his own good, but that of his neighbor." The NKJV renders "wealth" (KJV) here as "well-being."

In the KJV Old Testament, the word "wealth" is used three times as a translation for the Hebrew *tob,* which means "good," either as an adjective or as a noun. The passages are Ezra's recital of the commandment not to intermarry with the people of the land, "nor seek their peace or their wealth" (Ezra 9:12); the praise of Mordecai as "seeking the wealth of his people" (Esther 10:3); and Job's description of the prosperity of the wicked who "spend their days in wealth" (Job 21:13).

The NASB, NKJV, NRSV, and RSV use "prosperity" in the passages from Ezra and Job, and "welfare" (RSV) and "good" (NASB, NKJV, NRSV) in the passage concerning Mordecai— "he sought the good of his people" (NRSV).

The KJV and the NASB, NRSV, and RSV use "welfare" as the translation for *tob* in Nehemiah 2:10, which tells how Sanballat and Tobiah were greatly displeased that Nehemiah had come "to seek the welfare of the people of Israel" (NRSV). The NKJV again uses the word "well-being."

The KJV "wealthy" occurs twice. At Psalm 66:12, "a wealthy place" in "thou broughtest us out into a wealthy place" is rendered in the contemporary versions as "a place of abundance" (NASB, NIV, NLT), "a spacious place" (NRSV, RSV), "rich fulfillment" (NKJV), "a land of plenty" (CEV), and at Jeremiah 49:31, "get you up unto the wealthy nation" is a nation that is "at ease" (NASB, NIV, NRSV, RSV); one that is "comfortable" (NCV); and

W

"self-sufficient" (NLT); the NKJV retains the KJV "wealthy."

WEIGHED IN THE BALANCE AND FOUND WANTING

If a person or thing has been "weighed in the balance and found wanting," they are considered not to have met a particular standard in their behavior, efficient working, etc. The expression derives from the writing on the wall to Belshazzar: "TEKEL; Thou art weighed in the balances and art found wanting" (Daniel 5:27, KJV). (See WRITING ON THE WALL)

The contemporary versions render this expression, which translates "Tekel," as: "you have been weighed on the scales and found wanting" [NASB, "found deficient"] (NASB, NIV, NRSV, RSV), "You have been weighed in the balances, and found wanting" (NKJV), "you have been weighed on the balances and have failed the test" (NLT), "You have been weighed on the scales and found not good enough" (NCV), and "He [God] has weighed you on his balance scales, and you fall short of what it takes to be king" (CEV).

WENT FOR

This expression appears in the KJV rendering of 1 Samuel 17:12, "Jesse . . . had eight sons; and the man went among men for an old man in the days of Saul." This seems to imply that he was regarded as an old man, though he was not really such. The KJV was the first to use "went for an old man." Tyndale and Coverdale had "was an old man." Geneva said "was taken for an old man," and was followed by the Bishops' Bible.

The CEV, NCV, and NLT return to the direct statement, "was an old man"; the NASB, NIV, NKJV, NRSV, and RSV simply say that Jesse "was old."

WHAT

The KJV uses "what" in the sense of "why" in 2 Kings 6:33, "what should I wait for the LORD any longer?" (KJV) and in Luke 22:71,

"What need we any further witness?" (KJV). In the first of these passages contemporary versions use "why," and they recast the second in closer touch with the Greek text: "What further need do we have of testimony?" (NASB); "What further testimony do we need?" (NKJV, NRSV, RSV). In *Paradise Lost* (II, 329) Milton wrote, "What sit we then projecting peace and war?"

"What time" (KJV) is used for "when" in Numbers 26:10, "what time the fire devoured two hundred and fifty men." Psalm 56:3, "What time I am afraid, I will trust in thee," is reworded by the NRSV as "When I am afraid, I put my trust in you."

Job 6:17 reads in the KJV, "What time they wax warm, they vanish: when it is hot, they are consumed out of their place." Job is comparing his deceitful friends to a wadi or a brook. The NRSV translates, "In time of heat they disappear; when it is hot, they vanish from their place." The NASB has "When they become waterless, they are silent"; the NKJV, "When it is warm, they cease to flow." (See WAX)

WHAT GOD HATH JOINED

See JOINED TOGETHER, LET NO MAN PUT ASUNDER.

WHAT IS TRUTH?

See TRUTH, WHAT IS?

WHATSOEVER THY HAND FINDETH TO DO

See HAND, WHATSOEVER.

WHEELS WITHIN WHEELS

The expression "wheels within wheels" is sometimes used in contemporary English to describe a complex series of several different interrelated influences or issues. This phrase comes from the description of Ezekiel's vision of the living creatures and the glory of the Lord: "The appearance of the wheels and their work was like unto the colour of a beryl: and they four had one likeness: and their appearance and their work was as it were a wheel in the middle of a wheel" (Ezekiel 1:16, KJV).

The KJV expression "as it were a wheel in the middle of a wheel" is rendered by the contemporary versions as: "as if one wheel were within another" (NASB), "as it were, a wheel in the middle of a wheel" (NKJV), "their construction being something like a wheel within a wheel" (NRSV, RSV), "like a wheel intersecting a wheel" (NIV), and "like one wheel crossways inside another wheel" (NCV).

The phrase is alluded to in literature, e.g., in Anthony Ashley Cooper, third earl of Shaftesbury's *Characteristics of Men, Manners, Opinions, and Times* (1711): "Thus we have Wheels within Wheels. And in some National Constitutions . . . we have one Empire within another."

WHEN AS

This expression is an archaism for "when," which is found just once in the KJV (Matthew 1:18): "When as his mother Mary was espoused to Joseph." Earlier English translations had "When his mother" and no subsequent translation has followed the KJV's wording at this point. The NKJV has "After His mother." The OED assigns to 1593 a quotation from Shakespeare's *King Henry VI, Part III* (V, 7, 34):

> "So Judas kiss'd his master.
> And cried 'all hail!' when as he
>   meant all harm."

It assigns to 1610 a quotation from Shakespeare's *The Tempest* (II, 1, 131–132):

> "you rub the sore,
> When you should bring the plaster."

Shakespeare's choice of "when as" in the one line and "when" in the other was probably determined by his sense of cadence.

The most famous use of "when as" in English poetry is Robert Herrick's lyric, *Upon Julia's Clothes,* beginning, "When as in silks my Julia goes . . ."

WHEREABOUT

In the KJV rendering of 1 Samuel 21:2, "whereabout" does not refer to place, but interest and concern. "The business whereabout I send thee" (KJV) is now translated as "your mission" (NIV), "the business on which I send you" (NKJV), and "the matter about which I send you" (NRSV, RSV).

WHEREBY

The word "whereby" appears thirty-nine times in the KJV, and is generally not used by the contemporary versions. In Acts 4:12 ("by which we must be saved") and 11:14 ("by which you will be saved"), and in ten other passages, the NRSV and RSV have "by which." "Whereby" asks a question, and means "how?" in Genesis 15:8 (Abraham) and Luke 1:18 (Zechariah, father of John the Baptist). In a number of cases some contemporary versions simply omit the word as unnecessary.

Jeremiah 33:8, for example, reads in the KJV: "I will cleanse them from all their iniquity, whereby they have sinned against me; and I will pardon all their iniquities, whereby they have sinned, and whereby they have transgressed against me." The NRSV reads: "I will cleanse them from all the guilt of their sin against me, and I will forgive all the guilt of their sin and rebellion against me."

In other cases, the meaning of the Hebrew or Greek is expressed with other words. Examples are Romans 8:15 (KJV, "whereby we cry, Abba, Father"), where contemporary versions have "by which we cry" (NASB), "by him we cry" (NIV), "by whom we cry" (NKJV), "When we cry, 'Abba! Father!'" (NRSV, RSV); and Ephesians 4:30 (KJV, "And grieve not the holy Spirit of God, whereby ye are sealed unto the day of redemption"), where contemporary versions have "by whom" (NASB, NKJV), "with whom" (NIV), "with which" (NRSV), and "in whom" (RSV).

The two occurrences of "whereby" in the

W

contemporary versions are Jeremiah 1:16 (NASB) and Psalm 68:9 (NKJV).

WHEREFORE

This is an adverb which may introduce a relative clause, "for which reason," or ask a question, "for what reason?" "Therefore" has demonstrative force, "for that reason," or the more general sense of "consequently." The KJV translators made liberal use of both words, often where there was no corresponding Hebrew or Greek expression.

Contemporary versions often substitute "therefore" for "wherefore"—for example, in 1 Corinthians 8:13: "Therefore, if food causes my brother to stumble, I will never eat meat again, so that I will not cause my brother to stumble" (NASB). In asking a question, they use "why"—for example, in Isaiah 55:2: "Why do you spend your money for that which is not bread?" (NRSV, RSV).

WHEREIN

"Wherein" is a formal adverb meaning "in which" or "where." It may be used interrogatively, meaning "in what?" or "how?" It occurs 167 times in the KJV. Of the contemporary versions, the RSV retains it only in the case of Samson ("wherein his great strength lies," Judges 16:5–6, 15, RSV) and Job ("Let the day perish wherein I was born," Job 3:3, RSV), the NKJV at Job 6:24, and the NASB at Ecclesiastes 8:9.

Other examples are: "all flesh, wherein is the breath of life" (Genesis 6:17, KJV); NASB, NKJV, NRSV, RSV, "in which." "The roll wherein thou hast read in the ears of the people" (Jeremiah 36:14, KJV); NCV, "the scroll that you read to the people"; "Wherein have we despised thy name?" (Malachi 1:6, KJV); NASB, NRSV, "How have we despised your [NASB, "Your"] name?"; "The bed wherein the sick of the palsy lay" (Mark 2:4, KJV); NIV, "the mat the paralyzed man was lying on"; "This grace wherein we stand" (Romans 5:2, KJV); NASB, NKJV, NRSV, RSV, "this grace in which we stand"; "For what is it wherein ye were inferior to other churches?"

(2 Corinthians 12:13, KJV); NRSV, "How have you been worse off than the other churches?"; "Wherein I suffer trouble, as an evil doer, even unto bonds" (2 Timothy 2:9, KJV); RSV, "the gospel for which I am suffering and wearing fetters, like a criminal."

WHEREINSOEVER

This word is now obsolete. It occurs once in the KJV, in 2 Corinthians 11:21: "Howbeit, whereinsoever any is bold, (I speak foolishly,) I am bold also." The rendering comes from Tyndale. In the NRSV this reads, "But whatever any one dares to boast of—I am speaking as a fool—I also dare to boast of that." The NASB and NKJV render the word as "in whatever."

WHEREINTO

"Whereinto" is an archaic word meaning "into what place." It occurs three times in the KJV.

"Every earthen vessel, whereinto any of them falleth, whatsoever is in it shall be unclean" (Leviticus 11:33, KJV) is now worded by the NRSV as "If any of them falls into any earthen vessel, all that is in it shall be unclean."

In Numbers 14:24 God promises to bring Caleb into the land "whereinto he went" (KJV). Contemporary versions have "the land which he entered" (NASB), "the land he went to" (NIV), "the land where he went" (NKJV), and "the land into which he went" (NRSV, RSV).

In John 6:22 the clause containing "whereinto" is a gloss which does not appear in the text of the more ancient manuscripts. It is rendered by the NKJV, which translates "whereinto" (KJV) as "which."

WHEREOF

"Whereof" is a formal or archaic word for "of which," and appears sixty-nine times in the KJV. Contemporary versions never use it. "Whereof I Paul am made a minister" (Colossians 1:23, KJV) reads in the NKJV and RSV, "of which I, Paul, became a minister."

A rather difficult rendering is 2 Corinthians 9:5: "Therefore I thought it necessary to exhort the brethren, that they would go before unto you, and make up beforehand your bounty, whereof ye had notice before, that the same might be ready, as a matter of bounty, and not as of covetousness." The NRSV has "So I thought it necessary to urge the others to go on ahead to you, and arrange in advance for this bountiful gift you have promised, so that it may be ready as a voluntary gift and not as an extortion."

WHEREON

This word means "on which." It appears twenty-four times in the KJV and only once in a contemporary version—in the RSV rendering of the poetic line "whereon hang a thousand bucklers" (Song of Solomon 4:4, RSV). Here and elsewhere the other versions use "on which" or "on it."

The word "whereon" is used interrogatively in 2 Chronicles 32:10: "Whereon do ye trust, that ye abide in the siege in Jerusalem?" (KJV). Contemporary versions render Sennacherib's taunt as "On what are you trusting?" (NASB), and "What are you trusting in?" (NLT); the NRSV has "On what are you relying, that you undergo the siege of Jerusalem?"

WHEREUNTO

This is an archaic adverb which may be used to ask a question or to introduce a relative clause. "Unto what is the kingdom of God like? and whereunto shall I resemble it?" (Luke 13:18) is now worded by the NKJV and RSV as "What is the kingdom of God like? And to what shall I compare it?" (cf. Luke 13:20; Matthew 11:16; Mark 4:30).

Jesus' question in Luke 7:31, "Whereunto then shall I liken the men of this generation" (KJV), reads in the contemporary versions: "What shall I say about the people of this time?" (NCV), "To what, then, can I compare the people of this generation?"

(NIV), and "How shall I describe this generation?" (NLT).

In Acts 5:24 we read that the authorities, on hearing of the apostles' miraculous release from prison, "doubted of them whereunto this would grow" (KJV). The NASB says that they "were greatly perplexed about them as to what would come of this"; the NKJV, that they "wondered what the outcome would be."

Introducing a relative clause, "whereunto" means "to which" (Numbers 36:4; 2 Chronicles 8:11; Esther 10:2; Jeremiah 22:27; Ezekiel 20:29; Acts 13:2; 1 Timothy 6:12).

Contemporary versions clarify some passages by making the relative clause a new sentence, beginning "For this" (Colossians 1:29, NRSV, RSV; 1 Timothy 2:7, NASB, NRSV, RSV; 2 Timothy 1:11, NRSV, RSV), "For this purpose" (Colossians 1:29, NASB; 1 Timothy 2:7, NIV; 2 Thessalonians 2:14, NRSV); "To this" (2 Thessalonians 2:14, RSV); "To this end" (Colossians 1:29, NIV, NKJV). In 2 Peter 1:19, "whereunto ye do well that ye take heed" (KJV) is now rendered by the NRSV and RSV as "You will do well to be attentive to this."

The wording in Ezekiel 5:9 may seem a little jumbled to contemporary readers: "I will do in thee that which I have not done, and whereunto I will not do any more the like, because of all thine abominations" (KJV). The NRSV reads: "Because of all your abominations, I will do to you what I have never yet done, and the like of which I will never do again."

The wording in the KJV rendering of 1 Peter 3:21 may also be a little confusing: "The like figure whereunto even baptism doth also now save us (not the putting away of the filth of the flesh, but the answer of a good conscience toward God) by the resurrection of Jesus Christ." The NLT paraphrases: "And this is a picture of baptism, which now saves you by the power of Jesus Christ's resurrection. Baptism is not a removal of dirt from your body; it is an appeal to God from a clean conscience."

W

"Whereunto thou hast attained" (1 Timothy 4:6, KJV) renders the Greek which contemporary versions translate as "which you have been following" (NASB, NCV) and "that you have followed" (NIV, NRSV).

WHEREUPON

"Whereupon" is an adverb "of place", meaning "on which"; or "of time," "immediately after which"; or "of reason," "in consequence of which." The KJV uses "whereupon" to translate the simple Hebrew word meaning "and," "so," or "then," which introduces 1 Kings 12:28 and 2 Chronicles 12:6.

"The glory of the God of Israel was gone up from the cherub, whereupon he was" (Ezekiel 9:3, KJV) is translated by the NRSV as "the glory of the God of Israel had gone up from the cherub on which it rested." "That whereupon they set their minds" (Ezekiel 24:25, KJV) is now "their heart's delight" (NASB), "their heart's desire" (NIV, RSV), and "their dearest treasure" (NLT).

Elsewhere contemporary versions use terms such as "so much" (Matthew 14:7, CEV, NASB, NRSV, RSV); "While thus occupied" (NKJV), and "With this in mind" (Acts 26:12, NRSV); and "hence" (NRSV, RSV), "This is why" (NCV, NIV), and "Therefore" (Hebrews 9:18, NASB, NKJV).

WHEREWITH

This word is slightly archaic; today we are more likely to say "with what" or "with which." The word appears 106 times in the KJV, and is retained by the contemporary versions only by the RSV in the language of the blessing which King Solomon invoked upon the assembly of Israel at the dedication of the house of the Lord (1 Kings 8:59). Examples of the KJV use of the word are: "Esau hated Jacob because of the blessing wherewith his father blessed him" (Genesis 27:41, KJV); NASB, NRSV, RSV, "with which his father had blessed him."

Gideon asks, "wherewith shall I save Israel?" (Judges 6:15, KJV); NCV, NIV, NKJV, "how can I save Israel?"

Jeroboam's apostasy is referred to as "his sin wherewith [RSV, "which"] he made Israel to sin" (1 Kings 15:34, KJV, RSV).

The Lord's question in Micaiah's vision, "Wherewith?" (1 Kings 22:22, KJV), is now phrased, "How?" (NASB, NRSV) and "By what means?" (NIV, RSV).

"Against the house wherewith I have war" (2 Chronicles 35:21, KJV) reads in the NASB, NRSV, and RSV, "against the house with which I am at war."

"Wherewith shall I come before the LORD?" (Micah 6:6, KJV) is now "With what shall I come before the LORD?" (NIV, NKJV, NRSV, RSV).

"Make ready wherewith I may sup" (Luke 17:8, KJV); NRSV, RSV, "Prepare supper for me."

"For all the joy wherewith we joy for your sakes" (1 Thessalonians 3:9, KJV); NKJV, "for all the joy with which we rejoice for your sake."

WHEREWITHAL

This word now means "the resources or supplies needed to do something" ("he didn't have the wherewithal to pay his rent"). The word appears only once in the KJV, in the Sermon on the Mount. "Wherewithal shall we be clothed" (Matthew 6:31, KJV) is now more simply translated as "What shall we wear?" (NIV, NKJV, RSV).

WHETHER

"Whether" is used nine times in the KJV as an interrogative pronoun, meaning "which of the two." This usage is archaic. "Whether is easier, to say, Thy sins be forgiven thee; or to say, Arise, and walk?" (Matthew 9:5, KJV) is now rendered by the NASB, NRSV, and RSV as "Which is easier, to say, 'Your sins are forgiven,' or to say, 'Rise [NASB, "Get up"; NRSV, "Stand up"] and walk'?" This form appears also in Luke 5:23, and in a more complicated form at Mark 2:9.

"Whether is greater" (KJV) is now translated, by most contemporary versions, as "Which is greater?" (Matthew 23:17, 19) and "who is greater"(Luke 22:27). "Whether of them twain" (Matthew 21:31, KJV) and "Whether of the twain" (Matthew 27:21, KJV) mean "Which of the two?"

The prayer of the apostles, "Thou, Lord, which knowest the hearts of all men, shew whether of these two thou hast chosen" (Acts 1:24, KJV) did not ask whether the Lord had chosen one of them, but "which one of these two You [NRSV, "you"] have chosen" (NASB, NRSV).

WHICH

As a relative pronoun, "which" is used in the KJV to refer to people as well as to things. "Lot also, which went with Abram" (Genesis 13:5, KJV) and "a new king over Egypt, which knew not Joseph" (Exodus 1:8, KJV) are renderings derived from Tyndale. So too is the wording of 1 Corinthians 15:57: "Thanks be to God, which giveth us the victory through our Lord Jesus Christ."

A count shows that in Genesis (KJV) "which" occurs 177 times and refers to people in thirty-seven of these instances, while "who" and "whom" as relative pronouns occur thirty-two times. In Galatians (KJV), "which" refers to people in eleven out of thirty-seven occurrences, while "who" and "whom" occur twenty times. Contemporary versions use the words "who" or "whom" to refer to persons.

The opening words of the Lord's Prayer, "Our Father which art in heaven, Hallowed be thy name" (Luke 11:2, KJV), are variously rendered by contemporary versions according to which Greek texts they use. The NKJV has "Our Father in heaven, hallowed be Your name," but adds in a marginal note that the words "Our" and "in heaven" are omitted in some Greek texts.

The NASB, NIV, and NRSV have "Father, hallowed be your [NASB, "Your"] name"; the NCV has "Father, may your name always be kept holy"; the CEV, "Father, help us to honor your name"; the NLT, "Father, may your name be honored."

WHILE AS

"While as" is an obsolete idiom for "while." It appears in the KJV rendering of Hebrews 9:8, "while as the first tabernacle was yet standing." Contemporary versions here use "while" (CEV, NASB, NCV, NKJV) and "as long as" (NIV, NLT, NRSV, RSV). Shakespeare uses it just once:

"While as the silly owner of the goods
Weeps over them and wrings his
    hapless hands."
—*King Henry VI, Part II* (1, 1, 225)

WHILES, WHILST

These are obsolete forms of the conjunction "while." The KJV translators used "whiles" ten times and "whilst" ten times, but "while" over two hundred times. There is no difference in meaning between the three terms. In Shakespeare's plays, "while" appears thirty-four times, "whiles" thirteen times, and "whilst" ten times.

WHISPER, WHISPERING, WHISPERER

These words are used in the KJV in senses still current and readily understood (2 Samuel 12:19; Psalm 41:7; Isaiah 29:4). Occasionally the contemporary versions use "slander" and "slanderer," and "gossip" and "gossips," to render these words.

The Hebrew word *nirgan* is translated as a "slanderer" by the NASB and as a "gossip" by the NCV, NIV, and NLT, in Proverbs 16:28 (KJV, "a whisperer separates close friends.") "Where there is no whisperer, quarreling ceases" (26:20, KJV) is rendered by the NKJV as "Where there is no talebearer, strife ceases."

In the New Testament, "whisperings" and "whisperers" translate the plural of Greek words which sound like whispers, *psithurismos* and *psithuristes* (2 Corinthians 12:20; Romans 1:29). These words are immediately linked in these verses with the Greek words for "slander" and "slanderers."

The NASB, NCV, NIV, NLT, NRSV, and RSV use "gossip" and "gossips"; the NKJV retains "whisperings" and "whisperers." In classical mythology, *psithuristes* was an epithet of Hermes (Mercury) and Eros (Cupid), and in its feminine form was an epithet of Aphrodite (Venus).

WHIT

The noun "whit" is used sometimes today to refer to a very small or the smallest part, "a bit" (e.g., in the negative "not a whit" meaning "not at all"). It is used in the KJV in the sense of "bit," "part," or "thing." Examples are: 1 Samuel 3:8, "And Samuel told him [Eli] every whit, and hid nothing from him. And he said, It is the LORD: let him do what seemeth him good"; where all the contemporary versions render the KJV "every whit" as "everything";

John 7:23, "If a man on the sabbath day receive circumcision, that the law of Moses should not be broken; are ye angry at me, because I have made a man every whit whole on the sabbath day?" (KJV) where the contemporary versions render the KJV "made a man every whit whole" as "making someone [NLT, "making a man"; NKJV, "made a man"] completely well" (CEV, NKJV, NLT), "made an entire man well" (NASB), "healing the whole man" (NIV), and "healed a man's whole body" (NRSV). (See WHOLE);

John 13:10, "Jesus saith to him [Simon Peter], He that is washed needeth not save to wash his feet, but is clean every whit: and ye are clean, but not all" where the contemporary versions render the KJV "is clean every whit" as: "[NASB, NRSV, "is"] entirely clean" (NASB, NLT, NRSV), "is completely clean" (NKJV), "his whole body is clean" (NCV, NIV), and "clean all over" (CEV);

2 Corinthians 11:5, "For I suppose I was not a whit behind the very chiefest apostles" (KJV) where the contemporary versions render the KJV "I suppose I was not a whit" as: "I think I am not in the least" (NRSV, RSV), "I do not think I am in the least" (NIV), "I don't think I am" (NLT), "I consider that I am not at all" (NKJV), and "I consider myself not in the least" (NASB).

WHITED SEPULCHRE

A "whited sepulchre" is a "hypocrite," a person who pretends to be holy and righteous but in reality is not. The phrase derives from one of the woes with which Jesus denounced the scribes and Pharisees: Matthew 23:27, "Woe unto you, scribes and Pharisees, hypocrites! for ye are like unto whited sepulchres, which indeed appear beautiful outward, but are within full of dead men's bones, and of all uncleanness" (KJV).

The contemporary versions render the KJV's "whited sepulchres" as "whitewashed tombs" (NASB, NIV, NKJV, NLT, NRSV, RSV) and "tombs that are painted white" (NCV). The whole verse is rendered by the CEV as: "You Pharisees and teachers are in for trouble! You're nothing but show-offs. You're like tombs that have been whitewashed. On the outside they are beautiful, but inside they are full of bones and filth."

As William Hendriksen comments: "Passover was just around the corner. This meant that the pilgrims, streaming into Jerusalem from every direction, near the city was many a whitewashed tomb. With powdered lime dust a few weeks earlier the burial places had been made to look spick-and-span, neat and trim. They had been made conspicuous, lest any pilgrim should render himself ceremonially 'unclean' by inadvertently coming into contact with a corpse or a human bone. . . . Yet, on the inside such graves were full of dead men's bones and all kinds of dirt and debris" (*New Testament Commentary: Matthew*).

The phrase at Matthew 23:27 may be linked to Acts 23:3, Paul's words to Ananias, "God shall smite thee, thou whited wall: for sittest thou to judge me after the law, and commandest me to be smitten contrary to the law?"

The expression is found in literature, e.g., in Milton's *Tetrachordon* (1.16.40), which says of a hypocrite:

"his owne house, and the whole
neighbourhood

Sees his foule inside through his
whited skin."

WHO

In the KJV, "who" is used in several ways which may seem odd to the modern reader but which were common speech around 1600. "Who steals my purse steals trash," wrote Shakespeare in *Othello* (III, 3, 157). Matthew 13:9–43 has the same construction, "Who hath ears to hear, let him hear." This was an innovation of the KJV; Tyndale and his successors had "Whosoever hath" and Rheims had "He that hath."

Moreover, the KJV itself, for the same Greek wording of the sentence, had "He that hath ears to hear, let him hear" in Matthew 11:15 and Luke 8:8; 14:35. Contemporary versions use "He who has" (NASB, NIV, NKJV, RSV) "Let anyone with ears listen!" (NRSV).

Acts 21:37 has an archaic usage. Paul "said unto the chief captain, May I speak unto thee? Who said, Canst thou speak Greek?" The NRSV translates as "Paul . . . said to the tribune, 'May I say something to you?' The tribune replied, 'Do you know Greek?' "

The cry of the unclean spirit, "I know thee who thou art, the Holy One of God" (Mark 1:14; Luke 4:34, KJV) is a literal translation of the Greek. As an English sentence, it may be compared to Cordelia's farewell to her sisters:

"I know you what you are;
And, like a sister, am most loath to
    call
Your faults as they are named."
               —*King Lear* (I, 1, 272)

WHOLE

The word "whole" has two basic meanings: (1) sound, unimpaired, in good condition; (2) complete, entire, undivided. The KJV uses "whole" in the second of these meanings eighty-one times, and "wholly" sixteen times. It uses "whole" in the first of these meanings thirty-four times, in almost all of which it is applied to persons, in the sense of "healthy," "well," "healed," or "made well." The OED regards this usage as archaic or "biblical."

The NKJV and RSV retain "whole" in Matthew 12:13, when Jesus told the man with the withered hand to stretch it out and "it was restored as whole like the other" (NKJV); other contemporary versions say that "it was restored to normal" (NASB) and "it become well again" (NCV).

In Matthew 15:31, the NKJV, NRSV, and RSV say that the crowds were amazed to see "the maimed whole [NKJV, "made whole"], the lame walking, and the blind seeing."

Elsewhere contemporary versions use "heal," "well," or "make well," depending upon the Hebrew or Greek word. "When they had finished circumcising all the nation, they remained in their places in the camp until they were healed" (Joshua 5:8, NASB). "Those who are well have no need of a physician, but those who are sick" (Matthew 9:12, NKJV, NRSV, RSV). "Daughter, your faith has made you well; go in peace, and be healed of your disease" (Mark 5:34, NRSV, RSV).

An interesting case is John 7:23, where the KJV reads: "If a man on the sabbath day receive circumcision, that the law of Moses should not be broken; are ye angry at me, because I have made a man every whit whole on the sabbath day?" The expression "every whit whole" goes back to Tyndale. The Greek word represented by "every whit" is not an adverb modifying the adjective represented by "whole," but is itself an adjective which modifies the word for "man."

The Greek is literally translated, "I have made a whole man well." The Latin Vulgate has *totum hominem sanum feci*; Wycliffe translated this "I made al a man hool." Martin Luther's translation was *ich den ganzen Menschen habe gesund gemacht*.

Contemporary versions render Jesus' words as "I made an entire man well" (NASB), "I made a man completely well" (NKJV), "I

W

healed a man's whole body" (NRSV). The verse reads in the NCV, "If a baby can be circumcised on a Sabbath day to obey the law of Moses, why are you angry at me for healing a person's whole body on the Sabbath day?" (See WHIT)

WHOLESOME

The word "wholesome" is likely to make us think of health foods or home cooking. The word occurs twice in the KJV in the sense of "healing" or "health-giving." "A wholesome tongue" (Proverbs 15:4, KJV) translates Hebrew which literally means "the healing of the tongue."

Contemporary versions render it as "A soothing tongue" (NASB), "The tongue that brings healing" (NIV), and "A gentle tongue" (NRSV, RSV). The CEV paraphrases as "Kind words are good medicine."

In the Pastoral Epistles the participle of the Greek verb which means "to be healthy or sound" is applied to Christian teaching. "Wholesome words" (1 Timothy 6:3, KJV) are "sound words" (KJV) in 2 Timothy 1:13. In the other passages the KJV has "sound doctrine" (1 Timothy 1:10; 2 Timothy 4:3; Titus 1:9; 2:1); "sound speech" (Titus 2:8); "sound in the faith" (Titus 1:13); "sound in faith, in charity, in patience" (Titus 2:2).

WHOSESOEVER

This is an archaic genitive of "whosoever." In the KJV it appears in one verse, John 20:23: "Whosesoever sins ye remit, they are remitted unto them; and whosesoever sins ye retain, they are retained." The remoteness of this form from present English is indicated by the fact that many present editions of the KJV print it as though it were two words, "whose soever sins," which may awaken curiosity as to what a "soever sin" is.

The NRSV translates as "If you forgive the sins of any, they are forgiven them; if you retain the sins of any, they are retained."

WHOSO

"Whoso" is an archaic form of "whosoever," which is itself on the way toward becoming archaic. "Whoso" appears fifty-one times in the KJV, twenty-five of which are in the Book of Proverbs. "Whosoever" appears 169 times, eighty-one of which are in the Gospels. "Whomsoever" appears twenty times. Contemporary versions use "whoever" and "whomever."

"Whoso sheddeth man's blood, by man shall his blood be shed" (Genesis 9:6, KJV) is worded in the NKJV, "Whoever sheds man's blood, By man his blood shall be shed." "Whoso looketh into the perfect law of liberty" (James 1:25, KJV) is now "one who looks intently at the perfect law, the law of liberty" (NASB), and "those who carefully study God's perfect law that makes people free" (NCV).

"Whosoever" is replaced in contemporary versions by terms such as "whoever," "every one who," "anyone," "if any one," and "someone." A simple test of the variety of usage is to examine the verses in the Sermon on the Mount which have "whosoever" in the KJV.

"Whoever" replaces it in Matthew 5:19 (NASB, NCV, NKJV, NRSV, RSV), 5:21 (NASB, NKJV, NRSV, RSV), 5:22 (NASB, NKJV, RSV), 5:31 (NASB, NKJV, NRSV, RSV), 5:32 (NKJV, RSV); "everyone [RSV, "every one"] who" in 5:22 (NASB, RSV), 5:28 (NASB, NRSV, RSV), 5:32 (NASB, RSV); 7:24 (NASB, NIV, NRSV, RSV); "anyone" in 5:28 (NCV, NIV, NLT), 5:31–32 (NCV, NIV; v. 32, NRSV); "if any one" (NRSV, RSV) and "someone" (NCV, NIV) in 5:39.

WIDOW'S CRUSE

The expression "the widow's cruse" is sometimes used in contemporary English to refer to a small supply of something, especially food or money, that seems inexhaustible.

The expression alludes to 1 Kings 17:10–16: "So he [Elijah] arose and went to Zarephath. And when he came to the gate of the city, behold, the widow woman was there gathering of sticks: and he called to her, and said, Fetch me, I pray thee, a little water in a vessel, that I may drink. And as she was going to fetch it, he called to her, and said, Bring me, I pray thee, a morsel of bread in thine hand. And she said, As the LORD thy God liveth, I have not a cake, but an handful of meal in a barrel, and a little oil in a cruse: and, behold, I am gathering two sticks, that I may go in and dress it for me and my son, that we may eat it, and die.

"And Elijah said unto her, Fear not; go and do as thou hast said: but make me thereof a little cake first, and bring it unto me, and after make for thee and for thy son. For thus saith the LORD God of Israel, The barrel of meal shall not waste, neither shall the cruse of oil fail, until the day that the LORD sendeth rain upon the earth. And she went and did according to the saying of Elijah: and she, and he, and her house, did eat many days. And the barrel of meal wasted not, neither did the cruse of oil fail, according to the word of the LORD, which he spake by Elijah" (KJV).

In the contemporary translations the KJV "cruse" is rendered "jug" (NCV, NIV, NRSV; the NLT for verse 12 reads "But she said, 'I swear by the LORD your God that I don't have a single piece of bread in the house. And I have only a handful of flour left in the jar and a little cooking oil in the bottom of the jug. I was just gathering a few sticks to cook this last meal, and then my son and I will die'"), "jar" (NASB, NKJV), and "bottle" (CEV); the RSV retains the KJV "cruse."

WIDOW'S MITE
See MITE.

WILL

As a verb, "will" is often used by the KJV in the obsolete sense of "desire," "wish for," "want," without implying, as it does today, a definite determination. Caleb's question to his daughter Achsah is translated as "What wouldest thou?" (KJV) in Joshua 15:18,

and "What wilt thou?" (KJV) in Judges 1:14. The Hebrew is identical in the two passages, and is now translated as "What do you want?" (NASB, NCV) and "What do you wish?" (NKJV, NRSV, RSV).

Salome's answer to Herod, "I will that thou give me by and by in a charger the head of John the Baptist" (Mark 6:25, KJV), now reads, "I want you to give me at once the head of John the Baptist on a platter" (NRSV, RSV). Peter's suggestion to Jesus on the Mount of Transfiguration is now rendered as "If You wish, I will make three tabernacles here, one for You, and one for Moses, and one for Elijah" (Matthew 17:4, NASB).

Festus's question to Paul, "Wilt thou go up to Jerusalem?" (KJV), now reads "Do you wish [NASB, NIV, "Are you willing"] to go up to Jerusalem?" (Acts 25:9, NASB, NIV, NRSV, RSV).

"To whomsoever the Son will reveal him" (Matthew 11:27, KJV) is now translated as "to whom the Son wills to reveal Him" (NASB), "those whom the Son chooses to tell" (NCV), and "to whom the Son chooses to reveal him" (NRSV, RSV). "Herod will kill thee" (Luke 13:31, KJV) is "Herod wants to kill you" (NASB, NCV, NIV, NKJV, NRSV, RSV). "Ye will not come to me" (John 5:40, KJV) is "you refuse [NASB, "you are unwilling"] to come to me" (NASB, NCV, NIV, NLT, NRSV, RSV).

In these and other cases the KJV "will" may seem to be an auxiliary verb denoting futurity, but in the Greek it stands for the main verb of the clause, which is followed by an infinitive. In 1 Timothy 5:11 the KJV reads, "But the younger widows refuse: for when they have begun to wax wanton against Christ, they will marry." This is not a prediction of the future; it is the statement of a present general condition.

The NRSV translates as "But refuse to put younger widows on the list; for when their sensual desires alienate them from Christ, they want to marry."

"If any man will do his will" (John 7:17, KJV) is a compacting and easing of the clause which reads in the NKJV, "if anyone wants to do His will." The reference is to the will of God, as the whole sentence, verses 16–17, makes clear.

The outstanding example of the use of the verb "will" in the sense of "desire" is in Paul's great chapter on sin, Romans 7:19: "For the good that I would I do not; but the evil which I would not, that I do" (KJV). The NRSV reads, "For I do not do the good I want, but the evil I do not want is what I do." (See WANT)

WILL-WORSHIP

This expression conjures up the idea of self-worship, but the OED defines it as "Worship according to one's own will or fancy, or imposed by human will, without divine authority." The word is a literal reproduction in English of a Greek compound word *ethelothreskeia*, which occurs in Colossians 2:23. Paul is here warning against the misdirected zeal and practices of ascetics. The KJV translates: "Which things have indeed a shew of wisdom in will worship, and humility, and neglecting of the body; not in any honour to the satisfying of the flesh."

The NKJV translates, "These things indeed have an appearance of wisdom in self-imposed religion, false humility, and neglect of the body, but are of no value against the indulgence of the flesh."

WIND BLOWETH WHERE IT LISTETH

See LIST.

WINEBIBBER

From the Latin verb *bibere*, "to drink," are derived the English verb "bib," "to drink" or "to tipple," and the nouns "bibation" and "bibber." "Winebibber" occurs three times in the KJV. It is retained by the NKJV, NRSV, and RSV in Proverbs 23:20–21:

"Do not mix with winebibbers,
Or with gluttonous eaters of meat;

For the drunkard and the glutton
will come to poverty,
And drowsiness will clothe a man
with rags" (NKJV).

Here "winebibbers" is rendered by the NASB as "heavy drinkers of wine," and "drunkard" stands for the Hebrew word which appears also in Deuteronomy 21:20.

"Winebibber" is retained only by the NKJV in the comment which Jesus quoted concerning himself: "Look, a glutton and a winebibber, a friend of tax collectors and sinners!" (Matthew 11:19 and its parallel Luke 7:34, NKJV).

WINEFAT

See FAT.

WINGS LIKE A DOVE

In Psalm 55:6 the psalmist wants to retreat from those who are hostile and threatening toward him: "And I said, Oh that I had wings like a dove! for then would I fly away, and be at rest." This is rendered as follows by the contemporary versions: "O that I had wings like a dove!" (NRSV, RSV), "Oh, that I had wings like a dove!" (NASB, NKJV), "Oh, that I had the wings of a dove!" (NIV), "I wish I had wings like a dove" (CEV, NCV).

The phrase is alluded to in literature. For example in *Don Juan*, Byron said that Don Juan, at the court of Queen Catherine was youthful, energetic, and beautiful,

"and those things
Which for an instant clip
enjoyment's wings.
But soon they grow again and leave
their nest.
'Oh!' saith the Psalmist, 'that I had
a dove's Pinions to flee away,
and be at rest!' "

The phrase "wings like a dove" also occurs in the KJV at Psalm 68:13: "yet shall ye be as the wings of a dove covered with silver, and her feathers with yellow gold."

WINGS OF THE MORNING

In the words of Psalm 139:9–10, "If I take the wings of the morning, and dwell in the uttermost parts of the sea; Even there shall thy hand lead me, and thy right hand shall hold me" (KJV), the psalmist is declaring that God's guidance and care are everywhere. The expression "take the wings of the morning" is included, in Coverdale's translation, in the OED, which notes that wings are "attributed to inanimate or abstract things represented as flying, or as carrying one swiftly along."

The contemporary versions render the expression "If I take the wings of the morning" as: "If I take the wings of the dawn" (NASB), "If I rise on the wings of the dawn" (NIV), "If I ride the wings of the morning" (NLT), "If I rise with the sun in the east" (NCV), and "Suppose I had wings like the dawning day" (CEV); the NKJV, NRSV, and RSV retain the KJV wording.

WINK AT

The verb "wink" is used in contemporary English to refer to closing and opening one eye quickly. The verb occurs in the KJV in this sense, with a malicious purpose or with insinuations, at Psalm 35:19; Proverbs 6:13; 10:10; and Job 15:12. It also occurs in the KJV with "at" in the rather archaic sense of "overlook." This usage occurs at Acts 17:30: "And the times of this ignorance God winked at; but now commandeth all men every where to repent."

The KJV "winked at" is rendered "overlooked" by the NASB, NIV, NKJV, NLT, NRSV, and RSV and "ignored" by the NCV; the CEV has "In the past, God forgave all this because people did not know what they were doing."

WISDOM OF SOLOMON

King Solomon was noted for his great wisdom and wealth. His wisdom has become proverbial, and is alluded to in such contemporary expressions as "one needs the wisdom of Solomon" and "as wise as Solomon."

First Kings 3:5 records the Lord appearing to Solomon in a dream and saying, "Ask what I shall give thee" (KJV). In Solomon's answer, he says: "Give therefore thy servant an understanding heart to judge thy people, that I may discern between good and bad: for who is able to judge this thy so great a people?" (1 Kings 3:9, KJV).

The Lord was pleased at Solomon's request: "lo, I have given thee a wise and an understanding heart; so that there was none like thee before thee, neither after thee shall any arise like unto thee" (1 Kings 3:12, KJV; "I will do what you asked. I will give you wisdom and understanding that is greater than anyone has had in the past or will have in the future," NCV).

This wisdom was demonstrated when two women came to Solomon, each claiming that a particular baby was her own. The king's suggestion that the baby be divided in two revealed the true mother—she was the woman who would rather let her rival have the baby than see him killed (1 Kings 3:16–28).

The people's response is noted: "And all Israel heard of the judgment which the king had judged; and they feared the king: for they saw that the wisdom of God was in him, to do judgment" (1 Kings 3:28, KJV); "Word of the king's decision spread quickly throughout all Israel, and the people were awed as they realized the great wisdom God had given him to render decisions with justice" (NLT).

His wisdom is also seen in the organizing of the kingdom and court and the building of the temple. Solomon also composed proverbs and other wisdom literature, and described plant and animal life. As 1 Kings 4:34 records, "People came from all the nations to hear the wisdom of Solomon; they came from all the kings of the earth who had heard of his wisdom" (NRSV).

W

WISE

This is an old noun which means "way," "manner," "fashion." "On this wise" was a common phrase which meant "in this way." Since the sixteenth century the use of "wise" in this sense has tended to disappear; it survives chiefly as a suffix in such words as "crosswise," "lengthwise," "likewise," "otherwise," "sidewise."

The OED quotes from a publication of 1677, "Let us try once more to argue Cardinalwise," and from one of 1916, "We trod the pilgrim road in pilgrim wise." The comment, "He spoke Coolidge-wise," refers to the laconic speech of Calvin Coolidge, President of the United States, 1923–1929.

The noun "wise" appears thirty-one times in the KJV, in the phrases "on this wise," "in any wise," "in no wise," "in like wise." In the place of "on this wise" contemporary versions use expressions such as "in this way" (NRSV, RSV) and "as follows" (Matthew 1:18, NKJV, NASB); "this is how" (NCV, NLT), and "in this way" (John 21:1, NASB, NRSV, RSV); "thus" (Acts 13:34, NKJV).

"Spake . . . on this wise" (Hebrews 4:4; Acts 7:6, KJV) is now "spoken . . . in these words" (Hebrews 4:4, NIV) and "spoke to this effect" (Acts 7:6, NASB, RSV; NRSV, "spoke in these terms"). In Romans 10:6, "speaketh on this wise" (KJV) is now rendered simply as "says" by the NIV, NLT, NRSV, and RSV.

In Luke 13:11 we read that the woman with the crippling spirit could "in no wise lift herself up" (KJV). Contemporary versions say that she "could not straighten up at all" (NASB, NIV) and was "quite unable to stand up straight" (NRSV). In Romans 3:9 "No, in no wise" (KJV) is now "No, not at all" (NLT, NRSV, RSV).

These eight passages are the only ones in which the Greek text contains an adverb or clause to allow for the use of a "wise" clause in English. In the other twenty-three passages there is no corresponding Hebrew or Greek term. The "wise" clauses are either periphrastic, like the word "manner," or an attempt to reproduce an emphasis which in Hebrew is conveyed by repetition of the verb, and in Greek by a double negative. (See GENERALLY; MANNER; SURELY)

In Leviticus 19:17, "Thou shalt in any wise rebuke thy neighbour, and not suffer sin upon him" (KJV), the clause "in any wise" represents the Hebrew absolute infinitive. A literal translation would be, "To rebuke thou shalt rebuke thy neighbour." The revised versions of 1881–1901 had "Thou shalt surely rebuke thy neighbour." The NASB and NRSV change "rebuke" to "reprove" and the RSV has "reason with" In the NKJV the verse reads: "You shall not hate your brother in your heart. You shall rebuke your neighbor, and not bear sin because of him."

Other examples are Deuteronomy 17:15; 21:23; 22:7. In 1 Samuel 6:3 the NASB, NIV, NKJV, NRSV, and RSV use "by all means," and in 1 Kings 3:26, 27 the NASB, NKJV, and RSV use "by no means."

"He shall in no wise lose his reward" (Matthew 10:42, KJV) represents Greek which is now translated more directly as "he shall not lose his reward" (NASB, RSV) and "he shall by no means lose his reward" (NKJV). "Shall in no wise enter therein" (Luke 18:17, KJV) means "will never enter it" (NCV, NIV, NRSV, RSV).

Peter's words to Jesus, "If I should die with thee, I will not deny thee in any wise" (Mark 14:31, KJV), are stronger when translated literally, "Even though I must die with you, I will not deny you" (NRSV). See also Matthew 5:18; John 6:37; Acts 13:41; Revelation 21:27.

WISE AS SERPENTS, HARMLESS AS DOVES

When Jesus sent out the twelve apostles, he said to them, "Behold, I send you forth as sheep in the midst of wolves: be ye therefore wise as serpents, and harmless as doves" (Matthew 10:16, KJV).

The contemporary versions render the expression as: "be wise as serpents and innocent as doves" (NRSV, RSV), "be shrewd as serpents and innocent as doves" (NASB), "be as shrewd as snakes and as innocent as doves" (NIV), "be wise as snakes and as innocent as doves" (CEV), "be as smart as snakes and as innocent as doves" (NCV), and "be as wary as snakes and harmless as doves" (NLT; the NKJV retains the KJV "be wise as serpents and harmless as doves."

The expression is sometimes referred to in literature, e.g., in Herman Melville's *Billy Budd, Foretopman* (written 1891, published 1924), it is said of Billy that "with little or no sharpness of faculty or any trace of wisdom of the serpent, nor yet quite a dove, he possessed that kind and degree of intelligence which goes along with the unconventional rectitude of a sound human creature" (chap. 2).

Jesus likened the kingdom of heaven to "ten virgins, which took their lamps, and went forth to meet the bridegroom. And five of them were wise, and five were foolish. They that were foolish took their lamps, and took no oil with them: But the wise took oil in their vessels with their lamps. While the bridegroom tarried, they all slumbered and slept.

"And at midnight there was a cry made, Behold, the bridegroom cometh; go ye out to meet him. Then all those virgins arose, and trimmed their lamps. And the foolish said unto the wise, Give us of your oil; for our lamps are gone out. But the wise answered, saying, Not so; lest there be not enough for us and you: but go ye rather to them that sell, and buy for yourselves. And while they went to buy, the bridegroom came; and they that were ready went in with him to the marriage: and the door was shut. Afterward came also the other virgins, saying, Lord, Lord, open to us. But he answered and said, Verily I say unto you, I know you not" (Matthew 25:1–12, KJV).

The contemporary versions render the words "wise," "foolish," and "virgins" as fol-lows: all the contemporary versions except the NASB retain the KJV "wise"; the NASB has "prudent"; all the contemporary versions retain the KJV "foolish"; and the KJV "virgins" (retained by the NASB, NIV, and NKJV) is rendered "bridesmaids" (NCV, NLT, NRSV), "girls" (CEV), and "maidens" (RSV).

The parable is often alluded to in literature. For example, Tennyson considers the aspect of belatedness in *Idylls of the King* where Queen Guinevere fled to a convent in an attempt to escape from her enemies and hears a young girl in a convent singing:

> "Too late, too late! ye cannot enter now.
> No light had we: for that we do repent;
> And learning this, the bridegroom will relent.
> Too late, too late! ye cannot enter now."

WISH

As a verb, "wish" is used only eight times in the KJV, partly because its meaning is often assigned to "will" and "would." (See WILL) It stands for "feelings of desire" in Psalm 40:14. In Psalm 73:7 the KJV rendering "they have more than heart could wish" is retained by the NKJV; the NLT paraphrases the whole verse as "These fat cats have everything their hearts could ever wish for!" The NRSV and RSV, however, translate the second clause as "their hearts overflow with follies" (CEV, "their minds are flooded with foolish thoughts").

In Job 31:30 and Jonah 4:8, "wish" (KJV) represents the Hebrew verb which means "ask." The KJV says that Jonah not only "wished in himself to die"; contemporary versions use stronger terms (NASB, "he . . . begged with all his soul to die"; NIV, "He wanted to die"; NRSV, RSV, "he asked that he might die"). The Hebrew is identical with the statement concerning Elijah in 1 Kings 19:4, which the KJV translates as "he requested for himself that he might die."

W

In three New Testament passages the KJV uses "wish" for the Greek verb which also means "to pray."

In Acts 27:29 the KJV says of the storm-tossed sailors that "they wished for the day"; the CEV, NIV, and NLT say that "they prayed for daylight."

John begins his letter to Gaius with the words, "Beloved, I wish above all things that thou mayest prosper" (3 John 2, KJV); the NRSV and RSV translate his greeting as "Beloved, I pray that all may go well with you."

In 2 Corinthians 13:7 all versions translate this Greek verb as "pray," but in verse 9 of this chapter the KJV renders it as "wish." "This also we wish, even your perfection" (KJV) is rendered by the NASB as "this we also pray for, that you be made complete."

The one occurrence of "wish" as a noun is in Job 33:6, where the KJV reads, "Behold, I am according to thy wish in God's stead." Contemporary versions translate this as "Behold, I belong to God like you" (NASB), "I am just like you before God" (NCV, NIV), "Truly I am as your spokesman before God" (NKJV), and "See, before God I am as you are" (NRSV).

WIT

As a noun, "wit" is used only once in the KJV, in the vivid description of the sailors' plight in a storm at sea (Psalm 107:27): "They reel to and fro, and stagger like a drunken man, and are at their wit's end."

The adjective "witty" appears in Proverbs 8:12, "I wisdom dwell with prudence, and find out knowledge of witty inventions." The rendering "witty inventions" was used by the KJV translators to represent a Hebrew word for which the earlier versions had "counsel" or "understanding,"; contemporary versions have "sound judgment" (CEV), "discretion" (NASB, NIV, NKJV, NRSV, RSV), "good sense" (NCV), and "discernment" (NLT).

The author of the Wisdom of Solomon, one of the books of the Apocrypha, says of himself, as translated by Coverdale and the Bishops' Bible, "I was a lad of ripe wit" (8:19). The Geneva Bible said, "I was a witty child," and the KJV adopted this.

The Greek adjective refers to good natural gifts, both of body and mind. The RV puts it, "I was a child of parts"; the RSV has "As a child I was by nature well-endowed"; and the NRSV, "As a child I was naturally gifted."

WIT, WIST, WOT

The Old English verb "wit" means "to know" or "to find out." Without inflection, it appears twenty times in the KJV; its present tense, "wot," eleven times; and its past tense, "wist," thirteen times.

While Rebekah drew water for his camels, Abraham's servant "wondering at her held his peace, to wit whether the LORD had made his journey prosperous or not" (Genesis 24:21, KJV). The NRSV translates as "The man gazed at her in silence to learn whether or not the LORD had made his journey successful."

When the baby Moses was put in a basket of bulrushes and left by the river's brink, "his sister stood afar off, to wit what would be done to him" (Exodus 2:4, KJV). The NKJV reads, "his sister stood afar off, to know what would be done to him."

The most familiar example of the use of the past tense "wist" is the answer of the twelve-year-old Jesus to his mother's reproach: "Wist ye not that I must be about my Father's business?" (Luke 2:49, KJV) The NRSV and NKJV translate this as "Did you not know that I must be in my Father's house?" (NKJV, "be about My Father's business?").

"Do you to wit" is an idiom which means "cause you to know." It was in common use in the thirteenth to the seventeenth centuries, but is now obsolete. Tyndale used it at 1 Corinthians 15:1 and 2 Corinthians 8:1, and the KJV retained it in the latter passage as "we do you to wit of the grace of God."

The expression "to wit," meaning "that is" or "namely," is used seventeen times in the KJV, and in all but one case has been inserted by the translators in the interest of clarity, without any corresponding Hebrew or Greek term. The one which has a corresponding Greek word is 2 Corinthians 5:18–19: "And all things are of God, who hath reconciled us to himself by Jesus Christ, and hath given to us the ministry of reconciliation; To wit, that God was in Christ, reconciling the world unto himself" (KJV).

The passages where "to wit" has been inserted are Joshua 17:1; 1 Kings 2:32; 7:50; 13:23; 2 Kings 10:29; 1 Chronicles 7:2; 27:1; 2 Chronicles 4:12; 25:7, 10; 31:3; Esther 2:12; Jeremiah 25:18; 34:9; Ezekiel 13:16; Romans 8:23.

WITCH

This word appears twice in the KJV: "Thou shalt not suffer a witch to live" (Exodus 22:18); "There shall not be found among you . . . an enchanter, or a witch" (Deuteronomy 18:10). The Hebrew word denotes a woman in the first of these passages, and a man in the second. The KJV translates the masculine plural of this word by "sorcerers" in Exodus 7:11, Daniel 2:2, and Malachi 3:5.

While it is true that the word "witch" was formerly applied to men as well as to women, the contemporary versions use "sorceress" (NRSV, "female sorcerer") in Exodus 22:18 (NASB, NIV, NKJV, NLT, NRSV, RSV), and "sorcerer" in Deuteronomy 18:10 (NASB, NKJV, NRSV, RSV).

WITHAL

As a preposition, "withal" is an archaic form of "with," which was used at the end of a relative clause or a question. The prize exhibit of its use and meaning is Rosalind's speech in Shakespeare's *As You Like It* (III, 2, 328–329): "I'll tell you who Time ambles withal, who Time trots withal, who Time gallops withal and who he stands still withal." The word occurs in the KJV twenty-four times

as a preposition, but is not retained by contemporary versions.

A typical passage is Job 2:8, "he took him a potsherd to scrape himself withal" (KJV), where the NKJV and RSV read, "he took a potsherd with which to scrape himself." Contemporary versions use "with which" in place of "withal" in Exodus 30:4 (NASB, NKJV, NRSV, RSV); 37:27 (NASB, NKJV, NRSV, RSV); Leviticus 5:3 (NASB, NKJV, RSV, NRSV, "by which"); 11:21 (NASB, NKJV, NRSV, RSV); Isaiah 30:23 (NKJV, RSV); Mark 10:39 (NASB, NRSV, RSV).

The KJV rendering of Exodus 25:29 is: "thou shalt make the dishes thereof, and spoons thereof, and covers thereof, and bowls thereof, to cover withal." The NRSV translates as "you shall make its plates and dishes for incense, and its flagons and bowls with which to pour drink offerings" (cf. Exodus 37:16). "To wash withal" (Exodus 30:18; 40:30, KJV) means "for washing" (NASB, NCV, NIV, NKJV, NRSV, RSV), and "to overlay the walls of the houses withal" (1 Chronicles 29:4, KJV) is translated by the NRSV as "for overlaying the walls of the house."

In Leviticus 6:30 "to reconcile withal" (KJV) means "to make atonement" (NASB, NIV, NKJV, NLT, RSV), and in Judges 7:20, 2 Chronicles 26:15, and Esther 6:9 most contemporary versions simply drop the "withal" which the KJV translators had inserted (cf. Exodus 36:3; 2 Chronicles 24:14).

"Withal" as an adverb means "with everything else," "in addition," "also." It occurs eight times, and is not retained by contemporary versions. "Now he was ruddy, and withal of a beautiful countenance" (1 Samuel 16:12, KJV) represents Hebrew which the NASB translates as "Now he was ruddy, with beautiful eyes."

In Proverbs 22:18, "they shall withal be fitted in thy lips" (KJV), the NRSV has "if all of them are ready on your lips" and the NKJV has "Let them all be fixed upon your lips."

"Withal" is omitted by contemporary versions in 1 Kings 19:1 and Acts 25:27. It is rendered as "and" (NIV, RSV), "meanwhile"

W

(NKJV), and "At the same time" (NRSV) in Colossians 4:3. The statement about the younger widows, "withal they learn to be idle" (1 Timothy 5:13, KJV), reads in the NRSV, "Besides that, they learn to be idle."

The closing request of Paul's letter to Philemon, "But withal prepare me also a lodging" (KJV), is literally translated by the RSV as "At the same time, prepare a guest room for me."

WITHHOLDEN

"Withholden" is the old past participle of "withhold." The NASB, NKJV, NRSV, and RSV replace it by "withheld" in Job 22:7; 38:15; Psalm 21:2; Jeremiah 3:3; Joel 1:13; and Amos 4:7. "The LORD hath withholden thee from coming to shed blood" (1 Samuel 25:26, KJV) reads in the NRSV and RSV, "the LORD has restrained you from bloodguilt."

Job's answer to the Lord, "I know . . . that no thought can be withholden from thee" (Job 42:2, KJV) means "I know . . . that no purpose of yours [NASB, "Yours"] can be thwarted" (NASB, NRSV). Again, "hath not withholden the pledge" (Ezekiel 18:16, KJV) now reads "retain a pledge" (NASB), "withheld a pledge" (NKJV), "exacts no pledge" (NRSV, RSV).

WITHOUT

As an adverb or preposition, "without" is frequently used in the KJV in the sense of "outside." In these cases contemporary versions usually use this word instead.

Examples are: "wherefore standest thou without?" (Genesis 24:31, KJV); NASB, NKJV, NRSV, RSV, "Why do you stand outside?" "Thou shalt set the table without the veil" (Exodus 26:35, KJV); NASB, NKJV, NRSV, RSV, "you shall set the table outside the veil" (NRSV, "outside the curtain"). "Peter sat without in the palace" (Matthew 26:69, KJV); NASB, NRSV, RSV, "Peter was sitting outside in the courtyard." "But them that are without God judgeth" (1 Corinthians 5:13, KJV); NIV, NRSV, "God will judge those outside."

Hebrews 13:12–14 reads in the KJV:

"Wherefore Jesus also, that he might sanctify the people with his own blood, suffered without the gate. Let us go forth therefore unto him without the camp, bearing his reproach." The NRSV translates as "Therefore Jesus also suffered outside the city gate . . . Let us then go to him outside the camp and bear the abuse he endured."

In 2 Corinthians 10:13 "without" (KJV) is used in the archaic sense of "beyond." "We will not boast of things without our measure" (KJV) means "we . . . will not boast beyond measure" [NIV, "beyond proper limits"] (NIV, NKJV) (cf. 10:15).

The KJV translates 2 Corinthians 11:28 as "Beside those things that are without, that which cometh upon me daily, the care of all the churches." The NRSV reads, "And, besides other things, I am under daily pressure because of my anxiety for all the churches."

WITHS

In Judges 16:7–9, we read how Delilah tried to bind Samson using "seven green withs which had not been dried" (v. 8). These were seven fresh bowstrings. Contemporary versions refer to them as "new bowstrings" (CEV, NLT), "fresh bowstrings" (NKJV, NRSV, RSV), "fresh cords" (NASB), and "fresh thongs" (NIV).

The Hebrew word clearly refers to a bowstring in Psalm 11:2: "For, lo, the wicked bend their bow, they make ready their arrow upon the string" (KJV; NKJV, "For look! The wicked bend their bow, They make ready their arrow on the string").

In Job 30:11, the KJV and RSV have "loosed my cord"; the NKJV and NRSV, "loosed my bowstring." The NIV reads, "Now that God has unstrung my bow and afflicted me, they throw off restraint in my presence." The first line of this verse from the book of Job is probably to be understood as the opposite of the second line of 29:20, which reads in the NKJV:

"My glory is fresh with me,
And my bow is renewed in my hand."

WOE IS ME

The lament "woe is me" occurs seven times in the KJV: at Psalm 120:5, Isaiah 6:5, in Jeremiah 4:31, 10:19, 15:10, 45:3, and Micah 7:1. At the most well-known reference, Isaiah 6:5, as a response to the vision of God's holiness, Isaiah says, "Then said I, Woe is me! for I am undone; because I am a man of unclean lips, and I dwell in the midst of a people of unclean lips: for mine eyes have seen the King, the LORD of hosts."

The NASB, NKJV, NRSV and RSV retain the KJV expression, while the other contemporary versions have: "Woe to me!" (NIV), "I'm doomed" (CEV), "Oh, no! I will be destroyed" (NCV), and "My destruction is sealed" (NLT).

Other contemporary renderings for the KJV expression at the other references include: "How terrible it is for me" (Psalm 120:5, NCV), "I'm dying!" (Jeremiah 4:31, CEV), "Alas" (Jeremiah 4:31 and 15:10, NIV), "What sadness is mine" (Jeremiah 15:10, NLT), "I am overwhelmed with trouble" (Jeremiah 45:3, NLT), "Poor me" (Micah 7:1, NCV), and "What misery is mine" (Micah 7:1, NIV, NLT).

WOE WORTH

This is an archaic lamentation or curse. It occurs only once in the KJV, in Ezekiel 30:2: "Son of man, prophesy and say, Thus saith the Lord GOD; Howl ye, Woe worth the day!" Today we might take "woe worth" to mean "worthy of woe," whereas "worth" is here an archaic verb meaning "come to be," "become," "happen." Contemporary versions have "Alas for the day!" (NASB, NRSV, RSV) and "Woe to the day!" (NKJV).

Scott's *Lady of the Lake* (1, 9) has a couplet with two appearances of this idiom:

"Woe worth the chase, woe worth
    the day,
That costs thy life, my gallant grey."

WOLF IN SHEEP'S CLOTHING

In contemporary English, the expression "wolf in sheep's clothing" is sometimes used to describe a person who appears to be friendly, harmless, or ordinary but in reality is malicious or dangerous. The expression derives from Jesus' teaching in the Sermon on the Mount: "Beware of false prophets, which come to you in sheep's clothing, but inwardly they are ravening wolves" (Matthew 7:15, KJV). The expression also alludes to one of Aesop's fables, in which a wolf in a sheep's skin succeeds in getting into a sheepfold without being noticed and attacks and eats the sheep.

The contemporary versions generally reflect the KJV wording closely: the NIV has "ferocious wolves" for the KJV "ravening wolves"; the CEV has "They dress up like sheep, but inside they are wolves who have come to attack you"; the NCV, "They come to you looking gentle like sheep, but they are really dangerous like wolves"; and the NLT, "Beware of false prophets who come disguised as harmless sheep, but are really wolves that will tear you apart."

The phrase is alluded to in literature, e.g., Shakespeare's *King Henry VI, Part I* (I, 3, 53–55), Gloucester, angered by the betrayals of the Bishop of Winchester, says:

"Winchester goose! I cry, a rope! a
    rope!—
Now beat them hence; why do you
    let them stay?—
Thee I'll chase hence, thou wolf in
    sheep's array."

WORD AND DEED

The expression "in word and deed (or: in deed)" means "not only as one says but also as one does." The expression occurs twice in the KJV, at 2 Corinthians 10:11 and 1 John 3:18.

At 2 Corinthians 10:11 the KJV reads, "Let such an one think this, that, such as we are in word by letters when we are absent, such will we be also in deed when we are

W

present." The NASB and NKJV retain the KJV "in word" and "in deed"; the NIV has "what we are" and "in our actions"; the NRSV, "what we say" and "we will . . . do"; the CEV, "Those people had better understand that when I am with you, I will do exactly what I say in my letters"; and the NLT, "The ones who say this must realize that we will be just as demanding and forceful in person as we are in our letters."

At 1 John 3:18, the KJV reads, "My little children, let us not love in word, neither in tongue; but in deed and in truth"; the NKJV, NRSV, and RSV retain the KJV "in word" and "in deed" (NRSV, "in action"); the NASB has "with word" and "in deed"; the NIV, "with words" and "with actions"; the CEV has "Children, you show love for others by truly helping them, and not merely by talking about it"; and the NLT, "Dear children, let us stop just saying we love each other; let us really show it by our actions."

WORD IN SEASON

"A word in season" is a piece of advice, a warning, etc., given at a time when it is needed, appropriate, or useful. The expression derives from Isaiah 50:4: "The Lord GOD hath given me the tongue of the learned, that I should know how to speak a word in season to him that is weary: he wakeneth morning by morning, he wakeneth mine ear to hear as the learned."

Of the contemporary versions, the NKJV is the only one to retain this KJV expression. Most of the other contemporary renderings use the verb "sustain." Examples are: "That I may know how to sustain the weary one with a word" (NASB), "to know the word that sustains the weary" (NIV), "that I may know how to sustain the weary with a word" (NRSV) or have "the right words to encourage the weary" (CEV), "what to say to make the weak strong" (NCV), and "what to say to all these weary ones" (NLT).

The phrase "in season" also occurs in Paul's charge to Timothy (2 Timothy 4:2): "Preach the word; be instant in season, out

of season; reprove, rebuke, exhort with all longsuffering and doctrine" (KJV).

The NASB, NIV, and NKJV retain the KJV "in season" and "out of season"; the NLT and NRSV have "whether the time is favorable or not" (NRSV, "or unfavorable"); the CEV for 2 Timothy 4:1–2 reads: "I command you to preach God's message. Do it willingly, even if it isn't the popular thing to do. You must correct people and point out their sins. But also cheer them up, and when you instruct them, always be patient."

WORMWOOD AND THE GALL

See GALL.

WORSHIP

Up to the seventeenth century, the word "worship" meant "to show due honor and respect to human beings as well as to God." "Then shalt thou have worship in the presence of them that sit at meat with thee" (Luke 14:10, KJV) means simply "you will be honored" (NIV, NLT, NRSV, RSV; NKJV, "you will have glory").

The servant who "fell down, and worshipped" (KJV) his lord, who had commanded that he be sold, "fell on his knees and begged" (NCV) him to have patience (Matthew 18:26). To the church in Philadelphia the promise is given that "them of the synagogue of Satan . . . [will] come and worship before thy feet" (Revelation 3:9, KJV; NASB, NRSV, RSV, "bow down").

Wycliffe translated John 12:26, "If ony man serue me, my fadir schal worschip hym"; Tyndale changed the last clause to "him will my father honoure," and this is the wording of the subsequent versions.

The problem of translation in the Old Testament is complicated by the fact that the Hebrew verb *shahah* can mean "bow down," "make obeisance," or "worship." Coverdale rendered 1 Kings 2:19 as "The kynge stode up, and wente to mete her, and worshipped her." The KJV has "The king rose up to meet her, and bowed himself unto her." An Aramaic verb of similar range appears in Daniel 2:46, where the KJV says that "the king Nebuchadnezzar fell upon his face, and worshipped Daniel"; the NASB and RSV have "and did homage to Daniel," and the NIV, "paid him honor."

In the New Testament the Greek verb *proskuneo* means "to kneel or prostrate oneself in honor or supplication of a human being," or to do this in worship of God. The challenge facing the translator is to find the right English word in the light of the context.

For example, Cornelius fell down at Peter's feet and worshiped him as a messenger of God, but Peter lifted him up, saying, "Stand up; I am only a mortal" (Acts 10:25, NRSV).

Where homage is paid to Jesus Christ, contemporary versions translate *proskuneo* as "worship" in Matthew 2:2, 8, 11 (NRSV, "pay homage"), the visit of the wise men; Matthew 4:9–10 and Luke 4:7–8, the temptation by the devil; Matthew 14:33; Mark 5:6 (NASB, NRSV, "bowed down"; NIV, "fell on his knees"; NCV, NLT, "fell down"); John 9:38, explicit recognition that Jesus is the Son of God and the Son of Man; Matthew 28:9, 17, meetings with the disciples after Jesus' resurrection.

In cases of personal requests made of Jesus, the majority of contemporary versions translate *proskuneo* with terms such as "bow down before," "kneel before" (Matthew 8:2; 9:18; 15:25; 20:20). In the account of the mockery of Jesus by Pilate's soldiers, the NIV, NRSV, and RSV use the word "homage" (Mark 15:19); the NLT has "mock worship."

The older meaning of "worship" lingers in the title "your worship" or "his worship" applied to magistrates or mayors, and in the honorific adjective "worshipful" which appears in various rituals and lists of protocol. It is chiefly in these forms that the word appears in Shakespeare. An example of the older meaning is found in *King Henry IV, Part I* (III, 2, 150–151):

"he shall render every glory up,
Yea, even the slightest worship
of his time."

WORTHY

"Worthy" is an adjective which implies "worth," "excellence," "merit." But it is also used in the KJV in cases of fault or wrongdoing, deserving blame or punishment. In Deuteronomy 25:2, "If the wicked man be worthy to be beaten" (KJV), contemporary versions render "worthy" as "deserves" (NASB, NIV, NKJV, NRSV, RSV). Similarly, "did commit things worthy of stripes" (Luke 12:48, KJV) now reads, "committed deeds worthy of a flogging" (NASB) and "did what deserved a beating" (NRSV, RSV).

"A sin worthy of death" (Deuteronomy 21:22, KJV) is now rendered as "a crime punishable by death" by the NRSV and RSV, while the NASB, NCV, and NLT retain the KJV wording (NLT, "a crime worthy of death"). Solomon's judgment upon Abiathar, "thou art worthy of death" (1 Kings 2:26, KJV) reads in the NASB, NIV, NRSV, and RSV, "you deserve to die" (NRSV, "deserve death").

Pilate's statement concerning Jesus, "nothing worthy of death is done unto him" (Luke 23:15, KJV) is translated by the CEV, "This man doesn't deserve to be put to death!" The "worthy of death" idiom appears four times with respect to Paul, in Acts 23:29; 25:11, 25; 26:31.

The KJV rendering of Hebrews 10:29 is: "Of how much sorer punishment, suppose ye, shall he be thought worthy, who hath trodden under foot the Son of God, and hath counted the blood of the covenant, wherewith he was sanctified, an unholy thing, and hath done despite unto the Spirit of grace?" The NRSV has: "How much worse punishment do you think will be deserved by those who have spurned the Son of God, profaned the blood of the covenant by which they were sanctified, and outraged the Spirit of grace?"

In Revelation 16:6 the concluding clause may easily be misunderstood—"for they are worthy" (KJV). Contemporary versions translate it as "They deserve it" (NASB), "It is their [NKJV, "their just"] due" (NKJV, RSV), "It is their just reward" (NLT), and "it is what they deserve" (NRSV). Knox, Goodspeed, and Moffatt have, with the NCV and NIV, "as they deserve"; Phillips, "They have what they deserve."

In 1 Samuel 1:5 we read that, because Elkanah loved Hannah, he made a point of giving her "a worthy portion" (KJV) of meat from the yearly sacrifice. Contemporary versions say that she received "a double portion" (NASB, NIV, NKJV, NRSV), "a special share" (NCV), and "a special portion" (NLT), but the RSV reads, "although he loved Hannah, he would give Hannah only one portion, because the LORD had closed her womb."

WOULD GOD

This is an obsolete or archaic expression of "earnest desire" or "longing." The little captive maid from Israel said to her mistress, Naaman's wife, "Would God my lord were with the prophet that is in Samaria! for he would recover him of his leprosy" (2 Kings 5:3, KJV). The NKJV has "If only my lord were with the prophet who is in Samaria! For he would heal him of his leprosy."

The expression "would God" (KJV) also appears in Numbers 11:29; 14:2; 20:3; Deuteronomy 28:67 (twice); 2 Samuel 18:33. In the form "would to God," it appears in Exodus 16:3; Joshua 7:7; Judges 9:29; 2 Corinthians 11:1. In these cases the Hebrew or Greek contains no reference to God, and contemporary versions translate with expressions such as "I [we] wish," "if only," "would that."

In the form "I would to God" the expression appears in Acts 26:29, Paul's response to Agrippa's sneer in verse 28, "Are you so quickly persuading me to become a Christian?" (NRSV). The NRSV reads, "Whether quickly or not, I pray to God that not only you but also all who are listening to me

today might become such as I am—except for these chains."

The NIV and NLT similarly translate "I would" here as "I pray," while the NKJV and RSV retain the KJV rendering (NASB, "I would wish to God") (cf. 1 Corinthians 4:8).

In its simplest form, "would God" is an English idiom that had little currency later than the sixteenthth century and its use in the KJV. Of six occurrences in Shakespeare, five are in the longest form, "I would to God"; the one "would God" is in *King Richard II* (IV, 1, 117). A free translation of the Latin hymn *Beata urbs Hirusalem*, written about 1600, has as the last of its twenty-six stanzas:

"Hierusalem! my happie home!
Would God I were in thee!
Would God my woes were at an end,
Thy joyes that I might see!"

WRATH TO COME

The expression "the wrath to come" (sometimes preceded by the verb "flee") is used in contemporary English to refer to (escaping from) punishment or revenge that is imminent. The expression occurs three times in the KJV: Matthew 3:7, Luke 3:7, and 1 Thessalonians 1:10.

The first two references describe John the Baptist's words: "But when he saw many of the Pharisees and Sadducees come to his baptism, he said unto them, O generation of vipers, who hath warned you to flee from the wrath to come" (Matthew 3:7, KJV). The contemporary versions render the KJV (retained by the NASB, NKJV, NRSV) expression "flee from the wrath to come" as: "flee from the coming wrath" (NIV), "flee God's coming judgment" (NLT), "run away from God's coming judgment" (NCV), "run from the coming judgment" (CEV). At Luke 3:7 the same wordings are used in each version.

First Thessalonians 1:10 reads in the KJV, "And to wait for his Son from heaven, whom he raised from the dead, even Jesus, which delivered us from the wrath to come"; for the KJV "wrath to come" (retained by the NASB and NKJV) the contemporary versions have "the coming wrath" (NIV), "the wrath that is coming" (NRSV), "the terrors of the coming judgment" (NLT), "God's angry judgment" (NCV), and "God's anger" (CEV).

WREST

As a verb, "wrest" is to "twist," "deflect," "misapply," "pervert." The prohibition, "Thou shalt not wrest judgment" (Deuteronomy 16:19, KJV), is now rendered as "You shall not pervert justice" (NKJV, RSV), "You shall not distort justice" (NASB), "You must never twist justice" (NLT); other references are Exodus 23:2, 6.

"Every day they wrest my words" (Psalm 56:5, KJV) is now translated by the NASB, "All day long they distort my words." Other contemporary versions use "twist" (NCV, NIV, NKJV) and "twisting" (NLT), but the NRSV and RSV adopt a differing rendering: "All day long they seek to injure my cause."

Writing concerning Paul's letters, Peter said, "There are some things in them hard to understand, which the ignorant and unstable twist to their own destruction, as they do the other scriptures" (2 Peter 3:16, NRSV, RSV).

WRITING ON THE WALL

The expression "the writing on the wall" is used in contemporary English to refer to ominous signs which warn of imminent collapse, failure, or disaster.

The phrase itself does not appear in the KJV text but is an allusion to the mysterious inscription that appeared on the wall of the royal palace of King Belshazzar: "In the same hour came forth fingers of a man's hand, and wrote over against the candlestick upon the plaister of the wall of the king's palace: and the king saw the part of the hand that wrote" (Daniel 5:5, KJV).

The words that were written were "MENE, MENE, TEKEL, U-PHARSIN" (Daniel 5:25), which Daniel interpreted as warning of the king's downfall (vv. 26–28): "MENE; God hath numbered thy kingdom, and finished it. TEKEL; Thou art weighed in the balances, and art found wanting. PERES; Thy kingdom is divided, and given to the Medes and Persians" (KJV).

Although the expression "writing on the wall" is not found in the KJV, it is in the NCV at Daniel 5:12, 16–17 and the NLT at Daniel 5:15.

The expression is often alluded to in literature: the OED quotes the *Poetic Works* of Jonathan Swift (1736), "A baited Banker thus desponds, From his own Hand foresees his Fall; They have his Soul who have his Bonds; 'Tis like the Writing on the Wall" and J. G. Lockhart's *Memoirs of the Life of Sir Walter Scott* (1837–38), "He pointed out to me this hand which, like the writing on Belshazzar's wall, disturbed his hour of hilarity." (See WEIGHED IN THE BALANCE AND FOUND WANTING)

Y

YESTERNIGHT

This old form appears in the KJV in Genesis 19:34 and 31:29, 42, and is rendered "last night" by contemporary versions. We retain "yesterday" but have dropped "yestermorn" and "yestereve." D. G. Rossetti is credited with coining "yester-year" for "last year." There is even a record of "yesterdayness," which would be a good name for a widespread affliction.

YET

This word occurs 683 times in the KJV, and in 332 of these cases Strong's *Concordance* records no corresponding Hebrew or Greek word. In these cases the translators inserted "yet" for stylistic reasons—for clarification, emphasis, elaboration, perhaps even for euphony. Contemporary versions occasionally do the same, but generally stay closer to the Hebrew or Greek text.

In Judges 9:5, "notwithstanding yet Jotham the youngest son of Jerubbaal was left" (KJV), contemporary versions use a simple "but" in place of "notwithstanding yet." In 1 Samuel 8:9, "howbeit yet protest solemnly unto them" (KJV), "yet" is dropped by the contemporary versions. The NASB has "however, you shall solemnly warn them"; the NIV, "but warn them solemnly"; the NRSV, "only—you shall solemnly warn them."

So also in 2 Chronicles 32:15, "neither yet believe him" (KJV), where the RV and ASV have "neither" and the NASB, NKJV, NRSV, and RSV have "and do not believe him."

In the KJV the word "yet" is often used to intensify the conjunction "nor." The most familiar example is Matthew 6:25, "Take no thought for your life . . . nor yet for your body." Other examples are Luke 14:35, "nor yet for the dunghill"; John 4:21, "nor yet at Jerusalem"; Acts 25:8, "nor yet against Caesar." Contemporary versions omit the word "yet" in all these cases.

The NASB and NKJV retain "yet" in Genesis 8:10, 12, where the KJV says that Noah "stayed yet other seven days." Other versions say that he "waited seven more days" [NRSV, RSV, "another seven days"] (NIV, NRSV, RSV). All contemporary versions omit the word in Esther 8:3, where the KJV has "Esther spake yet again before the king," and the NASB, NKJV, NRSV, and RSV translate more simply as "Esther spoke again to the king."

"Yet a little sleep, a little slumber" (Proverbs 6:10, KJV) has no word for "yet" in the Hebrew, and the contemporary translation omit it. Verses 10–11 read in the CEV, "Sleep a little. Doze a little. Fold your hands and twiddle your thumbs. Suddenly, everything is gone, as though it had been taken by an armed robber."

YOURSELVES

In the KJV "yourselves" is used in the nominative case, as subject of a verb, without the implied "ye" or "you," in 1 Thessalonians 2:1; 3:3; 5:2; and 2 Thessalonians 3:7. In each of these verses the KJV has "yourselves know," which in the 1611 edition was written as three words "your selues know." But in each of these cases Tyndale and his sixteenth-century successors had "ye youre selves knowe."

The KJV translators took their rendering from the Rheims New Testament. It is not clear why they accepted the Rheims rendering at these four passages, since they did not accept the same idiom at other points where Rheims had it: Luke 11:46; John 3:28; Acts 20:34; 1 Thessalonians 4:9.

The use of a reflexive pronoun as the subject of a verb is not uncommon in Shakespeare. The 1608 edition of *King Lear* (II, 4, 194) had "If you doe loue old men . . . if your selues are old." Later editions printed "yourselves" as one word. Examples of this use of other reflexive pronouns are:

"Myself hath often heard them
  say."
  —*Titus Andronicus* (IV, 4, 74)

"Thyself is self-misused."
  —*King Richard III* (IV, 4, 376)

"Ourselves will hear
The accuser and the accused freely
  speak."
  —*King Richard II* (I, 1, 16)

"O could their master come and
  go as lightly,
Himself would lodge where
  senseless they are lying!"
  —*Two Gentlemen of Verona*
  (III, 1, 143)

Recommended for Additional Reading

Barker, Kenneth L. *The NIV: The Making of a Contemporary Translation.* Grand Rapids: Zondervan, 1986.

Bois, John. *Translating for King James,* translated and edited by Ward Allen. London: Allen Lane, 1970.

Caird, G. B. *The Language and Imagery of the Bible.* London: Duckworth, 1980.

Cowie, A. P., R. Mackin, and I. R. McCaig. *Oxford Dictionary of Current Idiomatic English,* volume II. Oxford, Oxford University Press, 1983.

Douglas, J. D., et al. *The Illustrated Bible Dictionary.* Leicester: Inter-Varsity Press; Wheaton, Ill.: Tyndale House, 1980.

Ehrlich, Eugene and David H. Scott. *MENE, MENE, TEKEL: A Lively Lexicon of Words and Phrases from the Bible.* New York: Harper Collins, 1990.

Fulghum, Walter B. *A Dictionary of Biblical Allusions in English Literature.* New York: Holt, Rinehart and Winston, 1965.

Hammond, Gerald. *The Making of the English Bible.* Manchester: Carcanet, 1982.

Jeffrey, D. L. (ed.). *A Dictionary of Biblical Tradition in English Literature.* Grand Rapids: Eerdmans, 1992.

Kohlenberger, John R. III. *The Contemporary Parallel New Testament.* New York and Oxford: Oxford University Press, 1997.

Lewis, C. S. *The Literary Impact of the Authorised Version.* London: The Athlone Press, 1950.

Lewis, Jack P. *The English Bible from KJV to NIV,* Second Edition. Grand Rapids: Baker Book House.

Metzger, B. M., R. C. Dentan, and W. Harrelson. *The Making of the New Revised Standard Version.* Grand Rapids: Eerdmans, 1991.

Norton, David. *A History of the Bible as Literature.* Cambridge: University Press, 1993.

Opfell, Olga S. *The King James Bible Translators.* Jefferson & London: McFarland, 1982.

Partridge, A. C. *English Bible Translation.* London: André Deutsch, 1973.

Prickett, Stephen. *Words and The Word.* Cambridge, University Press, 1986.

Prickett, Stephen and Robert Barnes. *The Bible.* Cambridge: University Press, 1991.

Scrivener, F. H. A. *The Authorized Edition of the English Bible (1611).* Cambridge: University Press, 1884.

Stevenson, W. H. (ed.). *King James's Bible: A Selection.* Harlow: Longman, 1994.

Vance, Lawrence M. *Archaic Words and the Authorized Version.* Pensacola: Vance, 1996.

Index

Key words and phrases, printed in CAPITAL AND SMALL CAPITAL letters in this Index, are discussed in alphabetical order in the text.